Every
MAN
in the Bible

Every

MAN

in the Bible

LARRY RICHARDS

Illustrated by
Paul Gross

THOMAS NELSON PUBLISHERS
Nashville

Published in Nashville, Tennessee, by Thomas Nelson, Inc.

Library of Congress Cataloging-in-Publication Data

Richards, Larry, 1931-
    Every man in the Bible / Larry Richards; illustrated by Paul Gross.
        p.   cm.
Includes biographical references and indexes.
ISBN 0-7852-1439-9
    1. Men in the Bible--Biography. 2. Bible--Biography. 3. Christian life--Biblical teaching. I. Title.
BS574.5.R53   1999
220.9'2'081—dc21   99-046499
                                                                        CIP

Printed in the United States of America

1 2 3 4 5 6 7 8—04 03 02 01 00 99

CONTENTS

See Expository and Scripture Indexes for Complete Topical and Scripture Listings

INTRODUCTION

Welcome to *Every Man in the Bible,* a companion to *Every Woman in the Bible* and to the other books in Nelson's "Everything in the Bible" series. Like the other books in this series, these books are intended to serve as resource tools that those studying Scripture can turn to for scholarly studies of important biblical themes. However, these books are also written for personal enrichment. Each book brings out the exciting relationship of great Bible truths to each reader's life. These books not only inform, they enrich.

This is especially true of *Every Man in the Bible.* It is a resource book which identifies every man named in Scripture. In fact, pages 216-354 are devoted to brief sketches of the famous, the little-known, and the obscure men mentioned in God's Word. The first ten chapters, however, are devoted to lengthier biographical studies of men who played significant roles in the unfolding of God's purposes in history. Through their lives the significance of great Bible themes such as covenant, law, faith, and loyalty are shown in the context of human experience. Also through these biographical studies the roles of prophets, priests, and kings in the Old Testament, and of apostles and evangelists of the New Testament, are unveiled in a vital, living way. In studying the men of the Bible each reader will gain fresh insight into the significance of the great themes and truths of God's Word.

While the biographical studies featured in *Every Man* instruct and inform, they also enrich. The men of Scripture, from Adam and Abraham to Paul and Timothy, are displayed as totally human individuals, each with strengths and weakness, each seeking to respond to God, and while succeeding, still failing at times. Rather than portraying the Bible's great men as stereotypical "saints," we discover ways that they are like you and me. As their lives and relationships are carefully examined we discover that their experiences can serve men today as examples to follow—or to avoid. Most readers will find the "An Example for Today" feature that concludes the biographical studies one of the most helpful and one of many distinctive features of this very special study of Bible men.

FIRST FATHERS

The word "greatest" here is deceiving. Many saints of old exhibited qualities that place them in the ranks of history's most admirable men. Yet certain towering figures simply must be recognized as the greatest. They are not the greatest because of their personal qualities. They are the greatest because they became turning points in salvation history. In a sense they *are* the Old Testament; the Old Testament's central message is summed up in them.

In Adam, we discover the true nature of human beings as persons created in God's image but now flawed by a terrible Fall. In Abraham, we identify the role of faith in reestablishing relationship with God and are given our first glimpse of God's plan to repair the damage done by Adam's sin. In Moses, we see God redeem Israel and set the Hebrew race on course to become the channel through whom He will reveal Himself to humans and through whom a Savior will come to redeem all. In David, we have God's ancient covenant promises further defined as we're told that through David's line a ruler will appear who will reign over an everlasting kingdom.

Each of these four men is pivotal in setting the course of the Old Testament. Each of these four is central to our understanding of what God has done and is going to do in human history. And, for this reason, these four truly are the "greatest men of the Old Testament."

ADAM
Scripture references:
Genesis 2:1—5:5; 1 Chronicles 1:1;
Luke 3:38; Romans 5:12–17;
1 Corinthians 15:21–23,45;
1 Timothy 2:13,14

Date:	*Unknown*
Name:	*Adam [AD-uhm; "human being"]*
Greatest accomplishment:	*Adam was the direct creation of God, the prototype human being.*

God designed every feature of Eden to enable Adam to use the gifts the Lord had given him.

ADAM'S ROLE IN SCRIPTURE

The Hebrew word *'adam* is used over 500 times in the Old Testament in the sense of "human being" or "humanity." Only in early Genesis and 1 Chronicles 1:1 is *'adam* the proper name of Adam, the first man. Early Genesis defines Adam's role in history. Any insight we're given into Adam as an individual is found there.

The significance of Adam's creation by God (*Gen. 1:26, 27; 2:7–25.*) Some argue that Genesis 1 and 2 are two contradictory creation accounts, spliced together by ancient editors. In fact, what we have in these two chapters are "establishing" and "close up" views of creation.

We see this same technique used daily on television. The camera gives us a look at the outside of an apartment building—and then shifts inside to focus on the featured individuals. The view of the building is the establishing shot; it tells us where the action takes place. The view focuses our attention on the hero and heroine of the writer's tale.

Genesis 1 is God's "establishing shot." Genesis 1 overviews the universe in which the action will take place. That brief overview establishes the fact that the material universe is the work of a Person. All that exists was consciously designed and brought into being by One whose power and wisdom are utterly awesome. That brief overview also establishes that all living creatures owe their existence to Him, yet draws our attention to "man." Only man will God fashion "in Our image, according to our likeness." And only to man will God give "dominion over the fish of the sea, over the birds of the air, and over the cattle, over all the earth and over every creeping thing that creeps on the earth" (Gen. 1:26–27).

Genesis 1 provides the framework in which we understand the universe and man's place in it. No one who ignores Genesis 1, God's "establishing shot," can hope to understand human nature or the meaning of human life.

Then, with the framework fixed, Genesis 2 takes us "inside." We're led to one spot on the surface of the earth, a place called Eden, and introduced to the pair who became the parents of our race.

Grasping the teaching of these two chapters is essential if we are rightly to understand the men we meet in the Bible—as well as any human being. What, then, do these chapters teach us?

Man was created in God's image and likeness (Gen. 1:26–27). In this text, two Hebrew words, *image* and *likeness*, are linked to convey a single powerful truth. Human beings, and human beings alone, have been given the "likeness-image" of God. *The Expository Dictionary of Bible Words* (1985) notes:

The creation story makes it clear that the likeness-image is not of physical form: material for man's creation was taken from the earth. It is the inner nature of human beings that reflects something vital in the nature of God. Thus theologians generally agree that the likeness is rooted in all that is required to make a human being a person: in our intellectual, emotional, and moral resemblance to God, who has revealed Himself to us a personal being.

It is this likeness-image that sets human beings apart from [the rest of] the animal creation, and it is transmitted through the process of reproduction to succeeding generations (Gen. 5:1–3). It is this likeness-image of God that makes each human life so precious that nothing of however great value can possibly be offered in compensation for the taking of another's life (Gen. 9:5–6)(p. 351).

According to Genesis then, human life is unique, and each human being is special.

Man was given dominion (Gen. 1:26). Three Hebrew words convey the idea of rule or dominion. *Masal,* found over 80 times in the Old Testament, is a general word denoting authority. *Sapat* and *mispat* are translated either "rule" or "judge," and are linked with various functions of human government. But the Hebrew word in Genesis 1 is *radah.* Its twenty-five uses in the Old Testament refer to human's governance of nature, and particularly animal creation, as God's surrogate. In stating His intention to give man dominion over animal creation, God charged human beings to *care for* what He has made. The gift of God's likeness-image carries with it the responsibility to guard God's handiwork rather than to exploit it.

Adam's creation was intimate and personal (Gen. 2:7). In Scripture's close up of Adam's creation, we note a striking departure. In describing the creation of the universe and the shaping of earth, Genesis 1 repeatedly records, "Then God said . . . and it was so." In describing Adam's creation, Genesis 2:7 says "the LORD God formed man of the dust of the ground, and breathed into his nostrils the breath of life; and man became a living being."

What a difference! "Then God said . . . and it was so" suggests emotional distance. The picture of God stooping to form Adam's body from the dust of the earth and then breathing life into his still form is warm and personal. God was emotionally involved. He stepped into His creation; He fashioned Adam's body and held it in His arms; He gently breathed His own breath into Adam's nostrils that Adam might become a living soul. God watched as Adam stirred. When Adam sat up, we can imagine God stepping back, deeply satisfied with this being who is the crown of His creation.

Adam was something totally new. His body is from earth, and in his possession of biological life Adam shared his earthly nature with the animals. But his *life* is from

God. As a "living soul" Adam shared something of the nature of his Creator. In time, Adam's body would grow old and die. But Adam himself, a self-aware and unique individual in whose essence God's breath had planted eternity, would exist for evermore. Adam would forever be an object of God's love.

In Genesis 1 and 2, we are taught foundational truths about man's essential nature, and we catch a glimpse of man's relationship with God.

- Man [both male and female] was created by the God who brought the universe into being.
- Man [both male and female] was given God's likeness-image, and in this gift was set apart from the animals.
- Man [both male and female] has been granted dominion over God's creation. We are God's caretakers.
- Man [both male and female] is a living soul, possessing biological life but also destined for eternity.

The men we meet in Scripture have been called to live their earthly lives in relationship with the God who created them. No human being's achievements or character can be rightly evaluated without considering how well his life reveals a whole and healthy relationship with the Lord.

BIBLE BACKGROUND:

Genesis provides a unique framework in which to understand humankind. No ancient culture saw human beings as Scripture portrays them, nor viewed human creation as the conscious act of a loving deity. Take the account of man's creation found in Egyptian Pyramid texts, reflecting concepts from 3000

B.C. After describing Khepri's creation of other deities by masturbation, the text describes his loss of an eye, to which Kephri was later reunited. He then said:

"After I had united my members, I wept over them, and that was the coming into being of mankind, from the tears which came forth from my Eye."

There is no intentionality here, no love. In commenting on this story, Joseph Kaster, in *The Wisdom of Ancient Egypt* (1968) observed, "ordinary man is nothing" (p. 46).

It is striking that the framework in which moderns view human origins is quite similar to that of ancient pagan cultures. True, evolution posits no deities. But the framework presented by evolutionists—an impersonal material universe in which humans emerged by chance through a series of unlikely accidents—leads inevitably to the same conclusions the ancients reached. In either framework, "ordinary man is nothing."

Only Scripture's account of Adam's intentional creation in God's likeness-image makes each "ordinary man" special and gives an ordinary person's life eternal significance.

The significance of Adam's early life in Eden (Gen. 2:8–20). While two of the rivers mentioned in Genesis as the boundaries of Eden are known, the location of the other two remain mysteries. While we can say with confidence that the biblical Eden lay somewhere in what is now Iraq or Turkey, between the Tigris and Euphrates, we do not know exactly where.

But knowing the location of Eden isn't crucial for discerning its significance in the Genesis account.

Genesis 2:8 tells us that "the Lord God planted a garden eastward in Eden, and there He put the man whom He had formed." As God had carefully designed the universe, He now just as purposefully designed Eden. He filled the garden with trees that were "pleasant to the sight and good for food." He enriched it with natural resources. He filled it with all kinds of wildlife, and at one place set out the "tree of the knowledge of good and evil."

We can understand God's care in designing Eden when we remember that God had given Adam the gift of His likeness-image. Adam, like God, was a person with all the capacities of personhood. Eden was designed to give Adam the opportunity to explore the wonderful capacities God had granted him.

In Eden, Adam discovered beauty (Gen. 2:9). God had planted there "every tree . . . that is pleasant to the sight." The God who has "made everything beautiful in its time" (Eccl. 3:11) filled Eden with beauty, and that beauty resonated in the heart of Adam.

In Eden, Adam discovered the satisfaction of meaningful work (Gen. 2:15). Genesis tells us that God "put him [Adam] in the garden . . . to tend and keep it." God had worked, and He looked over what He accomplished in each of creation's days and "saw that it was good." God had made Adam in His likeness-image, and thus Adam's nature cried out for something significant to accomplish, some work of his own he could look on and say, "this is good."

In Eden, Adam experienced the joy of discovery (Gen. 2:19). Scripture tells us that God showed Adam "every beast of the field and every bird of the air," and gave Adam the task of naming them. Here we need to understand the Hebrew concept of *name.* In Hebrew thought, a name was more than a label. The name was intended to capture and express something of the essence of the thing named. To "name" the animals and birds, Adam would have had to study each kind, to observe its ways and catalog its habits. Only when he understood each creature could he name it. Adam discovered another joy rooted in sharing God's likeness-image. Adam discovered the joy of learning, of thinking, of classifying, of identifying that which was unique.

In Eden, Adam discovered the peace that comes from doing what is right (Gen. 2:17). God had planted the tree of the knowledge of good and evil in Eden, and told Adam that of this one tree: "You shall not eat." Some have viewed the tree as a trap, and pondered why God should want Adam to fail. But there is a different explanation for the existence of the tree. God had created Adam in His own likeness-image. And God is a moral being, committed to doing what is right. If Adam was to explore this aspect of personhood, he must be given the opportunity to make moral choices. And so the tree. And so too, for the uncountable months or years or decades that Adam lived in Eden and worked and studied there, Adam must have frequently passed by the forbidden tree. He did not eat. And in this Adam found inner peace, for in obeying God he had done what was right.

In Eden, Adam discovered his need for companionship (Gen. 2:18). There was one dimension of personhood that Adam had not and could not experience. Adam was alone, with no one like him whom he could love and with whom he could share life's experiences. In this need, too, Adam shared God's likeness-image. As Three-in-One—Father, Son, and Holy Spirit—God had always possessed, within Himself the "helper comparable."

God knew what Adam lacked, and said, "It is not good that man should be alone." God had always planned to "make him a helper comparable to him" (Gen. 2:18). But Adam did not realize how lonely he was until he studied all the animals and birds, and the realization dawned that he truly was alone. As wonderful as the animals were, Adam found no "helper comparable to him" (2:20). Only when Adam recognized his need did God form Eve from Adam's rib.

In Eden, God gave Adam Eve as a helper truly comparable to him (Gen. 2:21–24). The significance of the account of Eve's creation lies in the fact that God used a rib taken from Adam as Eve's source. If God had begun again with earth's dust, it might have been argued that woman was a second and subordinate creation. But God used Adam's own substance. And when the Lord brought Eve to Adam, he immediately recognized the significance of God's act. Adam said,

> This is now bone of my bones
> And flesh of my flesh;
> She shall be called Woman,
> Because she was taken out of Man.
>   (Gen. 2:23)

Eve shared with Adam the likeness-image God granted to humankind. Each was fully a person as God is a Person. At last, Adam had a companion with whom he could share life fully and completely.

The insights to be gained from Genesis 2 further help us as we consider what it means to be a real man. Like Adam, we men are made in God's likeness-image, and real men follow the pattern Adam set in Eden.

- Real men look for and appreciate the beautiful.
- Real men find satisfaction in accomplishing meaningful work.
- Real men develop their capacity to think and explore the nature of the universe.
- Real men make moral commitments and find deep satisfaction in choosing to do what is right.
- Real men build relationships with others, valuing interdependence more than independence.
- Real men invest in their relationship with their spouse, finding joy in sharing all of life on earth with her.

The story of Adam's creation reminds us that a man's life is to be rich and varied and that we find fulfillment in developing all the wonderful capacities of personhood with which God so graciously gifted humankind.

The significance of Adam's fall (Gen. 3:1–19). The fairy tales we learned to love as children typically ended with marriage and the formula, "and they lived happily ever after." We have no idea how many years Adam and Eve lived together happily in Eden. But Genesis moves quickly to describe an incident that made the fairy-tale ending impossible.

We're familiar with what happened. Satan, in the guise of a serpent, deceived Eve and encouraged her to eat the forbidden fruit of the Tree of the Knowledge of Good and Evil. We're not told where Adam was as Eve and Satan conversed. We do know that after Eve had eaten, "she also gave to her husband with her, and he ate" (Gen. 3:6). The phrase "with her" has been taken by some to indicate that Adam silently observed the conversation between Satan and Eve, and rather than step in, he abdicated his leadership responsibility. While this view might be debated, it is clear that Scripture holds Adam responsible. Throughout Scripture, the fault is ascribed to Adam, not Eve. Paul tells us in 1 Timothy 2:14 that "Adam was not deceived, but the woman being deceived, fell into transgression." Rather than blame Eve, this verse makes it clear that Adam had no excuse. He consciously chose to eat the forbidden fruit, intentionally violating God's command. And thus the Fall is Adam's Fall, not Eve's nor even Adam's and Eve's. And that Fall had a dire impact on the human race, on nature itself, and on all of Adam's sons as males.

The impact of Adam's fall on the human race (Gen. 2:17). When God introduced Adam to Eden, He clearly defined the consequences of violating His command: "You shall not eat [of the tree]," God said, "for in the day that you eat of it you shall surely die" (2:17). At first, it might seem this was an empty threat. Adam and Eve ate the fruit, but did not drop dead!

The answer is found in the three senses in which Scripture uses the concept of *death*. In one sense, death is simply the cessation of

Biological death is a symbol of the spiritual death which overtook humanity when Adam sinned.

biological life. In this sense, the day Adam and Eve ate the forbidden fruit they *began to die*. Those processes that lead to biological death were set in operation, and the grave prepared to welcome the first pair and all their offspring.

In another sense, death is a theological concept depicting the spiritual state of those who are separated from God by sin. In this sense Adam and Eve did die "in the day" that they ate. This death is powerfully depicted in *The Expository Dictionary of Bible Words* (1985).

Death, then, is a biological concept that is applied theologically to graphically convey the true state of humankind. The death that grips mankind is moral and spiritual. Death warps and twists man out of the pattern of original creation. Every human potential is distorted, every capacity—for joy, for relationships, for harmony with God, for true goodness—is tragically misshapen. And because each ugly twist and turn gives expression to sin, man—intended to reflect God's image and likeness—falls instead under God's condemnation. The striking and terrible image of death is designed to communicate how desperately we need God and how hopeless we are without him (p. 409).

Human beings have not been stripped of the likeness-image, but the likeness-image has been distorted, and every human capacity is now bent toward sin.

There is a third sense in which *death* is used in Scripture. Death describes the eternal state of those who fail to be reconciled to God during their days on earth. The eternal punishment to which they condemn themselves by unbelief is called the "second death" (Rev. 20:14).

BIBLE BACKGROUND:

NEW TESTAMENT PASSAGES ON DEATH AND THE FALL

ROMANS 5:12–17

Therefore, just as through one man sin entered the world, and death through sin, and thus death spread to all men, because all sinned; (For until the law sin was in the world, but sin is not imputed when there is no law. Nevertheless death reigned from Adam to Moses, even over those who had not sinned according to the likeness of the transgression of Adam, who is a type of Him who was to come. But the free gift is not like the offense. For if by the one man's offense many died, much more the grace of God and the gift by the grace of the one Man, Jesus Christ, abounded to many. And the gift is not like that which came through the one who sinned. For the judgment which came from one offense resulted in condemnation, but the free gift which came from many offenses resulted in justification. For if by the one man's offense death reigned through the one, much more those who receive abundance of grace and of the gift of righteousness will reign in life through the One, Jesus Christ.)

1 CORINTHIANS 15:21–22

For since by man came death, by Man also came the resurrection of the dead. For as in Adam all die, even so in Christ all shall be made alive.

EPHESIANS 2:1–3

And you He made alive, who were dead in trespasses and sins, in which you once walked according to the course of this world, according to the prince of the power of the air, the spirit who now works in the sons of disobedience, among whom also we all once conducted ourselves in the lusts of our flesh, fulfilling the desires of the flesh and of the mind, and were by nature children of wrath, just as the others.

Because of the Fall, all human beings have been born spiritually dead, with all those wonderful capacities given us by God bent toward sin.

The impact of Adam's Fall on nature (Gen. 3:17–18). After their sin, Adam and Eve tried to hide from God (3:8). Ultimately they responded to God's call, and in the confrontation that followed God explained the specific consequences of their disobedience. The consequences to Eve are explained in 3:16, and the consequences to Adam in 3:17, 18. (For a thorough discussion of woman in the original creation and the stunning consequences of the Fall on woman's relationship to man, see the companion volume, *Every Woman in the Bible.*)

God's first words of explanation to Adam were, "Cursed is the ground for your sake" (3:17). This theme is repeated in verse 18: "Both thorns and thistles it shall bring forth for you."

Just as the principle of death and decay were introduced into the human genetic code, so death and decay would now establish their grip on nature itself. The unalloyed beauty and glory of original creation and its essential friendliness toward man were transformed, and earth became a hostile environment that humans must tame. Eden was lost, and as a consequence of the Fall:

> In the sweat of your face you shall eat
>   bread
> Till you return to the ground.
> For out of the ground you were taken;
> For dust you are,
> And to dust you shall return. (Gen. 3:19)

A NEW TESTAMENT PASSAGE:

ON THE IMPACT OF THE FALL ON NATURE

ROMANS 8:20–22

For the creation was subjected to futility, not willingly, but because of Him who subjected it in hope; because the creation itself also will be delivered from the bondage of corruption into the glorious liberty of the children of God. For we know that the whole creation groans and labors with birth pangs until now.

Genesis gives us the answer to challenges skeptics raise based on the observed "cruelty" of nature. It wasn't always so. The Fall, not God, introduced death and decay into our world.

The impact of Adam's fall on males (Gen. 3:17–19).

In *Every Woman in the Bible,* we explored the striking impact of the Fall on male/female. The Fall disrupted the partnership of equals that had existed originally in Eden, and shifted woman's orientation, originally toward seeking to please God, to become an orientation toward seeking to please males. The subordination and oppression of women common to most civilizations is not rooted in any innate superiority of men but is a consequence and expression of sin.

In explaining further consequences of the Fall to Adam, the Lord spoke of a reorientation of male life as well. "Cursed is the ground for your sake," God said, and went on: "In toil you shall eat of it all the days of your life" (Gen. 3:17). The same thought is repeated in verse 19: "In the sweat of your face you shall eat bread." The human race would now have to wrest a living from an uncooperative earth. And even as the Fall refocused women's priorities to create a need for male approval, so the Fall reoriented men's priorities, and created a need for personal achievement. The great vulnerability of women is to focus on gaining the approval of men rather than God, but the great vulnerability of men is to focus on being successful in their work rather than on doing God's will.

The man who becomes a workaholic, the man who measures his worth by his accomplishments, the man whose whole goal in life is to build up his business has fallen into the trap set in Adam's Fall. For men, a commitment to accomplishment and a drive toward success is the siren's song that draws us away from God.

Significantly, God chose the word "toil" to describe man's work after the Fall. While some Bible words for work convey a positive sense of the joy to be found in meaningful work, other words focus on work's dark side. Here the Hebrew word indicates painful toil, and emphasizes the unpleasant and frustrating aspects of work as "drudgery that never yields satisfaction or profit" (*Expository Dictionary*, p. 636). In choosing this word, God reminds us that while the work that provides for our families has value, when work becomes the focus of a man's life, he is doomed to frustration and ultimate failure. Our focus is to be on God and on serving Him. Work is an idol at whose feet all too many men bow down.

Genesis's teachings on the Fall help us better understand ourselves as men.

- Because of the Fall we often find ourselves driven by corrupt impulses and desires. We will find in ourselves the weaknesses we see in the men of the Bible. By studying their lives, we can be warned away from similar tendencies in ourselves.

- Because of the Fall, spiritual death has gained its grip on our personalities. Only through faith in God's promises and in commitment to His Word can we find our way successfully through life. Here, too, the men of Scripture give us guidance and encouragement.

- Because of the Fall, we men are especially vulnerable to giving first place to our work rather than to God. When we do give first place to God, work, wife, children, and all those other aspects of our lives can exist in harmony. When we give first place to work, every other relationship will suffer.

ADAM: AN EXAMPLE FOR TODAY

Genesis treats Adam as the prototype human being, and this he is. But Genesis gives us little biographical material about

Adam. We learn much from early Genesis about human beings, but little about Adam, the man. The biographical material available to us is after the Fall.

In Genesis 3, we get a sense of Adam's human side. We see his sudden discovery of guilt and shame (Gen. 3:7). We see his anxious attempts to cover up his sin, and the sudden fear that drove him to flee from the God who had always treated him with love (3:8,10). We see his frantic attempt to shift the blame from himself to Eve and even to God rather than take responsibility for his choices (3:12). In this we see more clearly flaws that reflect our own failings, and indeed the failings of every human being. Adam becomes a man with whom we can sympathize, for we know intimately the weaknesses he displays.

What comfort we take then as, after telling Adam and Eve the consequences of their sin, God "made tunics of skin and clothed them" (Gen. 3:21). For here we have history's first sacrifice. Here we begin to learn the repeated lesson of the Old Testament that, while sin deserves death, God will accept the death of another in our place, and so will cover our sin. In the flaws of Adam, we see ourselves, but in God's gracious act, we see foreshadowed an ultimate sacrifice offered by One who will pay the penalty for all the sins of humankind.

Through early Genesis, and Adam's story, we learn these important lessons.

- All human beings are special, created in God's own likeness-image. Every person is to be valued and treated with respect as one who is precious to God.
- All human beings have God-given capacities rooted in our relationship to God as persons. We need to nurture these capacities, whether that is the ability to appreciate beauty, the ability to do meaningful work and find satisfaction in it, the ability to build significant relationships with others, and so

forth. Let's not be satisfied to be one-dimensional individuals, but let us develop and find joy in all the gifts God has given us.

- All human beings are terribly flawed by sin, and the likeness-image gifts of God are twisted. Let's remain aware of our fallibility, and humbly respond to the guidance God gives us in His Word.
- Men are especially vulnerable to the temptation to focus on work and on achievement at the expense of commitment to God and the nurturing of other relationships. We need to live a balanced life in which we place God first and let the other aspects of our lives fall into place as He directs us.

While little is known of Adam the man, his story in early Genesis is foundational to our understanding of ourselves as human beings, and as men.

ABRAHAM
Scripture references:
Genesis 12—24; Romans 4;
Galatians 3

Date:	2100 B.C.
Name:	Abram [AY-bruhm; "exalted father"]
	Abraham [AY-bruh-ham; "father of a multitude"]
Main contribution:	Abraham stands in Scripture as the prime example of saving faith, and the covenant promises given him reveal God's plans and purposes.

ABRAHAM'S ROLE IN SCRIPTURE

Abraham is a towering figure in history. God chose Abraham to receive a unique revelation of Himself and gave him a series of stunning covenant promises. And Abraham responded to God with faith. These two themes—covenant and faith—sum up Abraham's unique role in Scripture's story of people's relationship with God.

God's Covenant promises to Abraham (*Gen. 12:1–3, 7*). God spoke to a man named Abram, a citizen of Ur in what is now Iraq. Genesis 12 records what God said to him, revealing in a series of "I will" statements what God intended to accomplish in and through this wealthy but otherwise ordinary man.

The covenant promises stated (*Gen. 12:1–3, 7*). Here are God's statements, understood as promises and later confirmed by the making of a formal covenant [a legally binding agreement]:

> Get out of your country,
> From your family

BIBLE BACKGROUND:

THE COVENANT PROMISES FULFILLED

In a companion volume in this series, *Every Covenant and Promise in the Bible*, the significance of the Genesis 12 promises and their fulfillment is traced through the entire Bible (pp. 23–27). This chart summarizes how God has or will fulfill His ancient promises.

The Promise Stated: I will	The Promise Fulfilled
. . . make you a great nation	Millions (both Arabs and Jews) have descended from Abraham.
. . . bless you	Throughout Abraham's long life God protected and cared for him.
. . . make your name great	Millions in three world religions—Islam, Judaism, and Christianity—revere Abraham as founder of their faith.
. . . you shall be a blessing	Abraham's faith-response to God revealed the key to personal relationship with God (Gen. 15:6).
. . . bless those who bless you and curse those who curse you	Ancient and modern history shows that nations that have persecuted the Jewish people have paid a terrible price.
. . . in you all the families of the earth shall be blessed.	Both the Scriptures and the Savior have been given to humanity through Abraham's descendants.
. . . and to your descendants I will give this land.	The promise was partially fulfilled in Israel's history, and according to Bible prophecy will be entirely fulfilled at history's end.

Abraham's first great act of faith was to leave the city of Ur for an unknown land at God's command.

And from your father's house,
To a land that I will show you.
I will make you a great nation;
I will bless you
And make your name great;
And you shall be a blessing.
I will bless those who bless you,
And I will curse him who curses you;
And in you all the families of the earth
   shall be blessed. (Gen. 12:1-3)

Later, when Abraham had obeyed God and arrived in the land God showed him, God added this promise: "To your descendants I will give this land" (Gen. 12:7).

Starting in chapter 12, the Book of Genesis tells the story of Abraham and the story of his sons, grandsons, and great-grandsons. While their stories are rich in spiritual lessons, Isaac, Jacob, and Jacob's twelve sons are significant primarily because the covenant-promises God gave Abraham were passed on to them, and through them to the Hebrew people. In a real sense, the rest of the Bible is a demonstration of God's faithfulness to the covenant promises He gave to Abraham long ago. As the Bible's story unfolds, we understand more and more of God's plan for the redemption of humankind, a plan stated first in the promises He made to Abraham.

The covenant promises expanded and explained. As the Bible unfolds, the covenant promises made to Abraham are both expanded and explained. Later, God promised David that a ruler would emerge from his descendants, who would establish an everlasting kingdom. Still later, God announced that one day he would make a new covenant with Israel that would make Old Testament law obsolete. In that covenant, signed and sealed by Jesus' death on the cross, God promised complete forgiveness of sins and inner transformation. Each of these historic events—giving of covenant promises to David, and the formal entry at Calvary into what Scripture calls the "New Covenant"—reveals more of how God intended to keep His original covenant with Abraham.

BIBLE BACKGROUND:

THE NEW COVENANT

G od revealed to Jeremiah that one day He would make a new covenant with His people (Jer. 31). That covenant, instituted by Jesus' death and resurrection, tells us God's plan for reversing the impact of the Fall by the transformation of those who have a personal relationship with God. The writer of Hebrews quotes Jeremiah, showing us this plan for the blessing of all the families of earth in Abraham's greatest descendant, Jesus Christ:

For this is the covenant that I will make with the house of Israel after those days, says the LORD: I will put My laws in their mind and write them on their hearts; and I will be their God, and they shall be My people. None of them shall teach his neighbor, and none his brother, saying 'Know the LORD,' for all shall know Me, from the least of them to the greatest of them. For I will be merciful to their unrighteousness, and their sins and their lawless deeds I will remember no more (Heb. 8:10–12)

Nearly a hundred times Scripture refers to God as "the God of Abraham" or to Abraham as the father of the Hebrew people. Each reference looks back to Abraham as the man to whom God made covenant promises. Each reference reminds us that what we know of God has been channeled to us through Abraham and his descendants.

The covenant promises: a foundation for our hope (Heb. 6:13–18). The writer of Hebrews reminds us that the significance of the promises to Abraham is not merely historical or theological. In looking back to Abraham and the promises made to him, we discover a firm basis for our own faith in God. In the promises given to Abraham and in their working out in history, we see a God who is utterly faithful to His word. The writer of Hebrews said:

For when God made a promise to Abraham, because He could swear by no one greater, He swore by Himself, saying, "Surely blessing I will bless you, and multiplying I will multiply you." And so, after he had patiently endured, he obtained the promise. For men indeed swear by the greater, and an oath for confirmation is for them an end of all dispute. Thus God, determining to show more abundantly to the heirs of promise the immutability of His counsel, confirmed it with an oath, that by two immutable things, in which it is impossible for God to lie, we might have strong consolation, who have fled for refuge to lay hold on the hope set before us. This hope we have as an anchor of the soul, both sure and steadfast, and which enters the Presence behind the veil, where the forerunner has entered for us, even Jesus (Heb. 6:13–29).

In looking back to Abraham and God's promises to him, the writer of Hebrews reminds us that God made an absolute and immutable commitment. All that we know of God, we know through events that unfolded through millennia, and these events have demonstrated that *God keeps His promises.* It is unthinkable that the God who kept His promises to Abraham would go back on the promises He made to us in Jesus Christ.

Summing up, Abraham's significance in Scripture is rooted first in the fact that he was the recipient of covenant promises made to him by God. Those promises give shape to salvation history, and indeed the rest of Scripture is the story of how God has kept commitments first made to Abraham. That God is still keeping those ancient covenant promises serves as a revelation of God's character. God is ever faithful to His Word. And because God is faithful to His commitments, we who look to Jesus for salvation can be utterly confident that we are secure in Him.

Abraham's faith in God *(Gen. 15:6; Rom. 4).*
Abraham is also significant in Scripture for
his modeling of saving faith. Abraham followed God's instructions and traveled from
Ur to Canaan. Some ten years after he
arrived, God spoke to Abraham again,
repeating and expanding the promise of
many descendants (Gen. 15:5). Although
Abraham was old, and his wife Sarah had
gone through menopause and was no longer
fertile, Scripture says that Abraham "believed
in the LORD, and He accounted it to him for
righteousness" (Gen. 15:6).

*Abraham's need for righteousness (Gen.
15:6).* Unlike hagiographies, the Bible never
glosses over the sins and failures of its
heroes. In saying God counted Abraham's
faith "for [or as] righteousness," the Bible
makes it clear that Abraham *had no righteousness of his own.*

This is clear to anyone who reads the
Bible's account of Abraham's life. Originally
Abraham was a pagan who, with his family,
"served other [pagan] gods" (Josh. 24:2-3).
In Canaan, Abraham twice was so terrified of
what strangers might do to him that he had
Sarah lie about being his wife. While some
have attempted to explain away Abraham's
moral failures, it is important to see that
Abraham was as flawed by sin as any human
being.

Why is this important? In three places
the New Testament portrays Jesus refusing
to permit His opponents to take comfort in
the notion that they have Abraham as their
father (Matt. 3:9; Luke 3:8; John 8:33,39).
While the claim by Jesus' opponents that
Abraham is their father rests on acknowledged physical descent from Abraham, far
more is implied. First-century rabbinic
Judaism, like Judaism today, tended to glorify Abraham. One modern Jewish commentary on Genesis stated:

God Himself was indebted to Abraham because,
until he proclaimed Him as Master, the purpose
of Creation had been frustrated. . . . What was
more, he would be father to a nation that

would carry on his mission of standing up to
skeptics and enemies until the day when all
would acknowledge its [creation's] message
and accept its teaching. Of course, Abraham
could be called master of mankind because,
whether they realized it or not, they owed their
existence to him. But that was not all. God
called him *My master,* because he had presented God with a gift that even He, in His infinite power, could not fashion for Himself. For
even God cannot guarantee that man's mind
and heart would choose truth over evil, light
over darkness, spirit over flesh, love of God
over love of pleasure, recognition that the
Master is God and not whatever inexorable
force happens to find favor in the eyes of any
current generation of non-believers (*Bereishis,*
Vol. 1, p. 376 [1988])

The glorification of Abraham led to the
doctrine that personal salvation was possible
through keeping Moses' Law and *participa-
tion in the merits of Abraham.* That is, God
owed such a great debt to Abraham that
Abraham's merits were endlessly available to
make up for any personal failures on the part
of his descendants!

Christ decisively rejected any such
claim, for Genesis clearly teaches that
Abraham was saved by faith rather than by
works. God accepted the sinner Abraham's
faith in place of a righteousness he did not
have, and his faith was credited to him *as if it
were* righteousness.

*Abraham as the prototype man of faith
(Rom. 4).* In arguing for a salvation won for
us by Jesus Christ and appropriated by
faith, the apostle Paul pointed back to
Abraham.

What shall we say that Abraham our father has
found according to the flesh? For if Abraham
was justified by works, he has something to
boast about, but not before God. For what does
the Scripture say? "Abraham believed God, and
it was accounted to him for righteousness." Now
to him who works, the wages are not counted as
grace but as debt. But to him who does not work

but believes on Him who justifies the ungodly, his faith is accounted for righteousness.

And not being weak in faith, he did not consider his own body, already dead (since he was about a hundred years old), and the deadness of Sarah's womb. He did not waver at the promise of God through unbelief, but was strengthened in faith, giving glory to God, and being fully convinced that what He had promised He was also able to perform. And therefore "it was accounted to him for righteousness." Now it was not written for his sake alone that it was imputed to him, but also for us. It shall be imputed to us who believe in Him who raised up Jesus our Lord from the dead, who was delivered up because of our offenses, and was raised because of our justification (Rom. 5:1–5,19–25).

Paul's point is that *faith in God's promises* has always been the key to a personal relationship with God (see also Gal. 3:6–14). This truth, lost in first-century Judaism, is clearly established in Abraham's experience with God. Abraham's true offspring are not his biological descendants but rather those who have an Abraham-like faith in the God who makes wonderful promises to humankind.

Abraham's role as one of Scripture's greatest—in the sense of significant—men is firmly established. Abraham received covenant promises that revealed God's fixed purposes and plans. In responding to God's promises with faith, Abraham showed us the way to a personal relationship with God.

A "contradiction" (James 2)? One passage in Scripture seems to contradict Paul's emphasis on salvation by faith. The apostle James also looked back to Abraham, but he emphasized Abraham's works! In chapter 2 of his New Testament book, James wrote,

Was not Abraham our father justified by works when he offered Isaac his son on the altar? Do you see that faith was working together with his works, and by works faith was made perfect? And the Scripture was fulfilled which says, "Abraham believed God, and it was accounted to him for righteousness." And he was called the friend of God. You see then that a man is justified by works, and not by faith only (James 2:21–24).

The apparent conflict is resolved when we realize that James was contrasting two kinds of "faith," one of which exists as mere intellectual assent. James pointed out that the demons also believe in God—and tremble (2:19). No, the kind of faith the Bible calls for is *trust*, a true commitment of oneself to God.

The question James asked is how can one justify a claim to have this kind of faith? Indeed, how can God Himself show that Abraham had a "trust" kind of faith so that He was right in counting it for righteousness? The answer James gave is simple: true faith works. A true trust in God will be expressed in the believer's daily life.

Here James pointed to one incident in Abraham's life—his willingness to sacrifice his son Isaac in response to God's command—as evidence that Abraham's faith was real. A claim that any man has faith, whether the claim is made by God or by the individual, is justified [vindicated, shown to be true] by his actions. For faith produces works.

In this brief paragraph, James gave us a key to use in studying Abraham's life. Abraham, the prototype man of faith, had to learn faith's walk step by step. He had no Scriptures to refer to, no believing parent to serve as a model. And so day by day, event by event, Abraham had to learn how to live out his faith. This is exciting for us, because you and I as men today do have a model—in Abraham! We can walk with him and learn from him how to build a faith lifestyle of our own.

ABRAHAM'S LIFE OF FAITH

First steps of faith (Gen. 12—15). Faith usually isn't something that springs into existence full-blown. This was certainly true in Abraham's case. Abraham's first steps of faith were faltering.

Abraham left Ur (Gen. 12:1–5). Genesis 12:1–3 harks back to a time when Abram lived in Ur, then a major and cosmopolitan city. There God had given Abram His wonderful covenant promises, and there God had commanded:

> Get out of your country,
> From your family
> And from your father's house
> To a land that I will show you.
>   (Gen. 12:1)

Abram did leave Ur. But Genesis 11 tells us that rather than go "from your family," Abram brought his family along (11:31)! And rather than go directly to the land God would show him, Abram settled in Haran until his father Terah died. Even then when Abram set out for Canaan, he brought his nephew Lot along.

Abram's first steps of faith were faltering ones, and his obedience to God was incomplete. Abram simply could not find the courage to set out alone in complete dependence on God. Abram tried so hard to hold on to the dear and the familiar.

Letting go is hard for us, too. What do we struggle to hold on to despite God's call? What are we afraid to release—that we might learn to rely on God alone? Whatever it is, the day will come when we, like Abram, do set out to complete our journey of faith. How good to see that despite Abram's failure, God's commitment to him remained firm. However long you and I may delay, God will remain committed to us, too.

God added promise to promise (Gen. 12:6–8). It is significant that the promise "to your descendants I will give this land" was not added to the covenant until Abram actually arrived in Canaan. God has more for us than we can imagine. Yet, we'll not discover the full riches of His provision until we act in faith and respond to God's call.

Abram responded to circumstances rather than wait on God's Word (Gen. 12:10). God had sent Abram to Canaan. But when the rains ceased to fall and a famine developed, Abram hurried off to Egypt in search of food. Abram reacted to circumstances rather than inquire concerning God's will.

God may guide us through circumstances. However, God expects us to use common sense in making decisions. God had specifically led Abram to Canaan, and God had not told Abram to leave.

We're naturally tempted to wonder, should things go wrong, if God has really led us into a difficult situation. But such situations are often intended to increase our faith, and it is important for those learning to walk by faith to discover that God has a solution already planned.

In this case, Abram relied on himself rather than God. And this led him into potential disaster.

Abram was gripped by fear (12:11–20). When Abram entered Egypt he became afraid. His wife Sarai was still beautiful, and he feared that some powerful Egyptian would kill him in order to possess her. Abram's solution was to beg Sarai to lie about their relationship, and claim that she was merely his sister.

Unrealistic fears are one sign that we have strayed away from God's will. Another is a strong temptation to do wrong—whatever our motive may be.

In this case, God protected Sarai and Abram from the possible consequences of his lie. God may well protect us as well. But how much better to remain in our Canaan rather than hurry to some Egypt when troubles come.

Abram risked being gracious to others (Gen. 13). When Abram was still in Ur, he built up the herds and flocks that were the wealth of nomads. As Abram and Lot now wandered through Canaan, it became clear that their herds were simply too large for them to remain together. As the eldest, Abram had the right to take his pick of the land when they separated. Instead, Abram gave Lot first choice. Lot selfishly (and foolishly) chose the verdant Jordan River valley where the cities of Sodom and Gomorrah lay.

Abram had risked offering Lot first choice, and his nephew had taken advantage of him. But shortly afterward God appeared to Abram and promised, "All the land which you see I give to you and your descendants forever" (13:15). Abram learned that making himself vulnerable was no risk at all, for God was for him. Whatever he lost, God would repay many fold.

This is an important lesson to learn early in our Christian life. We, too, can trust God. Rather than act in a self-protective way, we can risk showing concern for others. Even should others take advantage of us, God will bless.

Abram rescued Lot (Gen. 14). Archaeology has documented the route taken by the raiding kings described in this chapter, and documented the natural resources they sought to obtain. In this case, the kings also stripped Sodom and Gomorrah of their wealth and their populations, taking Abram's nephew Lot captive as well.

Abram immediately set out to rescue Lot, and succeed in retrieving all the goods and people of the fallen cities. When the king of Sodom offered to turn the recovered wealth of his city over to Abram, Abram refused. "I have raised my hand to the LORD, God Most High, the Possessor of heaven and earth, that I will take nothing . . . lest you should say, 'I have made Abram rich'" (Gen. 14:22–23).

Abram showed himself not only ready to depend on God completely, but he was also concerned for God's reputation. Abram wanted the world to see that any blessing he experienced came from God, not from favor shown by others.

The promise formalized (Gen. 15). God's response to Abram's fresh affirmation of faith was to appear to Abram again, telling Abram not to be afraid and saying, "I am your shield, and your exceeding great

Abraham failed as a husband when he begged Sarah to pretend that they were not married and then let her be taken into the king's household.

❖

reward" (15:1). In turning his back on Sodom's wealth, Abram had lost nothing. God would guard him. No reward on earth could compare with what God had planned for him.

Abram's response was a complaint. What could possibly have any value to Abram, seeing he still had no son? God made an utterly amazing promise to this aged, childless man. "Look now toward heaven, and count the stars if you are able to number them. . . . So shall your descendants be" (Gen. 15:5). And Abram responded with total and complete trust in God. He believed God.

In this we see how much Abram has grown in his walk of faith. From a man hesitant and uncertain about relying fully on God, Abram has been freed by his trust in God to be vulnerable to his nephew, bold in confronting danger, and more concerned with God's glory than with earthly wealth.

Abram has come to have complete faith that God can and will do the impossible for him!

The message for us is a wonderful one. Our young faith may falter as Abram's did. But as the years pass and we experience more and more of God's goodness, our faith, like Abram's, will grow. The doubts that trouble us will dissipate, to be replaced by an unshakable confidence in the Lord.

Challenges to a mature faith (Gen. 16—24). One of the things that we learn from Abraham's life is that faith is no guarantee of a stress-free existence. In fact, men of faith experience just as many if not more trials than others. This was certainly true for Abram.

The challenge of awaiting God's timing (Gen. 16). When Abram and Sarah had been in Canaan for ten years, Sarah began to urge her husband to seek a child through a surrogate. It was common in Mesopotamia two thousand years before Christ for marriage contracts to include a provision that should a wife not produce an heir within as little as two years, she should procure a servant girl who would serve as a surrogate to be impregnated by her husband. Sarai had waited ten years, and she had ceased menstruating. So Abram gave in to her urgings, and had sex with Sarai's maid Hagar, who almost immediately became pregnant.

The child Hagar bore Abram was named Ishmael, and although Abram loved him, he was not destined to inherit the covenant. Once again Abram had run ahead of God, and the consequences were disastrous. For the Islamic peoples trace their roots back to Ishmael, and the conflict between Arab and Jew has been bitter indeed.

Even those whose faith is great need to learn to wait on God. Sensing His timing, and resisting the temptation to run ahead of Him, is a challenge indeed.

The challenge of testifying to the impossible (Gen. 17:1–9). Thirteen years passed before God spoke to Abram again. This time He promised specifically that Sarah would bear

Abram a son. At that time God also told Abram, "your name shall be called Abraham" (17:5).

It must have been difficult enough for the childless Abram to bear a name that meant "exalted father." But to have his name changed to Abraham, "father of a multitude," must have seemed a burden. In a culture where a man's name was expected to reflect something of his essence, for a childless man nearly a hundred years old to be called Abraham was an object of ridicule. Yet from this point on, Abram *is* Abraham. We can imagine him returning to his tents and announcing the change to all. Abraham believed God. And He was willing to bear the ridicule in the firm confidence that God would vindicate him in due time.

Today, we live in a world that laughs at the most basic truths taught in Scripture and at Christians' moral commitments. Like Abraham we are called to testify boldly to what seems impossible to most, in the sure and settled belief that God will vindicate us too, in His own time.

The challenge of maintaining unity (Gen. 17:9–27). On this occasion, the last statement of His covenant promises, God instituted the rite of circumcision. Throughout the Old Testament era, circumcision remained a vital symbol of membership in the covenant community.

Abraham's challenge and that of his offspring was to see himself as a member in a community of faith. Relationship with God, while personal, is not merely individual. The faith that bonds us to God bonds us to all others who profess the same allegiance. If we are to grow to maturity we need to commit ourselves to develop nurturing relationships with other believers, for worship, fellowship, and ministry.

The challenge of appropriate prayer (Gen. 18). When God next visited Abraham, this time as the Angel of the Lord and accompanied by two angels, it was to inform him that within the year Sarah would bear the promised son. God also informed Abraham that Sodom and Gomorrah were about to be judged. For fascinating insights into the role of investigator angels and the place of angels in carrying out divine judgment, see the companion volume, *Every Angel and Demon in the Bible* (1998).

The announcement troubled Abraham. His concern was expressed in a series of prayers. Abraham did not object to God judging sin, but Abraham was worried that some who were innocent might die with the guilty. This would tarnish God's reputation. Abraham won a promise from God that if even ten good men could be found in Sodom and Gomorrah, God would withhold judgment. In fact, only one good man could be found in the cities: Lot. God saw to it that Lot and his family were brought out before He destroyed the cities.

We're reminded of several things about prayer in this incident. We're reminded that our prayers are to be driven by a desire to see God glorified. And we're reminded that our prayers for others are welcome. God has a far deeper love for them than we do.

The challenge of continuing temptation to sin (Gen. 20). Abraham's faith had matured. But Abraham remained a sinner, subject to the pull of his old nature. This is revealed in another incident. Again, fearing that he might be killed for the sake of his wife, Abraham asked Sarah to lie about their relationship. Again, God protected Abraham. But Scripture records Abraham's confession—and his weakness. "I thought, surely the fear of God is not in this place" (20:11).

How easy it is for us to look away from God for a moment and be overwhelmed by circumstances. Had Abraham taken a moment to consider, he would have realized that whether or not the people he feared respected God, God was present there. We are not to be confident because others believe in God but because we know God is ever present with us.

The challenge of personal heartbreak (Gen. 21:1–14). Isaac, the child of Abraham and Sarah, had now been born and, at age three

or four, was being weaned. At the celebration marking this transition from infant to child, Isaac's half-brother Ishmael teased Isaac. Sarah exploded and insisted that Abraham send Ishmael and his mother away.

Abraham refused, not only because such an act was morally wrong and legally wrong in that culture, but also because Abraham loved his son Ishmael (Gen. 21:11). Only when God confirmed that this was His will as well as Sarah's did Abraham consent to send Ishmael away.

The separation from his son broke Abraham's heart. All too many today, in our age of broken families, share Abraham's pain. Yet, God's words to Abraham can comfort us. God promised, "I will also make a nation of the son of the bondwoman, because he is your seed" (Gen. 21:13). Abraham could no longer care for his son, but God would take care of Ishmael. When events beyond our control shatter a precious relationship, we need to remember those words. We may not be able to be with our loved one, but God is with him or her. If for no other reason than that the loved one is ours, God will care for him or her.

The challenge of surrendering all (Gen. 22). All Abraham had left was his son Isaac. But when Isaac was a young teenager, God claimed Isaac too. He commanded Abraham to take his son to Mount Moriah [later to be known as Mount Zion], and to sacrifice Isaac there.

The text tells us that Abraham "rose early in the morning" (22:3) and set out with his son. How stunning! Despite the awful import of the command, Abraham did not wait to obey. What a difference from the man whose reluctant journey to Canaan had taken so many years!

Years later, the writer of Hebrews recalled Abraham's words to two servants who accompanied father and son on their journey: "The lad and I will go yonder and worship, and we will come back to you" (Gen. 22:5). The New Testament interprets this in a fascinating way. Abraham's faith in

Abraham was willing to offer his son Isaac because he was convinced that God could raise Isaac from the dead if that were necessary to keep His promises.

❖

God's promise that "in Isaac your seed shall be called" was so firm that he concluded "God was able to raise him up, even from the dead" (Heb. 11:18).

At times, we too are called to surrender what is nearest and dearest to us. Faith reminds us that, no matter how great the loss may seem, God will never take away more than He gives.

The challenge of the death of loved ones (Gen. 23). Sarah, who had shared Abraham's life for well over half a century, now died. Abraham went about the sad task of arranging for the burial of this one he had loved so long. Of all the ills human beings are subject to, the loss of loved ones may be the most painful. Yet faith looks beyond the

loss to a grand reunion in God's future, dawning day.

The challenge of relying on others (Gen. 24). It was now time for Isaac to wed. Abraham, unwilling for his son to marry one of the women of Canaan, sent the most responsible servant in his household on a mission to find a bride for Isaac. Quieting the servant's doubts, Abraham quietly said, "The LORD God of heaven, who took me from my father's house and from the land of my family . . . He will send His angel before you" (24:7).

It's hard for most men to delegate responsibility. We feel confident in what we do ourselves but less sure of others. Abraham's example helps us understand how to approach situations in which we must rely on others. First, choose the right person. Abraham selected "the oldest servant of his house, who ruled over all that he had" (Gen. 24:2). Second, instruct him carefully. Abraham made his expectations clear (Gen. 24:3–4). And third, Abraham trusted God to work in and through the man he had chosen (Gen. 24:7).

We need to be wise in who we select to take on responsibilities for us, and careful to prepare them. But then we need to trust God to work through them.

The challenge of aging and death (Gen. 25:1–11). Abraham's last challenge was to face his own mortality. As Abraham drew near the end of his life, he was forced to realize that his day was past. His descendants would play their part in fulfilling God's purposes, but Abraham's moment on history's stage was drawing to an end.

It's hard for men of action to come to grips with inactivity. It's hard for those who have done great things to realize that nothing remains for them to do. As life draws near its end, each of us must focus anew on our relationship with God, and realize afresh that knowing Him is the most significant thing of all.

CHALLENGES TO A MAN'S MATURE FAITH

- Awaiting God's timing
- Testifying to the impossible
- Maintaining unity with others
- Praying appropriately
- Resisting continuing temptations
- Trusting despite heartbreak
- Being willing to surrender all
- Loss of loved ones
- Relying on others
- Facing personal mortality

EXPLORING ABRAHAM'S RELATIONSHIPS

As we read the chapters in Genesis devoted to Abraham, we can clearly see that he had several significant relationships.

Abraham's relationship with Lot *(Gen. 12— 14; 18; 19).* Lot was Abraham's nephew, the son of Abraham's brother Haran. Haran had died years before in Ur (Gen. 11:27–28); it's likely that Abraham looked on his nephew almost as a son. It's no wonder that despite God's command to leave family behind, Abraham took Lot with him when he came to Canaan.

Competition develops (Gen. 13). In letting his emotions rather than God guide him, Abraham did his nephew no favor. Lot had inherited his herds and flocks along with servants to care for them. The trouble was that when Abraham and Lot traveled together, "the land was not able to support them" (Gen. 13:6). The conflict began with the herdsmen as they competed for grass and water, but soon the hard feelings infected Lot's and Abraham's relationship too (Gen. 13:8).

Lot's selfish choice (Gen. 13). Abraham took the initiative to restore peace. In doing so, he surrendered his rights as eldest and offered Lot first choice of the whole land. Lot looked over the land and selfishly chose the best for himself: "all the plain of Jordan . . . well watered everywhere" (Gen. 13:10). This left the less desirable highlands for Abraham, but Abraham neither complained nor resented Lot's choice. What neither grasped then was that the men of the cities of the plain "were exceedingly wicked and sinful against the LORD" (13:13). In disobeying God and bringing Lot with him to Canaan, Abraham had inadvertently placed his nephew in a danger neither could imagine.

Abraham's loyal love (Gen. 14). The first hint of danger came when raiding kings overwhelmed the cities of Sodom and Gomorrah and took their populations captive. When Abraham heard that Lot was among the captives, he quickly organized a nighttime raid that startled the enemy into flight. Lot was rescued from the most obvious danger, and then he returned to Sodom!

Lot's compromise (Gen. 18; 19). The real danger, however, was moral. Lot had settled among a wicked and immoral people. He was wealthy and comfortable, but the society he lived in was corrupt. Yet Lot, knowing the character of the men of the land, chose to remain among them, not imagining that God was about to destroy the wicked cities.

Abraham's intercessory prayer (Gen. 18). When God told Abraham of His intent to destroy Sodom and Gomorrah, Abraham must have thought immediately of Lot. Although not stated in Scripture, Abraham's concern for Lot must have been in Abraham's mind as he pleaded with God on behalf of any "righteous" among the wicked men God was determined to destroy. God too was concerned for Lot, and the angels sent to investigate Sodom's sins carried Lot and his family to safety. Yet in the process, Lot lost his wife and all his wealth. The riches Lot had compromised his convictions to enjoy were burned to ashes, and he was reduced to poverty, living with his two daughters in a cave.

Genesis makes it clear that Abraham was intensely loyal to Lot and remained loyal to the end. Even when Lot behaved selfishly, Abraham was committed to his nephew. Loyalty is an admirable trait in any man, but in this case, Abraham's loyalty to Lot had moved him to disobey God's command. In the end, Abraham's loyalty did Lot far more harm than good.

You and I may be so loyal to our sons or daughters that we act protectively even when we know deep down that we should release them to mature on their own. Should God lead us to release our loved ones to find His path for them without us, we need to let them go.

Abraham's relationship with Sarah *(Gen. 13—21).* Sarah was Abraham's companion for many decades. Yet only four incidents involving her directly are recorded in the text.

Abraham's shocking requests (Gen. 13; 20). We're told of two incidents in which Abraham asked Sarah to lie about their relationship. In each case, the lie resulted in Sarah's being taken from Abraham's tents and installed in a pagan ruler's harem. In each case, God protected Sarah's virtue despite Abraham's betrayal of their relationship.

It is hard to view Abraham's actions, motivated as they were by fear, as anything but betrayal. Husbands are supposed to love their wives, to protect and sacrifice for them. Abraham asked his *wife* to sacrifice for *him.* Surely Abraham's actions damaged their relationship, robbing Sarah of trust in her husband, and burdening Abraham with a load of shame.

Sarah's suggestion of a surrogate (Gen. 16:1–6). After years of childlessness, Sarah urged Abraham to give her a child through a surrogate, her maid Hagar. This was common practice in the ancient East, and any child Hagar bore would legally be considered Sarah's (see 16:2).

Strikingly, this incident is reported immediately after the account in Genesis 15 in which God reaffirmed His promise of descendants to Abraham. Did Abraham share what God had told him with Sarah? If he had, wouldn't the two have found grace to wait for God to act, rather than taking matters into their own hands? We cannot know, but the juxtaposition of these two stories is suggestive indeed. Sarah, without the reassurance God had given Abraham, panicked. But rather than relate his experience to his wife to give her perspective, Abraham "heeded [her] voice" (16:2).

Nothing turned out as expected. When Hagar became pregnant, she showed contempt for Sarah, as the couple's childlessness was clearly not due to Abraham's impotence. The hostility between Sarah and Hagar poisoned any possibility that Sarah might love and accept Hagar's child as her own. And Sarah blamed Abraham, saying, "My wrong be upon you!" (16:5).

Sarah's angry demand (Gen. 21). When Ishmael, the son Hagar bore Abraham, was a teenager, Sarah had her own son, Isaac. When Ishmael teased [NKJV "scoffing"] Isaac, Sarah demanded that Ishmael and Hagar be sent away. This time Abraham refused. Abraham truly cared for his son Ishmael. Only when God intervened and told Abraham to do as Sarah had said did Abraham agree.

In this case, despite Sarah's selfish motives, she was in harmony with God's purposes. Isaac and Ishmael represented two contrasting principles: promise, which depends entirely on God's work in and for us; and works, which rely on what human beings can do for themselves. Only the miracle-child Isaac could truly symbolize the outcome of Abraham's faith in God.

Ultimately Abraham's relationship with Sarah can only be described as flawed but fruitful. We cannot doubt that a true love existed between these two saints, or that their love enabled each to overlook flaws in the other. However, we cannot explain away Abraham's cowardly sacrifice of Sarah to his fears. Yet, Sarah out of love was willing to risk herself to protect her husband. Concern for his childless wife as well as his own desire for offspring led Abraham to have sex with Hagar. Sarah had desperately wanted a son; Abraham was willing to take this means to give her one. Yet Abraham was wrong not to share more openly with Sarah about his meetings with God.

As in most marriages, each spouse hurt the other, not intentionally, but nevertheless painfully. And as in most marriages, each

forgave, and Abraham and Sarah continued to build a life together. Perhaps this is the most basic message for us from Abraham's relationship with Sarah. Their marriage wasn't perfect, but they remained committed to each other. The life they shared was a fruitful one indeed.

Whatever our spouse's flaws, we need to remember that we, too, are imperfect, and trust that through mutual forgiveness and commitment our marriages will be fruitful too.

Abraham's relationship with Ishmael (*Gen. 21; 25:7–8*). Our insight into Abraham's relationship with Ishmael comes first from chapter 21. Abraham was eighty-six when Ishmael was born (Gen. 16:16) and had fourteen years to bond with his boy before Isaac's birth. And bond Abraham did! When Sarah demanded that he send the then nineteen-year-old Ishmael away, Abraham was distressed "because of his son" (Gen. 21:11). When God confirmed Sarah's demand and told Abraham to send Ishmael away, Abraham must have been heartbroken. Yet, he did as God said. And God promised that He Himself would watch over Ishmael and make him a great people for Abraham's sake.

In this day of easy divorce and broken homes, many fathers share Abraham's pain. They are separated from their children, for whatever reason. And not only do many of them hurt; many must wonder whether their children will ever understand or forgive. In such cases one can only follow Abraham's course and trust the children into God's loving hands. And this is good. Yet Scripture adds a word of additional comfort.

Years later, when Abraham died, the Bible tells us that "his sons Isaac and Ishmael buried him in the cave of Machpelah" (Gen. 25:9). Ishmael had understood after all! In the years after Sarah's death, father and son must have been reconciled. What a relief to know that if we continue to love our children, in time they will understand.

Abraham paid in pain for the lack of faith shown when he fathered a son by Hagar, Sarah's maid. Later his heart was broken when he had to send this son, Ishmael, away.

Abraham's relationship with Isaac (*Gen. 22*). Genesis tells us that God tested Abraham telling him to "take now . . . your only son Isaac, whom you love" (Gen. 22:2). Abraham was to take Isaac to Mount Moriah (Zion) and sacrifice him there.

The description of the incident records touching words exchanged by the two. After reaching the foot of the mountain, Abraham and his son set out together, bringing wood for the burnt offering and a knife. Isaac looked up at his father trustingly and asked, "Where is the lamb for a burnt offering?" Abraham could only reply: "God will provide for Himself the lamb."

Reaching the top of the mountain, Abraham built an altar and then bound his son Isaac, and laid him on the altar. Isaac trustingly let his father tie him, and then looked up as Abraham picked up the knife. Only then did a voice from heaven call Abraham and point out a ram caught in a nearby thicket. God had provided the sacrifice. Abraham had demonstrated his trust in God—and Isaac had demonstrated trust in his father.

We can find many lessons in this brief story. Abraham had shown himself willing to surrender what he loved most should God require it. Only as complete a trust in God as Abraham's will enable us freely to give up to God what we love, confident that He has something better in mind for us.

Isaac also demonstrated a remarkable trust in Abraham. Isaac knew his father loved him. A healthy father-son relationship marked by love and trust makes the son's transition to trust in God a natural and easy one.

But the story of these two tells us even more about God. In the end, God could not ask Abraham to sacrifice his only and dearly loved son. Yet, one day God would lead His own beloved Son to Calvary's cross, and Jesus Christ would die there for us. For Christ there would be no reprieve. God the Father would fully experience the pain that for a few brief days Abraham had looked forward to but from which he had been spared.

ABRAHAM: AN EXAMPLE FOR TODAY

Abraham is truly one of Scripture's towering figures. Yet he lived his life as a nomad far from any ancient seat of power. What made Abraham so significant was not, as some have suggested, his "invention" of monotheism, but the fact that the God of the universe spoke to Abraham—and Abraham responded with faith.

Abraham's long life was marked by challenges that required him to exercise faith. At times, Abraham's faith failed. Yet, we can see the growth in his faith as Abraham experienced more and more of God.

Abraham's relationships involved long-term commitments to the others in his life. While Abraham may not have been wise in his relationships with either Lot or Sarah, he most surely was loyal. Perhaps considering our many failings, loyalty and commitment are the most important gifts we can give to those we love.

All in all, Abraham was a man to be respected and admired. We can hardly describe him more appropriately than did the writer of the Book of Hebrews, who said in chapter 11:

By faith Abraham obeyed when he was called to go out to the place which he would receive as an inheritance. And he went out, not knowing where he was going. By faith he dwelt in the land of promise as in a foreign country, dwelling in tents with Isaac and Jacob, the heirs with him of the same promise; for he waited for the city which has foundations, whose builder and maker is God (Heb 11:8–10).

What lessons can a man take away from a study of Abraham's life? Certainly the following:

- Trust in God and His promises is the only sure foundation on which a man can build his life.

- As we meet each new challenge, we need consciously to rely on God for guidance and for strength.

- We need to remain aware of our fallibility, and live humbly in the sight of others and of God.

- Like Abraham, we need to invest in our long-term relationships with spouse, family, and friends. We must set aside time and energy to nurture our relationships with those who are important in our lives.

BUILDERS OF A NATION

MOSES

Scripture references:
Exodus-Deuteronomy;
The Gospels, Hebrews 2; 11

Date:	*About 1520–1400 B.C.*
Name:	*Moses [MOH-zuhs;* *"drawn-out"]*
Greatest accomplishment:	*Moses was God's agent in delivering the Israelites from slavery in Egypt and in giving them His Law.*

MOSES' ROLE IN SCRIPTURE

We cannot praise Moses' significance too highly. Moses' name is mentioned some 850 times in the Old Testament in 787 verses. His name is found 80 times in the New Testament, in 79 verses. He is the traditional author of the first five books of the Bible and the dominant figure in four of them. His ministry during a definitive period of Old Testament history is absolutely unique.

Moses' role in Scripture can be summed up under four headings. Moses was a *miracle worker*, a channel through whom God's power was revealed to Israel, to Egypt, and to us today. Moses was the prototype *prophet*, a spokesman for God through whom God revealed Himself and His will. Moses was the *lawgiver*, who at Sinai recorded God's commandments and the precepts that were to shape the lives of the Israelites. And Moses was a *leader*, whose struggles with the Israelites and whose prayers to God for them both have encouraged and guided those in spiritual leadership ever since.

Without question, Moses is one of the dominant figures of the Old Testament and remains the central figure in Judaism to this day.

MOSES IN JUDAISM

In *The Book of Jewish Knowledge*, Nathan Ausubel writes of Moses:

To the persecuted Jewish people—rootless human beings feeling the need for emotional as well as physical security—Moses appeared as a powerful father-image. He was the indomitable, the wise, the righteous, the comforting father who had been protectingly, in times of crisis, like a shield and a buckler for their ancestors, the children of Israel, and had led them into freedom when they were slaves in Egypt. And whenever God had lost patience with them on account of their backsliding, Moses had stood between them and His wrath and had pleaded their wretched cause for them—his straying sheep. . . .

To this day, after thirty-two centuries, Moses remains an exemplar of social morality, law, and justice not only to the adherents of three world religions—Christianity, Islam, and Judaism—but also to countless millions of the religiously uncommitted or even downright skeptics and unbelievers. His greatness transcends the sectarian limits of theological dogma or institutional separation. By his intellectual power and moral will, and with his organizational genius to serve both, he was able to hammer a self-respecting people out of a brutalized conglomeration of former slaves. He taught them to abide by a system of morality and law—not a philosophical or utopian system like that described in Plato's theorizing blueprint for an ideal Republic of *superiors*, but one realistic and practical enough to enable a people who lived by it to cope with the daily problems of living; working, suffering and striving to create under it a happier and more just society of *equals*. Therein lies his achievement in the history of human progress (p. 306).

MOSES' LIFE AND TIMES

Moses was born into a family of Hebrew slaves. Some twenty years earlier, about 1540 B.C., West Semitic peoples known as the Hyksos had finally been driven from Egypt by Ahmose I. Before that, the Hyksos had supplanted the Egyptian rulers and had governed as pharaohs some one hundred years.

Boats made of bundles of papyrus reeds carried cargo on the Nile River from before the time of Moses well into New Testament times.

Perhaps partly because the Hebrews were also a Semitic people, Pharaoh intended to take no chances that the Israelites would support his enemy (see Ex. 1:10). Pharaoh enslaved the Israelites and set them to forced labor. He also determined to limit severely the Hebrew population, and ordered the midwives of Egypt to kill any male children born to the Israelites. When this attempt at population control failed, Pharaoh commanded "all his people" to see that every male Hebrew infant should be thrown in the River Nile.

Moses' childhood (Ex. 2:1-10). When Moses was born about 1520 B.C. his parents obeyed Pharaoh's command. Only they first placed their boy child in a basket-boat, woven of papyrus reeds! Every Sunday school child has heard the story of baby Moses found floating in his basket boat by Pharaoh's

Was this the princess who rescued Moses? *The Nelson Illustrated Bible Handbook* comments on the possibility:

It is possible that the daughter of Pharaoh who finds him is Hatshepsut, only living child of Thutmose I. . . .

As a woman, Hatshepsut could not take the throne in her own right. So she married a brother, born to one of her father's lesser wives. On his death, the throne passed to one of her younger brothers, who was then about 10. Hatshepsut seized the throne and ruled for another 22 years. After her death the long suppressed and bitter king, Thutmose II, ordered every mention of Hatshepsut obliterated. Throughout all Egypt her statues were defaced and her name chiseled from stone inscriptions. Undoubtedly Thutmose, who went on to become the greatest ruler in Egyptian history, would have hated Moses, and welcomed any excuse to kill him (p. 73).

daughter. Moses was adopted by the princess, who hired Moses' own mother as his wet nurse. As children in biblical times frequently were not weaned until age four, Moses would have heard the stories of his people from his mother during his most impressionable years. Later when Moses was an adult, he identified himself with the Israelites rather than the Egyptians and dreamed of freeing them from slavery.

Moses' education. As the adoptive child of an Egyptian princess, Moses would have received the best education Egypt had to offer. Interestingly, attendance records from the royal schools of the era list the names of other Semitic boys being trained for roles in Egypt's bureaucracy.

Moses' formal education would have lasted for about twelve years. Afterward, he would probably have received additional training in diplomacy and the military. Some have suggested that Moses was probably fluent in some four or five languages of the time.

A reference in Hebrews 11:24 speaks of Moses as "the son of Pharaoh's daughter." Some have speculated that this is in fact a title, reflecting the fact that in Egypt the royal line was passed through the daughter, rather than directly to the son. If Moses was considered the "son of Pharaoh's daughter" and was in line for the throne, we can understand why Moses would have received the best education Egypt had to offer!

Moses' rash act (Ex. 2:11-22). When Moses was forty, he noticed an Egyptian taskmaster brutalizing a Hebrew slave. Looking around to see that he was unobserved, Moses killed the Egyptian and hid his body.

Later when Moses tried to intervene in a dispute between two Hebrews, he discovered that the killing was known! Before long, word of what Moses had done came to Pharaoh, and the text says that Pharaoh "sought to kill Moses" (Ex. 2:15). It may well be that Moses' rash act had given the Pharaoh an excuse to rid himself of someone he already hated! At any rate, Moses realized his only hope was to flee. And he did.

Moses in the Sinai (Ex. 2:15–25). In the time of Moses, the Sinai Peninsula was largely

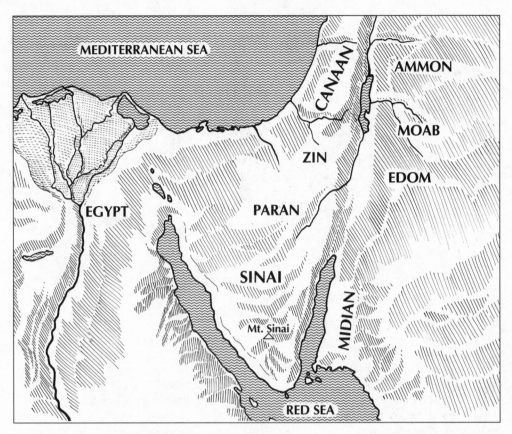

Moses wandered the Sinai desert as a shepherd, and later he led Israel to Mount Sinai, modern Jebel Musa.

❖

uninhabited, although the Egyptians had long mined it for semi-precious stones. In that desolate wilderness, Moses found a small group of Midianite shepherds whom he joined. In time, he married the daughter of Jethro, the Midianite clan and religious leader. Moses himself became a shepherd, and the text tells us that for the next forty years Moses "was content to live" there (Ex. 2:21).

For forty years, Moses lived the quiet life of a wilderness shepherd, so different from his life in the court of Egypt. During that forty years, Moses' dream of delivering his people died. His grand vision of himself gradually shrank until, finally humbled, Moses was fitted for the task God had in mind all along.

Moses' call by God (*Ex. 3—4*). When Moses was eighty years old, God appeared to him in a burning bush and commissioned Moses as His people's deliverer.

Reading the text, it's clear that Moses didn't want to go. "Who am I that I should go to Pharaoh, and that I should bring the children of Israel out of Egypt?" (3:11) was Moses' immediate response to the Lord. Rather than being unwilling, Moses was uncertain. He had at last become fully aware of his own inadequacies, and seeing his limitations more clearly, Moses was understandably hesitant. Even though God promised to go with Moses, Moses still made excuses. Moses wouldn't know what to say (Ex. 3:13). He didn't know enough about God to represent Him (Ex. 3:13). Moses was

Pharaoh's response to Moses' demand for freedom was to increase the workload of the Hebrew slaves.

sure that even the Israelites wouldn't believe him (Ex. 4:1). He was "slow of speech and slow of tongue" (Ex. 4:10). Despite the fact that God had an answer for every excuse, Moses begged, "O my LORD, please send by the hand of whomsoever else You may send" (4:13).

In this, Moses was very much like many of us today. We hesitate when called by God to act for Him; we fix our eyes on our inadequacies rather than on His sufficiency. The later accomplishments of Moses, who finally did obey the Lord, are a healthy reminder to you and me. We may be utterly correct in our assessment of our weaknesses, but to those whom God lends His strength, weaknesses are irrelevant. We are not to plead, "Send someone else." We are to respond, and set out in faith to obey.

Moses' confrontation of Pharaoh (Ex. 5—15). Moses finally responded to God's commission and did confront Pharaoh. The biblical text tells us that those who had sought Moses' life were now dead (Ex 4:19). The arrogant Pharaoh with whom Moses had to deal was likely a young man, filled with

himself and with the foolish confidence of youth.

The familiar story of the miracle plagues that finally drove Pharaoh to his knees is told in chapters 7—13. In the end, Pharaoh changed his mind once again about his slaves, and set out with his army to recapture the Israelites. This choice doomed the Egyptian forces, for they followed the Israelites into a sea whose waters God had parted, only to have the same waters close on the pursuing Egyptians.

For a detailed study of the plagues and associated miracles, see the companion book in this series, *Every Miracle and Wonder in the Bible.*

Moses as Lawgiver (Ex. 18—Deut.). Moses had succeeded in bringing some two and a half million Israelites out of Egypt (see Num. 1:46, which numbers only males of military age). God Himself provided a cloudy-fiery pillar that led the Israelites deep into the Sinai peninsula to Mount Sinai. It was there that Moses was given not only the Ten Commandments but also the various regulations that would govern the daily lives of the Israelites from that time forward. It is a mistake to think of "the Law" only as the Ten Commandments, for it also details worship regulations, criminal law, and civil law, defines acceptable sexual relationships and diet, and much more. Moses' role in the giving of the Law is so central that both Testaments frequently refer to the Sinai revelation as the "Law of Moses."

In this context, Moses is not only called a prophet, but He serves as the model prophet. Simply put, a *prophet* serves as God's spokesman, delivering a message from God to human beings. Deuteronomy 18 forbade Israel to consult with any occult source. There Moses promised that God would "raise up for [Israel] a Prophet like [Moses] from among their brethren, and will put My words in His mouth" (Deut. 18:18). The Prophet like Moses to whom this verse *refers* is Jesus Christ. Yet the verse also *relates* to the many prophets who, throughout Israel's history, appeared at critical times to serve as God's spokespersons.

In what way, however, were the prophetic ministries of Moses and Christ parallel? The revelation given through these two set sacred history on a new and unexpected course. The revelation given through Moses served as the basis for the founding of a people and a nation; a basis that established the identity of Old Testament Israel as God's own people. The revelation given through Jesus Christ, which supplanted the Mosaic revelation, served as the basis for the founding of another people of God; not a nation, but the very body of Christ in which we Christians find our identity as God's Own.

Moses as leader (Ex. 16—Deut.). In the Pentateuch, we discover a Moses who was a leader as well as a miracle worker, lawgiver, and prophet. In these aspects, Moses proved very human indeed. The people whom Moses led were troublesome and rebellious, and Moses felt all the frustration, anger, and

pain that can accompany the struggle to lead an unresponsive people. Yet, Moses remained faithful to his task, and frequently interceded with God on the Israelites' behalf. Moses' prayers on Israel's behalf merit intense study on their own, as a challenge and an encouragement for pastors and for parents.

For forty years, Moses led two generations of Israelites. Those who failed to respond to God and rebelled against Moses' leadership died in the wilderness outside the promised land. Moses then led their sons and daughters, a purified and responsive people, to the borders of the land God had promised to Abraham's offspring. There, finally, Moses died, but only after seeing from a distance the land he had dreamed of from childhood. Moses' dream had come true in the most unexpected way.

For forty years, Moses was a privileged prince of Egypt, picturing himself as his people's deliverer. For the next forty years, Moses was a humble shepherd isolated in an empty wilderness, finally aware of his own inadequacies. And for his last forty years, Moses was an agent of God on earth, accomplishing far more in his old age than he could ever have imagined. By God's grace and sovereign choice, Moses had become the miracle worker, lawgiver, prophet, and leader who towers over every other Old Testament character, the greatest of the Old Testament's great men.

EXPLORING MOSES' RELATIONSHIPS

The biblical account describes several sustained relationships maintained by Moses. Moses' mother had a significant impact in shaping Moses' sense of personal identity. He grew up seeing himself as a Hebrew rather than as a member of Egyptian royalty. Yet, we have no description of the interaction between mother and son. It is also clear that Moses' sister Miriam played a significant role in his life, not only during

Moses' infancy but also in his later ministry as a leader. [Miriam is discussed in depth in the companion volume in this series, *Every Woman in the Bible*.] We have much more information on Moses' relationship with his older brother, Aaron. That relationship is explored in the chapter on notable priests of the Old Testament (see page 140). Similarly, Moses' relationship to the young Egyptian Pharaoh of the Exodus will be explored in the article on that Pharaoh, on page 134. The two most important relationships, each of which receives extensive attention in the biblical text, must be examined here. These are Moses' relationship with God, and Moses' relationship with the Israelites.

MOSES' RELATIONSHIP WITH GOD

The relationship begins: the burning bush (*Ex. 3:1—4:17*). We might argue that Moses knew God before the incident at the burning bush. The stories of Abraham, Isaac, and Jacob and of their God that Moses had heard from his mother had such an impact on Moses that he identified with the Hebrew people despite his privileged position in the Egyptian royal family. Yet Moses' *personal* relationship with God clearly began when he was some 80 years old and was caring for sheep in the Sinai wilderness. There God spoke to him from a bush that burned yet was not consumed. And there three significant things occurred.

God commissioned Moses for his mission (*Ex. 3:6–10*). When God had identified Himself to Moses as the God of Abraham, Isaac, and Jacob, the Lord told Moses He had seen the oppression of His people and heard their cries. God revealed Himself to Moses at this time because He intended to deliver the Israelites and bring them home to the Promised Land. Moses must have been utterly nonplused when God told him, "Come now, therefore, and I will send you to Pharaoh that you may bring My people, the children of Israel, out of Egypt" (3:10).

God revealed His personal name to Moses (*3:11–22*). The forty years Moses had spent in the wilderness had taken away his native arrogance and pride as well as his early dream of being Israel's deliverer. Now when God appeared to commission Moses for the task he had once yearned to accomplish, Moses resisted. His self-effacing "Who am I that I should go to Pharaoh" (3:11) revealed a man who had come to face his inadequacies and to know himself all too well. The depth of his humbling is further revealed in the series of objections he raised during this conversation with God:

- "What shall I say to them" (3:13).
- "But suppose they will not believe me" (4:1).
- "O my Lord, I am not eloquent . . . I am slow of speech and slow of tongue" (4:10).
- "O my Lord, please send . . . whomever else You may send" (4:13).

God's initial response to the hesitant Moses was to promise to be with him, and then to reveal His personal name, Yahweh, which is represented in our English versions by "LORD." That most significant of God's biblical names, rendered "I AM" in our English text, may be better translated as "The One Who Is Always Present." Moses and all Israel were about to come to know God as the Ever-Present One whose closeness guaranteed their release. The events about to take place in Egypt and at the Red Sea would forever shape Israel's and the world's image of God. No wonder God told Moses, "This is My name forever" (3:15). [For a thorough exposition of the significance of the name Yahweh, see the companion volume in this series, *Every Name and Title of God in the Bible*.]

Moses would succeed, not because of his personal gifts or endowments, but because God was with Him. The humility Moses had learned during the forty years he had been in the desert would enable him to remain completely dependent on God. That dependence on the Lord was the key to Moses' greatness.

What a wonderful lesson here for each of us. Spiritual significance is not a matter of our abilities, our talents, or even our gifts. God can and will use those who have learned humility and who as a consequence remain totally, trustingly dependent on Him.

God equipped Moses for his ministry (Ex. 4:1–17). The essential equipment for any successful ministry is a dependence on God, expressed as a ready response to His leading. Moses however was given two unusual gifts.

The first was knowledge of what God intended to do. The Lord plainly told Moses that Egypt's Pharaoh would resist releasing his slaves and that the Lord would then "stretch out My hand and strike Egypt with all My wonders" (Ex. 3:19–20). It is fascinating that with both Abraham and Moses God announced His intentions beforehand. Just as fascinating is that through Abraham and Moses God announced His intentions *to us.* The great "I will" statements to Abraham set the course of redemption history, and God's promise of a Prophet like Moses set the stage for the coming of Christ and His totally unexpected revelation of the cross and Christianity.

But God also equipped Moses with two simple "signs." This word for miracles emphasizes that such interventions by God authenticate both His presence and His prophet. The word reminds us that when God so chooses, He can intervene in our world in ways that simply cannot be explained by reference to either trickery or to natural law's reliance on cause and effect. The two simple signs God gave Moses—the ability to turn his staff into a snake and back to staff again, and the ability to turn his arm leprous and restore it to health—were enough to convince both Moses and the Israelites of God's presence. It would take far greater and more devastating signs to convince Pharaoh, but these signs, too, would be present when the occasion required.

This is worth meditating on. God goes with His own. He equips us with whatever we need to accomplish His purpose in our lives.

Moses' relationship with God is tested *(Ex. 5:1—7:7).* Moses' first approach to Pharaoh on behalf of Israel proved to be a disaster. The young Pharaoh was understandably contemptuous of Moses and of his God. In the ancient world, one measure of the power of a people's deities was assumed to be that people's relationship with other nations. At the time Egypt was not only wealthy but also the dominant power in the region. The Hebrews were an oppressed population of slaves. Weighed in Pharaoh's balance, the God of slaves seemed weak and feeble indeed.

In utter contempt, Pharaoh increased the burden placed on the Hebrews, causing the Israelites to accuse Moses of putting "a sword" (5:21) in Pharaoh's hand to kill them. Moses, stunned by this turn of events, turned to God with a complaint of his own. "Lord, why have You brought trouble on this people? Why is it You have sent me? For since I came to Pharaoh to speak in Your name, he has done evil to this people; neither have You delivered Your people at all" (Ex. 5:22,23). The pattern seen here would be followed throughout Moses' last forty years. When things seemed to go wrong, the Israelites would murmur and complain to Moses. Moses would take his own frustrations and uncertainties to God (see Ex. 17:1).

In this, the Israelites sinned, while Moses showed respect for God. The Israelites failed to look beyond circumstances and realize that a sovereign God had His hand on every event. Moses understood that however he might feel about an event and however in the dark he might be about God's purposes,

God *was* at work in the situation. The Israelites' failure to look to God as Moses consistently did is a stunning revelation of their spiritual insensitivity, while Moses' immediate acknowledgment of God's responsibility for what was happening demonstrated a true faith in the Lord.

Here, too, is a vital lesson for Christians today. Events will often test the quality of our relationship with God. It will be so easy to complain about others or about our circumstances. All too often we complain *to* others. This is an ungodly response. The godly follow Moses' example, recognize God's hand in events, and bring their complaints to Him.

God responded to Moses' complaint by giving him the perspective he needed. Pharaoh would resist, but God would "multiply My signs and wonders in the land of Egypt" (Ex. 7:3) and so convince Israel, Egypt, and future generations that He, the Lord, surely is God.

Moses' relationship with God is revealed (Ex. 7:8–15). Moses had been called by God and given a mission. He was to win the release of the Israelite slaves. In a most significant interchange the Lord told Moses, "See, I have made you as God to Pharaoh, and Aaron your brother shall be your prophet. You shall speak all that I command you" (7:1–2).

This statement was made in response to yet another of Moses' expressions of inadequacy: "Behold, I am of uncircumcised lips, and how shall Pharaoh heed me" (6:30). God's answer was that Moses would represent Him to Pharaoh. Through Moses' words and actions, God would be revealed to the disbelieving Egyptians.

Moses did represent God before Pharaoh, and when Pharaoh ridiculed the God Moses represented, devastating plagues struck Egypt at Moses' word. Those same plagues departed at Moses' word. The reality of Moses' relationship with God was displayed in the works God performed through Him. The reality of Moses' relationship with God was revealed. Through His relationship with Moses, God revealed Himself.

This remains true today. God *will* communicate His reality through the walk and the words of believers who love Him and live close to Him. Spiritual power and effectiveness are as dependent today on maintaining a close relationship with the Lord as they were in Moses' time. When we maintain this relationship, God will be able to use us as He did Moses. He will use us, not to carry out Moses' mission, but rather to fulfill His purpose in *our* lives. The reality of our relationship with God will be revealed in the works God does in us; works that in truth will reveal Him.

Moses' relationship with God transforms (Ex. 32:1–14). Moses led the Israelites away from Egypt into the Sinai peninsula. When they reached Mount Sinai, God gave Israel the law through Moses. Exodus 32 tells one of the darker stories of the period. While Moses was on Mount Sinai receiving the Ten Commandments, the Israelites camped on the plains below Sinai. They came to Aaron, Moses' brother, and demanded: "Make us gods that shall go before us; for as for this Moses, the man who brought us up out of the land of Egypt, we do not know what has become of him" (Ex. 32:1). Aaron gave in to them and fashioned a golden calf. The Israelites imagined an invisible deity sat astride this calf. God informed Moses of what was happening below, and said, "I have seen this people, and indeed it is a stiff-necked people! Now therefore, let Me alone that My wrath may burn hot against them and I may consume them. And I will make of you a great nation" (Ex. 32:9–10).

What is significant for us here is not any theological questions the verse raises, but rather Moses' response. For Moses pleaded with God, saying:

"LORD, why does Your wrath burn hot against Your people whom You have brought out of the land of Egypt with great power and with a mighty hand? Why should the Egyptians speak, and say, 'He brought them out to harm them, to kill them in the mountains, and to consume them from the face of the earth'? Turn from Your fierce wrath, and relent from this harm to Your people. Remember Abraham, Isaac, and Israel, Your servants, to whom You swore by your own self, and said to them, 'I will multiply your descendants as the stars of heaven; and all this land that I have spoken of I give to your descendants, and they shall inherit it forever' " (Ex. 32:11–13).

There are several things to note about this prayer. First, Moses expressed a concern for God's glory. To turn against the Israelites at that point would have exposed God as a failure, unable to accomplish His stated purpose (32:12). Second, Moses reminded God of His Word. Surely the Lord would not go back on the covenant commitments He had made to the patriarchs.

In this prayer, we see into Moses' heart. Whatever His motives were as a youth when he dreamed of freeing the Israelites, His motives at this point were pure. Moses sought not fame for himself; rather, he sought glory for his God.

This same motivation was expressed in a similar prayer uttered just after the Israelites rebelled at Kadesh Barnea and refused to enter the promised land (Num. 14). There, too, Moses prayed for a rebellious people, and there, too, Moses' intent was to glorify God.

The text adds a fascinating insight. After Moses' prayer was granted on Mount Sinai, he went down the mountain. But when he saw the golden calf idol and the "dancing" [orgy] taking place around it, "Moses' anger became hot, and he cast the tablets [stones, on which the Ten Commandments had been recorded] out of his hands and broke them" (32:19).

God had preserved Moses' perspective by reporting what was happening while Moses was still on the mountain. Isolated from the awful offenses, Moses retained his perspective, and was able to plead with God. If Moses had first seen the people sinning, in His anger He might well have responded as God had, and determined on extermination.

It's hard for us, being human, to be balanced in our responses to sin. On the one hand, the godly feel revulsion and anger at humanity's inhumanities. On the other hand, we are to be concerned for the honor of God who is glorified as much in His displays of grace as in His righteous judgments. All we can do is keep our desire focused on glorifying God, and our thoughts purified by a knowledge of His Word.

Scripture's own evaluation of Moses makes it clear how completely his relationship with God transformed Moses. The Bible tells us that "the LORD spoke to Moses face to face, as a man speaks to his friend" (Ex. 33:11). Hebrews 3:5 praises Moses as a man who was "faithful in all His [God's] house as a servant." Moses, at times referred to as "the man of God" (Deut 33:1; Josh. 14:6), had been transformed indeed by his personal relationship with God.

Moses yearns to know God better (Ex. 33:13–23). Despite Moses' godly response to the Israelites' sin with the golden calf, the incident shook Moses to his core. Yet, Moses prayed that the people's sin might be forgiven. God did announce that He would punish the individuals who had engaged in the idolatry. He forgave the rest and promised that despite the Israelites' sins He would bring them into the Promised Land. Moses warned the Israelites that God could easily destroy them, and Moses himself continued to meet with the Lord. This intimate relationship with God sustained Moses during the difficult years ahead—years during which the Israelites again and again revealed a hostile and angry spirit and caused Moses, as well as God, intense pain.

God sustained His prophet with a promise: "My Presence will go with you, and I will give you rest" (Ex. 33:14). To Moses it

Israel worshiped at the portable tabernacle for some 400 years after the Exodus.

was increasingly clear that God's Presence was Israel's only hope—and his own only support.

Eager to know God even better, Moses begged the Lord, "Please, show me Your glory" (Ex. 33:18). Here "glory" refers to the divine essence. Moses yearned to see God as He truly is, fully revealed. God refused, for "no man shall see Me, and live." But God did promise to "make all My goodness pass before you" (33:19). The Lord then placed Moses in a fissure in the rock wall of Mount Sinai until His glory had passed by. And then God allowed Moses to see His back, not His face.

The imagery here is metaphoric, not anthropomorphic. God's "face" stands for His essential being; His "back" for that which He reveals of Himself to human beings. With this, Moses had to be—and surely was—content. For God showed Moses more of Himself than he had revealed to any human being up to that time. This revelation by God of Himself sustained Moses through the difficult and painful years that lay ahead. Moses could not imagine the stress he would experience in trying to lead God's obstinate people. But through it all, God's Presence would

go with Moses. And through it all, Moses would learn more about the grace and goodness of God.

This thought is important to you and me today. We need God's presence in our lives if we handle the pressures that stress all people. For us, as for Moses, the ultimate revelation of God's essence awaits. In the meantime, we can learn more of God, both through Scripture and by responding to His revealed will. As we follow Him closely, we will experience His presence. And this will enable us, as it did Moses, to overcome.

Flaws in Moses' relationship with God (Ex. 34:29–34; Num. 20:1–12). Whether or not the first incident constitutes a flaw is debatable. But the second kept Moses from entering the promised land.

The veil on Moses' face (Ex. 34:29–34). God spoke to Moses in the Israelite camp as well as on Sinai. When this happened, the cloudy-fiery pillar that accompanied the Israelites in the wilderness came down and hovered over the tabernacle, which the text also calls the "tent of meeting." Moses entered the tabernacle to converse with the Lord, and when Moses left the divine presence, his face literally shone.

Exodus tells us that after exiting the tabernacle following his meetings with the Lord, Moses would come out and speak to the Israelites, who were clearly impressed with the radiance that shone from his face. Moses would then put a veil over his face until the next time he met with the Lord. Again Moses would exit the tent unmasked, but soon once again slip on his veil.

Nahum M. Sarna, in the Jewish Publication Society's commentary on Exodus, rightly notes that the shining face "functions to reaffirm and legitimate the prophet's role as the peerless intimate of God, the sole and single mediator between God and His people" (p. 221). And certainly, in view of the Israelites' intransigence, such a symbol must have been comforting to Moses. But why did Moses put on a veil? Why not simply leave it off? The answer is provided by the apostle Paul, who told us that Moses "put a veil over his face so that the Israelites might not see the end of the fading splendor" (2 Cor. 3:13, R.S.V.).

While each meeting with God seemed to recharge the supernatural effulgence, Moses truly was merely a man. He did not wish the Israelites to see the splendor fade and be reminded of his humanity. Strikingly, the apostle urged Christians to abandon similar efforts to mask our mortality, and thus our flaws. He urged us in 2 Corinthians 3 to be bold, "not like Moses," and to remove the masks. Yes, people will see our flaws. But as we live open and honest lives, people will also see Jesus' face, for "we are being transformed" (2 Cor. 13:18) by God's Spirit. Witnessing *the process of our transformation*—not a pretense of perfection—convinces others that God is in our lives and that He is real!

Was Moses wrong to veil his face so that the Israelites would not realize that the radiance faded away? Certainly given the characteristics of the people whom Moses led, his actions were understandable. Yet, it would seem that Moses might have better glorified God and better set us an example if he had chosen simply to be himself, without any pretense or deceit.

Striking the rock (Num. 20:1–13). The Israelites had rebelled against God, and God had condemned them to wander in the wilderness until the entire unbelieving generation died out. In their wanderings, they came again to the region of Zin [called "Sin" in Ex. 17:1]. The land was parched and waterless, and as at the earlier time, the people were desperate for water. As usual, they complained bitterly against Moses and Aaron and against [but not *to*] God. And as usual, Moses went immediately to God.

This time God told Moses to "speak to the rock" before the eyes of the Israelites and the rock would produce water for humans and animals. "The rock" is undoubtedly the same rock which, at an earlier time, Moses had been told to strike with his staff and had at that time produced water (Ex. 17:5–7). But this time Moses, upset and angry with the Israelites and undoubtedly worn down by their unresponsiveness, failed to heed God's words. Rather than speak to the rock, he struck it twice, angrily complaining to the rebels and asking, "Must we bring water for you out of this rock?"

The rock did produce abundant water. But God was displeased.

Then the Lord spoke to Moses and Aaron, "Because you did not believe Me, to hallow Me in the eyes of the children of Israel, therefore you shall not bring this assembly into the land which I have given them" (Num. 20:12).

God had told Moses to speak to the rock. Moses failed to heed God's word, and struck the rock instead.

Some have felt that the punishment God decreed hardly fit Moses' crime. But there are two possible reasons why such critics are wrong. The first reason is theological; the second is practical.

Because Moses disobeyed God by striking rather than speaking to the rock to produce water, he was not allowed to lead Israel into the promised land.

❖

The theological reason is based on Paul's statement in 1 Corinthians 10:4 that the Rock represented Christ. When Moses struck the rock, the first time on the way to Mount Sinai, the rock provided life-saving water, even as when Christ died on Calvary He provided a life-giving salvation for all who believe in Him. Jesus died once for all for sins: His sacrifice was complete and fully efficacious. Hebrews says that by His one sacrifice He perfected forever those who are sanctified (cf. Heb. 10:10). In striking the rock on this second occasion, Moses distorted the typology, for Christ was smitten *once* for all. It was not necessary for Jesus to be stricken twice or three times.

The practical reason is expressed in the Numbers text. Moses had failed to believe God. This statement rests on the principle that trust in God leads to obedience, a theme developed in Hebrews 3 and 4. Israel had

disobeyed God through unbelief and rebelled at Kadesh Barnea; in a similar way Moses disobeyed God through unbelief and failed to follow His instructions. We might argue that Moses' failure can hardly be compared to that of the Israelites *in degree*, but we must admit that Moses' failure was the same *in kind*. The consequences to Moses and to the Israelites were the same. Like the Israelites, Moses died outside the promised land, unable to set foot on territory God had promised to Abraham's seed.

Before we assume that God was overly hard on Moses, let's consider. Moses was an intimate of God's. Moses knew far more of the Lord than did the Israelites he led. With Moses' privileges, there came weighty responsibility. As James reminds us, "Let not many of you become teachers, knowing that we shall receive a stricter judgment" (James 3:1).

Unlike the Israelites of the Exodus generation, however, God did permit Moses to stand on heights across the Jordan and see the promised land. There Moses died, and God Himself buried His faithful prophet and His friend.

MOSES' RELATIONSHIP WITH THE ISRAELITES

One might almost say that Moses had a love-hate relationship with Israel. His early dream of delivering God's people was shattered when an Israelite rejected Moses' intervention in a quarrel and revealed that people knew about Moses' earlier murder of an Egyptian slave-master (Ex. 2:11–15). Forty years later when Moses returned to Egypt he was first welcomed by the Israelite community, but with the very first setback the Israelites turned on Moses and blamed him for their misfortunes (Ex. 5:1–22). This pattern was repeated for most of the forty years that Moses led Israel, with almost all hostility in the relationship expressed by the Israelites.

Yet through the years, Moses not only remained faithful to his mission; he also remained committed to care for and to pray for the Israelites. What an example he set for parents of strong-willed children and for shepherds of God's sometimes-contentious flock.

The pattern of the relationship foreshadowed *(Ex. 5)*. When Moses first appeared in Egypt, he went to the Hebrew community's leaders with the good news that God intended to win their release from slavery. When Moses performed the signs God had given him, the Israelites expressed thanks to God for the prospect of freedom (Ex. 4:31). However, when Moses delivered God's demand to Pharaoh, the Egyptian ruler's response was to increase his slaves' workload. Understandably, the Israelites blamed Moses (Ex. 5:21). Puzzled, Moses turned to God for an explanation. When Moses understood that God would use Pharaoh's hostility as an occasion to display His power, and would win Israel's freedom in time, Moses believed God. But when Moses reported God's intentions to the Israelites, "they did not heed Moses, because of anguish of spirit and cruel bondage" (Ex. 6:9).

In this initial story, we can see elements that would mark this generation of Israelites' relationship with God and with Moses for the next forty years. Moses obeyed God. Difficulties arose. The Israelites criticized Moses. Moses prayed. God acted.

While the nature of the difficulties, the intensity of the criticisms, the content of the prayers, and the nature of God's responses varied, these elements remained constant.

The character of the relationship displayed *(Ex. 16—17)*. It was one thing for the Israelites to react with unbelief after the setback described in Exodus 5. Their reactions as they left Egypt and traveled toward Mount Sinai were much more difficult to explain.

Before that journey had begun, the land of their servitude had been devastated by a wondrous series of judgments through which God had unmistakably demonstrated His power. On that journey a massive cloudy-fiery pillar that hung in the heavens above them led the Israelites. Even more, the Israelites had seen God part the waters of a sea so they might pass safely through and then had seen the waters close to wipe out their pursuers. God was obviously, unmistakably with them, and Moses was marked as God's appointed spokesman and leader.

Yet, just three days after being led safely through the sea, when confronted with undrinkable water, "the people complained against Moses" (15:24). Moses prayed, and God responded by showing Moses how to purify the waters so the people could drink.

Some days later, food ran out and again, rather than look to God to provide, the Israelites "complained against Moses and Aaron" (Ex. 16:2). Again the Lord provided. Yet when the water ran out once again, "the people contended with Moses" and demanded water, continuing to "complain" against him.

What the English text does not reveal is that in the original languages the *intensity* of the complaints increases incident by incident. We can sense Moses' increasing frustration as we read Exodus 17:4: "Moses cried out to the LORD, saying, 'What shall I do with this people? They are almost ready to stone me!'" Once again God provided water.

The sequence of events in these chapters is striking and significant. With each difficulty the hostility of the Israelites toward Moses and their insensitivity to God increased—despite the fact that God continued to meet their every need immediately. In this we see both the pattern and the consequences of "permissive parenting." In permissive parenting, wrong behavior is not corrected nor are the children disciplined. Rather, they are given whatever they demand. The product is not a mature, self-disciplined and responsible adult, but an individual or a people ever more selfish and insensitive.

All this however was about to change. For the Israelites were journeying toward

Mount Sinai. Soon they would become subject to a law that not only set standards but also called for sin to be disciplined.

The rebelliousness of the Israelites unveiled (Num. 11). It is striking to compare the events of Numbers 11 with those recorded in Exodus 16—17. The circumstances are parallel, the responses of the Israelites are the same, but God's actions are totally different. We see it in the very first verse of Numbers 11:

Now when the people complained, it displeased the LORD; for the LORD heard it, and His anger was aroused. So the fire of the LORD burned among them, and consumed some in the outskirts of the camp (Num. 11:1).

This incident introduced Moses' role as an intercessor, for "when Moses prayed to the LORD, the fire was quenched" (Num. 11:2).

But the Israelites did not learn from discipline any more than they had learned from unmixed grace. They craved a change in diet, and soon the spirit of dissatisfaction and complaint swept through the camp. Again the Lord was angry, and Moses began to feel the weight of leading an unspiritual and selfish people. We can sense Moses' frustration in his prayer:

So Moses said to the LORD, "Why have You afflicted Your servant? And why have I not found favor in Your sight, that You have laid the burden of all these people on me? Did I conceive all these people? Did I beget them, and You should say to me, 'Carry them in your bosom, as a guardian caries a nursing child,' to the land which You swore to their fathers? . . . I am not able to bear all these people alone, because the burden is too great for me" (Num. 11:11, 12, 14).

Despite the tone of Moses' prayer, and Moses' failure to remember that God was with him so he did not "bear all these people alone," Moses was right to bring his complaint directly to the Lord. In this, Moses showed a great respect for God and acted quite differently than the Israelites, who directed their complaints against Moses.

God's response was to provide the meat the Israelites craved, but with it He sent a "very great" plague that must have killed thousands of Israelites. The psalmist commented on this event:

So they ate and were well filled,
For He gave them their own desire.
They were not deprived of their craving;
But while the food was still in their mouths,
The wrath of God came against them,
And slew the stoutest of them,
And struck down the choice men of Israel.
In spite of this they still sinned,
And did not believe in His wondrous works.
Therefore their days He consumed in futility,
And their years in fear. (Ps. 78:29–33)

Here too we find an important lesson. God had provided in manna all that the Israelites needed to sustain life and health. Yet, they craved what God had not seen fit to provide. Rather than be thankful and satisfied with God's gracious provision, they were dissatisfied and focused on what they did *not* have. Finally, God gave them what they craved—and it destroyed them. How foolish not to find satisfaction in the gracious gifts God has given us, and how foolish to crave more. Should God give us what we crave rather than what He chooses for us, we too might be destroyed.

The ultimate act of rebellion (Num. 14). When the Israelites reached Canaan, a representative of each tribe was sent to explore the land and bring back reports. Ten of the explorers emphasized the military strength of the Canaanites. This terrified the people. Despite the miracles of deliverance and the terror of the divine judgments they had experienced, they still refused to take account of God's power or to trust Him. Numbers 14:2, 3 tells us:

All the children of Israel complained against Moses and Aaron, and the whole congregation said to them, "If only we had died in the land of Egypt! Or if only we had died in this wilderness! Why has the Lord brought us to this land to fall by the sword, that our wives and children should become victims? Would it not be better for us to return to Egypt?

Despite the urgings of Moses, Aaron, and the two faithful explorers Caleb and Joshua, the Israelites rebelliously refused to obey God's command to go up and take Canaan. The Israelites' response is described in verse 10: "All the congregation said to stone them with stones."

At this point God again threatened totally to destroy the Israelites and begin anew with Moses. Moses again interceded for the Israelites, pleading God's glory and reminding the Lord of His covenant commitment to the descendants of Abraham, Isaac, and Jacob. [See the discussion of this similar prayer, page 35.]

Moses' prayer for pardon was granted (Num. 14:20), yet the disobedient and unbelieving Israelites would have to face some consequences. The Israelites had proclaimed that they would rather die in the wilderness than face the Canaanites. God would give them what they had chosen. God announced through Moses:

"Just as you have spoken in My hearing, so will I do to you: the carcasses of you who have complained against Me shall fall in this wilderness, all of you who were numbered, according to your entire number, from twenty years old and above" (Num. 14:29).

And so it was.

We can learn several lessons from this incident. First, leaders, like Moses, are both to represent their people before God and represent God before their people. On the one hand, faithfulness in ministry calls for earnest prayer on behalf of others even when they sin. On the other hand, faithfulness calls for announcing God's judgments even

when we know they will be unpopular. In each of these aspects of spiritual leadership, Moses provides us with an exceptional example.

The second lesson is that our choices have consequences. When we refuse to follow God's Word, we can be sure that disaster will follow—whatever our motives for disobedience may have been. Whether it is a fleshly craving or fear that moves us to disobey, abandoning God's will provides neither satisfaction nor security.

The Israelites' unbelieving hearts further revealed (*Num. 16*). The Israelites' rebellion at Kadesh Barnea destined the Exodus generation to decades of wandering in the wilderness until God's sentence had been carried out. Yet, clearly the Israelites still failed to understand or to trust the Lord. This is made abundantly clear in the story of Korah's rebellion.

Korah and his followers argued that in a faith community where each individual had been redeemed and set apart to God, it was inappropriate for Moses and Aaron to exalt themselves "above the assembly of the Lord" (Num. 16:3). They felt that this was especially true for them, for they were Levites, set apart to serve God at the tabernacle. So Korah and his followers argued that where all are holy [in the sense of being set apart to God], no individual should be responsible to a mere human leader.

In this, of course, Korah and his followers totally ignored the fact that God Himself had commissioned Moses to lead His people and that while Moses had consistently been faithful to the Lord, Korah and all the rest had proven rebellious and unbelieving. So Moses proposed a test: let Korah and his followers appear before the Lord ready to lead in worship, and let the Lord decide.

But Korah's coleaders in this rebellion, Dathan and Abiram, refused to listen to Moses. They accused Moses of being responsible for the failure to take Canaan, and they blamed him for the wilderness death they now faced. Whatever Moses suggested, they would refuse to do! Angry then, Moses prayed *against* these rebels, asking God not to respect their offering. How could they treat Moses in this way; Moses who had never done one thing to exploit his position as a leader or to harm a single individual (Num. 16:15)?

When the day of the test came, Korah with Dathan and Abiram and their followers, some 250 men in all, marched up to the tabernacle bearing censers filled with incense to offer to the Lord. They were followed by the entire congregation of Israelites, who supported them in their stand against Moses!

Again, God threatened to destroy the Israelites. Again, Moses prayed for the people. This time, however, Moses made a distinction in his prayer between the congregation and the leaders of the rebellion. God then told Moses to warn the Israelites to get away from the tents of the rebel leaders. Moses then established the parameters of the test: The people would know that God had chosen Moses as their leader if the ground opened and swallowed the tents and families of the rebels. A great chasm opened and swallowed the households and possessions of Korah's clan, and fire blazed from the tabernacle and consumed the 250 men who had arrogantly violated God's Word and taken on themselves the priestly role reserved for Aaron's descendants.

The terrible fate of Korah and his family and followers was unmistakably the result of an act of God. Yet "on the next day" all the Israelites complained against Moses and Aaron and accused *them* of killing "the people of the Lord!" (Num. 16:41). Again, God threatened to wipe out His rebellious people, and a plague struck. This time Moses sent the true priest, Aaron, to make atonement for the Israelites, and the plague was stopped.

The incidents reported in this chapter fully demonstrate why the Lord had no choice but to replace the Exodus generation with their children. The adults who left Egypt simply refused to respond to the Lord, no matter what God did. This generation could not enter the promised land, for only people who trusted God enough to obey Him would win the victories that would establish the Hebrew's dominance of the Holy Land.

Moses leads the new and responsive generation (Num. 26—36). Taking the census described in Numbers 26 marks the passing of the Exodus generation. The census revealed that just as some 600,000 men of military age had left Egypt four decades earlier, there were now some 600,000 men of the new generation, ready to succeed where their fathers had failed.

These last chapters of Numbers tell of Moses' travels with the new generation, travels marked by military victories and preparations for entering the promised land. What a relief and joy it must have been for Moses, now well over a hundred years old, at last to be able to guide a people who were respectful, responsive, and willing to trust the Lord. It is so much easier for leaders when those they lead willingly follow! The Lord had given Moses a wonderful gift near the end of his life.

At the same time, we must appreciate that Moses' travails are more instructive for us. Moses' experience with the Israelites remind us that leadership is burdensome, a ministry not to be sought lightly or for self-aggrandizement. A person who accepts the mantle of leadership must accept with it the care of persons who will often misunderstand, criticize, and complain. A person who accepts the mantle of leadership must faithfully pray for the hostile, and just as faithfully honor and communicate God's Word, regardless of whether others accept that Word. Yet, a person who accepts the mantle of leadership will find in that ministry great and wonderful rewards. Leadership's challenges will drive the leader closer to God. When at last the leader sees God's people respond and grow, it will all seem worthwhile.

MOSES: AN EXAMPLE FOR TODAY

We rightly hesitate to compare ourselves to the greatest or even *great* men of faith. Yet, we can learn much from their lives. Perhaps the most significant quality Moses modeled was humility. No person full of himself would have been so totally dependent on God or so patient with the Israelites. Both these aspects of humility are required in anyone who aspires to spiritual leadership. Only the person who acknowledges and who acts in total dependence on the Lord will experience God's full working in and through his life. And only the truly humble person will remain loving despite the unmerited complaints and hostility that seem so typically associated with leading God's people.

It is striking that in a world where people assume that the self-confident, assertive individual is the leader type, that in God's economy it is the humble and self-effacing who achieve great things. It took Moses forty years in the wilderness to learn humility. May we learn humility from him, in far less time, and far less painfully.

There are also other lessons a person can take away from a study of Moses' life.

- Moses was eighty years old before he was ready to be used by God. Never despise the time it takes to prepare yourself for ministry. And never assume that it's too late to serve. The church and the world are well able to wait until God has fully equipped you.

- Moses performed miracles—and even so those God called him to lead abused him. Few of us will ever perform miracles, so we should not be surprised when we are treated unfairly.

- Moses brought his complaints to God, not to the neighbors. We will often be tempted to tell friends and fellow believers when we feel we have been mistreated. This will only make matters worse. We need to recognize God's hand in all that happens and honor Him by bringing our complaints as well as our praises to Him.

- Moses continued to pray for his congregation, despite their lack of spirituality and the personal abuse he suffered. We are not called to treat others as they treat us, but rather to treat others as God for Christ's sake has treated us.

- Moses remained obedient to the Lord, even when obedience seemed to lead to disaster. The "success" of what we do does not indicate God's pleasure. What pleases the Lord is our obedience, whatever may come.

DAVID

Scripture references:
1 Samuel 16—2 Samuel;
1 Chronicles; 1 Kings 1;
Numerous psalms

Date:	Reigned 1010–970 B.C.
Name:	David [DAY-vid; "beloved"]
Greatest accomplishment:	David built a powerful Hebrew kingdom, greatly expanded Israel's territory, and instituted major religious and political reforms.

DAVID'S ROLE IN SCRIPTURE

Moses is Scripture's prototype prophet; David is Scripture's prototype king. Christ fulfilled the promise of a Prophet like Moses in His first coming when He introduced the new covenant era. In Christ's Second Coming, He will fulfill the promise of a King like David, of David's line, destined to rule over all. The Old Testament prophets spoke of the coming of a promised Ruler to spring from David's line who would fulfill the promise implicit in the historic reign of Israel's greatest king.

In his own day, David had a powerful impact on the political life of the Hebrew people. Prior to David, the Israelites had remained loosely associated tribes governed for centuries by charismatic judges, and then for a time by a flawed king, Saul. During these centuries, the Israelites were an oppressed minority in Canaan, squeezed into a narrow strip of the broad land God had promised to Abraham, Isaac, and Jacob. When David finally won the allegiance of the twelve Hebrew tribes, he was able to weld them into the most powerful Middle Eastern kingdom of his era. The *Nelson Illustrated Bible Handbook* summarizes David's accomplishments as Israel's ruler:

The years of David complete Israel's transition from a loose tribal structure, under which God's people lived in the days of the judges, to a monarchy. A number of important aspects of the transition are accomplished under David's leadership:

- Transition from government by judges to an established monarchy.
- Transition from a loose confederation of tribes to a united nation.
- Transition from anarchy to a strong central government.
- Transition from bronze-age poverty to iron-age economy and wealth.
- Transition from a subject people to conquerors. David expanded Israel's territory some ten times!
- Transition from decentralized worship to centralized worship, with one city as both political and religious capital.

While David proved to be a military and political genius whose accomplishments in

Israel are unmatched, David's contributions to Israel's spiritual life are just as impressive. David himself was deeply committed to God and spiritually sensitive. The passion and intensity of David's personal relationship with God are revealed in the seventy-three poems in the Book of Psalms attributed to him. In these psalms, David fully exposed his inner spiritual life, freely expressing his hopes and fears, his failures and his abiding confidence in the goodness of the Lord. David's psalms, along with the others in this book of 150 religious poems, have served believers ever since as a pattern for praise and worship. They have led untold millions of people into a deeper relationship with the Lord.

DAVID'S SHEPHERD PSALM

The Lord is my shepherd;
I shall not want.
He makes me to lie down in green
    pastures;
He leads me beside the still waters.
He restores my soul;
He leads me in the paths of righteousness
For His name's sake.

Yea, though I walk through the valley of
    the shadow of death,
I will fear no evil;
For You are with me;
Your rod and Your staff, they comfort me.

You prepare a table before me in the
    presence of my enemies;
You anoint my head with oil;
My cup runs over.
Surely goodness and mercy shall follow
    me
All the days of my life;
And I will dwell in the house of the LORD
Forever.

David also expressed commitment to worship by desiring to construct a temple in Jerusalem. While God did not permit David to fulfill this dream, David spent his declining years laying out plans for its design and developing detailed organizational plans for the duties of the priests and Levites who would lead worship there. David also committed his personal wealth and much of the kingdom's income to stockpiling the materials his son Solomon would use to build the temple of which David had dreamed.

David fell short in many ways, particularly in his family life. Yet, David's military, political, and spiritual accomplishments cannot be overstated. David founded a dynasty that ruled in Judah, the southern Hebrew kingdom, from 1010 B.C. to its fall to the Babylonians in 586 B.C. And, as the prophets announced, Israel's Deliverer and future Ruler of all was to emerge from David's family line.

And so He did, when the babe destined to be both Savior and King was born to Mary in Bethlehem, the hometown of David, nearly a thousand years after David died.

❖

SAMPLING "DAVID" IN PROPHECY

"Of the increase of His government and peace
There will be no end,
Upon the throne of David and over His kingdom,
To order it and establish it with judgment and justice
From that time forward, even forever. The zeal of the LORD of hosts will accomplish this." (Isa. 9:7)

"In mercy the throne will be established;
And One will sit on it in truth, in the tabernacle of David,
Judging and seeking justice and hastening righteousness." (Isa. 16:5)

"Behold, the days are coming," says the LORD,
"That I will raise to David a Branch of righteousness;
A King shall reign and prosper,
And execute judgment and righteousness in the earth." (Jer. 23:5)

"But they shall serve the LORD their God,
And David their king,
Whom I will raise up for them." (Jer. 30:9)

"David My servant shall be king over them, and they shall all have one shepherd; they shall also walk in My judgments and observe My statutes, and do them." (Ezek. 37:24)

"Afterward the children of Israel shall return and seek the LORD their God and David their king." (Hos. 3:5)

"The book of the genealogy of Jesus Christ, the Son of David . . . " (Matt. 1:1)

All the multitudes were amazed and said, "Could this be the Son of David?" (Matt. 12:23)

"I, Jesus, have sent My angel to testify to you these things in the churches. I am the Root and the Offspring of David, the Bright and Morning Star." (Rev. 22:16)

See the companion book in this series, *Every Covenant and Promise of the Bible*, for a complete explanation of this theme.

❖

DAVID'S LIFE AND TIMES

David was born at a time when his people's fate hung in the balance. Israel's primary enemies at the time were the Philistines, who dominated their weaker neighbors. The Philistines had mastered the secrets of smelting iron, and they carefully guarded this new technology. When David was a youth, only King Saul and his son Jonathan carried iron

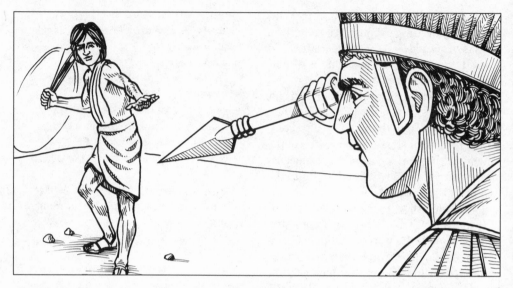

The stone in slings used by Israelites in David's time were about the size of tennis balls, plenty large enough to fell even a giant like Goliath.

weapons; the other members of Israel's citizen militia were forced to use bronze knives and farm implements when they fought. During David's lifetime, and largely due to his own efforts, this situation was transformed, and all of Israel's neighboring enemies were subdued.

We can trace the transformation by looking at the differing period of David's life.

David's early life as a shepherd *(1 Sam. 16:11).* David was the youngest son of a man named Jesse, who lived in Bethlehem, a small town about six miles from the future site of David's capital, Jerusalem. As the youngest, David was assigned the task of guarding his father's sheep. Alone in nature, David experienced a growing awe of God as Creator. David's sense of wonder is frequently expressed in the psalms. As David would one day write,

> The heavens declare the glory of God;
> And the firmament shows His handi-
>   work.
> Day unto day utters speech,
> And night unto night reveals knowledge.

> There is no speech nor language
> Where their voice is not heard.
>   (Ps. 19:1–3)

As David cared for his sheep, he listened to nature's testimony. During those quiet years, David developed a sense of God's greatness that never left him. David's later confidence in God's power rested in large part on the lessons David learned as a shepherd.

David also learned to act on his confidence in God. Later, when asked how he dared challenge a giant Philistine warrior, David replied simply:

Your servant used to keep his father's sheep, and when a lion or a bear came and took a lamb out of the flock, I went out after it and struck it, and delivered the lamb from its mouth; and when it arose against me, I caught it by its beard, and struck and killed it. Your servant has killed both lion and bear; and this uncircumcised Philistine will be like one of them, seeing he has defied the armies of the living God (1 Sam. 17:34–36).

When Saul, Israel's first king, proved weak and untrusting, God sent the prophet

Samuel to Bethlehem to anoint David as his successor. At first, Samuel assumed that one of David's older brothers, impressively tall, was God's choice. But God pointed out David, who was handsome but rather small of stature, as His choice. In one of the Bible's most telling verses, the Lord reminded Samuel that "the Lord does not see as man sees; for man looks at the outward appearance, but the LORD looks at the heart" (1 Sam. 16:7). It was David's heart for the Lord, nurtured during his shepherd years, that more than anything else equipped David for greatness.

David's emergence as a military hero (1 Sam. 17—19). An invasion of Israelite territory by the Philistines created the opportunity for David's emergence from obscurity. As the two armies lay camped on hillsides opposite each other, a Philistine warrior some nine feet tall strode out each morning to challenge the Israelites to send out a champion to fight him. Saul, the tallest and most powerful man in Israel's army as well as king, cowered in his tent, promising to reward anyone who would venture out to do battle.

When David, then a teenager, came to camp to bring provisions to his brothers, David was shocked that no one was willing to fight the giant. In David's eyes, the Philistine's challenge demeaned the living God who would surely give victory to anyone who stepped out to represent Him and His people. So David volunteered, and the cowardly king permitted a stripling to attempt what no soldier in Saul's army was willing to try.

As every Sunday school student knows, David killed the giant, Goliath. He was quickly accepted into Saul's army as a junior officer, and immediately began to display the courage and brilliance that marked his entire military career. David was so successful, and so honored by the Israelites, that Saul grew jealous. Saul undoubtedly recognized in David that true faith and courage that he

himself lacked. In the end, when several plots to rid himself of David failed, Saul attempted to kill David whom he now saw as a rival to the throne. David, although at the time the king's son-in-law as well as a military officer, fled for his life.

David's outlaw years (1 Sam. 20—31). David was alone when he fled from Saul; however, others soon joined him. Before long, David had assembled a band of some 600 fighting men and their families; fierce warriors, many of whom became the core of his army after David became king.

During these outlaw years, Saul often pursued David. Saul was determined to see David dead. Many close calls and last-minute escapes are described in these chapters. Particularly notable however is David's refusal to assassinate Saul on two occasions when he had the opportunity. Saul had been anointed king by the prophet Samuel and thus appointed by God. God, not David, must remove him.

Only once during these years did David become discouraged. Convinced that sooner or later Saul would massacre his little band, David moved into Philistine territory and offered himself and his men as mercenaries to the king of Gath. God overruled however, and David was preserved from fighting against his own people when Philistia and Israel went to war again. Despite this one lapse, David generally maintained his confidence in God and realized that in time he would fulfill his destiny as Israel's king.

David's rule over Judah (2 Sam. 1—4). When at last Saul was killed in a battle with the Philistines, the tribes of Judah and Benjamin invited David to become their king. A son of Saul, Ishbosheth, was propped up as king of the other ten tribes by Abner, who had been Saul's commanding general. For seven years the north [the ten tribes] and the south [David's two tribes] skirmished. In the end, a perceived insult moved Abner to make peace with David and

David ruled Judah and Dan for seven years before the other Hebrew tribes acknowledged him as king.

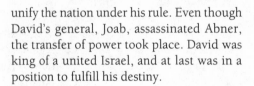

unify the nation under his rule. Even though David's general, Joab, assassinated Abner, the transfer of power took place. David was king of a united Israel, and at last was in a position to fulfill his destiny.

David builds a nation (2 Sam. 5—10; 1 Chron. 11—16). David's first act as king was to establish a new capital. He chose Jerusalem, a city that lay between north and south and had been occupied by neither. David drove out the Canaanites who held the heights. David also set out to break the power of the enemy nations that surrounded the Israelites. In a series of wars, many of which were started by the enemy, David defeated all of Israel's foes. In the process, David expanded Israelite-held territory ten times. During David's reign, God's people occupied nearly all the lands promised to Abraham long before.

With his borders secure, David organized his government, setting up an efficient administrative system. David also instituted religious reforms. Since the conquest of Canaan, some four hundred years earlier, the Israelites had offered their sacrifices and worshiped at the tabernacle, the portable worship center constructed under Moses' supervision. Now David brought the ark of the covenant, the most holy object in Israel's religion, to Jerusalem, and laid plans for the construction of a magnificent temple in which to house it. In this, David provided a third unifying symbol for his nation. Israel now had a common capital, a common king, and a common faith. The Israelites were at last a unified nation, no longer merely a loose confederation of tribes who shared a common heritage.

David's declining years (2 Sam. 11—24; 1 Chron. 20—29). David's faith and energy had enabled him to build a powerful and stable kingdom. But with this accomplished, a strange lethargy seems to have gripped David. All of life's challenges seemed to have been met successfully; David had arrived at the top. Now David would face a different kind of challenge, a moral and interpersonal challenge.

David's moral challenge (1 Sam. 11—20). One spring when David's armies went out to do battle, David stayed in Jerusalem. There he chanced to see a beautiful woman bathing. Inflamed with desire, he sent for the woman and took her, and then tried to hide what was essentially a rape. David's detour into sin caused him real anguish; likewise, it harmed others and outraged the Lord. David's anguish is clearly expressed in Psalm 32, as well as being reflected in his great prayer of confession recorded in Psalm 51. When the prophet Nathan finally confronted David, he confessed his sin and was forgiven. But David's moral failure had a terrible impact on his family. When his son Amnon followed his father's example and raped his half-sister, Tamar, David did nothing. Robbed of moral authority by his own sins, David seemed strangely silent over the crimes committed by his children. Later Absalom, the brother of Tamar, murdered Amnon and fled the country. Again David said and did nothing. Still later Absalom returned to Jerusalem. Again David said and did nothing, despite the fact that Absalom sought to alienate the northern tribes from David. Absalom succeed in fomenting a rebellion, but he was killed in the battle between north and south.

David, so brilliant in building the nation, was strangely helpless to guide or govern his own family. How tragic when our sins impact our children so. We need to learn from David's mistakes and guard our hearts against the attractions of sin.

David's enthusiasm restored (1 Chron. 17—28). The challenges of kingdom building had all been met successfully. David had learned by painful experience that however attractive sin might appear, its consequences could be devastating.

In his declining years, David found a better way to invest his energies, and his enthusiasm for life was restored. Essentially David turned his thoughts and his efforts to preparing for the construction of God's temple and to working out the details of how temple worship would be conducted. David also dedicated his own personal wealth to temple building and urged the wealthy in his kingdom to follow his example. First Chronicles describes in detail David's plans; and, here again, we see David's organizational genius displayed.

It is striking that the emphases in Second Samuel and 1 Chronicles, which cover the same periods of David's life, differ so significantly. But there is a good explanation. The Books of Samuel and the Kings are historical reports of events in the kingdoms of Israel and Judah. The books of Chronicles are divine *commentary* on those events. Second Samuel emphasizes David's failure and its impact on David's family, faithfully reporting conditions in the kingdom. But 1 Chronicles skips over David's sin and its consequences to focus on evidence of his interior life with God. His sins like ours had been forgiven; his service remembered and celebrated.

Whatever else can be said of David, he was a human being who truly had a heart for God. Yes, David was flawed, as we all are. Nevertheless David loved and trusted God, and those qualities enabled him to use his many gifts to the fullest and mark him as one of the Old Testament's greatest men.

EXPLORING DAVID'S RELATIONSHIPS

DAVID'S RELATIONSHIP WITH GOD

Scripture testifies that God chose David to succeed Saul because David was a man after God's "own heart" (1 Sam. 13:14). This does not mean that David was perfect. Far from it. It does mean that with all his flaws, David loved the Lord and was responsive to him.

David was responsive to God's revelation of Himself in nature. David was deeply moved by the evidence of God's greatness in nature and profoundly awed that God could care about human beings. His pondering is reflected in Psalm 8:

> When I consider Your heavens, the work
> of Your fingers,
> The moon and stars, which You have
> ordained,
> What is man that You are mindful of
> him,
> And the son of man that You visit him?
> (Ps. 8:3–4)

> In praise and wonder David exclaimed,
> O LORD, our LORD,
> How excellent is Your name in all the
> earth." (Ps. 8:9)

David displayed confidence in God's promises *(1 Sam. 17).* While all in Saul's army quaked before the Philistine champion, Goliath, young David was merely surprised. Why hadn't anyone been willing to fight Goliath? The Philistine wasn't simply challenging men; he was challenging the forces of the living God. David was utterly convinced that the God of the covenant, the God of Israel's deliverance from Egypt, would fight for His people. Only David counted on God's commitment to His people and looked beyond the giant foe to Israel's far greater and more powerful God. All David's life he displayed confidence in the Lord and counted on Him to keep His promises. As a result, He won great victories for his people.

David looked to God for guidance *(1 Sam. 23:2).* The historical books that tell the story of David's life report some eleven times that David "inquired of the Lord" when facing difficult decisions. In David's day this typically involved an appeal to the Urim and Thummim held by the high priest, as described in Exodus 28:30. It is significant that although a brilliant strategist and a decisive leader of men, David was also a humble believer, deeply aware of his need for divine guidance. David's dependence on God is reflected in Psalm 31:3–5:

> For You are my rock and my fortress;
> Therefore for Your name's sake
> Lead me and guide me.
> Pull me out of the net which they have
>   secretly laid for me,
> For You are my strength.
> Into Your hand I commit my spirit;
> You have redeemed me, O LORD, God of
>   truth.

David encouraged others to honor and worship God. We see this ministry of David's reflected in several ways.

David set a personal example (1 Sam. 26:1–12). On one occasion when King Saul pursued David and his band, David had an opportunity to assassinate Saul. Abishai, one of David's men, urged him to kill Saul, arguing that God had delivered Saul into David's hand. David refused: "The LORD forbid that I should stretch out my hand against the LORD's anointed." God would remove Saul in His own time. David had too great a respect for God to kill a man the Lord had appointed to royal office.

David emphasized the importance of worship (2 Sam. 6). As soon as David had established himself as king and made Jerusalem the capital of a united Israel, he brought the ark of the covenant to Jerusalem. David himself led the celebration honoring God, again setting an example for his people and demonstrating his own passionate desire to honor and worship the Lord.

David devoted himself to producing a worship liturgy for his people. David's psalms expressed his personal relationship with God. They also were intended to serve as guides to personal and corporate worship for David's people. David knew it was vitally important for the Israelites to become a worshiping people. Many of the psalms David wrote have in their superscription the phrase "to the chief musician." The "chief musician" was responsible for leading worship. David intended these psalms to become part of Israel's worship liturgy.

David committed his later years to prepare for constructing the temple (1 Chron. 21—27). David's deepest desire was to encourage worship of God. In his later years, he committed all his energies to raising the money and assembling the materials needed to construct a temple to the Lord in Jerusalem. While Solomon actually built the temple, David drew up the temple plans, organized the tasks of the priests and Levites who would ministered there, and energized the nation to undertake the project.

DAVID'S RELATIONSHIP WITH GOD REFLECTED IN HIS PSALMS

Psalm	The relationship expressed	Psalm	The relationship expressed
3, 4	David finds inner peace during Absalom's rebellion.	40	David praises God for His loving kindness.
5	David begins his day with prayer.	41	David honors God for his mercy and goodness.
6	David entreats God for mercy.	51	David confesses his sin with Bathsheba.
7	David examines his own heart before the Lord.	52	David warns the wicked.
8	David expresses awe at God's concern for people.	53	David ponders the foolishness of the wicked.
9	David rejoices in the Lord and sings His praises.	54	David affirms God as his helper in a time of great stress.
11	David expresses trust in God.	55	David turns to God when fearful and pained.
12	David calls on God to judge the wicked.	56	David begs for mercy when captured by the Philistines.
13	David expresses trust despite unanswered prayer.	57	David cries out to God when pursued by Saul.
14	David ponders the foolishness of the wicked.	58	David calls on God to judge the wicked.
15	David describes the ways of those who fear God.	59	David calls on God to scatter his enemies.
16	David rejoices in the blessings of knowing God.	60	David cries out for help.
17	David begs God to intervene.	61	David expresses trust in God when overwhelmed.
18	David praises God as his rock and salvation.	62	David commits himself to wait for God.
19	David rejoices in God's revelation in nature and Scripture.	63	David longs to know God better.
20	David prays for others and encourages trust.	64	David expresses confidence that God will preserve him.
21	David expresses trust in God's sovereign control.	65	David praises God's awesome deeds.
22	David laments over God's seeming silence.	68	David reviews history in praise of God.
23	David rests in God as his shepherd.	69	David begs God's help against those who hate him.
24	David looks forward to the coming of the King of glory.	70	David appeals to God to deliver him.
25	David trusts God to guide and to deliver.	86	David cries out to God "all day long" for help.
26	David begs God to vindicate him.	101	David praises God for His mercy and justice.
27	David praises God as an antidote to fear.	103	David blesses God for his mercy and love.
28	David urgently seeks God's aid against enemies.	108	David reaffirms his commitment to the Lord.
29	David worships.	109	David seeks God's help against enemies.
31	David expresses trust in God as rock and fortress.	110	David foresees the work of God's Messiah.
32	David contemplates sin, forgiveness, and guidance.	122	David rejoices in the privilege of worship.
33	David calls on the righteous to praise God.	124	David praises God for past deliverance.
34	David praises God and urges all to trust Him.	131	David bows as a child before the Lord.
35	David calls on God to defend him against enemies.	133	David affirms the blessings of unity.
36	David praises God's loving kindness and mercy.	138	David praises God with his whole heart.
37	David encourages delight in the Lord.	139	David sees his life totally exposed to God's scrutiny.
38	David shares his pain when God disciplined him.	140	David begs God to keep him from the hand of the wicked.
39	David expresses frustration and begs for relief.	141	David expresses commitment to God in evening prayers.
		142	David contemplates answered prayers.
		143	David expresses reliance on the Lord as he prays for deliverance.
		144	David sings God's praises.
		145	David meditates on God's splendor and works.

David refused to strike when King Saul was in his power, for God had made Saul king and David believed only God should remove him.

❖

David relied on God's grace to create in him a clean heart and restore the joy of his salvation. God restored David, encouraging each of us to turn quickly to the Lord when we sin. Even in David's great failure God used David to teach transgressors God's ways and to convert sinners to Him.

David was a man after God's own heart not because he was sinless but because David trusted how God responded to Him. For most of his life, David sought to honor and obey God. His psalms remind us that David freely shared his inner life and emotions with the Lord and was as eager to commune with the Lord as to depend on Him. Even when David sinned, he relied on God's grace and forgiveness to restore him to a right relationship with the Lord. In all this, David is an example of true godliness.

DAVID'S RELATIONSHIP WITH SAUL

In many ways, Saul was the opposite of David. Saul had been anointed king of Israel, but the pressures of leadership revealed that Saul was unwilling to trust God. As Saul became more and more alienated from the Lord, he grew erratic, fearful, and paranoid. All of Saul's weaknesses are displayed in David's relationship with the unworthy king.

David repented when he sinned (2 Sam. 12). The Old Testament records more than one sin committed by David. Although David's love for God was real, he was a fallible human being whose sins seem as great as his accomplishments. While Scripture records David's sin in numbering Israel (2 Sam. 24), the sin all remember is his sexual assault on Bathsheba and his subsequent murder of her husband, Uriah. Even remembering that these actions were out of character, there is no excuse for David's actions.

However, David's deep sense of guilt, revealed in Psalm 32, and his public repentance, expressed in Psalm 51, remind us that David truly responded to God. In repentance,

David as a musician in Saul's court (1 Sam. 16:14–23). After Saul had been rejected by the Lord and condemned by Samuel, he was frequently depressed. David was called to court to play the harp for Saul and cheer him. Saul liked the young man and made him his armor bearer, an official court position.

David as victor over Goliath and as an army officer (1 Sam. 17:1—18:16). David, a teenager, was at home from court when the Philistines invaded. His father sent him to carry supplies to his brothers, who were with the Israelite forces. There David volunteered to meet Goliath in single combat, and Saul reluctantly agreed. Saul's question to his general, Abner, "Whose son is this youth," (17:55), has been taken to contradict the story that David was already known to Saul. However, Saul's question related to David's lineage. Saul had promised his daughter in marriage to whoever killed Goliath, and understandably, he wondered about David's family.

After David killed Goliath, Saul failed to give David his daughter, but he made David an officer in his army. David proved himself a gifted and successful military man, and rapidly became a hero to the people of Israel. David's popularity aroused Saul's resentment. Saul was both jealous and fearful, for Saul sensed that God, who had deserted him, was with David.

David as the king's son-in-law *(1 Sam. 18:17—19:24).* When Saul's daughter Michal fell in love with David, Saul saw a way to rid himself of the young army officer. He set David to earn Michal's hand by killing Philistines, hoping that David would be the one killed. When David succeeded, Saul permitted the wedding, but soon was asking his servants and even his son Jonathan, David's friend, to murder David.

During this time, David simply could not credit the reports that Saul was out to kill him. David had proven himself loyal to Saul, and he was the king's son-in-law! Finally Saul moved openly against David, and David was forced to flee.

David as a fugitive *(1 Sam. 20—30).* For a number of years, Saul, who was still intent on seeing David dead, harried David and those who joined him. Twice while David and his men were being pursued, David had opportunities to kill Saul. Each time, David refused, but took tokens from Saul that revealed how close to death the king had come. Each time, Saul was forced to acknowledge that David was more righteous than he was, and each time Saul promised David a pardon. David, however, was too

wise to trust Saul, and he continued to live as a fugitive. During those years Saul served as a grindstone, whose pressure strengthened David's faith and honed his trust in the Lord.

Even so, it is not surprising that after years of narrow escapes even a person with as much trust in God as David displayed should become discouraged. Convinced that sooner or later Saul would take him, David left Israelite territory and enrolled his men as mercenaries with the king of Philistine Gath. David pretended to the Philistine ruler to lead raiding parties into Israelite territory, but instead David raided Israel's enemies. This lapse of David's faith created a serious situation. When the Philistines went to war with Israel, David, now a subject of the king of Gath, was expected to battle his own people! God extricated David from this situation, and in the battle that followed, Saul and his son Jonathan were both killed.

Saul had been God's instrument to test David's faith and his loyalty. David had passed the test; now it was time for a maturer David to lead God's people.

How often God uses those who make themselves our enemies to strengthen and mature us. We need to be sure, however, that we follow the course David took, refusing to strike back, and treating our enemies with consideration and respect (see Matt. 5:44).

DAVID'S RELATIONSHIP WITH HIS WIVES

While David maintained an exemplary relationship with Saul, the same cannot be said for his relationship with his wives. We shall explore his relationship with three of the women David married.

David's relationship with Michal, Saul's daughter *(1 Sam. 18—19; 2 Sam. 3, 6).* Saul's younger daughter, Michal, fell in love with the young and handsome army officer who had killed Goliath. Her father saw her love as an opportunity to strike at David. Saul established a dowry of one hundred Philistine foreskins, hoping his enemies would kill David. When David brought Saul the required dowry, Saul permitted the marriage. Later when Saul's hostility became open and the threat to David's life became clear, Michal helped David escape. After David fled, Saul married Michal to another man. In this manner, Saul callously used his daughter, showing no concern at all for her feelings.

There is no evidence that David tried to contact Michal during his fugitive years. But much later, when David was offered the throne of Israel, he demanded that Michal be returned to him. The Israelite general who was negotiating turning the northern tribes over to David went to Michal's home and simply took her away from her husband and brought her to David.

To suppose that David was eager to have his first love restored to him would be romantic. However, the text suggests that David's insistence on the return of Michal was a political rather than a loving act. Marriage to Saul's daughter would help to legitimize David's rule over the northern tribes that had remained loyal to Saul's family. Michal's expression of hostility toward David seen in 2 Samuel 6:16–23 reveals no affection between them.

David's relationship with Michal reveals him to be as much an exploiter of women as Saul had been. The text tells us that Michal loved David; it never suggests that David loved Michal. Many years later when David demanded her return without consulting her, David showed a callous disregard for her feelings.

While some might excuse David's actions by noting that women in the royal houses of the ancient world were universally regarded as pawns of public policy, such a heartless disregard of the feelings of a woman who had shown David such love and loyalty was inexcusable.

David's relationship with Abigail (1 Sam. 25). Once when he was a fugitive, David's men camped near the land of a wealthy rancher named Nabal. David's men never stole a sheep to eat, but rather helped the shepherds guard the flock. Yet, at harvest time when David sent a delegation to ask Nabal for a gift, Nabal insulted David and sent the delegation away.

David's anger flared, and he set out with his men to kill Nabal and his herdsmen. Warned by the herdsmen, who were appalled at what Nabal had done, Nabal's wife Abigail quickly assembled some supplies and set out to intercept David.

Not only did Abigail intercept David, but she spoke so wisely that David realized his intent to take revenge was both wrong and politically unwise. He accepted Abigail's gifts, and returned to his camp. When Nabal suffered a stroke and died a few days later, David sent for Abigail and married her. David recognized and appreciated Abigail's strength of character and her wisdom.

Too many men today are threatened by strong women. David, a strong man himself, realized that a woman of strength and character is of great worth, and he took the opportunity to join her life to his. In this relationship, at least we can admire David's choice and seek to emulate him.

David's relationship with Bathsheba (2 Sam. 11—12; 1 Kings 1). David's initial attraction to Bathsheba was purely sensual. She was beautiful; David wanted her; David took her. The fact that Bathsheba was another man's wife was something that David, driven by passion and power, simply ignored.

The text of 2 Samuel makes it clear that Bathsheba was a victim here; she was not the temptress some in their efforts to excuse David have tried to cast her (see 2 Sam. 11:1–6). It was night when Bathsheba was bathing in the privacy of the inner court of her own home, when David looked down from the palace roof and saw her. He "sent messengers and took her" and when she arrived at the palace, "he lay with her." And then David simply sent Bathsheba home.

Weeks later when she let him know she was pregnant, David called her husband home from the war, hoping to mask his responsibility for her condition. In the end, David arranged to have Bathsheba's husband killed in battle, and then he married her himself, perhaps to further hide his rape of a young woman who was helpless in the hands of Israel's king.

David and Bathsheba's marriage was likely not a loving one at first. David's lust, so shocking in a king who had a reputation for godliness, must have shaken Bathsheba. When she discovered she was pregnant by David, she clearly had lost control of her own life and was utterly powerless.

Yet we learn in the Chronicles that she later bore David four sons, and that one of those sons, Solomon, was David's successor. Even more fascinating, as David lay dying and one of his sons acted to usurp the throne, the prophet Nathan enlisted the aid of Bathsheba to appeal to the king. Bathsheba reminded David of his promise to see Solomon crowned, but it was her reminder that after David died the lives of both herself and Solomon would be in danger (1 Kings 1:21) that moved David to act.

Something had happened to transform a relationship initiated in lust into a loving commitment of these two to each other.

In Psalm 51, we learn what happened. After David was confronted by the prophet Nathan and acknowledged his sin to the Lord, David took another significant step. David penned a confession and delivered it to the chief musician to be used in public worship. That confession, Psalm 51, is headed by a superscription that bluntly describes the occasion of its writing: "A psalm of David when Nathan the prophet went to him, after he had gone in to Bathsheba."

In this public confession David took full responsibility for what happened, and wrote: "I acknowledge my transgressions" (51:3).

The public confession not only restored David's relationship with the Lord, but also

David showed himself a truly strong man when he listened to the advice of Abigail and changed his mind despite publicly stating he would take revenge.

❖

laid a foundation on which to build a loving relationship with Bathsheba.

All too many women today are in abusive relationships. The first reaction of most victims is to hide the abuse out of a sense of guilt and shame, while the first reaction of the abuser is to his victim. Typically these relationships are marked by repeated expressions of contrition and promises never to do it again—all too soon followed by repeated abuse. Such relationships can be healed in only one way: David's way. The abuser must take full responsibility for his actions and publicly exonerate the abused—just as David did in writing Psalm 51.

When we examine David's relationships with his wives, what we find is not pretty. David showed a disregard for women that we rightly find repugnant. And yet, David also showed appreciation for the strong woman who repels rather than attracts so many men today. And in his relationship with Bathsheba, David did display a willingness to accept responsibility for the wrong he committed. In this, David pointed the way to the healing of many relationships today.

We can never study David without realizing how complex human beings are. And how greatly we need the grace, forgiveness, and guidance that can be ours through a personal relationship with David's God.

DAVID'S RELATIONSHIP WITH HIS CHILDREN

It was not unusual in the ancient Middle East for kings to have a number of children. Nor was it common for kings to be close to their children while they were young. We know that David had a number of sons and daughters (cf. 1 Chron. 3:1–9). We also know that several of David's children featured in Scripture came to a tragic end.

David's relationship with Amnon and Tamar (*2 Sam. 13*). David's son Amnon developed a consuming lust for his half-sister, David's daughter Tamar. Amnon feigned illness and asked for Tamar. When Amnon got Tamar alone, he raped her. As soon as he had sex with her, his lust changed to hatred, and he sent her away, weeping bitterly. The text tells us that "when King David heard of all these things, he was very angry" (13:21). But David did nothing.

According to Old Testament law, Amnon should have married Tamar, a marriage she herself suggested before the rape. Surely David, whose relationship with Bathsheba had begun the same way and yet had been healed, could at least have advised his son. Yet rather than deal with the situation, David remained silent. Tamar hid herself in her brother Absalom's home, and the pain and the anger the rape created festered. David's failure to act made a tragic situation worse and made resolution impossible.

David's relationship with Absalom (*2 Sam. 13—15*). Tamar was the full sister of Absalom, and her rape by Amnon kindled Absalom's hatred. Absalom waited for two years, pretending to remain Amnon's friend, and then arranged for Amnon to be assassinated. Absalom then fled to a friendly nation, where he remained in exile for some time. Finally, David was prevailed on to recall Absalom, but even then the king refused to see him. In this, David neither judged Absalom for his fratricide, nor confronted him as Nathan had confronted David, nor forgave him as God had forgiven David.

Nor did David act when Absalom set out on a carefully crafted campaign to win the allegiance of the northern Hebrew tribes. Soon it was too late: Absalom and a group of David's old advisors led rebel forces into Jerusalem, forcing David to flee.

In the civil war that followed, Absalom was killed, and David wept inconsolably over his son. David had loved Absalom. But David's failure to deal with the sin contributed to the tragedy and deaths that followed.

David's relationship with Solomon (*1 Chron. 29*). Like many a dad whose children go into the family business, David had his doubts about Solomon's readiness. Near the end of his life David commented in public, "My son Solomon, whom alone God has chosen, is young and inexperienced" (29:1). This may explain in part why David held on to the throne long after he was physically and mentally unable to rule. Even on his death bed David failed to confirm Solomon as his successor until another of his sons, Adonijah, took a chance and attempted to have himself crowned Israel's ruler. Only then did David act and fulfill his pledge to see Solomon, God's choice, crowned.

How easy it is to see our children as "young and inexperienced," never realizing that until we let them step out on their own they will never gain the experience they need.

Yet David's relationship with Solomon clearly mirrors his relationship with his other children. David was at best a passive parent. David cared deeply but he was never willing to step forward. David neither disciplined nor counseled. He neither confronted nor forgave. David's inaction seems to have been perceived by David's children as indifference; an indifference that left them free to cross the boundary between right and wrong.

David's failures as a father warn us all. More than anything else our children need us to be involved in their lives. They may rebel as they grow up; they may seem to reject our values. But loving involvement gives a father an influential role in shaping a child that detachment never can.

Why did David detach himself from these intimate family matters? Some assume it was the press of great affairs—for David had a kingdom to manage. But I suspect that the underlying reason was David's earlier failure with Bathsheba, which despite God's forgiveness and her forgiveness too, robbed him of that moral authority that every parent needs. Seeing his own flaws repeated in his children, David seems to have drawn back, feeling helpless.

DAVID: AN EXAMPLE FOR TODAY

The more closely we examine David's life, the more we realize how complex an individual David was. On the one hand, David was a mystic, deeply in awe of and in love with God. On the other hand, David was a military genius, a gifted leader.

On the one hand, David was deeply committed to the Lord, so concerned with doing right that he remained loyal to King Saul even when Saul betrayed David again and again. On the other hand, David was a man who casually exploited a woman who loved him, and who surrendered to lust for another man's wife.

On the one hand, David was consumed with a desire to honor God and to lead his people to worship the Lord. On the other hand, David was a failure as a father; he proved unable to control, guide, or discipline his children.

Perhaps the best we can say of David was that he was a human being, writ large. Both David's sins and his sanctity come across boldly, so much greater than either our sins or our meager efforts to nurture our relationship with the Lord. And so from David the lessons we can learn are great ones, too.

- David came to know and love God early in life. The earlier we can introduce our children to God, the more significant their lives will be.

- David was responsive to God's self-revelation. David not only wished to honor God; David was eager to know God better and to glorify Him. A passion for the Lord will not keep us from sin by itself, but it will bring us back to Him should we fall.

- David gave significant attention to worship. If we would know God better, we too will spend time in personal and corporate worship.

- David's flaws stand as warnings, signposts erected by God for our benefit. We are not to succumb to lust, nor are we to demean or exploit women. And we are not to withdraw from involvement with our children.

- Yet David's sterling qualities also point us toward significant lives. We are to be loyal to God and to others, faithful under persecution, trusting when things go wrong, captivated by the vision of serving God in whatever way He chooses. We are to be ready to confess our sins and quick to turn to the Lord when in need. In these things David can be our example. And for these things we rightly honor him today.

PATRIARCHS AND PIONEERS

NOAH

Scripture references:
Genesis 5—9; Ezekiel 14:14–20;
Hebrews 11:7; 1 Peter 3:20

Date:	Unknown
Name:	Noah [NOH-uh; "rest" or "comfort"]
Greatest accomplishment:	Noah built the giant ship in which his family and land animals survived the Genesis Flood.

NOAH'S ROLE IN SCRIPTURE

When God determined to wipe out a corrupt human society, He chose Noah to build an ark in which his own family and representatives of all animals would be preserved. Genesis describes the cataclysmic Flood that then scoured the entire earth, radically changing earth's ecology. After a year in the great ship, the waters receded, and Noah and his family were deposited in a fresh, new world to begin again the process of populating earth.

Most references to Noah are found in the Genesis 6—9 account of the Flood and its aftermath. However, other references to Noah help us sense his significance in the Old and New Testament.

Noah is an example of a righteous man (*Ezek. 14:14–20*). The prophet Ezekiel was among the Jewish captives taken to Babylon in an early invasion of his homeland. There he received a message from God. Judah and Jerusalem soon would be crushed by the Babylonians, the city and its temple destroyed, and the people either killed or taken into captivity. Ezekiel emphasized that there was no hope that God would relent. Not even Noah, Daniel, or Job would be a shield against the coming judgment. The three righteous men would survive, but they would be unable to shield even their own

Noah and his family labored on the ark for 120 years, undoubtedly earning the ridicule of neighbors for miles around.

❖

children—something Noah had done in the time of the Flood.

This reference to Noah underlines the utterly corrupt character of moral and religious life in Judah at the time of the Babylonian invasion. As in the days of Noah, the wickedness of the people was so great (cf. Ezek. 8—11) that nothing could turn aside the divine judgment.

Noah is an example of a man of faith (Heb. 11:7).
The writer of Hebrews said of Noah, "By faith Noah, being divinely warned of things not yet seen, moved with godly fear, prepared an ark for the saving of his household, by which he condemned the world and became heir of the righteousness which is according to faith." This brief mention makes several significant points. When God warned Noah of a coming Flood, Noah believed God. This faith—not any innate moral goodness—made Noah different from the people of his time. Noah's faith, as all faith, was exercised as a response to God's revelation. Noah did not seek God; God spoke to Noah. Noah's response to the divine warning "condemned the world" (Heb. 11:7). Noah's response to God revealed what was right and exposed the unbelief of those around him as wrong. In the same way today, the Christian's faith and life condemns those who refuse to trust the Lord.

Noah's experience foreshadowed our salvation in Christ (1 Pet. 3:18—4:3).
The 1 Peter passage is often misunderstood, even though the text makes it clear that Noah's experience is a type, or foreshadowing, of salvation. The points of comparison are these: Noah was preserved from waters of the Flood in the ark, and deposited in a fresh new world. Believers are preserved from divine judgment in Christ, and given a new life as citizens in Jesus' kingdom. The analogous points are:

The waters = Divine judgment

The ark = Christ

The new earth = Christ's kingdom

The "baptism" mentioned by Peter is not water baptism, as some have mistakenly assumed, but rather spiritual baptism, by which the Holy Spirit bonds the believers of Jesus so that we are united to Him in

God caused the animals to enter the ark Noah had prepared.

His death and in His resurrection (Rom. 6:1–14).

Noah's times symbolize godlessness and wickedness *(Matt. 24:37; Luke 17:26–27).* Jesus warned that when He returns, human beings will be just as indifferent to God and just as wicked as were the people of Noah's day. Human nature remains corrupt despite the passage of many centuries. This condition will call for divine judgment when Jesus returns to rule, just as when Noah lived.

From references to Noah in the rest of Scripture, we see that this man is of more than historical interest. Noah and his times are also a metaphor, reminding us that in our day too we must deal with issues of faith, judgment, and redemption in Jesus Christ.

NOAH'S LIFE AND TIMES

When Noah lived human society was totally corrupt. Genesis states that "the wickedness of man was great in the earth, and every intent of the thoughts of his heart was only evil continually" (Gen. 6:5). God was grieved and determined to destroy humankind. Verse eight then states, "but Noah found grace in the eyes of the Lord" (Gen. 6:8). Of all his generation, only Noah was sensitive to the Lord or concerned about a personal relationship with Him (Gen. 6:9).

The making of the ark (Gen. 6:11–22). When God spoke to Noah and warned him of the coming flood, Noah immediately set out with his sons to construct a giant vessel. God provided the plans, and the rationale. The ark must be large enough to house members of each animal kind, Noah's family, and food for them all.

Genesis 6:3 suggests that it took Noah 120 years to build the ark, something possible because of the long life-spans of those who lived before the Flood (cf. Gen. 5). Interestingly, the proportions of the ark are in harmony with modern ship building practice, as the giant vessel was 450-by-75-by-45 feet.

As this great vessel rose over the plains, people from miles around must have come to see and to laugh at "Noah's folly." Peter refers to this when he speaks of the spirit of Christ speaking to the people of Noah's day.

Along with the ark's powerful witness to the coming Flood, Noah must have urgently warned his neighbors of what God was about to do. Through Noah's words, God both invited faith and damned unbelief. By their ridicule of Noah and his message, the people of Noah's day condemned themselves.

WHICH ANIMALS WERE ON THE ARK?

Some have ridiculed the notion that Noah's ark could have been large enough to contain pairs of all kinds of animals and birds. The ridicule is based on the assumption that Noah took one of every species of animal and bird. But the Hebrew tells us that Noah took one of every "kind" of animal. On this point the *New International Encyclopedia of Bible Words* notes:

> Despite the often-stated truth that the Bible is "not a book of science," it is clear that Scripture is in conflict here with modern evolutionary thought. The conflict is even more clear when we explore other passages in which the word "kind" (*min*, 31 times in the OT) is used (particularly Gen. 6—7, Lev. 11, Deut. 14). In Scripture, *min* designates what biologists would identify as species, genus, family, and even order. And in each case the Bible affirms that God created and maintains the identity of the form within the creation order. Whatever we may conclude from Scripture's affirmation, we find no support for the evolutionary hypothesis that calls at the least for development and change across kingdoms and phyla (p. 375).

Riding out the great Flood (Gen. 7:1—8:14). When the ark was finished and supplied, God caused representatives of each animal kind to come to the ark. When all were aboard God himself shut and sealed the door.

In the surging waters that flooded earth, all human and animal life on earth was wiped out. [For a fascinating examination of the Genesis Flood, and comparison of Scripture's account with other ancient flood stories, see the companion volume in this series, *Every Miracle and Wonder of the Bible.*] Adjusting the dates given in Genesis to our calendar, Noah and his family would have been in the ark for over a year, from 10 May (Gen. 7:10) to 27 May the next year (Gen. 8:14).

The Flood's aftermath (Gen. 8:15—9:29). When Noah and his sons and their wives left the ark, Noah's first act was to build an altar and worship the Lord. Several themes in these chapters are significant.

God's promise (8:20–22; 9:8–17). God promised that He would never again destroy the world by water, even though man's heart remains evil.

God's commission (9:1–7). The divine permission God gave Noah and his descendants to use fish and animals for food suggests that before the Flood human beings were vegetarians. Even more significant however is the responsibility that God imposed on human beings in Genesis 9:6–7. Noah's descendants were charged with once again populating the earth, and they were also given the responsibility of governing themselves. This responsibility is implied in the call for capital punishment: "whoever sheds man's blood, / by man his blood shall be shed; / For in the image of God He made man" (Gen. 9:6). It would now be up to humankind to restrain one another's evil impulses. And should a person take a human life, murdering an individual made in God's image, the penalty must be forfeiture of his or her own life.

Sin's persistence (Gen. 9:8–28). Genesis makes it clear that despite the purging of the pre-Flood population, our world was hardly purified from sin. Noah and his family carried within themselves the sin nature that was a consequence of Adam's fall. This is illustrated in an incident that happened after Noah had become a farmer. One day he drank too much wine, and as he lay in a stupor one of his sons, Ham, "saw the nakedness of his father" (9:22). While many have speculated just what this phrase implies, it is clear that Ham's shameless *attitude* was far different from that of his two brothers. These two hurried and carefully covered their father.

The predictive curse recorded here on one of Ham's offspring, Canaan, is suggestive. Later Canaanite religion was shameless in its exploitation of sex and violence.

The main point of the incident, however, is to remind us that human beings remain flawed after the Flood. Even a Noah can sin unintentionally, while a Ham will take a perverse delight in what others view as shameful.

NOAH: AN EXAMPLE FOR TODAY

Noah's relationship with God is emphasized throughout Scripture. Genesis depicts Noah as a man who believed God despite the bizarre content of God's revelation. Who would have believed, in a land without seas, that it was necessary to build a giant boat? Who would have persisted in the task for 120 years, rallying his family to the work, despite the certain ridicule of all around him. There can be no doubt that Noah was a truly exceptional man who challenges us in our own walk with God.

- Noah challenges us to commit to the unseen. There was no visible evidence of a coming flood. Yet, Noah considered God's Word far more trustworthy than what he could taste and touch and see, and he made his choice accordingly.
- Noah challenges us to persistence. It's easy to undertake a task we can finish in a few minutes or a few days. It is far

more difficult to remain committed to tasks that we must faithfully perform for years before we derive any benefits.

- Noah challenges us to withstand peer pressure. So many of our choices are made so we will fit in with others, to please them or to avoid their criticism. Noah was so committed to his God-given course that he could not be influenced to abandon it, even though the entire world thought him a fool. We need to determine in our hearts to please God, whether we please others or not.

JOB
Scripture references:
The Book of Job;
Ezekiel 14:14–20; James 5:11

Date:	*Unknown*
Name:	*Job [JOHB; meaning uncertain]*
Greatest accomplishment:	*Job endured suffering despite his inability to understand God's purpose.*

JOB'S ROLE IN SCRIPTURE

Job's story and his struggle challenge us to contemplate the mystery of human suffering. Job was an innocent man, a man whom God loved. Yet, all that Job himself loved was taken from him, and Job was forced to endure intense physical and psychic pain. The Book of Job traces his tormented thoughts as Job tries to puzzle out what God could possibly intend by permitting him to endure such anguish.

Job is mentioned in the Old Testament, along with Noah and Daniel, as one of three righteous men whose presence in a city might normally avert God's judgment. Ezekiel refers to the three to underline the certainty of the judgment about to befall Jerusalem in his day. Not even the presence of all three would cause God to withhold His punishing hand (Ezek. 14:14–20).

Job is also referred to in the Book of James as an encouragement for believers who also were suffering despite living righteous lives. James called on his readers to be patient and reminded them, "You have heard of the perseverance of Job and seen the end intended by the Lord—that the Lord is very compassionate and merciful" (James 5:11).

JOB'S LIFE AND TIMES

Job's date. The Book of Job may be the oldest book in the Bible. Many commentators place Job in the patriarchal era as a contemporary of Abraham. The following are some of the reasons cited for this. The Hebrew in which the book is written is archaic, with many words that do not appear in other Old Testament writings. The book makes no reference to God's covenant with Abraham or to Mosaic Law. Instead, reference is made to revelations received in dreams and to long-held traditional beliefs about God. It seems clear from these elements that Job predates the giving of the written revelation and quite possibly preceded God's special revelation of Himself to Abraham.

Job's character (1:1; 31:1–24). The first verse of the book introduces Job as a man who was "blameless and upright, and one who feared God and shunned evil." The Lord Himself confirmed this in His dialogs with Satan (1:8; 2:3).

Perhaps even more significant is Job's own characterization in chapter 31 of his moral commitments. Throughout the book Job argued with three of his friends who were convinced that Job's suffering must be punishment for some secret sin. Job, sure that he had lived a godly life, rejected their argu-

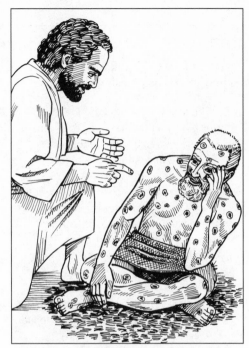

Job showed his despair by tearing his clothing and sitting in ashes.

ments. While Job did not know God's reasons for apparently causing his suffering, Job was sure that God couldn't be punishing him.

Job 31 is significant in that it reminds us that God has created human beings with a moral nature and an innate knowledge of right and wrong. Long before the Ten Commandments, nomadic peoples in the legendary land of Uz were fully aware of God's moral expectations, and knew how they should live. Job's problem is that while he has lived by commonly accepted moral precepts, he is still suffering. The puzzle is, Why should such bad things happen to a truly good person?

Job's problem (Job 3—31). On the surface it would seem that Job's problem lay in the disasters that had befallen him. On a single day, Job had suffered the loss of his wealth and the deaths of his children. Shortly after this, excruciatingly painful boils tormented him.

CHAPTER 31: JOB DEFENDS HIS MORALITY

In none of the following ways did Job fail to live a moral life. Job's conclusion is that God simply cannot be punishing him for sin.

If I have walked with falsehood,
Or if my foot has hastened to deceit,
Let me be weighed on honest scales,
That God may know my integrity.

If my heart has been enticed by a woman,
Or if I have lurked at my neighbor's door,
Then let my wife grind for another . . .
For that would be wickedness;
Yes, it would be iniquity deserving of
   judgment.

If I have kept the poor from their desire,
Or caused the eyes of the widow to fail,
Or eaten my morsel by myself,
So that the fatherless could not eat of it;

If I have raised my hand against the
   fatherless,
When I saw I had help in the gate,
Then let my arm fall from my shoulder,
Let my arm be torn from the socket.

Or if I have made gold my hope,
Or said to fine gold, "You are my confidence";
Or if I have rejoiced because my wealth
   was great, And because my hand had
   gained much.

If I have rejoiced at the destruction of him
   who hated me,
Or lifted myself up when evil found him
(Indeed I have not allowed my mouth to sin
By asking for a curse on his soul);

If I have covered my transgressions as
   Adam,
By hiding my iniquity in my bosom,
Because I feared the great multitude
And dreaded the contempt of families,
So that I kept silence
And did not go out of the door.
      (Job 31:5, 6, 9–11, 16–17, 21–22,
      24, 25, 28, 30, 33, 34)

Yet, it was neither the disasters nor the pain that unnerved Job. What deeply troubled Job was that he could not explain *why* he was suffering. Job's understanding of God reflected the view of others of his time. God was a moral judge who expected human beings to live up to commonly accepted moral standards. And God rewarded those who did so and punished those who did not.

Job, however, had lived an exemplary life. So the question of why God was letting him suffer tormented Job. In a lengthy dialog with three friends Job over and over asserted his innocence, and implied that God was being unfair. Yet, Job could not bring himself to believe that God is unfair. The conflict of his beliefs about God over against what he was experiencing frustrated and tormented righteous Job.

Job's end *(Job 42)*. In the end, God restored Job's wealth two times over and gave him another family. God commended Job for facing the problem of suffering with honesty and integrity. God rebuked the three friends who, in their efforts to be on what they thought was God's side, tried to coerce Job into confessing sins he did not commit.

EXPLORING JOB'S RELATIONSHIPS

Job's relationship with Satan *(Job 1,2)*. The first chapters of Job take us behind the curtain that hangs between material and spiritual realms. We are shown a dialog between God and Satan, in which God pointed Job out to Satan as a blameless and upright man.

Satan immediately complained that God had erected a hedge around Job that Satan cannot penetrate. If only God would permit Satan to attack Job, Job would deny God to His face. God permitted Satan to attack Job, and Satan stripped Job of his wealth and family and inflicted Job with intensely painful boils. But Satan's efforts to move Job to deny God failed utterly (Job 2:10).

Job himself was unaware of Satan's involvement in his experience, and saw God as the direct cause of his pain. However, with the insight provided in chapters one and two, we note several things about the relationship between this believer and the devil.

Satan was innately hostile to God's own. Satan's desire is to harm God's people, never to do them good. The means Satan chose to attack Job shows how wicked this fallen angel truly is.

Satan is limited in his ability to harm believers. Satan's complaint that God had placed a hedge around Job should comfort us. Only with God's permission can our great enemy aim his attacks against us. We are not to take Satan lightly. But neither are we to fear him as though his powers were unlimited. [For a thorough study of Satan, see the companion volume in this series, *Every Good and Evil Angel in the Bible.*]

Satan can be defeated when resisted in faith. Even Job's wife urged him to give up, to curse God, and to die. She seemed convinced that death was preferable to continued suffering. Job however remained faithful in his commitment to the Lord. And, after the notation of Satan's defeat in Job 2:10, this fallen angel is not mentioned again in the book. Despite his pretensions, Satan is but a bit player on sacred history's stage, destined to be set aside in eternity.

Job's relationship with God. We have noted that Job was a godly person who lived a moral life out of respect for the Lord. When tragedy struck, Job did not blame God, even though he assumed that God was responsible for his sufferings. Job's problem was that he could not *understand* what God was doing in his life.

Job's inadequate knowledge of God. While rejecting the idea that God was punishing Job for sin, Job agreed with his three friends that this was what God did. The wicked were supposed to suffer, for God simply must be fair! As Job's dialog with his friends developed, Job questioned this assumption. Finally Job argued, correctly, that all four of them knew of wicked people who seem to prosper, and apparently godly individuals who struggle. It is dangerous for any of us to "put God in a box," and to assume from what we know of Him that God must act in this way or that.

Job's confrontation by God (Job 38—40). God spoke to Job and his friends following an insight shared by a younger man named Elihu. Elihu had listened as Job and his friends argued endlessly. Now Elihu pointed out that suffering isn't always punishment. Suffering may serve a corrective purpose; God may be seeking to turn a sinner from his ways rather than punishing him. While this did not apply to Job, it did break the impasse. God need not punish Job! So Job can preserve his integrity, and his friends need not "defend God" by accusing Job.

When God appeared to the little company, He did not explain the reason for Job's suffering. Instead the Lord urged Job to consider how far above His creation God is. Job cannot even explain the wonders of nature; how can he expect to explain God's purposes?

Job acknowledged the rightness of what God had said, and humbled himself. Job had heard about God, but now that he had confronted God, Job realized how little right he had to question God's acts. Whatever God's purposes might be in permitting Job to suffer, Job's role was simply to continue to trust and honor the Lord.

Job's restoration by God (Job 42). God commended Job for facing the mystery of God's actions honestly without retreat to theological hair splitting. God restored all of Job's goods twice over. And, God gave Job another seven sons and three daughters. Why not fourteen sons and six daughters? Because unlike the material wealth which had been taken from Job, his children were not really lost to him. In the resurrection Job will be reunited with them. The seven new sons and three new daughters do, in fact, give Job twice as much as he had lost.

JOB: AN EXAMPLE FOR TODAY

Job never learned why God permitted him to suffer. Job did come to know God better, and perhaps this is an underlying purpose in all suffering. Through suffering, we are forced to face the mystery of God, and challenged to trust Him deeper. The Job who emerged from the crucible of pain had a deeper trust in God than the Job who entered it. May it be the same for us, when we, too, face the hurts that are a part of every human life. In the meanwhile, there are other lessons we can learn from Job as well.

- Job's story reminds us of God's watch-care. God does put a hedge around His own, and only what He permits is allowed to pass through. In this we can take comfort. Knowing God's love, we can be certain any pain He permits is for our good.
- Job's story reminds us that experiences we cannot understand provide the greatest opportunities to exercise faith. Faith is proven to be genuine only when it is tested. As Peter reminded us, a faith that passes the test is more precious than gold (1 Pet. 1:7).

- Job's story reminds us that God has multiplied blessings in store for us. We may not find these blessings in this life, as Job did, but they are there for us. They are reserved in heaven, awaiting only the coming of our Lord (James 5:7–11).

ISAAC
Scripture references:
Genesis 17:19–21; 21:3–12;
22; 24—28; 31; 35

Date:	*2066 B.C.*
Name:	*Isaac [I-zik; "laughing"]*
Greatest accomplishment:	*Isaac inherited God's covenant promises from Abraham and passed them to his son Jacob.*

ISAAC'S ROLE IN SCRIPTURE

Isaac is significant primarily as a transitional figure. He inherited the covenant promises God gave to Abraham, and he passed those promises on to his son Jacob. He is frequently named where the Bible speaks of patriarchs, and for generations the Israelites knew God simply as "the God of Abraham, Isaac, and Jacob."

ISAAC'S LIFE AND TIMES

Isaac lived his life as a nomad in the Promised Land, living in tents, leading his flocks and herds to pasture as the seasons changed, and now and then pausing to plant and harvest grain. By the standards of the time, Isaac was a wealthy person.

Most references to Isaac portray him in a passive role, being acted upon rather than acting. God predicted his birth and gave him his name (Gen. 17:19–21). When Isaac was weaned, his mother insisted that his older half-brother Ishmael be sent away to protect Isaac's inheritance rights (Gen. 21:3–12). Perhaps as a teenager, his father took Isaac to Mount Horeb where Abraham prepared to offer him as a sacrifice at God's command (see pages 19–20). When Isaac was forty years of age, his father sent a servant to find a bride for him (Gen. 24). Later when a dispute with local peoples over water rights erupted, Isaac's response was to move again and again rather than engage in conflict (Gen. 26). And, like his father Abraham, Isaac got his wife Rebekah to pretend they were not married out of fear that he might be killed by a king of the Philistines who desired her (Gen. 26).

Isaac is not known for bold actions or great achievements. Yet, Isaac played a vital role in God's plan and His calling into being a people through whom He intended to reveal Himself and through whom Christ would come.

EXPLORING ISAAC'S RELATIONSHIPS

The relationships developed in the text are Isaac's relationships with his family members.

Isaac's relationship with his wife. The text tells us that Isaac loved Rachel (Gen. 24:67). Certainly she was a strong woman as well as a beautiful one, as displayed in her willingness to leave her homeland for an unknown future with a man she had just met. Yet, the relationship between Rachel and Isaac apparently was not especially close. Each of the two had a favorite son, and Rachel plotted to trick Isaac into giving his blessing to her favorite rather than his. Perhaps Isaac was rigid and unwilling to dialog with his wife, but whatever the reason for Rachel's actions they suggest that husband and wife were not as close as they might have been.

It is tragic when spouses feel they cannot discuss significant family issues with each other but must go behind one another's backs to gain a personal "win."

Isaac's relationship with his sons. Isaac and Rachel both fell into the trap of having favorites—and favoring them. It may not be humanly possible for a parent not to feel more affection for one child than for others. However it is possible, and right, to refrain from showing favoritism. Isaac liked the outdoorsman Esau, even though he was a materialistic individual with no spiritual sensitivity. Rachel liked the quiet and contemplative Jacob, who felt more comfortable staying near the family tents. How much better it is for parents to praise the strengths of each child rather than to favor the child whose strengths we appreciate most.

Isaac's relationship with God. Surprisingly, little is said of Isaac's personal relationship with God. We know that Isaac was a believer who worshiped the Lord (Gen. 26:23–25). Jacob once referred to "the LORD your God" when addressing his father (Gen. 27:20). At the same time nothing in the text suggests that Isaac's relationship with the Lord was as close as that of his father Abraham.

However, one action indicates that Isaac chose to submit to God's will despite his own desires. Jacob had come to his blind and aged father, and, pretending to be Esau, tricked Isaac into blessing him. In Old Testament times, this final parental blessing had legal as well as prophetic force. When Esau himself appeared before his father, Isaac realized that Jacob had tricked him. Jacob, whom God had indicated before his birth would be preferred over his older twin Esau, now had the old man's blessing even though it was stolen. Realizing what had happened, Isaac said, "and indeed he shall be blessed" (Gen. 27:33). This simple statement, seemingly an afterthought, is significant. Isaac accepted that God had chosen Jacob and that his favorite, Esau, had been set aside. At last Isaac was willing to submit to God's will.

ISAAC: AN EXAMPLE FOR TODAY

Isaac reminds us that it's not necessary for a son to be as great as his father to have a significant role in God's plan. Nor is it necessary for a father to be as great as his son. In a real way, both his father Abraham and his son Jacob overshadowed Isaac. Even so, we have much to learn from him.

- Isaac is a model for the quiet among us who neither want nor need the limelight. He reminds us that it is less important to be great than to be faithful and that the apparently insignificant people play a greater role in God's plan than we imagine.

- Isaac encourages us to love our wives—but also to share with them. Neither children nor any other thing should be permitted to divide us in our willingness to do God's will together.

- Isaac reminds us that it is better to submit to God's will later than never. Isaac truly favored Esau and loved him much better than he loved Jacob. But Jacob was God's choice as the one to whom the covenant should pass. In the end, Isaac submitted to God's will and so decreed, "Indeed, he shall be blessed."

JACOB
Scripture references:
Genesis 25—35; 48—49
Romans 9:6–13

❖

Date: About 2006–1859 B.C.
Name: Jacob [JAY-kuhb; "supplanter"]

Greatest accomplishment: *Jacob, renamed Israel, fathered the twelve men from whom the Jewish people sprang.*

JACOB'S ROLE IN SCRIPTURE

It's tempting to skip over Jacob in our discussion of great men of the Old Testament. Jacob is hardly a savory character. Yet, in God's economy Jacob fathered twelve sons who are the source of the twelve tribes of Israel, and thus of God's Old Testament people. Jacob's significance is reflected in the fact that his names (Jacob, and later Israel) are found 2,549 times in our Bible!

Yet, it simply is because Jacob gave his second name, "Israel," to a people that his name is mentioned so often. Both Isaac and Jacob are significant primarily because their histories permit us to trace the passage of the covenant God made with Abraham from Abraham to the Jewish people as a whole. The covenant passed from Abraham, to his son Isaac, and then to his son Jacob, whose name was changed to Israel.

In Romans 9, Paul made an important point concerning the passage of the covenant to these sons. Isaac had an older half-brother, Ishmael. Yet the covenant promises were passed to Isaac. Jacob had an older twin brother, Esau. Yet the covenant promises were passed to Jacob, and God decisively rejected Esau. According to the apostle Paul, this demonstrates an important truth. God is Sovereign, and is free to act as He chooses without reference to human conventions. While in ancient culture the older son was to inherit the tangible and intangible property of the father, God saw fit to do things His way. That Jacob was in many ways an unsavory character simply reminds us that the bestowing of God's gifts do not depend on our righteousness but rather on the grace and unmerited favor of our God.

JACOB'S LIFE AND TIMES

Jacob spent his youth living a nomadic life with his parents and twin brother Esau. A rivalry developed between the two brothers, fostered by the fact that their father favored the outdoorsman, Esau, while their mother favored Jacob. The rivalry and the parents' favoritism introduced discord and hostility into the family.

Jacob supplanted his brother (*Gen. 25:27–34; 27:1–41*). In biblical times, the oldest son inherited twice the amount of younger sons, as well as family headship. Despite the fact that Esau was minutes older than Jacob, and thus the eldest, God intended Jacob to inherit the covenant promises He had given to Abraham, which were the family's true legacy. Rather than be patient and wait for God to work this out in His own way, Jacob took matters into his own hands.

One day when Esau came in from hunting and was hungry, he asked Jacob for some stew Jacob was cooking. Jacob proposed a trade: the stew for Esau's birthright. Esau's easy acquiescence showed how little concern he had for spiritual things; Jacob's proposal showed how little Jacob cared for integrity.

Years later, when Isaac felt that his death was near, he determined to bless his boys. In that era, the "blessing" of a father had the force of a will and was also thought to fix the future of the sons he blessed. When his wife Rebekah learned that Isaac intended to give his blessing to Esau, Rebekah urged Jacob to pretend to be his brother. Jacob deceived the now blind Isaac, who gave Jacob the blessing he had intended for Esau. When Isaac learned what had happened, he bowed to God's will and confirmed passage of the covenant promise and other blessings to Jacob.

Jacob's offer to trade his stew for Esau's birthright provides significant insight into the character of each.

❖

Rebekah and Jacob's deceit gained their objective but at a terrible cost. Esau now hated his brother and planned to kill Jacob when their father died. When Rebekah learned what Esau intended to do, she sent Jacob away, ostensibly to obtain a bride from her own family back in Haran. Little did Rebekah realize when she plotted with Jacob that once her best loved son left home, she would never see him again. Jacob was gone from Canaan for twenty years, during which time his mother died.

Jacob in Haran (*Gen. 28—31*). In Haran Jacob located his uncle Laban's family. There he fell deeply in love with Laban's younger daughter, Rachel. However in Laban, Jacob found his match as a trickster. Lacking a dowry, Jacob promised to work for Laban for seven years for Rachel. Documents from the period show that an exchange of service in place of the payment of money as a bride price was not unusual. But at the wedding Laban substituted Rachel's older sister Leah. When dawn came, Jacob discovered the trick, and stormed out to confront his uncle. The slippery Laban made excuses, and Jacob was forced to work an additional seven years for Rachel.

With this obligation met, Laban, realizing that God had blessed him because of Jacob, worked out other agreements to keep Jacob in his employ. To Jacob's frustration Laban kept changing the terms of the agreement. Jacob learned by experience the frustration his brother Esau must have felt when Jacob tricked Esau! Finally, after twenty years, God directed Jacob to return to the promised land.

The journey home (Gen. 32—35). During his years in Haran, Jacob had sired eleven boys and one girl, and through God's intervention had gained large flocks and herds. On his way home, Jacob was terrified of the possible reaction of his brother, Esau. Jacob sent gifts of sheep and cattle on ahead to pacify his brother. When Esau met Jacob, however, he greeted him gladly. During the years Jacob was away, Esau had become rich. To Esau, the original "material man," all he had ever cared about were material possessions. Since he was now wealthy, Esau cared nothing about Jacob's possession of God's covenant promises.

The Genesis text tells us of several adventures of Jacob's family in Canaan, but the essence of the story is that Jacob was again in the land that God had promised to Abraham and his offspring. There Jacob was content to live a nomadic lifestyle as his father and grandfather before him.

Jacob's great tragedy (Gen. 37). For many years Jacob's great love, Rachel, had remained childless. Finally she had a son, Joseph, who became his father's favorite. Just as favoritism had ruined the harmony of Jacob's childhood family, so the favoritism he now showed toward Joseph destroyed his happiness.

Jacob's other sons grew to resent Joseph. They plotted to kill him, but instead sold him as a slave to traders bound for Egypt. They then took Joseph's distinctive coat, sprinkled it with goat's blood, and let Jacob conclude that wild animals had killed his son.

Jacob's resettlement to Egypt (Gen. 39—50). Jacob mourned for years for his lost son, never dreaming that Joseph was alive and had risen to head the government of Egypt. When a famine struck Canaan, and Joseph's brothers went to Egypt to buy grain, the family was reunited. Jacob and the seventy-five members of his clan were welcomed in Egypt, where their offspring remained for several hundred years, multiplying to a population of some two million persons.

Jacob ended his life in Egypt, content to be reunited with Joseph and Joseph's two sons. But when Jacob died his body was returned to Canaan, and he was buried there beside Abraham and Sarah, with his parents Isaac and Rebekah, and his wife Leah.

E S A U :   T H E M A T E R I A L I S T I C   M A N

Jacob and Esau were twins, but they were quite different individuals. We rightly criticize Jacob for defrauding and cheating Esau of his birthright; yet we need to be aware of Esau's total indifference to spiritual realities.

The "birthright" in ancient times was the right of the eldest son to leadership of the family, to the bulk of the tangible and to all of the intangible family assets. Isaac's intangible asset was the covenant of promise God had given to Abraham and his descendants. When the hungry Esau readily traded this birthright for a bowl of Jacob's stew, he showed his contempt for spiritual realities and for God. Esau was a truly material man; for him this world of sight and touch and taste and feel was all that counted.

Later, after Jacob stole Esau's blessing by tricking their father Isaac, Esau planned to murder his brother. Esau was angry with his brother for defrauding him, but what moved Esau to consider murder was the fear that Jacob would now take possession of the bulk of the family's wealth.

Years later, when Jacob returned to Canaan from the land to which he had fled from Esau's wrath, Esau met his brother graciously. The threat to Esau's wealth had not materialized; Esau had in fact taken possession of their father's entire estate! Esau's remark, "I have enough, my brother" (Gen. 33:9) explains his lack of rancor. All Esau had ever wanted was to be wealthy in this world's goods. And Esau, the material man, was wealthy indeed. Jacob could keep God's covenant promises, and even keep the little flocks and herds he had offered as a gift to win his brother's favor. Since Jacob did not ask the one-third of the family estate to which he was entitled, Esau could afford to be generous!

How tragic is the fate of the materialistic man. Like Esau, he may gain wealth beyond his dreams. But like Esau, he will never grasp the significance of the spiritual and will enter eternity as a truly poor man.

EXPLORING JACOB'S RELATIONSHIPS

Jacob's relationship with God. The biblical text traces the development of Jacob's personal relationship with God.

God's choice of Jacob (Gen. 25:19–26). The apostle Paul made it clear that Jacob was God's choice to inherit the covenant promises. This choice was announced to his mother, Rebekah, before Jacob's birth. The apostle drew an important lesson from this fact. He wrote in Romans 9:10 that "when Rebecca also had conceived by one man, even by our father Isaac (for the children not yet being born, nor having done anything good or evil, that the purpose of God according to election might stand, not of works but of Him who calls)." Paul's point is simply that God's choice of Jacob did not depend on what Jacob had done or would do, or on Jacob's character. God was and is free to choose. And, when He chooses, God intends to do us good, no matter how flawed our nature might be.

God was involved in Jacob's life before Jacob was born as He is in ours.

Jacob's desire for Esau's birthright (Gen. 25:29–34). It would be wrong to suppose at this point that Jacob had a conscious personal relationship with God. What Jacob did have was enough faith to see the value of the spiritual. In this he contrasts with Esau, to whom the notion of a spiritual realm beyond what he could see and taste and feel seemed nonsense. Today, too, some seem more aware of and open to the spiritual, while others are utter materialists who are blind to every spiritual reality. How important it is to cultivate spiritual sensitivity, for such may prove to be the door though which God enters our life.

Jacob's initial meeting with God (Gen. 28:10–22). When Jacob was forced to flee from his home he had an experience with God at a site he named Bethel ["house of God"]. In a dream, Jacob saw angels passing back and forth between heaven and earth. The vision stunned Jacob, and before he left the next morning he made a pledge:

> If God will be with me, and keep me in this way that I am going, and give me bread to eat and clothing to put on, so that I come back to my father's house in peace, then the Lord shall be my God (Gen. 28:20).

For Jacob, this was a first step in welcoming God into his life. Like our own first steps, this one seems to have been taken for selfish reasons. Jacob was willing to commit

Jacob's vision of angels at Bethel convinced him to trust himself and his future to the Lord.

himself to the Lord in exchange for protection, food, clothing, and a safe return home. One day, Jacob would learn that the greatest benefit of any relationship with the Lord is His presence and that the greatest reason to seek Him is to praise and enjoy Him forever. But for now, this was as far as Jacob could see.

This first step was acceptable to the Lord, even as our first faltering steps of faith are acceptable to Him.

God's intervention on Jacob's behalf (Gen. 30:25–43). During the years that Jacob worked for Laban, God blessed Jacob's every effort. Laban was becoming rich!

When Laban schemed to defraud Jacob, God taught Jacob how to transfer much of Laban's wealth in herds to himself, while always dealing honestly with his uncle. In time, Laban and his sons saw their wealth dwindle and Jacob's wealth increase. At that point, God told Jacob it was time to return to the Promised Land.

Jacob prayed to God (Gen. 32:1–12). Despite his fear of Esau, Jacob set out for home. When he reached the borders of Canaan, Jacob saw an encampment of angels waiting to accompany him home. Despite this vision, Jacob was afraid. He took all the precautions humanly possible to secure his family should Esau attack, and then turned to prayer. Jacob's prayer showed a maturity and spiritual depth lacking in his early years.

I am not worthy of the least of all the mercies and the truth which You have shown Your servant; for I crossed over this Jordan with my staff, and now I have become two companies. Deliver me, I pray, from the hand of my brother, from the hand of Esau; for I fear him, lest he come and attack me and the mother with the children. For You said, "I will surely treat you well, and make your descendants as the sand of the sea, which cannot be numbered for multitude" (Gen. 32:10–12).

This prayer demonstrated an appreciation for the Lord and a reliance on His promises of which Jacob was not capable earlier in his life.

Jacob wrestled with God (Gen. 32:22–32). That night, Jacob sent his herds and family across the river while he remained behind. There he wrestled with a "Man" whom Jacob identified as a theophany— a pre-incarnation appearance of God in human form. Jacob refused to release his hold on his supernatural opponent, and the Lord blessed Jacob and changed his name to Israel. The nature of this encounter remains a mystery, but the new name God gave Jacob echoed throughout Old Testament history.

Jacob/Israel's mature faith (Gen. 48:15–16). The last incident in which we gain a sense of Jacob's relationship with God occurred in Egypt. Jacob was near death, and he called for his sons and grandchildren. He blessed Joseph's two sons, and said:

> God, before whom my fathers Abraham
>   and Isaac walked,
> The God who has fed me all my life long
>   to this day,
> The Angel who has redeemed me from all
>   evil,
> Bless the lads. (Gen. 48:15, 16)

To Joseph he said, "Behold, I am dying, but God will be with you and bring you back to the land of your fathers" (Gen. 48:21).

Jacob, who began life relying on tricks and on his wits to gain spiritual ends, had finally come to the place where he acknowledged God's hand in all, and where he encouraged his son to wait, trustingly, on the Lord.

It took a long journey to bring Jacob/Israel to this point. May you and I accomplish that journey from self-reliance to complete reliance on God more quickly.

Jacob's relationship with his wives (Gen. 29, 30). Jacob had children by four women. Two were wives, Rachel and Leah. The other two, Bildad and Zilpah, were surrogates forced on Jacob by the two wives in a competition to give their husband sons. Little is said of the impact of this arrangement on Jacob, but the text reveals much about its impact on the women. [For a study of that impact, see the companion book in this series, *Every Woman in the Bible.*]

Clearly, Jacob had a deep and abiding love for Rachel, and just as clearly, Jacob put up with, but did not love, Leah. We sense Leah's pain in the names she gave her sons, names that reflect her dwindling hope to win her husband's affection.

> Reuben: "now therefore, my husband
>   will love me" (29:32)

> Simeon: "because the Lord has heard I
>   am unloved" (29:33)
> Levi: "now this time my husband will
>   become attached to me" (29:34).

At last, Leah realized that whatever she did, her husband would never truly care for her, so she named her next son Judah: "Now I will praise the Lord."

We can sense something of the pressure on Jacob that his wives' competition for sons caused. But the real tragedy is that in this polygamous family one wife was loved and the other unloved, and the two slave girls the wives forced on Jacob were treated as objects, with no say in what happened to them.

For those who imagine that God's intent that marriage involve one man and one woman somehow limits human beings, a study of Jacob and his wives is revealing indeed. How tragic for the man who seeks relationships with many women, to be deprived of the blessings of growing toward oneness with his wife. And how tragic for the women, to be in a relationship which at best depersonalizes and devalues them as human beings.

Jacob's relationship with Esau. See the sketch of Esau on pages 70–71.

JACOB: AN EXAMPLE FOR TODAY

Jacob is honored as one of the patriarchs through whom God's covenant promises were transmitted to His Old Testament people, the Jews. In a sense Jacob is most significant as a conduit of both revelation and grace.

At the same time, Jacob's experiences can teach us much about ourselves and our relationship with God. How clearly we see in Jacob our own tendency to take matters into our own hands, even when God has promised to act in His own time. How clearly we see our own willingness to cut corners when we think it will bring us closer to some goal. Yet Jacob also reminds us of our potential for spiritual growth and transformation. If we are spiritually sensitive and value a relationship with God, as Jacob did, God will speak to our open hearts. God will graciously and gradually work within us, until like Jacob we reach a point in which we have learned to value grace.

What specific lessons can we learn from Jacob?

- Jacob teaches us to look past material gain and value the spiritual. We must never lose sight of the fact that God is there and that the reality He inhabits is far more important than the shadow world we know through our senses.

- Jacob reminds us that God intends to correct our character flaws. Often, He does this by making us victims of the same kind of hurt we inflict on others. God is not willing to leave His chosen ones unchanged. We can correct ourselves. Or He will correct us.

- Jacob reminds us that the purpose we serve is greater than we are. Jacob was the conduit through which God intended to bless the world. That God uses us to bless others is far more important than that we live happy and prosperous lives.

- Jacob's life journey reminds us that God never deserts His own. God was with Jacob before Jacob knew him. He ventured with Jacob on all his travels. He stayed close to Jacob as his life drew to an end. There is no place we can go, no time we can inhabit, where God is absent. His presence is, and will ever remain, our hope.

JOSEPH

Scripture references:
Genesis 37—50; Acts 7:9–18;
Hebrews 11:22

Date:	About 1880 B.C.
Name:	Joseph [JOH-suhf; "may God add"]
Greatest achievement:	Joseph rose to become vizier of Egypt and preserved the Israelites by settling his family there.

JOSEPH'S ROLE IN SCRIPTURE

Joseph played a vital role in the preservation of the Hebrew people. His little family lived in Canaan, the land bridge and buffer between the great powers of the north and Egypt in the south, and Canaan frequently became a battleground. There was no way the Israelites could have built the population needed to inhabit the Promised Land had God's people remained in Canaan. But resettled by Joseph in one of the richest of Egypt's agricultural areas, the Hebrew people multiplied greatly. Despite being later enslaved by the Egyptians, the sojourn in Egypt was an essential part of God's plan for fulfilling his promise to Abraham, "I will make you a great nation" (Gen. 12:2).

Joseph is also one of the most attractive of Old Testament characters. He maintained a steadfast trust in God, and despite suffering unjustly, he consistently made choices that honored the Lord. Some have suggested that Joseph is the single most Christlike figure in the Old Testament, a man whose life mirrors that of our Lord in significant ways.

JOSEPH'S LIFE AND TIMES

Joseph's early years (Gen. 37). Joseph was the son of Jacob and of Rachel, Jacob's best-loved wife. Unfortunately, his father showed him such obvious favoritism that Joseph's brothers resented him deeply. Joseph seems to have been naively unaware of their jealousy. When Joseph related two dreams that suggested that one day his parents and his brothers would bow down to him, he only deepened their animosity. While Joseph was still a teenager, his brothers sold him to merchants traveling to Egypt.

Joseph's suffering in Egypt (Gen. 39—40). In Egypt, Joseph was sold to a high official named Potiphar. Joseph soon became Potiphar's most trusted agent and was put in charge of his estate. When Potiphar's wife falsely accused Joseph of attempting to rape her, Potiphar imprisoned Joseph. In prison, Joseph's organizational gifts and trustworthiness again led to advancement. Soon he became the warden's agent, and ran the prison. This prison housed the king's prison, and when two high officials of the royal court were housed there, Joseph correctly interpreted their dreams. As Joseph had predicted, one official was hanged, while the other was restored to his office. Two years later when Pharaoh had disquieting dreams no one could interpret, the official whose dream Joseph had explained told Pharaoh about him.

Several things are significant about the decade or more during which Joseph lived first as a slave and later as a convict. First, Joseph made the most of his opportunities. Rather than become despondent, Joseph went to work. There is no better way to prepare for great things than to be faithful in small things.

Second, Joseph remained committed to God and godliness. We see this in Joseph's response to Potiphar's wife's attempts to seduce him: "How then can I do this great wickedness, and sin against God" (39:9). It's all too tempting, when life treats us unfairly, to take detours into sin. Joseph maintained his integrity through it all.

Joseph's exaltation as second ruler of Egypt (Gen. 41). God showed Joseph the meaning of Pharaoh's disquieting dreams.

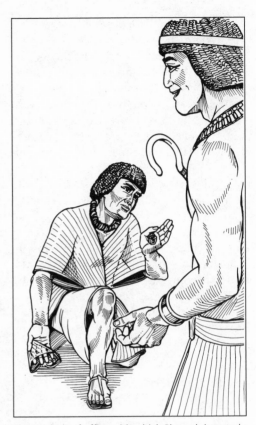

The symbols of office with which Pharaoh invested Joseph were those traditionally worn by the vizier of Egypt, as shown on ancient reliefs.

Joseph explained that Egypt would experience seven years of abundant crops, followed by seven years of famine. Joseph advised Pharaoh to prepare for the famine by storing grain during the seven good years. Pharaoh, impressed by the dream interpretation and the advice, made Joseph "second ruler" in Egypt. The symbols of Joseph's office described in Genesis 41:42 can be seen in wall paintings from the era. They suggest that Joseph was made vizier of Egypt, the highest administrative position in the kingdom. Applying the organizational skills he had developed in Potiphar's house and in the king's prison, Joseph set out energetically to prepare Egypt for the coming famine.

Joseph's reunion with his family (*Gen. 42—46*). When the famine struck, the entire Middle East was affected. Jacob sent his sons to Egypt to purchase grain so the family might survive. On each of their two trips they met with Joseph, but did not recognize him. Finally Joseph revealed himself, and wept with happiness. He forgave his brothers and invited the whole family to settle in Egypt.

The review in Acts 7 of Joseph's life reminds us that while Joseph is a fascinating individual, what is truly significant is the role Joseph played in God's plan. Joseph clearly understood this plan. Joseph explained his gracious attitude toward the brothers who had sold him into slavery by saying, "As for you, you meant evil against me; but God meant it for good, in order to bring it about as it is this day, to save many people alive" (Gen. 50:20).

EXPLORING JOSEPH'S RELATIONSHIPS

The most significant relationship in the Joseph story is that which he had with his brothers. Joseph's relationships with his brothers was complex, even though he was with them only during his youth and later as ruler of Egypt.

Joseph's early relationship with his brothers (*Gen. 37*). As a child and young teen, Joseph basked in his father's affection. He was dad's favorite and accepted the love lavished on him as his due. Not surprisingly, Joseph was naively unaware of the effect this obvious affection had on his older brothers. Joseph hardly understood how his brothers would feel when he related dreams that suggested he would be exalted above his parents as well as them.

But the dreams made his brothers even more hostile toward him. The hostility was so great that one day when Joseph was sent to find his brothers and their flocks, the brothers decided to kill Joseph. Instead of such drastic action, Joseph's brother Judah suggested that he be sold to a caravan of Ishmaelite merchants. Later, they led their father to believe wild beasts had killed Joseph.

When the brothers saw how utterly devastated their father Jacob was, they were sorry. By then, it was too late. In the coming years, witnessing their father's unresolved grief deeply troubled their consciences. But their sorrow—or ours over the wrong choices we make—could never repair the damage caused by their sin.

Joseph's later relationship with his brothers (*Gen. 42—50*). Joseph immediately recognized his brothers years later when ten of them came to Egypt to buy grain.

The first trip to Egypt (*Gen. 42*). When Joseph's brothers arrived in Egypt they failed to recognize him. Joseph at first accused them of being spies, and questioned them closely. Joseph had a younger full brother, Benjamin, who had remained in Canaan. He demanded that they bring Benjamin to him.

The brothers, deeply disturbed and unaware that Joseph could understand their language, exclaimed that the present disaster was a just consequence of their wickedness in selling Joseph into slavery. Joseph kept Simeon in Egypt, but gave the others grain and sent them home. First, however Joseph had the silver they had paid him slipped into their grain sacks. When the money was later discovered, the brothers were terrified, saying, "What is this that God has done to us?" (Gen. 42:28).

The second trip to Egypt (*Gen. 43*). When the purchased grain was gone the brothers simply had to return to Egypt, the only source of food in the region. Joseph welcomed his brothers, told them not to worry about the money they had found in their sacks, fed them, and sent them away. But this time Joseph had his staff hide a valuable cup in the sacks carried by Benjamin's donkey. Joseph's men then pursued the brothers, found the sack, and brought them back to Joseph. When Joseph threatened to keep Benjamin as a slave, Judah begged Joseph to enslave him in place of Benjamin, pleading that their father could not survive the loss. "He alone is left of his mother's children," Judah pled, "and his father loves him" (Gen. 44:20; see v. 31). This selfless act by Judah, who was willing to give up his own freedom and family, is in striking contrast to the earlier actions of the brothers. (Judah was also the one who had suggested selling Joseph into slavery instead of killing him.)

At this, Joseph could no longer restrain himself. He revealed himself to his brothers, weeping and hugging them, and urging them to bring their father to Egypt where Joseph would provide for them all.

Many have wondered about Joseph's motives in testing his brothers as he did. Was he simply taking revenge? Or did he have another reason? Knowing Joseph, we must assume that his motive was honorable. Joseph wanted to know his brothers' hearts before making himself known. Their actions revealed their hearts. On their first visit, Joseph learned that they still felt guilt for what they had done to him. On the second visit Joseph saw in his brother Judah's actions an inner transformation that was wonderful indeed. By the time Joseph revealed himself to his brothers, he knew that he could trust them at last!

Forgiveness is a wonderful thing. But often it is not enough to heal a relationship. The person who is offered forgiveness must be repentant, willing to acknowledge his fault and ready to accept the gift offered to him. Joseph's "tests" revealed that his brothers truly were ready to receive what Joseph had always been willing to extend—a full and complete forgiveness which put the past behind and restored trust and confidence for the future.

Perhaps it is this grace of forgiveness that most reminds us of Christ and makes Joseph a Christlike figure. Both Joseph and Jesus were treated unjustly by their own people. Both suffered great loss. Both were later exalted to a position of power. Both, through their suffering, were enabled to deliver their loved ones from certain death. And both *chose* to forgive.

JOSEPH: AN EXAMPLE FOR TODAY

Joseph is one of the few—and perhaps the only—biblical character who seems to have had no flaw. His actions as a young teen that so provoked his brothers reflect a certain naïveté, not arrogance. His behavior in the house of Potiphar, his industriousness and integrity, are beyond rebuke. As the second most powerful man in Egypt, Joseph selflessly dedicated himself to the well being of that land. And, as an abused brother, Joseph showed such grace in forgiving those who had injured him that we cannot help comparing him with Jesus Christ. No wonder we have much to learn from Joseph, one of the truly godly men of the Old Testament.

- Joseph teaches us to seek excellence in whatever situation we may find ourselves. What we achieve in life's small things will train and equip us for the greater challenges ahead.

- Joseph teaches us to live morally pure lives. We, too, live in a world filled with temptations. Keeping ourselves pure honors God and shows respect for others.

- Joseph teaches us to maintain a positive attitude when treated unfairly. Others often abused Joseph, but he never gave in to despair. He continued to do his best in every circumstance, and in so doing, he prepared himself for the future God had in mind.

- Joseph reminds us that while it is divine to forgive, we must also be wise in our relationship with those who have harmed us. We are always to be willing to forgive, but this does not mean we must foolishly trust ourselves to others who have proven untrustworthy before. Joseph's test of his brothers' character was not undertaken to help him decide whether they were worthy of forgiveness, but rather to determine whether they were worthy of trust.

- Joseph reminds us that fulfilling God's purpose in our lives is more significant than our experiences along the way. Many Christians have suffered for God's greater good, and found joy in doing so. We need to look beyond ourselves—beyond our own wants and desires–and take satisfaction in serving Him.

- Joseph reminds us of the wonder of forgiveness and its healing power. As God has forgiven us, so we are to forgive others, freely and completely. To the extent that others will receive the forgiveness we offer, the hurts of both culprit and victim can be healed.

JOSHUA

Scripture references:
Exodus 17; Numbers 14; 32;
Deuteronomy 1—3, 32; Joshua
Acts 7:45; Hebrews 4:8

Date:	*About 1480–1375* B.C.
Name:	*Joshua [JAHSH-oo-uh;*
	"Yahweh is salvation"]
Greatest	
achievement:	*Joshua was Moses'*
	successor and led Israel in
	the conquest of Canaan,
	beginning about 1400 B.C.

JOSHUA'S ROLE IN SCRIPTURE

Joshua was Moses' faithful assistant during the Exodus and succeeded him as Israel's leader after Moses died. Joshua not only was a great military leader, but he was also Israel's spiritual leader. During his years as commander of God's hosts, and as long as he lived, the Israelites remained faithful to the Lord.

EXPLORING JOSHUA'S RELATIONSHIPS

From the first mention of Joshua in the Old Testament, he clearly was destined for great things.

Joshua's relationship with Moses. From the beginning of the Israelites' exodus from Egypt, Moses depended on Joshua.

Moses depended on Joshua in time of war (Ex. 17:8–13). Just after Israel passed through the Red Sea on their journey into the Sinai, the Amalekites attacked the great mass of Israelite men, women, and children. Moses turned to Joshua, and told him to choose some men and lead them in the fight against Amalek. Joshua successfully defended God's people and defeated the Amalekites.

Our introduction to Joshua through this incident has led many to assume that Joshua was a trained military man, an officer in Pharaoh's army. While this may seem strange in view of the Israelites' position as slaves, it was not unusual for gifted individuals to find advancement in Egypt despite their origin.

Moses depended on Joshua to spy out Canaan (Num. 14). When the Israelites first approached Canaan, Moses sent a representative from each Hebrew tribe to explore the land. Although ten of the spies returned with horror stories about the Canaanites' power, Joshua and a man named Caleb urged the Israelites to trust God and to attack as God had commanded. Only four persons among the Israelite millions—Moses, Aaron, Joshua and Caleb—displayed this kind of trust in God. Only Joshua and Caleb, of all the adults who escaped from Egypt, lived to see the conquest of the promised land.

Moses depended on Joshua for spiritual support (Ex. 24:13; 33:11). When Moses went up Mount Sinai to meet with God, he took his "assistant" Joshua part way with him. Later, Joshua was with Moses in the tabernacle when Moses met with God, and Joshua remained inside when Moses went outside. Joshua is identified as Moses' "servant" (Ex. 33:11). Moses clearly viewed Joshua as a supporter, almost an apprentice. Moses carefully groomed Joshua to be his successor.

Moses appointed Joshua his successor (Num. 27:15–23). When it became clear to Moses that he would soon die, he prayed that the Lord would set another leader over the Israelites. God told Moses publicly to appoint Joshua as his successor. Moses continued to urge the Israelites to follow Joshua, promising them that "he shall cause Israel to inherit" (Deut. 1:38) the promised land.

God's words to Moses to "command Joshua, and encourage him and strengthen him; for he shall go over before this people, and he shall cause them to inherit the land which you will see" (Deut. 3:28) reflects the close relationship between the two.

The significance of the relationship (Deut. 34:9). It is truly a blessing to have as a mentor someone you can respect, who takes a deep and abiding interest in equipping you for the future. This is the kind of relationship that brings out the best in people and equips them for greatness.

Even more, Joshua's relationship with Moses eased the transition after Moses died.

The text tells us that "Joshua . . . was full of the spirit of wisdom, for Moses had laid his hands on him" and adds, "so the children of Israel heeded him" (Deut. 34:9). Joshua was a capable individual, but it was because Moses had appointed Joshua that the Israelites were at first willing to follow him. Later, Joshua would prove himself as a leader and a man of God. But at first, the Israelites followed Joshua for Moses' sake.

Joshua's relationship with God. Despite decades in Moses' shadow, Joshua had a significant relationship with God.

An early lesson (Ex. 17:8–13). During the first battle that Joshua commanded, Moses stood on a hillside and watched. When Moses' hands were lifted up to heaven, the Israelites won. When he tired and his hands were lowered, the Amalekites prevailed. Finally, two men stood by Moses and literally held his arms up in the air until the battle was won. While the text gives Joshua credit, it must have been clear to all that God was actively involved in the struggle. The dependence on God that Joshua learned that day would serve him well in the future.

A sound memory (Num. 14:8–9). When the spies returned from Canaan, Joshua was shocked at the terror ten of them spread by their description of the Canaanites. Joshua remembered what the others had forgotten: that the Lord is a God of power and might. In urging the Israelites to obey the Lord, Joshua and Caleb cried out, "Their protection has departed from them, and the LORD is with us. Do not fear them" (Num. 14:9). This trust in Yahweh nurtured by the memory of what God had done for Israel marked Joshua's relationship with the Lord.

Constant exposure (Ex. 24:13; 33:11). As noted above, it was Moses' practice to bring Joshua along when Moses went to meet with the Lord. In this way, Joshua was exposed to God's presence, helping to nur-

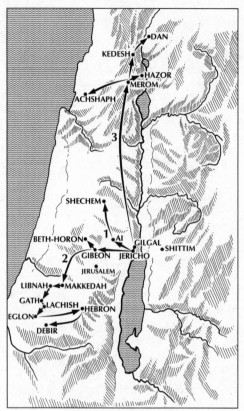

Joshua's military strategy is studied in modern war colleges. He first thrust deep into Canaan, dividing the territory, and then dealt separately with southern and northern coalitions of Canaanite kings.

❖

ture Joshua's faith. We need to remember this when our children object to accompanying us to church. No better place exists for the Lord to reach our children than a community of faith where God is loved and His word is taught.

God spoke to Joshua (Josh. 1:1–9). After Moses died the Lord spoke directly with Joshua. There is no more challenging passage of Scripture for leaders than the words of the Lord recorded in this first chapter of Joshua's book.

- God promised to be with Joshua (1:2–5).
- God promised Joshua success (1:6).

- God challenged Joshua to focus on observing His commands (1:7–8).
- God challenged Joshua to be "of good courage; do not be afraid, nor be dismayed" (1:9).
- God repeated His promise to be with Joshua wherever he would go (Josh. 1:9).

The significance of God's promises and His commands were reinforced when Joshua crossed the Jordan and stood outside the walls of the fortress Jericho. There the angel of the Lord appeared to Joshua and identified Himself as "Commander of the army of the LORD" (Josh. 5:14–15). Joshua was a leader. Like all spiritual leaders, he was also a follower, the secret of whose success would ever be his willingness to follow the Lord. The story of the conquest relates Joshua's faithfulness in fearlessly obeying God's commands.

Joshua's commitment to obedience (Josh. 7). When the walled city of Jericho fell, one of Joshua's troops disobeyed God's command and "liberated" some silver and a garment he coveted. As a result, the Israelites were defeated when they attacked a small city nearby. The defeat shook Joshua, who looked to God for the reason.

When the sin was known and sinner identified, Joshua ordered the man and his family executed. Because of Achan's sin, the Israelites had been defeated and thirty-six men had died! It seems likely that the family participated in Achan's sin, as the stolen wealth was buried beneath the family tent.

Joshua surely took no pleasure in demanding Achan's death, but Joshua determined that God must be obeyed at all costs. As long as the Israelites worshiped the Lord and honored His Word, the Israelites were victorious.

Joshua's unusual prayer (Josh. 10). One of the fascinating features of Moses' confrontation of Pharaoh is that the Lord told Moses what to pray for. Then God answered the prayer He had instructed His servant to make. In one of the battles Joshua fought with the people of Canaan, night began to fall before the enemy was destroyed. Realizing how vital it was to crush the enemy, Joshua spontaneously cried out to God and commanded the sun to stand still. The text tells us that the sun then shone on that valley for another whole day, as the Israelites wiped out their foe.

The text comments, "there has been no day like that, before it or after it, that the LORD heeded the voice of a man" (Josh 10:14). Joshua's relationship with God was so close that he felt free to speak in God's name, and God honored his faith.

Joshua's relationship with the Israelites *(Josh. 23, 24).* Joshua had served for many years as Moses' apprentice. At first after Moses' death, the Israelites followed Joshua because Moses had commissioned him. Soon however the Israelites saw that God was with Joshua (Josh. 3—5), and followed him because he had proven himself to be a successful leader.

It took the Israelites some seven years to break the Canaanites' power and settle in the land. Joshua then supervised the distribution of Canaan to the twelve tribes. When the land had been parceled out, the army was disbanded and the tribal groups settled on their inheritance. There were still pockets of Canaanites left in the land, but each tribe was now responsible to drive out the enemy left in their territory as they needed additional land.

Some years later, when Joshua was near death, he called all the Israelites together for a great covenant renewal ceremony. He challenged them to "choose for yourself this day whom you will serve" (Josh. 24:15). Unanimously the Israelites responded, "We also will serve the LORD, for He is our God" (24:18).

The text sums up Joshua's influence with this simple note: "Israel served the Lord all the days of Joshua, and all the days of the elders who outlived Joshua, who had known all the works of the LORD which He had done for Israel" (Josh. 24:31). No man could ask for a better epitaph.

JOSHUA: AN EXAMPLE FOR TODAY

Joshua as a leader was second only to Moses in his impact on the early Israelite generations. He had faithfully served God as Moses' assistant, and when the time came he served God just as faithfully as commander of all the Israelite forces. Joshua was noted not only for his commitment to obey the Lord fully, but also for the fact that he kept the Israelites—a people noted for backsliding—faithful to the Lord throughout his life. All in all, Joshua was a man about whom no negative facts are recorded; a man we can truly and fully admire. His life contains several lessons for us.

- Joshua demonstrates the value of mentoring. However great our gifts and abilities, they can be honed to a sharper edge by spending time with someone we admire.

- Joshua demonstrates the importance of obedience to the Lord. At Jericho, Joshua followed the Lord's instructions despite the fact that they made no military sense. He had confidence that God's Word could be trusted, whether he understood that word. We need to have a similar confidence in the Lord and a similar readiness to commit ourselves to live His Word.

- Joshua demonstrated the power of a good example. Joshua set a high standard for his people, and they lived up to that example. Let's be sure that we set a good example for our children, our employees, and our fellow Christians. We can never overestimate the impact of our godly living on those around us.

CHAPTER 4

SPOKESMEN FOR GOD

Men of the Old Testament filled three major offices: prophet, priest, or king. The prophet had a unique and vital role in the Old Testament era.

From the beginning, human beings have searched for help to make wise decisions in times of stress. For this the peoples of the ancient world looked to various occult sources. Deuteronomy 18:10–11 lists occult sources consulted by the Canaanites in Palestine: divination and sorcery, interpretation of omens, witchcraft, casting spells, mediums and spiritist and those who consult the dead. Each of these occult practitioners has a modern counterpart. Their horoscopes appear in the daily paper, palm readers place signs in their yard, and so-called psychic networks advertise on TV. But Scripture forbids all of these practices to God's people, for demonic forces often operate through the occult. [For an extended discussion of the occult, see the companion volume in this series, *Every Good and Evil Angel in the Bible*.]

However, God promised that He Himself would provide supernatural guidance for His people through prophets (Deut.

18:15). While Scripture laid out the way of life the Israelites were to follow, situations existed to which Scripture simply did not speak. And at times God's people strayed, and needed to be called back to the Lord. So God gave prophets special messages to deliver to Israel when the people needed a guiding word from Him.

Deuteronomy 13 and 18 identify tests the Israelites were to apply when a person claimed to have a message from God: (1) A prophet must be a Hebrew. (2) He must speak in the name of Yahweh. (3) His message must be authenticated, either by a prediction that comes true or by a miraculous sign, and (4) the prophet's message must be in harmony with God's written revelation.

Those who were authenticated as God's spokesmen were to be heeded, even as Scripture itself was heeded.

Today, believers have a different and more wonderful source of supernatural guidance. The Holy Spirit has taken up residence in each believer's life, and He guides us to apply and live by principles found in the Old and New Testaments. In Old Testament times the prophets of Israel had a vital role to play, a role that we'll examine through the lives of notable speaking and writing prophets.

SPEAKING PROPHETS

The title "speaking prophets" is given to Old Testament men and women whose ministries are recorded in Scripture but whose writings, if any, did not survive. Their messages were primarily for people of their own time.

NATHAN
Scripture references:
2 Samuel 7, 12; 1 Kings 1;
1 Chronicles 17, 29

Date:	*About 1000 B.C.*
Name:	*Nathan [NAY-thuhn; "gift"]*
Greatest accomplishment:	*Nathan served as court prophet to King David.*

NATHAN'S ROLE IN SCRIPTURE

We know little about Nathan's origins or background. When we first meet him, Nathan is already serving in the royal court, delivering God's messages to King David. Nathan announced the Davidic covenant in which God promised to confirm David's family line as the royal line in Israel and which would ultimately produce a King who would rule Israel forever. Nathan also confronted David after he sinned with Bathsheba and brought about David's repentance. And, when David was near death, Nathan rallied Solomon's supporters and made sure that Solomon succeeded David as king. On each

of these occasions, Nathan's ministry helped shape Old Testament history.

Nathan clearly portrays the challenging role of the Old Testament prophet. Old Testament prophets most often delivered God's message to kings. While some prophets like Ezekiel ministered primarily to the people, most were sent by God to guide or to confront the rulers of His people. While a few kings, like David, heeded the prophets sent to them, most rulers rejected the message and persecuted the prophet.

The relationship between David and Nathan shows us the ideal: prophet and king function together to carry out God's will.

EXPLORING NATHAN'S RELATIONSHIPS

Nathan was court prophet, and his primary relationship was with King David. Each of three major incidents involving the two men reveal much about their characters.

Nathan reported God's promise (2 Sam. 7; 1 Chron. 17). When David had defeated all the surrounding nations and Israel was at peace, David told Nathan his dream of building a temple for the Lord. At first, Nathan encouraged the king. But that night "the word of the Lord came to Nathan" (2 Sam. 7:4). The prophet had to return and tell David that he was not allowed to build a temple, but that God would build David a "house"—a permanent dynasty.

Any disappointment David felt at being denied the privilege of constructing a temple was swallowed up in his joy and wonder at God's promise. David accepted Nathan's message as the very word of God Himself. David had such confidence in Nathan that he trusted his words completely.

Nathan confronted David (2 Sam. 12). David had sinned with Bathsheba and had arranged for the death of her husband. He had then married Bathsheba. For some time afterward David lived with these sins, although Psalm

Nathan fulfilled a major role of Old Testament prophets when he confronted David concerning David's sin.

32 suggests that he suffered intense guilt. God sent Nathan to confront David. Nathan told David a story of a wealthy man who had taken a poor man's only lamb to feed a guest. David was furious over the injustice. (Like us, David found it far easier to be angry over another's sins than his own!) Nathan than denounced David, saying, "You are the man!" and delivering the Lord's blunt and harsh condemnation (12:7–12).

David immediately confessed to Nathan: "I have sinned against the LORD."

The incident tells us much about the courage it took to serve as a prophet in any royal court. Court prophets were charged not only with delivering good news but also with confronting men who had the power to punish or even kill them. In this case, we are amazed by Nathan's boldness, for his message was harsh indeed. But we are also impressed by David's reaction. David immediately humbled himself and confessed his sin. God's Word through the prophet had its intended effect.

All too often, as we read the Old Testament we meet rulers who ignored the words of God's prophets or who tried to kill the prophets. While Nathan models the ministry of prophets in the royal court, David models the appropriate response of kings to the messages delivered by God's spokespersons.

Nathan acted to preserve Solomon's rights *(1 Kings 1)*. When David was near death one of his sons attempted to usurp the throne. Nathan, aware of God's intent that Solomon succeed David, acted. He enlisted the help of Bathsheba and others and appealed to the king to crown Solomon immediately.

In this Nathan was not acting as a prophet but rather as an ordinary man who had been a trusted associate of the king. Through his years with David, Nathan had become a trusted advisor as well as a respected spokesman for God.

The respect that Nathan showed David, as revealed in the dialog in this chapter, makes it clear that Nathan did not confuse the roles of prophet and adviser. Too many of us would have presumed on our calling by God and, puffed up by our own importance, would have expected the king to give the same weight to our words as to God's. But not Nathan; he was aware that while he was a prophet he was also an ordinary man.

NATHAN: AN EXAMPLE FOR TODAY

Nathan was able to live near the center of power and remain uncorrupted. His close relationship with David was not only displayed in the incidents noted above, but Nathan also helped David reorganize Israel's worship (1 Chron. 29:25). Nathan also wrote a book, now lost, that may have been used to compile the record of David's life found in 2 Samuel and 1 Chronicles. Throughout his years in David's court, Nathan was utterly faithful to God, while at the same time being a loyal supporter and friend of David the king.

- Nathan reminds us that to be a true friend we need to be as willing to confront as to encourage.
- Nathan reminds us that we need to be willing to speak out for God even when that course might involve risk.
- Nathan reminds us to remain humble, especially when we have been given spiritual gifts that others recognize and honor.

ELIJAH
Scripture references:
1 Kings 17—19; 2 Kings 1—2;
Malachi 4; Matthew 11, 17;
Mark 9; Luke 1, 4, 9;
John 1; James 5:17

Date:	*About 875 b.c.*
Name:	*Elijah [ee-LI-juh; "Yahweh is my God"]*
Greatest accomplishment:	*Elijah checked the efforts of evil King Ahab and his wife Jezebel to replace the worship of Yahweh with worship of Baal in the northern Hebrew kingdom.*

ELIJAH'S ROLE IN SCRIPTURE

Elijah lived at a critical time in the history of the northern kingdom, Israel. From its origin in 930 B.C., Israel had been ruled by kings who refused to submit to God's will. The first ruler of the north, Jeroboam I, had designed a counterfeit worship system to keep his citizens from going to Jerusalem, the capital of the southern kingdom, Judah, to worship. In the 850s, King Ahab, encouraged by his wife Jezebel, initiated an active campaign to wipe out the worship of Yahweh in Israel and replace it with worship of Baal. Jezebel had imported some 850 pagan prophets from her homeland and at the same time had set out to exterminate any prophets of the Lord who remained in Israel. It was then that Elijah appeared, and demonstrated the power of the Lord first by bringing a three-and-a-half-year drought that devastated Israel, and then by defeating 450 prophets of Baal in a contest on Mount Carmel. The outcome was that the people of Israel, who had been wavering, affirmed that "the LORD, He is God!" (1 Kings 18:39). The efforts of Ahab and Jezebel were stymied, and while the counterfeit religious system existing in Israel was not changed, the Israelites were turned back to the Lord.

This confrontational ministry of Elijah and its great national impact serve in Scripture as a model for the ministry of a prophet predicted in Malachi 4:5–6.

Behold, I will send you Elijah the
    prophet
Before the coming of the great and dreadful day of the Lord.
And he will turn

The hearts of the fathers to the children,
And the hearts of the children to their
fathers,
Lest I come and strike the earth with a
curse.

Elijah and the Malachi prophecy are referred to frequently in the Gospels. A prophet with an Elijah-like ministry (or, some say, Elijah himself!) will appear before the Messiah sets up His kingdom. John the Baptist had this kind of ministry, but Israel did not respond, and so the Elijah prophecy was not fulfilled in John.

James 5 also contains a significant reference to Elijah. James encouraged his readers to pray and declared that "Elijah was a man with a nature like ours, and he prayed earnestly that it would not rain; and it did not rain on the land for three years and six months. And he prayed again, and the heaven gave rain, and the earth produced its fruit" (James 5:17–18). The inspired author focused on two matters: Elijah's humanity and his prayer.

EXPLORING ELIJAH'S RELATIONSHIPS

Elijah's relationship with Israel's rulers (1 Kings 17—19; 2 Kings 1). Elijah dealt with rulers who were utterly hostile to God and thus to him. Four incidents illustrate the antagonism that existed between the rulers and God's prophet.

Elijah announced a drought (1 Kings 17). God sent Elijah to Ahab to announce that for three years there would be neither rain nor dew in Israel. For those three years the prophet was hidden from the king, who searched for him as the land withered under the drought. Ahab had the largest chariot army in the region, and he was unable to find provisions for his horses.

Elijah proposed a test (1 Kings 18). After three and a half years, God sent Elijah to confront Ahab again. Elijah proposed a test of God's power versus Baal's power. Ahab, who seems actually to have had some confidence in Baal's powers, agreed. For hours, the prophets of Baal called on their deity with no response. But as soon as Elijah prayed, fire fell from heaven and consumed the offering Elijah had laid out. The people, who had been wavering, were convinced. At Elijah's words, the people killed the prophets of Baal. Elijah then prayed for rain, and the drought was broken.

Elijah pronounced Ahab's doom (1 Kings 21). Ahab's wife Jezebel arranged the judicial murder of Naboth, a man whose vineyard Ahab coveted. Although Ahab had not conspired to commit the murder, he gladly went down to inspect the property when Jezebel told him what she had done. Elijah confronted Ahab there, and announced God's judgment on the wicked pair. Ahab put on sackcloth, fasted, and wept to demonstrate his repentance. God put off the punishment He decreed on Ahab's dynasty. Later the king ignored the warning of another prophet and was killed in battle.

Elijah announced the death of Ahaziah, Ahab's son and successor (2 Kings 1). When King Ahaziah was injured, he sent messengers to inquire of a foreign deity whether he would survive. Elijah intercepted the messengers and announced that since Ahaziah had not seen fit to inquire of the Lord, he would surely die. The king sent several troops of soldiers to bring Elijah to him. Elijah called down fire from heaven on two of the companies, but when the captain of the third squad showed respect for the Lord and His power, God told Elijah to accompany them to the king.

In each of these situations Elijah was called to a ministry of judgment. Each placed Elijah in potential danger at the hands of a hostile king. Yet, Elijah faithfully carried out each mission and was protected by the Lord.

Elijah's relationship with Elisha *(1 Kings 19:19–21; 2 Kings 2)*. Near the end of his ministry Elijah became despondent and discouraged. It seemed to him that everyone had abandoned the Lord. At this point, God selected Elisha as a companion and an apprentice for Elijah.

When God took Elijah into heaven, Elisha became the premier prophet in Israel. While Elijah's ministry had been one of confrontation and judgment—as demonstrated in the miracles attributed to him—Elisha benefited from his predecessor's impact on the average Israelite. Elisha's ministry was marked by miracles that aided both the nation and godly individuals.

Elijah's relationship with the Lord *(1 Kings 19)*. When we read of Elijah's accomplishments, he comes across as a fierce and fearless individual. Whatever God called Elijah to do, he did boldly. Yet, James reminded us that Elijah was a "man with a nature like ours" (James 5:17).

God provided for Elijah (1 Kings 17). During the years of drought when Elijah was hiding from Ahab, God provided for him in supernatural ways. Ravens provided his food by the brook Cherith, and later God miraculously extended the supply of food of a widow with whom Elijah stayed.

God ministered to a despondent Elijah (1 Kings 19). Elijah's humanity came through most clearly after his victory on Mount Carmel. When Jezebel heard that Elijah had ordered the prophets of Baal killed, the queen sent a death threat to the prophet. Elijah was terrified, and ran for his life.

While terror gripped Elijah, the Lord supplied him with the strength he needed to flee. Finally exhausted after a forty-day journey, Elijah stopped running at Mount Sinai [called Horeb here]. God spoke to him there, and Elijah shared his despair:

"I have been very zealous for the LORD God of hosts; for the children of Israel have forsaken

Elijah's victory on Mount Carmel convinced the wavering Israelites that the Lord truly was God.

Your covenant, torn down Your altars, and killed Your prophets with the sword. I alone am left; and they seek to take my life" (1 Kings 19:10).

Often emotional highs are followed by emotional lows. This was surely Elijah's experience. In the grip of depression, Elijah could not see matters clearly.

Rather than rebuke Elijah, God ministered to His prophet in specific and gracious ways.

- God spoke to Elijah in a "still small voice" (1 Kings 19:12). Elijah needed to know God cared and the gentle response of the Lord communicated this reality powerfully.

- God gave Elijah a task to complete (1 Kings 19:15–17). Elijah was sent to anoint two future kings who would bring an end to Ahab and his line. A depressed person often feels overwhelmed. Elijah needed to have a clear and obtainable goal set for him.

- God gave Elijah a companion, Elisha (1 Kings 19:16). A depressed person typically feels isolated and alone. This certainly describes Elijah, who had complained, "I alone am left." Elisha would become Elijah's friend and companion as well as his successor.

- God gave Elijah perspective (1 Kings 19:18). Elijah was wrong in his belief that all except him had abandoned the Lord. God told him, "I have reserved seven thousand in Israel, all whose knees have not bowed to Baal."

Truly Elijah was "a man with a nature like ours" (James 5:17), and just as surely God graciously ministered to Elijah. Elijah had given his life to serve God, but God also was dedicated to serve Elijah.

ELIJAH: AN EXAMPLE FOR TODAY

Elijah provides us a picture of the prophet as a lonely man—a man dedicated to God in a hostile society. Elijah was bold and brave, but Elijah was merely human. His dedication to God placed strains on him that led to the recorded bout of fear and depression. Elijah's experience reminds us that while commitment to the Lord may increase the stress in our life, the Lord is committed to us and will meet us in our need. From Elijah we discover much about the cost and the rewards of commitment.

- Elijah reminds us that we may find ourselves in situations where we feel that we alone have remained faithful to the Lord. Should this happen, we are to be bold and speak up for Him as Elijah did.

- Elijah reminds us that when we feel weakest God may be the closest to us, ready to whisper to us in a still, small voice.

- Elijah reminds us that God is never critical of our human limitations. God understands us, and cares. He knows how to provide what we need to go on with life.

- Elijah reminds us that we need God's perspective always. However alone we may feel, many others love God equally and share our experiences.

- Elijah reminds us that we, too, need the companionship of like-minded believers. Today, you and I can find this companionship with others in the church, the body of Christ. Let's seek fellowship there, that we might offer and receive support.

ELISHA
Scripture references:
1 Kings 19; 2 Kings 2—13;
Luke 4:27

Date:	*About 850 B.C.*
Name:	*Elisha [ee-LI-shuh; "God is salvation"]*
Greatest accomplishment:	*Elisha was the successor of Elijah whose ministry confirmed God's active presence in Israel.*

ELISHA'S ROLE IN SCRIPTURE

Elisha had a very different ministry from that of Elijah. Elijah's role as a prophet of judgment was to display God's power in a time of apostasy. Elisha, his successor, seems to have focused his ministry on a display of God's grace toward those who would trust Him.

The Old Testament records fourteen miracles of Elisha compared with seven miracles performed by Elijah. These miracles help us sense the healing nature of Elisha's ministry and their promise of overflowing grace should the Israelites simply turn to Him completely. Here is a list of Elisha's miracles as reported in 2 Kings:

1. Elisha separated the waters of the Jordan (2:14)
2. Elisha healed bitter spring waters (2:21)
3. Elisha cursed young men who ridiculed God (2:24)
4. Elisha won a battle for Israel (3:15–26)
5. Elisha multiplied a poor widow's oil (4:1–7)
6. Elisha promised a good woman a child (4:14–17)
7. Elisha raised the good woman's child from the dead (4:32–37)
8. Elisha made poison stew edible (4:38–41)
9. Elisha multiplied loaves to feed many (4:42–44)
10. Elisha healed a Syrian general's leprosy (5:1–19)
11. Elisha made a borrowed ax head float (6:1–6)
12. Elisha trapped an Aramean army (6:8–23)
13. Elisha showed his servant an angel army (6:15–17)
14. Elisha predicted an excess of food for starving Samaria (6:24—7:20)

These miracles were certainly less spectacular than those performed by Elijah; they were also different in nature. Yet, each prophet's miracles displayed different aspects of God's character. God reveals himself in judgment; He also reveals Himself in gracious acts to nations, individuals, and even to enemy generals.

ELISHA: AN EXAMPLE FOR TODAY

Elisha replaced Elijah as God's premier prophet in Israel. When we compare Elisha with his mentor, we come to appreciate the lessons he has to teach us.

- Elisha had a less spectacular ministry than that of Elijah, but one that was as significant in its revelation of God's character to His people. He reminds us that we each have our calling and are not to measure ourselves or our mission against that of the great people of our time. The role we play in God's plan is the role He has designed for us, and this makes us significant indeed.

- Elisha had a ministry to common people as well as to kings. In every context, Elisha displayed God's grace and showed that the Lord cares about every detail of our lives. This is important to remember as we serve others. We should bring our ordinary needs to the Lord as well as the big things.

JONAH
Scripture references:
2 Kings 14:25; Jonah;
Matthew 12:39–41; 16:4;
Luke 11:29–32.

Date:	About 775 B.C.
Name:	Jonah [JOH-nuh; "dove"]
Greatest accomplishment:	Jonah predicted the resurgence of Israel and warned Assyria of impending judgment.

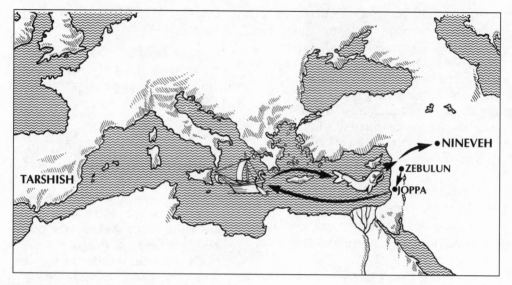

When told to go north to Nineveh, Jonah boarded a ship going west! It took a storm and a great fish to set Jonah back on God's path.

JONAH'S ROLE IN SCRIPTURE

Jonah lived in Israel and predicted the triumphs of Jeroboam II that led to a resurgence of the northern kingdom in the eighth century B.C. His little book relates the story of his reluctance to carry a warning of divine judgment to Nineveh, the capital of Assyria, and what happened when he did deliver the message. Jonah's famous three-day stay in the belly of a great fish is referred to in the Gospels as a symbol of Christ's stay in the tomb after His crucifixion.

JONAH'S LIFE AND TIMES

Jonah was a patriot who predicted the victories won by Jeroboam II (2 Kings 14:25). This king of Israel, who is given little space in the Old Testament, was one of the most successful rulers of the northern Hebrew kingdom. During his forty-year rule, Assyria was weak and Israel became the dominant power in the Middle East. Jeroboam II expanded his borders almost to the extent reached in Solomon's days, and, like Solomon, dominated the trade routes that ran through Damascus.

When God called Jonah to go to Nineveh and announce the destruction of the capital of Israel's most powerful enemy, he chose to run away instead. Jonah explained his motivation in the little four-chapter book that bears his name.

Ah, LORD, was this not what I said when I was still in my country? Therefore I fled previously to Tarshish; for I know that You are a gracious and merciful God, slow to anger and abundant in loving kindness, One who relents from doing harm (Jon. 4:2).

Jonah's attempted flight was thwarted, however. God sent two unusual elements: a storm that nearly destroyed the ship on which Jonah had taken passage and a great fish to return the fleeing prophet to land. The next time God spoke, Jonah obeyed. He went to Nineveh, and announced the coming judgment. As Jonah had feared, the people of Nineveh did repent! Jonah sat on a hill outside Nineveh waiting to see what would happen until it became clear that God had chosen to delay the judgment Jonah had announced. Angry and miserable, Jonah begged God to end his life.

Instead, Jonah rebuked his prophet, reminding him that the Lord had pity on "Nineveh, that great city, in which are more than one hundred twenty thousand persons who cannot discern between their right hand and their left—and much livestock" (Jon. 4:11).

Jonah missed the significance of God's warning and subsequent relenting. Amos, a prophet from Judah, would soon come to Israel and issue God's indictment of Israel's sins and call on His own people to repent. Nineveh's repentance and God's gracious failure to punish that city was an object lesson for Israel. Surely, if God would be gracious to an enemy of His people, God would be gracious to His own people if only they would repent! However, Israel did not repent. They persisted in their sins. The judgment of which Amos spoke came when Israel fell to Assyria and its people were carried away as captives and were swallowed up in that mighty empire.

JONAH: AN EXAMPLE FOR TODAY

Jonah is a prime example of a patriot who knew God well but whose first loyalty was to his nation. He was unwilling to do God's will when he feared that what God had in mind might conflict with his own hopes for his nation's future. We have much to learn from Jonah today.

- Jonah warns us against confusing God's purposes with our own political or national agendas. We are to be loyal to God and responsive to Him. We must avoid any temptation to "use" God to advance our own purposes.

- Jonah reminds us that we are to view others as God views them, being as gracious and merciful toward them as He Himself is. Compassion is a quality God values and which we are to nurture as well as express in our relationships with others.

- Jonah encourages us, in that God overlooked His prophet's rebellion and gave him a second chance to do His will. God is gracious to us as well as to others. When we rebel, we need to remember that we too can safely return.

WRITING PROPHETS

The ministry of the speaking prophets is described in narrative passages of Scripture. The ministry of the writing prophets, although several are mentioned in Old Testament narrative, is known primarily through the books of the Bible that bear their names. In most cases, we know little about the lives or personalities of the writing prophets other than what their books reveal. This may be little, indeed. For instance, we know that Amos was a rancher of Judah who was sent to Israel with a call for social justice and for Israel to return to the Lord. Aside from what we can sense from the concerns expressed in his little book, we know little about Amos as a person. We know more about other writing prophets, notably Daniel and Jeremiah.

ISAIAH
Scripture references:
2 Kings 19—20; 2 Chronicles 26:22;
32:30–32; Isaiah 20:2–3; 38:21

Date:	*Isaiah prophesied about 739–681 B.C.*
Name:	*Isaiah [I-ZAY-yuh; "Yahweh is salvation"]*
Greatest achievement:	*Isaiah penned the great Old Testament book bearing his name, filled with messianic prophecies.*

IMAGES OF CHRIST IN ISAIAH

- will be obedient (50:4, 5)
- will suffer injustice (53:7–9)
- will not raise his voice (42:2)
- will not reject the worthless (42:3)
- will be rejected by Israel (50:6)
- will be mocked and spit on (53:3)
- will die (53:9)

* will enforce obedience (11:3, 4)
* will blot out injustice (42:4)
* will exercise power (40:10)
* will redeem the earth (41:14, 15)
* will be welcomed by Israel (44:3, 6)
* will win mankind's allegiance (49:6)
* will establish an endless kingdom (9:7)

ISAIAH'S ROLE IN SCRIPTURE

Isaiah was a prophet of Judah, who ministered to the people of the southern kingdom. During his time Assyria's expansionist policies seriously threatened Judah. This threat, combined with the preaching of Isaiah and Micah and the leadership of godly king Hezekiah, led to a religious revival in Judah. God intervened to turn back the Assyrian forces after Judah was invaded and severely battered. Many of Isaiah's messages recorded in his book focus on Judah's sin and injustice and show how greatly the spiritual renewal was needed in Isaiah's time.

Isaiah's messages however looked beyond the immediate situation, and portrayed a future in which God, after punishing His people's sins, would restore and bless the redeemed. Because so many of Isaiah's images of the future feature the coming Messiah, Isaiah has rightly been called the evangelist of the Old Testament. His significance can be seen in the fact that Isaiah's words are quoted or referred to some 13 times in the Gospels, three times in Acts, and five times by the apostle Paul in Romans.

ISAIAH'S LIFE AND TIMES

Nelson's *Illustrated Bible Handbook* comments on how little we know of Isaiah the man.

He is often mentioned in Kings and Chronicles, and his name occurs several times in his own book. But his family background and social status remains a mystery. The fact that his great personal vision of God took place in the temple (Isa. 6) suggests he may have been a priest, as only priests were to enter the holy place. Isaiah was an intimate of King Hezekiah—probably a sort of court preacher. His mastery of Hebrew is as rich and great as Shakespeare's grasp of English, and shows he was a highly educated man (p. 282).

While Isaiah at times writes of events in which he played a significant part, Isaiah, unlike Jeremiah, does not go into detail about his emotions. For instance, Isaiah describes the following experience, but makes no comment on his emotions:

"Go, and remove the sackcloth from your body, and take your sandals off your feet." And he did so, walking naked and barefoot. Then the Lord said, ". . . My servant Isaiah has walked naked and barefoot three years for a sign and wonder against Egypt and Ethiopia." (Isa. 20:2, 3)

As Isaiah remained silent about his own feelings, he revealed little about his personal life. We know that Isaiah was married to an unnamed prophetess and that he had children (Isa. 7; 8), but we know nothing about them. Isaiah is the proverbial silent man, who although a very public figure, is at the same time a very private man.

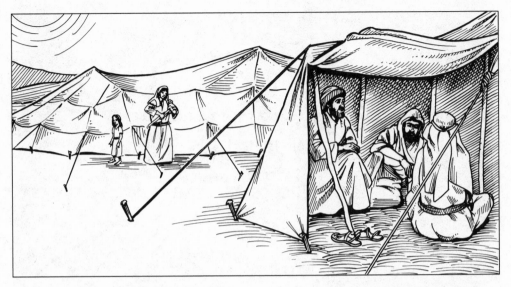

Today Bedouins still live in tents much like those that housed Jacob and his family 4,000 years ago.

ISAIAH: AN EXAMPLE FOR TODAY

Isaiah's prominence in his own time and in Scripture contrasts sharply with his reticence. He was a great man but one who felt no need to put himself forward. He had no need for public accolades or to be the center of attention. To serve God faithfully and selflessly was enough for him. We have much to learn from Isaiah.

- Isaiah reminds us that modesty is a virtue. Serving God is reward enough, without seeking or demanding public acclaim.
- Isaiah reminds us that while some freely share emotions, others are private individuals. Each personality style is valid and acceptable, and we are not to force others into a way of relating that may be uncomfortable for them.
- Isaiah encourages us to keep Christ in focus. We should seek to impress others with Him—not with ourselves.

EZEKIEL

Scripture references:
Ezekiel

Date:	*Prophesied between 593–571 B.C.*
Name:	*Ezekiel [ee-ZEE-kee-uhl; "God strengthens"]*
Greatest accomplishment:	*Ezekiel ministered to Jews in Babylon before the fall of Jerusalem.*

EZEKIEL'S ROLE IN SCRIPTURE

Ezekiel was taken to Babylon with many other Jews in 597 B.C. He was God's spokesman to the captive community before the final fall of Jerusalem in 586 B.C., and he warned the captives that Jerusalem and the temple would be destroyed. After the fall of Jerusalem, God gave Ezekiel a message of

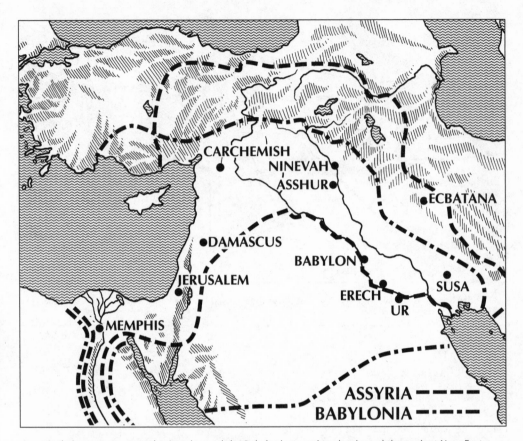

At their greatest extent the Assyrian and the Babylonian empires dominated the ancient Near East.

❖

hope and described a great new temple to be constructed in Jerusalem in the days of the Messiah (Ezek. 40–48).

One of the most striking aspects of Ezekiel's experience is the stunning visions of Himself that God granted to this prophet. These visions of a transcendent God, glorious and all-powerful, strengthened Ezekiel for the many personal trials that lay ahead.

EZEKIEL'S LIFE AND TIMES

Only two verses in the Old Testament identify Ezekiel by name. Each is in the prophet's own book (1:3; 24:24). At the same time many passages in Ezekiel's book describe his experiences. Ezekiel was not only given towering visions of God; he also

was called to act out God's messages to the Jewish captives. While some in Babylon held out hope that Judah might be preserved and that they might return home, God's words through Ezekiel emphasized the depths of Judah's sins (see Ezek. 8—11), and the certainty of divine judgment. While God would restore His people to the Promised Land in the future, there was no hope for the present generation.

Two incidents reflect ways in which Ezekiel's experiences were to mirror the fate God had in store for the people of Judah.

Ezekiel acted out the siege of Jerusalem (Ezek. 4; 5). God told Ezekiel to build a model city and lay siege works against it. Ezekiel then was to lie on his side for a fixed number of days and for over a year was to live on a daily ration of some eight ounces of food and a pint of water. Ezekiel's diet represented the starvation diet of those trapped in Jerusalem by the Babylonian forces.

At the end of this time, Ezekiel shaved his head and beard, and divided it into thirds. Each third represented the fate of Jerusalem's inhabitants when the city fell.

Ezekiel's wife died suddenly (Ezek. 24). The prophet was called to do more than act out the fate of others. He was also called to experience the pain of judgment. Ezekiel was warned that his wife, "the desire of your eyes," would die. God told His prophet, "you shall neither mourn nor weep, nor shall your tears run down. Sigh in silence, make no mourning for the dead; bind your turban on your head, and put your sandals on your feet; do not cover your lips, and do not eat man's bread of sorrow" (Ezek. 24:16, 17).

This strange behavior at the death of a loved one provoked the wonder of the Jewish community, and Ezekiel explained that this fate—a disaster so great that it was beyond mourning—awaited the Israelites as God's judgment on His people for their sins.

EZEKIEL: AN EXAMPLE FOR TODAY

Ezekiel reminds us that believers who live in times of national disaster will not be protected from the suffering associated with divine judgment. We may, in fact, be called to speak to our generation out of the pain of personal loss.

- Ezekiel challenges us to be faithful to God when everything in our life seems to go wrong. God guarantees us an eternity of blessing but not a life of ease or pleasure in this world.

- Ezekiel reminds us that we are citizens of heaven and of earth. We will not escape suffering when our nation

undergoes a purging judgment, but God can use us to speak to our contemporaries at such times.

- Ezekiel encourages us to keep our eyes fixed on the Lord. Only a clear vision of Him will give us the courage to face our own difficult times with peace and hope.

DANIEL
Scripture references:
The Book of Daniel;
Ezekiel 14:14, 20; 28:3;
Matthew 24; 25; Mark 13:14

Date:	About 600 B.C.
Name:	Daniel [DAN-yuhl; "God is my judge"]
Greatest Accomplishment:	Daniel rose high in the government of two world empires and had a personal impact on at least three of their rulers.

DANIEL'S ROLE IN SCRIPTURE

Daniel is perhaps best known to Bible students for the prophecies that compose the last half of the Book of Daniel. Fulfilled prophecies in this section outline the history of the East until the appearance of Jesus, and one stunning prophecy even relates Christ's triumphal entry into Jerusalem. Daniel's prophecies concerning events associated with history's end are yet to be fulfilled (Matt. 24 and Mark 13).

Boys and girls in Sunday School are more familiar with Daniel the man whose adventures, such as being thrown in the lion's den, have captured children's imaginations for centuries. As a young teen,

Daniel and three Jewish friends were taken from Judah to Babylon and enrolled in the school where future administrators of the Babylonian empire were trained. Daniel and his friends remained faithful to God's law while in Babylon and excelled in their studies. After Daniel successfully interpreted King Nebuchadnezzar's dream, Daniel became an influential advisor and administrator in his kingdom. Daniel also was influential when the Medo-Persians supplanted the Babylonians as rulers of the vast eastern empire.

Throughout his long life, Daniel remained totally committed to God despite serving a secular state. He was mentioned by Ezekiel, a contemporary, as one of three men noted for their righteousness (Ezek. 14:14,20), an unusual accolade for a still-living person. In a sarcastic remark addressed to the king of Tyre (Ezek. 28:3), Ezekiel also held up Daniel as the premier example of a truly wise man.

EXPLORING DANIEL'S RELATIONSHIPS

Daniel's relationship with pagan rulers (*Dan. 1—6*). Daniel served three different rulers of what was initially the Babylonian Empire.

Daniel and Nebuchadnezzar (Dan. 1; 2; 4). Nebuchadnezzar's first recorded exposure to Daniel was when Daniel and his friends graduated from the king's school. Graduation involved an interview with the great ruler himself, and Nebuchadnezzar found Daniel and his friends "ten times better" (Dan 1:10) than not only the other graduates but also his official advisers.

In the second year of his reign, Nebuchadnezzar had a troubling dream. When he awoke, he had forgotten it. The king demanded that his wise men tell him both the dream and its meaning. When none could, the king determined to put all of his advisors to death. When Daniel heard of the

king's decree, he prayed and God revealed the dream and its meaning. Daniel gave full credit to the Lord, and Nebuchadnezzar was deeply impressed, affirming that "your God is the God of gods" (Dan. 2:47). Nebuchadnezzar then "promoted Daniel and gave him great gifts. He made Daniel ruler of the whole province of Babylon and chief administrator over all the wise men of Babylon" (2:48).

Some time later Daniel interpreted another dream that warned Nebuchadnezzar against arrogantly giving himself credit for what God had done in exalting him. Nebuchadnezzar ignored the warning and God drove the ruler mad. For a time, he lived as a wild beast eating grass. When Nebuchadnezzar recovered he "blessed and honored the Most High and praised and honored Him who lives forever" (Dan. 4:34). Many see this response of Nebuchadnezzar as evidence of a true conversion to the Lord—a conversion in which Daniel's faithful witness played the critical part.

Daniel and Belshazzar (Dan. 5). After Nebuchadnezzar's death, Daniel's influenced waned. Belshazzar was regent in Babylon under his father Nabonidus when Medo-Persian forces attacked the city of Babylon. When writing miraculously appeared on a wall during a banquet, Belshazzar was urged to send for Daniel to interpret it. Daniel did interpret it, though it was a message of doom. That night the city fell to the invaders, who diverted a river that flowed through Babylon and entered it through the riverbed.

Daniel and Darius (Dan. 6). Cyrus the Great conquered Babylon, but the Bible identifies a man named Darius subsequently governing the empire from Babylon city.

Darius reorganized the administration of the empire into 120 districts and set Daniel over these high officials. The honest Daniel frustrated the governors, who traditionally relied on graft to enrich themselves, and they set out to rid themselves of Daniel. Through a clever trap they maneuvered Darius into ordering Daniel thrown in a den of lions. The deep concern Darius obviously felt for Daniel indicated how close Daniel had become to the ruler. When God delivered Daniel, Darius ordered all those who had plotted against Daniel to be thrown to the lions.

What is significant about these stories is that we see in Daniel a person of great integrity and faith whose utter honesty and loyalty won him the respect and affection of powerful pagan rulers. Daniel modeled one who lived his faith in the political arena.

Daniel's relationship with God. Daniel's story clearly reflects a lifelong and total commitment to the Lord.

Daniel in the king's school (Dan. 1). Daniel and his friends were Jews and thus subject to the Old Testament dietary laws. Daniel refused to eat the nonkosher diet served in the school, and respectfully requested the privilege of eating only that which was lawful. His commitment to God while still a young teen set the course of the next eighty or so years of Daniel's life.

Daniel and the king's dream (Dan. 2). When Daniel heard that all the kings' advisors were to be executed, he asked Nebuchadnezzar for time. Daniel returned to his three Jewish friends, and they went to prayer. When the secret was revealed, the first thing Daniel did was to praise God. Only then did he go to the king.

Daniel's confidence that God could do the humanly impossible, Daniel's reliance on prayer, and his emphasis on praise tell us much about the man. They also help us understand how Daniel could have functioned so effectively in a pagan environment.

When Daniel revealed the answer to the king, he made sure that God received all the credit. This true humility was part of the secret of Daniel's success.

Daniel's concern for Nebuchadnezzar (Dan. 4). When Daniel interpreted the dream that warned Nebuchadnezzar against his pride, Daniel was deeply concerned. Daniel's expression and his words showed that he cared about Nebuchadnezzar as a person (Dan. 4:19). Daniel also showed his concern by taking the risk of giving unsolicited advice to the king, something most rulers did not welcome (Dan. 4:27). Nebuchadnezzar accepted this from Daniel, for he knew that Daniel was not trying to manipulate him for personal gain but did truly care about him.

How important to care about people who have the power to benefit us—not because of what we can get from them, but because the Lord loves them.

Daniel's faithfulness in prayer (Dan. 6). Daniel made it a practice to pray three times daily with his window open facing Jerusalem. As his religion was the only possible "flaw" his enemies could find, they tricked Darius into promulgating a decree that no one could make a request to any god or man other than Darius for 30 days. The decree did not deter Daniel. Daniel continued his practice of daily, faithful prayer. He was rightly convinced that God could and would deliver him, and was unwilling to abandon time with the Lord for even a few days.

Daniel's prayers and prophecies (Dan. 9; 10). These chapters show a close link between prayer and prophecy. They make it clear that Daniel, intent on understanding Scripture, dedicated himself to "make request by prayer and supplications, with fasting, sackcloth, and ashes" (9:3). The most striking of Daniel's prophecies were revealed as responses to the prophet's commitment to prayer. Daniel's prayer recorded in 9:4–19 is one of the most beautiful and powerful in the Bible.

DANIEL: AN EXAMPLE FOR TODAY

Daniel was an exceptional individual. Throughout his life, he was a powerful and influential individual, unusually close to mighty rulers. Yet Daniel remained a humble believer whose honesty and integrity were unalloyed with greed or a lust for personal power. The intensity of Daniel's relationship with the Lord enabled him to live uncorrupted at the very center of worldly power.

Daniel was a man with essential lessons to teach us.

- Daniel teaches us to put God first, both privately and publicly. Daniel's commitment to the Lord and to nurturing a healthy relationship with Him was indispensable to the role he played in the government of world empires.

- Daniel reminds us to view every person as an individual, however exalted a position he or she might have. Much of Daniel's influence resulted from the fact that mighty rulers were aware that Daniel cared about them rather than what they could do for him.

- Daniel inspires us to remain faithful to the Lord whatever the difficulty. If our relationship with God is the only basis on which others can attack us, let them do so. But we are to remain faithful to the Lord in deed and in word.

- Daniel encourages us to be involved in government. True believers can have a role in politics without compromising their convictions. Such a person may impact an entire nation as well as influence many who need to know the Lord.

- Daniel encourages us to give prayer a central role in our lives. Daniel did not pray only in emergencies. Daniel prayed daily. Daniel not only brought his requests to the Lord; Daniel brought praise. When we see the impact Daniel had on those of his own time, we can hardly discount the role of prayer in his life or in ours.

JEREMIAH
Scripture references:
The Book of Jeremiah;
2 Chronicles 35

Date:	*About 652–567 B.C.*
Name:	*Jeremiah [JAIR-uh-MI-uh; "Yahweh lifts up"]*
Greatest Accomplishment:	*For the last forty years of Judah's existence, Jeremiah urged kings and people to submit to the Babylonians.*

JEREMIAH'S ROLE IN SCRIPTURE

Jeremiah was born during the forty-four-year reign of Manasseh, Judah's most wicked king. God called Jeremiah to his prophetic ministry during the reign of Josiah, who led the last great religious revival in Judah. For forty years, until the Babylonians swept into Judah to destroy both Jerusalem and Solomon's beautiful temple, Jeremiah waged a lonely and futile crusade to turn God's people back to the Lord and to urge the people to submit to the Babylonians whom God would send to discipline them.

During his lifetime, Jeremiah was persecuted as a traitor and his life was frequently threatened. Yet, he lived to see his predictions of judgment come true. Tradition says that after the destruction of Jerusalem Jeremiah found his way to Babylon, where he wrote the haunting poems of the Book of Lamentations.

Despite the dark cast of most of Jeremiah's prophecies, he was also given the privilege of recording God's promise that one day God would make a new covenant with the house of Israel (Jer. 31). Twice

Matthew quoted Jeremiah's prophecies that related to the Savior's birth and death (Matt. 2:17; 27:9).

EXPLORING JEREMIAH'S RELATIONSHIPS

Jeremiah's relationships with his people *(Jer. 16)*. Jeremiah is rightly known as the weeping prophet. He was called to live among God's people but to isolate himself from them. In summarizing chapter 16, the *Nelson Illustrated Bible Handbook* sums up this theme:

To communicate the grim reality of the approaching disaster, Jeremiah is told not to marry and have children. Children born in his day will only die of deadly disease and lie unburied in the streets (1–4). Also, the prophet is not to mourn the death of friends, for God has no compassion left for Judah. Nor is he to take part in any feasting (5–9). Instead, Jeremiah is told to speak words that condemn, and hold up the sin and faithlessness of God's people (10–13). A distant generation will know God's blessing once again (14–15). But for this people there is only death (16–18): disaster is assured (p. 323).

It is hardly surprising that the people to whom he ministered shunned Jeremiah, or that he felt isolated and alone.

Jeremiah's relationship with God *(selected Scripture)*. Without human companionship, Jeremiah constantly turned to God as friend and confidant. Jeremiah often expressed his pain and anguish to the Lord, and looked to him for strength to continue his unpopular mission.

Jeremiah's call (Jer. 1:5–19). When God first spoke to Jeremiah, He informed Jeremiah that before his birth God had set him apart for a special purpose. The Lord warned Jeremiah that his ministry would be unpopular, for he would announce the coming judgment of

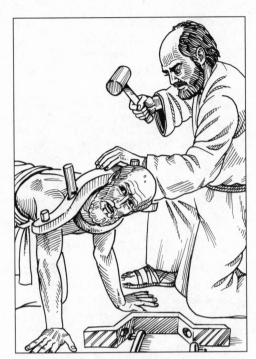

The wooden yoke the false prophet Hananiah broke off Jeremiah's neck was replaced with a yoke of iron, and shortly afterward Hananiah died, as Jeremiah had predicted.

Judah. " 'They will fight against you, / But they will not prevail against you / For I am with you,' says the LORD, 'To deliver you' " (Jer. 1:19).

Jeremiah's neighbors (Jer. 11:18–23). Jeremiah grew up in Anathoth. The Lord revealed to Jeremiah that his friends and neighbors were plotting to kill him because of his preaching against idolatry. Deeply shaken, Jeremiah called on God to judge them even as they threatened to kill him if he did not stop prophesying. God told Jeremiah that in the coming Babylonian invasion "there shall be no remnant of them, for I will bring catastrophe on the men of Anathoth" (11:23).

Jeremiah's wounds (Jer. 15:15–21). The prophet would not have been human had he not felt the antagonism of his people intensely. He cried out to the Lord:

Why is my pain perpetual
And my wound incurable,
Which refuses to be healed?
Will You surely be to me like an unreli-
    able stream,
As waters that fail? (Jer. 15:18)

God responded not by relieving the pressure but by assuring Jeremiah of His protective care:

And they will fight against you,
But they shall not prevail against you;
For I am with you to save you
And deliver you. (Jer. 15:20)

Jeremiah's only solace (Jer. 20.) Jeremiah lived under intense pressure for the forty years of his ministry in Jerusalem. His situation is summed up here: "I am in derision daily; / Everyone mocks me" (v.7).

Jeremiah tried to stop preaching, but "His word was in my heart like a burning fire / shut up in my bones; / I was weary of holding it back, / And I could not" (v. 9). Yet when Jeremiah spoke out, his listeners reported his words to the authorities and plotted revenge. The intensity of Jeremiah's pain is powerfully expressed in chapter 20:

Cursed be the day in which I was born!
Let the day not be blessed in which my
    mother bore me!
Let the man be cursed
Who brought news to my father, saying,
"A male child has been born to you!"
Making him very glad.
. . . .
Why did I come forth from the womb to
    see labor and sorrow,
That my days should be consumed with
    shame? (Jer. 20:14, 15, 18)

Through it all, only Jeremiah's relationship with the Lord sustained him, and he kept his heart and mind focused on God: "But the LORD is with me as a mighty, awesome One. / Therefore my persecutors will stumble, and will not prevail" (Jer. 20:11).

To the people of Jerusalem Jeremiah must have seemed harsh and bold, yet Jeremiah was a painfully sensitive person who suffered intensely. What sustained Jeremiah was that he was able to share his emotions with the Lord and in God find both reassurance and strength.

JEREMIAH: AN EXAMPLE FOR TODAY

Jeremiah lived in a time of apostasy. His society had abandoned the Lord and deeply resented Jeremiah for confronting their sins and affirming God's standards. Jeremiah's contemporaries not only rejected Jeremiah's message; they ridiculed and hated the man. Jeremiah couldn't help being deeply hurt by all the antagonism focused on him.

Despite the hostility of those around him, Jeremiah faithfully proclaimed God's Word and warned of judgment for forty years. Without human companionship for most of this time, Jeremiah was forced to turn to the Lord. Jeremiah poured out his heart to God, expressing his anger, his sorrows, and his anguish. God encouraged Jeremiah, but did not let the prophet draw back from his painful ministry.

In the end, Jeremiah's predictions of doom and destruction all came true. The prophet was vindicated, but never appreciated. Only after his death was Jeremiah given the respect and appreciation he always deserved. How striking that when the crowds of Jesus' day were asked who they thought Christ might be, their first response was that He was possibly Jeremiah or one of the other great prophets (Matt. 16:14)! What, then, do we learn from Jeremiah's example?

- Jeremiah reminds us that we too may be called to face opposition. If we are, we need to be as faithful in our ministry as Jeremiah was in his.

- Jeremiah challenges us to speak out against the evils in our day. We are likely to be labeled "intolerant" and our words may evoke hostile responses. But we are to be true to God whatever pressure others may bring to bear.

- Jeremiah prods us to share our inner life with the Lord. God understands and cares, even when no one else seems willing to listen. God will not only listen, but He will encourage and support us in our labors.

- Jeremiah encourages us to look beyond the present time to envision a future in which God's will is done. However dark the present may be, the future that God will bring is bright indeed.

LEADERS, KINGS, AND PRIESTS

The major offices that existed during Old Testament times were those of prophet, priest, and king. The prophet served as God's spokesman. The priest represented the people to God by offering sacrifices and leading in worship. The king, under God's leadership, was to rule the people. The Book of Deuteronomy laid down special regulations for kings, the most significant of which are stated in Deuteronomy 17:18–20:

Also it shall be, when he sits on the throne of his kingdom, that he shall write for himself a copy of this law in a book, from the one before the priests, the Levites. And it shall be with him, and he shall read it all the days of his life, that he may learn to fear the LORD his God and be careful to observe all the words of this law and these statutes, that his heart may not be lifted above his brethren, that he may not turn aside from the command- ment to the right hand or to the left, and that he may prolong his days in his kingdom, he and his children in the midst of Israel.

While Israel's king ruled God's people, he was himself to be ruled by the Lord and submit always to God's Law.

The Bible books that record the history of the Hebrews under kings describe good kings and evil ones—godly rulers who drew God's people closer to Him and ungodly rulers whose example of wickedness led God's people further from Him. We have much to learn from each of these rulers, especially the notable rulers introduced in this chapter.

NOTABLE JUDGES

In the first centuries after the conquest of Canaan (ca. 1390–1050 B.C.), the Israelite tribes shared a common heritage. However, they never functioned as a united people. During this era when there was no king "everyone did what was right in his own eyes" (Judges 17:6). When one or several tribes slipped into idolatry, God sent foreign enemies to oppress them. When their suffer- ing drove the people back to the Lord and they appealed to Him, God raised up a charismatic leader called a judge to defeat the enemy. Typically this leader then gov- erned in his tribe or area for the rest of his life. Also, typically, the people governed by

JUDGES AND THEIR RULE

	Name	Reference	Oppressor in Judges	Years of Oppression	Years of Rule
1.	Othniel	3:7–11	Mesopotamia	8	40
2.	Ehud	3:12–30	Moabites	18	80
3.	Shamgar	3:31			
4.	Deborah	4—5	Canaanites	20	40
5.	Gideon	6—8	Midianites	7	40
6.	Tola	10:1, 2			23
7.	Jair	10:3–5			22
8.	Jephthah	10:6—12:7	Ammonites	18	6
9.	Ibzan	12:8–10			7
10.	Elon	12:11–12			10
11.	Abdon	12:13–15			8
12.	Samson	13—16	Philistines	40	20

the judge remained faithful to the Lord during his lifetime.

In most ways, the judge functioned like a king. Judges were political, military, and religious leaders with judicial responsibilities. The primary difference was that while the monarchy was a hereditary institution, the judges were charismatic leaders whose mantle of authority was not passed on to their sons.

Just a glance at the chart above shows that some of the judges were given much more thorough treatment than others are given. We'll look at two of the more important judges and also at a man who is not mentioned in this Old Testament book, but who is the major figure marking the transition from the age of judges to the age of kings.

GIDEON
Scripture references:
Judges 6—8; Hebrews 11:32

Date:	*Ruled about 1169–1129*
Name:	*Gideon [GID-ee-uhn; "hewer" (i.e., "great warrior")]*
Greatest Accomplishment:	*He delivered his people from Midianite oppressors and maintained peace for forty years.*

GIDEON'S ROLE IN SCRIPTURE

Gideon was a very ordinary person. He was a younger son in a not-too-distinguished family when God called him to take the lead in defeating the Midianite raiders who swept into Israelite territory each year at harvest time, impoverishing God's people. Gideon,

Gideon put out the fleece not to learn God's will but because he needed reassurance.

empowered by the Spirit, rallied the men of the four tribes most affected—Manasseh, Asher, Zebulun, and Naphtali—and decisively defeated the Midianites, bringing peace to the tribes under Gideon's leadership for the next forty years.

GIDEON'S RELATIONSHIP WITH GOD

Gideon's story as recorded in the book of Judges clearly emphasizes Gideon's relationship with God. What is most striking in the account is Gideon's readiness to respond to God's commands and God's willingness to encourage Gideon along the way.

The Angel of the Lord appeared to Gideon (Judg. 6:11–23). When the Angel of the Lord addressed Gideon as a "mighty man of valor" and announced "the LORD is with you," Gideon almost laughed. If the Lord was with Israel, why were the Midianites allowed to oppress them? The Lord informed Gideon that he been chosen to save Israel. Gideon accepted what the Angel of the Lord told him, but asked for a sign. When Gideon brought meat and

bread for an offering, fire rose out of the rock and the Angel of the Lord departed.

It would be wrong to assume that Gideon was a skeptic. He had believed, but still found the experience hard to accept.

God gave Gideon his first command (Judg. 6:25–32). God then told Gideon to tear down the altar to Baal that his father had built for the town. Gideon was too timid to attack the shrine during the day, but under cover of darkness he did as the Lord commanded. When the men of the town demanded Gideon be killed for this sacrilege, his father defended him. If Baal was a god, his father suggested, he could take revenge on his own. The men backed down, and Gideon lived.

God's Spirit empowered Gideon (Judg. 6:33–35). Gideon was suddenly empowered by the Spirit, and he sent messengers to the affected tribes to join him in battling the Midianites. Amazingly, the men of Israel responded.

Gideon set out the fleece (Judg. 6:36–40). Gideon was still overwhelmed by all that had happened. He asked God for additional signs, first to have dew saturate a fleece (a lambskin) while the ground remained dry, and then for dew to saturate the ground while the fleece remained dry. God granted him both signs.

God reduced Gideon's army (Judg. 7:1–8). Some 32,000 men responded to Gideon's call, but God told Gideon he had too many men. God reduced Gideon's force to 10,000, and then to 300 men. With his 300 men, Gideon approached the Midianites' camp.

God further encouraged Gideon (Judg. 7:9–23). The evening before the attack, the Lord sent Gideon down to observe the enemy camp. There he overheard a man telling of a symbolic dream in which Gideon crushed the Midianites. A confident Gideon then ordered the attack, telling his men to suddenly appear waving torches, blowing trumpets, and shouting. The Midianites were so startled that in the dark they struck out at each other and fled. With the enemy in flight, the other Israelites pursued and killed them.

Gideon was offered the throne (Judg. 8:22–28). After the decisive victory, the Israelites were ready to make Gideon king. Gideon refused: "I will not rule over you, nor shall my son rule over you; the LORD shall rule over you" (8:23). Gideon did however serve God as judge. For the next forty years, the tribes he led remained faithful to the Lord.

GIDEON: AN EXAMPLE FOR TODAY

Some have misinterpreted Gideon's actions in setting out the fleece. They have taken what Gideon did as a means for discovering God's will, and they encourage believers to "put out the fleece" when faced with a difficult decision. But Gideon knew what God wanted, and was ready to obey. Gideon set out the fleece simply for encouragement, and this God graciously provided.

Gideon had shown himself willing to obey God *without* encouragement. Gideon had already raised his army before setting out the fleece. And Gideon had already reduced his army to 300 men before God let him overhear the Midianite's dream. Obedience had led to encouragement, and encouragement led to greater obedience still.

- Gideon's experience reminds us that we are to obey God without demanding "signs." While God may give signs to encourage us, He gives them to those who trust and have obeyed rather than to those who doubt and hold back.

- Gideon's experience reminds us that God uses ordinary people to accomplish His purposes. The one thing that distinguished Gideon was his willingness to risk obeying God, as when he tore down his father's altar of Baal.

- Gideon's experience reminds us that God leads us one step at a time. Gideon hardly knew from his first encounter with the Lord that he would be expected to face the Midianite masses with a mere three hundred men. But by the time Gideon had to face that challenge, he was ready for it. Let's not worry about what the future may hold when God asks us to step out for Him. One step at a time is enough for Him—and for us.

SAMSON

Scripture references:
Judges 13—16; Hebrews 11:32

Date:	*Judged about 1095–1075*
	B.C.
Name:	*Samson [SAM-suhn;*
	"distinguished"]

Philistine smiths knew the secret of working iron. This technological advantage enabled them to dominate the Israelites for decades.

| *Greatest Accomplishment:* | *He personally killed many of the Philistines who oppressed the Israelites.* |

SAMSON'S ROLE IN SCRIPTURE

Samson is the last of the judges whose story is told in the Book of Judges. With each repeated cycle of sin and deliverance reported in Judges 3—16, the Israelites seem to have sunk deeper into idolatry and adopted more and more of the religious concepts of the Canaanites. Samson showed us that the quality of the judges also declined.

EXPLORING SAMSON'S RELATIONSHIPS

We learn much about Samson by examining the various relationships he sustained.

Samson's relationship with his parents *(Judg. 13:1—14:3).* The Angel of the Lord appeared to Samson's parents before he was conceived. The angel instructed them on how to raise their special son. He was to be a Nazarite set apart to God from birth—a person set apart to God who would neither cut his hair nor use any product of the vine, nor touch any dead body (cf. Num. 6:2–10). Samson's parents carefully followed the Lord's directions, and God blessed Samson as he grew up (Judg. 13:25).

Samson soon showed himself to be a strong-willed youth. When he was attracted to a Philistine girl, Samson demanded that his father negotiate a marriage. Old Testament Law against intermarriage was clear (Ex. 34:12–16), and his parents urged him to seek a wife from among God's people. Samson refused.

While we think it appropriate that a young adult make his own decisions, in Bible times the father was to be heeded as long as he lived. Samson showed disrespect for his parents and for God's Law.

Samson's relationship with the Philistines *(Judg. 14—16).* As judge, Samson should have led his people against the Philistines. But Samson's relationship with the oppressors was personal, not political.

Samson first attacked the Philistines when Philistine guests at his wedding forced his bride-to-be to give them the answer to a riddle Samson had posed.

In Samson's time and even into David's early years, the Philistines maintained dominance over the Israelites. This was largely because the Philistines knew the secret of working iron and carefully guarded that secret to keep it from the Israelites. Remains of Philistine outposts have been found deep in Israelite territory. When King Saul led Israel into battle against the Philistines, only Saul and his son Jonathan carried iron weapons (1 Sam. 13:19–23)!

Samson then went to another district, killed thirty Philistines, and got the clothing to pay the gambling debt (Judg. 14:19).

When his Philistine father-in-law give his bride to another man, Samson burned Philistine grain fields in revenge (Judg. 15:1–5). When the Philistines demanded that Samson be turned over to them by the Israelites, Samson personally killed a thousand with the jawbone of a donkey.

Later Samson lost his strength temporarily and fell into Philistine hands. He was blinded and put to forced labor. Later his strength returned, and Samson cried out to God for power to take vengeance. Samson pushed over two key pillars in a Philistine temple, and killed more Philistines in his death than he had during his life (Judg. 16).

Through it all, Samson seems to have carried out a personal vendetta against the Philistines. He hated them, not because of their oppression of God's people, but because they had harmed *him*.

Samson's relationship with the Israelites *(Judg. 15:9–20)*. Although Samson judged Israel for twenty years, he was never the leader that Gideon, Jephthah, and the other judges had been. After Samson burned the Philistine grain fields, they sent an army against Israel, and demanded that Samson be turned over to them. Rather than follow Samson into battle, the Israelites bound Samson and turned him over to their enemies! Samson is the only judge of whom the biblical text does not state, "and the land had rest."

Samson killed Philistines, but the Philistines continued to oppress Israel throughout the twenty years of his rule.

Samson's relationship with women *(Judg. 16)*. Samson was a sex addict, and the text tells us of his visits to prostitutes as well as his passion for Philistine women. The most notorious relationship Samson had was with a prostitute named Delilah, who was well paid by the Philistine rulers to discover the secret of Samson's strength. When she finally learned that the secret lay in Samson's hair, uncut from birth, Delilah cut his hair off. Samson was then captured, blinded, and set to turning a millstone, typically work for an ox.

Some have expressed disgust at Delilah's "betrayal" of Samson. But why should a woman who sold herself be criticized for selling a man who exploited her vulnerability? The one who deserves our contempt is Samson, who used Delilah to feed his passion and was used in return.

Samson's relationship with God *(Judg. 13— 16)*. God gave Samson great strength that Samson employed against the Philistines. But Samson felt no obligation to use God's gift on behalf of God's people. Instead, Samson consistently used his strength to take revenge on the Philistines for what he perceived they had done to *him*.

In each crisis, God's Spirit gave Samson the supernatural strength he needed; yet, Samson ignored God's commands. The only prayers of Samson that are recorded are selfish prayers: a prayer-complaint demanding water and a cry to the Lord for strength to "take vengeance on the Philistines for my two eyes" (Judg. 15:18; 16:28). Clearly Samson was not a man who stayed close to the Lord. Samson was a man captive to his passions and his pride.

SAMSON: AN EXAMPLE FOR TODAY

Samson is not a man we want to emulate. Despite great gifts, he was a man of greater flaws. These flaws kept him from achieving as much for his people as earlier judges were able to achieve. Yet Samson, whatever his motives, served God's purpose in thwarting the total domination of the

Israelites by the Philistines. What can we learn from Samson?

- Samson warns us that we cannot equate gifts with godliness or success with spirituality.

- Samson reminds us that godly motives are as important as active service. Samson set himself against the Philistines for personal reasons, because he wanted to revenge himself for what Philistines had done to *him*. He was unmoved by the suffering of his people—concerned only with personal slights.

- Samson encourages us to use our gifts wisely. God will not judge us on how great our gifts are. He will judge us on how faithfully we have used those gifts to serve Him.

- Samson challenges us to live godly lives. How many spiritual leaders have fallen because of the pull of the flesh? When we choose to live by the standards God has laid out in His Word, we both honor our Lord and protect ourselves from unexpected disasters.

SAMUEL
Scripture references:
1 Samuel 1—8; 28; 1 Chronicles 6:27, 28
Psalms 99:6; Jeremiah 15:1; Acts 3:24;
13:20; Hebrews 11:32

Date:	About 1063–1000 B.C.
Name:	Samuel [SAM-yoo-uhl; "name of God"]
Greatest Accomplishment:	Samuel was Israel's last judge, who oversaw Israel's transition to a monarchy.

SAMUEL'S ROLE IN SCRIPTURE

Samuel was arguably Israel's greatest judge, who was also both a priest and a prophet. During his years as a judge, the Israelites were able to maintain relative independence from their greatest enemies, the Philistines. In his old age, Samuel anointed Saul as Israel's first king, and served as his counselor during the early years of his reign. When Saul failed to obey God's words spoken through the prophet, Samuel then anointed David to succeed Saul. In Jeremiah 15:1, the Lord linked Samuel with Moses as two men whose prayers had great influence with Him.

SAMUEL'S LIFE AND TIMES

When Samuel was born, the Israelites were in both spiritual and political depths. The spiritual leader, Eli, was well-meaning but had no control over his two sons, who used their position as priests to exploit their fellow Israelites (1 Sam. 2). For many years, no word had come from God through a prophet or any other source. In addition, the Philistines dominated the Israelites politically and economically. When Samuel was a young man, the Philistines not only defeated the Israelite militia at Aphek, but also capture the ark of the covenant (1 Sam. 4). The death of Eli's sons in that battle and Eli's subsequent stroke left Samuel as Israel's religious leader.

Samuel called for a return to the Lord, urging Israel to put away the foreign gods the people had been worshiping, and the people responded (1 Sam. 7). When another invading Philistine force approached, Samuel prayed for God's intervention, and the Israelites defeated the Philistines so completely that "they did not come anymore into the territory of Israel" in Samuel's time (1 Sam. 7:13).

When Samuel grew old, however, the people demanded a king. Tragically, Samuel's sons had "turned aside after dishonest gain, took bribes, and perverted justice" (1 Sam. 8:3). The demand for a king troubled Samuel, however, for he saw it as an implicit rejection of God in favor of a human ruler. When the Lord told Samuel to do as the people demanded, the aged prophet obeyed and anointed Saul as king.

Samuel invested much in King Saul and was bitterly disappointed when Saul proved to be a weak and ungodly ruler. Near the end of his life, God sent Samuel to anoint the youth David to succeed Saul. Samuel never got over his disappointment over Israel's first king, but died before Saul lost his life in battle.

EXPLORING SAMUEL'S RELATIONSHIPS

While Scripture focuses on two relationships of Samuel, at least two others are also significant.

Samuel's relationship with his mother *(1 Sam. 1; 2)*. The story of Hannah's passionate desire for a son and her gift of that boy to God is told and retold in Sunday School. During his first four years, until he was weaned, Samuel lived with his mother and father. We are told nothing of those early years, but undoubtedly Hannah told her son glowing stories of God's love for His covenant people and of the wonderful things God had done for them. In this, Samuel was like Moses with whom he is linked in Jeremiah 15:1. Each boy was taught by his mother; each boy was separated from her after being weaned. And each boy grew up to become a spiritual leader of God's people.

We can never underestimate the influence of mothers on their children when they are very young. Both Samuel and Moses should give parents pause before they choose day care over mother's care. Our first years of life are significant indeed!

Samuel's relationship with Eli *(1 Sam. 2)*. After Samuel was weaned his mother brought him to Eli the priest. Eli's sons were corrupt, but Eli himself was a dedicated although weak individual. Eli took Samuel under his care, and even as a child Samuel

God spoke to Samuel as a child, and Samuel was quickly recognized as a prophet.

❖

"ministered before the LORD" (1 Sam. 2:18). One of Samuel's most painful tasks as a child was to inform his mentor of God's judgment on his family because Eli had failed to restrain his wicked sons (1 Sam. 3:18).

Samuel's relationship with the Lord. Samuel's relationship with the Lord was close and personal throughout his life.

The foundation for Samuel's relationship with God was laid early (1 Sam. 2). Samuel's mother Hannah dedicated her son to the Lord before he was born and nurtured him carefully through his early years

Samuel proved responsive to God in his youth (1 Sam. 3). As a boy Samuel lived at the tabernacle, Israel's worship center. He helped in any way he could, and was daily exposed to the sacrifices and praises offered to the Lord there. While Samuel was exposed to the wickedness of Eli's sons, he bonded to Eli and chose to follow the path of godliness.

It is difficult to understand parents who fail to take their children to church, making the excuse that they want their children to make up their own minds when they are old enough. Without significant exposure to the Lord and His ways, young people have no basis on which to make that choice!

Samuel saw the right and the wrong, the godly and the ungodly. When he was just a youth, he made his choice to serve the Lord. That choice was so clear and its effect so powerful that "all Israel . . . knew that Samuel had been established as a prophet of the LORD" (1 Sam. 3:20).

Samuel influenced all Israel to recommit to the Lord (1 Sam. 7:1–9). After the death of Eli and his sons, Samuel became the recognized spiritual leader of the Israelites. Samuel used his influence to urge a return to the Lord. One of the most significant motivating factors was the Israelite's conviction that Samuel would pray for them if they returned to God (1 Sam. 7:5,8). Clearly Samuel was a man of prayer whose intimate relationship with God was known to all his people. We know nothing of Samuel's ability to preach, or his capacity to persuade. But we do know that Samuel was a man of prayer. This evidence of Samuel's close relationship with God gave the Israelites confidence in him.

Clearly, this should be as true today as it was then. The leader believers can trust and follow is a leader whose power rests in prayer and whose close relationship with God makes us confident that we can safely follow him.

Samuel led Israel to victory over the Philistines (1 Sam. 7:10–14). One of the roles of the judge in ancient Israel was to free God's people from dominance by foreign enemies. Samuel proved just such a leader, not in virtue of his military prowess, but in

virtue of his prowess in prayer. As Samuel prayed, Israel fought, and God provided the victory.

Samuel was jealous for God's honor (1 Sam. 8). In Samuel's old age, the Israelites begged for Samuel to give them a king. They did not want Samuel's son to rule them. He had not made the choice Samuel had, and he proved to be a corrupt and ungodly man. While this must have troubled Samuel deeply, when the Israelites called for a king Samuel was more concerned for God's honor. During the era of the judges, the Lord was viewed as Israel's King, and He was viewed as the One to turn to when it was necessary to fight foreign enemies. The call for a king was an implicit rejection of reliance on the Lord.

Samuel tried to dissuade the Israelites (1 Sam. 8:10–18), but finally the Lord told Samuel to do as the people asked.

How tragic it is when a spiritual leader knows what is best for the people he leads, but they simply will not consider his warnings.

God led Samuel to Israel's first two kings (1 Sam. 9; 16). God specifically led Samuel first to Saul and then to David whom the prophet anointed to become Israel's first two kings. During Saul's early years Samuel also served as court prophet and advisor, and he was bitterly disappointed when Saul refused to obey the Lord.

These must have been difficult years for Samuel. For years, he had been Israel's unquestioned leader, trusted because of his calling as judge and prophet and because of his personal relationship with God. Samuel then surrendered his authority to King Saul, and stepped into the role of an advisor. Saul should have heeded Samuel as God's prophet. Saul's failure to obey God's instructions pained Samuel deeply, not because it was an insult to him but because Samuel desperately wanted the king to be as loyal to the Lord as he himself had been.

For a person who is totally committed to the Lord to see the flaws in a successor who is committed only to his own self-interest is heart-breaking. In this situation Samuel could only trust God and wait to see what the Lord would do. When God told Samuel to anoint David as Saul's successor, Samuel obeyed despite his own deep disappointment.

Throughout his life, Samuel remained fully committed to God. In all he did, Samuel showed himself to be a man of faith and prayer who influenced his people to trust in God and who oversaw Israel's transition from the era of the judges to the monarchy.

Samuel's relationship with Saul. Even though Saul was Samuel's successor, the aged prophet-judge had a deep affection for him.

Samuel anointed Saul king (1 Sam. 9; 10). God clearly identified Saul to Samuel as the man He intended to become king of Israel. Samuel not only anointed Saul, but at a great convocation of the Israelites, Samuel presented Saul to them as king. Samuel like the rest of Israel seems to have been impressed by Saul's physical stature: he was "taller than any of the people from his shoulders upward" (1 Sam. 10:23).

Samuel rebuked Saul for disobedience (1 Sam. 13). When a Philistine army invaded, Saul had been told to wait seven days for Samuel to appear and pray for God's people. When the Israelite forces began to desert, however, and Samuel did not arrive during the first seven days, Saul himself sacrificed an offering. This sacrifice violated the commandment God had given him through Samuel (1 Sam. 10:8). Samuel was frustrated and angry and announced that God would not permit Saul to found a dynasty. Despite his personal disappointment, Samuel faithfully conveyed God's rebuke to Saul.

Samuel rejected Saul for rebelling against God (1 Sam. 15). Later, Saul directly disobeyed a command of God when going to war with the Amalekites. Samuel confronted the king and told him that the Lord had completely rejected him. After this incident, Samuel "went no more to see Saul until the day of his death. Nevertheless Samuel mourned for Saul" (1 Sam. 15:35).

Saul proved to be one of Samuel's greatest disappointments. Those who have labored a lifetime to establish something significant hurt when they see a successor undo what they have built or fall so far short of what they have dreamed!

SAMUEL: AN EXAMPLE FOR TODAY

Samuel is undoubtedly one of the great men of the Old Testament. He was significant because he was a transition figure. But his personal significance is rooted in his personal commitment to the Lord.

- Samuel's commitment was nurtured by Hannah's dedication of her son to the Lord. More often than not, a parent's love and prayers powerfully influence a child's future.
- Samuel's commitment was encouraged by his early exposure to worship at the house of the Lord. The more we learn of the Lord, and the earlier we learn His ways, the more willing we tend to be to respond when He speaks to us.
- Samuel's commitment involved a personal and decisive choice. Samuel saw both godly and ungodly ways of life, and he was mentored by a godly though weak individual. Samuel chose to take His stand with God. His mother's prayers and his exposure to God at the tabernacle helped him make this choice, but these did not determine the way he would go. Samuel made that choice

himself, freely and responsibly. Each of us makes his or her own choices in life, and the sooner we choose commitment to the Lord, the richer and more significant our lives will be.

- Samuel's commitment involved dedication to prayer. Samuel's intimate relationship with God and the power of his prayers helped give the Israelites confidence to trust the Lord. If we are to influence and move others to a deeper trust in God, prayer must have a significant place in our daily lives.

- Samuel's commitment was expressed as a concern for God's glory. Samuel clearly was more concerned that Israel honor God than that the people honor him or his sons. We, too, can make the chief end of our life to glorify God and to enjoy Him forever.

KINGS OF THE UNITED HEBREW KINGDOM

The most notable king of the united Hebrew kingdom was David, whose life we considered earlier (see page 44). In a sense David was the one who created the united kingdom, bonding the scattered tribes together to form a powerful nation. King Saul, who took some initial steps toward unification, preceded David. And David's son Solomon, who ruled during what has been called Israel's "golden age," followed David.

Only these three ruled a united Hebrew kingdom. After Solomon's death the nation was divided into northern and southern kingdoms.

SAUL
Scripture references:
1 Samuel 9—31; 1 Chronicles 10:1–13

Date:	*Ruled about 1043–1010* B.C.

Name:	*Saul [SAWL: "asked"]*
Greatest	
Accomplishment:	*He was Israel's first king.*

SAUL'S ROLE IN SCRIPTURE

Saul was a man who began well but who broke under the pressure of leadership. Saul was Israel's first king, and he began the process of unifying the Hebrew tribes and making them a nation. This task was finally accomplished by his far more famous successor, David.

SAUL'S LIFE AND TIMES

Samuel was the last prophet/judge to lead Israel. When Samson became old, the Israelites demanded a king. The people longed for a ruler like those in pagan nations—a military man who would fight to protect them. While the people's motives were wrong, God gave in to their demand. He gave them Saul, a physically imposing individual— a trait that was probably necessary if the Israelites were to accept him as their ruler.

Saul achieved early military successes that solidified his support among the people. But all too soon, Saul's flaws—an inability to trust God and an unwillingness to obey Him—led the Lord to reject Saul. Saul continued as Israel's ruler for many years, but his growing alienation from the Lord showed up in many ways. Saul suffered from deepening depression and paranoia. Saul cowered when challenged by the Philistine champion, Goliath. Saul became intensely jealous of David after he killed Goliath and achieved other military victories. Finally, Saul determined to kill David. His frequent attempts forced David to become a fugitive. Saul's hostility toward David never waned, and he pursued David throughout his life until Saul was killed in a great battle with the Philistines.

Saul's failure to stay close to the Lord led him to a spiritist in a desperate attempt to learn his future.

EXPLORING SAUL'S RELATIONSHIPS

Saul's relationship with David. See the biography of David, pages 43-57.

Saul's relationship with God. The text enables us to trace Saul's rapidly deteriorating relationship with the Lord.

Saul credited God with a victory (1 Sam. 11). When the Ammonites attacked an Israelite city, Saul raised a militia and defeated them. Appropriately, he announced that "today the LORD has accomplished salvation in Israel" (11:13). All Israel, then, pledged allegiance to Saul as king.

Saul's fear led to disobedience (1 Sam. 13). Saul established a small standing army. In his second year, he attacked a Philistine outpost. The Philistines raised a massive army to put down the upstart king and the Israelites. When the Israelites saw the size of the force gathered against them, the men who had responded to Saul's call earlier hid or fled the country! Even members of Saul's little army began to desert. Within a week, Saul had a mere 600 men left to support him.

Samuel had told Saul to wait seven days and promised he would then come to offer sacrifice to the Lord. Saul, desperate to hold the few men who remained, finally determined to offer the sacrifice himself even though he was not a priest. When Samuel did arrive he condemned Saul for doing "foolishly." The Hebrew term here portrays the "fool" as one who acts rebelliously. Samuel announced that because of Saul's act he would not be allowed to found a dynasty.

Saul's fears may be understandable. But Saul undoubtedly knew well the stories of the judges and of God's aid to men of the past. Fear had driven Saul to disobey God's prophet despite the fact that when he disobeyed he had twice as many soldiers as Gideon had when he defeated as large a force.

The fact that Saul's fear was groundless and showed a lack of faith was soon demonstrated. Saul's son Jonathan attacked a Philistine outpost, and routed a great army.

Saul disobeyed God again (1 Sam. 15). When God sent Saul to wipe out the Amalekites, Saul kept their king alive and took their cattle and other valuables as spoil. This was a direct violation of God's command. When Samuel confronted him, Saul first lied and said that he planned to offer the animals as sacrifices to the Lord. Saul then tried to excuse himself by pleading that he had feared people (1 Sam. 15:24). Finally Saul admitted to Samuel that he had sinned, but begged the prophet to "honor me" before the people. In this Saul was totally unlike David, who publicly confessed his sin and took responsibility for his actions.

Saul ordered the murder of the priests of Nob (1 Sam. 22). As David fled from Saul, the priest Ahimelech gave David food and Goliath's sword, which was kept at Nob. Despite the fact that the priests did not know that David was a fugitive, Saul ordered their murder. When no Israelite would touch a priest of the Lord, Saul ordered an Edomite by the name of Doeg to do the deed.

Saul consulted a spiritist (1 Sam. 31). Near the end of his reign, Saul was about to go to war with the Philistines once again. By now he was totally isolated from the Lord. Desperate for some hint of what the future held, Saul consulted a medium, whose contact was a demonic spirit. Saul knew this was a violation of God's law, for he himself had ordered all such persons driven from Israel. To the shocked surprise of the medium, Samuel himself appeared and told Saul that he would die in battle the next day.

THE ROLE OF THE OCCULT IN THE ANCIENT WORLD

The Book of Deuteronomy lists a number of occult practices common in Canaan in the second millennium B.C. Among them were "one who practices witchcraft, or a soothsayer, or one who interprets omens, or a sorcerer, or one who conjures spells, or a medium, or a spiritist, or one who calls up the dead" (Deut. 18:10–11). Each of these practices was common beyond Canaan as well. Roman augurs examined the entrails of animals and looked for signs in the flight of birds before conducting religious ceremonies or going into battle.

The Handbook of Life in Ancient Rome observes:

It was thought that the gods revealed their will to people in the form of signs or omens. Some might be fairly obvious, such as thunder, lightening, unusually natural phenomena or a causal word or phrase overheard in passing. But most signs were less obvious, and in any case needed proper interpretation. Divination was the art of reading such signs to predict the future (p. 279).

Similarly, the Greeks consulted oracles whose drugged mutterings were thought to contain guidance from the gods. In Mesopotamia lots were cast to determine the auspicious day for a new venture, while astrologers consulted the stars and spiritists served as channels through whom deities or the dead might speak.

The Old Testament clearly states that these occult religion-linked practices were channels through which demons worked to blind and to bind human beings (cf. Lev. 17:7; Deut. 32:17; 2 Chron.11:15; Ps. 106:37. For an extended discussion, see the volume in this series on *Every Good and Evil Angel in the Bible*).

Yet, the universality of these practices demonstrates a deep hunger of the human heart to find some source of guidance that will provide help in making potentially dangerous decisions.

SAUL: AN EXAMPLE FOR TODAY

Saul, despite his imposing physique, was a moral coward. In this, he serves as a negative example, warning us away from traps into which we, too, might fall.

- Saul warns us against a failure to trust God. However bleak our situation may seem, taking things into our own hands is foolish indeed.

- Saul warns us against failing to obey God. Too often, Christians are more concerned with what others think than with what God thinks. To fear humans is foolish when in the end all people will have to answer to the Lord.

- Saul reminds us that when our steps lead us too far from God, returning to God becomes more and more difficult. Saul had a chance to repent, but he was so concerned with appearances that he was unwilling to confess his sin openly and honestly and give God the glory. A way back to the Lord always exists, but we may be unwilling to take it.

- Saul reminds us that character counts. People's looks, their intelligence, their appeal to the crowds, their commanding presence, their skill with words, or their ability to move crowds should not be the only criteria we use in choosing a leader. We need men and women of character and principle who will do what is right no matter what the polls or the media may say.

SOLOMON
Scripture references:
1 Kings 1—11; 1 Chronicles 29;
2 Chronicles 1—9; Nehemiah 13:26;
Proverbs; Song of Solomon; Ecclesiastes;
Matthew 6:29; Luke 12:27;
Matthew 12:42; Luke 11:31

Date:	*Ruled 970–930 B.C.*
Name:	*Solomon [SAHL-uh-muhn; "peaceable"]*

Greatest Accomplishment:	*Solomon built the magnificent Jerusalem temple and ruled the united Hebrew kingdom for forty years.*

SOLOMON'S ROLE IN SCRIPTURE

Solomon succeeded his father David as Israel's king. He immediately set out to fulfill his father's dream of constructing a temple for the Lord. Solomon's wisdom was legendary. Solomon:

spoke three thousand proverbs, and his songs were one thousand and five. Also he spoke of trees, from the cedar tree of Lebanon even to the hyssop that springs out of the wall; he spoke also of animals, of birds, of creeping things, and of fish (1 Kings 4:32, 33).

Solomon's vast intellect was a wonder in his own time, and he was still referred to in New Testament times as the wisest of men (Matt. 12:42; Luke 11:31). Many of his wise sayings are preserved in the Book of Proverbs (Prov. 1:1; 10:1; 25:1). Solomon also is credited with writing the Song of Songs, a warm and beautiful poem in praise of married love.

In addition to his intellectual pursuits, Solomon undertook aggressive building programs throughout his kingdom. He maintained a large chariot army that was never used during his reign. Rather, Solomon relied on diplomacy to maintain peaceful relations with the surrounding nations. During this era, Solomon's control of land trade routes brought vast revenues into his kingdom that Solomon spent on his projects. Solomon was the only Hebrew king ever to maintain a fleet of trading vessels, and this venture also added to the kingdom's wealth. The New Testament also reflected on the

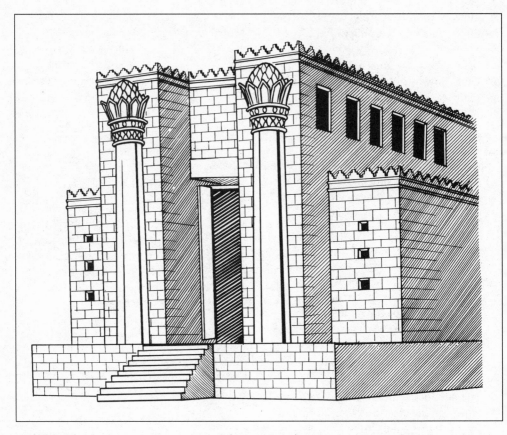

Solomon's Temple

glory of Solomon's kingdom, beautified by the great public projects he undertook (Matt. 6:29; Luke 12:27).

While Solomon saw vast funds flow into his kingdom, money always seemed to be in short supply. Solomon kept increasing the taxes on his people to the extent that, when he died, the northern tribes refused to submit to Solomon's son Rehoboam unless the young king promised to reduce taxes.

EXPLORING SOLOMON'S RELATIONSHIPS

Solomon's relationship with God. Solomon was granted several revelation experiences. Unfortunately, Solomon did not remain committed to the Lord throughout his life.

Solomon asked for wisdom (1 Kings 3). At the beginning of his reign, the biblical writers said Solomon "loved the LORD, walking in the statutes of his father David" (3:3). Just after Solomon had expressed his love by offering a thousand sacrifices, God spoke to Solomon in a dream, inviting Solomon to make a request. Solomon expressed his sense of inadequacy, and asked only for "an understanding heart to judge Your people, that I may discern between good and evil" (1 Kings 3:9). This request pleased God, and the Lord granted him not only wisdom but peace, wealth, and long life as well.

Solomon dedicated the temple (1 Kings 8; 2 Chron. 6). One of Solomon's first priorities was to construct the temple his father David had dreamed of building to honor the Lord. Solomon's prayer of dedication, recorded in these chapters, further reveals Solomon's heart for the Lord and his understanding of spiritual realities. Solomon concluded the dedication service by challenging his people: "Let your heart therefore be loyal to the LORD our God, to walk in His statutes and keep His commandments, as at this day" (1 Kings 8:61).

God's second appearance to Solomon (1 Kings 9). After the dedication of the temple, the Lord appeared to Solomon again, promising to bless the king if he continued to walk before Him and live a godly life.

Solomon's fall (1 Kings 11). In Solomon's later years, the foreign women he married "turned his heart after other gods; and his heart was not loyal to the LORD his God" (1 Kings 11:4).

Solomon paid a high personal price for his apostasy. The Book of Ecclesiastes, an anonymous book likely written by Solomon, reveals the misery he felt as he drifted further and further from God. After urgently seeking some meaning in life apart from God and apart from the perspective provided by divine revelation, Solomon concluded that all was meaningless—including his own accomplishments.

What a tragic ending this was to a life that had begun with such promise.

Solomon's relationships with women. The text tells us that Solomon had 700 wives and 300 concubines. It would be a mistake, however, to read into this the conclusion that Solomon was simply a sexual addict.

Solomon's marriages and public policy (1 Kings 3:1). Solomon made a treaty with Pharaoh king of Egypt "and married Pharaoh's daughter." Unlike David, who relied on his military, Solomon relied on diplomacy to maintain peace and national security. In the ancient world, treaties between nations were typically sealed by marriages between the royal houses. Many of Solomon's foreign wives were introduced into Israel through this route.

Solomon's love for his wives (1 Kings 11). Solomon did care for his foreign wives, however they came to him. But rather than expecting them to worship the Lord, Solomon built them shrines so they could worship their own deities. In time, these women moved Solomon to worship with them. In this way, Solomon fell into idolatry, and he "turned from the LORD God of Israel, who had appeared to him twice" (1 Kings 11:9).

God spoke to Solomon a third time and announced that because of Solomon's idolatry the kingdom would be divided after Solomon's death. Much later, Nehemiah referred to Solomon when insisting that Jews who returned to Judah after the Babylonian captivity divorce the foreign wives they had married. "Did not Solomon king of Israel sin by these things?" Nehemiah asked. The people of Judah had done "great evil, transgressing against our God by marrying these pagan women" (Neh. 13:26, 27).

SOLOMON: AN EXAMPLE FOR TODAY

Solomon is both a good and bad example. His youthful concern for his people is touching, and his prayer at the dedication of the temple shows great spiritual insight. But Solomon knowingly turned away from the Lord—motivated by his passion for the foreign wives he had married despite prohibitions against intermarriage in God's Law. What then do we learn from Solomon?

- Solomon's experience reminds us that concern for others truly does please the Lord. When we ask for gifts to minister more effectively, God is likely to grant our requests.

- Solomon's experience warns us not to grow lax in our commitment to the

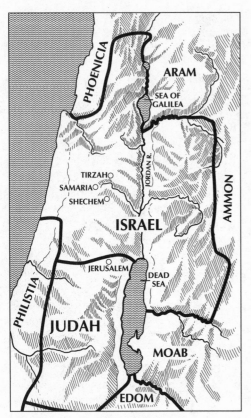

After Solomon's death his kingdom was torn in two. The north, Israel, was ruled by a series of wicked kings. In the south, Judah, each ruler descended from King David.

Lord. We cannot rest on zeal shown in our youth to carry us through maturity and old age. We must remain focused on pleasing the Lord.

- Solomon's experience compels us to reevaluate our relationship with our spouse. Each of us rightly wants to please his wife. This is one of the marks of a loving relationship. But our first allegiance must always be to the Lord. "I love my wife, and she wants me to spend Sunday morning with her" is no excuse for not going to church.

- Solomon teaches us that only as we continue to walk with the Lord will we find life meaningful and be fulfilled.

NOTABLE KINGS OF THE NORTHERN KINGDOM

When Solomon died in 730 B.C., his son Rehoboam succeeded him. The high taxes Solomon had imposed to support his vast building projects had placed great stress on his people. An agitator and ex-official named Jeroboam exploited this unrest, and the northern Hebrew tribes were ready to revolt. The men of the north informed Rehoboam that they would remain loyal only if he promised to reduce their taxes. The young king arrogantly informed his subjects that he would raise their taxes! At this the northern tribes did revolt and made Jeroboam king. Only the two southern tribes, Judah and Benjamin, remained loyal to David's line.

The northern Hebrew kingdom, called Israel, lasted from 930 to 722 B.C., when it was overrun by the Assyrians and its population was resettled. During Israel's two centuries as a nation not a single godly king ruled in the north. The best known king of the northern kingdom, Ahab, has been discussed in the article on Elijah (see pages 87–90). Two other rulers, Jeroboam I and Jehu, give us an accurate impression of the character of the northern kings.

JEROBOAM I
Scripture references:
1 Kings 11:26—14:20;
2 Chronicles 13

Date:	Ruled Israel 930–909 B.C.
Name:	JAIR-uh-BOH-uhm; "may the people increase"
Greatest Accomplishment:	Jeroboam was the first ruler of the northern Hebrew kingdom, Israel.

THE KINGS OF ISRAEL

Ruler	B.C. Date	Scripture
Jeroboam I	930–909	1 Kings 12:23—14:20
Nadab	909–908	1 Kings 15:25–31
Baasha	908–886	1 Kings 15:33—16:7
Elah	886–885	1 Kings 16:6–20
Zimri	885	1 Kings 16:9–20
Tibni	885–880	1 Kings 16:21–22
Omri	880–874	1 Kings 16:23–28
Ahab	874–853	1 Kings 16:29—22:40
Ahaziah	853–852	1 Kings 22:51–53
Joram	852–841	2 Kings 1:1—9:26
Jehu	841–814	2 Kings 9:1—10:36
Jehoahaz	814–798	2 Kings 13:1–9
Jehoash	798–782	2 Kings 13:10–25
Jeroboam II	793–753	2 Kings 14:23–29
co-regent	793–782	
Zechariah	753	2 Kings 15:8–11
Shallum	752	2 Kings 15:13–16
Menahem	752–742	2 Kings 15:17–22
Pekahiah	742–740	2 Kings 15:23–26
Pekah	740–732	2 Kings 15:27–31
Hoshea	732–723	2 Kings 17

JEROBOAM'S ROLE IN SCRIPTURE

After Rehoboam's foolish first actions as king of the united Hebrew kingdom built by David and Solomon, Jeroboam was largely responsible for the establishment of the breakaway northern kingdom of Israel. Jeroboam was also responsible for setting the sinful course for the northern kingdom. The Bible frequently condemns the kings of Israel by saying that they followed "the way of" or committed the "sins of" Jeroboam (1 Kings 15:30; 16:2, 19, 26, 31; 2 Kings 3:3; 10:29). Jeroboam is a powerful example of a man who had a great opportunity but consciously abandoned God's ways and by his choice condemned not only himself but future generations.

JEROBOAM'S LIFE AND TIMES

Jeroboam was an industrious and talented young man. Solomon recognized his ability and made him supervisor of the labor force engaged in all public works. When Solomon heard that the prophet Ahijah had predicted that Jeroboam would become ruler of ten of the twelve Hebrew tribes, Solomon tried to kill Jeroboam. After Solomon died, Jeroboam became the spokesman for the northern tribes, urging Solomon's son Rehoboam to lighten the tax load Solomon had imposed. When Rehoboam arrogantly refused, the rebel tribes crowned Jeroboam.

The north possessed a larger population and controlled most of the land of the old united kingdom. Jeroboam immediately took steps to consolidate his power. But in a

As Jeroboam dedicated the worship center he intended to replace God's temple at Jerusalem, his arm was paralyzed when he attempted to kill the young prophet who condemned his action.

war with Judah in his eighteenth year, Jeroboam lost territory. Jeroboam died three years later.

EXPLORING JEROBOAM'S RELATIONSHIPS

The relationship that is key to understanding Jeroboam is his relationship with the Lord.

Jeroboam commissioned by God (1 Kings 11:26–40). Jeroboam was a responsible official in Solomon's service when the prophet Ahijah announced that God would give Jeroboam ten of the twelve Hebrew tribes. God made Jeroboam a promise: "If you heed all that I command you, walk in My ways, and do what is right in My sight, to keep My statutes and My commandments, as My servant David did, then I will be with you and build for you an enduring house, as I built for David, and will give Israel to you" (11:38). The Lord gave Jeroboam a tremendous opportunity he might easily have grasped.

Jeroboam's choice (1 Kings 12:25–33). When Jeroboam became king of the ten northern tribes, he began to worry. The temple, where the Lord was to be worshiped, was in Jerusalem. Jerusalem was the capital of the southern kingdom, Judah. Jeroboam did not want his citizens to go to Jerusalem to worship, as the Law stated that they must. Despite God's promise Jeroboam was sure that religious unity would lead to political reunion.

So Jeroboam set up his own sect, a religious system that counterfeited elements of the law God had given to Moses. Jeroboam intended his people to worship Yahweh. But they would worship at shrines in Bethel and Dan, not in Jerusalem. Jeroboam erected golden calves in Bethel and Dan. The Lord was assumed to stand or be seated on these calves. Rather than keeping the religious festivals established in the law, Jeroboam implemented a religious calendar that "he had devised in his own heart" (12:33). Rather than have descendants of Aaron offer sacrifices, Jeroboam sold priesthood positions to anyone who could pay.

God's response (1 Kings 13). God sent a prophet from Judah to confront Jeroboam on the day he dedicated the altar at Bethel. The prophet condemned what Jeroboam had done as sacrilege and predicted that a future king of Judah named Josiah would one day burn human bones on that altar, so polluting it that the site could never again be used for worship. As a sign that the prophet spoke in God's name, the altar at Bethel shattered.

Rather than repent, Jeroboam ordered the young prophet killed. Only paralysis of the arm he lifted to point at the prophet stopped him. The prayer of the prophet restored the arm, but Jeroboam had made his choice. Jeroboam determined to go his own way rather than rely on the promise of the God who had given him his kingdom.

God helps Judah (2 Chron. 13:20). In Jeroboam's eighteenth year, he went to war with Abijah, king of Judah. Jeroboam had 800,000 men, Abijah 400,000. But the young King Abijah challenged Jeroboam:

"Have you not cast out the priests of the Lord, the sons of Aaron, and the Levites, and made for yourselves priests, like the peoples of other lands . . . But as for us, the LORD is our God, and we have not forsaken Him; and the priests who minister to the LORD are the sons of Aaron, and the Levites attend to their duties. . . .Now look, God Himself is . . . our head, and His priests with sounding trumpets to sound the alarm against you. O children of Israel, do not fight against the LORD God of your fathers, for you shall not prosper" (13:9–12).

Jeroboam refused to listen to the young king. He relied on his numbers and on an ambush that surprised Judah's forces. Despite Jeroboam's strategic and numerical advantages, Abijah decisively defeated Jeroboam. He had abandoned God, and his destiny was sealed.

JEROBOAM: AN EXAMPLE FOR TODAY

Jeroboam was an energetic leader. God had promised to make him ruler of ten of the Hebrew tribes, and God had kept His promise. God had also promised that if Jeroboam was faithful to Him, Jeroboam's kingdom would be established. But in a conflict between reason and faith, Jeroboam was unwilling to rely on God's promises. It was *reasonable* to assume that if his people went to Jerusalem to worship, he would lose his throne. It was *reasonable* to invent his own national religion. When it came time to do battle with Judah, it was *reasonable* that the larger force would win, and *reasonable* that superior strategy and tactics would route the enemy. But in every choice, Jeroboam was wrong. So, what do we learn from Jeroboam?

- Jeroboam reminds us that we are wise to trust God's promises, and utterly foolish to discount them.

- Jeroboam alerts us to the limitations of human reason. Yes, we are to be reasonable in making decisions. However, we need to remember that to submit our reason to God and to walk always in His ways is truly reasonable.

- Jeroboam demonstrates the impact one person's choices can have on others. Jeroboam's sins corrupted generations of Israelites. No telling how our own sinful choices may affect the lives of those we love. How much better to do what is right and trust God to bless.

AHAB
Scripture references:
1 Kings 16—18; 20—22;
2 Chronicles 18

Date: **Ruled Israel 874–854 B.C.**

Name:	*Ahab [AY-hab; "father is brother"]*
Greatest Accomplishment:	*Although one of Israel's most wicked kings, he was one of the most successful.*

mony in which they were burned alive while drums beat loudly to drown out the children's anguished screams.

The struggle between Elijah and the royal family to establish which deity would be the God of Israel, the Lord or Baal-Melqart, was truly a matter of life and death.

AHAB'S ROLE IN SCRIPTURE

Ahab and his queen, Jezebel, aggressively promoted the worship of Baal-Melqart in an attempt to replace worship of the Lord in the northern Hebrew kingdom, Israel. The prophet Elijah thwarted Ahab's efforts by demonstrating decisively that the Lord is God and turning the populace back to Him (see Elijah, page 87). The religious struggle between the royal family and Elijah was so significant that no other king of either Judah or Israel was given as much space in the Old Testament account of the history of the divided kingdom.

AHAB'S LIFE AND TIMES

Nelson's *Illustrated Bible Handbook* fills in details about Ahab's political accomplishments that are not recorded in Scripture.

The biblical record focuses on the religious conflict. But from OT hints and other historical sources we can reconstruct other elements of Ahab's long rule. In general, he was a capable leader. He continued to build (1 Kings 22:39). Twice he defeated the Aramean forces of Ben-Hadad II. He also joined a coalition of kings who temporarily stopped the advance of the Assyrians under Shalmaneser II at Qarqar in 853 B.C. Ahab also made an alliance with Jehoshaphat of Judah, maintaining the peace that had existed between the two nations since the time of Omri (p. 197).

BAAL-MELQART

The particular form of idolatry Ahab and Jezebel sought to introduce into Israel had its origins in Phoenicia, Jezebel's home. Worshipers of Baal-Melqart seem to have possessed a missionary zeal, although the primary motivation may have been political. Like other Canaanite religions, the worship of Baal-Melqart was morally degrading and included religious prostitution.

The deity was also worshiped in the Phoenician colony of Carthage. Findings by archaeologists in a sacred garden in Carthage demonstrate just how depraved this religion was. There, in thousands of burial urns, the remains of children ranging in age from infants to four-year-olds have been found. These were children offered to Baal in a cere-

EXPLORING AHAB'S RELATIONSHIPS

Ahab's relationship with the prophet Elijah is explored in the article on Elijah (p. 87). Two of the king's other relationships are significant.

Ahab's relationship with Jezebel *(1 Kings 21).* Jezebel was from Sidon, a center of the worship of Baal-Melqart. When Jezebel came to Israel, she influenced her husband to worship her deity; in time, Ahab converted to her religion. The text tells us that Ahab "set up an altar for Baal in the temple of Baal, which he had built in Samaria" (the capital of the northern kingdom), and that Ahab "made a wooden image" (1 Kings 16:32, 33). Together Ahab and Jezebel set out to replace worship of the Lord in Israel with the worship of Baal. To accomplish this, Jezebel attempted to kill off all prophets of the Lord (1 Kings 18:4) and imported hundreds of prophets of Baal to spread the new religion. Jezebel was the driving force behind these efforts, but Ahab was her willing accomplice.

First Kings 21 provides special insight into the relationship between these two. Ahab wanted a plot of land near his palace for a vegetable garden. When the owner refused to sell or trade the land, Ahab went home and sulked. When Jezebel found what was wrong, she promised to take care of the matter. She organized a plot in which the owner was killed, and she then presented the field to her husband. The incident suggests that Ahab while wicked was also weak and in many ways depended on his wife. He might have been a gifted military commander, but he clearly lacked the strength of character which Jezebel, a truly evil woman, possessed. No wonder Jezebel had been able to win Ahab over to the worship of Baal and to her plans for turning the Israelites away from the Lord.

Ahab's relationship with God. Early in his reign Ahab turned from God to the worship of his wife's deity, Baal-Melqart. Yet God did not leave the apostate king alone, nor did God abandon efforts to turn him back to the true faith.

Elijah predicted God's judgment (1 Kings 17). Elijah confronted Ahab and announced that there would be neither rain nor dew in Israel except at his word for three years. Elijah then dropped out of sight. Although Ahab sent officials to scour the kingdom, they could not find Elijah. Ahab clearly blamed Elijah for the drought that brought economic disaster on Israel rather than acknowledging his own responsibility for the divine judgment.

Ahab accepted Elijah's challenge (1 Kings 18). After three years had passed, Elijah again met Ahab. Elijah proposed a contest between himself and the 450 prophets of Baal who owed allegiance to Ahab. The king's acceptance of the challenge suggested that Ahab truly did believe in Baal and expected that deity to respond to the prayers of Baal's prophets. In contrast, Jezebel was unwilling to expose the four hundred prophets of Asherah (Baal's consort) that she controlled to the contest. Apparently Jezebel viewed promotion of her nation's religion more as a political than a religious mission!

When God answered Elijah's prayers and decisively demonstrated that He is God, Ahab did not attempt to intervene when Elijah ordered the death of Baal's prophets. But Jezebel expressed her determination to see Elijah dead!

God assisted Ahab against the Syrians (1 Kings 20). When Ben-Hadad of Syria attacked Samaria, God sent a prophet to instruct Ahab on how to defeat his enemy. The prophet announced that the Lord intended to deliver the enemy into his hand, "and you shall know that I am the LORD" (1 Kings 20:13). Ahab followed the prophet's instruction, and the Syrians were defeated. The same prophet continued to inform Ahab of Syrian plans, enabling Ahab to block every effort of the enemy. However, when Ahab again defeated the Syrians and captured Ben-Hadad, the defeated Syrian offered a treaty. Ahab, without consulting the Lord or his prophet, agreed! The prophet then announced that Ahab would now suffer the fate God had intended for the Syrian enemy.

Ahab had been shown God's ability to help as well as to judge, but Ahab continued to be unresponsive to God.

Ahab feared God's judgment (1 Kings 21). After Jezebel arranged the murder of the owner of the land Ahab coveted, the king hurried to take possession of the property.

He met Elijah, who pronounced a terrible judgment on the king and Jezebel.

This time Ahab took the prophet's word seriously, and displayed some repentance in the traditional way. He "tore his clothes and put sackcloth on his body, and fasted and lay in sackcloth, and went about mourning" (1 Kings 21:27). God then told Elijah that since Ahab had humbled himself before the Lord, the terrible judgment pronounced on Ahab's line would be delayed until after Ahab's death.

Ahab disregarded the warning of the prophet Micaiah (1 Kings 22). Later Ahab, in alliance with the king of Judah, laid plans to attack Syria. Ahab's court prophets predicted victory, but the king of Judah asked Ahab to inquire of a prophet committed to the Lord. Ahab responded: "I hate him, because he does not prophecy good concerning me, but evil" (1 Kings 22:8).

When Micaiah appeared he told the king plainly that an evil spirit inspired his prophets and that if he fought the Syrians he would die in battle. Ahab had Micaiah imprisoned, to be dealt with when he returned from the conflict. Ahab did not return, but was killed in battle as God's prophet had foretold.

AHAB: AN EXAMPLE FOR TODAY

Ahab is a complex figure whose weaknesses made him vulnerable to domination by his wife, Jezebel, and whose tendency toward sin made him unresponsive to God despite the many opportunities God gave him to repent.

Ahab demonstrated many traits against which believers must be on guard.

- Ahab warns us against choosing a spouse whose faith is at odds with God's Word. Ahab not only chose Jezebel but also succumbed to her influence. He adopted her faith and her

ways, and in the end brought judgment on himself and his people.

- Ahab warns us against showing contempt for God's grace. God helped Ahab against the Syrians despite Ahab's abandonment of the Lord in favor of Baal. Ahab showed contempt for this gracious revelation of God's willingness and ability to come to his aid. When Ahab showed contrition, God relented and put off the judgment decreed against the king and his line. Even after this, Ahab showed himself unwilling to respond to the Lord by his hatred for Micaiah, God's prophet. The only valid responses to God's grace are gratitude and faith.

JEHU
Scripture references:
1 Kings 19:16, 17; 2 Kings 9:1—10:36;
2 Chronicles 22; Hosea 1:4

Date:	Ruled Israel 841–814 B.C.
Name:	Jehu [JEE-hoo; "he is Yahweh"]
Greatest Accomplishment:	Jehu exterminated Ahab's line and wiped out Baal worship in Israel.

JEHU'S ROLE IN SCRIPTURE

Jehu was the commander of Israel's army, but the prophets Elijah and Elisha anointed him king. He proceeded to wipe out the remaining members of Ahab's family. To further strengthen his position, Jehu also wiped out the adherents of Baal worship, a faith that the house of Ahab had aggressively promoted. Jehu's descendants ruled Israel for four generations.

Jehu had a reputation for driving "furiously." His real drive, however, was to win the kingdom by whatever means necessary.

EXPLORING JEHU'S RELATIONSHIPS

The relationship that is emphasized in the text is Jehu's relationship with God. However, it is clear that the relationship was indirect, not intimate or personal.

Jehu anointed by God's prophets *(1 Kings 19:16, 17; 2 Kings 9:1–10).* Elijah had anointed Jehu some time before Elisha sent a young prophet to commission him. The prophet declared that God had chosen Jehu to be king "over the people of the Lord, over Israel" (2 Kings 9:6). The prophet then specifically commissioned Jehu to wipe out Ahab's family and put an end to Baal worship. When Jehu reported the prophet's words to his officers, they immediately acclaimed Jehu king. Jehu set out on God's mission.

Jehu fulfilled God's word *(2 Kings 9:11—10:28).* Jehu not only aggressively carried out God's command, but he also quoted the prophet's words to explain his actions.

Jehu killed members of Ahab's family (2 Kings 9:11—10:17). Jehu killed the ruling king, Ahab's son. He saw to the death of Jezebel, Ahab's queen. Jehu then ordered the execution of Ahab's remaining seventy sons by the heads of the families with whom the seventy had been living. When the sons were dead, Jehu announced, "Know now that nothing shall fall to the earth of the word of the LORD which the LORD spoke concerning the house of Ahab; for the LORD has done what He spoke by His servant Elijah" (2 Kings 10:10).

Jehu ended Baal worship (2 Kings 10:18–28). Jehu then announced publicly that he would actively promote Baal worship. He called all worshipers of Baal to a conference at the temple of Baal in Samaria, Israel's capital. When all had assembled, he ordered soldiers to murder every devotee of the pagan faith. Jehu then tore down the temple of Baal and turned it into a garbage heap. "Thus Jehu destroyed Baal from Israel" (10:28).

Jehu's incomplete obedience and reward (2 Kings 10:29–33). Despite Jehu's habit of quoting the Lord and his zealous attack on Ahab's royal house and the worshipers of Baal, Jehu "took no heed to walk in the law of the LORD" (10:31). Instead, he followed the politically motivated religious practices established by Jeroboam (see page 121).

God then spoke to Jehu and told him that "because you have done well in doing what is right in My sight" in carrying out God's judgment on the house of Ahab, "your sons shall sit on the throne of Israel to the fourth generation" (10:30). However, Jehu's failure to completely commit himself and his people to the Lord resulted in the loss of territory to Syria.

JEHU: AN EXAMPLE FOR TODAY

Jehu seems a puzzling character until we note one important thing. He was zealous in carrying out God's will—as long as God's purposes were in harmony with Jehu's ambitions! If Jehu were to establish a dynasty of his own, he had to wipe out every descendant of Ahab around whom others might rally. And, as the worshipers of Baal had been Ahab's strongest supporters, it made sense to break their power and influence once and for all. Jehu quoted God's prophets to justify his actions. But Jehu was zealous to fulfill God's word only so long as God's will promoted Jehu's goals!

Once Jehu had obtained his objectives, he had no more interest in submitting to the Lord, and so "took no heed to walk in the law of the LORD God" (10:31). As a result Jehu, like those before him, continued to lead Israel down the path of disaster.

What can we learn from Jehu?

- Jehu alerts us to the danger of self-centered obedience. We are to do God's will not because it conforms to what we want, but because we trust God and are committed to obey him.

- Jehu warns us not to take everyone who quotes Scripture at face value. We are to judge people by the way they live, not simply by what they say.

- Jehu confirms the importance of complete obedience. We are not to pick and choose between Bible teachings we like and those we do not. Jehu's defeats after he gained his kingdom and refused to walk with the Lord remind us that continued blessings are possible only as we remain close to the Lord.

NOTABLE KINGS OF THE SOUTHERN KINGDOM

When the united kingdom was broken into northern and southern nations, in the south, David's descendants ruled Judah. Davidic rulers continued in an unbroken line from the division in 930 B.C. to the nation's destruction by Babylon in 586 B.C.

Even though the rulers of Judah were David's descendants, only six of them can be considered godly men. While the godly rulers encouraged worship of the Lord and actively promoted His Law, the common people often drifted into idolatry with all its associated sins. All too often, the other kings

KINGS OF THE SOUTH (JUDAH)

Ruler	Dates	Good/Evil	Scripture
Rehoboam	930–913	Neutral	1 Kings 14:21–31; 2 Chronicles 11:5—12:16
Abijam	913–910	Neutral	1 Kings 15:1–8 2 Chronicles 13:1—14:1
Asa	910–869	Good	1 Kings 15:9–24 2 Chronicles 14:2—16:14
Jeoshaphat	872–848	Good	1 Kings 22:41–50
co-regent	872–869		2 Chronicles 17:1—21:3
Jehoram	853–841	Evil	2 Kings 8:16–24
co-regent	853–848		2 Chronicles 21:4–20
Ahaziah	841	Evil	2 Kings 8:25–29 2 Chronicles 22:1–9
Athaliah	841–835	Evil	2 Kings 11:1–16 2 Chronicles 23:10–15
Joash	835–796	Mixed	2 Kings 11:1–12 2 Chronicles 23:1—24:27
Amaziah	796–767	Evil	2 Kings 14:1–22 2 Chronicles 25:1–28
Azariah	792–740	Good	2 Kings 15:1–7
overlap	792–767		2 Chronicles 26:1–23
Jotham	750–732	Good	2 Kings 15:32–38
co-regent	750–735		2 Chronicles 27:1–9
Ahaz	732–715	Evil	2 Kings 16 2 Chronicles 28
Hezekiah	715–686	Good	2 Kings 18—20 2 Chronicles 29—32
Manasseh	697–642	Evil	2 Kings 21:1–18
co-regent	697–686		2 Chronicles 33:1–20
Amon	642–640	Evil	2 Kings 21:19–26 2 Chronicles 33:21–25
Josiah	640–609	Good	2 Kings 22:1—23:30 2 Chronicles 34, 35
Jehoahaz	609	Evil	2 Kings 23:31–34 2 Chronicles 36:1–4
Jehoiakim	609–598	Evil	2 Kings 23:33—24:6 2 Chronicles 36:5–8
Jehoiachin	598–597	Evil	2 Kings 24:6—25:30 2 Chronicles 36:9–10
Zedekiah	597–586	Evil	2 Kings 24:18—25:7 2 Chronicles 36:11–23

of Judah abandoned God's ways and worshiped pagan deities.

It is not surprising then that the southern kingdom knew alternating times of prosperity and decline. Under godly kings, the Lord typically blessed the nation. During that time, the nation maintained its boundaries or gained back lost land. Under wicked rulers, foreign enemies frequently defeated the nation. Two of Judah's kings illustrate the influence that a strong and godly leader can have on a people.

HEZEKIAH

Scripture references:
2 Kings 18—20; 2 Chronicles 29—32;
Isaiah 36—39

Dates:	Ruled Judah 715–686 B.C.
Name:	Hezekiah [HEZ-uh-KI-uh; "Yahweh is my strength"]
Greatest Accomplishment:	He preserved Judah when Assyria conquered and deported the people of Israel.

HEZEKIAH'S ROLE IN SCRIPTURE

When Hezekiah became king, the great Assyrian Empire was forcing its way into the Middle East. Syria had fallen and the massive Assyrian army was a threat to Israel and Judah. Hezekiah refused to submit to Assyria. To prepare for the invasion, he defeated the Philistines and built fortress cities along his borders. In Hezekiah's fourth year, the Assyrians invaded the northern kingdom Israel and defeated them after a three-year struggle. In Hezekiah's fourteenth year, Assyria attacked Judah. While the border fortresses were taken, the Lord answered Hezekiah's prayer and miraculously intervened to throw back the Assyrians. This was a pivotal event in the history of Judah, and the story is told and retold in Scripture. The nation was preserved, and the people were given a powerful example of the efficacy of prayer offered by a ruler in right relationship with God.

EXPLORING HEZEKIAH'S RELATIONSHIPS

Hezekiah's relationship with God. Hezekiah's relationship with God was by far the most significant relationship to the writers of sacred history. They focused on Hezekiah's true devotion to God, and related three spiritual challenges faced by the godly king. The three challenges were not recorded in the text in the order they occurred, but in the order of their significance. We take them in chronological order, below.

Hezekiah's focus on worship (2 Chron. 29—31). Hezekiah was twenty-five years old when he became king. In the first year he reinstituted worship at the temple that had been closed during the reign of evil King Ahaz, his father. Hezekiah called the priests and Levites back into service and set them to offering sacrifices and singing psalms. With the temple purified, Hezekiah called all the people of Judah to celebrate the Lord's Passover, that important annual religious festival that had not been kept for decades. Hezekiah even sent messengers into Israel to invite Jews from the northern kingdom to participate. The joy was so great that the seven-day worship festival was extended another week. The people went home and destroyed the idols and shrines that had infested the land.

Hezekiah's emphasis on worship set the tone for his reign, and restored Judah to a place where God could and did bless the land.

Hezekiah's first challenge (2 Chron. 32:24; 2 Kings 20:1–11; Isa. 38). In 701 B.C. the king became seriously ill, and the prophet Isaiah announced that he would die. The king pleaded with God for added years: "Remember now, O LORD, I pray, how I have walked before You in truth and with a loyal heart, and have done what was good in your sight" (2 Kings 20:3). God answered Hezekiah's tearful appeal and gave him fifteen more years. Thus Hezekiah lived to beg God to intervene when the Assyrians attacked a few years later.

Hezekiah's second challenge (2 Chron. 32:27–31; 2 Kings 20:12–19; Isa. 39). After the miraculous healing, Hezekiah became proud. The text does not tell us why, but we can speculate that not only Hezekiah's growing wealth but also his status as the recipient of a miracle fed the king's pride. When ambassadors from Babylon visited Hezekiah to congratulate him on his recovery, the king showed off all the kingdom's treasures—without consulting God or one of His prophets.

Isaiah rebuked Hezekiah and told him that one day all that he and his predecessors had accumulated would be carried away to Babylon—but not in his time. The king's response has often been criticized. He said, "The word of the LORD which you have spoken is good! . . . Will there not be peace and truth at least in my days?" But in view of the constant threat from Assyria, word that the nation would one day fall to a world power that did not yet exist must have seemed good news indeed!

Hezekiah's third challenge (2 Chron. 32:1–23; 2 Kings 18:9—19:37; Isa. 36; 37). The Assyrians attacked Judah in Hezekiah's fourteenth year. The border fortress-cities the king had constructed fell, and Jerusalem was endangered. An Assyrian emissary appeared outside Jerusalem's walls and called for the city's surrender. The emissary ridiculed Hezekiah's military weakness and

Hezekiah turned to God in prayer when he received an Assyrian demand that he surrender his nation and accept deportation.

❖

scoffed at Hezekiah's reliance on Judah's God. The gods of other nations had proven powerless before the might of Assyria; so would the Lord.

Hezekiah took the matter to the Lord. In his prayer Hezekiah affirmed God as the maker of heaven and earth and begged God to act. Surely the Lord would not permit the Assyrians to hold Him in such contempt.

Hezekiah's prayer was answered. The prophet Isaiah reported God's promise to save the city and send the Assyrian king home without having launched a single arrow into Jerusalem. That night 185,000 Assyrian soldiers died in their sleep, and the Assyrian king returned home, where he was assassinated by two of his sons. (For an extended treatment of this event, see the companion volume in this series, *Every Miracle and Wonder in the Bible.*)

Hezekiah's relationship with prophets. The accounts of Hezekiah's reign frequently mention the prophet Isaiah. Hezekiah clearly listened to, depended on, and trusted the prophet's utterances.

Hezekiah's relationship with his people. Hezekiah's driving motive was to reestablish worship of the Lord in Judah. His enthusiasm was contagious, and after the people celebrated the Passover, the people themselves purged the land of idols and idolatry. Hezekiah's success in motivating his people to turn to the Lord was almost unique in the nation's history.

HEZEKIAH: AN EXAMPLE FOR TODAY

Hezekiah was a godly person whose zeal for worship led to a national revival. The priority he placed on worship was evident from his first year as king. His personal blessings and the deliverance of his nation were both rooted in Hezekiah's passion for worshiping God. We have much to learn from Hezekiah.

- Hezekiah motivates us to make worship a priority in our own lives. Both private and corporate worship have an essential role in any transforming relationship with the Lord.
- Hezekiah encourages us to expect God to answer prayer. God answered Hezekiah's prayers for his nation and for personal well being in wonderful ways.
- Hezekiah reminds us that God's blessings are rooted in His grace, not our goodness. Hezekiah's pride that God would answer *his* prayers was misplaced, and that was his primary fault.
- Hezekiah shows us the significance of being always responsive to God's Word. As Hezekiah was committed to follow the precepts of Scripture and the words of God's prophets, so are we

to be committed to doing God's Word today.

JOSIAH
Scripture references:
1 Kings 13:2; 2 Kings 22—23;
2 Chronicles 34—35

Date:	Ruled Judah 640–609 B.C.
Name:	Josiah [joh-SI-uh; "Yahweh supports"]
Greatest Accomplishment:	He led the last great religious revival in Judah.

JOSIAH'S ROLE IN SCRIPTURE

Josiah was only eight years old when he was crowned king of Judah. Josiah was the grandson of Manasseh, the most evil of Judah's kings, who had ruled for fifty-five years. During that time, Manasseh destroyed all the copies of God's Law he could find and closed the Jerusalem temple. At age sixteen, Josiah experienced a personal conversion; at twenty, he began his efforts to purge Judah of idolatry. During repair of the temple a copy of the lost Law was found, and Josiah discovered how far from God his nation had strayed. Josiah immediately sent to Huldah, a prophetess, to learn God's intent. Josiah learned that judgment would come, but after Josiah's time.

Now totally dedicated to the Lord, Josiah revived Passover celebration, and set out to destroy local shrines. Josiah not only purged Judah of centers of idolatry, but he also went into Israel and tore down the idol and altar erected by Jeroboam, fulfilling a prophecy identifying him by name uttered nearly four centuries earlier (1 Kings 13:2).

During Josiah's later years, the Assyrian empire was being crushed by the Babylonians. In 609 B.C. a decisive battle seemed to be taking shape, and Pharaoh Necho of Egypt planned to intervene in support of the Assyrians. Josiah, eager for the destruction of Judah's ancient enemy, set out to stop the Egyptians. Josiah was killed in the battle. With Josiah's death, the nation quickly slipped back into idolatry. In less than thirty years, the nation fell to the Babylonians.

EXPLORING JOSIAH'S RELATIONSHIPS

As was true for other godly kings, Josiah's relationship with God is the key to evaluating his rule.

Josiah's commitment to worship (2 Kings 22:1–7; 23:1–30; 2 Chron. 34—35). Josiah's conversion to Yahweh at age sixteen was evidenced by the young king's orders to purge Judah and Jerusalem of idolatry. The king personally supervised the destruction of altars and idols throughout the land.

Josiah then set out to repair God's temple in Jerusalem. When the repair was complete, Josiah called all his people to Jerusalem to celebrate the Passover.

Josiah's commitment to God's Word (2 Kings 22). During repair of the temple the lost Book of the Law (possibly Deuteronomy) was discovered. Josiah immediately discerned that Israel had strayed far from God and that God would punish sins such as his people had committed. The king immediately contacted Huldah, a prophetess, to inquire into God's intentions. The Lord reassured Josiah. Because he had shown himself humble and eager to serve God, judgment would be delayed until after his time. Josiah then set out aggressively to carry out God's will as revealed in Scripture.

When Josiah burned human bones and desecrated the altar Jeroboam had erected, he fulfilled a prediction made hundreds of years earlier which mentioned him by name.

JOSIAH: AN EXAMPLE FOR TODAY

While Josiah himself was completely dedicated to the Lord, the revival he led was superficial. The hearts of the Israelites were never turned to the Lord. We see this in the complaint of the prophet Habakkuk (1:1–5) concerning the corruption of justice after the "revival." We see it in the sermons Jeremiah gave during the reign of Josiah (see references to "in the days of Josiah" in the Book of Jeremiah). We also see it in Judah's immediate return to idolatry after Josiah's death. Yet, Josiah himself remains one of the Old Testament's truly model men.

- Josiah demonstrates that one godly man in a position of influence can impact a nation. While the hearts of the people were not changed, Josiah's reforms helped hold off the nation's destruction.

- Josiah reminds us that whatever the spirit of the times, we are to be fully committed to the Lord. Once Josiah came to know the Lord, he showed himself willing to do God's will whatever the cost.

- Josiah highlights the relationship between worship and Scripture. In worship, we speak to the Lord; in Scripture, God speaks to us. Josiah was concerned that the Word of God guide his worship of the Lord. And so must we be.

FOREIGN KINGS

PHARAOH

Scripture references:
Exodus 3—15; Deuteronomy 7; 11; 29;
1 Samuel 6:6; Psalm 135:9; 136:15;
Romans 9:17

Date:	1450 B.C.
Name:	*Pharaoh [FAIR-oh, "great house"]*
Greatest Accomplishment:	*The pharaoh of the Exodus refused to permit God's people to leave Egypt until forced to do so by a series of miraculous judgments announced by Moses.*

PHARAOH'S ROLE IN SCRIPTURE

Pharaoh is the title borne by rulers of Egypt rather than a proper name. A number of pharaohs are mentioned in Egyptian history. By far the most significant pharaoh biblically is the pharaoh of the Exodus whom Moses confronted and finally forced to submit to God's will and release the Israelite slaves. The pharaoh of the Exodus is referred to frequently in Deuteronomy and in the Old Testament historical books, in Psalms, and in the Book of Romans.

PHARAOH'S LIFE AND TIMES

The pharaoh of the Exodus was young when Moses came out of the desert to demand the release of his Israelite slaves. Thutmose III, who had forced Moses to flee Egypt some forty years earlier, had just died. The Scriptures portray the new pharaoh, certainly a youth, as arrogant and proud. And proud he might well have been. This young man ruled over one of the wealthiest and most powerful empires of his era. He had confidence in the deities of Egypt. In ancient times the power of a nation was thought to reflect the potency of its gods. Who then could be greater than the gods of Egypt which was a truly great world power? Certainly, the young pharaoh would have nothing but contempt for the God of slaves!

Additional pressure on the young pharaoh caused him to react as he did to Moses. In Egyptian theology, the pharaoh was the mediator between the people of Egypt and their gods. He was responsible to see that the respect due the gods was shown, so that the gods might look with favor on Egypt and cause the land to prosper. Deeply aware of this duty, Pharaoh honored the gods of Egypt, and resisted honoring another deity.

Only after a series of miraculous plagues devastated Egypt and impoverished the once wealthy land did Pharaoh bow before the God of Israel and let his Israelite slaves go.

PHARAOHS OF THE BIBLE

Reference	Biblical name	Secular name	Significance
Genesis 12:14–20	Pharaoh	A ruler of the 12th dynasty	Added Sarah to his harem, unaware she was married
Genesis 37—50	Pharaoh	A Hyksos 15th dynasty ruler	Made Joseph vizier of Egypt
Exodus 1—2	Pharaoh King of Egypt	Thutmose II (?) (1504–1450)	Oppressed the Israelites
Exodus 3—15	Pharaoh (1450–1425)	Amenhotep II (?)	Forced to release the Israelite slaves
1 Kings 3:1; 7:6 9:16–24; 11:1	Pharaoh	Siamun (978–959)	Solomon wed his daughter
1 Kings 11:18–22	Pharaoh King of Egypt	Amenemope 993–984	Welcomed Hadad when David crushed Edom
1 Kings 11:40; 2 Chronicles 12:1–12	Shishak	Sheshonq I (945–924)	Invaded Judah and sacked Jerusalem
2 Kings 17:4	So, king of Egypt	Osokorn IV (?) (727–716)	Hoshea of Israel ally against Assyria
2 Kings 19:9	Tirhakah	Taharqa (690–664)	Unsuccessfully fought Sennacherib of Assyria
2 Kings 23:29 2 Chronicles. 35:20–24	Pharaoh Necho	Necho II (610–595)	Josiah killed in 609 in battle with Necho
Jeremiah 44:30 Ezekiel 17:11–21; 29:1–16	Pharaoh Hophra	Waibre (589–570)	His fall to Nebuchadnezzar was predicted

EXPLORING PHARAOH'S RELATIONSHIPS

Two relationships are emphasized in the biblical account: Pharaoh's relationship with Moses and his relationship with God.

Pharaoh's relationship with Moses. First, let us consider Pharaoh's relationship with Moses.

Pharaoh rejected Moses' first appeal (Ex. 5:1–9). Moses apparently gained access to Pharaoh first as the accredited representative of the Israelites (Ex. 4:29–31). Moses presented himself as Yahweh's servant, and requested that Pharaoh give the Israelites time off to go three days into the wilderness to worship the Lord. This request displayed God's grace; it would have been far easier for

Pharaoh to give his slaves time off than to free them completely. However, Pharaoh refused. He was so incensed that his slaves should even think of stopping work that he increased their workload. Moses was shaken by this reaction, but God reassured him that He had taken Pharaoh's response into account. Pharaoh's rejection would lead to a series of miracles through which "the Egyptians will know that I am the LORD" (Ex. 7:5).

Pharaoh rejected Moses' signs (Ex. 7:8–25). When God commissioned Moses, He had empowered him with the miraculous signs as evidence that Moses spoke for God. When Moses showed these signs to Pharaoh, the young ruler turned to Egypt's magicians, who duplicated the signs "with their enchantments." We do not know whether the Egyptian magicians used trickery or drew on demonic sources to duplicate Moses' miracles. The success of his magicians gave Pharaoh all the excuse he needed to dismiss Moses and his signs.

Pharaoh's reaction to the miracles of judgment (Ex. 8—11). At this point, Moses brought a series of plagues on Egypt the magicians could neither duplicate nor halt. Again and again, Pharaoh begged Moses to provide relief, promising to do as Moses asked. But when each plague was lifted Pharaoh went back on his word. It was galling for the young Pharaoh to be forced to confess his sin and ask Moses for forgiveness. Finally Pharaoh revealed his true feelings and threatened Moses, "Get away from me! Take heed to yourself and see my face no more! For in the day you see my face you shall die!" (Ex. 10:28).

In a sense Pharaoh's relationship with Moses grew to become like that of a rebellious son with his father. The more frequently the son was coerced to submit to his father's authority, the more his inner anger and resistance grew. Finally, he could contain himself no longer. He would not give in, no matter what the cost.

In Pharaoh's case, the cost was devastating; the final plague took the lives of the firstborn in all Egypt. And the young Pharaoh, broken, was finally ready to submit and let the Israelites go.

Pharaoh's relationship with God. Pharaoh's relationship with God reveals much about Pharaoh and God.

God's self-revelation. Through Moses and through the judgments Moses announced, the Lord revealed to Pharaoh that He, not the deities of Egypt, was God. Pharaoh refused to accept that the God of Israel was superior to the deities of Egypt who proved powerless to protect their land. While Pharaoh was forced to bow to God's power, Pharaoh continued to be hostile to God to the end. Pharaoh would bow his knee when he had no other choice, but Pharaoh would never bow his heart.

Pharaoh's hard heart. Many have been troubled by the Old Testament's description of Pharaoh's hard heart. Several times the text simply states that Pharaoh's heart was or grew hard so that he resisted God's will (Ex. 7:13, 14; 8:19; 9:7, 35). Other times the text states that Pharaoh hardened his own heart (Ex. 8:15, 32; 9:34), implying a conscious determination to resist God's will. But at other times the text indicates that the Lord hardened Pharaoh's heart. These verses have troubled many who wonder how God could then blame Pharaoh for doing what God seemingly caused him to do.

To resolve the issue, we need to note just what the text says.

- Exodus 7:3: "I will harden Pharaoh's heart."
- Exodus 9:12: "the LORD hardened the heart of Pharaoh."
- Exodus 10:1: "I have hardened his heart."

- Exodus 10:20: "the LORD hardened Pharaoh's heart."
- Exodus 10:27: "the LORD hardened Pharaoh's heart."
- Exodus 11:10: "the LORD hardened Pharaoh's heart."
- Exodus 14:4: "I will harden Pharaoh's heart"
- Exodus 14:8: "the LORD hardened Pharaoh's heart."

Looking at these texts, we note that the first reference is a revelation to Moses of what will happen, not a report of any action taken by God.

The second reference to God hardening Pharaoh's heart took place after Egypt had experienced six of the ten plagues and after no less than four statements that Pharaoh hardened his own heart! It is appropriate here to ask *how* did God harden Pharaoh's heart? Clearly God did not cause Pharaoh to act contrary to his nature, for the writer had already mentioned Pharaoh's hard heartedness toward God. The best answer to "how" is that God hardened Pharaoh's heart externally. In revealing more of His power in the plagues on Egypt, God forced Pharaoh to react to him, and Pharaoh reacted by hardening his heart. Much like the heat of the sun hardens clay but melts wax, so God's increasing self-revelation hardened Pharaoh's clay-like heart while it would have softened the heart of a believer.

What then about the last four references? Each of them refers to a time after the ninth plague, when Pharaoh threatened the life of Moses. These four references are to *judicial* hardening. Pharaoh had for so long and so fiercely refused to submit to God that the Lord now shut the door. Pharaoh had had multiple opportunities to respond to God and had refused to submit each time. It was now too late; as a judgment on Pharaoh for his multiplied sins, God locked the already-closed door of Pharaoh's heart.

PHARAOH: AN EXAMPLE FOR TODAY

The pharaoh of the Exodus was so full of himself that he was closed to every evidence of God's presence and power. In his arrogance, he refused to submit to God, and both he and his people suffered as a consequence. The young pharaoh serves as a warning and example for people today.

- Pharaoh reminds us to remain humble and teachable. We cannot afford to assume that we know it all; nor can we have contempt for others.
- Pharaoh reminds us that we are responsible for our own reactions. God never *caused* Pharaoh to act against his nature or character. Pharaoh made his own choices, freely and responsibly. We can't blame circumstances, God, or others for the choices we make in life. Therefore, we need to consider our choices carefully.
- Pharaoh reminds us that the central issue in life is how we relate to God— not our position or role in society. If we keep our hearts tender toward the Lord and are responsive to Him, we will do well.
- Pharaoh reminds us that there are limits to any person's rebellion against God. We can reject God's revelation of Himself again and again, and be given yet another chance. But the time will come when God in judgment will lock the heart that is shut tight against Him. May we repent before it is too late.

NEBUCHADNEZZAR
Scripture references:
2 Kings 24; 25; 2 Chronicles 36;
Jeremiah 21—52; Ezekiel 26; 29; 30;
Daniel 1—4

Date:	*Ruled Babylon 605–562 B.C.*
Name:	*Nebuchadnezzar [NEB-uh-kuhd-NEZ-uhr; "Nabu had protected the boundary stone"]*
Greatest Accomplishment:	*Nebuchadnezzar ruled the Babylonian Empire at its most powerful stage, dominating the ancient world.*

NEBUCHADNEZZAR'S ROLE IN SCRIPTURE

Scripture understandably views world history from the point of view of God's people and God's purposes. The Old Testament views the Holy Land as the center of its universe, and other lands are discussed only as they relate to God's people. Thus we see Nebuchadnezzar primarily as the conqueror of Judah, which in fact was a rather tiny land in view of the vast territories that made up Nebuchadnezzar's empire. Nebuchadnezzar was also noted as a builder, and the hanging gardens he constructed in Babylon were one of the wonders of the ancient world.

Nebuchadnezzar was God's instrument of judgment on His people, fulfilling the warning issued by Moses in Deuteronomy 28 of what would befall His people if they abandoned the Lord. God used the decades that the Jewish people were captives in Babylon for His good purposes. During the captivity, the Israelites were at last cured of their tendency toward idolatry. The synagogue movement had its roots in the Babylonian captivity as did zeal for the study of God's written Word.

EXPLORING NEBUCHADNEZZAR'S RELATIONSHIPS

Nebuchadnezzar brought a number of promising young Jewish captives to Babylon to train them with young men from other nations as administrators of his empire. Through his relationship with Daniel, one of these captives, and with Daniel's friends, Nebuchadnezzar was exposed to the Lord and gained an appreciation for Him. The king's relationship with Daniel and with God are discussed in the article on Daniel (see page 96). Nebuchadnezzar's final declaration of belief in God, and his affirmation that "now I, Nebuchadnezzar, praise and extol and honor the King of heaven, all of whose works are truth, and His ways justice" (Dan 4:37) has led many to believe that the Babylonian ruler truly was converted.

NEBUCHADNEZZAR: AN EXAMPLE FOR TODAY

Nebuchadnezzar was the ruler of a pagan land. He was named after his nation's principle deity, Nebo. He was also a persecutor of God's chosen people and a brutal conqueror. Yet, God was especially gracious to the great king, reminding us that God has always had a concern for all peoples. Nebuchadnezzar's experiences also serve as examples to us today.

- Nebuchadnezzar's experience reminds us of the influence that godly individuals can have on even powerful persons. Daniel showed respect and concern for the king, and his witness gradually convinced Nebuchadnezzar to put his trust in the Lord.

- Nebuchadnezzar's experience reminds us not to expect "instant conversions." Daniel's influence and that of his friends was exerted over a number of years before the king finally surrendered to the Lord.

- Nebuchadnezzar's experience further emphasizes God's grace, which He extends toward all. The king was not a member of God's covenant people but their persecutor. Nevertheless, God showered grace upon grace on the autocratic ruler. Often the most unlikely candidates for conversion are those in whom God chooses to display the riches of His grace.

CYRUS

Scripture references:
2 Chronicles 36:22; 23; Ezra;
Isaiah 44:28; 45:1–7; Daniel 1:21;
6:28; 10:1

Date:	*King of Persia 558–530 B.C.*
Name:	*Cyrus [SI-ruhs; meaning unknown]*
Greatest Accomplishment:	*He unified the kingdoms of Media and Persia and in 539 B.C. took over the Babylonian Empire.*

CYRUS'S ROLE IN SCRIPTURE

The Babylonian Empire dominated the Mesopotamian valley and the Middle East after Assyria's fall in 609 B.C. The Babylonians followed a policy instituted by Assyria of resettling conquered peoples outside their homeland. This had led to the Israelites' removal from the northern Hebrew kingdom in 722 B.C., and the exile of the people of Judah after the fall of Jerusalem in 586 B.C.

When Cyrus the Persian took the Babylonian capital and gained control of the Babylonian Empire, he reversed this policy.

Cyrus permitted conquered peoples to return to their homeland and encouraged them to rebuild their worship centers. He even returned the religious items taken from their temples, asking only that those he returned to their homelands pray for him and his empire.

One of the groups affected by Cyrus's decree was the Jews, and some 50,000 set out for Judea, determined to rebuild the temple there. Their story is told in the Book of Ezra, the setting for the ministry of the prophets Haggai and Zechariah. Strikingly, Cyrus's ascendancy and his permitting the return of the Jews to their homeland was predicted by Isaiah a century before Cyrus was born (Isa. 44:28; 45:1)! Although a pagan who did not know or worship God (Isa. 45:4), the Lord said of Cyrus,

"He is My shepherd,
And he shall perform all My pleasure,
Saying to Jerusalem, 'You shall be built,'
And to the temple, 'Your foundation shall
be laid.' " (Isa. 44:28)

CYRUS: AN EXAMPLE FOR TODAY

Cyrus reminds us of God's sovereign control of history and His ability to move individuals to carry out His purposes. Anyone who understands Cyrus's significance can never speak of being "under the circumstances." Our God is one who shapes circumstances so that His purpose, and our blessing, will be achieved.

NOTABLE PRIESTS OF THE OLD TESTAMENT

The third role a man could play in Old Testament faith and life was that of priest. The priesthood was reserved for descendants of Aaron, a Levite. The men of the other Levitical families were assigned to assist the priests in their ministry, to maintain the worship center, and to serve as singers and worship leaders. The Nelson *Illustrated Bible Handbook* describes the Old Testament priesthood:

Three institutions dominate the life of Israel as she developed within the Promised Land. These are expressed in the persons of prophets, priests, and the king. Of the three, two originate in the exodus period. Moses is the prototype prophet. Aaron is the prototype Levitical priest.

What was the role of the priesthood in Israel, and what are we to learn from this institution?

The word "priest" appears more than 700 times in the Old Testament. While the root meaning of the word itself is uncertain, the role of the priest is carefully explained. The priest was to represent the people before God, and to represent God to the people.

As a representative of the people of Israel, priests appeared before the Lord to make sacrifices and offerings. As God's representative, the ministry of the priests was more complex. They were to instruct in the law (Deut. 33:8–10; Hos. 4:1–10), to give judgment on legal issues (Deut. 33:7–11), and to discover the will of God, using the Ephod (1 Sam. 23:6–12). The priests also watched over matters of ritual cleanness associated with disease (Lev. 13—15).

There were several orders of Old Testament priests. At the top of the hierarchy was the high priest, who alone could enter the inmost chamber of the tabernacle or temple. He officiated on the Day of Atonement. The second level included the sons of Aaron, who were the hereditary priests. These served at the temple altar and officiated at regular sacrifices. There was also a priestly role for the rest of the tribe of Levi (of which Aaron's family was a part). Although the Levites never served the altar, they did carry the parts of the portable tabernacle during the wilderness years. In David's time they provided worship music, and later served as wandering law teachers in time of revival. Like the priests, the offerings and tithes given by the people supported the Levites.

After the Babylonian exile there was a change in the teaching function. Men like Ezra dedicated themselves to study and teach the Scriptures. By Jesus' time, the class of rabbis (teachers) was set apart as students and teachers of the Bible and Jewish traditions. By then the priests focused entirely on ceremonial matters.

The great institutional significance of the priesthood was mediatorial. In the priests who stood daily at the tabernacle or temple, making the prescribed sacrifices to the Lord, the average Israelite had living evidence that a way of approach to God was open and available to him (pp. 103–104).

We'll look at two men who represent the basic ministries of the priests in the Old Testament.

AARON
Scripture references:
Exodus—Deuteronomy;
various references

Date:	*About 1517–1410 B.C.*
Name:	*Aaron [AIR-uhn; meaning unknown]*
Greatest Accomplishment:	*Aaron was Moses' brother and companion through the Exodus era and Israel's first high priest.*

AARON'S ROLE IN SCRIPTURE

Aaron was with Moses when Moses confronted Egypt's pharaoh, often serving as Moses' spokesman. While clearly secondary to Moses, Aaron was viewed as a coleader of the Exodus. When the Israelites complained, they criticized both Moses and Aaron. Most of the 322 references to Aaron associate him with Moses. He is referred to independently only when Moses

Each garment worn by Israel's high priest had spiritual significance.

is not present or when the subject is Aaron's role as high priest.

Aaron's role as high priest and founder of the family that became Israel's priests gave Aaron his significance. As long as Old Testament Law was in force, from Mount Sinai to the death of Christ, the Aaronic priesthood was an essential element of Hebrew faith and life.

EXPLORING AARON'S RELATIONSHIPS

In a way, Aaron can almost be viewed as a man lost in Moses' shadow. He was with Moses at critical junctures of the history of the Exodus. Yet, Aaron never seemed central or even essential. The spotlight clearly was on Moses. Aaron was almost insubstantial, standing beside his brother, taking each stand with him, but all too easy to ignore.

Two incidents, however, portray Aaron out of Moses' shadow. And neither is flattering.

Aaron and the golden calf (Ex. 32). At Mount Sinai God called Moses up the mountain to meet with Him alone. God gave Moses the Ten Commandments and the rest of the Law under which the Israelites were to live for the next 1,400 years.

While Moses was on the mountain, Aaron was in charge. And when the people demanded that Aaron make them a golden calf as a visible representation of deity, Aaron complied. Not only did Aaron comply; he constructed an altar where sacrifices might be offered and announced that the next day they would hold a worship feast to the Lord! When Moses, alerted by God to what was happening, returned, he confronted Aaron. Aaron cowered and said, "You know the people, that they are set on evil" (Ex. 22:22). Aaron explained that he had given in to the people's demand, had simply thrown gold into a fire, "and this calf came out."

The incident reveals Aaron as a truly weak man. He realized that the people's desire was evil, yet he did what they asked. Like so many "leaders," Aaron saw which way the crowds were surging and hurried to get out in front of them. Aaron would have been the first to take political polls in our day to determine his personal convictions!

Aaron and Miriam criticized Moses (Num. 12). After leaving Sinai, Moses' brother and sister became jealous. They criticized Moses, using the excuse that he was married to an "Ethiopian woman." Their added question, "Has the LORD indeed spoken only through Moses? Has He not spoken through us also?" (Num. 12:2) was a clear attempt to undermine Moses' authority and ultimately to replace him.

God intervened and confronted the two, confirming Moses' priority. As a punishment, Miriam became leprous and was forced to live outside the camp for seven days. As leprosy would have disqualified Aaron from his priesthood, he was spared. But the rebuke to the two was sharp and clear.

AARON: AN EXAMPLE FOR TODAY

In each incident, we see Aaron as a weak individual. He was easily influenced by his sister and easily swayed by the Israelites. Yet, when Moses was present, Aaron consistently stood with him against the complaints and sins of the people. Aaron seems to be a classic example of a person who is willing to make right choices as long as there is a stronger personality nearby to provide the backbone. But when faced with going against the urgings of others on his own, Aaron was too weak to take a stand.

Perhaps this trait made Aaron an ideal choice for high priest. The writer of Hebrews points out that a high priest "can have compassion on those who are ignorant and going astray, since he himself is also subject to weakness" (Heb. 5:2). If ever a high priest was subject to weakness, Aaron was. He must have been extremely sensitive to the need for those sacrifices through which a person might confess sin and be restored to right relationship with the Lord.

- Aaron reminds us to be gentle with the weak. Some men need to draw strength from others if they are to make the choices they know they should. God has compassion for the weak, and so should we.

- Aaron reassures us that our failures do not disqualify us from significant roles in God's plan. Aaron could never have been a Moses, but we need our Aarons as well.

- Aaron alerts us to the necessity of evaluating our own strengths and weaknesses. We need to be honest with ourselves so we will avoid situations

we simply are not equipped to handle on our own.

- Aaron encourages us to be faithful followers. Not everyone is called to be a leader. But not every follower is as faithful as Aaron was in support of Moses. A congregation of faithful followers is as necessary as a visionary leader if we are to have an impact for the Lord on our world.

EZRA
Scripture references:
Ezra 7—10; Nehemiah 8

Date:	*About 450 B.C.*
Name:	*Ezra [EZ-ruh; "Yahweh helps"]*
Greatest Accomplishment:	*Ezra led a second group back to Judah after the Babylonian captivity and taught God's Law there.*

EZRA'S ROLE IN SCRIPTURE

Cyrus, the king of Persia who replaced the Babylonians as the dominant eastern power, permitted Jews to return to their homeland. Ezra led a second group back to the homeland some eighty years after a first contingent from Babylon arrived in 538 B.C. Ezra was a priest who had dedicated himself in Babylon to "seek the Law of the LORD, and to do it, and to teach statutes and ordinances in Israel" (Ezra 7:10). While Aaron represents the priestly ministry of sacrifice, Ezra represents the priestly ministry of teaching.

Later when Nehemiah came to Judah as governor, the two initiated a return to the Law, elements of which the settlers in

Jerusalem and Judah had ignored. Many credit Ezra with launching the scribal movement with its commitment to study the Scriptures and especially the Law—a commitment that has marked Judaism for over two millennia.

EXPLORING EZRA'S RELATIONSHIPS

As a teacher of God's Word, Ezra maintained a relationship with God and at the same time a relationship with the people he instructed.

Ezra's relationship with the Lord *(Ezra 8:21–35; Nehemiah 8; 9).* Ezra 7:10 reveals Ezra's priorities. An incident recorded in chapter 8 demonstrates his faith. When Ezra received permission to go to Jerusalem to return wealth taken from the temple a hundred fifty years before, he was ashamed to asked the ruler for a military escort. He would travel through dangerous lands, but he was determined to seek God's help alone. Ezra and his companions "fasted and entreated our God for this, and He answered our prayer" (Ezra 8:23).

When Ezra arrived, he discovered that some of the Jews, including priests and Levites, had intermarried with their pagan neighbors. Ezra was deeply shaken. These were the very sins for which the Jews had been driven from the land! Rather than rail at the people, Ezra again fasted and prayed, confessing his shame and the iniquity of God's people. Ezra's obvious heartbreak and appeals to the Lord moved the community so much that soon all were weeping and confessing. The guilty then voluntarily determined to separate from their pagan wives and to be faithful to the Lord.

Later, after Nehemiah had arrived and rebuilt the walls of Jerusalem, Ezra gave a seven-day public reading and exposition of the Scriptures after which the people celebrated with worship.

Ezra's relationship with the people *(Ezra 8:21–35; Neh. 8; 9).* From the beginning, Ezra led by example. He demonstrated his trust in God by fasting and praying before his group set out for Judah. Once there, he demonstrated his anguish over the Jews' disobedience in public prayer and confession. While Ezra's commission granted him the right to administer God's Law judicially (7:25), Ezra was concerned with the hearts of the people he had come to teach. Rather than force conformity to God's Laws, Ezra showed by his own behavior how totally committed he was to doing God's will and how deeply he felt the Jews' disobedience.

EZRA: AN EXAMPLE FOR TODAY

Ezra serves as an ideal model for those who would teach God's Word. He was committed to study, to obey, and to teach. Ezra taught by example and by showing how deeply he cared that God's people lived in right relationship to Him.

- Ezra set his heart on learning, doing, and teaching God's Word. Each element is important. Teaching the Bible as information is dry and irrelevant. Teachers need to be doers of the Word if they are to have an impact on others.

- Ezra relied on God's power not only to protect him on his dangerous journey to Judah but also to move the hearts of persons living in sin. We are unable to change a single person's heart, but God can—and will.

- Ezra identified with the people he was called to teach. It would have been easy for Ezra to stand aside and condemn the sinners of Judah. Instead, Ezra took their sins to heart and wept for them before the Lord. Teachers who move others will identify with and weep for their students.

- Ezra was unwilling to compromise the truths taught in God's Word. There was no room for "reinterpreting" the teachings of Scripture to better fit modern times. We, too, are to hold fast to Scripture as our authority on faith and morals, and to take our stand with God's Word whatever the world around us may say.

A NOTABLE LAY LEADER

NEHEMIAH
Scripture references:
The Book of Nehemiah

Date:	450 B.C.
Name:	Nehemiah [NEE-uh-MI-yuh; "Yahweh comforts"]
Greatest Accomplishment:	He governed Judah for two lengthy terms and rebuilt the walls of Jerusalem.

Ancient monarchs feared assassination, by poison as well as other means. A "cupbearer" such as Nehemiah was a trusted official who was especially close to the king.

NEHEMIAH'S ROLE IN SCRIPTURE

Nehemiah stimulated yet another return to God and His ways while he was governor of Judah, then a province in the Persian Empire. He also motivated and organized the rebuilding of Jerusalem's wall. He is another example of the influence a godly and committed leader can have on the people of God.

NEHEMIAH'S LIFE AND TIMES

Nehemiah was an important official in the Persian Empire, with direct access to the king, when he heard that Jerusalem's walls still lay in ruins. In Old Testament times cities without protecting walls were viewed with contempt, and Nehemiah was ashamed that God's holy city should lie in such a state. Nehemiah then applied to the king for permission to go to Judah as governor, intending to restore the reputation of Jerusalem and of the Lord.

The Book of Nehemiah tells of his struggles with hostile neighbors and with a reluctant Jewish population that had grown cold toward following God's laws. His little book has been looked to ever since as a guide to principles of spiritual leadership.

Nehemiah had a vision (Neh. 1). Nehemiah was deeply moved when he heard Jerusalem lay unwalled. For many days he mourned and prayed, deeply aware that this situation had been caused by his people's sins. Out of his awareness of the need and his immersion in prayer, Nehemiah developed the conviction that God's people, now returned to the holy land, must honor Him and rebuild the city walls. As the vision formed, Nehemiah realized that he himself had been called to carry it out.

Nehemiah committed himself to the vision (Neh. 2). Nehemiah held a key post in the administration of the Persian Empire and was a confidant of the king. Nevertheless he was ready to abandon his power and position to fulfill the vision. When Nehemiah asked the king for the governorship of the tiny district of Judah, his request was granted. This was a definite demotion as far as the world was concerned. But Nehemiah was committed to his vision of what must be done to honor the Lord.

Nehemiah shared his vision (Neh. 3). Nehemiah needed to motivate others if his vision was to be fulfilled. In Judah he shared his vision with the people and motivated them to join him in sacrificing to rebuild the city wall.

Nehemiah persisted despite opposition (Neh. 4). The peoples around Jerusalem opposed the plan to rebuild the walls and even plotted to attack the Jewish workers. Nehemiah refused to be intimidated. He armed the workers and continued to rebuild.

Nehemiah set a personal example of self-less dedication (Neh. 5). The rebuilding effort kept many from working their fields. Some of the wealthy loaned the poor money at interest and took their fields when they could not repay. Nehemiah, who had personally paid the governor's expenses rather than take tax money from the people, confronted the guilty and forced them to restore the lands they had taken and cancel interest charges (which were condemned by the Law—see Deut. 23:19, 20).

Nehemiah saw to it that God's Law was taught and obeyed (Neh. 8—10). Nehemiah was committed to seeing to it that's God's people honored the Lord by their lives, as well as that the city of God honor the Lord by restoring the wall. He called for a national convocation so that Ezra might teach the people God's Law, and then saw to it that violations of the Law were corrected.

While the people strayed when Nehemiah later took a leave of absence to report to the king of Persia, when Nehemiah returned he again insisted on and obtained obedience to God's Law.

NEHEMIAH: AN EXAMPLE FOR TODAY

Nehemiah is rightly honored for his strong spiritual and political leadership. From Nehemiah we learn that to be effective leaders, we need to:

- Become aware of a need, pray about it, and form a vision for meeting the need. Frequently those who form such a vision will be called by God to fulfill it.

- Commit ourselves to the vision God gives us. Often we may have to set aside other perfectly valid concerns and give ourselves to carrying out the vision given by God.

- Share our vision with others. One test for the validity of a vision is our ability to form a team of others motivated to see that the vision is carried out.

- Persist in our efforts to fulfill the vision should opposition develop. Satan has an active interest in thwarting God's purposes, so that opposition should not be unexpected.

- Provide a personal example of dedication to the vision, bearing the burden of any personal sacrifices that may be called for.

- Demonstrate a concern that all involved in the enterprise maintain a close personal relationship with God. God is to be honored in the workers as well as in the work.

LESSER-KNOWN HEROES AND VILLAINS

Most of us have some familiarity with the major figures of Scripture. But the Bible also contains stories of many lesser-known men. Some appear as heroes, some as villains. But there is much we can learn from each.

HEROES

BARUCH

Baruch [BAIR-uch; "blessed"] was the friend and secretary of Jeremiah the prophet. Baruch's father and his brother were officials in the royal court, and Baruch dreamed of becoming an influential person himself. The trouble was, Jeremiah was out of favor at court and an object of hostility for the entire nation. Because Baruch was associated with Jeremiah, he too was an outcast and in danger of arrest.

Baruch felt torn. On the one hand he was loyal to the Lord and to Jeremiah; on the other hand he was both ambitious and driven. To Baruch's credit, he remained loyal to Jeremiah. The prophet was given a special word for Baruch from the Lord. "'Do you seek great things for yourself? Do not seek them; for behold, I will bring adversity on all flesh. . . . But I will give your life to you as a prize in all places, wherever you go'" (Jer. 45:5).

When we find ourselves torn between ambition and loyalty, we need to remember Baruch. Baruch chose loyalty, and the Lord rewarded him with the "prize" of life. When we get our priorities straight, we please God. And we learn the lesson that Baruch learned long ago: people are more important than success. In the end, serving others provides the far greater prize.

BOAZ

Boaz [BOH-az; "strength"] lived during the era of the judges, possibly around 1100 B.C. Conditions in his time were grim. The Hebrews had lost their spiritual moorings. Religion was corrupted by the infusion of pagan concepts, and many people had abandoned basic moral principles. When the Moabitess Ruth came to glean in Boaz's fields, he had to warn his workmen not to molest (rape) her!

But Boaz himself was a man of quality and character. The Book of Ruth tells us that Boaz was attracted to Ruth, not because she

The godly farmer Boaz sheltered the young widow Ruth and protected her from the many wicked men who lived during the age of the judges.

❖

may have been beautiful, but because "all the people of my town know that you are a virtuous woman" (Ruth 3:11). Boaz did wed Ruth, and the two had a child who became the great-grandfather of David the king.

It's hard in a society that emphasizes sex and physical beauty to keep focused on the qualities that are truly important in a wife or husband. Too many fall in lust—not in love. Others ascribe to the person they're attracted to qualities she or he simply does not possess. How important to remember that if we are to have a truly blessed marriage, we need to choose as a spouse someone "all the people of my town" know to be a truly virtuous individual.

CALEB

In 1439 B.C., when Moses sent out scouts to explore Canaan, one of the twelve men selected was Caleb. Caleb [KAY-leb; "rabid"], like Joshua, came back with a glowing report of the riches of the land and with total enthusiasm for going up and taking it. When the people refused to move forward, frightened by the other scouts' report of the enemy's strength, Caleb was one of just four men who urged trusting and obeying the Lord.

Caleb and Joshua were the only adults of the Exodus generation left alive when the Israelites finally did enter Canaan some forty years later.

But Caleb was not one to rest on his laurels. Although an old man, he was in the forefront of the fighting. When the power of the enemy was broken, Caleb asked for land that was still occupied by Canaanites! Not surprisingly, Caleb soon drove them out and occupied his land (Josh. 15).

Caleb kept his eyes on the Lord when nearly everyone around him refused to trust. Caleb sought and accepted personal responsibility. He was not one to sit back and let others do the job that needed doing. Nor was he one to look for an easy way out.

Caleb lacks the fame of Moses or Joshua, but Caleb and men like him made the conquest of Canaan possible. It's the same in the church today. Many men and women of character and quality live their entire lives in the background. People outside their own congregation do not know their names, but the qualities that bring others fame are qualities the Calebs among us possess in just as great a degree. In the end, our Calebs are as important as the more famous in carrying on God's work.

ENOCH

We don't know a lot about Enoch [EE-nuch; "initiated"]. He lived long before the Genesis Flood, and all that Scripture tells us about him is that "Enoch walked with God three hundred years," and that "he was not, for God took him" (Gen. 5:21, 24).

The Jewish sages had an inventive interpretation of "God took him." They suggested simply that Enoch died. "God took him" because he lived in an evil time, and so the Lord caused his death before Enoch could turn to sin! Most Christian commentators believe that "God took him" indicates that Enoch, like Elijah, was snatched up into glory without passing through death.

What is more fascinating about Enoch is that at age sixty-five something happened to turn Enoch to the Lord. For the next three hundred years, faithful Enoch continued to walk with God.

This is what makes Enoch a hero: not that God took him, but that for three hundred years Enoch lived in a corrupt society and remained faithful to the Lord. Enoch walked with God *for centuries*. How challenging for us! Our life span is much shorter than Enoch's, and in Christ, we know God better and even have the support of our brothers and sisters in the Lord. In our few short years, let's emulate Enoch and walk with God.

GEDALIAH

After Nebuchadnezzar took most of the Jewish population to Babylon, the King appointed Gedaliah [ged-uh-LI-uh; "Yahweh is great"] governor of Judah. Judah now was a Babylonian province. His story is told in Jeremiah 40; 41.

The Babylonians had left Gedaliah with only the poorest of the citizens of Judah. But Gedaliah urged them to take an oath to obey Nebuchadnezzar. Gedaliah pledged to care for them as they worked the land. Many of the Jews who had fled before the Babylonians invaded Judah returned to their homeland. Gedaliah was not only a caring person; he was also trusting. Even though he was warned that a certain man intended to assassinate him, Gedaliah refused to credit the man with such an evil intent. So Gedaliah welcomed the assassin, who then killed him and his companions.

This action so terrified the remaining Jews that they fled to Egypt, despite Jeremiah's warning that if they left the holy land they would perish.

Gedaliah was a truly good man who had his people's well-being at heart. Like many good men, others hated him. And also like many good men, Gedaliah simply could not believe that anyone would be evil enough to harm him.

While Gedaliah is in many ways a hero, he was also foolish in a way that we must be careful not to emulate. How many Christians have been defrauded by con men who have pretended to share our faith, and then taken all their savings and fled? How many well-meaning believers have been taken in by leaders who talk the talk, but fail to walk the walk? We are to be as good and harmless as Gedaliah was. But we are not to assume that everyone is as harmless as we are.

HUSHAI

Hushai [HOO-shi] was a friend of David on whom the king frequently relied for advice. When Absalom led a rebellion of the ten northern tribes against his father David, Hushai made a courageous offer. He would stay in Jerusalem and pretend to be on Absalom's side. He would then try to sabotage the rebellion by giving advice that might give David an edge.

Absalom accepted Hushai as an advisor. When Ahithophel urged Absalom to pursue David immediately and kill him, Hushai counseled against that course. Absalom followed the advice of Hushai, giving David time to raise an army in the south. The northerners were defeated, Absalom was killed, and David's kingdom was saved.

Hushai was willing to risk his life in the camp of the enemy to gain a possible advantage for David. His bold gamble paid off and proved to be the key to David's final victory. There are times when we also need to be ready to take risks to help others. It's easy to draw back rather than to get involved in the causes of others—especially when our involvement might cost us time, money, or even risk our reputation. Yet how many battered women, how many abused children might be saved if Christians took a chance and intervened?

ITTAI

Ittai was a Philistine mercenary. In Old Testament times, bands of military men often offered their services to foreign kings. Such mercenaries were frequently valued highly. They were unlikely to be involved in local politics and thus were considered "safe" troops for a ruler's personal guard.

When Ittai and his men came to David, David enrolled them in his service. But the next day, Absalom led a rebel army into Jerusalem, and David had to flee! David graciously released Ittai and his men from their oath of service. "Return, and take your brethren back," David said, "Mercy and truth be with you" (2 Sam. 15:20). But Ittai refused, and pledged to follow the king whatever happened. "As the LORD lives, and as my lord the king lives, surely in whatever place my lord the king shall be, whether in death or life, even there also your servant will be" (2 Sam. 15:21).

The utter faithfulness of this foreigner to his oath of loyalty must have both encouraged David and caused him deep pain. Here was a Philistine just entering his service who was loyal while the people David had loved and led so well for decades had rebelled.

Ittai is certainly one of the unknown heroes of Scripture. He sets a challenging example. For Ittai, his word was his bond. When he pledged his service to David, he had not expected a rebellion the very next day. Even though circumstances changed, Ittai's commitment was unchanging.

May we, too, be people of our word, without excuses and without the all-too-common search for loopholes.

JONATHAN

Jonathan [JAHN-uh-thuhn; "Yahweh has given"], the son of Saul, is one of the most attractive figures in the Old Testament. Jonathan was a military hero (1 Sam. 14) who had a deep faith in God. Like Saul's, Jonathan's feats were eclipsed by those of David. But unlike Saul, Jonathan did not become jealous of the younger man. Saul saw David as a threat to Jonathan's succession to Israel's throne; Jonathan saw David as a friend. When Saul raged against David, Jonathan defended him. Finally, when Jonathan became convinced his father was set on seeing David dead, Jonathan warned David so he might escape.

What is so striking about Jonathan's friendship is that it was totally unselfish. Jonathan's personality had no room for envy or selfish ambition. Jonathan exemplifies Proverbs 17:17: "A friend loves at all times."

A friend like Jonathan is truly special. But perhaps it is more special to *be* a friend like Jonathan. To offer consistent, loving support to others may be hard, but it is a rewarding and truly godly thing to do.

PHINEHAS

Phinehas [FIN-ee-uhs; "mouth of brass"] was a second-generation priest who lived during the time of the Exodus. As the Israelites finally approached the promised land after nearly four decades of wandering in the wilderness, they camped on the plains of Moab. There some of the men fell into a trap set by the Moabites (Num. 25:7–11). Today we call the trap a "honey pot." Moabite women seduced Israelite men and involved them in highly erotic pagan religious rites. The Moabites' intent was to turn the Lord against Israel so he would punish them rather than fight for them.

When an Israelite man brought a Moabite woman into camp in front of all the people, Phinehas, burning with anger and zeal for the Lord, went into the man's tent.

With a single thrust of his javelin Phinehas killed the two, who were entwined on the tent floor. Phinehas's bold action stopped a plague God had begun in the camp, and the Lord rewarded Phinehas with a "covenant of peace." He and his descendants would always have a place in Israel's priesthood.

Years later, after the Israelites had conquered Canaan, Phinehas filled a different role. The Hebrew tribes who settled east of the Jordan River had constructed an altar at the riverside (Josh. 22:13–34). The leaders in Canaan were concerned. God had commanded that sacrifices be offered only on the altar that stood before the tabernacle. In fact, the leaders were ready to go to war with their brothers over the altar if indeed it was intended to be used for illicit sacrifices. But first they organized a fact-finding mission. Who better to send on a fact-finding mission than Phinehas, who had proven his zeal for God?

Phinehas discovered that the Trans-Jordan tribes had been afraid that as the years passed some in Canaan might deny their right to share in the worship of God. So the Trans-Jordan tribes had constructed the altar, following the rules laid out in Moses' writings, as a witness that they, too, were God's people. Phinehas accepted their explanation, and civil war was avoided.

On occasions, commitment to the Lord calls for what might seem like harsh discipline in the church. At such times, we need our Phinehases. But we also need Phinehases who are willing to listen and eager to keep peace when misunderstandings come between brothers. Phinehas was one of those unusual men who was harsh only when harshness was appropriate and compassionate when it was fitting to listen and make peace.

Phinehas won a lasting priesthood for his line when he honored God by killing an Israelite who brought a Moabite prostitute into the Israelite camp.

❖

The three came to Babylon with Daniel and like him were enrolled in the king's training school to become officials in the Babylonian Empire. Like Daniel, they faithfully observed Jewish dietary law. And like Daniel, they excelled in their studies and were promoted to important posts.

However, when Nebuchadnezzar erected a gigantic idol and ordered all present at the dedication to bow down before it, the three remained standing. When this was reported to the king, he was furious. He again commanded them to bow down, and again the musical fanfare was played. But the three remained standing. They were convinced, they told the ruler of history's most vast empire, that "our God whom we serve is able to deliver us from the burning fiery furnace, and He will deliver us from your hand, O king. But if not, let it be known to you, O king, that we do not serve your gods, nor

SHADRACH, MESHAK, AND ABEDNEGO

Probably most Sunday school students know the stories of these heroes of the faith.

will we worship the gold image which you have set up" (Dan. 3:17, 18).

The three were cast into the flames and were seen walking there accompanied by a fourth figure. They were then brought out of the furnace totally unharmed. Nebuchadnezzar acknowledged God's power, and he made a decree that no one in the empire should speak a word against the God of Shadrach, Meshak, and Abednego on pain of death.

What impresses us about these three is not so much the miracle they were confident God could work. What is impressive is that they were determined to remain faithful to the Lord, miracle or not. They did not demand a miracle or even expect one. They honored God as Sovereign, free to act as He chose.

This is the kind of faith we need today: a faith that is convinced God *can* deliver us from any difficulty. Yet, this faith is committed to do God's will and honor Him whether God chooses to perform a miracle for us. How much more honoring to the Lord this is than to suppose, as some teach, that God *must* do miracles for us if we believe strongly enough. Let's remember that God is God and is free to do what He knows is best.

URIAH

Uriah [yoor-I-uh; "Yahweh is light"] was an officer in David's army. He was also a husband, married to a beautiful woman named Bathsheba.

While Uriah was at the front fighting Israel's battles, David happened to see Bathsheba. He desired her and took her. When Bathsheba became pregnant, David called Uriah back to Jerusalem, ostensibly to report on the progress of the war. David expected Uriah to sleep with his beautiful wife so that when she had her child Uriah would suppose that the baby was his own.

But Uriah was a dedicated soldier. It didn't seem right to Uriah to enjoy the benefits of home while his troops were in the field. So Uriah slept outdoors that night on the steps of the king's palace. Despite David's urgings, Uriah remained true to his principles and would not go home to his wife.

Desperate, David sent back sealed orders to his commanding general. Uriah was to be given a dangerous mission so that he might fall in battle. David's orders were carried out. Uriah died in battle. And David, quite possibly to further disguise his rape of Bathsheba, married her. (For a discussion of this event from David's perspective, see pages 49 and 55).

Military service does demand extraordinary sacrifice. We rightly honor the dedication of soldiers who carry out their orders in the face of mortal danger. And all too often we suspect that the political leaders who placed them in harm's way are as crass and selfish as was David. The Uriahs who live and die with honor are more blessed than those who manipulate them for personal gain.

VILLAINS

The Bible gives us heroes of faith to emulate. It also contains the stories of villains whose negative qualities we are to avoid. These, too, teach us practical lessons about living in this world.

ABIHU

Abihu [uh-BI-hoo; "father is majesty"] was a son of Aaron. Abihu and his brothers were ordained as Israel's first priests—a great honor and responsibility. God had with great care and in considerable detail defined their duties and how these duties were to be carried out. Each step to be followed as a priest appeared before the Lord had deep symbolic and spiritual significance, and each step was to be carried out just as God had commanded.

Shortly after being ordained, Abihu and his brother Nadab ignored God's instructions. They "offered profane fire before the

Lord, which he had not commanded them" (Lev. 10:1). Immediately, fire from God consumed the two priests. Moses explained why God had reacted in this way to Aaron, their father:

> By those who come near Me
> I must be regarded as holy;
> And before all the people
> I must be glorified. (Ex. 10:3)

The priests in Israel not only represented the people before God but also were charged with teaching God's Law to the people. The priests were nearest to God; they had to set an example of faithfully carrying out his Word. Abihu and Nadab were worse than careless. They were disobedient in a way that might infect the entire community.

It is serious when any believer consciously disobeys God. Abihu reminds us that when those who are teachers in the Christian community disobey, it is serious indeed.

ABIMELECH

A number of men mentioned in the Bible were named Abimelech. The name means "my father is king," and quite possibly was used by the Philistines as a royal title. But the Abimelech who ranks a place among the villains of Scripture was a son of Gideon, the judge.

Gideon had refused the crown when the Israelites offered to make him king after he defeated the Midianites. Gideon piously and correctly reminded the Israelites that God alone was to be their king. For many years, Gideon led the Israelites as a judge, not as a ruler intent on founding a dynasty.

But then Gideon named one of his sons Abimelech, "My father is king." Whether this name was intended to stake a subtle claim to royalty or was simply another name to be given to one of Gideon's seventy sons, we do not know. But we do know that Abimelech decided that *he* should be king.

Abimelech gained support in a few towns and proceeded to murder his brothers. Only Jotham, Gideon's youngest son, escaped (Judg. 9). But Abimelech failed to gain the support of the rest of Israel. In the end, dissension among those whom he supposedly governed led to a minor civil war in which Abimelech was killed.

Abimelech made the basic mistake of all who are too eager to gain wealth or power: he tried to construct a kingdom on wickedness. In the end, he reaped the evil he had sown.

Anyone who seeks to gain at the expense of others makes the same mistake. We are to be ambitious to do good. But we are not to be so ambitious for our own advancement that we harm others in our rush to the top.

ABSALOM

Absalom [AB-suh-lum; "father of peace"] was one of David's best-loved sons. Despite good looks and many gifts, however, Absalom was not a good man.

We see the seeds of Absalom's destruction in his response to the rape of his sister, Tamar, by a half-brother Amnon (2 Sam. 13). When Absalom learned what had happened, he advised Tamar to keep quiet, and He took her into his home. Even though Absalom named a daughter after Tamar, he was hardly sensitive to the anguish of the distraught young woman.

What Absalom was sensitive to was the insult. While he pretended to be friends with Amnon, Absalom hated him. Two years after the rape, Absalom engineered Amnon's death and fled Israel.

Some time later, David permitted Absalom to return. Once in Jerusalem, Absalom began an active campaign to win the allegiance of the northern tribes and of some of David's advisers. Absalom's campaign was successful, and David's son threw the nation into a bitter civil war. Absalom was killed in the final battle of the war. But thousands of others lost their lives because of this bitter young man's ambition.

Cain's murder of Abel was a vivid demonstration of the reality of Adam's fall. Evil truly had entered the hearts of humankind.

❖

David handled the situation poorly, yet that does not excuse Absalom for what he did. His hatred of Amnon, his pretense, his murder of his half-brother, and his rebellion against his father were Absalom's responsibility alone.

Today our society seems too quick to excuse. Pleas that people had a difficult childhood or that someone had harmed them is presented to excuse them of their crimes. Yet, two wrongs still do not make a right. Whatever others may have done to us never releases us from the obligation to do what is right and good.

BALAAM

Balaam [BAY-luhm; "devourer"] had a reputation for controlling occult powers.

When the king of Moab realized the Israelites were approaching his territory, he sent for Balaam to curse them (Num. 22—24). God warned Balaam not to go, but the vast wealth the king offered Balaam enticed him.

In the end, Balaam won God's permission to do what he intended to do anyway. But the Lord sternly warned Balaam to say only what God told him to say. As a result, despite repeated attempts to curse Israel, all Balaam could do was to bless them. Needless to say, this did not please the king of Moab.

Balaam was still eager to earn his fee, and so he gave the Moabites some advice. There was nothing *he* could do against Israel. So something must be done to make God so angry with Israel that the Lord himself would destroy them. Balaam suggested that the Moabites place their most attractive women just outside the Hebrew camp. These women would seduce Israelite men, and then get them to engage in the erotic rites associated with the Moabites' pagan religion. This, Balaam thought, would make God so angry that He would turn on His own people.

The Moabites followed Balaam's advice, and the strategy seemed to work. Many Israelite men fell into the trap, and God was angered and sent a plague to wipe out Israel. But Phinehas (one of the lesser-known heroes described above) acted quickly and the plague was stopped.

Subsequently, the Israelites overran the territory of Moab and Balaam was killed. Whatever reward he gained by counseling sin was something he left behind.

Balaam is mentioned in the New Testament as an example of a foolish as well as wicked and greedy man (2 Pet. 2:15; Jude 11; Rev. 2:14). Those who counsel another to act wickedly in the hope of personal gain follow Balaam's way—and deserve what they later receive.

CAIN

Cain was one of the sons of Adam and Eve. He became history's first murderer when he killed his brother, Abel.

It wasn't that Abel had done anything to harm Cain. All Abel did was to be faithful to the Lord. God had taught Adam and Eve about sacrifice in Eden when He himself had slain animals with which to clothe the first pair. Abel followed the pattern set then, and sacrificed an animal from his flocks. But Cain, a farmer, felt that his produce was good enough to bring to the Lord. Cain may well have brought the very best of what he had grown. But in doing so Cain rejected the example God had set and the teaching he had undoubtedly received from his parents. God required a blood sacrifice.

God rejected Cain's offering, but told him that if he brought an animal sacrifice it would be accepted. Cain, furious at the rejection, refused. Cain's anger at God was redirected against his brother. Cain invited Abel to walk with him in his gardens, and there Cain murdered Abel and buried his body.

Some people simply will not take direction—even from God. They insist on doing everything their own way. If their way is rejected, they become hostile and angry. All too often, this hostility is directed against a totally innocent person. We see it today in "road rage," an irrational anger directed against another motorist who somehow offends, often completely innocently. And we see it in families where individuals take out their frustration by doing violence to a child or a spouse.

The angry man still carries the mark of Cain.

Of all the meaningless excuses a person may offer, "I got angry" is one of the worst.

DOEG

Doeg [DOH-eg; "anxious"] was an Edomite hanger-on in the court of King Saul. When David, fleeing the court, asked for help from a community of priests, Doeg happened to be near. He informed on the priests to King Saul (1 Sam. 21; 22). Even though the priests had not suspected that David was out of favor with Saul, Saul demanded they be executed. When no Israelite would harm one of the Lord's priests, Doeg did the deed. For Doeg, the favor of the king and what he might gain by it was far more important than the lives of blameless men.

Few today would be willing to pick up a weapon and murder innocent men. However, far too many delight in spreading rumors that ruin reputations. In many ways, a man's good name is his life.

HAMAN

Haman was a high official in the Persian court. When a Jew named Mordecai failed to bow to him, the insulted Haman determined to take revenge. He planned to kill Mordecai and exterminate his entire people!

A young Jewish girl, Esther, whose story is told in the Book of Esther, thwarted Haman's plot. In the end, Haman was hanged on the scaffold on which he had intended to execute Mordecai.

Haman alerts us to one of the dangers of pride. The arrogant man, protective of his own self-image, is a dangerous companion. In the end, he is the one who is brought low.

JEZANIAH

The Babylonians had devastated Judah, destroyed Jerusalem and its temple, and had taken most of the Jews into captivity. Nebuchadnezzar appointed a governor for the ruined province, but when this governor was executed, the few remaining Jews were terrified. Surely the Babylonian ruler would send an army and kill them all!

Jezaniah was a military officer, and the leadership of the remaining Jews fell to him. Jezaniah felt that the Jews' best hope was to flee to Egypt, Babylon's enemy, and seek shelter there. But first, Jezaniah asked the prophet Jeremiah for a word from God. He and all the people agreed to do whatever God told them (Jer. 42:1–6). Soon Jeremiah communicated God's message. The Jews were to stay in their homeland. God would see to it that they would not be punished for their governor's murder. Jezaniah reacted angrily to the message. He even blamed Jeremiah for the destruction of the city. The people rejected God's guiding word. They announced that they had been comfortable when they worshiped pagan deities; they would go back to worshiping them rather than Yahweh.

One of the most foolish things a person can do is to seek God's will, find it, and then refuse to do it. We are not to use God to get our way; we are to submit to God so that we can go His way.

MICAH

Micah [MI-kuh; "who is like Yahweh?"] might be called an innocent villain. A number of men in Scripture bear this name, but the Micah in view here was an ordinary landholder who lived during the era of the judges. Some might call him a villain because he stole his mother's silver, her life savings. He probably qualifies on this account. But Judges 17 tells us much more.

When Micah heard that his mother had cursed the thief (an act of witchcraft intended to harm another person), Micah quickly confessed. Mom removed the curse with a blessing, and let Micah keep the silver. Mom had dedicated the silver to the Lord, so she made household idols from it to be kept in the family shrine. Micah made one of his sons the family priest. When a wandering Levite passed through, Micah hired him to be the family priest, sure that since his family priest was a Levite God would bless him.

What enables Micah to make our list of villains is that nearly everything he did directly violated a command of God! God's people were not to steal or resort to witchcraft. God's people were to have no idols, no family shrines. And only the sons of Aaron were to serve as priests. Micah's religious views had been so corrupted by pagan notions that he did not even know when he sinned.

We might make excuses for Micah, the innocent villain. However, it's difficult to make excuses for people today whose beliefs are corrupted by notions that have no root in Scripture at all. Today God's Word is readily available to us. And we are responsible to search the Scriptures to see whether the things we believe are true.

THE LEVITE

The last chapters of Judges describe conditions in Israel when the faith was corrupt and morality a casualty. The consequences of losing touch with God and His ways are illustrated powerfully in the story of the Levite and his concubine (Judg. 19).

The young woman had run away and returned to her parents. After a time, the Levite went to retrieve her. The parents were cooperative, and the Levite and his concubine set out for his home. When it was getting dark the Levite hurried to find shelter in an Israelite village. He stopped in a town belonging to the tribe of Benjamin. An old man offered him shelter in his home, but when dark fell the home was surrounded by men intent on homosexual rape. They demanded the Levite be sent out. Instead, the Levite thrust his concubine out the door. The men of the town gang raped and tormented her all night.

The next morning the Levite found her body in front of the home, her hand stretched out as if reaching desperately for the door and safety.

The Levite was incensed. He took his concubine's body home, cut it into pieces, and sent pieces to all the other tribes. This shocked everyone, and the tribes assembled to take revenge on the guilty villagers. But the men of the tribe of Benjamin were unwilling to surrender the perpetrators. The result was civil war.

What shocks us, of course, is not simply the readiness of Israelites to commit gang rape. What shocks us is that the Levite so callously turned his young concubine over to the men and that later he was eager to see *them* punished for molesting and killing her. Apparently, the Levite felt no personal responsibility—despite his utter disregard for his partner or for his act in exposing her to them.

Of course, this is the point of the story and the reason it is included in the Bible. Where knowledge of God is lost, erosion of conscience is sure to follow. Where relationship with God is abandoned, personal responsibility for one's actions will be denied as well. The Levite is a villain indeed, yet at the same time he is a victim of his times.

We, of course, have no excuse. We have every opportunity to get to know God better. We have an increased sensitivity to the wrongs of chauvinism and to the value of the rights of women. Whatever the condition of the world around us, we are to be fully dedicated to God and to good.

There are many more little-known heroes and villains in the Scriptures. And there are lessons for life in the story of each one.

❖

THE MAN AT THE HEART OF THE BIBLE

JESUS CHRIST

Scripture references:
Old Testament prophecy;
the Gospels;
New Testament Epistles;
Revelation

Date:	*Eternity to eternity*
Name:	*Jesus [JEE-zuhs; "Yahweh is salvation]*
Greatest Accomplishment:	*As God the Son incarnate as a human being, Jesus fully revealed the Father, won our salvation on Calvary, was raised from the dead, and is now seated in glory where He will remain until He comes again to judge humankind.*

JESUS' ROLE IN SCRIPTURE

It is impossible to treat Jesus Christ merely as another man of the Bible. Jesus was and is unique. John's Gospel opens with the introduction of a Person John calls the Word who has existed from eternity past with God and as God. John tells us that this Person became flesh in Jesus and lived for a while among us (John 1:14). John, who knew Jesus well and who was with Him from the inception of His public ministry, said: "We have seen his glory, the glory of the One and Only, who came from the Father, full of grace and truth" (John 1:14 NIV).

Implications of Jesus' deity. As God incarnate, Jesus is the fulfillment of the covenant promises that shape the Old Testament. He is the focus of the New Testament revelation. History turns on the few brief years that Jesus Christ lived on earth, and time itself is measured before and after His coming. While it is popular these days to imagine a variety of "historical" Jesuses who can be cast as mere men, the historical documents that are the source of our knowledge about Jesus present him as God and man. Nor is there any question that Jesus represented Himself as God. The Nelson *Illustrated Bible Handbook* sums up this evidence:

Each Gospel affirms many times that Jesus is the Son of God. John makes it clear that this means "making himself equal with God" (John 5:18). More than once Jesus states His deity in an absolute way (Mark 14:61, 62; John 9:35–37; 10:36). Jesus also claims to be the preexistent "I AM" (Yahweh) of the Old Testament (John 8:58). He claims that He existed with God "before the world was" (John 17:5). He claims a oneness with the Father so complete that "he that has seen Me has seen the Father" (14:9). Nor does Jesus hesitate to claim God's prerogative to forgive sins (Mark 2:10). The people of Jesus' day clearly understood His claim to be God, and that claim was one of the charges against Him at His trial (cf. Matt. 14:33; 26:63–65). Even demons trembled before Him and acknowledged Him as the Most High God (Matt. 8:29; Mark 3:11; 5:7; Luke 4:41). There is no doubt that Jesus claimed to be—and is shown to be—God Himself. It is as God that He promises "I am with you always, even to the end of the age" (Matt. 28:20) (p. 540–41).

It was as God/Man that Jesus spoke; as God/Man that Jesus acted; as God/Man that Jesus brought God's gifts to human beings.

THE PERSON OF JESUS

The orthodox definition of the Person of Jesus was given final form at Chalcedon in A.D. 451 in a document that summed up convictions held by Christians from the beginning.

Therefore, following the holy Fathers, we all with one accord teach men to acknowledge one and the same Son, our Lord Jesus Christ, at once complete in Godhead and complete in manhood, truly God and truly man, consisting also of a reasonable soul and body; of one substance with the Father as regards His Godhead, and at the same time of one substance with us as regards his manhood; like us in all respects, apart from sin; as regards His Godhead, begotten of the Father before the ages, but yet as regards His manhood begotten, for us men and for our salvation, of Mary the Virgin, the God-bearer; one and the same Christ, Son, Lord, Only-begotten, recognized in TWO NATURES, WITHOUT CONFUSION, WITHOUT CHANGE, WITHOUT DIVISION, WITHOUT SEPARATION; the distinction of natures being in no way annulled by the union, but rather the characteristics of each nature being preserved and coming together to form one person and subsistence, not as parted or separated into two persons, but one and the same Son and Only-begotten God the Word, Lord Jesus Christ; even as the prophets from earliest times spoke of Him, and our Lord Jesus Christ himself taught us, and the creed of the Fathers has handed down to us. [Henry Bettenson, *Documents of the Christian Church* (London: Oxford University Press, 1959), 73.]

The statement of the Chalcedon Council illustrates why it is impossible to deal with Jesus just as another man. While we can look at the Gospels and describe Christ's life here on earth, what we cannot do is "separate out" His humanness from His deity. On the other hand, we cannot correctly attribute some actions to His deity in isolation from His humanity. Jesus simply is unique, God and Man at the same time; a Person who cannot be treated as a human being without remaining fully aware of His deity, yet who cannot be treated as God without fully appreciating His humanity.

Telling the story of Jesus. At the end of his Gospel, John noted that Jesus did many things not recorded in his account, and he observed, "I suppose that even the whole world would not have room for the books that would be written" should all Jesus did be written down (John 21:25). The four

Gospels that relate the story of Jesus take up nearly half of the entire New Testament. The writers of Acts, the Epistles, and Revelation constantly refer to Jesus. As John noted, telling the story of Jesus can hardly be contained in a single book, much less a single chapter of a book on Bible men.

Yet, Jesus' very uniqueness guarantees that He will be more carefully studied than any other Bible character. This is certainly true in the "Everything in the Bible" series. Jesus is so central to the message of the Bible that each book in this series must and does highlight a different dimension of the meaning of His life. In *Every Covenant and Promise,* we see Jesus as the One on whom the fulfillment of God's covenants and promises depends. In *Every Miracle and Wonder,* we see Jesus authenticate His claim of deity by wonderful works of mercy and healing—works no other individual in history has performed. In *Every Good and Evil Angel,* we see Jesus' pre-incarnate appearances as the Angel of the Lord, and observe His power over demons and Satan himself. In *Every Prayer and Petition,* we explore Jesus' teachings on prayer and discover what it means to pray in Jesus' name. In *Every Woman in the Bible,* we explore Jesus' relationships with women and discover how Christ's attitude toward women initiates the restoration of an equality with men that women lost in the Fall. Even in this book, we must understand the men whose lives are portrayed in the New Testament by examining their relationship with Jesus Christ and noting His transforming influence on their lives.

Simply put, it is impossible to develop a single theme in Scripture without discovering that Jesus Christ is central to our understanding of that theme! In every case, the Jesus who gives form and meaning to the theme is the Jesus of Scripture, God the Son, incarnate as a true human being.

Clearly then it is impossible even to survey the life and ministry of Jesus in a brief chapter. Yet, Jesus did live a human life during the thirty-three years of His earthly sojourn. So what we can do is to provide some insight into what Christ's life on earth may have been like.

In looking at Jesus' life on earth, we need to be careful not to be drawn into unfounded speculation. For instance, we know that Jesus was seen as a carpenter by the people of His hometown of Nazareth (Mark 6:3). So it is valid to seek to understand what life was like for a carpenter in first-century Palestine. On the other hand, while we know that Joseph took his family to Egypt when Jesus was about two years old, we have no idea where the family stayed in Egypt or how long that stay was. So it would not be valid to imagine that they might have lived in the great city of Alexandria, and go on to describe life in its Jewish quarter in the first century.

We will give a picture of the life Jesus would have lived in first-century Palestine. Life would have been much the same for Jesus' contemporaries.

JESUS' CHILDHOOD AND YOUTH

Jesus' birth and infancy. Little is known of Jesus' birth and infancy. Several elements of the birth story give insight into the culture into which Jesus was born.

The date of Jesus' birth (Luke 2:1–3). Luke carefully pinpoints the date Christ was born, using as markers the rule of the Roman emperor Augustus, and a well-known census held when Quirinius was governor of Syria (Luke 2:2). These markers remind us that the world of the first century was dominated by a Roman Empire which, while it maintained law and order and made travel safe throughout the then-known world, also heavily taxed the peoples of the empire and maintained peace by Roman military might.

While Luke pinpointed the time of Jesus' birth, one of the events he used as a marker is uncertain. Our English versions erroneously identify the census that called

Mary and Joseph to Bethlehem as the one ordered by Quirinius. We know this census took place in A.D. 6, and it could not have marked Jesus' birth date. However, the Greek word *prote,* which is rendered "first" in our English versions, is better rendered "previous to." Thus Luke indicated a census taken *before* that of Quirinius. Today, we do not know just when that census took place. We do know, however, from copies of similar censuses ordered in Egypt that the Romans took censuses for purposes of taxation, and in a Roman census, people were required to return to their cities of origin to be counted.

The best evidence suggests that Jesus was most probably born in what we call 4 B.C., and ended His life on earth around A.D. 30 at the age of thirty-three.

Jesus' birth announced to shepherds (Luke 2). The night Jesus was born, angels appeared to shepherds in the fields near Jerusalem.

It was particularly significant that this good news was first given to shepherds. To most Christians, shepherds seem positive, caring figures. We focus on the image of God as our shepherd portrayed in David's twenty-third psalm, and imagine that all shepherds were caring, loving persons. But in first-century Judaism, shepherds were scorned as untrustworthy and as thieves. Their reputation was so bad that shepherds were singled out with women as unqualified to testify in court cases!

When the angels announced the good tidings of Jesus' birth, and said, "There is born to you this day in the city of David a Savior," those words "born *to you*" must have thrilled the shepherds. The Christ child was born not just for the wise men of Matthew's Gospel, but for the shepherds of Luke's Gospel as well. Christ was born to be Savior of the great—and to be the Savior of the outcast. The promised Messiah of the Old Testament truly would care for those who were sinners and for those who in the eyes of their own society were beneath contempt.

When we look again at the angel's words from the perspective of those first hearers, we sense in a fresh way just what the lead angel meant when he proclaimed, "I bring you good news of great joy that will be for all the people" (Luke 2:10 NIV). If the birth of the Savior was Good News for first-century shepherds, it surely must be Good News for all!

Jesus visited by the Magi (Matt. 2). The wise men of Matthew 2 were "Magi," members of a Persian scholar class that had existed in the East for over 600 years. While we know much about their role in ancient times as advisors to Persian royalty, we know much less about their role in the first century. However, that they were familiar with the Old Testament prophecies of a mighty Ruler destined to be born to the Jews is clear. Many people believe that the Magi recognized the bright star that appeared at Jesus' birth as the fulfillment of a prophecy found in the Book of Numbers: "A star will come out of Jacob; a scepter will rise out of Israel" (Num. 24:17).

It's not surprising that the Old Testament should be available to these wise men from the East. The Scriptures had been carried to Babylon in the captivity of 586 B.C. and were intensively studied there by the Jewish captives. When Cyrus of Persia later gave the Jews their freedom, most Jews remained in Babylon and in other major cities of the Babylonian/Persian Empire. One of the two great ancient rabbinic biblical studies is the Babylonian Talmud, developed in the East, while the other is the Jerusalem Talmud, developed in the Holy Land. The ancient East, then, had for centuries been a center of Bible study. So we should not be surprised that Magi from the East, guided by the Holy Spirit, understood the significance of the bright star that hung over the western horizon. Nor is it a surprise that some of them—the Bible does not give us a number—determined to brave the long journey to Judah to find, and to worship, the promised Child King. Based on Herod's command to kill all children two years old and younger (Matt. 3:16), Jesus was probably a toddler when the Magi arrived in Jerusalem.

What else might the Magi have understood about Jesus' birth from the Old Testament? For one thing, they might have understood that Jesus was to be virgin born (Isa. 7:14; Matt. 1:23). Isaiah declared: "The virgin will be with child and will give birth to a son, and will call him Immanuel." While the Hebrew word indicates a "young unmarried woman, usually a virgin," the Greek text of Matthew settles the question of whether a virgin is intended in the Old Testament. The Greek word, *parthenos,* unquestionably indicates a virgin, one who is not only unmarried but who has not had sexual relations with any man. In this same prophecy, the true nature of the child was unveiled in the name He was to be given: Immanuel. That name, preserving the emphasis of the Hebrew, is "WITH US is GOD." The virgin's child was to be God Himself, come as a human being to be with us in every sense.

The Magi might also have understood that the child born was at the same time a Son given (Isa. 9:6–7). Isaiah declared: "For to us a child is born, to us a son is given, and the government will be on his shoulders. And he will be called Wonderful Counselor, Mighty God, Everlasting Father, Prince of Peace. Of the increase of his government and peace there will be no end. He will reign on David's throne and over his kingdom." Here, too, the text gives striking testimony to Christ's deity. While He was to be born a child, He was also to be God's Son. His names are titles of deity: Wonderful Counselor, Mighty God. Even the phrase, "Everlasting Father" affirmed the Child's deity, for the Hebrew might better be translated "Source of Eternity." Before time, and prior to the existence of the universe, Jesus existed and was Himself the source of eternity.

It is no wonder, then, that the wise men, familiar as they must have been with the Old Testament, sought the Christ child to *worship* Him. They did not travel for months to honor a mere human being. They did not bring their rich gifts to win the favor of a mere human monarch. They came because they knew that in the Babe of Bethlehem God Himself entered our world. And this One the wise men were eager to bow before, in worship and in adoration.

Jesus' life as a child (Luke 2:41–52). The Gospels are silent about Jesus' childhood years. The only incident they report took place when Jesus was twelve and marked His religious coming of age when Jewish boys were considered responsible to keep the Law of Moses. That year, Jesus accompanied Joseph and His mother to Jerusalem to attend the Passover festival. When His parents and their neighbors set out to return to Nazareth, Jesus stayed behind, discussing the Scriptures with the sages who during festival times shared their wisdom with the common people. The text tells us that those who heard Jesus were "amazed at his understanding and his answers" (Luke 2:47 NIV). When Jesus' parents missed Him, they returned and found Him at the temple. Afterward, the text tells us, Jesus returned with them to Nazareth "and was obedient to them" (Luke 2:51 NIV) Beyond that the only reference to His childhood is the remark that Jesus "grew in wisdom and stature, and in favor with God and men" (2:52 NIV). This account, although very sketchy, raises two questions. Where did Jesus learn the Scriptures to discuss them with the rabbis on His first trip to the Jerusalem temple? And, what are the implications of Jesus' "obedience" to His parents.

Jesus' education. In first-century Judaism, education was understood to be primarily training in righteousness, with the Scriptures themselves as the sole sourcebook. The rabbis insisted that as soon as a child could speak his father should instruct him in the Law (The Talmud, *Sukkah* 42a). Instruction was woven into the very fabric of Jewish life. Each Sabbath, the synagogue services emphasized instruction in the Old Testament. Various religious festivals gave structure to the Jewish year, and each added its own testimony to the grace and nature of the God of Israel. In addition every town with over twenty-five boys was expected to have an elementary school. Before the destruction of Jerusalem in A.D. 70, Jerusalem had 480 synagogues, and each had its own school. William Barclay, in *Educational Ideals in the Ancient World*, reports that the community paid teachers' salaries and that teachers were to have the highest moral qualifications. Sayings collected from the Talmud required the teacher to use kindness, never to lose patience, but to explain over and over again if necessary to make a matter plain.

The child Jesus would have received instruction from Mary and Joseph before beginning school. Sometime between the age of five and seven, Jesus would have been enrolled for formal education. Typically school met before 10:00 A.M. and after 3:00 P.M. Class size was regulated; the ideal was one teacher for twenty-five boys. The only textbook was the Scripture, and during the first years of schooling, instruction was largely oral, although during these years children were taught to read. In most schools, the essentials of arithmetic were taught, and many children—but not all—learned to write as well as to read.

A later addition to the *Sayings of the Fathers* sums up the educational process: "At five years old, Scripture; at ten years, Mishnah; at thirteen, the Commandments; at fifteen, Talmud." While few children went beyond what the local school could provide, it is clear that Jesus would have been taught the Scriptures as a child. When he amazed the sages on His first visit to the temple at age twelve, it would not have been because He knew the Old Testament, for all school children were expected to have a basic knowledge of the Scriptures. Jesus would have

amazed the sages because of His ability to interpret and to apply the Scriptures and to relate one passage to another, for these skills were not emphasized in an educational approach that was essentially the memorization of passages by rote repetition.

Jesus' obedience to Joseph and Mary. The *IVP Bible Background Commentary* notes:

The commandment to honor one's father and mother was regarded as one of the most important in the law, and children not yet considered adults were to express this honoring in part by obedience (p. 196).

As the oldest child in the family, Jesus would set the example for his younger half-brothers and sisters.

JESUS' YOUNG ADULTHOOD

Up to about age thirty (Luke 3:23), Jesus worked as a carpenter in the little town of Nazareth in the district of Galilee (Mark 6:3). Yet, history and Scripture are silent about these years, so we can only suggest what life was like for any young adult in the province of Galilee.

Jesus' family life. Each of the Gospels relates an incident in which Jesus' mother and His brothers and sisters came seeking Him. Matthew 13:55 names His four brothers (James, Joses, Simon, and Judas) and mentions unnamed sisters. Jesus obviously grew up as the eldest in a relatively large family. Large families were considered a blessing in Judaism, so God had clearly blessed Joseph and Mary.

Typically, houses in villages like Nazareth were small, containing only a few rooms. Family members generally ate and slept in the same main room. The modern ideal proposing that each family member have his or her own room and personal space was never imagined by the poor in first-century Palestine. The people of Nazareth were

Carpenters in the ancient world used a variety of tools, even as do carpenters today. Saws, bow drills, chisels, and mallets were commonplace.

relatively poor, even though the town was large enough to support a synagogue (Matt. 13:54).

The Gospels' failure to mention Joseph after Jesus began His public ministry has been taken to indicate that Joseph had died earlier. In this case Jesus, as the eldest son, would have been responsible for his mother Mary's well-being as head of the little family. He would undertake with His mother to negotiate marriages for His brothers and sisters and to provide dowries for His sisters. On the cross Jesus asked the apostle John to take on the care of His mother (John 19:27). This important responsibility of the eldest as well as the other sons weighed on Jesus' mind even as He hung dying on the cross.

While Jesus lived a sinless life in the family as in every other relationship, His siblings simply viewed Him as their brother.

When Jesus became famous, the other members of the family seem to have resented it. According to John 7:5, during most of Jesus' life on earth His own brothers did not believe in Him. Later, Jesus' half-brother James became a significant leader in the Jerusalem church and authored the book that bears his name in the New Testament. We can assume that Jesus' other half-brothers and half-sisters also became believers after His resurrection.

Jesus' occupation. The ideal in Judaism was that every man have a trade at which to work and that he also be a student of Scripture. Few in first-century Galilee, laboring under the heavy burden of maintaining their families and paying the taxes required by local government, the religious establishment, and the Roman occupation forces, found time for intensive study. However, the ideal of the workman/student was encouraged through two institutions.

The first institution was the synagogue, which served as a study center for the men of a community. The second institution was apprenticeship. Normally, the older son in a family adopted the father's trade. Other sons might be apprenticed to other tradesmen unless they spent all their time in farming. The former course was taken by Jesus, for Jesus' contemporaries spoke of Him both as the "carpenter's son" (Matt. 13:55) and as "the carpenter" (Mark 6:3). Clearly, Joseph plied the trade of a carpenter, and as a youth Jesus worked with Joseph and learned the trade.

Some have speculated that Jesus might have been a "finish carpenter" or a cabinetmaker. Yet most tradesmen in the villages of Galilee also maintained plots where they grew crops to feed their families and supplement the income that could be earned from their trade. *The Revell Bible Dictionary* notes:

Wood was generally scarce in Palestine, and most homes were constructed of stone, but roof beams and often doors were made of wood. The many fishing boats that crossed the Sea of Galilee were wooden, and fashioning them called for special skills. Probably Joseph and Jesus, working in Nazareth some miles from the water, made farm tools like plows and sickles, and furnishings for the homes of their neighbors; chairs, tables, and bed frames (p. 195).

The romantic speculation that imagines Jesus was a master craftsman, or even one who shaped crosses on which criminals might be hung, is hardly likely to reflect the reality of Christ's very ordinary daily life and work.

The very ordinariness of Jesus' life is significant to our realization that Christ lived a truly human life. He came to be one with us, and He blended in perfectly among the poor with whom He lived.

Life in Nazareth of Galilee. In the first century most Jews in the ancient homeland lived in either Judea or Galilee. The two were separated by the district of Samaria (see the map on page 162), so intercourse between them was difficult. While the Jews of Galilee were faithful to temple worship, they tended to be less strict in observing regulations imposed by the rabbis. The Jews of Judea considered themselves the elite, and took pride in their more strict approach to their common religion. There was also a definite distinction in dialect (see Luke 22:59), and Galileans were looked down on by the people of Judea.

It would be wrong, however, to assume that Jesus grew up in a backwater town, isolated from the larger society and speaking only Aramaic. Just an hour's walk from Nazareth was the city of Sephoris, a vital city of 30,000. It is more than likely that Joseph and Jesus found work in this Galilean center of Greek culture. Excavations there indicate that Greek influence was far more pervasive in Galilee than was once thought, and Jesus and His family would most likely have spoken that language as well as Aramaic. Jesus would have been far more aware of the issues that concerned His fellow countrymen than

if He had lived in the rural isolation that commentators once assumed.

POLITICAL AND RELIGIOUS FACTIONS

Albert A. Bell Jr., in *Exploring the New Testament World,* sketches influential groups and movements active in Jesus' world.

Sadducees. This religious and political elite group controlled the temple and derived their support from the rich; they sought to maintain the status quo with Rome.

Pharisees/Scribes. This scholar class emphasized the application of the written and oral law to everyday life. Despite piling up rules the religious were to follow, they were greatly respected by the common people.

Herodians. This political party campaigned for the restoration of one of Herod's descendants to the throne as ruler of the Jews under Rome.

Zealots. This radical faction called for rebellion against Rome and the reestablishment of a Jewish state under God.

Essenes. This religious faction called for withdrawal from society in favor of an ascetic and self-disciplined life in wilderness communities.

Jesus was not associated with any of these factions. There is no evidence of contact with the Essenes or the Zealots in the Gospels, although one of Jesus' disciples was called "Simon the Zealot." When Jesus first began His miracle working and teaching ministry, many people expected Him to fulfill their

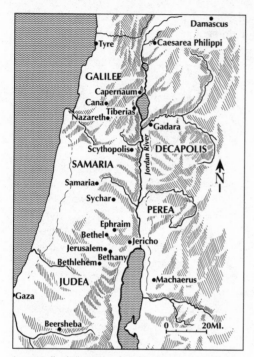

Jesus walked throughout Galilee and Judea, but the distances were not great.

❖

apocalyptic expectations. When Jesus did not do so, many people became confused about how to understand Him. While many Pharisee actively opposed Jesus (who showed little respect for them or their legalism), factions within their own movement made the Pharisees more open to various interpretations of the Law than we might expect. The Sadducees, however, saw Jesus as a definite threat to their position and power. They feared He might become the focal point of a rebellion against Rome. In the end, the Sadducees arrested Jesus, organized His trial, and urged the Roman governor Pilate to execute Him.

JESUS' PUBLIC MINISTRY

For some three years, Jesus traveled through Galilee and Judea healing and teaching. He was accompanied by a number of adherents, among whom twelve were des-

ignated as His disciples. The miracles Jesus performed during these years have been discussed in *Every Miracle and Wonder in the Bible* and in *Every Good and Evil Angel in the Bible*. His teaching will be explored in a future book in this series, *Every Parable and Teaching of Jesus in the Bible*. Here we note only the several details about what life would have been like for Jesus during those ministry years.

An itinerant ministry. It comes as a surprise to most to learn how small the territories of Galilee and Judea were in Jesus' time. Galilee was only some forty-four miles long by twenty-five miles wide, and according to Josephus contained 204 villages as well as larger cities such as Sephoris and Capernaum. Judea was even smaller, with a population of approximately 200,000, half of whom lived in or near Jerusalem. These two districts were isolated from each other by Samaria, populated by a mixed-race people who were generally hostile to the Jews. Many Jews traveling between the districts chose to take the longer route, crossing the Jordan and traveling through Perea. While the Romans maintained several roads that ran through Galilee and from Jerusalem to the Mediterranean coast, narrower pathways linked the villages to one another. Nearly everyone traveled on foot, and the typical distance that could be covered per day was only about fifteen or twenty miles. As Jesus and His disciples traveled through Galilee and Judea, they would have taken a more leisurely approach, pausing frequently to teach and to heal.

At the same time, an itinerant ministry was demanding. There were no motels or inns at which the travelers could stay at night. Most often they would be invited to stay in the homes of villagers and would be dependent on those they visited for food. Jesus summed up the challenges of such a ministry when sending out His disciples two by two:

Do not take along any gold or silver or copper in your belts; take no bag for the journey, or extra tunic, or sandals or a staff; for the worker is worthy of his keep. Whatever town or village you enter, search for some worthy person there and stay at his house until you leave. . . . If anyone will not welcome you or listen to your words, shake the dust off your feet when you leave that home or town (Matt. 10:9-11, 14 NIV).

While Jesus received financial gifts from those who wished to support His ministry (Mark 15:40, 41), most of the time, He and His disciples were dependent on the generosity of the poor among whom they ministered. As Christ once remarked to one who offered to follow Him, "Foxes have holes and the birds of the air have nests, but the Son of Man has no place to lay his head" (Matt. 8:20 NIV).

A discipling ministry. As Jesus began His public ministry, He chose twelve men to be His disciples.

In first-century Judaism, discipleship was the well-defined path to spiritual leadership. Those who sought to become teachers of the Law (rabbis), attached themselves to a recognized expert in biblical law and its interpretation. The disciple committed himself to be with his master for a period of years, with the goal of learning all the master knew and, more than that, becoming like his teacher in moral character (cf. Luke 6:40).

When Jesus began to teach, the establishment criticized Him because He had never gone through this discipleship process. Yet, when Jesus began to speak publicly, He also performed miracles of healing and even cast out demons that were the cause of many disabilities. Even Nicodemus, a member of the Jewish high court, addressed Jesus as rabbi, and stated: "We know you are a teacher who has come from God. For no one could perform the miraculous signs you are doing if God were not with him" (John 3:2 NIV).

Jesus' teaching ministry had one other unique quality. By the first century, the rabbis taught by referring to the rulings concerning God's Law that had been made by other rabbis generations earlier. What others had said that they had learned from their masters during their own discipleship was the basis of their authority. People were amazed when Jesus taught, because "he taught as one who had authority, and not as their teachers of the law" (Matt. 7:29).

Despite the scribes' and Pharisees' differences with Jesus, and despite the fact that He had not followed the established path to become a teacher, most of the common people in Galilee and Judea quickly realized that Jesus was a teacher who possessed intrinsic authority. The Twelve were understood to be His disciples, who would one day become leaders in the school of thought Jesus founded.

JESUS' CRUCIFIXION AND RESURRECTION

The bulk of each Gospel is given to an account of Jesus' final week on earth, with each event portrayed leading inexorably to Jesus' crucifixion and, after three days, His resurrection.

The crucifixion. Crucifixion was such a terrible form of execution that no Roman citizen in the first century was subject to it. Crucifixion was reserved for slaves, pirates, and brigands, and those involved in rebellion. *The Revell Bible Dictionary* describes the death Jesus experienced.

By the first century, the Romans had perfected this form of punishment. As an official known as the *carnifix serarum* supervised, the victim was beaten with a leather whip containing shreds of metal or bone that tore the flesh. Weakened by the pain and loss of blood, the victim was then forced to carry the crossbar to the place of crucifixion. The crossbar was fixed to the top of the imbedded pole, and the victim was either tied or nailed with his arms stretched along it.

In Jesus' case, nails were probably driven through the palms near the fleshy part of the thumb, the only part of the hand that could bear the body's weight (if indeed the wrist and forearm are not included in "hand"). Archaeologists have discovered remains of a young man crucified in Jerusalem in the first century; these show that the victim's feet were probably nailed to the sides of the fixed post by spikes driven through the heel.

Suspended in this awkward position, the victim died slowly, from extreme shock or from the gradual weakening of the two sets of muscles used for breathing. When it was desirable to hasten death, the Romans increased the stress on the body by breaking the leg bones of the victim (p. 268, 269).

The Gospels tell us that in Jesus' case death came before the legs were broken, and the fact of death was confirmed when a soldier drove a spear into Jesus' side.

The resurrection. It is possible that the tomb where Jesus was laid is preserved in Jerusalem today. The site is known as the Garden Tomb, nearby Gordon's Calvary, so-called after the British general who identified it. In the first century, burial sites of the wealthy were hewn in soft limestone. The bodies were laid on benches cut from the stone in a main room. Later the bones were stored in stone boxes (ossuaries) in narrow chambers called *kokhim* which ran off the main room. These complex tombs were intended as the final resting-place for several generations of the same family.

Frequently these tombs of the wealthy were sealed by large round stone slabs that rolled along a track cut in the limestone. Frequently also a garden was maintained at the tomb site.

The Gospel account describes Jesus' burial in a new tomb belonging to the wealthy Joseph of Arimathea, which he had just cut out of rock and sealed with a large rolling stone (Matt. 27:57–60). According to the Gospels, this tomb was near the place of execution (John 19:38–42). John adds an important detail: when John arrived at the tomb to check a report that Christ's body was gone, he bent down to look inside and was able to see the empty slab where the body had been laid (John 20:5).

Those who visit the garden tomb today can see the track along which the stone that sealed the tomb rolled. They can bend down and look inside and see, in the light that passes through a small window cut in the rock, the empty slab in the main chamber of what was clearly a new tomb, for *kokhim* side chambers had not yet been cut. For many, these and other details about the site are convincing evidence that they stand in a garden outside the very tomb where Jesus' body was laid, where He experienced a resurrection which is promised to all who trust in Him.

These details help us understand the earthly life Jesus of Nazareth experienced. But only Scripture helps us understand the meaning of His life, His death, and His resurrection. Only in looking back over the human life Jesus lived here on earth do we understand its significance. In the resurrection, Jesus, "who was born of the seed of David according to the flesh," was "declared to be the Son of God with power according to the Spirit of holiness, by the resurrection from the dead" (Rom. 1:3, 4).

CHURCH BUILDERS

A side from the Son of God, two New Testament figures tower above all others: Peter, the "prince of the apostles," and Paul, the apostle to the Gentiles.

PETER

Scripture references:
the Gospels; 1, 2 Peter;
Acts 1—5; 10—12;
Galatians 2:11–21

Date:	About 5 B.C.–A.D. 65
Name:	Peter [PEE-tuhr; "rock"]
Greatest Accomplishment:	Peter was the acknowledged leader of Jesus' twelve disciples and preached the first gospel sermons to Jews and Gentiles.

PETER'S ROLE IN SCRIPTURE

Peter was a central figure in the Gospel narrative and the most quoted figure of the disciples. He was clearly the spokesman for the Twelve, the first to see spiritual truths and express them, and at the same time the first to blurt out his unformed thoughts. Peter played a central role in the three great transitions from Old to New Testament realities. Peter's confession of Jesus as the Christ, recorded in Matthew 16, marked the shift in Jesus' teaching from an emphasis on the kingdom to an emphasis on the cross. Peter's sermon on the Day of Pentecost (Acts 2; 3) defined the gospel message and led to the forming of the first local church. Peter's visit to the home of the Roman centurion Cornelius (Acts 10; 11) initiated the first Gentiles into what had been a purely Jewish church. Peter's prominence in these three critical transition stages identifies him as one of the most significant men of the New Testament.

PETER'S LIFE AND TIMES

We can divide Peter's life into four periods. Peter began life as a fisherman, became

Fishing Boat

a disciple, then a preacher, and finally a missionary.

Peter the fisherman. Peter began his life as a fisherman in Bethsaida (John 1:44). Nathaniel and Philip, two other disciples of Jesus, were also from this little fishing village that lay on the shores of upper Galilee. Peter's fishing business prospered. By the time we meet him in the Gospels, he had moved to Capernaum, the leading city of Galilee, and had gone into partnership with James and John, two other members of the Twelve.

Remains of what is believed to be Peter's house in Capernaum have been uncovered by archaeologists and, in harmony with the Gospel account, they suggest that his residence was relatively large. Peter was not simply a fisherman; he was involved in a successful fishing enterprise. Some commentators have suggested that Peter's business caught, salted, and transported fish to Jerusalem, where the disciple John oversaw their sale and distribution. While we cannot tell just how dominant Peter's fishing cooperative was, we do know that it was a successful enterprise. And we know that Peter, who was older than the others, was the acknowledged leader of a team of men who were already friends and co-workers when Jesus called them to follow Him.

The historian Josephus stated that some 330 fishing boats operated on the Sea of Galilee in the first century. One such boat, cradled in mud for some 2,000 years, was recovered in the 1980s along Galilee's shore. The boat, sketched here, was 27 feet long, and is undoubtedly the kind of boat Peter and his fishermen friends used.

Peter the disciple. It is striking that the team of fishermen Peter led responded to Jesus' call to follow Him together. They left their fishing business, and for the next three to three and a half years they accompanied Jesus everywhere.

In New Testament times, the role of the "disciple" was well defined. A person trained for spiritual leadership not by enrolling in a seminary but by becoming the disciple of a recognized rabbi. The disciple literally lived with his master, learned by listening and discussing matters with him, and also learned by observing his life. As Luke 6:40 indicates, the goal of discipleship was to produce a person who, when fully trained, "will be like his teacher."

The time Peter and the other disciples spent with Jesus was designed to prepare them for a life of ministry which, at the time, they could not envision. The time spent with Jesus was to prepare them not only to communicate what Jesus taught but to be Christlike.

Peter the preacher (*Acts 2:22–39; 3:12–26*). After Jesus' resurrection, Peter was the first to preach a gospel sermon. Two of Peter's sermons are recorded in Acts, and from them we can reconstruct the basic elements in the early preaching of Christ's disciples:

- Jesus, the historic person (2:22)
- Was crucified and raised from the dead (2:23, 24; 3:13–15)
- in accordance with Scripture (2:25–35; 3:18)
- He is God's Messiah (2:36; 3:20)
- All who believe on Him will have remission of sins and receive the Holy Spirit. (2:37, 38; 3:19, 21–26)

Peter also was the first to present the gospel to Gentiles (Acts 10; 11). The later New Testament letters, written to predominantly Gentile believers, make it clear that the core gospel Peter preached remained central to Christian preaching throughout the New Testament era.

Peter the missionary. While the Book of Acts follows Peter's ministry for only a few chapters, firmly established tradition tells us that Peter spent the rest of his life—some three decades after the resurrection—traveling and sharing Christ. Apparently, Peter focused on the Jews scattered throughout the Roman Empire (Gal. 2:8), while Paul focused on reaching Gentiles. Early tradition states that John Mark, who traveled with

Peter, wrote the Gospel of Mark and that Mark's Gospel reflected the stories Peter told about the Savior.

Another generally accepted tradition tells us that Peter died in Rome in the mid-60s, crucified upside down by the Roman government within a year or two of the execution of the apostle Paul.

EXPLORING PETER'S RELATIONSHIPS

Peter's relationship with the other disciples. Several facts indicate that the Twelve looked to Peter as their leader, although all looked to Jesus as Lord. Wherever the Gospels list the Twelve disciples, Peter's name is listed first (Mark 14:13). Peter's name occurs over 150 times in the Gospels and Acts—far more than any other disciple's name.

The Gospel accounts also make it clear that three of the Twelve were closer to Jesus than the others, and at times they accompanied Him while the others waited behind. Not only was Peter one of the three, but again when the three are named Peter's name is given first (Mark 5:37).

Peter served as the disciple's spokesman. When a disciple's dialog with Jesus is recorded, it is almost always Peter who speaks up. Peter's influence over the others is reflected in John 21, which recounts that while the disciples waited in Galilee for Christ to visit them after His resurrection, Peter said, "I am going fishing." And the others said, "We are going with you also" (John 21:3).

Peter was clearly the leader, not only by virtue of his outspokenness, but also because he could galvanize others to action by his example.

Peter's relationship with Jesus. Peter shared with the other eleven disciples the privilege of traveling with Jesus and learning from Him. Yet, the Gospels make it abundantly clear that Peter was something more than another member of a group that had gathered around the

Lord. A number of incidents recorded in the Gospels relate one-on-one interactions between Peter and our Lord. Several of them are beneficial in helping us understand Peter as a person and as a disciple.

Peter's first contact with Jesus (John 1:41, 42). When John the Baptist began his exciting ministry in the Jordan Valley wilderness, many people came to hear his preaching. Among them was the team of fishermen headed by Peter. It happened that the fishermen were there the day Jesus was baptized, and two of them, Andrew and probably Philip, overheard John speak of Jesus as the "Lamb of God." Intrigued, the two followed Jesus and spent the day with Him. That evening, or perhaps the next morning, they told their companions that they had found the Messiah prophesied in the Old Testament. This exciting message delivered by his brother Andrew introduced Peter to Jesus.

Jesus was from Nazareth, a hamlet not far from Capernaum. So the fishermen traveled back to Galilee with Jesus. On the way they stopped at a wedding in Cana, and there the future disciples witnessed the first of Jesus' miracles (John 2). They then went on together to Capernaum, where Jesus visited with the fishermen for some time, apparently staying as a guest in Peter's house (Mark 1:29). While the first story about Jesus and the fishermen pictures their call to discipleship, Peter and the others had come to know Jesus earlier. By all accounts, months after meeting Jesus, He called them to follow Him.

Peter's call to discipleship (Matt. 4:18–22; Mark 1:16–18; Luke 5:1–11). Matthew and Mark gives quite sparse accounts of the disciples' call. Luke fills in many details and relates the special role Peter played.

Jesus had been preaching to large crowds that kept pressing in on Him. Jesus borrowed Peter's boat, put out from the shore, and taught from there. Afterward Jesus told Peter to launch into deeper water and let down his nets. Peter was skeptical. Fishermen on Galilee worked at night, not during the day, and the night before they'd caught nothing. Peter, who knew the ways of the fish, was sure there was nothing there to catch. "Nevertheless," Peter said, "at Your word I will let down the net" (Luke 5:5). When a great school of fish swarmed into the net, Peter was stunned. When they returned to shore with boats almost sinking from the weight of the fish, Peter fell on his knees and begged Jesus, "Depart from me, for I am a sinful man, O Lord!" (5:9). This simple nature miracle convinced Peter as nothing else had that Jesus truly was Lord. Moreover, seeing Jesus in this way made Peter deeply aware of his own sinfulness. It was not that Peter felt *unworthy* to be in Jesus' company; Peter felt *uncomfortable*.

Peter's reaction is a common one for those who possess spiritual sensitivity. The presence of the holy makes spiritually sensitive people recognize their own lack and makes them aware that they deserve God's judgment. Jesus immediately put this fear to rest, for Jesus intended to make Peter His companion. "From now on you will catch men" (Luke 5:10).

Today, we have only the same two choices Peter faced. We can invite Jesus to leave us alone or we can accept His invitation to become His followers. That day on Galilee, Peter and his friends made the right choice. "They forsook all and followed Him" (Luke 5:11).

Peter's budding faith (Matt. 14:22–33). The disciples had been with Jesus for some time and seen many miracles when, one evening, they found themselves trapped in a storm on the Sea of Galilee.

The Sea of Galilee rests between high hills that often funnel winds across the water. The storms that toss the sea come up suddenly, and are often fierce. This storm was exceptionally violent, and row as they would, the disciples could make little progress. Unexpectedly, they saw a figure walking on the water toward them. The disciples' first thought was that the figure was a ghost, a supernatural apparition. Then Jesus spoke to them, and they recognized Him. Excited, Peter shouted out, "Lord, if it is You, command me to come to You on the water." And when Jesus said, "Come," Peter unhesitatingly stepped over the side of the boat and walked on the water toward Jesus. But then Peter realized what he had said and where he was. Shifting his gaze from Christ to the white-capped waves, Peter began to sink.

Immediately Peter cried out to Jesus, "Lord, save me," and Christ lifted him up and helped him into the boat.

Much has been made of Christ's mild rebuke in which He called Peter a "little-faith" and asked, "Why did you doubt?" More should be made of the insight the incident gives into Peter. Peter was impetuous, yes. Peter may have had little faith, but Peter had more faith than the others did who stayed in the boat and watched! When Peter began to sink, his first thought was to call out to Christ. Today the faith still needs men who are willing to step out into life's storms and who, even though they may begin to sink, will quickly call on Jesus to save.

Peter's confession of Christ (Matt. 16:13–28). For at least eighteen months, Jesus traveled through Jewish territory in Galilee and Judea. His preaching and His miracles were now well known, and wherever Jesus went He drew crowds. Yet the crowds viewed Jesus merely as a prophet, albeit a great prophet. When Jesus asked His disciples who they said He was, Peter spoke: "You are the Christ, the Son of the Living God" (Matt. 16:16).

Jesus attributed Peter's correct response to God's work in Peter's heart: "This was not revealed to you by man, but by My Father in heaven" (16:12 NIV). Then Jesus went on to say two things to Peter that have been greatly misunderstood: "You are Peter, and on this rock I will build my church" (16:18). The modern Roman Catholic Church views this statement as Peter's commissioning to be the church's first pope. However, even the church fathers to whom the Catholic Church appeals differ on what Jesus was saying. Three views have been argued:

- Peter is the rock.
- Christ is the rock.
- Peter's confession is the rock.

Part of the confusion comes from the name "Peter," *petros,* which means *stone* in Greek. But the term here for "rock" is *petra.* While the similarity between *petros* and *petra* is obvious, the words are not the same, and the verse might be best understood as "You are Pebble, and on this boulder I will build my church." The chances are that Peter the Pebble is not the boulder Christ referred to!

Noting this, some of the church fathers argued that the boulder on which the church rests is the confession of Christ as the Son of God. This has much to commend it, for acknowledging Christ as God the Son lies at the heart of the New Testament revelation. Even so, it is more likely that the boulder is Christ Himself, the subject of Peter's confession. The gates of hell will not prevail against the church because Jesus *is* God, and His power is fully invested in protecting His own. As Paul writes in 1 Corinthians 3:11, "No other foundation can anyone lay than that which is laid, which is Jesus Christ."

"I give unto you the keys to the kingdom" (Matt. 16:19). This verse, too, is important in Roman Catholic theology. The church assumes that the "keys" passed from Peter to pope after pope. Thus the Catholic Church claims to hold the keys that open heaven's door to the faithful through the sacraments. Protestants have, however, pointed out that Peter used his keys in preaching the gospel first to the Jews (Acts 2; 3) and then to the Gentiles (Acts 10; 11). In using the keys Peter, by articulating the gospel, threw open the door of salvation to all who believe. With the door flung open, never to be shut, "keys" become irrelevant.

While Matthew 16 is important in the study of theology, we look at the passage to learn more of Peter the man. Peter had already displayed spiritual sensitivity; now we see him grow in his responsiveness to God's will. But, at the same time, we see a person who has a long way to go!

Immediately after Peter's bold confession of Christ as the Son of God, Peter rebuked Jesus for predicting His death on the cross! When Jesus spoke of His coming death, Peter blurted out, "Far be it from You!" (Matt. 16:22). The very idea seemed unthinkable!

And Jesus, who had just praised Peter, now rebuked him: "Get behind Me, Satan." Peter, who had so quickly taken God's part, now promoted a course that would have delighted Satan, not the Lord.

How like Peter we all seem to be. We have insights into God's will and His ways. At the same time, we all too frequently take a course that runs counter to God's. We may be motivated, as Peter was, by a love for Jesus. But good motives are no substitute for an understanding of and submission to God's will.

At the same time, we need to recognize Peter's quickness to speak and act as one of his strengths. Peter was not one of those persons who hesitate until the opportunity for action passes. Peter was ready to act, wisely or unwisely, on what he believed right.

Christ is still able to correct those who in their zeal for Him act unwisely. But it is the immovable, the waiting, and the hesitant who pass on life's opportunities and accomplish nothing for the Lord.

Peter spoke too quickly (Matt. 17:24–26). One day Peter was approached by those who collected the temple tax—an annual payment due the Jerusalem temple from every adult Jewish male. The tax collectors asked if Christ paid the tax, and Peter blurted out, "Of course!" Later, Christ spoke with Peter

about it, asking whether rulers collected taxes from sons or from strangers. Peter gave the obvious answer: from strangers.

Jesus' question communicated a fascinating insight. That all Jewish males were to pay a temple tax demonstrated the truth that mere physical descent from Abraham did not make anyone a child of God! The temple tax was collected from strangers, not sons! But should Jesus then pay the temple tax? Again the lesson was no. Peter had confessed that Jesus was the Son of the living God!

Jesus sent Peter to the seashore where he caught a fish in whose mouth was a coin large enough to pay the temple tax for both Peter and Christ. Peter was again reminded that despite being one of Jesus' disciples, Peter was not qualified to answer questions that should have been addressed to Christ Himself. Again, we see Peter as impetuous, perhaps even unthinking. We see him as a person who despite spiritual sensitivity still lacked insight into the underlying significance of issues on which he too readily spoke.

Peter denied Christ (Matt. 26). As the day of Christ's crucifixion approached, Jesus warned His disciples that He was soon to die. He also warned them that in that hour they would desert Him. Peter couldn't believe Christ's words. Didn't Jesus know how committed he and the others were to their Master? So Peter blurted out, "Even if I have to die with You, I will not deny You" (Matt. 26:35). The others followed Peter's lead and protested their loyalty. And even when Jesus told Peter that before morning came Peter would deny Him three times, Peter couldn't imagine anything that would make him deny His Lord.

Later than night, a mob led by Judas found Christ in Gethsemane. As usual, Peter showed himself braver than the others. He tried to protect Jesus, and even cut off the ear of one of the high priest's servants with his knife (the same word in Greek is translated both "knife" and "sword") (John 18:10).

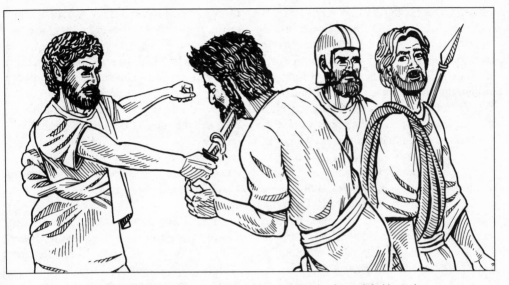

Peter boldly tried to defend Jesus when He was taken by the mob led by Judas.

Jesus told Peter to put his weapon away, and, powerless, Peter fled as the others had done. But even then, Peter followed the mob that led Jesus away, and slipped into the courtyard of the high priest's home.

When a servant girl said she recognized Peter as one of Jesus' followers, Peter vehemently denied any association with Christ. Later, he repeated his denial when recognized by another girl, and finally denied Jesus a third time when some bystanders commented on Peter's Galilean accent. Only when the cock crew, and Jesus, being led out of the house, looked across the courtyard and caught Peter's eye, did Peter realize what he had done.

Then he went out and wept bitterly (Matt. 26:75).

In this we see Peter at his best and his worst. He was so full of self-confidence that he rejected Christ's words of warning. He was bold and fearless, but at the same time cowardly. He was ready to face a mob with nothing but a fisherman's knife, yet caved in before the accusations of a slave girl. Despite his gifts of leadership and his willingness to risk, Peter seems surprising unstable, and all too quick to act without giving serious thought to what he said and did.

Peter's recommissioning by Christ (John 21). Events associated with the earliest days after the resurrection show that Peter was as eager as anyone to establish Christ's return to life. Peter and John both ran to the tomb when they heard it was empty, and although the younger John outran Peter, Peter was the first to enter the empty tomb and discover the grave cloths in which Jesus had been wrapped, lying there empty.

Later the disciples were fishing in Galilee, and Jesus appeared on the shore. When Peter realized it was Jesus, he tore off his outer cloak and plunged into the sea to swim to Him. Despite this evidence of Peter's continuing love for the Lord, Peter seems to have held back on that occasion. While the others crowded around Jesus, Peter dragged a net filled with fish up on the shore (John 21:11). But after they had all shared breakfast, Jesus singled Peter out.

Three times Jesus asked Peter if Peter loved him, and three times Peter professed his love for Christ. There is an interplay in the Greek that is not reflected in our English versions. The first two times Christ asked Peter, "Do you love me," He used the Greek word *agape*. This word, a rather neutral word in secular Greek, is used in Scripture to express the utterly amazing love of God seen in Jesus' sacrifice of Himself for us. God's love is a love that consciously, purposefully, acts for the benefit of the one loved whatever the cost to the lover.

When Peter answered Jesus' questions, "Do you love me?" with "Yes, Lord, You know that I love you," Peter used a different word for "love." That word was used in both secular and biblical Greek to represent a deep affection for the one loved, but not the total commitment of *agape* love.

Finally, when Jesus asked Peter a third time, "Do you love me," Jesus used Peter's word for love. And Peter responded with that same affirmation of a "deep affection" love for His Lord.

Much has been made of the interchange of the words for love used here. But perhaps the best explanation is that Peter had at last recognized his own fallibility. Peter had been so sure that His commitment to Jesus would carry him victoriously through any test. But Peter had failed. Now Peter, deeply aware of his weakness, was unwilling to profess a depth of commitment that he might not be able to maintain. Peter knew he loved Jesus as Lord. But Peter also knew that without a supernatural source of power, his love, however great, would not enable him to be the man he wanted to be.

Jesus accepted Peter's three professions of love. And Jesus commissioned Peter to "feed my lambs." Peter's denial of Christ had not disqualified him from the leadership role Christ intended Peter to fill. For failure there is forgiveness. And, as Peter was about to learn, for our weaknesses there is God's own strength.

Peter's leadership after the ascension (Acts 1). Despite the fact that Peter's companions must have been well aware of his weak-

nesses, he remained their acknowledged leader in the days following Christ's ascension. Peter's name is first on the list of the disciples turned apostles (Acts 1:13), and it was Peter who stood up and, applying Psalm 109:8, called for the selection of a man who had been with the disciples from the beginning to take the traitor Judas's place. Peter took the lead. The others followed.

Whatever we may say about Peter's flaws, he was a man others looked up to, a man of influence.

Peter's first sermons (Acts 2; 3). On the Day of Pentecost, when the Spirit Jesus had promised to His disciples filled the little company of believers and gave birth to the church, Peter took public leadership of the little band. Miraculous signs that amazed the people of Jerusalem marked the Spirit's coming. Peter stepped forward to announce that Christ, the promised Messiah, had died and risen again that all who believe in Him might be forgiven. Peter's sermon was powerful, not because he was a great orator, but because the truth of his words was borne to the hearts of many by the Holy Spirit. Acts tells us that 3,000 were saved that day. Acts goes on to report another powerful sermon preached by Peter after the healing of a man who had been lame from birth.

Peter, the man who had been such a natural leader despite his glaring weaknesses, was now filled and empowered by the Holy Spirit. The disciple had become an apostle, not only sent by God but also equipped by God for ministry.

Peter's mission to Cornelius (Acts 10; 11). The earliest Christian church was a Jewish church, and no one at that time expected Gentiles to become believers on a spiritual par with Jews. Peter, like the other earliest believers, was convinced that the Jews were God's chosen people and that Jesus was the Jews' Messiah. But Peter was both teachable and willing to take a stand for what God taught him.

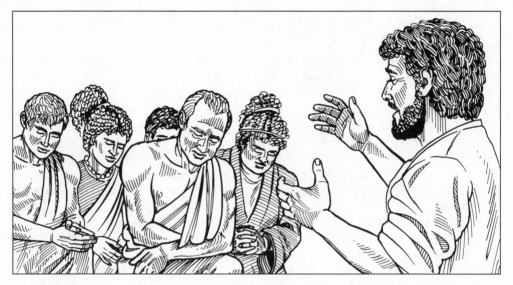

The first large-scale conversion of Gentiles to Christ took place in the home of the retired Roman centurion, Cornelius.

❖

God showed Peter a vision: a group of animals that Old Testament dietary laws classified as unclean, and God commanded Peter to kill and eat them. Shocked, the apostle refused, only to hear God's voice telling him not to classify as "unclean" what God had cleansed. The vision was repeated, and as Peter puzzled over its meaning, messengers from a Roman centurion named Cornelius knocked on the door of the home where Peter was staying.

In the first century, pious Jews considered Gentiles unclean and would not enter a Gentile's home for fear of being ritually polluted. Peter immediately realized that God had sent the vision to show him that he was to go to Cornelius's home. Once there, Peter spoke of Jesus, and the entire company was not only converted but began to speak in tongues as the disciples themselves had on the Day of Pentecost.

When Peter returned to Jerusalem, he told what had happened, and argued that since the Gentiles had not only trusted in Christ but that the Holy Spirit had also shown His presence in them, these Gentiles must be considered believers, full members in Christ's church. The apostles and elders agreed, glorifying God that "God has also granted to the Gentiles repentance to life" (Acts 11:18).

Clearly Peter had become more teachable. At the same time, he had maintained his influence as a leader.

Peter's failure in Antioch (Gal. 2:11–21). Some time later, Peter visited a Gentile church in the city of Antioch that Paul and several elders and prophets led. Peter fit in well, enjoying his fellowship with Gentile believers—until a group of Jewish Christians came down from Jerusalem to visit. When they arrived, Peter stopped eating with the Gentiles that he might follow the strict Jewish dietary laws. Paul immediately confronted Peter. Peter's actions implied that Gentile believers were second-class Christians. Peter's actions were hypocritical. Worse than that, they cast doubt on the gospel message that salvation was by faith apart from works, a free gift to all who would place their trust in Christ. While Paul did not say so, it's clear that Peter accepted the rebuke and changed.

Peter's stand at the Jerusalem council (Acts 15). It had been relatively easy for the church in Judea to accept the few Gentiles who believed. As the gospel spread beyond the Jewish homeland, tensions emerged. More and more Gentiles came to Christ until the church outside Palestine was predominantly Gentile, drawn from a population with customs that differed radically from Jewish customs. Soon a faction emerged that insisted that Gentile Christians should adopt the Law of Moses and follow Jewish customs.

The apostle Paul fought this movement, convinced that any who relied on keeping the Law as a means for living in vital relationship with God denied grace and misunderstood the implications of the gospel. The matter became so divisive that finally a council was held to settle the matter. Paul reported on God's work among the Gentiles, arguing against the position that the Gentile believers must be circumcised and keep the Law of Moses. Peter, now clearly grasping the significance of this issue, supported Paul's position. Peter argued strongly that since God "made no distinction between us and them, purifying their hearts by faith" that there was no reason to test God by "putting a yoke on the neck of the disciples which neither our fathers nor we were able to bear" (Acts 15:9,10). Salvation was and must remain a matter of "the grace of our Lord Jesus Christ" (15:11).

Paul, Peter, and James the brother of Jesus who chaired the council carried the day, and the council officially rejected any confusion of faith with works.

We know little from Scripture about Peter's later life. We have two letters written by Peter preserved in the New Testament. The letters are addressed to Jewish Christians scattered throughout the Roman Empire and the East. Yet, from the material we have in the Gospels and in Acts we can draw a rather accurate picture of Peter, the prince of the apostles, who truly was the leader among Jesus' disciples and later one of the most influential leaders of the early Christian church.

PETER: AN EXAMPLE FOR TODAY

Peter was a successful businessman and a natural leader. He was enthusiastic and impulsive, quick to speak and quick to act. While driven by the best of motives, Peter was not always wise in what he said and did. Yet, Peter was open to God and teachable. He was the acknowledged leader of the disciples and of the earliest church, and the man God chose to open the door of the gospel to Jews and Gentiles alike. We truly have much to learn from Simon Peter.

- Peter reminds us that men who are willing to step out and take risks have great value in God's kingdom. Men who are willing to put themselves on the line and who will lead by example are at a premium today as in the first century.

- Peter challenges those who come to Christ later in life. Peter was mature and a successful businessman when called to follow Jesus. Many like Peter today seek second careers in ministry.

- Peter encourages us not to expect too much from our leaders. Peter was a man with flaws as great as his strengths. Yet his commitment to Christ shines through. Our leaders, too, will be imperfect. We need to encourage them, not judge them or gossip about their flaws.

- Peter alerts us to the dangers of too much self-confidence. None of us is immune to temptations or to failure. None of us is so strong that we can follow Jesus in our own strength.

- Peter encourages us to believe in growth and change. Peter made mistakes, but he increasingly displayed a teachable spirit and a desire better to carry out God's will. And Peter matured! In this, Peter is an encouragement to all.

• Peter focuses our attention on trust in Christ and empowerment by His Spirit as the secret of spiritual accomplishment. Peter's natural gifts were great, but they were not enough. When Peter kept his eyes on Christ and relied on the Spirit, He did his greatest work for the Lord.

PAUL
Scripture References
Acts 9; 13—28; Paul's epistles

Date:	About A.D. 1–67
Name:	Paul [PAWL, "little"]
Greatest Accomplishment:	Paul led the first-century expansion of the church and was its greatest theologian and minister.

To some, the apostle Paul seems the corrupter of Christianity, a man who took the "simple" religion of Jesus and made it something entirely different. To the student of Scripture, however, the apostle Paul is history's premier theologian and missionary, the man God chose to reveal the deepest significance of the new covenant instituted in Christ's death, and the nature of the life to be lived "in Christ." As the writer of thirteen of the twenty-one New Testament letters, Paul is undoubtedly the most influential Christian of our era.

PAUL'S LIFE AND TIMES

Paul, the zealous *(Acts 9:1–2)*. The apostle Paul was a Jew from the city of Tarsus. As a young man, he came to Jerusalem to study under Gamaliel (Acts 22:3), perhaps the most notable of first-century sages. Paul, known then as Saul, was totally committed to the Law as interpreted and understood by the rabbis, and was a member of the sect of the Pharisees. When Stephen, the bold Christian evangelist, was stoned to death in Jerusalem by a mob, Saul stood watch over the cloaks of the killers, fully supporting their action (Acts 7:58). Later, when official persecution developed, Saul took a leading role in rounding up Jesus' followers. To this young persecutor, the followers of Christ were heretics, and their faith an affront to the God he served, an aberration that must be purged from Judaism.

Saul's conversion *(Acts 9:3–30)*. Saul was on his way to Damascus with a commission from the high priest charging him to return Christian Jews to Jerusalem when his conversion took place. This event was so significant that the story is repeated three times in the New Testament (Acts 9; 22; 26).

SAUL'S COMMISSION

In the Roman Empire each national and ethnic group was granted the privilege of living under its own laws. This meant that the Sanhedrin in Jerusalem had authority over Jews living anywhere in the Roman Empire insofar as Jewish law was concerned. Pairs of rabbis from Jerusalem typically traveled to Jewish communities in foreign lands to adjudicate difficult cases according to Mosaic and rabbinic law. Saul's commission, which allowed him to capture Jews who followed Christ and return them to Jerusalem, was an extension of this legal principle.

As the party traveled, Saul was blinded by a flash of brilliant light and heard the voice of Jesus speaking to him from heaven.

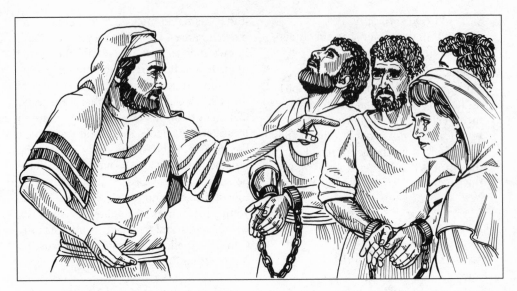

Before his conversion, Saul—later the apostle Paul—showed his zeal for God by binding Christians and bringing them before the court at Jerusalem.

Saul was totally stunned, and realized that those he had been persecuting were right: Jesus *was* the Son of God!

Saul, still blind, was led to a house in Damascus. The Lord sent a Christian named Ananias, who prayed for Saul and restored his sight. Immediately, Saul became as bold and zealous in preaching Christ as he had been in persecuting Christians! Saul's aggressive preaching soon aroused so much hostility that the believers in Damascus were able to save his life only by lowering him over the wall of the city in a basket. Apparently, angry Jews lay in wait at every exit to the city, eager to kill Saul.

Saul returned to Jerusalem, where at first the believers were fearful of approaching him. Although they had heard of Saul's conversion, they feared he had simply gone "undercover" to identify them. Even when the Christian community accepted Saul, he was a problem for them. Saul remained totally zealous and bold. He so outspokenly preached Christ that he further aroused hostility in Jerusalem too. Finally, Paul had stirred up such opposition that a delegation of Christians took Saul to Caesarea and put

him on a boat for Tarsus. He was simply too contentious to keep around!

Saul's maturing (Gal. 1:17). Later, in reference to Saul's years after leaving Jerusalem, he spoke of spending his time in Arabia. Whether the apostle was speaking literally or using "Arabia" as symbolic of a desert experience, the years Saul spent isolated from the church in Jerusalem were critical ones. It was during these years that Paul, immersing himself in the Old Testament and open to the teaching of the Holy Spirit, began to work out the overwhelming significance of Christ's death and resurrection. Later, Paul asserted that the gospel he proclaimed, while the same gospel as that preached by Peter and the other apostles, he had "neither received it from man, nor was I taught it, but it came through the revelation of Jesus Christ" (Gal. 1:12).

Some years later, Barnabas, who had befriended Saul in Jerusalem and was then a leader of a predominantly Gentile church in Antioch, looked for Saul and recruited him to join the Antioch leadership team.

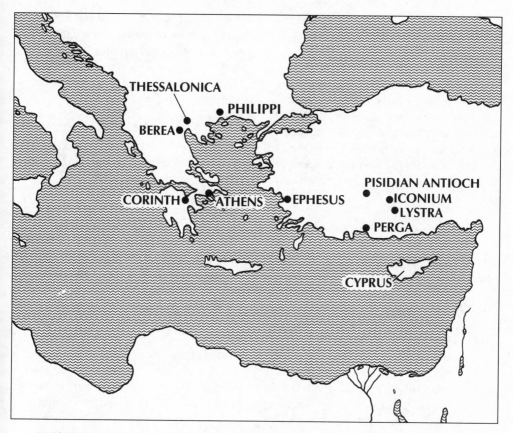

THESSALONICA
PHILIPPI
BEREA
PISIDIAN ANTIOCH
CORINTH   ATHENS   EPHESUS   ICONIUM
LYSTRA
PERGA
CYPRUS

Paul founded churches in each of these New Testament cities, and quite probably in Spain as well.

Paul's missionary ministry (*Acts 13—28*). Around AD. 46, approximately a decade after his conversion, Saul set out with Barnabas to carry the gospel to the major cities of the Roman Empire. For the rest of his life, Saul, soon to be known by his Roman name of Paul, would plant churches throughout Asia Minor and Europe.

Paul developed a simple but effective missions strategy. He would go to one of the major population centers located along established travel routes. He would first go to the Jewish synagogue and present Christ as the Messiah. Not only Jews would hear his message, but also many Gentile "God fearers" who had been attracted to Judaism's high vision of God and of morality and who attended synagogue services heard him. From this group of listeners, a core of converts would be won. At times, this core represented a mixture of Jew and Gentile, but all too often it was predominantly Gentile. Paul would then instruct this core of believers in the faith, and, after a time, move on to another city where he would repeat the process.

Paul kept in touch with the congregations he founded. His associates would often visit the young churches, and Paul wrote letters of instruction to the churches. When possible Paul would return to visit the churches himself, and give official sanction to the leaders who emerged in these congregations. Paul himself, however, kept on the move, leaving the task of evangelizing the districts beyond central cities to the Christians there.

This process is beautifully reflected in words Paul wrote to the Christians at Thessalonica:

And you became followers of us and of the Lord, having received the word in much affliction, with joy of the Holy Spirit, so that you became examples to all in Macedonia and Achaia who believe. For from you the word of the Lord has sounded forth, not only in Macedonia and Achaia, but also in every place (1 Thess. 1:6–8).

In Paul, God had chosen not only a man who was totally committed to sharing the gospel, but a man who was a true innovator and missions strategist.

Paul, the theologian (the Epistles). Paul, while a profound theologian. was essentially a *practical* theologian. He wrote his letters to real men and women struggling with real-life issues. Thus, Paul's challenge was to explain the great truths about God and His relationship to humankind in such a way that their implications for daily life would be clearly understood.

In Romans, which has rightly been called the greatest theological treatise of all times, Paul took the theme of righteousness. He pointed out that human beings are sinners who lack righteousness, but that God has chosen to give human beings righteousness as a gift, made possible by Jesus Christ in His death on Calvary. Cloaked in a righteousness that God provides, human beings now have peace with God. But the righteousness God provides is no mere legal fiction. It has dramatic and life-changing potential. For God gives believers the Holy Spirit who works within to enable Christians to live righteous lives here and now. Paul explains how this is possible, and in the last chapters of his letter describes how a people of God infused with the righteousness of God will live in society and in the faith community.

In each of his letters, Paul taught truths that shape lives—realities about knowing and walking with God that put every relationship in fresh, transforming perspective. As a theologian and a pastor Paul was without peer.

EXPLORING PAUL'S RELATIONSHIPS

Paul was a complex individual. His complexities are clearly seen in the various relationships he maintained.

Paul's relationship with young Christians (1 Thess. 2; 2 Cor.). In his first letter to the Thessalonians, Paul recalls the time he spent with his converts and speaks of the relationship he had with these new Christians.

But we were gentle among you, just as a nursing mother cherishes her own children. So, affectionately longing for you, we were well pleased to impart to you not only the gospel of God, but also our own lives, because you had become dear to us. For you remember, brethren, our labor and toil; for laboring night and day, that we might not be a burden to any of you, we preached to you the gospel of God. You are witnesses, and God also, how devoutly and justly and blamelessly we behaved ourselves among you who believe; as you know how we exhorted, and comforted, and charged every one of you, as a father does his own children (1 Thess. 2:7–11).

Clearly the best way to describe Paul's relationship with young Christians is "nurturing." Taking the role of both mother and father, the apostle totally invested himself and his love in new believers.

The New Testament book that best displays this investment throughout is 2 Corinthians. There we see Paul's willingness to be open and sharing (chap. 1), his heartbreak over misunderstandings (chap. 2), his commitment despite disappointments (chap. 4), and his deeply rooted confidence that God will keep working in the believers' lives until they mature in righteousness (chap. 5).

While some have miscast the great apostle as a legalistic and harsh man, his own words, written to those who know him well and could not be deceived, reveal a man with a great and tender heart. He loved and kept on loving, nurtured and kept on nurturing, however his loved ones might respond to him.

Paul's relationship with his coworkers. Despite the fact that we tend to view Paul as a towering individual, he was in the best sense of the phrase a "team player." From his first missionary journey through the end of his life, Paul traveled with a team of believers. While Paul was the acknowledged leader, he was never without companions whom he valued as fellow-workers and partners in ministry.

Paul as a team player (Acts 13; Rom. 16). The team that set out from Antioch on the first missionary journey (Acts 13) was initially led by Barnabas, since his name was mentioned first (Acts 13:2). Soon, however, Paul's great gifts made him the accepted leader of the team (13:46), which included Barnabas and several others. Along the way, Paul was quick to recruit others to travel with him, notably Timothy (Acts 16:1) and Luke, who wrote Acts as well as the Gospel that bears his name.

What is particularly notable is that as new churches were planted, Paul drew others into his inner circle to share his ministry. Romans 16, in which Paul mentioned a number of individuals by name, makes it clear that Paul saw both men and women as "fellow workers in Christ Jesus" (Rom. 16:3).

Paul as a demanding leader (Acts 15:36–41). While Paul was a nurturing individual, he was also a demanding leader. Paul never spared himself in his commitment to reach, win, and equip men and women for Christ. Paul had little sympathy with others who were unwilling to make a similar commitment. This trait was illustrated when

Barnabas wished to bring John Mark along on their second missionary journey. Paul refused. John Mark had abandoned them on their first missionary venture, and Paul had no room on his team for a quitter. The disagreement between the two long-time friends and teammates was so great that Paul and Barnabas parted, with Barnabas taking John Mark along on a missionary journey of his own.

History proved Barnabas wiser than Paul. Years later, Paul wrote from prison asking that Mark be sent to him, "for he is useful to me for ministry" (2 Tim. 4:11).

Paul's relationship with those he mentored *(Acts 16:1; 1, 2 Timothy).* While Paul had little sympathy with quitters, he had infinite patience with those who were willing to keep trying. Paul had recruited Timothy in Lystra on his second missionary journey and invested years in training Timothy to be among the next generation of church leaders. Paul's mentoring style followed a classic pattern: Timothy spent years traveling with Paul and learning from him; Timothy was then given assignments to carry out on his own under Paul's tutelage. In time and after Paul's death, Timothy would himself follow the same pattern with others, as described in 2 Timothy 2:2: "The things that you have heard from me among many witnesses, commit these to faithful men who will be able to teach others also."

Paul's two letters to Timothy reflected Paul's deep affection for his "beloved son" (2 Tim. 1:2) whom he urged to "be watchful in all things, endure afflictions, do the work of an evangelist, fulfill your ministry" (2 Tim. 4:5). While the letters suggest that Timothy was far from being bold and in some instances had been ineffective, Timothy was a committed Christian. Paul was willing to invest whatever it took to shape Timothy into the leader Paul was sure he could become.

Paul's relationship with the Roman Empire *(Acts 16; 22—28; Rom. 13).* The apostle Paul was a complex individual. Although a Jew and a Pharisee, Paul was also thoroughly trained in secular philosophy and was a Roman citizen.

In the first century, Roman citizenship was not common outside of Italy. Wherever the various peoples in the empire might travel, they retained citizenship in their homeland. They were subject to its laws and its courts. Roman citizens were subject to Roman laws and might bring civil and criminal cases to Roman courts. Roman citizens also enjoyed many other privileges. For instance, Roman citizens could not be examined by torture or condemned without trial.

In Paul's travels, he never hesitated to identify himself as a Roman citizen or to claim the rights of a citizen when brought before Roman authorities. When the Jews accused Paul in the court of the Roman governor of Judea, Paul exercised his right as a citizen and appealed to the emperor's court in Rome to avoid being taken back to Jerusalem, where Paul knew he would be assassinated (Acts 28:17–19).

While Paul never hesitated to assert his rights as a Roman citizen, he also fully accepted a citizen's responsibilities. Paul taught and urged Christians to be good citizens, "subject to the governing authorities" (Rom. 13:1). Paul saw government officials as God's servants who had been placed in office to maintain an orderly society. Paul was deeply concerned that Christians live as good citizens, for they were to represent Christ and carry His message to all. Paul agreed wholeheartedly with Peter, who also urged submission to "every ordinance of man for the Lord's sake," that through the Christian's honorable conduct "they may, by your good works which they observe, glorify God in the day of visitation" (1 Peter 2:12).

During most of Paul's lifetime, the Roman government viewed Christianity as a sect of Judaism, and thus as a licit (approved) religion. Later, Christians would come under persecution for no other reason than their commitment to Jesus Christ. Even then, for conscience sake, most Christians sought to live as good citizens under oppressive regimes. Like Christ Himself, they chose to suffer for doing right rather than for doing wrong.

Paul's relationship with God. Before his conversion to Christ, Paul, then known as Saul, was both zealous and dedicated. He lived as a Pharisee, dedicated to following the most minute commandments as interpreted and defined by the rabbis. Paul, intensely hostile to all who seemed to him to violate God's will, was undoubtedly a fiercely religious individual.

The totality of Paul's commitment (Phil. 3). When Paul became a Christian, all his zeal was poured into his commitment to Jesus Christ. His own words perhaps best convey the totality of his dedication.

If anyone else thinks he may have confidence in the flesh, I more so: circumcised the eighth day, of the stock of Israel, of the tribe of Benjamin, a Hebrew of the Hebrews; concerning the law, a Pharisee; concerning zeal, persecuting the church; concerning the righteousness which is in the law, blameless. But what things were gain to me, these I have counted loss for Christ. Yet indeed I also count all things loss for the excellence of the knowledge of Christ Jesus my Lord, for whom I have suffered the loss of all things, and count them as rubbish, that I may gain Christ and be found in Him, not having my own righteousness, which is from the law, but that which is through faith in Christ, the righteousness which is from God by faith; that I may know Him and the power of His resurrection, and the fellowship of His sufferings, being conformed to His death (Phil. 3:3–10).

The expression of Paul's commitment (1 Thess. 2:19). Earlier, we looked at Paul's loving, nurturing relationship with new converts. In his early life, Paul's expression of

Paul's life as a missionary was filled with hardship and danger, as in the three shipwrecks he experienced.

commitment to God was a rigorous attention to keeping the law as interpreted and expanded by generations of rabbis. After his conversion, Paul changed. While we might correctly say that his commitment was expressed in preaching the gospel, it is more accurate to say that Paul suddenly began to care about *people*. Paul realized that God loves all people. The Holy Spirit quickened this same love in Paul's heart. Paul could write early in his missionary ministry: "What is our hope, or joy, or crown of rejoicing? Is it not even you in the presence of our Lord Jesus Christ as His coming?" (1 Thess. 2:19).

This passion for seeing people saved and growing in Christ is beautifully expressed in prayers recorded in Paul's letters. One of the most beautiful is found in Ephesians 3:16–19, and expresses the yearning of the great apostle for his converts. Paul prayed:

that He would grant you, according to the riches of His glory, to be strengthened with might through His Spirit in the inner man, that Christ may dwell in your hearts through faith; that you, being rooted and grounded in love, may be able to comprehend with all the saints what is the width and length and depth and height; to know the love of Christ which passes knowledge; that you may be filled with all the fullness of God.

The cost of Paul's commitment (2 Cor. 10). In this passage, Paul compares himself to some who had come to Corinth claiming to be apostles and contradicting his teaching. Even though Paul was the founder of the church and had lived among the Corinthians for some three years, a number of believers were deceived by the intruders who made much of their supposed credentials. In his response, Paul briefly revealed how foolish the Corinthians had been. In the process Paul mentioned some of his own credentials.

Are they ministers of Christ?—I speak as a fool—I am more: in labors more abundant, in stripes above measure, in prisons more frequently, in deaths often. From the Jews five times I received forty stripes minus one. Three times I was beaten with rods; once I was stoned; three times I was shipwrecked; a night and a day I have been in the deep; in journeys often, in perils of waters, in perils of robbers, in perils of my own countrymen, in perils of the Gentiles, in perils in the city, in perils in the wilderness, in perils in the sea, in perils among false brethren; in weariness and toil, in sleeplessness often, in hunger and thirst, in fastings often, in cold and nakedness; besides the other things, what comes upon me daily: my deep concern for all the churches (2 Cor. 11:23–28).

Paul was not so foolish as to think that such things are true credentials of an apostle (2 Cor. 3:1–3). But the terrible personal cost Paul had gladly paid to share the gospel and serve God's people gives unmistakable witness to the sincerity and depth of Paul's commitment.

PAUL: AN EXAMPLE FOR TODAY

Paul was a truly unique man. He possessed great intellectual gifts and an unusually strong will. Paul also was fully dedicated to God even before his conversion to Christ. The biblical text suggests that in his first years as a Christian he also possessed an abrasive personality. Yet as God worked in Paul's life, the great apostle grew into an individual motivated by a passionate love both for Christ and for people. It is most unusual to find a person with both absolute strength of character and a capacity for tenderness and nurturing. In a significant sense, Paul may be viewed as a primary example of a "real man."

- Paul shows us that a real man has a commitment to God that gives direction and focus to his life.

- Paul shows us that a real man will face opposition with courage, taking stands for what is right no matter how powerful the opposition.

- Paul shows us that a real man can be tender and nurturing. Too often, we view nurture as a woman's role, and picture real men as emotionally detached. Paul reveals how wrong this impression is.

- Paul shows us that a real man is willing to pay a price to serve God and others—even when that price is personal suffering and pain.

- Paul shows us that a real man has deep convictions and is committed to live by them. A real man will not compromise his convictions but will stand up for them when he is convinced they are right.

- Paul shows us that real men will invest themselves in others, building a mentoring relationship with those younger than themselves.

- Paul shows us that a real man is a team person, not a rugged individualist. A real man links his energies with others who have similar goals, builds a close relationship with them, and works together with them.

- Paul shows us that a real man is a people person, committed to the task but ever sensitive to the concerns of others, ever encouraging to draw the best from them.

- Paul shows us that a real man models what God wants all His people to become. Paul had lived the faith, becoming an example that others gladly followed.

MEN WHO KNEW JESUS

NOTABLES AMONG THE TWELVE

We know the names of the twelve men Jesus chose to be His disciples, but we know very little about most of them. We know most about Peter, clearly one of the greatest men of the New Testament. While James the brother of John is mentioned frequently, it is invariably in association with his brother John. And even though there are traditions that tell of the ministries of the disciples after Jesus' resurrection, these traditions are uncertain at best. We know that Judas, the traitor, committed suicide after he betrayed Jesus. We know that the apostle James was executed by Herod (Acts 12:1, 2) a few years after Jesus' resurrection. We know that John lived well into his nineties, ministered in Asia Minor, and wrote five of our New Testament books. We know that Peter traveled and ministered for many years until his execution in Rome in the mid- to late-60s. A relatively strong tradition tells us that Thomas traveled to India and established a church there that has continued into the twenty-first century. Other than that, most of Jesus' Twelve remain shadowy fig-

ures, both in the Gospels and in church history. We can, however, learn much from the several notables among the disciples.

JOHN
Scripture references:
The Gospels; 1, 2, 3 John;
Revelation

Date:	*About A.D. 5–97*
Name:	*John [JAHN; "Yahweh is gracious"]*
Greatest Accomplishment:	*John was an intimate of Jesus. He lived the longest of the apostles and wrote five New Testament books.*

JOHN'S LIFE AND TIMES

John with his brother James and their father Zebedee was a partner in Peter's fishing cooperative. Like Peter he lived in Capernaum, the capital of the district of Galilee.

John's familiarity with key people in Jerusalem has led many scholars to presume that John not only fished, but also handled the marketing of fish in the Judean capital. In New Testament times, fish from Galilee were dried or salted and transported to many cities. The fish were a primary source of protein in a land where meat was eaten only on special occasions.

John was with the others who came to listen to John the Baptist and who met Jesus by the Jordan River. When the group of fishermen headed back to Capernaum, Jesus, who lived in nearby Nazareth, traveled with them. John witnessed Jesus' miracle of changing water into wine, and afterward Jesus stayed with the group for a time. Later, when John and the other fishermen disciples had come to know Him well, Jesus called John and his brother James to become His disciples.

For the next three years, John, like the others, traveled with Jesus and learned from Him. After Jesus' resurrection, tradition tells us that John settled in Ephesus in Asia Minor, and ministered to the churches of the region. Sometime during the reign of the Emperor Domitian (A.D. 81–96), John was exiled to the small island of Patmos where he received the vision recorded in the Book of Revelation.

EXPLORING JOHN'S RELATIONSHIPS

John's relationship with Jesus. John—along with Peter and James—was a member of Jesus' inner circle of three disciples. Christ often took these three with Him while the other nine stayed behind (Mark 5:37; 9:2; Luke 8:51). Most scholars agree that John's reference to a disciple "whom Jesus loved" in John 13:23 is biographical. Of the twelve, the deepest bond of affection seemed to exist between Christ and John, who made it a point to stay close to Him.

Yet, as we trace specific references to John through the Gospels, we're struck with the fact that John himself does not appear particularly lovable. Three incidents reported in the Gospels illustrate.

John was protective of his privileges (Mark 9:38–41). One day John remarked to Jesus, "Teacher, we saw someone who does not follow us casting out demons in Your name, and we forbade him because he does not follow us." Jesus gently rebuked John, "Do not forbid him."

John might have had a valid reason to raise this issue, for Jewish exorcists often used names in formulas supposed to control supernatural powers, a practice forbidden in God's Law. But John had quite a different reason. "We forbade him *because he does not follow us!*" John was a member of a select group, and he was not about to see the uniqueness of his position eroded by others using Jesus' name who were not followers of His party.

Party spirit has often distorted Christianity as individuals have claimed a corner on God's truth for their group. John's complaint, "he does not follow us," is far from the spirit of Jesus.

John was easily angered (Luke 9:51–56). On another occasion Jesus led His friends along the short route between Galilee and Judea. This route lay through Samaria, and most pious Jews would take the longer route, crossing the Jordan River to avoid Samaritan lands. A long history of hostility existed between the two races, and because Jesus' party was traveling toward Jerusalem, they were refused hospitality at a Samaritan village. This so infuriated John that he and James asked, "Lord, do You want us to command fire to come down from heaven and consume them, just as Elijah did?"

The question was in reality a disguised suggestion, for James and John knew they had no authority to command fire. But they were sure Jesus did. In effect, the two disciples let

Every famous picture of the Last Supper shows the apostle John leaning close to Jesus.

Jesus know they thought He should not stand for this kind of treatment from Samaritans. Those Samaritans deserved to be burned alive!

This incident earned James and John the nickname, Boanerges, "Sons of Thunder" (Mark 3:17). It also earned them Jesus' rebuke: "You do not know what manner of spirit you are of. For the Son of Man did not come to destroy men's lives but to save them."

John was motivated by selfish ambition (Mark 10:35–39). After spending nearly two years with Jesus, James and John approached Jesus with a request. (Matthew tells us that they first sent their mother to speak for them!) The request was, "Grant us that we may sit, one on Your right hand and the other on Your left, in Your glory." The two disciples were sure Jesus the Messiah would soon rule not only the Jewish homeland but also the world. In the imagery of the Middle East, those sitting to a ruler's right and left were the most powerful individuals in his kingdom!

The two didn't want much! They simply yearned for power and glory. If that meant they had to step on their companions to gain this end, so be it.

Naturally the other disciples were upset and angry when they heard what James and John had done (Mark 10:41). But the incident gave Jesus an opportunity to share a vital leadership principle. In Christ's kingdom, "whoever desires to become great among you shall be your servant, and whoever of you desires to be first shall be the slave of all" (Mark 10:43, 44). Once again John and his brother James had displayed a spirit totally out of harmony with the spirit of Christ.

John's later relationship with believers. John's attitudes displayed in the synoptic Gospels provide a striking background for one feature of John's own Gospel and his three letters. In these writings the apostle again and again emphasizes love.

John is the one who wrote, "God so loved the world that He gave His only begotten Son, that whoever believes in Him should not perish but have everlasting life" (John 3:16). John also urged Christians to love one another, saying: "We know that we have passed from death to life, because we love the brethren. He who does not love his brother abides in death" (1 John 3:14).

John, the protective, the angry, the selfish, became the apostle of love who not only taught love but also lived it for some sixty years after Christ's resurrection!

JOHN'S GOSPEL

The Gospel of John was the last written of the four accounts of Christ's life. It is unique in that unlike the others it does not take a chronological approach. It is also unique in that it begins the story of Jesus before creation, when Christ existed as and with God as the Second Person of the Trinity.

John organized his material around seven miracles performed by Jesus, each of which was associated with an extended dialog reporting Jesus' teaching and actions. An especially important feature of John's Gospel is John's report of Jesus' teaching during the Last Supper (John 13–16) and his report of Christ's final prayer for His followers (John 17). The Last Supper discourse has been called the "seedbed" of the New Testament, for most of the major doctrines developed in the New Testament epistles can be found there.

John likely wrote his Gospel in the 80s with the intent of making it utterly clear that Jesus truly is God the Son. John also clearly intended to make plain the basic issues in life that every person must resolve. In this book, he clearly compared and contrasted life/death, light/darkness, belief/unbelief, truth/falsehood, and love/hate.

JOHN: AN EXAMPLE FOR TODAY

John reminds us of the transforming power of a personal relationship with Jesus.

During John's years as a disciple he frequently displayed his all-too-human flaws. Yet, Christ loved John for who he was and for the person he was to become. Truly, John was transformed, for in place of an ambitious and defensive young man, a caring, selfless individual emerged. How much we have to learn, not simply from John, but from what a personal relationship with Jesus did for him.

- John's transformation reminds us that Christians are to be a "before and after" people. Our relationship with Christ is to make a difference not simply in our beliefs but in our attitudes and our character as well.

- John's transformation encourages us to set aside our own selfish ambition and realize that Christ calls us to serve rather than be served.

- John's transformation shows us that God is willing to invest time and effort in us. We do not come to Christ fully equipped with Christ-like attitudes and values. We are often riddled with sinful thoughts and desires. But the God who made John into a truly godly man is also at work in us, and He will work His wonders in us as He did in John.

MATTHEW
Scripture references:
Matthew 9:9; 10:3; Mark 2:14;
Luke 5:27–29

Date:	*About* A.D. *5—?*
Name:	*Matthew [MATH-you; "gift of God"]*
Greatest Accomplishment:	*He authored the Gospel of Matthew.*

MATTHEW'S LIFE AND TIMES

We know little about Matthew other than that before he was invited to become a disciple, Matthew collected taxes. In New Testament times, tax collectors were among the outcasts of society. They worked with an oppressive government and often extorted more than was due to line their own pockets. Matthew, who is also called Levi, was among this outcast group.

Because respectable members of society, and especially the religious, did not associate with tax collectors, Matthew had an unusual circle of friends. The New Testament tells us that after Matthew left his office to follow Jesus, Christ ate at his home and was joined there by many "tax collectors and sinners" (Matt. 9:9–10). That Jesus would share a meal with such folk scandalized the Pharisees, who were careful never to risk pollution by associating with any "unclean" person or thing.

Matthew reported the Pharisees' criticism, and He also reported Jesus' reply. "Those who are well have no need of a physician, but those who are sick" (Matt. 9:12; cf. the accounts in Mark 2:13–17; Luke 5:27–29).

Even the poorest farmer bringing produce to market was taxed by men like Matthew.

Matthew's answers are, first, that Jesus did not set up the promised kingdom because God's people rejected and killed their Messiah (Matt. 16). This too should have been understood from the Old Testament prophets. Isaiah and others indicated that the Messiah would suffer and die for sin (Isa. 53). Second, Matthew indicates that God will yet set up the kingdom envisioned by the prophets, but not until Jesus returns (Matt. 24; 25). The Suffering Servant and the triumphant Ruler envisioned by the prophets are one and the same Person. What the Old Testament prophets did not know was simply that the Messiah's death and His rule would be separated by an unspecified period of time.

In harmonizing these divergent themes found in the Old Testament, Matthew helped Jews steeped in the Old Testament see Jesus in a new light. They could accept Him in His first-coming mission as Savior

MATTHEW'S GOSPEL

Matthew's Gospel is the most Jewish of the four portraits of Jesus found in our New Testament. Matthew frequently quotes or alludes to the Old Testament to demonstrate that Jesus fulfilled prophecies about the Messiah.

Matthew carefully deals with questions that would concern any Jew who was told that Jesus Christ is the Messiah: If Jesus is the Messiah, why didn't He set up the kingdom promised in the Old Testament? If Jesus is the Messiah, what happened to the promised kingdom?

without stumbling over His failure to set up an earthly kingdom.

MATTHEW: AN EXAMPLE FOR TODAY

Each of the synoptic Gospels tells the story of Matthew's call, the feast Matthew gave afterward to introduce Jesus to his "sinner" friends, and the reaction of the Pharisees. Clearly, important lessons are imbedded in a story that is repeated three times in the New Testament.

- Matthew is referred to as "Matthew, the tax collector" even when listed with the other disciples (Matt. 10:3). He reminds us that even the outcasts of society have a place in Christ's kingdom and may well have a significant place!

- Matthew's eagerness to expose his friends to Jesus challenges us to resist an enclave mentality. When our only friends are fellow-Christians, it is difficult to see how we can penetrate society with the gospel.

- Jesus' choice of Matthew reminds us never to assume that any person, whatever his history, is not a candidate for salvation. Jesus was comfortable in the company of sinners because He truly cared for them. When we show Jesus' love, even sinners will be comfortable with us.

THOMAS
Scripture references:
John 11:16; 14:5; 20:24–29

Date:	About A.D. 5—?
Name:	Thomas [TAHM-uhs; "twin"]

Greatest Accomplishment:	*Thomas was a disciple, then apostle, of Christ.*

THOMAS'S LIFE AND TIMES

Thomas's name appears on the several lists of disciples found in the Gospels, often with the added phrase, "the twin." However, only John's Gospel reports incidents in which Thomas is an actor.

***Thomas's loyalty** (John 11:16)*. Jesus had left Jerusalem because the growing hostility of the religious leaders placed him in deadly peril. While Jesus was away, a close friend, Lazarus, became seriously ill. His sisters, Mary and Martha, immediately sent for Jesus. When Jesus received the message He waited several days. Then Jesus announced He was returning to Bethany, which lay just outside of Jerusalem. The disciples were reluctant to return, for the danger to Christ was real. Thomas "said to his fellow disciples, 'Let us also go, that we may die with Him.' "

Jesus had become so significant to Thomas that he was unwilling to live if Christ were killed.

***Thomas's uncertainty** (John 14:5)*. The second incident featuring Thomas took place during the Last Supper. Jesus was explaining why it was to His disciple's benefit for Him to leave, and said, "Where I go you know, and the way you know" (John 14:4). This saying puzzled all of the disciples, but Thomas spoke up and said, "Lord, we do not know where You are going, and how can we know the way?" Christ's response is one of the most significant of His sayings recorded in the New Testament: "I am the way, the truth, and the life. No one comes to the Father except through me" (John 14:6).

Thomas and the others did know, for the key to understanding heaven is not that it is a location, but a relationship. Christ was going to be with the Father, and knowing Christ is our passport to where He is.

Thomas's expression of doubt (John 20:24–29). The first time after His resurrection that Jesus showed Himself to His disciples, Thomas was absent. When the others told Thomas that they had been with Christ, Thomas announced: "Unless I see in His hands the print of the nails . . . I will not believe."

Remembering Thomas's readiness to die with Jesus rather than be without Him, we can perhaps understand. Thomas's life had been turned upside down by Jesus' death. Hope that Jesus was alive was simply too painful to entertain. Hope might be dashed, and the disappointment would be too great to bear.

Eight days later, Jesus came to His disciples again. This time, Thomas was present! When Jesus invited Thomas to explore the wounds in His hand and side, Thomas simply fell to the floor and said, "My Lord and my God!"

There is an unhealthy skepticism that refuses to believe, and there is an eager skepticism that wants desperately to believe but is afraid to hope. It was this skepticism that possessed Thomas. At the first sight of his Lord, the skepticism disappeared.

THOMAS: AN EXAMPLE FOR TODAY

Thomas, although briefly portrayed in the New Testament, comes across as a person with qualities we would do well to emulate.

- Thomas exemplifies both love and loyalty. He was willing to go with Christ to Jerusalem because he could not face the prospect of life without Him. Christ needs this kind of follower today, too.

- Thomas exemplifies an inquiring spirit. When puzzled by Christ's reference to "the way," Thomas spoke up with his question. Today truly honest Christians question matters of faith, not because they doubt, but because they yearn to know what God's Word means.

- Thomas exemplifies the right kind of skepticism. Thomas wanted what the disciples reported to be true, but at the same time he was afraid of further disappointment. As soon as Thomas saw Jesus, his doubts dissolved and he acknowledged Christ as Lord and God. When we have doubts, we need to remain open to belief so that when Christ's Spirit speaks to us we will be as ready as Thomas to respond with faith.

JUDAS
Scripture references:
Matthew 10:4; 26; 27; Mark 14;
Luke 22; John 13; 18

Date:	*About* A.D. *1–33*
Name:	*Judas [JOO-duhs; "praise"]*
Greatest	
Accomplishment:	*Judas betrayed Christ.*

JUDAS'S LIFE AND TIMES

Our knowledge of Judas is limited to the account in each of the Gospels of his terrible act of betrayal and references to his attachment to money. When a woman once poured expensive ointment on Jesus, Judas objected. John reported that Judas complained, "Why was this fragrant oil not sold for three hundred denarii and given to the poor?" And then John added, "Not that he cared for the poor, but because he was a thief, and had the money box; and he used to take what was put in it" (John 12:1–6).

Only after Jesus was condemned did Judas show any remorse. He threw the money the high priests paid him on the floor.

It was entirely in character for Judas later to approach the high priests and conspire to deliver Christ to them for money.

Each of the Gospels relates what happened, although John adds poignant detail. While the disciples shared their last meal with Jesus, Christ predicted one of them would betray Him. Each of the disciples voiced the question, "Is it I?" Yet when Jesus offered Judas a choice morsel from their serving dish, and told him to do what he intended to do quickly, the others did not realize the significance of Christ's act.

Jesus showed that He knew what Judas planned. Yet, in the offering of a choice morsel, a sign in that culture of special favor, Jesus was giving Judas a last opportunity to repent. If only Judas would repent he was not yet lost. But Judas would not change his mind and lose the thirty pieces of silver for which he had bargained, for Satan now had a firm grip on Judas's heart and mind.

Later that night, Judas led a mob that included temple guards and soldiers to Gethsemane, a favorite spot of Jesus', and Christ was taken away.

Matthew added a vital piece of information. After Christ was sentenced to death, Judas, "seeing that He had been condemned, was remorseful and brought back the thirty pieces of silver to the chief priests and elders, saying 'I have sinned by betraying innocent blood.' " The chief priests scornfully sent Judas away. Judas left, and hanged himself (Matt. 27:1–50). In the act of hanging, the rope broke and Judas's body fell, tearing open his belly (Acts 1:18).

JUDAS: AN EXAMPLE FOR TODAY

Judas's story, terrible as it is, contains lessons for us.

- Judas illustrates that mere association does not make anyone a believer or a godly person. For all those who have gone to church all their lives, the fact that Judas was an intimate of Jesus Himself carries a definite warning. Not association with—but commitment to—Jesus Christ makes the difference.

- Judas reminds us of Paul's warning that a love of money is a root of all kinds of evil (1 Tim. 6:10). Judas's love of money effectively blinded him to the significance of Jesus' words and acts. Those whose consuming interest is money will be blind to what really counts in life.

- Judas warns us not to miss God-given opportunities to change our life's direction. If we persist in doing evil, a time will come when we will be too hardened to repent. When Judas finally realized the enormity of what he had done, it was too late.

- Judas teaches us not to rationalize wrong decisions. Judas's reaction after Christ was condemned suggests that he thought Christ would be able to overcome His enemies. What harm could there be in making a profit while giving Jesus the opportunity to show up the religious establishment once again? When Judas realized that Christ was to be executed, he was so filled with remorse he could no longer stand to live. Yet whatever its outcome, Judas's choice was history's most terrible betrayal. Let's never try to justify sinful choices by assuming that what we do won't make any difference anyway.

OTHER FRIENDS AND FOES OF JESUS

The twelve disciples were the closest to Jesus, but He came in contact with many other men who played significant roles in the Gospel stories. Several individuals and groups require special treatment.

JOHN THE BAPTIST
Scripture references:
Matthew 3; 11; Mark 1; 6;
Luke 1; 3; 7; John 1; 3

Date:	About 4 B.C.–A.D. *28*
Name:	John *[JAHN; "Yahweh is gracious"]*
Greatest Accomplishment:	*The last and greatest of the Old Testament prophets, John announced the arrival of the Messiah.*

JOHN'S LIFE AND TIMES

Jesus called John the last and greatest of the prophets (Matt. 11:11, 13). He was a relative of Christ's, born some three months before our Lord. In every way, his life was unusual.

John's birth was announced by an angel (Luke 1). The angel Gabriel announced the coming birth of a child to a priest named Zacharias and his wife, Elizabeth. The angel predicted that John would be filled with the Holy Spirit and that his ministry would "turn many of the children of Israel to the Lord their God" (Luke 1:16). The angel also stated that John would "go before Him [the Lord] in the spirit and power of Elijah" (Luke 1:17). This was most significant because the prophet Malachi had foretold that Elijah would return before God's anointed Savior appeared.

John had a prophetic ministry (John 1). As an adult, John lived in the wilderness, dressed in animal hides, and ate what he could scavenge from the land (Matt. 3:4). He then appeared near the river Jordan and began to preach. His ministry had two main themes: the promised Messiah was about to appear, and his listeners must repent and change their ways to be ready for Him.

John's preaching was blunt and confrontational. He respected neither the wealthy nor the religious leaders. One time, he noticed a number of Pharisees and Sadducees listening, and John boldly shouted, "Brood of vipers! Who warned you to flee from the wrath to come? Therefore bear fruit worthy of repentance, and do not think to yourselves, 'We have Abraham as our father' " (Matt. 3:8–9).

While the religious people scoffed at John, he was popular with common people. His call for moral reform combined with his promise that the Messiah would soon come was a compelling message.

John was the first to recognize Jesus (John 1). When Jesus came to be baptized, John objected (Matt. 3:13–15). John was baptizing sinners who needed to change their ways, and John knew his cousin to be a godly individual. But Jesus insisted on identifying Himself with John's message, and so John baptized our Lord. During the baptism, John saw the Holy Spirit descend on Jesus in the form of a dove and heard God's voice announcing Christ as His beloved Son (John 1:11). Later, John pointed out Jesus to his disciples as the Son of God (John 1:34), and a day later as "the Lamb of God" (John 1:36). John continued preaching, but within months the crowds that he once gathered began to follow Jesus. John's response when questioned by his followers was "He must increase, but I must decrease" (John 3:30). John's mission had been to prepare the way for Christ's appearance. Once Christ appeared, the spotlight rightly shifted to Him.

John later had doubts (Luke 7:18–24). Later, John himself began to doubt. He, like other pious Jews, expected God's Coming One to lead Israel back to glory and set up an eternal kingdom here on earth. So John sent disciples to ask Jesus if He were indeed the One. As John's messengers watched, Jesus healed many, and then quoted from Isaiah 35:5, 6, a passage that describes a unique healing ministry to be performed only by the

John the Baptist's bold preaching identified the sins of every segment of society and moved many to repent.

❖

Messiah. John might not understand God's present program, but Jesus' works of healing were proof positive that He was indeed the promised Messiah of the Old Testament.

John was executed by Herod (Matt. 14:3–10). Herod Antipas, a son of Herod the Great, had married his brother Philip's wife in violation of Old Testament Law. John preached openly against Herod, who then imprisoned John. Herod feared John and was unwilling to take further action against him, but his wife Herodias determined to see John dead. When Herod rashly promised Herodias's daughter a reward after she danced for his guests at a banquet, Herodias had the girl ask for the head of John the

Baptist. Herod reluctantly granted the request, fearful of how it would look if he went back on his promise. Later, when Jesus became more prominent, Herod imagined that Christ might be John the Baptist, come back from the dead to haunt him.

Jesus' evaluation of John (Luke 7:24–28). After John's messengers returned to report Christ's proof of His messiahship, Jesus called John "more than a prophet." Christ said that "among those born of women there is not a greater prophet than John the Baptist."

JOHN: AN EXAMPLE FOR TODAY

John was a man with a specific mission to fulfill, and he carried it out faithfully. It was his great privilege to fulfill the Elijah role, if not the Elijah prophecy, and prepare his generation for the appearance of Jesus Christ.

In John's mission and in his attitude believers can find several important lessons for today.

- John was called to a specific mission and dedicated his life to it. John clearly modeled the kind of commitment to ministry believers are to display, whatever our individual ministry may be.
- John was equipped by God's Spirit to carry out His mission. God never asks us to do anything for Him without providing the spiritual resources that will enable us to succeed.
- John was bold in confronting sin, whether the corrupt were great or small. We may not have the same prophetic calling John had, but we need His boldness in sharing Christ with our generation.
- John was ready to step aside when a greater than he arrived. From John, we

need to learn the grace of humility; we need to be as willing as John to give center stage to another God may have called to a ministry more significant than ours. Rivalry or jealousy has no room in the church of Jesus Christ.

NICODEMUS
Scripture references:
John 3; 7:50; 19:39

Date:	A.D. *30s*
Name:	*Nicodemus [NIK-uh-DEEM-uhs; "conqueror of the people"]*
Greatest Accomplishment:	*His visit to Jesus elicited the statement, "You must be born again."*

NICODEMUS'S LIFE AND TIMES

We know little of Nicodemus other than that he was a member of the Sanhedrin, the ruling body of Judaism and its highest court. Nicodemus would have been influential and wealthy and close to those who became Jesus' most vicious enemies. In view of the group of which he was a part, his relationship with Jesus was truly fascinating.

EXPLORING NICODEMUS'S RELATIONSHIP WITH JESUS

***Nicodemus's night visit to Jesus** (John 3).* Relatively early in Jesus' ministry, Nicodemus visited Christ privately and at night. Many have speculated that the visit took place at night because Nicodemus was unwilling to be seen with Christ for fear of his companions. However, he may well have come at night because Jesus was so surrounded by crowds during the day that no private meeting was possible.

Nicodemus began the meeting with a confession: "We know that You are a teacher come from God; for no one can do these signs that You do unless God is with him" (John 3:2). This admission is striking, for the "we" indicates that the religious leaders privately recognized that Christ spoke with divine authority, although they publicly tried to undermine His mission!

Christ quickly shifted the focus of the conversation to the issue of rebirth: a person must be "born again" even to see the kingdom of God. The saying either puzzled Nicodemus, or he attempted to dismiss it. Christ rebuked him. As a ruler of Israel, he must be familiar with Jeremiah's new covenant teaching and God's promise to give His people a new heart and character. Jesus had come into the world as a gift of God's love, "that whoever believes in Him should not perish but have everlasting life" (John 3:16).

John tells us nothing more of the interview or of Nicodemus's reaction. John does mention this ruler of the Jews two additional times in his Gospel.

Nicodemus took Jesus' part in a council meeting (John 7:50). As Jesus continued to preach and heal, people everywhere began to wonder if He were the Messiah. Jesus' impact on the people was so great that the Pharisees and chief priests sent officers to take him. But Jesus continued to speak in public, and the officers returned without Jesus, offering as their reason, "No man ever spoke like this Man!" (John 7:46). The Pharisees angrily responded, "Have any of the rulers or the Pharisees believed in Him?" They were certain that not one of their members would take Jesus' part.

Nicodemus, identified in the text as "one of them," timidly raised a legal question: "Does our law judge a man before it hears him and knows what he is doing?" (John 7:51). Nicodemus certainly did not confess that he had himself gone to hear Jesus to find out what he was doing! Nor did Nicodemus confess any belief in Christ. And, after the rebuke of his companions, Nicodemus remained silent.

Nicodemus provided spices for Jesus' burial (John 19:39). After the crucifixion, Nicodemus provided expensive spices with which to anoint Jesus' body. The hundred pounds of spices mentioned by John would have cost a fortune. Did Nicodemus act out of love for Christ, or was he trying to assuage his own feelings of guilt for remaining so long a secret adherent of Jesus?

In any case, Nicodemus's expensive gift would not have gone unnoticed. By his gift, Nicodemus took a stand with the crucified Messiah: a stand he may have believed was too late—at least until after resurrection morning.

NICODEMUS: AN EXAMPLE FOR TODAY

Nicodemus teaches us several important lessons.

- Nicodemus warns us that our choice of associates is important. Nicodemus was a member of a prestigious group, and his position was important to him. Even though he knew Jesus was a teacher sent by God, he was unwilling to follow Jesus openly for fear of his peers.

- Nicodemus's experience alerts us to an important warning sign. When any group of which we are a part refuses to do what group members themselves know is right, it's time to part company with that group! Our membership in it is not as important as the cost of moral compromise.

- Nicodemus reminds us that there may be many secret believers among our friends and coworkers. When we openly express our faith, we encourage such persons more boldly and freely to confess their faith as well.

- Nicodemus shows us that while late is better than never, early is best. During Jesus' life, the active hostility of Nicodemus's peers had silenced him, but regret caused Nicodemus to display his allegiance after Christ's death. What Nicodemus did was bold, but it would have been more to Nicodemus's credit if he had taken a stand while Jesus was still living.

TAX COLLECTORS AND SINNERS

When we consider men who were friends of Jesus, we need to remember that Jesus was especially close to ordinary persons and that He had great affection for "tax collectors and sinners." Most of the population despised tax collectors as collaborators with oppressive foreign or local governments. "Sinners" was a term broadly applied in New Testament times by the religious elite. It included such persons as prostitutes, but at times was applied to the mass of ordinary people who were not as rigorous in keeping the rulings of the rabbis.

Jesus, who attended parties given by the tax collectors Matthew and Zaccheaus for their friends (Matt. 9:10–13; Mark 2:15–17; Luke 5:30–32; 19:1–10), was strongly criticized for being a "friend of tax collectors and sinners" (Matt. 11:19; Luke 7:34). Yet, it was sinners Jesus had come to save, and those who knew they were sinners were most responsive to Christ. Jesus not only felt comfortable with them; they felt comfortable with Him.

What a challenge for us today to be as loving and accepting as Christ was so we can communicate love for sinners while in no way countenancing their sin.

THE PHARISEES

The Pharisees, along with the Sadducees, chief priests, and scribes (experts in rabbinic interpretation of Moses' Law) stand in stark contrast with publicans and sinners. These groups were the religious elite, noted for and proud of their piety. Rather than welcome Jesus and His message, these men were maliciously hostile to Christ. They viewed Jesus as a threat to their position and power, and they used every means possible to oppose Him. While not every Pharisee was like those portrayed in the Gospels, several incidents involving the religious elite reveal their flaws.

THE PHARISEES' ROLE IN SCRIPTURE

The hypocrisy of the Pharisees (Matt. 15:1–9). When some scribes and Pharisees challenged Jesus because His disciples did not follow a rabbinic tradition and wash their hands in the ritually prescribed manner before eating, Jesus struck back. He pointed to a rabbinic practice called corban, which permitted a person to dedicate possessions to the temple while retaining lifetime use. They used this "gift to God" as an excuse for not providing for parents! How hypocritical it was for men who used rabbinic traditions to contravene God's clear command to honor parents to criticize others for failure to keep a minor tradition!

Near the end of Christ's life on earth, He openly confronted the Pharisees and religious elite concerning their hypocrisy. We can read His condemnation of them in Matthew 23.

The heartlessness of the Pharisees (Matt. 12:9–14). When Jesus entered a synagogue where there was a man with a withered hand, the Pharisees used the cripple to try to get at Jesus. They asked Christ if it was legal to heal on the Sabbath. As the rabbis considered giving medical treatment to be work, doctoring was allowed on the Sabbath only if

Public prayer was one way in which many Pharisees sought to impress others with their piety.

a person's condition was life-threatening. But Jesus pointed out that the elite themselves called for helping a farm animal that fell into a pit on the Sabbath. How much more valuable a human being is to God than an animal!

Jesus then healed the cripple, an act that showed viewers how heartless the so-called shepherds of Israel really were. Shamed and angry, "the Pharisees went out and plotted against Him, how they might destroy him" (Matt. 12:14).

The Pharisee's deceptions (*Matt. 12:22–32*). When Jesus healed a demon-possessed man, the religious leaders were unable to deny the miracle. As such miracles were understood to be signs by which God authenticated a prophet, the Pharisees would logically be forced to assume that Jesus truly had been sent by God. To avoid admitting the obvi-

ous, the Pharisees began a whispering campaign against Jesus, charging him with being in league with the devil. Yes, Jesus had cast out demons, but that was because the devil had helped Him—not because Jesus acted in God's power and overcame the demons!

Christ not only exposed the ridiculous nature of this argument, but He also warned His accusers. To recognize supernatural acts performed by the Holy Spirit and then credit those acts to the devil was committing a sin that would not be forgiven. The religious leaders had demonstrated a hardness to revelation that nothing could overcome.

JOSEPHUS ON THE PHARISEES

Not all Pharisees were like the hypocrites Jesus condemned in Matthew 23. Some, like Nicodemus (see page 193), believed in Jesus, although secretly. Many were completely earnest men who honestly sought to honor God. The Pharisees themselves condemned the hypocrites among them. The Babylonian Talmud (tractate *Sotah, 22B*) denounced six types of hypocritical Pharisees, leveling many of the same criticisms Jesus leveled. However, the Pharisees of the Gospels were those who took the leadership in openly opposing Christ. Jesus identified and condemned their underlying motives.

The generally positive view held in the first century of the Pharisees is reflected in the historian Josephus, who wrote in his *Antiquities,* (18:12–15):

The Pharisees simplify their standard of living, making no concession to luxury. They follow the guidance of that which their doctrine has selected and transmitted as good, attaching the chief importance to the observance of those commandments that it has seen fit to dictate to them. They show respect and deference to their elders, nor do they rashly presume to contradict their proposals.

Though they postulate that everything is brought about by fate, still they do not deprive the human will of the pursuit of what is in man's power, since it was God's pleasure that there should be a fusion and that the will of man with his virtue and vice should be admitted to the council-chamber of fate. They believe that souls have power to survive death and there are rewards and punishments under the earth for those who have led lives of virtue or vice, eternal imprisonment is the lot of evil souls, while the good souls receive an easy passage to a new life.

Because of these views they are, as a matter of fact, extremely influential among the townsfolks; and all prayers and sacred rites of divine worship are performed according to their exposition. This is the great tribute that the inhabitants of the cities, by practicing the highest ideals both in their way of living and in their doctrine, have paid to the excellence of the Pharisees.

THE PHARISEES: AN EXAMPLE FOR TODAY

The Gospels record several other incidents that show Jesus' steadily deteriorating relationship with the religious elite. Christ threatened the foundations of their power, and they were determined to rid themselves of Him. They remain today tragic figures whose lives teach us what *not* to do if we would be true followers of Jesus.

- The Pharisees were dedicated to maintaining their position of influence and power. Influence and power can be as addictive as a love for money, and they are often chosen over commitment to the Lord.
- The Pharisees were so committed to their beliefs that they lost sight of God's love for people. To do what we

believe is right is important, but we must always remain aware that God's priority is people and that we need to reevaluate our convictions when those lead us to be unloving.

- The Pharisees possessed clear evidence that God had sent Jesus, but they chose to reject that evidence. They searched desperately for biblical texts and for arguments to use against Jesus and to support their already-formed decision to oppose Him. We need to remember that a closed mind is as great a barrier to truth as it is a defense against error.

CAIAPHAS
Scripture references:
Matthew 26:3, 57; Luke 3:2;
John 11:49; 18:13–28;
Acts 4:6

Date:	About 15 B.C.–A.D. 45
Name:	Caiaphas [KAY-uh-fuhs]
Greatest Accomplishment:	As high priest, he presided over Jesus' trial before the Sanhedrin, which condemned Christ to death.

CAIAPHAS'S LIFE AND TIMES

The Revell Bible Dictionary provides this brief overview of Caiaphas's character and his significance in the gospel story. Extrabiblical sources reveal much about this man.

Caiaphas was the son-in-law of Annas, who for many years dominated the priesthood and the Sadducean party. Extra-biblical sources establish this family's greed and its exploitation of the Jewish people. At that time, the high priesthood was no longer hereditary—the eldest son of Aaron's family—but was a Roman political appointment given because of graft. Christ's remarks about "thieves and robbers" who pretended to be shepherds (John 10:8–10) would have been clearly understood by his hearers—and by the family of Annas. This vindictive and selfish motive for Jesus' capture and trial before Caiaphas's court is reflected in a discussion held after Jesus raised Lazarus. The Jewish leaders expressed fear that, if Jesus sparked a popular uprising, the Romans might come and take away "both our place and our nation." Caiaphas then remarked how expedient it would be for just one man to die, rather than the whole nation (p. 184)!

CAIAPHAS: AN EXAMPLE FOR TODAY

Knowing something of Caiaphas's character and the family he represented helps us understand his hidden motives in seeking Jesus' death. The family of Annas controlled buying and selling in the temple, and the rate of exchange for purchasing the Tyran Duodrachma that they decreed was the only coinage acceptable as temple money. Their control of the temple generated vast wealth for the family— wealth extorted from the poor who came to the temple to worship God. No wonder Caiaphas was unwilling that anyone threaten his place, which was far more important to Caiaphas than the nation. Yet, we can learn from him.

- Caiaphas reminds us we are not to take individuals at face value, especially where money is involved. Christians tend to be trusting, especially of others who present themselves as believers. Religion has been used as a cloak by the greedy for centuries.
- Caiaphas warns us that evil men will go to any lengths to achieve their ends. The trial over which Caiaphas presided

was illegal, held in secret at night. Caiaphas feigned shock at Jesus' "blasphemy" when Christ stated that He was the Son of God. Evil men use religion and believers without concern for what God must think. You and I are to be too concerned with pleasing God either to have evil ends in mind or to use evil means.

PILATE
Scripture references:
Matthew 27; Mark 15;
Luke 13:1; 23; John 18; 19

Date:	Governor of Judea A.D. 26–36
Name:	Pontius Pilate [PON-shus Pi-luht; "javelin-carrier"]
Greatest Accomplishment:	He allowed himself to be pressured into ordering Jesus' crucifixion.

PILATE'S LIFE AND TIMES

Pilate served as prefect and later procurator of Judea. His position gave him command of the Roman military forces that occupied the Jewish homeland, the power to order the death sentence, and the right to appoint the Jewish high priest. He even exercised control over the temple funds.

Pilate is known from both Jewish and Roman literary sources. The Jews saw him as a hostile and insensitive ruler who cared nothing for the people he governed. Both Josephus and Philo accused Pilate of being corrupt and cruel and of slaughtering hundreds of Jews illegally as well as misappropriating temple funds. Even so, the Romans left Pilate in Judea for ten years rather than the typical three or four, apparently considering Pilate an effective administrator. When seeking the death penalty, the high priest was forced to bring Jesus to Pilate, who was no friend of the Jews he governed. Only Pilate could condemn a person to death.

EXPLORING PILATE'S RELATIONSHIPS

Pilate's relationship with Jesus (John 18; 19). Pilate may well have known about Jesus before the high priest and his party brought Christ to him. Yet, the interview Pilate had with Jesus left him uncomfortable. John gives us details of Pilate's talk with Christ, and Jesus' statement that while He was, as accused, the "King of the Jews," His kingdom was "not of this world" (John 18:36). Pilate finally announced that he found no fault in Christ, and attempted to have Jesus released. The Jews, however, shouted out so loudly that Pilate decided to have Christ examined by torture. After Christ was beaten and ridiculed, Pilate showed him to the crowd, which loudly demanded that Jesus be crucified. It was unthinkable that one who "made Himself the Son of God" should live (John 19:7).

This revelation frightened Pilate, and he held another private interview with Jesus. When Christ refused to defend himself, Pilate again expressed his intention to release Him. In the end, Pilate gave in and ordered the crucifixion. But first, Pilate publicly washed his hands and announced that all blame for the execution must fall on his accusers, thus declaring himself "innocent of the blood of this just Person" (Matt. 27:24). The crowd mobbing Pilate's court shouted, "His blood be upon us and on our children." (Matt. 27:25).

Pilate did have one last statement to make. He ordered that the cross bear an inscription stating "THIS IS JESUS, THE KING OF THE JEWS" (Matt. 27:37). Even though the high priest complained, Pilate remained firm.

Pilate's relationship with the Jews (John 19:12–13). Pilate's relationship with the Jews was described by Philo, a Jewish philosopher and writer, who complained about "his corruptions, his acts of insolence, his rapine, his habit of insulting people, his cruelty, and his continual murders of people untried and uncondemned, and his never-ending, gratuitous and most grievous inhumanity." Clearly, Pilate did not like or respect the people he governed. Why then did he give in to their insistence that Christ be crucified?

The answer lies in the danger to Pilate of a threat implicit in the Jewish shouts, "If you let this Man go, you are not Caesar's friend" (John 19:12). The text says that *"when Pilate . . . heard that saying"* (italics mine) he delivered Christ to the Jews to be crucified.

Back in Rome, the emperor Tiberius had recently come out of retirement and executed the commander of his Praetorian Guard, Sejanus. For years Sejanus had in effect run the empire, but his request to be allowed to marry into the royal family aroused Tiberius's suspicions. After the execution, Tiberius also put to death a number of officials Sejanus had appointed. Pilate had been one of Sejanus's appointments! While Pilate seemed safe in Judea, an out-of-the-way backwater in Rome's vast empire, the Jews' threat to denounce Pilate as no friend of Caesar was something Pilate felt he could not afford to risk. So Pilate weighed in the balance the certain death of an innocent man and a possible threat to his future, and he made his choice: Jesus must die.

PILATE: AN EXAMPLE FOR TODAY

Pilate was hardly a savory character. Interestingly, early Christian writers treat him more kindly than did first-century Jewish historians. It would be hard to argue that Pilate possessed any admirable traits. Yet, we can learn from Pilate as well.

- Pilate represents every individual who wavers when finally confronting Jesus Christ. What to do with Jesus remains the most important choice any person can make. Pilate had his opportunity, but he made the wrong choice.

- Pilate reveals the futility of blaming others for our own choices. Pilate made a great show of washing his hands and announcing that Christ's blood was on His accusers. Yet, Pilate was the one with the authority to permit an execution. He was the one who permitted Jesus to die. Nothing he said or did can obscure the fact that he was personally responsible for that choice.

- Pilate reminds us that those choices that seem clear are in fact often the most complex. Should Pilate let Jesus die or risk his own future? The eternal risk to Pilate was far greater than any possible temporal threat from the Roman emperor. We do not know whether Pilate later became a Christian. One ancient document may suggest that Pilate's wife became a believer, but of Pilate's fate we know nothing. How much wiser to choose risk in this world and certain gain in the world to come.

NAMELESS MEN IN THE GOSPELS

When considering every man in the Bible, we must note the many nameless men mentioned in the Gospel accounts. While a number of Pharisees or scribes are identified only by their title, they each fit the profile provided. As the chart below indicates, the majority of the nameless men who came in contact with Jesus were supplicants, whose desperate need for healing and help Jesus generously met. Each of them, too, has a story, and although space does not permit us to look at them closely here, each has lessons to teach us. We can mine these lessons for ourselves if we prayerfully approach the Scriptures that portray them.

There are also men featured in stories Jesus told. There is the rich fool, the Good Samaritan, the wise and foolish builders, the unjust judge, the prodigal and his family, and others. Space makes it impossible to treat them here, but they will be treated in a future volume, *Every Parable and Teaching of Jesus in the Bible*.

UNNAMED MEN IN THE GOSPELS

The men	Matthew	Mark	Luke	John
Shepherds in the fields			2:8–20	
Herod's wise men	2:7			
Wise men from the East	2:1–12			
Wise men at the temple			2:45–48	
Tax collectors, soldiers			3:12–14	
Men at the wedding in Cana				2:1–10
Merchants in the temple				2:14–16
Demonized man		1:23–26	4:33–36	
Man with withered hand		3:1–5		
A leper	8:2	1:40–45	5:12–14	
Samaritans				4:39–43
A centurion	8:5–13	7:1–10		4:46–54
Cripple at the pool of Bethesda				5:1–15
The widow's dead son			7:11–17	
Demon-possessed men	8:28–34	5:1–20	8:22–39	
A paralytic and friends	9:2	2:3–5	5:18–20	
Disciples of John the Baptist	11:1–7		7:18–24	
Tax collectors and sinners		2:15–18		
Two blind men	9:27–31	8:22–26		
Deaf and mute man of Decapolis		7:31–36		
Blind and demonic man	12:22–33			
Jesus' brothers	12:46–47; 13:55–56		8:19–21	7:1–5
An epileptic's father	17:14–18	9:17–29	9:38–43	
Men who failed to follow Jesus			9:57–62	
The seventy			10:1–20	
The man with an inheritance dispute			12:13	
Ten lepers			17:11–19	
Man blind from birth				9:1–41
A rich young ruler	19:16–22	10:17–22	18:18–23	
A "certain young man"		14:51–52		
A blind man			18:35–43	
Two robbers	27:38–44	15:27, 32		
Soldiers who abused Jesus	27:27–31			
Centurion at the cross	27:54	15:39		
Soldiers at the cross				19:23–24
Guards at Jesus' tomb	28:4, 11–15			

NEW TESTAMENT MEN OF ACTION

While a number of men are mentioned in the Book of Acts and in the Epistles, several are so significant that they require additional discussion here.

BARNABAS

Scripture references:
Acts 4:36; 9:27; 11:22–30;
13; 14; 15; 1 Corinthians 9:6;
Galatians 2:1–13; Colossians 4:10

Date:	About A.D. 1–55
Name:	Barnabas [BAHR-nuh-buhs; "son of encouragement"]
Greatest Accomplishment:	He was a loving man and active missionary of great influence in the early church.

BARNABAS'S LIFE AND TIMES

Barnabas was one of the first members of the Jerusalem church formed after the Day of Pentecost. He set an example of selfless generosity in keeping with his name (Acts 4:36). Barnabas's life was soon interwoven with that of the apostle Paul. Barnabas was the first person in the Jerusalem church to risk contact with Paul after his miraculous conversion on the road to Damascus (Acts 9:27). Later, the Jerusalem elders entrusted Barnabas with a mission to Antioch to check out a Gentile church that had formed there (Acts 11:22). Barnabas teamed with Paul on the first missionary journey reported in Acts (Acts 13), and after he and Paul separated, Barnabas led his own missionary team (Acts 15:39).

Throughout his life as a Christian Barnabas lived up to his name, for in Hebrew idiom "son of consolation" simply means "consoler," or "encourager."

EXPLORING BARNABAS'S RELATIONSHIPS

Whenever we see Barnabas portrayed in Scripture, he is seen in relationship with others. Barnabas was not a loner but found his fulfillment in ministering to others.

Barnabas's relationship with the first church *(Acts 4:36).* Luke reports that the first

Barnabas showed a generous and caring spirit from his earliest days as a Christian. He brought proceeds of a land sale to the apostles to be distributed to those in need.

Christians in Jerusalem were bound together in such love that they not only met and prayed together, but also sacrificed to meet each other's needs. Our first introduction to Barnabas is as one of those who "having land, sold it, and brought the money" to the apostles to be used to care for the destitute. This was necessary because, while Jewish widows and orphans were cared for by a fund established at the temple, those who became Christians were quickly cut off from this major source of support.

Barnabas's relationship with the apostle Paul.
Barnabas was intimately linked with Paul in the Book of Acts, and he played a significant role in the apostle's acceptance in Jerusalem and in Paul's calling to ministry.

Barnabas reached out to Paul (Acts 9:27). Paul had been actively persecuting Christians when he was converted. When Paul returned to Jerusalem from Damascus, the Christians were unwilling to contact him, afraid that his "conversion" was a trick to infiltrate their movement and betray its leaders. Barnabas was the one who first reached out to Paul and, convinced that Paul's conversion was real, brought him into the fellowship of the church.

Barnabas found Paul and invited him to minister (Acts 11:22). When Barnabas was sent to Antioch to check out reports of a predominantly Gentile church there, he discovered a vital work of God. Barnabas stayed and became one of the leadership team of prophets and elders who guided the Antioch church. After a time, Barnabas realized that Paul's gifts could be used in this situation, and Barnabas went to Tarsus to find him. Barnabas brought Paul with him to Antioch, and Paul became a member of the church's leadership team. Galatians 2:1–13 tells something of the situation at Antioch and mentions Barnabas. Only there can the slightest criticism of Barnabas be found. Paul noted that "even Barnabas" temporarily withdrew from table fellowship with Gentile churches under the critical eye of Christian Pharisees visiting from Jerusalem.

Barnabas was with Paul on the first missionary journey (Acts 13—14). Luke went into considerable detail about the adventures Barnabas and Paul shared on this mission trip. While initially Barnabas was the team's leader, Paul's gifts soon made it clear that he was to lead. Barnabas displayed no hint of any jealousy at this turn of events, and it is characteristic in these chapters for Luke to link "Paul and Barnabas."

Barnabas and Paul argued for grace at the Jerusalem council (Acts 15). When converted Pharisees argued that Gentile Christians must be circumcised and keep the Law of Moses to be saved, Barnabas joined Paul at the Jerusalem council of the church in arguing for a salvation by grace totally apart from works.

Barnabas and Paul split up (Acts 15:35–39). When the two planned a return visit to the churches they had founded, Barnabas wanted to take his cousin (Col. 4:10) John Mark along. Because Mark had abandoned the missionary team earlier, Paul refused to consider it. The disagreement was so sharp that, despite their years of friendship and shared ministry, the two separated and each set out with his own missionary team. Characteristically, Barnabas would risk Paul's friendship on behalf of a young man who needed to be salvaged. John Mark was salvaged, and Paul was reconciled to him and, we assume, to Barnabas as well (see 2 Tim. 4:11).

BARNABAS: AN EXAMPLE FOR TODAY

Barnabas is one of the most admirable men mentioned in the New Testament. He truly merited his name, "Comforter" or Encourager." His truly selfless commitment to ministry was an inspiration in his day and in ours.

- Barnabas inspires us to give priority to people, not possessions. Barnabas quickly responded when Christian widows and orphans were refused food by temple authorities, and he sold his own land to meet the emergency need.

- Barnabas inspires us to reach out to others who claim Christ even when we are unsure of their sincerity. Only Barnabas in the church at Jerusalem was willing to reach out to Saul after his conversion. The others may have been afraid that Saul was faking and would turn them over to the Jewish authorities.

- Barnabas inspires us to draw promising young people into ministry. When Barnabas became a leader in the church at Antioch, he left to find Saul of Tarsus, and bring him to Antioch, where Paul's gifts and talents were honed for greater future ministry.

- Barnabas inspires us to take delight when our disciples surpass us. When Barnabas and Saul started on their first missionary journey, Barnabas was team leader. On the trip, it quickly became apparent that God had given Paul greater gifts, and the leadership passed to him. The two continued to serve together in complete harmony.

- Barnabas inspires us to make a commitment to those whose flaws or past failures have led others to write them off. Barnabas's investment in John Mark salvaged a young man who became a second-generation leader in the church whom God used to write the second Gospel. It cost Barnabas significantly to break with his companion Paul over John Mark.

STEPHEN
Scripture references:
Acts 6:1—8:2

❖

Date:	*Died about* A.D. *35*
Name:	*Stephen [STEE-vuhn; "crown"]*

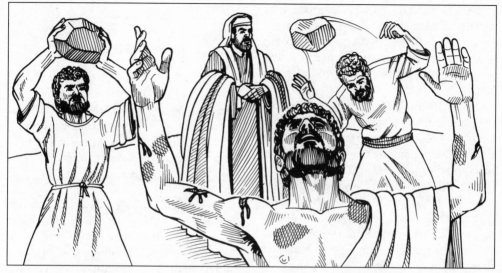

As Stephen was being stoned he saw a vision of Jesus in glory and prayed for his persecutors.

❖

| Greatest Accomplishment: | Stephen was the first Christian martyred for his faith. |

❖

STEPHEN'S LIFE AND TIMES

Stephen was a member of the first Christian church in Jerusalem and a bold witness for Christ. He played two important roles in the early church.

Stephen's role as deacon *(Acts 6)*. In Jerusalem the temple authorities distributed food to the city's needy, primarily widows and orphans. However, they soon cut from their rolls those who followed Jesus. The church quickly organized its own distribution system, relying on gifts of the better-off members to meet the needs of the destitute.

Jerusalem was a magnet to which Jews from all over the empire came, and many stayed in the Holy City. The population included native, Aramaic-speaking Jews, and also a large number of Hellenistic or Greek-speaking Jews. Acts 6 tells us that the Hellenists began to complain that their widows were not getting their fair share when food was distributed, and hard feelings developed. The apostles recommended that the congregation choose six godly men filled with the Holy Spirit whom they could trust to be fair, and turn the distribution over to these deacons. (The word "deacon" in Greek means "servant.") The elected men would serve the church by tending to the details of collecting money, buying food, and seeing that it was distributed fairly.

Acts 6 lists the six men chosen. Strikingly, the church chose six men with Hellenistic names, displaying trust that those who felt they had been treated unfairly would themselves be totally fair! Stephen was one of these six godly, Spirit-filled men the whole church knew they could trust.

Stephen's role as evangelist *(Acts 6; 7)*. Stephen was a bold evangelist, "full of faith and power," whose words were supported by "great wonders and signs among the people" (6:8). He focused on reaching others of

Hellenistic heritage, and in the process, he debated fanatical Jews from a Hellenistic synagogue (6:9). When they were unable to refute his preaching, they lined up false witnesses and accused him of religious crimes.

When taken before the Sanhedrin that had condemned Jesus to death, Stephen preached boldly, showing from history that Israel had consistently resisted rather than responded to God. He argued that in their crucifixion of Christ they, too, "always resist the Holy Spirit" (7:51). The accusation, with Stephen's report of a sudden vision of Christ standing at the right hand of God, turned the council into a mob that dragged Stephen into the streets and stoned him to death. With his last breath, Stephen prayed that God would "not charge them with this sin."

STEPHEN: AN EXAMPLE FOR TODAY

Stephen truly is an example to us in several ways.

- Stephen is an example of trustworthiness. We need to be the kind of person whose integrity others will respect even though they may be suspicious of the group to which we belong.
- Stephen is an example of humility. Although he clearly had great spiritual gifts, Stephen did not think it beneath him to pass out food to the needy.
- Stephen is an example of courage. Few of us risk our lives when we speak up for Christ, yet many seem unwilling to risk possible ridicule or rejection. We need Stephen's kind of courage to share the gospel's good news in our day.

PHILIP THE EVANGELIST
Scripture references:
Acts 6:5; 8:5–40; 21:8

Date:	*About A.D. 35*
Name:	*Philip [FIL-ip; "lover of horses"]*
Greatest Accomplishment:	*One of the seven deacons in the Jerusalem church, Philip became one of the earliest Christian missionaries.*

Several Philips are mentioned in the New Testament, including one of Jesus' twelve disciples. Our Philip, however, was one of the early converts in Jerusalem in the first days after Pentecost. That he retained his Greek name indicates he was a Diaspora Jew—a Jew who had lived outside of Palestine but had probably come to Jerusalem to attend one of the religious festivals and stayed on after his conversion to Christ. Unlike the disciple Philip, Philip the evangelist was an "ordinary" Christian whose conversion launched him on a course that gave special significance to his life.

PHILIP'S ROLE IN SCRIPTURE

Philip was one of seven men who had so gained the trust of the Christian community that they were appointed to oversee the distribution of food to Christian widows and orphans. When most Christians were forced out of Jerusalem by persecution, Philip preached Christ to the people of Samaria and started a revival there. Later, God led him away from the revival he had started, to speak with one individual, an official of the queen of Ethiopia. Later, Philip traveled and preached in the coastal cities along the Mediterranean and settled in Caesarea, the seat of the Roman governor. The apostle Paul stayed briefly with Philip, who by then had four daughters who prophesied.

EXPLORING PHILIP'S RELATIONSHIPS

While relatively little space is given to Philip in the New Testament, we can tell much about the man from the relationships he had with others.

Philip's relationship with other Christians (*Acts 6*). Jerusalem was noted for its care of widows and orphans, which was administered through the temple. As the Christian movement grew, the temple authorities cut off Christian widows from this support. The believers rallied, and, through gifts provided by individuals, they set up their own system to care for the needy Christians. Trouble developed when the newcomers felt that their widows were being treated unfairly and that the long-time residents of Jerusalem were receiving favorable treatment.

The apostles suggested that the Christian community select seven men "of good reputation, full of the Holy Spirit and wisdom" (Acts 6:3) to supervise the distribution. Strikingly, each of the seven chosen, including Philip, bore a Greek name. These men were Greeks and would be expected to be most sensitive to the problem.

Philip's relationship with the Samaritans (*Acts 8:1–25*). After Stephen's martyrdom at the hands of an angry mob, the Christians of Jerusalem were actively persecuted, and most of them were forced to leave the city. Acts tracks the impact of this dispersion through the story of Philip, who traveled to Samaria proclaiming Christ. Despite the deep hostility that existed between the Jews and Samaritans, Philip eagerly shared the gospel with them. Through Philip's preaching, many Samaritans believed; so many believed that Peter and John came to check out the reports of mass conversions.

Although Philip was not one of the apostles, and was in effect a layperson, Philip felt an urgency to share Christ with others. That he was so willing to preach the gospel

to the Jews' ancient enemies tells us much about the kind of man Philip was.

Philip's relationship with the Ethiopian eunuch (Acts 8:26–39). God led Philip away from the revival he had begun so he could meet one man. The man was a high official in the court of Ethiopia, and possibly a Jew who had also come to Jerusalem to attend one of the festivals. While called the "Ethiopian eunuch," this title does not necessarily mean that he had been castrated. In the ancient Middle East, rulers tended to rely on men who had been castrated to fill important posts, reasoning that without families they would not have divided loyalties. By the first century, "eunuch" often functioned as a title of high court officials and might be borne by those not physically mutilated.

Whatever the case, Philip struck up a conversation with the Ethiopian official who was reading Isaiah 53. Philip explained the meaning of the passage and showed how Jesus Christ had fulfilled Isaiah's every prediction. The Ethiopian believed, was baptized, and returned to his homeland a believer.

All too many would have resented being called away from a great movement he had initiated to witness to one man—and a stranger at that. Philip, however, was as happy to have a part in helping one individual turn to Christ as to be the well-known focus of a mass movement.

Philip's continuing witness (Acts 8:40). The text tells us that after his meeting with the Ethiopian, Philip "preached in all the cities" along the Mediterranean coast until he reached Caesarea, and settled there. There is no indication in Acts that the major revival Philip had stimulated was ever duplicated. Yet, Philip remained an active witness wherever he went. This witness was so active that in later years he was known as "Philip the evangelist" (Acts 21:8).

PHILIP: AN EXAMPLE FOR TODAY

Philip is best understood as an ordinary Christian. Much of what he did was exceptional, but what made him special was his commitment to godliness and an eagerness to share the gospel with others. We may never achieve the ministry of someone like the apostle Paul, but every Christian can realistically aspire to be like Philip the evangelist.

JOHN MARK
Scripture references:
Acts 12:12, 25; 15:39;
Colossians 4:10;
2 Timothy 4:11; 1 Peter 5:13

Date:	About A.D. 45
Name:	Mark [MAHRK; "large hammer"]
Greatest Accomplishment:	Mark became Peter's companion and wrote the Gospel of Mark.

MARK'S LIFE AND TIMES

As a teen, Mark may have witnessed the capture of Jesus in Gethsemane (Mark 14:51–52). After the resurrection, Mark participated in prayer meetings of the young church held in his mother Mary's home (Acts 12:12). He had another important Christian connection; his cousin Barnabas was one of the young church's most notable leaders (Col. 4:10). It was not surprising that Mark should accompany Paul and Barnabas as a member of their team on their first missionary journey. However, for some reason, young Mark abandoned them and returned to Jerusalem (Acts 15:38). Later, when Barnabas wanted to take Mark on another missionary journey, Paul refused. Paul and Barnabas separated, and each led a separate missionary team. John Mark went with Barnabas.

Under Barnabas's gentle tutelage Mark matured as a Christian. Years later, Paul asked Timothy to send Mark to him because "he is useful to me for ministry" (2 Tim. 4:1). Tradition tells us that Mark became the companion of Peter, who described him as "my son" (1 Pet. 5:13). The same tradition states that Mark related in his Gospel the stories he heard from Peter.

MARK'S GOSPEL

Mark's Gospel reflects the stories told by Peter in his ministry to the Jewish Diaspora (the Jews living outside the Holy Land). Yet Mark's Gospel had a special appeal to the Roman mind.

The Romans who built and maintained an empire that surrounded the Mediterranean Sea—incorporating Europe and England, Egypt, and Asia Minor—were an eminently practical people. The Romans were people of action who appreciated decisiveness and strength of character. Mark's portrait of Jesus, which tells His story briefly but with vivid scenes frequently linked by "then immediately," appealed to the Roman mind. This Jesus was a Man of strength and honor, a Man of action, a Man with power and authority.

While Mark's Gospel is the shortest of the four accounts of Jesus' life and closely parallels Matthew's Gospel in structure, it has a very different tone. Matthew presents Jesus the Messiah. Mark presents Jesus, the Man of action and authority, stripped of those details that were necessary to answer questions Jewish readers might ask. The Jesus of Mark's Gospel was an attractive figure to the first-century Roman, a Man to whom one might confidently pledge allegiance and become His client, confident that Jesus would be able to protect and care for His own.

MARK: AN EXAMPLE FOR TODAY

Mark at best is a peripheral character as far as the Gospels and Acts are concerned. Yet, he seems representative of many young people who come to faith early but grow into commitment only after a number of false starts or failures. From Mark we learn several important lessons about nurturing faith in young people.

- Mark had many family and other links to Christian faith. Through them he was exposed to the gospel early in life. Mature believers need to help young people establish relationships with as many committed believers as possible.

- Mark, in Barnabas, had a Christian friend who would not give up on him. Young people may fall short of our and their own expectations. We need not only to support them but also to give them additional opportunities to succeed.

- Mark had a more significant role in God's plan than anyone might have expected. When we invest in a young person, we never know how significant that investment might become!

LUKE
Scripture references:
Colossian 4:14; 2 Timothy 4:11;
Philemon 1:24; "we" passages in Acts

Date:	*About* A.D. *50*
Name:	*Luke [LUKE; "light"]*
Greatest accomplishment:	*A companion of the apostle Paul, Luke wrote Acts and the Gospel that bears his name.*

LUKE'S LIFE AND TIMES

Paul speaks of him as the "beloved physician" (Col. 4:14) and as a "fellow laborer" (Philem. 1:24). From earliest times, Luke has been identified as the author of the third Gospel and of Acts, in part because each book features medical language and refers often to illnesses, diagnoses, and to the details of sickness, cures, and marks of recovery. In Acts 16, for the first time the author shifts from describing what "they" (Paul and his companions) did to what "we" (Paul, with Luke now among his companions) did (16:11). It becomes clear that Luke joined the missionary team at Troas, just before Paul crossed into Europe for the first time.

What we know of Luke as a person must be inferred from the books he wrote. First, Luke used the most educated and beautiful Greek of any Gospel writer. He was clearly given a classical education as well as medical training. While his name is Greek, he may well have been a Jew, as Jews often bore Greek as well as Jewish names. We also know from the emphases in Luke's Gospel that Luke was especially concerned with the poor, the oppressed, and with women. His Gospel contains many stories depicting Jesus' involvement with the poor, and Luke frequently contrasted the responses of women to the Lord with the responses of men. The themes developed in Luke's writings show that he was an unusually sensitive and caring man as well as a careful historian.

LUKE: AN EXAMPLE FOR TODAY

Luke was by all indications a true intellectual as well as a dedicated physician and caring person. The term "beloved" used by Paul to describe Luke tells us much about his character. He combined a sharp mind with a loving and mild disposition and an unusual sensitivity for those whom society largely ignored.

Someone once commented that God must love the common people because He made so many of them. It is just as true to say that God must love the uncommon, because men like Luke so wonderfully glorify Him.

JAMES THE BROTHER OF JESUS
Scripture references:
Matthew 13:55; Mark 6:3;
Acts 12:17; 15:13; 21:18;
Galatians 1:19; 2:9, 12

Date:	A.D. *30*
Name:	*James [JAYMZ; "supplanter"]*
Greatest Accomplishment:	*James emerged as the leader of the church in Jerusalem and wrote the Book of James.*

JAMES'S ROLE IN SCRIPTURE

James the brother of Jesus emerged as the leader of the church in Jerusalem. He apparently chaired the first council of the church, held to discuss the relationship between Gentile Christians and Moses' Law (Acts 15). Paul's reference to James in Acts 21:18 also suggests that he was first among the elders of the Jerusalem church.

Later, James wrote a letter of exhortation to believing Jews, urging them to maintain a lifestyle appropriate to the faith. James's letter, preserved in Scripture as the Book of James, may be the first written of the New Testament books.

JAMES'S LIFE AND TIMES

James was the son of Mary and Joseph, the half-brother of Jesus Christ. According to the list of brothers in Matthew 13:55 and Mark 6:3, James was the eldest after Jesus. While they grew up in the same family, John's Gospel makes it clear that throughout much of Christ's earthly ministry "his brothers did not believe in him" (John 7:5).

After the death of the apostle James (Acts 12:2), James the brother of Jesus quickly emerged as the spiritual leader of the church in Jerusalem. He actively supported the apostles Peter and Paul, who urged that Gentile converts not be forced to keep Jewish Law. James's statement of consensus expressed the decision of "the apostles, the elders, and the brethren" (Acts 15:23).

Tradition ascribes great piety to James, whose nickname was "camel-knees," because of the calluses on his knees caused from spending so much time in prayer. James's commitment to the practical expression of a true faith in Christ is clearly seen in the way of life taught in the book that carries his name.

JAMES: AN EXAMPLE FOR TODAY

James reminds us of Jesus' observation that the last shall be first. James, despite or perhaps because of his intimate relationship with Jesus, found it hard to accept his half-brother as the Messiah and Son of God. But once the doubts were settled, James's commitment was unmatched, and he quickly emerged as the most respected church leader in Jerusalem.

- James reminds us that leadership in the church is earned, not passed on from father to son. It was not James's relationship with Jesus but his commitment to Jesus that won him respect.

- James demonstrates collegial leadership. In the Jerusalem council, he did not impose a decision but rather summarized the consensus worked through by all.

- James exhorts us to live out our faith and makes it plain that a "faith" that does not produce works is dead—mere intellectual assent rather than a heartfelt commitment to Jesus Christ.

AQUILA

Scripture references:
Acts 18:2, 18, 26; Romans 16:3
1 Corinthians 16:19; 2 Timothy 4:19

---------------- ----------------

Date:	*About A.D. 50*
Name:	*Aquila [AK-wh-luh; "eagle"]*
Greatest Accomplishment:	*He and his wife Priscilla were close friends and coworkers of the apostle Paul.*

---------------- ----------------

AQUILA'S LIFE AND TIMES

The *Revell Bible Dictionary* provides a good summary of Aquila's life and times.

Acts 18 identifies Aquila as a Jew. Like other Jews living outside of Palestine, he and his wife adopted Roman names in addition to their Jewish names, which are not given in Scripture. Expelled from Rome by edict of the Emperor Claudius (about A.D. 49), they settled in Corinth. Paul, who shared their trade of tent making (that is, leather working), stayed with Aquila and Priscilla there. Aquila was apparently well off: he owned property, and the couple was free to travel with Paul to Ephesus (Acts 18:24–26). According to 1 Cor. 16:19, a house-church was established in their home. Later, after Claudius's edict expelling Jews was revoked in A.D. 54, the couple apparently returned to Rome and became leaders of the Christian community there (Rom. 16:3–5a) (p. 80).

What is perhaps most fascinating about references to Aquila in the New Testament is that in each case his wife is mentioned with him, and in half the references Priscilla is named first. What an appropriate reminder that in ministry as in life husbands and wives are to be partners, and that in some partnerships the wife's gifts may be greater than those of her husband.

AQUILA: AN EXAMPLE FOR TODAY

We know little about Aquila. Yet we know enough to view him as an example for Christians today.

- Aquila was a businessman who used the flexibility of business ownership to minister. Aquila provided work for the apostle Paul. Aquila and his wife relocated to Ephesus to be part of Paul's missionary team. Aquila is a good example of a person who sees ministry rather than profit as his objective, and who uses his business to create opportunities to serve God.

- Aquila was a husband who was not threatened by having a wife with gifts and abilities that may have exceeded his own. Their partnership in life and ministry challenges every man to reevaluate his attitude toward women and especially toward his spouse.

TIMOTHY

Scripture references:
Acts 16:1; 17:14–15; 18:5; 19:22; 20:4;
Romans 16:21; 1 Corinthians 4:17; 16:10;
Philippians 1:1; 2:9; 1 Thessalonians
1:1; 3:2; 2 Thessalonians 1:1; 1 Timothy;
2 Timothy

Date:	A.D. *50*
Name:	*Timothy [TIM-uh-thee; "honored by God"]*
Greatest Accomplishment:	Timothy was a second-generation leader of the church, trained by the apostle Paul.

TIMOTHY'S ROLE IN SCRIPTURE

In the early church, itinerant ministers who traveled from place to place maintained communication between the apostles and local congregations and between congregations. Timothy frequently fulfilled this role as he went to various churches on missions for Paul.

Timothy is named with Paul in the salutation of four New Testament letters (Philippians, 1, 2 Thessalonians, and Philemon), but most of what we know about Timothy comes from the two letters of instruction and encouragement Paul wrote to him. Indeed, the letters to Timothy have had a more lasting impact on the church than did Timothy himself.

TIMOTHY'S LIFE AND TIMES

Paul enlisted Timothy as a companion on his second missionary journey. Luke noted that Timothy was the son of a Jewish woman and a Greek father. According to Jewish custom that traces Jewishness through the mother rather than the father, this meant that Timothy was a Jew. Timothy became a believer at an early age, taught by his mother Eunice and grandmother Lois (2 Tim. 1:5). Timothy may have been in his early twenties when he began traveling with

Paul, who would have been closer to fifty. Paul obviously valued Timothy, and referred to him as "my fellow worker" in Romans 16:21, and three times mentioned sending Timothy to churches as his representative (Phil. 2:9; 1 Thess. 3:2; 2 Thess. 1:7).

At the same time it is clear from the letters Paul wrote to Timothy that Timothy lacked the confidence and the powerful presence of the apostle. In urging Timothy to let "no one despise your youth" (1 Tim. 4:12), Paul seems to have had Timothy's timidity in view, as well as the fact that in the first century wisdom and authority were associated with age. It must have been difficult for the relatively youthful Timothy to represent the apostle Paul and expect churches to respond to his authority.

In a real sense, anyone who is expected to step into the shoes of giants, as the second generation of Christian leaders surely was expected to do, faces a daunting task. Yet Timothy, Titus, and others like them maintained the integrity of the church, helped to preserve its deposit of truth, and continued the spread of the gospel throughout the world.

For a deeper insight into Timothy see the discussion of Paul as a mentor of young, future leaders, on page 180.

TIMOTHY: AN EXAMPLE FOR TODAY

Timothy can be a great encouragement for young men and women who appear to be thrust into leadership before they have matured sufficiently. God not only calls but also enables those whom he intends to serve him.

- Timothy reminds us of the importance of having a relationship with a mature believer who can mentor us in the faith.
- Timothy encourages us, for in Timothy we see that even the young

can play an important part in carrying out God's purposes in the church and the world.

- Timothy challenges us to provide young people with opportunities for truly significant ministry. When youth are denied opportunities to put their faith into practice, they will not catch a vision for what God is able to do in and through them. Young people may need guidance, but they *can* minister, as Timothy surely did.

EVERY MAN NAMED IN THE BIBLE IN BRIEF

A

AARON [AIR-uhn]. 1450 B.C. Israel's first high priest. A weak man, he was faithful when led by Moses, his brother. See page 141.

ABADDON [uh-BAD-uhn: "destroyer"]. Hebrew name for the demon king of the abyss in Revelation 9:11. The Greek form of the name is Apollyon.

ABAGTHA [uh-BAG-thuh: "happy, prosperous"]. 475 B.C. One of the seven eunuchs who served king Ahasuerus. Esther 1:10.

ABDA [AB-duh: "servant, worshiper"]. Shortened form of Obadiah.

1. 975 B.C. Father of Adoniram, an official whom Solomon put in charge of the forced labor building the temple. 1 Kings 4:6.

2. 450 B.C. A Levite who served in Jerusalem after the exile. Nehemiah 11:17; called Obadiah in 1 Chronicles 9:16.

ABDEEL [AB-dee-el: "servant of God"]. 62? B.C. The father of Shelemiah, an official of King Jehoiakim who was instructed to arrest Jeremiah and his scribe Baruch. Jeremiah 36:26.

ABDI [AB-di: "servant of Jehovah"]

1. 1075 B.C. The grandfather of Ethan who was a minister of music at the tabernacle. 1 Chronicles 6:44.

2. 750 B.C. The father of Kish, a Levite who served in the temple during Hezekiah's reign. 2 Chronicles 29:12.

3. 450 B.C. A Jew forced to divorce a foreign wife after the exile. Ezra 10:26.

ABDIEL [AB-dee-el: "servant of God"]. B.C. date unknown. The head of a family in the tribe of Gad. 1 Chronicles 5:15.

ABDON [AB-dahn: "servile"]

1. B.C. date unknown. A Benjamite who lived in Jerusalem. 1 Chronicles 8:23.

2. 1075 B.C. A little-known judge who led Israel for eight years. Judges 12:13–1?

3. 1075 B.C. The older brother of Ner, the father of King Saul. 1 Chronicles 8:30.

4. 625 B.C. An officer in the court of King Josiah. 2 Chronicles 34:20. He is called Acbor in 2 Kings 22:12.

ABED-NEGO [uh-BED-nuh-goh: "servant of Nego" (a Babylonian deity)]. 600 B.C. The name given the Hebrew youth Azariah when he became an official in the government of Nebuchadnezzar. This companion of Daniel was one of three Jews thrown into a fiery furnace for refusing to worship an idol the king erected. Daniel 1:7; 3:12–30.

ABEL [AY-buhl: "breath, vapor"]. B.C. date unknown. The second son of Adam and Eve, who was killed by his brother Cain. Genesis 4.

ABI-ALBON [AY-bi-AL-buhn: "father of strength"]. 1000 B.C. One of David's thirty top military men. 2 Samuel 23:31. Called Abiel in 1 Chronicles 11:32.

ABIASAPH [uh-BI-uh-saf: "my father has gathered"]. B.C. date unknown. The founder of a Levite family whose descendants served as musicians and gatekeepers in the tabernacle. Exodus 6:24. Called Ebiasaph in 1 Chronicles 6:23, 37; 9:19.

ABIATHAR [uh-BI-uh-thahr: "father of abundance"]. 1000 B.C. The sole survivor of Saul's massacre of a family of priests, he became high priest during David's reign as king. 1 Samuel 22:22; 2 Samuel 15:27; 1 Kings 1—4; 1 Chronicles 15:11. See page 116.

ABIDAH [uh-BI-duh: "father of knowledge"]. 2000 B.C. Fourth son of Midian, a son of Abraham. Genesis 25:4.

ABIDAN [uh-BI-duhn: "father is judge"]. 1450 B.C. The leader of the tribe of Dan in Moses' time. Genesis 25:4.

ABIEL [Ay-bee-el: "father is God"]

1. 1100 B.C. An ancestor of Saul. 1 Samuel 9:1. Possibly the same as Jeiel, father of Kish, in 1 Chronicles 9:35.

2. 1000 B.C. A military commander and member of David's top thirty. 1 Chronicles 11:32. Called Abi-Albon in 2 Samuel 23:31.

ABIEZER [AY-bih-EE-zuhr: "father is help"]

1. B.C. date unknown. A descendant of Manasseh, and ancestral head of his clan. Joshua 17:2; Judges 8:2; 1 Chronicles 7:18. Called Jeezer in Numbers 26:30

2. 1000 B.C. A Benjamite who was one of David's top thirty military commanders. 2 Samuel 23:27.

ABIHAIL [AB-uh-hayl: "father is strength"].

1. 1475 B.C. The father of Zuriel, a leader of the tribe of Levi. Numbers 3:35.

2. B.C. date unknown. A man listed only as a descendant of Gad in 1 Chronicles 5:14.

3. 500 B.C. The father of Esther and uncle of Mordecai. Esther 2:15; 9:29.

ABIHU [uh-BI-hoo: "father is he"]. 1450 B.C. Second of Aaron's four sons. He was destroyed by fire when he approached God's altar with "profane fire." Leviticus 10.

ABIHUD [uh-BI-hud: "father is majesty"]. 1825 B.C. The third son of Bela, the firstborn of Benjamin. 1 Chronicles 8:3.

ABIJAH [uh-BI-ah: "my father is Yahweh"]. Also ABIA.

1. 1825 B.C. Seventh son of Becher, son of Benjamin. 1 Chronicles 7:8.

2. 1050 B.C. The corrupt son of Samuel, Israel's last judge. 1 Samuel 8:1–5.

3. 1000 B.C. The head of the eighth of twenty-four priestly divisions organized by David to conduct worship at the temple. Zechariah, the father of John the Baptist, belonged to this division. 1 Chronicles 24:10; cf. Luke 1:5.

4. 925 B.C. The son of evil Jeroboam I, Abijah's death in childhood was an exhibition of divine grace. 1 Kings 14:1–6.

5. 913–910 B.C. ruled Judah. 1 Kings 15; 2 Chronicles 13. He is also called Abijam.

6. 525 B.C. Head of a priestly family who returned to Judah from exile with Zerubbabel. Nehemiah 12:1, 4, 17.

7. 450 B.C. A priest who signed the renewed covenant made during Nehemiah's time. Nehemiah 10:7.

ABIJAM [uh-BI-juhm: "father of the sea"]. Ruled Judah from 913–910 B.C. 1 Kings 15:2. Called Abijah in 2 Chronicles 13.

ABIMAEL [uh-BIM-ay-el: "my father is God"]. B.C. date unknown. Ninth son of Joktan, a descendant of Shem the son of Noah. Genesis 10:28; 1 Chronicles 1:22.

ABIMELECH [uh-BIM-uh-lek: "my father is God"]. A title of Philistine kings.

1. 2050 B.C. A Philistine king of Gerar who established a treaty with Abraham. Genesis 20:1–18; 21:22–34.

2. 1950 B.C. Another king of Gerar who made an alliance with Abraham's son, Isaac. Genesis 26:1–33.

3. Ruled 1129–1126 B.C. over part of Israel. A son of Gideon who assassinated seventy of his brothers in an effort to establish himself as king. Judges 9. See page 107.

4. 1025 B.C. Achish, king of the Philistine city of Gath, referred to as Abimelek in Psalm 34, title.

5. 975 B.C. Another name of the priest Ahimelech, son of Abiathar. See Ahimelech, below.

ABINADAB [uh-BIN-uh-dab: "father is generous"]

1. 1025 B.C. A man from Kirjath Jearim, where the ark was kept for twenty years after its return by the Philistines. 1 Samuel 7:1; 2 Samuel 6:3.

2. 1025 B.C. The second son of Jesse, an older brother of David. 1 Samuel 16:8; 17:2; 1 Chronicles 2:13.

3. 1025 B.C. A son of Saul who was killed fighting the Philistines. 1 Samuel 31:2; 1 Chronicles 8:33.

4. 950 B.C. The father of Ben-Abinadab, one of Solomon's district governors. 1 Kings 4:11.

ABIRAM [uh-BI-ruhm: "father is exalted"]

1. 1450 B.C. One of the leaders of a rebellion against Moses and Aaron. Numbers 16:1, 12, 24–27.

2. 850 B.C. The first son of Hiel, who rebuilt Jericho in the time of Ahab. In accord with a prophecy uttered 550 years earlier by Joshua (Josh. 6:26), he died during construction. 1 Kings 16:34.

ABISHAI [uh-BEE-shi: meaning unknown]. 1000 B.C. A loyal warrior who fought with David, as did his brothers Joab and Asahel. 2 Samuel 2; 1 Chronicles 2.

ABISHALOM [uh-BISH-uh-lohm: "father of peace"]. 975 B.C. Father (or grandfather?) of Maacah, the wife of Rehoboam and mother of Abijah. 1 Kings 15:2, 10. Also called Absalom, another form of the name, in 2

Abner supported a son of Saul as king rather than David. He defended his choice during a seven-year conflict with David's forces.

❖

Chronicles 11:20, 21, and Uriel in 2 Chronicles 13:2. Possibly the same as Absalom, the rebel son of King David.

ABISHUA [uh-BISH-oo-uh: "father of deliverance"]

1. 1825 B.C. Fourth son of Bela, the first son of Benjamin. 1 Chronicles 8:4.

2. B.C. date unknown. A descendant of Aaron, and an ancestor of Ezra the scribe. 1 Chronicles 6:5, 50; Ezra 7:5.

ABISHUR [uh-BI-shur: "father is a wall"]. B.C. date unknown. A descendant of Judah listed in the genealogy of Jerehmeel. 1 Chronicles 2:28, 29.

ABITUB [uh-BI-tub: "my father is good"]. B.C. date unknown. Listed in the genealogy of Benjamin. 1 Chronicles 8:11.

ABIUD [uh-BI-ud: "father is majesty"]. 525 B.C. A son of Zerubbabel and an ancestor of Christ. Matthew 1:13.

ABNER [AB-nuhr: "father is a lamp"]. 1025 B.C. The commander of Saul's armies. 1 Samuel 17:55; 2 Samuel 2:8.

ABRAHAM [AY-bruh-ham: "father of a multitude"]. Known as Abram (exalted father) until his name was changed by God. 2100 B.C. God gave Abram special covenant promises, the working out of which in history give shape to Old and New Testaments. He is also the Scripture's prime example of faith.

ABSALOM [AB-suh-luhm: "father of peace"]

1. The rebellious son of David who tried to take his father's throne about 975 B.C.

2. 975 B.C. Father (or grandfather?) of Maacah, the wife of King Rehoboam and mother of Abijah. 2 Chronicles 11:20, 21. Called Abishalom, another form of the same name, in 1 Kings 15:2, 10, and Uriel in 2 Chronicles 13:2. May be the same as 1, above.

ACHAICUS [uh-KAY-uh-kuhs: "belonging to Achaia," a Roman province, possibly indicating he was a slave]. A.D. 55. One of three men from the church in Corinth who visited Paul in Ephesus. 1 Corinthians 16:17.

ACHAN [AY-kuhn: "troubler"]. 1400 B.C. An Israelite who violated God's command by taking loot from Jericho, causing a military defeat at Ai. Joshua 7; 8.

ACHBOR [AK-bohr: "mouse"]

1. B.C. date unknown. The father of the Edomite King Baal-Hanan. Genesis 36:38, 39,

2. 625 B.C. Father of Elnathan. Jeremiah 26:22; 36:12.

3. 625 B.C. An official sent by Josiah to inquire of the prophetess Huldah concerning the rediscovered Book of the Law. 2 Kings 22:12. Called Abdon in 2 Chronicles 34:20. Probably the same as Achbor 2.

ACHIM. See Akim.

ACHISH [AY-kish: "the king gives" or "serpent charmer"(?)]

1. 1025 B.C. A ruler of the Philistine city of Gath, to whom David fled to escape Saul. 1 Samuel 21:10–15; 27; 29:1–10.

2. 975 B.C. Also a ruler of Gath, to whom two of Shimei's slaves fled. Likely the same as Achish. 1 Kings 2:39, 40.

ADAIAH [uh-DAY-uh: "Yahweh has adorned"]

1. 1675 B.C. Father of Jedidah, the mother of Josiah. 2 Kings 22:1.

2. B.C. date unknown. A Levite, ancestor of Asaph, the psalm writer and minister of music in David's time. 1 Chronicles 6:41. Called Iddo in 1 Chronicles 6:21.

3. B.C. date unknown. Listed in the genealogy of Benjamin in 1 Chronicles 8:21.

4. 850 B.C. Father of Masseiah, a military officer who helped Jehoiada overthrow Queen Athaliah. 2 Chronicles 23:1.

5. 525 B.C. A descendant of Judah who settled in Jerusalem after the Exile. Nehemiah 11:5.

6. 450 B.C. A priest who settled in Jerusalem after the Exile. 1 Chronicles 9:12; Nehemiah 11:12.

7. 450 B.C. A Jew who took a foreign wife in Ezra's time. Ezra 10:29.

8. 450 B.C. He took a foreign wife after the Exile. Ezra 10:39.

ADALIA [uh-DAYL-yah]. 475 B.C. One of ten sons of Haman put to death by the Jews during the reign of Ahasuerus. Esther 9:8.

ADAM [AD-uhm: "human being" or "humanity"]. The first man, directly created by God in His own image and given dominion over the earth. Genesis 1–5. See page 1.

ADBEEL (AD-bee-el: "languishing for God"]. 2025 B.C. One of Ishmael's twelve sons. Genesis 25:13.

ADDAR [AD-dahr: possibly "honor"]. 1850 B.C. First of the nine sons of Bela, son of Benjamin in 1 Chronicles 8:3.

ADDI [AD-i: "my witness" or "pleasure"]. B.C. date unknown. An ancestor of Joseph, Jesus' stepfather. Luke 3:28.

ADIEL [AY-dee-el: "God is an ornament"]

1. 1025 B.C. Father of Azmaveth, an treasurer in David's kingdom. 1 Chronicles 27:25.

2. 700 B.C. A Simeonite clan leader who lived in Hezekiah's time. 1 Chronicles 4:36.

3. 450 B.C. A priest whose son, Masasi, resettled in Jerusalem after the Exile. 1 Chronicles 9:12.

ADIN [AY-din: "ornament"]

1. B.C. date unknown. Ancestor of a family who returned to Judah after the Exile. Ezra 2:15; Nehemiah 7:20.

2. 450 B.C. A Jewish leader who sealed the covenant renewal in Nehemiah's time, probably with the name of the family's ancestral head. Nehemiah 10:16. See Adin I.

ADLAI [AD-lay: "lax, weary"(?)]. 1025 B.C. Father of Shaphat, David's chief herdsman. 1 Chronicles 27:29.

ADMATHA [ad-MAY-thuh]. 475 B.C. One of the seven nobles of Persia who advised Ahasuerus to divorce Queen Vashti. Esther 1:14.

ADNA [AD-nuh: "pleasure"]

1. 525 B.C. Head of a priestly family who returned to Judah with Zerubbabel. Nehemiah 12:15.

2. 450 B.C. A Jew who took a foreign wife after the Exile. Ezra 10:30.

ADNAH [AD-nuh: "pleasure"]

1. 1000 B.C. A man who joined David's army at Ziklag. 1 Chronicles 12:20.

2. 875 B.C. A commander in the army of Jehoshaphat. 2 Chronicles 17:14.

ADONI-BEZEK [uh-DOH-ni-BEH-zek: "lord of Bezek"]. 1400 B.C. Title of a king of Bezek. He was defeated in battle and taken captive by Israelites. Judges 1:5–7.

ADONIJAH [AD-oh-NI-juh: "Yahweh is Lord"]

1. 975 B.C. David's oldest surviving son, a rival of Solomon whom David proclaimed king. 1 Kings 1, 2.

2. 875 B.C. A Levite whom Jehoshaphat sent to teach God's Law throughout Judah. 2 Chronicles 17:8.

3. 450 B.C. A Jewish leader who signed the covenant renewal in the time of Nehemiah, probably with the name of the family's ancestral head. Nehemiah 10:16.

ADONIKAM [ad-uh-NI-kuhm: "my lord has risen"]. B.C. date unknown. Ancestral head of a family that returned to Judah after the Exile. Ezra 2:13; 8:13; Nehemiah 7:18.

ADONIRAM [ad-uh-NI-ruhm: "my lord is exalted"]. 930 B.C. The official in charge of forced labor under David, Solomon, and Rehoboam, he was stoned to death during the Israelite revolt against Rehoboam. 2 Samuel 20:24; 1 Kings 4:6; 12:18.

ADONI-ZEDEK [uh-DOH-ni-ZEH-dek: "lord of righteousness"]. 1400 B.C. The king of Jerusalem who made a pact with four other Amorite kings to attack the Gibeonites for allying with Israel. Joshua defeated them and executed the five kings. Joshua 10:1–26.

ADRAMMELECH [uh-DRAM-muh-lek: "the lord is king" or "Adad is king"]

1. 725 B.C. A deity of the Sepharvites, who were settled in Samaria by the Assyrians. Child sacrifice was made to this pagan god. 2 Kings 17:31.

2. 675 B.C. Son of Sennacherib, king of Assyria, who with his brother Sharezer assassinated their father in the temple of Nisroch. 2 Kings 19:37; Isaiah 37:38.

ADRIEL [AY-dree-el: "my help is God"]. 1025 B.C. The man to whom Saul gave his daughter Merab in marriage. 1 Samuel 18:19; 2 Samuel 21:8.

AENEAS [eh-NEE-uhs: "praise"]. A.D. 35. A paralytic in Lydda who was healed by Peter. Acts 9:33, 34.

AGABUS [AG-uh-buhs: possibly "locust"]. A.D. 45. A Christian prophet from Jerusalem who predicted a severe famine throughout the Roman Empire. He also prophesied Paul's arrest in Jerusalem by the Roman authorities. Acts 11:28; 21:10.

AGAG [AY-gag: "high" or "warlike," probably a title]

1. B.C. date unknown. A powerful king mentioned by Balaam in his third attempt to curse Israel. Numbers 24:7.

2. 1025 B.C. The king of the Amalekites whom Saul spared in direct disobedience to God's command. 1 Samuel 15:8–33.

AGEE [AG-ee: "fugitive"]. 1025 B.C. Father of Shammah, one of David's top thirty military commanders. 2 Samuel 23:11.

AGRIPPA [uh-GRIP-uh]. Ruled A.D. 50–100. Agrippa II, the ruler of Galilee to whom the new Roman governor, Festus, turned for advice concerning his prisoner, Paul. Acts 25:13–26; 26:1–32.

AGUR [AY-guhr: possibly "hireling" or "gatherer"]. B.C. date unknown. The author of Proverbs 30.

AHAB [AY-hab: "father is brother"]

1. One of Israel's most wicked kings, who ruled the northern kingdom 874–853 B.C. 1 Kings 16–21; 2 Chronicles 18–22.

2. 600 B.C. A false prophet among the Jews in Babylon during the Exile. Jeremiah 29:21–23.

AHARAH [uh-HAR-uh: "brother's follower"] 1850 B.C. One of five sons of Benjamin listed in 1 Chronicles 8:1. Called Ahiram in Numbers 26:38. Possibly the same as Aher in 1 Chronicles 7:12 and Ehi in Genesis 46:21.

AHARHEL [uh-HAR-hel: "brother of Rachel"]. B.C. date unknown. Listed in the genealogy of Judah in 1 Chronicles 4:8.

AHASAL [UH-ah-zal: possibly a corruption of Ahaziah, "Yahweh sustains"]. B.C. date unknown. Ancestor of Amashasi, a priest in Nehemiah's time. Nehemiah 11:13.

AHASBAI [uh-HAS-bi: "blooming"]. 1025 B.C. Father of Eliphelet, another of David's top thirty military officers. 2 Samuel 23:34. The parallel passage reads "Eliphal son of Ur" (1 Chron. 11:35).

AHASUERUS [uh-HAZ-yoo-EE-ruhs]

1. 575 B.C. Father of Darius the Mede, mentioned in Daniel 9:1.

2. Notable in history as Xerxes, who ruled Persia 486–465 B.C. The king of the Book of Esther.

AHAZ [Ay-haz: "he grasped"]

1. 950 B.C. Great grandson of King Saul. 1 Chronicles 8:35, 36; 9:42.

2. 742–725 B.C. Son of the godly Hezekiah, this evil eleventh king of Judah burned a son as a human sacrifice. 2 Kings 16; 2 Chronicles 28; Isaiah 7.

AHAZIAH [AY-huh-ZI-uh: "Yahweh sustains"]

1. The evil ninth king of Israel who ruled from 883–852 B.C. He turned to Bael-Zebub rather than the Lord when he was injured. 1 Kings 22; 2 Kings 1; 2 Chronicles 20. He was a son of Ahaz and Jezebel.

2. Evil sixth king of Judah who ruled in 841 B.C. 2 Kings 8,9; 2 Chronicles 22. He is called Jehoahaz in 2 Chronicles 21:16, 17.

AHBAN [AH-bahn: "brother of intelligence"]. B.C. date unknown. Listed only in the genealogy of Jerehmeel, 1 Chronicles 2:29.

AHER [AY-huhr: "another"(?)]. B.C. date unknown. The Benjamite ancestor of the Hushites. 1 Chronicles 7:12.

AHI [AY-hi: "my brother"]

1. B.C. date unknown. Listed only in the genealogy of Asher in 1 Chronicles 7:34. Possibly a mistranslation of "his brother Shomer."

2. B.C. date unknown. Head of a family listed in the genealogy of Gad in 1 Chronicles 5:15.

AHIAM [uh-HI-uhm]. 1000 B.C. One of David's top thirty military leaders. 2 Samuel 23:33; 1 Chronicles 11:35.

AHIAN [uh-HI-uhn: "brotherly"]. B.C. date unknown. Listed in the genealogy of Manasseh in 1 Chronicles 7:19.

AHIEZER [AY-hi-EE-zuhr: "brother is help"]

1. 1450 B.C. Leader of the tribe of Dan in Moses' day. Numbers 1:12.

2. 1000 B.C. Benjamite military leader and kinsman of Saul, he defected to David's army at Ziklag. 1 Chronicles 12:3.

AHIHUD [uh-HI-hud: "brother is majesty"]

1. B.C. date unknown. Son of Gera, a descendant of Benjamin. 1 Chronicles 8:7.

2. 1400 B.C. Leader from the tribe of Asher appointed by Moses to help divide the land upon entering Canaan. Numbers 34:27.

AHIJAH [uh-HI-juh: "Yahweh is brother"]

1. B.C. date unknown. A son of Jerahmeel, a descendant of Judah. 1 Chronicles 2:25.

2. 1025 B.C. Son of Ahitub, a priest with Saul's army who served the ark at Gibeah. Likely the same as Ahimelech 2. 1 Samuel 14:3, 18.

3. 1000 B.C. A Levite in charge of the temple treasures in David's day, according to the KJV and RSV. The NIV reads the name as an adjective, in 1 Chronicles 26:20.

4. 1000 B.C. A military officer, one of David's thirty mighty men listed in 1 Chronicles 11:36. A parallel text (2 Samuel 23:24) gives his name as Eliam.

5. 950 B.C. A secretary to Solomon. 1 Kings 4:3.

6. 935 B.C. The prophet of Shiloah who foretold the division of Solomon's kingdom. He later predicted the death of Jeroboam's son and the fate of Jeroboam's dynasty. 1 Kings 11:29–39; 14:1–18.

7. 925 B.C. Father of Baasha, a king of Israel. 1 Kings 15:27–39.

8. B.C. date unknown. KJV Ahiah. A descendant of Benjamin deported to Manahath, listed in 1 Chronicles 8:7. Possibly a scribal error duplicating v. 4.

AHIKAM [uh-HI-kuhm: "my brother has risen"]. 625 B.C. An official Josiah sent to inquire of prophetess Huldah concerning the rediscovered Book of the Law. 2 Kings 22:12,14: Jeremiah 26:24; 40:5–16.

AHILUD [uh-HI-luhd: "a brother born"(?)]. 1025 B.C. Official recorder under David and Solomon. Probably same as Ahilud, the father of Basna, one of Solomon's twelve district governors. 2 Samuel 8:16; 20:24; 1 Kings 4:3, 12.

AHIMAAZ [uh-HIM-ay-az: "brother" is wrath"(?)]

1. 1050 B.C. Father of Ahinoam, Saul's wife. 1 Samuel 14:50.

2. 975 B.C. Son of Zadok the high priest who remained loyal to David during Absalom's revolt. 2 Samuel 15:27, 17:17, 20; 18:19–29.

3. 950 B.C. One of Solomon's twelve district governors who married Solomon's daughter, Basemath. 1 Kings 4:15.

AHIMAN [uh-HI-muhn: "brother of fortune"]

1. 1400 B.C. Descendant of Anak, among the Canaanites driven from Hebron by Caleb. Numbers 13:22; Joshua 15:14.

2. 450 B.C. A gatekeeper at the temple in Jerusalem after the Exile. 1 Chronicles 9:17.

AHIMELECH [uh-HIM-eh-lak: "my brother is king"]

1. 1025 B.C. He fled with David from Saul. 1 Samuel 26:6.

2. 1025 B.C. The priest at Nob who aided David and was executed on Saul's orders with his fellow priests and family. 1 Samuel 21:1–9; 22:9–20.

3. 975 B.C. Son of Abiathar, and grandson of Ahimelech 2 Samuel 8:17; 1 Chronicles 24:6. Called Abimelech in 1 Chronicles 18:16.

AHINADAB [uh-HIN-uh-dab: "brother is noble"]. 950 B.C. one of Solomon's twelve district governors. 1 Kings 4:14.

AHIO [uh-HI-oh: "his brother"]

1. B.C. date unknown. Listed only in the genealogy of Benjamin in 1 Chronicles 8:14.

2. 1075 B.C. An uncle of Saul. 1 Chronicles 8:3; 9:37.

3. 1000 B.C. A son of Abinadab who helped move the ark from his father's house in Kirjath Jearim to Jerusalem. 2 Samuel 6:3, 4; 1 Chronicles 13:7.

AHIRA [uh-HI-ruh: "brother is evil"]. 1450 B.C. Leader of the tribe of Naphtali in Moses' day. Numbers 1:15; 2:29; 10:27.

AHIRAM [uh-HI-ruhm: "brother is exalted"]. 1850 B.C. Also called Aharah, in 1 Chronicles 8:1. Third of the five sons of Benjamin listed in Numbers 26:38. Possibly the same as Aher in 1 Chronicles 7:12 and Ehi in Genesis 46:21.

AHIROTH [uh-HI-roth: "brother is death"]. B.C. date unknown A Levite from whom Samuel is descended. 1 Chronicles 6:25.

AHISAMACH [uh-HIS-uh-mahk: "brother supports"]. 1475 B.C. A Danite craftsman who helped build the tabernacle and its furnishings. Exodus 31:6; 35:34; 38:23.

AHISH [uh-HISH: "Yahweh is brother"]. Probably a shortened form of Ahimelech.

1. B.C. date unknown. A son of Jerahmeel, a descendant of Judah. 1 Chronicles 2:25.

2. 1025 B.C. Son of Ahitub, he served as a priest with Saul's army. Likely the same as Ahimelech. 1 Samuel 14:3, 18.

3. 1000 B.C. A military commander, one of David's top thirty listed in 1 Chronicles 11:38. Parallel text in 2 Samuel 23:34 reads: "Eliam son of Ahithophel."

4. 1000 B.C. A Levite in charge of the temple treasuries in David's day. 1 Chronicles 26:20.

5. 950 B.C. A secretary of Solomon. 1 Kings 4:3.

6. 925 B.C. A prophet of Shiloh who foretold the division of the kingdom of Israel after the reign of Solomon. He later predicted the death of Jeroboam's son, and the end of Jeroboam's dynasty. 1 Kings 11:29–39; 14:1–18.

7. 925 B.C. Father of Beasha, who became king of Israel after killing Nadab, son of Jeroboam. 1 Kings 15:27, 33.

8. B.C. date unknown. A descendant of Benjamin listed in 1 Chronicles 8:7. Possibly a scribal error, duplicating v. 4.

AHISHAHAR [uh-HISH-uh-hahr: "brother of the dawn"]. B.C. date unknown. Listed in the genealogy of Benjamin in 1 Chronicles 7:10.

AHISHAR [uh-HI-xhshr: "brother has sung"]. 950 B.C. A chief official of Solomon in charge of the palace. 1 Kings 4:6.

AHITHOPHEL [uh-HITH-oh-fel: "brother of foolishness"]

1. 1025 B.C. Father of Eliam, a military commander. 2 Samuel 23:34.

2. 975 B.C. The advisor of David, who joined David's son Absalom in a revolt against his father. 2 Samuel 15–17. Some think he is the grandfather of Bathsheba (cf. 2 Sam. 23:34; 11:3), who joined Absalom because of David's adultery with Bathsheba (2 Sam. 11; 12).

AHITUB [uh-HI-tub: "brother is good"]

1. 1050 B.C. A priest, the father of Ahimelech 2 (see also Ahijah 2) the priest of Nob. 1 Samuel 14:3; 22:9.

2. 1050 B.C. Grandfather of Zadok, the high priest in David's day, as indicated by 1 Chronicles 9:11. See 2 Samuel 8:17; 1 Chronicles 6:7, 8, 52; 9:11; Ezra 7:2; Nehemiah 11:11. Possibly the same as Ahitub 1.

3. B.C. date unknown. A Levite, also father of Zadok, descended from Ahitub 2. 1 Chronicles 6:11, 12.

AHLAI [AH-li]. 1025 B.C. Father of Zabad, one of David's mighty men. 1 Chronicles 11:41.

AHOAH [uh-HO-uh]. 1825 B.C. Possibly an error for "Ahijah" in v. 7. Sixth of the nine sons of Bela, firstborn son of Benjamin. 1 Chronicles 8:4.

AHOLUAB. See Oholiab.

AHOUBAMAH. See Oholibamah.

AHUMAI [uh-HOO-mi]. B.C. date unknown. Clan leader listed in the genealogy of Judah in 1 Chronicles 4:2.

AHUSH [uh-HUSH: "Yahweh is brother"]. 450 B.C. A Jewish leader who sealed the covenant renewal in Nehemiah's day. Nehemiah 10:26.

AHUZAM [uh-HUZ-uhm: "possessor"]. B.C. date unknown. Listed in the genealogy of Judah in 1 Chronicles 4:6.

AHUZZATH [uh-HUZ-ath: "held fast"]. 2025 B.C. Advised Abimelech, king of the Philistines, when making a treaty with Isaac. Genesis 26:26–31.

AKIM [AY-kim: "woes"; possibly a shortened form of Jehoiakim]. B.C. date unknown. KJV, RSV—Achim. An ancestor of Jesus. Matthew 1:14.

AJAH [AY-juh: "vulture"]

1. 1975 B.C. Son of Zibeon and brother of Anah who lived in the land of Seir during Esau's time. Genesis 36:24.

2. 1075 B.C. Father of Rizpah, Saul's concubine. 2 Samuel 3:7; 21:8–11.

AKKUB [AK-ub: "pursuer"(?)]

1. B.C. date unknown. Ancestor of a family of gatekeepers after the Exile. Ezra 2:42; Nehemiah 7:45.

2. B.C. date unknown. Ancestor of a family of temple servants after the Exile. Ezra 2:45.

3. 450 B.C. A gatekeeper at the temple in Jerusalem, after the Exile. 1 Chronicles 9:17; Nehemiah 11:19; 12:25.

4. 450 B.C. A Levite who in Jerusalem instructed the people in the Law with Ezra. Nehemiah 8:7.

5. B.C. date unknown. A descendant of Zerubbabel listed in the genealogy of David's line. 1 Chronicles 3:24.

ALEMETH [AL-uh-meth: "hidden"]

1. 1825 B.C. A son of Becher, son of Benjamin. 1 Chronicles 7:8.

2. B.C. date unknown. A descendant of Jonathan, son of Saul. His father is given as Jehoaddah in 1 Chronicles 8:36 and Jarah in 1 Chronicles 9:42.

ALEXANDER [al-ig-ZAN-duhr: "defender of man"]

1. "The Great" king of Macedon from 336–323 B.C. He conquered the Persian Empire and spread Greek culture and language throughout the eastern world.

2. A.D. 30. A member of the Sanhedrin and kinsman of Annas the high priest. Acts 4:6.

3. A.D. 50. A son of Simon, the man from Cyrene who was forced by soldiers to carry the cross for Jesus. Mark 15:21.

4. A.D. 55. A Jewish spokesman at the time of the riot in Ephesus. Acts 19:33, 34.

5. A.D. 65. A teacher ejected by the apostle Paul for teaching false doctrine. 1 Timothy 1:20.

6. A.D. 65. A metalworker in Ephesus who opposed Paul's ministry. 2 Timothy 4:14.

ALIAH. See Alvan.

ALLON [AL-luhn: "large tree"]. B.C. date unknown. Listed in the genealogy of Simeon. 1 Chronicles 4:37.

ALMODAD [al-MO-dad: "agitator" or Elmodad, "God is friend"]. B.C. date unknown. A son of Joktan descended from Shem. Genesis 10:26; 1 Chronicles 1:20.

ALPHAEUS [al-FEE-uhs: "leader"]

1. A.D. 1. Father of Levi the tax collector, who became Matthew, one of the twelve apostles. Mark 2:14.

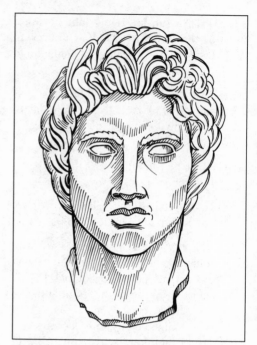

Alexander's vision of one world kingdom led to the spread of the Greek language across the East and provided the common tongue which made the gospel accessible to all in the first century.

2. A.D. 1. Father of the apostle James (the Less), not to be confused with James, son of Zebedee. Possibly the same as Alphaeus 1, which would make James and Matthew brothers. Matthew 10:3; Mark 3:18; Luke 6:15; Acts 1:13.

ALVAH [AL-vuh: "sublime"(?)]. B.C. date unknown. A descendant of Esau. Genesis 36:40; 1 Chronicles 1:51.

ALVAN [AL-vun: "sublime"(?)]. 1950 B.C. A Horite chief in the land of Seir when Esau settled there. Genesis 36:23; 1 Chronicles 1:40.

AMAL [AY-mahl: "laborer"]. B.C. date unknown. Listed in the genealogy of Asher. 1 Chronicles 7:35.

AMALEK [AM-ah-lek: "warlike"]. 1900 B.C. The grandson of Esau and ancestral source of the Amalekites. The name is also used of the people and of the land they lived in. Genesis 36:12; 1 Chronicles 1:36.

AMARIAH [am-uh-RI-uh: "Yahweh has said"]

1. 1100 B.C. Grandfather (or possibly great-grandfather) of Zadok, high priest in David's time. 1 Chronicles 8:7; Ezra 7:3.

2. B.C. date unknown. Descendant of Amariah 1, listed in the genealogy of Levi. 1 Chronicles 6:11.

3. B.C. date unknown. A descendant of Kohath, son of Levi. 1 Chronicles 23:19; 24:23.

4. 875 B.C. High priest during Jehoshaphat's reign. 2 Chronicles 19:11.

5. B.C. date unknown. Ancestor of Zephaniah the prophet. Zephaniah 1:1.

6. 725 B.C. A Levite who helped disburse offerings to the priests in Hezekiah's time. 2 Chronicles 31:15.

7. 525 B.C. Head of a priestly family that returned with Zerubbabel to Judah after the Exile. Nehemiah 10:3; 12:2, 13.

8. 450 B.C. A man who took a foreign wife after the Exile. Ezra 10:42.

9 B.C. date unknown. An ancestor of Athaiah, who remained in Jerusalem after the Exile. Nehemiah 11:4.

AMASA [uh-MAS-uh: "burden-bearer"(?)]

1. 975 B.C. The commander of Absalom's army. After Absalom's death he replaced Joab as commander of David's army, only to be murdered by Joab. 2 Samuel 17:25; 19:13; 20:4–13; 1 Chronicles 2:17.

2. 750 B.C. An Israelite who opposed enslavement of captured men of Judah. 2 Chronicles 28:12.

AMASAI [uh-MAS-i: "burden-bearer"(?)]

1. B.C. date unknown. A temple minister of music in David's time. 1 Chronicles 6:25, 35; 2 Chronicles 29:12.

2. 1000 B.C. Chief of David's thirty mighty men, possibly the same as Abishai, the brother of Joab; or possibly the same as Amasa 1. 1 Chronicles 12:18.

3. 1000 B.C. A priest who blew the trumpet as David brought the ark of the covenant to Jerusalem. 1 Chronicles 15:24.

AMASHAI [uh-MASH-i]. 450 B.C. A priest who resided in Jerusalem in Nehemiah's day. Nehemiah 11:13.

AMASIAH [am-ah-SI-uh: "Yahweh bears"]. 875 B.C. A military commander under Jehoshaphat. 2 Chronicles 17:16.

AMAZIAH [AM-uh-ZI-uh: "Yahweh is mighty"]

1. 1000 B.C. One of David's temple musicians. 1 Chronicles 6:45.

2. Ruled 798–767 B.C. The eighth king of Judah, who began well but turned from God and was assassinated. 2 Kings 14.

3. 775 B.C. A priest at Bethel who opposed Amos and was cursed by God's prophet. Amos 7:10–17.

4. 725 B.C. A clan leader in Hezekiah's day. 1 Chronicles 4:34.

AMI [AY-mi: "faithful"]. 950 B.C. A servant of Solomon whose descendants returned to Judah after the Exile. Ezra 2:57. Called Amon in Nehemiah 7:59.

AMITTAI [uh-MIT-i: "truthful"]. 775 B.C. Father of Jonah the prophet. 2 Kings 14:25; Jonah 1:1.

AMMIEL [AM-ee-el: "God is kinsman"]

1. 1450 B.C. A Danite assigned by Moses to explore Canaan. Numbers 13:12.

2. 1025 B.C. Father of Makir, who aided David when he fled from Absalom. 2 Samuel 9:4, 5; 17:27.

3. 1025 B.C. The father of Bathsheba, wife of David and mother of Solomon. 1 Chronicles 3:5. Called Eliam in 2 Samuel 11:3.

4. 1000 B.C. One of eight sons of Obed-Edom, all of whom were temple gate-keepers in David's day. 1 Chronicles 26:5.

AMMIHUD [uh-MI-hud: "my kinsman is glorious"]

1. 1450 B.C. Leader of the tribe of Ephraim in Moses' day. Numbers 1:10; 1 Chronicles 7:26.

2. 1400 B.C. The Simeonite appointed by Moses to help divide the land of Canaan. Numbers 34:20.

3. 1400 B.C. The Naphtalite appointed by Moses to help divide the land of Canaan. Numbers 34:28.

4. 1025 B.C. Father of the king of Geshur, where Absalom fled after assassinating his half-brother Amnon. 2 Samuel 13:37.

5. 450 B.C. Descendant of Perez the son of Judah, who resettled in Jerusalem after the Exile. 1 Chronicles 9:4.

AMMINADAB [uh-MIN-uh-dab: "my kinsman is noble"]

1. B.C. date unknown. A descendant of Levi, identified as father of Korah in 1 Chronicles 6:22.

2. 1500 B.C. Father of Nahshon and his sister Elisheba, Aaron's wife. He led the tribe of Judah in Moses' day, and was an ancestor of David. Exodus 6:23; Numbers 1:7; Ruth 4:19, 20; Matthew 1:4; Luke 3:33.

3. 1000 B.C. Head of a Levite family, he helped carry the ark when David

brought it to Jerusalem. 1 Chronicles 15:10, 11.

AMMISHADDAI [am-mi-SHAD-i: "Almighty is kinsman"]. 1500 B.C. Father of Ahiezer, head of the tribe of Dan in Moses' day. Numbers 1:12.

AMMIZABAD [uh-MIZ-uh-bad: "my kinsman has given"]. 975 B.C. Son of Benaiah, captain of David's bodyguard. He was a commander of his father's division. 1 Chronicles 27:6.

AMNON [AM-nahn: "faithful"]

1. B.C. (date unknown). Listed in the genealogy of Judah. 1 Chronicles 4:20.

2. 1000 B.C. Firstborn son of David, who raped his half-sister Tamar. Later Tamar's brother Absalom assassinated him. 2 Samuel 3:2; 13:1–39; 1 Chronicles 3:1.

AMOK [AY-muhk: "deep"]. 525 B.C. A priest who returned to Judah with Zerubbabel after the Exile. Nehemiah 12:7, 20.

AMON (UH-muhn: "trustworthy")

1. B.C. date unknown. The Egyptian deity of Thebes. Jeremiah 46:25.

2. 950 B.C. A servant of Solomon whose descendants returned to Judah with Zerubbabel after the Exile. Nehemiah 7:59. Called Ami in Ezra 2:57.

3. 875 B.C. Governor of Samaria during Ahab's reign. 1 Kings 22:26.

4. Ruled 542–640 B.C. Son and successor of the evil king Manasseh. His own officials assassinated him. 2 Kings 21:18–26; 2 Chronicles 33:21–25.

AMOS (AY-muhs: "burden-bearer")

1. 775 B.C. A prophet during the reigns of Uzziah and Jeroboam II, his message is contained in the Book of Amos.

2. B.C. date unknown. An ancestor of Christ. Luke 3:25.

AMOZ [AY-mahz: "strong"]. 775 B.C. Father of Isaiah the prophet. 2 Kings 19:2, 20; Isaiah 1:1.

AMPLIAS [AM-plee-AY-uhs: "large"]. A.D. 55. A Roman Christian to whom Paul sent greetings. Romans 16:8.

AMRAM [AM-ram: "the kinsman is exalted"]

1. 1525 B.C. A descendant of Levi and father of Moses, Aaron, and Miriam. Exodus 6:18, 20; Numbers 26:58, 59.

2. 450 B.C. A Jew who took a foreign wife in Ezra's day. Ezra 10:34.

AMRAPHEL [AM-rah-fel: meaning uncertain]. 2100 B.C. A king of Shinar, who with other kings defeated the kings of Sodom and Gomorrah, only to be defeated by Abraham and his allies. Genesis 14.

AMZI [AM-zi: "my strength"]

1. B.C. date unknown. A Levite who served as a minister of music in David's time. 1 Chronicles 6:46.

2. B.C. date unknown. Ancestor of Adaiah, a priest who settled in Jerusalem in Nehemiah's time. Nehemiah 11:12.

ANAH [AY-nuh]

1. 1975 B.C. The father of Oholibamah, one of Esau's wives. Genesis 36:14, 24–29; 1 Chronicles 1:40. Probably the same as Beeri, father of Judith. Genesis 26:34

2. 1950 B.C. The uncle of Anah 1, a Horite chief in Esau's time. Genesis 36:20, 29: 1 Chronicles 1:38.

ANAIAH [uh-NI-uh: "Yahweh has answered"]

1. 450 B.C. He stood with Ezra when he read the Law to the people. Nehemiah 8:4.

2. 450 B.C. A signer of the covenant renewal with God in Nehemiah's time. Nehemiah 10:22. Possibly the same as Anaiah 1.

ANAK [AY-nak: "long-necked") B.C. date unknown. Ancestral source of the Anakites. Numbers 13:22, 28, 33.

ANAN [AY-nuhn: "cloud"]. 450 B.C. A signer of the covenant renewal in Nehemiah's time. Nehemiah 10:26.

ANANI [uh-NAY-ni: "my cloud"(?)]. B.C. date unknown. A descendant of Zerubbabel, listed in the genealogy of David's line. 1 Chronicles 3:24.

ANANIAH [AN-uh-NI-uh: "Yahweh has covered"(?)]. 500 B.C. Grandfather of Azariah, who helped reconstruct the walls of Jerusalem in Nehemiah's time. Nehemiah 3:23.

ANANIAS [AN-uh-NI-hus: "protected by Yahweh"]

1. A.D. 30. A believer who was struck dead for plotting with his wife Sapphira to deceive the early church. Acts 5:1–11.

2. A.D. 35. A Christian in Damascus, noted for healing Saul after he was stricken with blindness. Acts 9:10–19; 22:12.

3. A.D. 60. High priest at Paul's trial before the Sanhedrin in Jerusalem. Acts 23:2; 24:1.

ANATH [AY-nath]. 1225 B.C. Father of Shamgar, a minor judge of Israel. Judges 3:31; 5:6.

ANATHOTH [AN-uh-thoth]

1. 1800 B.C. A son of Becher, son of Benjamin. 1 Chronicles 7:8.

2. 450 B.C. A leader who signed the covenant renewal in Nehemiah's time. Nehemiah 10:19.

ANDREW [AN-droo: "manly"]. A.D. 25. One of Jesus' twelve disciples. This brother of Peter operated a fishing business with him near their home in Capernaum, in partnership with James and John. The church historian Eusebius says Andrew later ministered in Scythia, an area in southern Russia north of the Black Sea. Matthew 4:18–22; Mark 1:16–18; John 1:40.

ANDRONICUS [an-DRON-uh-kuhs: "conqueror"]. A.D. 55. A male relative Paul greeted in Romans 16:7.

ANER [AY-nuhr: "sprout" or "waterfall"(?)]. 2100 B.C. One of the three Amorite brothers allied with Abraham against the invaders who had taken Lot captive. Genesis 14:13, 24.

ANIAM [uh-NI-uhm: "lamentation of the people"]. B.C. date unknown. Listed in the genealogy of Manasseh in 1 Chronicles 7:19.

ANNAS [AN-uhs: "grace"]. High priest from 6 B.C. to A.D. 15. He questioned Jesus after his arrest. Caiaphas, the acting high priest at the time, was his son-in-law. John 18:13, 24; Acts 4:6.

ANTIPAS [AN-ti-puhs]. A.D. 80. A Christian martyr from the church in Pergamum. Revelation 2:13.

ANTOTHIJAH [AN-thoh-THI-jah: "belonging to Anathoth"(?)]. B.C. date unknown. Listed in the genealogy of Benjamin in 1 Chronicles 8:24.

ANUB [AY-nub: "ripe"]. B.C. date unknown. Listed in the genealogy of Judah in 1 Chronicles 4:8.

APELLES [uh-PEL-eez]. A.D. 55. A Christian whom Paul greeted in Romans 16:10 as "approved in Christ."

APHIAH [uh-FI-uh: "striving"(?)]. B.C. date unknown. An ancestor of Saul. 1 Samuel 9:1.

APOLLOS [uh-PAH-lohs: "a destroyer"(?)]. A.D. 50. A scholarly Jewish Christian who became an influential teacher in the early church. Acts 18:24–25; 1 Corinthians 1:12; 3:4–6, 22.

APOLLYON [uh-PAHL-ee-ahn: "the destroyer, destruction"]. Greek name of Abaddon, the angel of the abyss and demon king of the "locusts" of Revelation 9:11.

APPAIM [AP-ay-im: "faces: nostrils"]. B.C. date unknown. Listed in the genealogy of Jerahmeel, a descendant of Judah. 1 Chronicles 2:30, 31.

AQUILA [AK-wih-luh: "eagle"]. A.D. 50. An early friend and coworker of the apostle Paul. Acts 18.

ARA [AR-uh]. B.C. date unknown. Listed in the genealogy of Asher. 1 Chronicles 7:38.

ARAD [AIR-ad: "fugitive"]. B.C. date unknown. Listed in the genealogy of Benjamin in 1 Chronicles 8:15.

ARAH [AIR-uh: "wanderer, traveler"]

1. B.C. date unknown. Listed in the genealogy of Asher. 1 Chronicles 7:39.

2. B.C. date unknown. Ancestor of a family that returned to Judah with Zerubbabel after the Exile. Ezra 2:5; Nehemiah 6:18; 7:10.

ARAM [AIR-uhm: "high, exalted"]

1. B.C. date unknown. Last of the five sons of Shem and ancestor of the Arameans. Genesis 10:22, 23; 1 Chronicles 1:17. The name is frequently used to refer to the people or the land of the Arameans.

2. 2000 B.C. Son of Kemuel, the nephew of Abraham. Genesis 22:21.

3. B.C. date unknown. Listed in the genealogy of Asher in 1 Chronicles 7:34.

ARAN [AIR-ahn: "wild goat"]. 1950 B.C. Son of a Horite chief. Genesis 36:28.

ARAUNAH [uh-RAH-nuh: possibly "noble"]. 1000 B.C. The Jebusite whose threshing floor David purchased to build an altar and end a plague. Later Solomon built the temple on this site. 2 Samuel 24:16–25; 1 Chronicles 21:18–28; 2 Chronicles 3:1.

ARBA [AR-buh: "four"]. Ancestor of Anak and founder of Kirjath Arba (Hebron). Joshua 14:15; 15:13; 21:11.

ARCHELAUS [ahr-kuh-LAY-uhs: "people's chief"]. Reigned 4 B.C.–A.D. 6. This son of Herod the Great succeeded his father as ethnarch of Judea. Matthew 2:22.

ARCHIPPUS [ahr-KIP-uhs: "chief groom"]. A.D. 60. A Christian Paul encouraged (1 Cor. 4:17) and mentioned in his letter to Philemon (v. 2).

ARD [AHRD]. 1825 B.C. Last of the ten sons of Benjamin and father of his own clan. Genesis 46:21; Numbers 26:40. Probably same as Addar, son of Bela, in 1 Chronicles 8:3.

ARDON [AHR-dahn: "descendant"(?)]. B.C. date unknown. Listed in the genealogy of Judah, 1 Chronicles 2:18.

ARELI [uh-REE-li]. 1850 B.C. Last of seven sons of Gad and head of his own clan. Genesis 46:16; Numbers 26:17.

ARETAS [AHR-uh-tuhs: "goodness, excellence"]. A.D. 35. Aretas IV, the Nabatean king, tried to capture Paul. 2 Corinthians 11:32.

ARGOB [AHR-gahb: "a mound"]. 750 B.C. An Israelite official assassinated with Pekahiah by Pekah. 2 Kings 15:25.

ARIDAI [AIR-uh-di]. 475 B.C. One of the ten sons of Haman who were executed by the Jews during the reign of Ahasuerus. Esther 9:9.

ARIDATHA [AHR-uh-DAY-thuh]. 475 B.C. Another of the ten sons of Haman killed by the Jews during Ahasuerus's reign. Esther 9:8.

ARIEH [AIR-yah: "lion (of Yahweh?)"]. 750 B.C. An official slain with Pekahiah by Pekah. 2 Kings 15:25.

ARIEL (AIR-ee-el: "lion of God"]. 450 B.C. He was sent by Ezra to reclaim temple servants from Iddo, leader at Casiphia. Ezra 8:16.

ARIOCH [AHR-ee-ahk: possibly "lion-like"]

1. 2100 B.C. King of Ellasar who attacked Sodom and Gomorrah and took Lot captive. Abraham defeated them and rescued Lot. Genesis 14:1, 9.

2. 600 B.C. Commander of Nebuchadnezzar's guard, instructed by the king to execute the wise men of Babylon. Daniel 2:14, 15, 24, 25.

ARISAI [AHR-uh-si]. 475 B.C. One of the ten sons of Haman executed by the Jews during Ahasuerus's reign. Esther 9:9.

ARISTARCHUS [AIR-uhs-TAHR-kuhs: "best ruler"]. A.D. 55. A Christian from Thessalonica who traveled with Paul and shared his imprisonment. Acts 19:29; 20:4; 27:2; Colossians 4:10: Philemon 24.

ARISTOBULUS [air-is-TOB-yuh-luhs: "best advisor"]. A.D. 55. A Roman whose household Paul greeted. Romans 16:10.

ARMONI [ahr-MOH-nee]. 1000 B.C. Son of Saul and his concubine Rizpah. 2 Samuel 21:8.

ARNAN [AHR-nuhn: "joyous"(?)]. B.C. date unknown. A descendant of Zerubbabel listed in the genealogy David. 1 Chronicles 3:21.

ARODI [AIR-oh-dee]. 1900 B.C. One of seven sons of Gad. Genesis 46:16: He is also called Arod. Numbers 26:17.

ARPHAXAD [Ahr-FAKS-ad]. B.C. date unknown]. A son of Shem and an ancestor of Christ through Joseph. Genesis 10:22, 24; Luke 3:36.

ARTAXERXES [AHR-tuh-ZERK-sees]. The title of four Persian kings. Artaxerxes I Longimanus, who reigned 464–424 B.C., is the Artaxerxes of the Bible. He authorized rebuilding Jerusalem's walls under Nehemiah. Ezra 4:7; 7:1—8:1; Nehemiah 2:1; 5:14.

ARTEMAS [AHR-teh-muhs: possibly contracted form of Artemidorus, "gift of Artemis," the Greek goddess]. A.D. 55. A Christian mentioned in Paul's letter to Titus. Titus 3:12.

ARZA [AHR-zuh]. 900 B.C. The steward in whose house Elah was slain by his successor, Zimri. 1 Kings 16:9.

ASA [AY-suh: "healer"]

1. 910–869 B.C. The third king of Judah, and its first godly ruler. 1 Kings 15:9–33; 2 Chronicles 14—16.

2. B.C. date unknown. Ancestor of Berechiah, a Levite who lived in Jerusalem after the Exile. 1 Chronicles 9:16.

ASAHEL [AS-uh-hel: "God has made")

1. 1025 B.C. Brother of Joab and Abishai, the sons of Zeruiah, David's sister. One of David's military commanders killed by Abner. 2 Samuel 2:18–23, 30, 32; 3:27, 30; 23:24; 1 Chronicles 2:16; 11:26; 27:7.

2. 875 B.C. A Levite sent by Jehoshaphat to teach the Law to the people of Judah. 2 Chronicles 17:8.

3. 725 B.C. A supervisor overseeing the collection of contributions to the temple in Hezekiah's time. 2 Chronicles 31:13.

4. 450 B.C. A man who opposed Ezra's plan to rid the land of foreign wives. Ezra 10:15.

ASAIAH [uh-ZAY-uh: "Yahweh has made"]

1. 1000 B.C. A Levite who helped David return the ark to Jerusalem. 1 Chronicles 6:30; 15:6, 11.

2. 725 B.C. A Simeonite clan leader in Hezekiah's time. 1 Chronicles 4:36.

3. 825 B.C. An official whom Josiah sent to inquire of the prophetess Huldah. 2 Kings 22:12, 14.

4. 450 B.C. A man who settled in Jerusalem after the Exile. 1 Chronicles 9:5. Called Masseiah in Nehemiah 11:5.

ASAPH [AY-Saf: "collector"]

1. B.C. date unknown. A descendant of Korah whose descendants were temple gatekeepers in David's time. 1 Chronicles 26:1.

2. 1000 B.C. A chief minister of music in David's time. Asaph is credited with authoring Psalms 50 and 72—83. 1 Chronicles 6:39; 15:17, 19.

3. B.C. date unknown. A descendant of Shemaiah, who settled in Jerusalem after the Exile. 1 Chronicles 9:15.

4. 725 B.C. Father of Joah, a historian in the court of Hezekiah. 2 Kings 18:18, 37; Isaiah 36:3.

5. 450 B.C. Keeper of the king's forests in Judah. Artaxerxes sent him a letter authorizing him to supply the timber needed by Nehemiah to rebuild Jerusalem. Nehemiah 2:8.

ASAREL [AS-uh-rel]. B.C. date unknown. Listed in the genealogy of Judah in 1 Chronicles 4:16.

ASHARELAH [AS-uh-REH-luh] 1000 B.C. A son of Asaph who ministered with music. 1 Chronicles 25:2.

ASHBEL [ASH-bel: "man of Baal"(?)]. 1850 B.C. One of the ten sons of Benjamin, listed in Genesis 46:21, Numbers 26:38, and 1 Chronicles 8:1.

ASHER [ASH-uhr: "happy"]. 1900 B.C. Second son of Jacob and Zilpah, the maidservant of his first wife, Leah. Ancestral head of the tribe of Asher. Genesis 30:13; 35:26; 46:17: 49:20; 1 Chronicles 2:2; Luke 2:36; Revelation 7:6.

ASHHUR [ASH-uhr: "happy"(?)]. B.C. date unknown. A descendant of Judah and chief of the people of Tekoa. 1 Chronicles 2:24; 4:5.

ASHKENAZ [ASH-keh-nahz]. B.C. date unknown. First son of Gomer and a great-grandson of Noah. Genesis 10:3; 1 Chronicles 1:6.

ASHPENAZ [ASH-peh-naz]. 600 B.C. Chief official over Nebuchadnezzar's school for training the bureaucrats who administered the Babylonian Empire, who was responsible for the training and instruction of Daniel and his companions. Daniel 1:3.

ASHURBANIPAL [ash-uhr-BAHN-uh-pahl: "Asahur has created an heir"]. 669–626 B.C. This son of Esarhaddon was the last of the great kings of Assyria. Ezra 4:10.

ASHVATH [ASH-vath: "fashioned"(?)]. B.C. date unknown. Listed in the genealogy of Asher. 1 Chronicles 7:33.

ASIEL [AS-es-el]. B.C. date unknown. An ancestor of Jehu, a Simeonite clan leader in Hezekiah's time. 1 Chronicles 4:35.

ASNAH [AS-nah]. B.C. date unknown. Ancestral head of a family of temple servants who returned to Judah with Zerubbabel after the Exile. Ezra 2:50.

ASPATHA [as-PAY-thok: "horse-given"(?)]. 475 B.C. One of the ten sons of Haman executed by the Jews in the time of Esther. Esther 9:7.

ASRIEL [AS-ree-el]. 1400 B.C. A descendant of Manasseh and head of his own clan. Numbers 26:31; Joshua 17:2; 1 Chronicles 7:14.

ASSHUR [ASH-uhr: "level plain"(?)]. B.C. date unknown. Second of the five sons of Shem, possibly the ancestor of the Assyrians. Genesis 10:22; 1 Chronicles 1:17.

ASSIR [AS-uhr: "Captive"]

1. B.C. date unknown. A Levite descended from Korah. Exodus 6:24; 1 Chronicles 6:22.

2. B.C. date unknown. Listed in genealogy in 1 Chronicles 6:23, 37.

ASYNCRITUS [uh-SING-krih-tuhs: "incomparable"]. A.D. 55. A Roman Christian to whom Paul sent greetings. Romans 16:14.

ATER [AY-tuhr: "bound"]

1. B.C. date unknown. Ancestral head of a family that returned to Judah with Zerubbabel after the Exile. Ezra 2:16; Nehemiah 7:21.

2. B.C. date unknown. Ancestor of a family of gatekeepers who returned to Judah with Zerubbabel. Nehemiah 7:45.

3. 450 B.C. A leader who signed the covenant renewal in Nehemiah's time, possibly with the name of his family's ancestral head. Nehemiah 10:17.

ATHAIAH [uh-THAY-uh: "Yahweh is helper"]. 450 B.C. A Judahite who lived in Jerusalem after the Exile. Nehemiah 11:4.

ATHALIAH [ATH-uh-LI-uh: "Yahweh is great"]

1. B.C. date unknown. One of six sons of Jeroham, a Benjamite who lived in Jerusalem. 1 Chronicles 8:26.

2. B.C. 841–835. The evil queen who murdered her grandchildren to secure the throne, and the only woman to reign over Judah. 2 Kings 11; 2 Chronicles 22; 23.

3. 475 B.C. Father of Jeshaiah, head of a family which returned to Judah with Ezra after the Exile. Ezra 8:7.

ATHLAI [ATH-li: shortened form of Athaliah, "Yahweh is great"]. 450 B.C. A descendant of Bebai who took a foreign wife in Ezra's time. Ezra 10:28.

ATTAI [AT-ti: "timely"]

1. B.C. date unknown. Listed in the genealogy of Jerahmeel, a descendant of Judah. 1 Chronicles 2:35, 36.

2. 1000 B.C. A Gadite warrior who joined David at Ziklag. 1 Chronicles 12:11.

3. 900 B.C. Second son of Rehoboam and Maacah, the daughter of Absalom. 2 Chronicles 11:20.

AUGUSTUS CAESAR [uh-GUST-uhs: "august"]. 63 B.C.–A.D. 14.]. Title of Octavian, nephew and successor of Julius Caesar. Christ was born during his reign. Luke 2:1.

AZALIAH [AZ-uh-LI-uh: "Yahweh has set aside"]. 650 B.C. Father of Shaphan, the secretary of Josiah. 2 Kings 22:3; 2 Chronicles 34:8.

AZANIAH [AZ-uh-NI-uh: "Yahweh has heard"]. 475 B.C. Father of Jeshua, a Levite who sealed the covenant renewal with God in Nehemiah's time. Nehemiah 10:9.

AZAREL [AZ-uh-rel: "God has helped"].

1. 1000 B.C. A Korahite who joined David's army at Ziklag. 1 Chronicles 12:6.

2. 1000 B.C. A son of Heman and a musician in David's time. 1 Chronicles

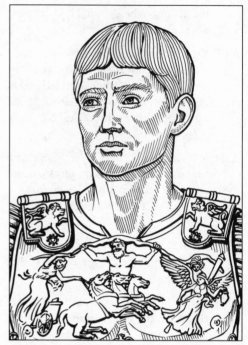

Augustus put down piracy and enforced peace throughout the Roman Empire, enabling Christian missionaries to travel freely as they spread the gospel everywhere.

25:18. Called Uzziel in 1 Chronicles 25:4.

3. 1000 B.C. Son of Jeroham and officer of David from the tribe of Daniel 1 Chronicles 27:22.

4. 475 B.C. Father of Amashai, a priest who settled in Jerusalem after the Exile. Nehemiah 11:13.

5. 450 B.C. A descendant of Binnui who took a foreign wife in Ezra's time. Ezra 10:41.

6. 450 B.C. A priest who played music at the dedication of the walls of Jerusalem in Nehemiah's time. Nehemiah 12:36.

AZARIAH [AZ-uh-RI-uh: "Yahweh has helped"]

1. B.C. date unknown. Listed in the genealogy of Judah in 1 Chronicles 2:8.

2. B.C. date unknown. Ancestor of Samuel the prophet, named in the genealogy of Heman the musician in David's time. 1 Chronicles 6:36.

3. B.C. date unknown. Listed in the genealogy of Jerahmeel, a descendant of Judah, in 1 Chronicles 2:38, 39.

4. B.C. date unknown. Ancestor of Zadok the high priest named in the genealogy of Ezra the scribe. Ezra 7:3. He is excluded from the list of high priests in 1 Chronicles 6:7.

5. 975 B.C. Son of Ahimaaz and grandson of Zadok the high priest. 1 Chronicles 6:9.

6. 950 B.C. Chief priest in Solomon's time. 1 Kings 14:21; 1 Chronicles 6:10, 11.

7. 950 B.C. Son of Nathan and the official of Solomon in charge of the twelve district governors. 1 Kings 4:5.

8. 900 B.C. A prophet during the reign of Asa. 2 Chronicles 15:1–8.

9. 850 B.C. A son of Jehoshaphat, king of Judah, killed by his brother Jehoram. 2 Chronicles 21:2.

10. 850 B.C. A military commander who helped Jehoiada overthrow Athaliah and place Joash on the throne of Judah. 2 Chronicles 23:1.

11. 850 B.C. Another military commander, a son of Obed, who aided Jehoiada. 2 Chronicles 23:1.

12. 792–740 B.C. The tenth king of Judah. Also called Uzziah. 2 Kings 14:21; 15:1–8; 1 Chronicles 3:12.

13. 775 B.C. The high priest who opposed Uzziah king of Judah. 2 Chronicles 26:17–20.

14. 750 B.C. An Israelite leader who opposed enslavement of captured men of Judah. 2 Chronicles 28:12.

15. 750 B.C. Father of Joel, a Levite who helped purify the temple in Hezekiah's time. 2 Chronicles 29:12.

16. 725 B.C. A Levite, son of Jehalelel, who helped purify the temple during the reign of Hezekiah. 2 Chronicles 29:12.

17. 725 B.C. A descendant of Zadok and high priest in Hezekiah's time. 2 Chronicles 31:10, 13. Possibly the same as Azariah 15.

18. 600 B.C. Son of Hilkiah, high priest in Josiah's time, and ancestor of Ezra. 1 Chronicles 6:13, 14; Ezra 7:1.

19. 600 B.C. Original name of Abednego, one of the three companions of Daniel who refused to worship Nebuchadnezzar's idol. Daniel 1:7; 2:17, 49; 3:12–30.

20. 575 B.C. A son of Hoshaiah who ignored the advice of Jeremiah. Jeremiah 43:2. Called Jezaniah in Jeremiah 42:1.

21. 525 B.C. One of those who returned to Judah with Zerubbabel after the Exile. Nehemiah 7:7. Called Seraiah in Ezra 2:2.

22. 450 B.C. A son of Masseiah who helped rebuild the walls of Jerusalem in Nehemiah's time. Nehemiah 3:23, 24.

23. 450 B.C. A Levite who with Ezra instructed the people in the Law. Nehemiah 8:7.

24. 450 B.C. A priest who sealed the covenant renewal with God in Nehemiah's time. Nehemiah 10:2. The name is likely that of a family's ancestral head, perhaps Ezra in Nehemiah 12:1, 13 (not Ezra the scribe).

25. 450 B.C. A leader of Judah at the time of the dedication of the walls of Jerusalem in Nehemiah's time. Nehemiah 12:33.

26. 450 B.C. Head of a priestly family who settled in Jerusalem after the Exile; descendant of Azariah 18. 1 Chronicles 9:11. Properly called Seraiah, as in 1 Chronicles 6:14; Nehemiah 11:11.

AZARYAHU [AZ-uh-RI-uh-hoo: "God has helped"]. 850 B.C. A son of Jehoshaphat killed by his brother Jehoram, successor of Jehoshaphat. 2 Chronicles 21:2–4.

AZAZ [AY-zaz: "powerful"]. B.C. date unknown. Listed only in the genealogy of Reuben in 1 Chronicles 5:8.

AZAZIAH [AZ-uh-ZI-uh: "Yahweh is strong"]

1. 1025 B.C. Father of Hoshea, leader of the tribe of Ephraim in David's day. 1 Chronicles 27:20.

2. 1000 B.C. A Levite who played the harp as David brought the ark back to Jerusalem. 1 Chronicles 15:21.

3. 725 B.C. A supervisor overseeing collection of contributions to the temple in Hezekiah's time. 2 Chronicles 31:13.

AZBUK [AZ-buk]. 475 B.C. Father of Nehemiah (not the governor of the same name), who helped rebuild the wall of Jerusalem. Nehemiah 3:16.

AZEL [AY-zel: "noble"]. B.C. date unknown. A descendant of Jonathan, son of Saul, listed in 1 Chronicles 8:37, 38; 9:43, 44.

AZGAD [AZ-gad: "Gad is strong"]

1. B.C. date unknown. Ancestral head of a family whose descendants returned from Exile with Zerubbabel and, a later group, with Ezra. Ezra 2:12; 8:12; Nehemiah 7:17.

2. 450 B.C. A leader who signed, probably with the name of his family's ancestor (see Azgad 1), the covenant renewal with God in Nehemiah's time. Nehemiah 10:15.

AZIEL [AY-zee-el: "God is power"]. 1000 B.C. Shortened form of Jaasiel (1 Chron. 15:18). A Levite who played the lyre as David returned the ark to Jerusalem. 1 Chronicles 15:20.

AZIZA [ah-ZI-zuh: "strong"]. 450 B.C. A Jew who took a foreign wife during the Exile. Ezra 10:27.

AZMAVETH [AZ-muh-veth: "strength of death"]

1. 1000 B.C. One of David's thirty top military men. 2 Samuel 23:31; 1 Chronicles 11:33.

2. 1000 B.C. Father of Jeziel and Pelet, warriors who joined David at Ziklag. 1 Chronicles 12:3. Probably same as Azmaveth 1.

3. 1000 B.C. A chief official of David, in charge of the royal storehouses. 1 Chronicles 27:25.

4. B.C. date unknown. A descendant of Jonathan, son of Saul, named in 1 Chronicles 9:42.

AZOR [AY-zor]. B.C. date unknown. An ancestor of Jesus listed in Matthew's genealogy of Jesus. Matthew 1:13, 14.

AZRIEL [AZ-ree-el: "God is helper"]

1. 1000 B.C. Father of Jerimoth, a leader of the tribe of Naphtali in David's time. 1 Chronicles 27:19.

2. 750 B.C. A family head of the tribe of Manasseh, taken captive by Tiglath-Pileser, king of Assyria. 1 Chronicles 5:24–26.

3. 625 B.C. Father of Seraiah, who was sent by Jehoiakim to arrest Jeremiah and Baruch. Jeremiah 36:26.

AZRIKAM [AZ-rih-kam: "help has risen"]

1. B.C. date unknown. A Benjamite descended from Jonathan, son of Saul. 1 Chronicles 8:38; 9:44.

2. 750 B.C. A chief official of Ahaz in charge of the palace. 2 Chronicles 28:7.

3. B.C. date unknown. Ancestor of Shamaiah, a Levite who resettled in Jerusalem after the Exile. 1 Chronicles 9:14; Nehemiah 11:15.

4. B.C. date unknown. A descendant of Zerubbabel listed in the royal line of David. 1 Chronicles 3:23.

AZZAN [AZ-zuhn]. 1450 B.C. Father of Paltiel, appointed by Moses to help divide the land upon entering Canaan. Numbers 34:26.

AZZUR [AZ-uhr: "helper"]

1. 825 B.C. Father of Hananiah, the false prophet who opposed Jeremiah. Jeremiah 28.

2. 575 B.C. Father of Jaazaniah, a Jewish leader seen by Ezekiel in a vision. Ezekiel 11:1.

3. 450 B.C. A leader who sealed the covenant renewal with God, probably with the name of his family's ancestor. Nehemiah 10:17.

B

BAAL [BAY-uhl: "master, lord"]

1. The title of the central Canaanite deity of Old Testament times. Local deities were also called "Baals" and were deemed to own and have power over specific locations. Numbers 25:1–5: 1 Kings 16:31, 32; 2 Kings 10:18–28; Jeremiah 19:5.

2. B.C. date unknown. Listed only in the genealogy of Reuben in 1 Chronicles 5:5.

3. B.C. date unknown. One of ten sons of Jeiel and a brother of Kish, Saul's ancestor. 1 Chronicles 8:30.

BAAL-HANAN [BAY-uhl HAY-nuhn: "Baal is gracious"]. B.C. date unknown.

1. A pre-Israelite king of Edom. Genesis 36:38, 39.

2. 1000 B.C. The overseer of David's olive and sycamore trees. 1 Chronicles 27:28.

BAALIS [BAY-uhl-is: "lord of joy"(?)]. 575 B.C. King of the Ammonites after the fall of Jerusalem. Jeremiah 40:14.

BAANA [BAY-ah-nuh: "son of oppression"]

1. 950 B.C. One of Solomon's twelve district governors. 1 Kings 4:12.

2. 950 B.C. Also one of Solomon's twelve district governors. 1 Kings 4:18.

3. 475 B.C. Father of Zadok, who helped repair the wall of Jerusalem in Nehemiah's time. Nehemiah 3:4.

BAANAH [BAY-ah-nuh: "son of oppression"]

1. 1050 B.C. Father of Heled, one of David's military elite. 2 Samuel 23:29; 1 Chronicles 11:30.

2. 1000 B.C. A military officer involved in the murder of Ishbosheth, Saul's son and successor. 2 Samuel 4:2–12.

3. 525 B.C. One who returned to Judah with Zerubbabel. Ezra 2:2; Nehemiah 7:7.

4. 450 B.C. A leader who signed the covenant renewal in Nehemiah's time, probably with the name of a family ancestor. Nehemiah 10:27.

BAARA [BAY-ah-ruh]. B.C. date unknown. A divorced wife of Shaharaim, listed only in the genealogy of Benjamin in 1 Chronicles 8:8.

BAASEIAH [BAY-uh-SEE-yuh: "Yahweh is bold" or "work of the Lord"]. B.C. date unknown. An ancestor of Asaph, the chief minister of music in David's time. 1 Chronicles 6:40.

BAASHA [BAY-ah-shuh: "boldness"(?)]. 908–888 B.C. He became the third king of Israel by assassinating his predecessor. 1 Kings 15:18—16:13; 2 Chronicles 16:1–6.

BAKBAKKAR [bak-BAK-uhr: "searcher"]. 450 B.C. A Levite who resettled in Jerusalem after the Exile. 1 Chronicles 9:15. Called Bakbukiah in Nehemiah 11:17.

BAKBUK [BAK-buk: "wasted" or "flask"]. B.C. date unknown. Ancestor of a family of temple servants who returned to Judah after the Exile. Ezra 2:51; Nehemiah 7:53.

BAKBUKIAH [BAK-buh-KI-uh: "wasted by Yahweh" or "Yahweh's flask"]

1. 525 B.C. A Levite who returned to Judah with Zerubbabel. Nehemiah 12:9.

2. 475 B.C. A Levite gatekeeper who guarded the temple storehouse. Nehemiah 12:25.

3. 450 B.C. A Levite who resettled in Jerusalem after the Exile. Nehemiah 11:17. Called Bakbakkar in 1 Chronicles 9:15. Possibly the same as Bakbukiah 2.

BALAAM [BAY-luhm: possibly "devourer"]. 1400 B.C. A famous pagan practitioner of the occult hired by King Balak of Moab to curse Israel. Numbers 22–24; 31:8, 16.

BALADAN [BAL-uh-duhn]. 750 B.C. Father of Merodach-Baladan, king of Babylon. 2 Kings 20:12; Isaiah 39:1.

BALAK [BAY-lak: "devastator"]. 1400 B.C. The king of Moab when Israel journeyed toward Canaan. He hired Balaam to curse Israel. Numbers 22—24; Revelation 2:14.

BANI (BAY-ni: "posterity"]

1. B.C. date unknown. A Levite whose descendant, Ethan, was a minister of music in David's time. 1 Chronicles 6:46.

2. 1000 B.C. One of David's mighty men. 2 Samuel 23:36.

3. B.C. date unknown. A man whose descendant, Uthal, settled in Jerusalem after the Exile. 1 Chronicles 9:4.

4. B.C. date unknown. Head of a family that returned to Judah with Zerubbabel after the Exile. Ezra 2:10; 10:29. Called Binnui in Nehemiah 7:15.

5. B.C. date unknown. His descendants took foreign wives after the Exile. Ezra 10:34. Possibly the same as Bani 4.

6. 475 B.C. Father of Rehum, a Levite who helped repair the wall of Jerusalem. Nehemiah 3:17.

7. 475 B.C. A descendant of Asaph and father of Uzzi, chief of the Levites in Jerusalem. Nehemiah 11:22.

8. 450 B.C. A Levite who with Ezra instructed the people in the Law. Nehemiah 8:7; 9:4.

9. 450 B.C. A Levite worship leader. Nehemiah 9:4, 5.

10. 450 B.C. A Levite who signed the covenant renewal with God. Nehemiah 10:13. Possibly the same as Bani 7 or 8.

11. 450 B.C. A Jewish leader who signed the covenant renewal with God after the Exile. Nehemiah 10:14.

BARABBAS [buh-RAB-uhs: "father's Son" or "Son of Abba"]. A.D. 30. The criminal Pilate released instead of Jesus, who was crucified. Matthew 27:18–28; Mark 15:7–15; Luke 23:18; John 18:40.

BARACHEL [BAHR-uh-kel: "God blesses"]. B.C. date unknown. Father of Elihu, one who instructed with Job. Job 32:2, 6.

BARAK [BAIR-uhk: "lightning"]. 1225 B.C. The general who defeated the forces of the Canaanite King Jabin. Judges 4, 5.

BARIAH [buh-RI-uh: "fugitive"]. B.C. date unknown. A descendant of Zerubbabel in the royal line of David after the Exile. 1 Chronicles 3:22.

BAR-JESUS [BAHR-JEE-suhs: "son of Jesus"]. A.D. 45. A Jewish sorcerer and false prophet with temporary blindness pronounced by Paul. Acts 13:8–11. Also called Elymas.

BARKOS [BAHR-kuhs]. B.C. date unknown. Ancestor of a family of temple servants who returned to Judah with Zerubbabel. Ezra 2:53; Nehemiah 7:55.

BARNABAS [BAHR-nuh-buhs: "son of encouragement"]. A.D. 35. A significant early church leader renamed by the apostles who also traveled with Paul on some of his missionary journeys. Acts 4:36, 37; 9:26, 27; 11:22–30; 13:1–7; 15:22–26, 36–40; Galatians 2:1, 9–13.

BARSABAS [bahr-SAHB-uhs: "son of Saba" or "son of the Sabbath"]

1. A.D. 30. Nickname of Joseph, one of the two men proposed to replace Judas Iscariot as the twelfth apostle. Acts 1:23. Also known as Justus.

2. A.D. 50. Nickname of Judas who was sent with Paul and Barnabas to Antioch by the apostles. Acts 15:22.

BARTHOLOMEW [bahr-THAHL-uh-muoo: "son of Taimal"]. A.D. 25. One of the "unknown" among the twelve disciples of Jesus, who appears only in lists which name them all. Matthew 10:3; Mark 3:18; Luke 6:14; Acts 1:13. Some suggest he is Nathanael of John 1:45–51.

BARTIMAEUS [BAHR-tuh-MAY-uhs: "son of Timaeus"]. A.D. 25. A blind beggar whom Jesus healed at Jericho. Mark 10:46–52.

BARUCH [BAIR-ukh: "blessed"]

1. 600 B.C. The friend and secretary of the prophet Jeremiah. Jeremiah 32; 36; 43; 45.

2. 475 B.C. Father of Masseiah, settled in Jerusalem after the Exile. Nehemiah 11:5.

3. 450 B.C. One who helped rebuild the wall of Jerusalem. Nehemiah 3:20.

4. 450 B.C. A priest who signed the covenant renewal in Nehemiah's time. Nehemiah 10:6. Probably the same as Baruch 3.

BARZILLAI [bahr-ZIL-i: "of iron"]

1. 1050 B.C. Father of Adriel, the husband of Saul's daughter Merab. 2 Samuel 21:8.

2. 1000 B.C. A wealthy Gileadite who aided David as he fled from Absalom. 2 Samuel 17:27; 19:31–39. David provided for his sons. 1 Kings 2:7.

3. 975 B.C. Ancestor of a family that could not prove its priestly ancestry. Ezra 2:61; Nehemiah 7:63.

BAZLUTH [BAZ-luth]. B.C. date unknown. Ancestral head of a family of temple servants that returned to Judah with Zerubbabel after the Exile. Ezra 2:52; Nehemiah 7:54.

BEALIAH [BEE-uh-LI-uh: "Yahweh is lord"]. 1000 B.C. A kinsman of Saul who defected to David's army at Ziklag. 1 Chronicles 12:5.

BEBAI [BEE-bi: "fatherly"]

1. B.C. date unknown. Head of a family that returned to Judah after the Exile. Ezra 2:11; 8:11; 10:28; Nehemiah 7:16.

2. 450 B.C. A Jewish leader who signed the covenant renewal pact, probably with the name of his family's ancestral head (see Bebai 1). Nehemiah 10:15.

BECHER [BEE-kuhr: "youth" or "young camel"]

1. 1850 B.C. A son of Benjamin listed in Genesis 46:21; 1 Chronicles 7:6, 8.

2. B.C. date unknown. A descendant of Ephraim listed in Numbers 26:35. Called Bered in 1 Chronicles 7:20.

BECHORATH, [beh-KOHR-ath: "firstborn"]. B.C. date unknown. An ancestor of Saul. 1 Samuel 9:1.

BEDAD [BEE-dad: "alone"]. B.C. date unknown. Father of Hadad, a pre-Israelite king of Edom. Genesis 36:35.

BEDAN [BEE-dan]. B.C. date unknown. Listed in the genealogy of Manasseh in 1 Chronicles 7:17.

BEDEIAH [beh-DEE-yuh: "servant of Yahweh"]. 450 B.C. A descendant of Bani who took a foreign wife after the Exile. Ezra 10:35.

BEELIADA [BEE-uh-LI-ah-duh: "the lord knows"]. 1000 B.C. A son of David. 1 Chronicles 14:7. (Called Eliada in 2 Sam. 5:16.) 1 Chronicles 3:8.

BEERA [BEER-uh: "well"]. B.C. date unknown. Listed in the genealogy of Asher in 1 Chronicles 7:37.

BEERAH [BEER-uh: "well"]. 750 B.C. A Reubenite leader taken captive by

Tiglath-Pileser, king of Assyria. 1 Chronicles 5:6.

BEERI [BEER-ee: "man of the springs"]

1. 1975 B.C. Father of Judith, a wife of Esau, Genesis 26:34. Probably the same as Anah in Genesis 36:24, 25.

2. 725 B.C. Father of Hosea the prophet. Hosea 1:1.

BELA [BEE-luh: "consumer"]

1. 1850 B.C. Firstborn son of Benjamin, listed in Genesis 46:21; 1 Chronicles 7:6, 7; 8:1, 3.

2. B.C. date unknown. A pre-Israelite king of Edom, listed in Genesis 36:32, 33.

3. B.C. date unknown. A clan leader listed in the genealogy of Reuben in 1 Chronicles 5:8.

BELSHAZZAR [bel-SHAZ-uhr: "Bel protects the king"]. Son of Nabonidus and coregent of Babylon from 550–539 B.C., notable as king for whom Daniel interpreted handwriting on the palace wall. Daniel 5.

BELTESHAZZAR [BEL-tuh-SHAZ-uhr: "protect his life"]. 600 B.C. Babylonian name given to Daniel upon his entrance into the service of Nebuchadnezzar. Daniel 1:7.

BEN-ABINADAB [BEN-ah-BIN-uh-dab]. 950 B.C. One of Solomon's twelve district governors, married to a daughter of Solomon. 1 Kings 4:11.

BENAIAH [beh-NAY-yuh: "Yahweh has built"]

1. 1025 B.C. Father of Jehoiada, successor of Ahithophel. 1 Chronicles 27:34.

2. 1000 B.C. The son of Jehoiada the priest, notable as Solomon's executioner of Adonijah and Joab. He served as commander of David's bodyguard and later as commander of Israel's

army under Solomon. 2 Samuel 20:23; 23:20–22; 1 Kings 1:8, 10, 26, 36; 2:25, 29–35, 46; 4:4.

3. 1000 B.C. Benaiah the Pirathonite, one of David's top thirty mighty men. 2 Samuel 23:30; 1 Chronicles 27:14.

4. 1000 B.C. A temple musician who played the lyre. 1 Chronicles 15:18, 20.

5. 1000 B.C. A priest assigned to blow the trumpet before the ark. 1 Chronicles 15:24; 16:6. Probably the same as Benaiah 4.

6. 925 B.C. Descendant of Asaph and grandfather of Jahazial, a priest in Jehoshaphat's time. 2 Chronicles 20:14.

7. 725 B.C. A Simeonite clan leader in the time of Hezekiah. 1 Chronicles 4:36.

8. 725 B.C. A financial officer supervising the collection of contributions to the temple in Hezekiah's time. 2 Chronicles 31:13.

9. 625 B.C. Father of Pelatiah, a Jewish leader seen in a vision by Ezekiel. Ezekiel 11:1–3, 13.

10–13. 450 B.C. Four Jews who took foreign wives after the Exile. Ezra 10:25, 30, 35, 43.

BEN-AMMI [ben-AM-ee: "son of my people"]. 2025 B.C. Son of Lot by his younger daughter and ancestor of the Ammonites. Genesis 19:38.

BEN-DEKER [ben-DEE-kuhr: "son of Dekar"]. 950 B.C. One of Solomon's twelve district governors. 1 Kings 4:9.

BEN-GEBER [ben-GEE-buhr: "son of Geber"]. 950 B.C. One of Solomon's twelve district governors. 1 Kings 4:13.

BEN-HADAD [ben-HAY-dad: "son of Hadad"]. Dynastic name of Syrian kings.

1. 875 B.C. Ben-Hadad I, king of Syria with whom King Asa established a treaty. 1 Kings 15:16–20. Son of Tabrimmon.

2. 850 B.C. Ben-Hadad II, also a Syrian king, probably son of Ben-Hadad I. He was defeated by Ahab. 1 Kings 20; 2 Kings 6:24; 8:7–15.

3. 800 B.C. The son and successor of Hazael who had killed Ben-Hadad II and usurped the throne. With his father, Ben-Hadad III oppressed Israel during the reign of Jehoahaz. He was defeated three times by Jehoash, son of Jehoahaz. 2 Kings 13:3, 24, 25.

BEN-HAIL [ben-HAYL: "son of strength"]. 875 B.C. An official sent by King Jehoshaphat to teach the Law throughout Judah. 2 Chronicles 17:7.

BEN-HANAN [ben-HAHN-an: son of grace"]. B.C. date unknown. Listed only in the genealogy of Judah in 1 Chronicles 4:20.

BEN-HESED [BEN-HEH-sed: "son of lovingkindness"]. 950 B.C. One of Solomon's twelve district governors. 1 Kings 4:10.

BEN-HUR [ben-HUHR: "son of Hur"]. 950 B.C. One of the twelve district governors under Solomon. 1 Kings 4:8.

BENINU [buh-NI-noo: "our son"]. 450 B.C. A Levite who signed the covenant renewal with God. Nehemiah 10:13.

BENJAMIN [BEN-juh-min: "son of my right hand"]

1. 1875 B.C. Jacob's youngest son; the ancestral source of the tribe of Benjamin. Genesis 35:18, 24; 42–45; 49:27.

2. B.C. date unknown. Noted only in the genealogy of Benjamin in 1 Chronicles 7:10.

3. 450 B.C. A man who took a foreign wife after the Exile. Ezra 10:32.

4. 450 B.C. He helped rebuild the wall of Jerusalem in Nehemiah's time. Nehemiah 3:23.

5. 450 B.C. He helped dedicate the reconstructed wall of Jerusalem. Nehemiah 12:34. Possibly the same as Benjamin 4.

BENO [BEE-noh: "his son"]. B.C. date unknown. Listed among the descendants of Merari in 1 Chronicles 24:26, 27.

BEN-ONI [ben-OH-nee: "son of my trouble"]. 1875 B.C. Name Rachel gave her second son; his father Jacob changed it to Benjamin. Genesis 35:18.

BEN-ZOHETH [ben-ZO-heth: "son of Zoheth"]. B.C. date unknown. Listed in the genealogy in 1 Chronicles 4:20.

BEOR [BEE-ohr: "shepherd"]

1. B.C. date unknown. Father of Bela, a pre-Israelite king of Edom. Genesis 36:32.

2. 1425 B.C. Father of Balam, the seer hired by Balak to curse the Israelites. Numbers 22:5.

BERA [BEER-uh]. 2100 B.C. The king of Sodom whom Abraham rescued from invaders. Genesis 14:2.

BERACHAH [BAIR-uh-kah: "blessing"]. 1000 B.C. A relative of Saul who joined David's army at Ziklag. 1 Chronicles 12:3.

BERAIAH [buh-RAY-yuh: "Yahweh has created"]. B.C. date unknown. Listed only in the genealogy in 1 Chronicles 8:21.

BERAKIAH [BAIR-uh-KI-uh: "Yahweh has blessed"]. B.C. date unknown. Father of Zechariah, a righteous man slain by the Jews. Matthew 23:35. Probably the same as Berechiah 4, father of Zechariah the prophet.

BERECHIAH [BAIR-uh-KI-uh: "Yahweh has blessed"]

1. 1025 B.C. Father of Asaph, a chief minister of music in David's time. 1 Chronicles 6:39; 15:17.

2. 1000 B.C. A doorkeeper in David's time. 1 Chronicles 15:23.

3. 750 B.C. A leader in Ephraim who opposed the enslavement of Jews from Judah during the reign of Ahaz. 2 Chronicles 28:12.

4. 550 B.C. Father of Zechariah the prophet. Zech. 1:1, 7. Probably the same as Berakiah, father of Zechariah referred to in Matthew 23:35.

5. 500 B.C. A son of Zerubbabel listed only in the genealogy of David's royal line. 1 Chronicles 3:20.

6. 475 B.C. Father of Meshullam, who helped repair the walls of Jerusalem. Nehemiah 3:4, 30; 6:18.

7. 450 B.C. A Levite who resettled near Jerusalem after the Exile. 1 Chronicles 9:16.

BERED [BEER-ed]. B.C. date unknown. A son of Ephraim. 1 Chronicles 7:20. Probably the same as Becher in Numbers 26:35.

BERI [BEER-ee: "wisdom"]. B.C. date unknown. Listed in the genealogy of Asher in 1 Chronicles 7:36.

BERIAH [buh-RI-uh: "misfortune")

1. 1850 B.C. One of four sons of Asher listed in Genesis 46:17; Numbers 28:44, 45.

2. 1825 B.C. A son of Ephraim listed in 1 Chronicles 7:23.

3. B.C. date unknown. Head of a family of Benjamites that lived in Aijalon. 1 Chronicles 8:13, 16.

4. B.C. date unknown. Listed in the genealogy of the Levites descended from Gershon. 1 Chronicles 23:10, 11.

BESAI [BEE-si: "downtrodden"]. B.C. date unknown. Ancestor of a family of temple servants that returned to Judah with Zerubbabel. Ezra 2:49; Nehemiah 7:52.

BESODEIAH [BEZ-uh-DEE-yuh: "in the confidence of Yahweh"]. 475 B.C. Father of Meshullam, who helped rebuild the wall of Jerusalem. Nehemiah 3:6.

BETHUEL [be-THOO-uhl: "dweller in God"]. 2050 B.C. A son of Abraham's brother Nahor, and the father of Rebekah and Laban. Genesis 22:22, 23; 24:15, 50.

BEZAI [BEE-zi]

1. B.C. date unknown. Head of a family who returned to Judah with Zerubbabel. Ezra 2:17; Nehemiah 7:23.

2. 450 B.C. A Jewish leader who sealed the covenant renewal of Nehemiah's time, probably with the name of his family's ancestral head (see Bezai 1). Nehemiah 10:18.

BEZALEL [BEZ-uh-lel: "protected by God"]

1. 1450 B.C. A Judahite chosen by God as designer and head craftsman of the tabernacle and its furnishings. Exodus 31:1–5; 35:30–36:2; 37:1.

2. 450 B.C. One who took a foreign wife after the Exile. Ezra 10:30.

BEZER [BEE-zuhr: "strong" or "gold"]. B.C. date unknown. Listed in the genealogy in 1 Chronicles 7:37.

BICHRI [BIK-ri: "youth, firstborn"]. B.C. date unknown. The ancestor of Sheba, who rebelled against David. 2 Samuel 20. Possibly the same as Becher, son of Benjamin (1 Chron. 7:6, 8).

BIDKAR [BID-kahr]. 850 B.C. A chariot officer of Jehu, king of Judah. 2 Kings 9:25.

BIGTHA [BIG-thuh: "gift of fortune"(?)]. 475 B.C. One of the seven stewards who served Xerxes. Esther 1:10.

BIGTHANA [BIG-thuh-nuh: called also Bigthan; "gift of fortune"(?)]. 475 B.C. An official who conspired to assassinate Xerxes and was executed. Esther 2:21; 6:2. Possibly the same as Bigtha.

BIGVAI [BIG-vi]

1. B.C. date unknown. Ancestral head of a family who returned to Judah with Zerubbabel. Ezra 2:2, 14; 8:14; Nehemiah 7:7, 19.

2. 450 B.C. Leader who signed the covenant renewal with God in Nehemiah's time, probably with the name of the family's ancestral head (see Bigvai 1). Nehemiah 10:16.

BILDAD [BIL-dad]. B.C. date unknown. One of three friends of Job who debated with him concerning the justice of God. Job 2:11; 8; 18; 25.

BILGAH [BIL-guh: "brightness"]

1. 1000 B.C. Head of the fourteenth of the twenty-four priestly divisions in David's time. 1 Chronicles 24:14.

2. 525 B.C. Head of a priestly family who returned to Judah with Zerubbabel. Nehemiah 12:5, 18.

BILGAI [BIL-gi: "cheerfulness"]. 450 B.C. Head of a priestly family who signed the covenant renewal with God. Nehemiah 10:8. Possibly the name used was that of an ancestor (see Bilgah 2).

BILHAN [BIL-han]

1. 1925 B.C. Son of a Horite chief living in the land of Seir when Esau settled

there. Genesis 36:27; 1 Chronicles 1:42.

2. B.C. date unknown. Son of Jediael listed in the genealogy of Benjamin in 1 Chronicles 7:10.

BILSHAN [BIL-shan: "inquirer" or "their Lord"]. 525 B.C. Head of a family who returned to Judah with Zerubbabel. Ezra 2:2; Nehemiah 7:7.

BIMHAL [BIM-hal: "circumcised"]. B.C. date unknown. In the genealogy of Asher in 1 Chronicles 7:33.

BINEA [BIN-ee-uh]. B.C. date unknown. A descendant of Jonathan son of Saul. 1 Chronicles 8:37; 9:43.

BINNUI [. BIN-noo-i: "built, building"]

1. B.C. date unknown. Ancestor of some who took foreign wives in Ezra's time. Ezra 10:38.

2. B.C. date unknown. Ancestor of a family that returned to Judah with Zerubbabel. Nehemiah 7:15. Called Bani in Ezra 2:10.

3. 525 B.C. A Levite who returned to Judah with Zerubbabel after the Exile. Nehemiah 12:8.

4. 450 B.C. Father of Noadiah, a Levite who helped weigh the sacred temple articles in Ezra's time. Ezra 8:33.

5. 450 B.C. A descendant of Pahath-Moab who took a foreign wife after the Exile. Ezra 10:30.

6. 450 B.C. A Levite who helped repair the walls of Jerusalem and signed the covenant renewal with God. Nehemiah 3:24; 10:9.

BIRSHA [BUHR-shuh]. 2100 B.C. King of Gomorrah in the time of Abram. Genesis 14:2.

BIRZAITH [buhr-ZAY-uhth: "well of olives"]. B.C. date unknown. Found in

1 Chronicles 7:31. It is possibly the name of a town founded by Malchiel.

BISHLAM [BISH-luhm: "peaceful"]. 475 B.C. One of three men who wrote a letter to Artaxerxes against the Jews. Ezra 4:7.

BIZTHA [BIZ-thuh: "eunuch"(?)]. 475 B.C. One of the seven stewards who served under Xerxes. Esther 1:10.

BLASTUS [BLAST-uhs: "bud," "sprout"]. A.D. 50. A servant of Herod Agrippa I. Acts 12:20.

BOAZ [BOH-az: "quickness; strength"]. 1100 B.C. The "kinsman redeemer" who married Ruth and became the grandfather of King David. Ruth 2—4; 1 Chronicles 2:11, 12.

BOHAN [BO-han]. B.C. date unknown. One of Reuben's sons whose lands served as a boundary between the lands of the tribes of Judah and Benjamin. Joshua 15:6; 18:17.

BOCHERU [BO-kuh-roo]. B.C. date unknown. A descendant from Jonathan, son of Saul. 1 Chronicles 8:38; 9:44.

BUKKI [BUHK-i: "proven"]

1. 1400 B.C. Danite leader appointed by Moses to help divide the land when Israel entered Canaan. Numbers 34:22.

2. B.C. date unknown. Descendant of Aaron and ancestor of Ezra the scribe. 1 Chronicles 6:5, 51; Ezra 7:4.

BUKKIAH [buh-KI-uh: "Yahweh has proven"]. 1000 B.C. A musician at the temple. 1 Chronicles 25:4, 13.

BUNAH [BOO-nuh: "intelligence"]. B.C. date unknown. Listed in the genealogy of Judah in 1 Chronicles 2:25.

BUNNI [BUHN-i]

1. B.C. date unknown. Ancestor of Shemaiah who settled Jerusalem after the Exile. Nehemiah 11:15.

2. 450 B.C. A Levite who led worship at Ezra's reading of the Law before the people. Nehemiah 9:4.

3. 450 B.C. A Jewish leader who sealed the covenant renewal with God after the Exile, possibly using the name of his family's ancestral head. Nehemiah 10:15.

BUZ [BUZ: "contempt"]

1. 2050 B.C. The second son of Nahor, brother of Abraham. Genesis 22:21.

2. B.C. date unknown. Listed in the genealogy of Gad in 1 Chronicles 5:14.

BUZI [BUZ-i: "contempt"]. 625 B.C. The father of Ezekiel the prophet. Ezekiel 1:3.

C

CAESAR [SEE-zuhr]. Title of Roman emperors. Matthew 22:17–21; Luke 2:1; 3:1; 23:2; Acts 17:7. See Claudius, Augustus, and Tiberius.

CAIAPHAS [KAY-uh-fuhs]. A.D. 30. High priest who presided at Jesus' illegal trial before the Sanhedrin. Matthew 26:3, 57–65; John 11:49.

CAIN [KAYN: "to acquire"]. The farmer son of Adam and Eve who killed his brother Abel. Genesis 4; 1 John 3:12.

CAINAN [KAY-nuhn]

1. B.C. date unknown. Son of Enos and great-grandson of Adam, listed in the genealogy of Jesus in Luke 3:37.

2. B.C. date unknown. Son of Arphaxad listed only in the genealogy of Christ in Luke 3:36.

CALCOL [KAL-kehl: "sustaining"]. B.C. date unknown. Listed in the genealogy of Judah. 1 Kings 4:31; 1 Chronicles 2:6.

CALEB [KAY-lab: "dog" or "rabid"]

1. B.C. date unknown. A son of Hezron, descendant of Judah. 1 Chronicles 2:9, 18.

2. 1400 B.C. Sent by Moses to spy out the land of Canaan, he survived the forty years in the wilderness to enter the Promised Land. Numbers 13:6, 30; 14; Joshua 14, 15.

CANAAN [KAY-nuhn: "merchant" or "lowly"]. B.C. date unknown. A son of Ham and grandson of Noah, he is the ancestor of the Canaanites. Genesis 9:18–27; 10:6, 15–18.

CARCAS [KAHR-kuhs: "vulture"). 475 B.C. One of the seven stewards of Ahasuerus. Esther 1:10.

CARMI [KAHR-mi: "fruitful" or "vineyard"(?)]

1. 1850 B.C. Last of the four sons of Reuben who went with him to Egypt. Genesis 46:9; Exodus 6:14.

2. 1425 B.C. The father of Achan, who at Jericho stole some of the things devoted to God and brought judgment on Israel. Joshua 7:1, 18; 1 Chronicles 4:1. Called Achar (which means "disaster") in 1 Chronicles 2:7.

CARPUS [KAHR-puhs: "fruit"]. A.D. 65. A resident of Troas with whom Paul left his cloak. 2 Timothy 4:13.

CARSHENA [kahr-SHEE-nuh] 475 B.C. One of seven nobles of Persia who advised Ahasuerus. Esther 1:14.

CEPHAS [SEE-fuhs: "rock"]. A.D. 25. The Aramaic equivalent of Peter, the name given to Simon by Christ. The leader of the disciples. John 1:42:1 Corinthians 1:12: 3:22. See Peter.

CHILEAB [KIL-ee-ab]. 975 B.C. A son of David and Abigail, born in Hebron. 2 Samuel 3:3.

CHRIST [KRIST: "anointed one"]. The name indicated appointment by God to a royal, priestly, or prophetic ministry, and was associated with the Messiah.

Matthew 1:18; 16:16–20; Mark 14:61; John 4:25.

CHUZA [KOO-zuh]. A.D. 25. Manager of Herod's household. Luke 8:3.

CLAUDIUS [KLAW-dee-uhs]. A.D. 41–54. The Roman Caesar who expelled the Jews from Rome for rioting. Acts 11:28;18:2.

CLAUDIUS LYSIAS [KLAW-dee-uhs LIS-ee-uhs]. A.D. 60. Commander of the Roman garrison in Jerusalem; he arrested Paul to prevent a mob from killing him. Acts 23:26.

CLEMENT [KLEM-uhnt: "mild: merciful"]. A.D. 60. A Christian at Philippi whom Paul identifies as a fellow worker. Philippians 4:3.

CLEOPAS [KLEE-uh-puhs: "renowned father"]. A.D. 30. One of the two disciples Jesus met along the road to Emmaus after his resurrection. Luke 24:13–35.

CLOPAS [KLOH-puhs]. A.D. 30. One who stood below the cross at the crucifixion. John 19:25.

COL-HOZEH [kohl-HOH-zuh: "all seeing"]

1. B.C. date unknown. An ancestor of Maaseiah, who lived in Jerusalem after the Exile. Nehemiah 11:5.

2. 475 B.C. Father of Shallun, who helped rebuild the wall of Jerusalem. Nehemiah 3:15.

CONANIAH [KOH-nuh-NI-uh: "Yahweh has founded"]

1. 725 B.C. A Levite in charge of temple contributions during Hezekiah's reign. 2 Chronicles 31:12, 13.

2. 625 B.C. A chief Levite during Josiah's reign. 2 Chronicles 35:9.

CORNELIUS [kohr-NEEL-ee-uhs]. A.D. 40. Roman centurion at Caesarea whose household was converted to Christ. Acts 10.

COSAM [KOH-suhm: "diviner"]. B.C. date unknown. An ancestor of Christ listed in Luke 3:28.

CRESCENS [KRES-uhnz: "increasing"]. A.D. 65. A companion of Paul during his imprisonment in Rome. 2 Timothy 4:10.

CRISPUS [KRIS-puhs: "curled"]. A.D. 55. Ruler of a Jewish synagogue in Corinth who converted to Christianity. Acts 18:8; 1 Corinthians 1:14.

CUSH (KOOSH]

1. B.C. date unknown. Firstborn son of Ham, son of Noah, and ancestor of the Cushites. Genesis 10:6–8; 1 Chronicles 1:8–10.

2. 1000 B.C. An enemy of David, mentioned only in the title of Psalm 7.

CUSHAN-RISHATHAIM [KOOSH-an RISH-uh-THAY-uhm]. 1382–1374 B.C. A king of Mesopotamia who dominated Israel for eight years during the period of the judges. Judges 3:8.

CUSHI [KOOSH-i]

1. B.C. date unknown. Ancestor of Jehudi and an official who brought the scroll of Jeremiah's prophecies to Jehoiakim, king of Judah. Jeremiah 36:14.

2. 675 B.C. Father of Zephaniah the prophet. Zephaniah 1:1.

CYRUS [SI-ruhs]. 558–529 B.C. Cyrus II, "the Great," founder of the Medo-Persian Empire. He allowed the Jews to return to Judah from exile in Babylon, and authorized rebuilding the temple. 2 Chronicles 38:20–23; Ezra 1:1–8; Daniel 6:28; 10:1.

D

DALPHON [DAL-fahn]. 475 B.C. One of the ten sons of Haman put to death by the Jews. Esther 5:7.

DAN [DAN: "he has vindicated"]. 1900 B.C. Fifth son of Jacob, born to Bilhah, Rachel's slave. Ancestor of the tribe of Dan. Genesis 30:6; 35:25; 49:16, 17.

DANIEL [DAN-yuhl: "God is my judge"]

1. B.C. date unknown. A wise man referred to by Ezekiel. Ezekiel 14:14, 20; 28:3. Possibly Daniel 2.

2. 975 B.C. Son of David and Abigail. 1 Chronicles 3:1. Called Chileab in 2 Samuel 3:3.

3. 600 B.C. The prophet whose life and prophecies are recorded in the Book of Daniel.

4. 450 B.C. Head of a priestly family who returned to Judah with Ezra. Ezra 8:2; Nehemiah 10:6.

DARDA [DAHR-duh: "full of wisdom" or "thistle"(?)]

1. B.C. date unknown. A noted wise man whom Solomon was said to surpass in wisdom. 1 Kings 4:31.

2. B.C. date unknown. Listed in the genealogy of Judah in 1 Chronicles 2:6. Probably the same as Darda 1.

DARIUS [duh-RI-uhs]. The name of three Persian kings.

1. 539–538 B.C. Darius the Mede, mentioned in the Book of Daniel. Probably another name for Gubaru, governor of Babylon by Cyrus the Great; or perhaps another name for Cyrus himself. Daniel 6.

2. 522–486 B.C. Darius the Great, who authorized completion of the temple as ordered by Cyrus. Ezra 5:6; Haggai 1:1; Zechariah 1:1.

3. 424–405 B.C. Darius II, mentioned only in Nehemiah 12:22.

DARKON [DAHR-kahn]. 950 B.C. A servant of Solomon whose descendants returned to Judah after the Exile. Ezra 2:56; Nehemiah 7:58.

DATHAN [DAY-thuhn]. 1450 B.C. A man who joined Korah in a rebellion against Moses. Numbers 16; 26:9; Deuteronomy 11:6: Psalm 106:17.

DAVID [DAY-vid: "beloved"]. Reigned 1010–970 B.C. Israel's greatest king, who initiated Israel's golden age and unified the Hebrew people. God's Messiah was born of David's family line and will ultimately rule God's never-ending kingdom. 1 and 2 Samuel; 1 Chronicles.

DEBIR [DEE-buhr: "back part" or "oracle"(?)]. 1400 B.C. King of Eglon defeated with other kings by Joshua during the conquest. Joshua 10.

DEDAN [DEE-duhn]

1. B.C. date unknown. A great-grandson of Noah, listed in the table of nations in Genesis 10:7.

2. 2000 B.C. A grandson of Abraham. Genesis 25:3.

DELAIAH [duh-LAY-uh: "Yahweh has raised up"]

1. 1000 B.C. Head of the twenty-third division of the priests in David's time. 1 Chronicles 24:18.

2. B.C. date unknown. Founder of a family that could not prove Israelite ancestry upon return from Exile. Ezra 2:60; Nehemiah 7:62.

3. 600 B.C. An official of Jehoiakim who was against burning the scroll containing Jeremiah's prophecies. Jeremiah 36:12, 25.

4. B.C. date unknown. Listed in the genealogy of the David's line after the Exile. 1 Chronicles 3:24.

5. 475 B.C. Ancestor of Shemaiah, who tried to deceive Nehemiah. Nehemiah 6:10. Possibly the same as Delaiah 2.

DEMAS [DEE-muhs]. A.D. 60. A friend of Paul who later deserted him. Colossians 4:14; 2 Timothy 4:10; Philemon 24.

DEMETRIUS [duh-MEE-tree-uhs: "belonging to Demeter"]

1. A.D. 55. A silversmith who started a riot in Ephesus to protest Paul's message. Acts 19:23–41.

2. A.D. 90. A Christian praised by John in 3 John 12.

DEUEL [DOO-uhl: "knowledge of God" or "God knows"]. 1475 B.C. Father of Eliasaph, leader of the Gadite tribe in Moses' time. Numbers 1:14; 7:42.

DIBLAIM [DIB-lay-uhm: "two cakes"]. 775 B.C. Father of Gomer, the adulterous wife of the prophet Hosea. Hosea 1:3.

DIBRI [DIB-ri: "wordy"(?)]. 1475 B.C. Father of Shelomith, whose son was stoned to death for blasphemy. Leviticus 24:10, 11.

DIDYMAS [DID-uh-muhs: "twin"]. A.D. 25. The name or nickname of the disciple Thomas. John 11:16; 20:24–29.

DIKLAH [DIK-luh: "place of palms"]. B.C. date unknown. Listed in the genealogy of Shem, son of Noah. Genesis 10:27; 1 Chronicles 1:21.

DIONYSIUS [DI-uh-NI-suhs]. A.D. 50. A member of the elite in Athens who became a Christian. Acts 17:34.

DIOTREPHES [Di-AH-truh-faaz: "nourished by Zeus"]. A.D. 90. A leader of a church who refused to welcome itinerant teachers. 3 John 9, 10.

DISHAN [DI-shan: "antelope" or "mountain goat"]. 1950 B.C. A Horite chief in Esau's time. Genesis 36:21, 28, 30.

DISHON [DI-shon: "antelope" or "mountain goat"]

1. 1950 B.C. A Horite chief. Genesis 36:21, 26, 30

2. 1950 B.C. Another Horite chief whose sister married Esau. Genesis 36:25.

DODAI [DOH-di: "beloved"]. 1025 B.C. Commander of a division of David's army and father of Eleazar, one of the three top commanders in David's army. 2 Samuel 23:9, 10; 1 Chronicles 27:4.

DODAVAHU [doh-duh-VAY-hoo: "beloved of Yahweh"]. 875 B.C. Father of Eliezer, who prophesied against Jehoshaphat. 2 Chronicles 20:37.

DODO [DOH-doh: "beloved"]

1. 1175 B.C. Grandfather of Tola, a judge who led Israel for twenty-three years. Judges 10:1.

2. 1025 B.C. Father of Elhanan, one of David's mighty men. 2 Samuel 23:24; 1 Chronicles 11:26.

DOEG [DOH-eg: "anxious"]. 1000 B.C. Saul's head shepherd who told Saul that Ahimelech, the priest of Nob, had aided David. At Saul's command, Doeg killed the priests of Nob and their families. 1 Samuel 21:7; 22:9–19.

DUMAH [DOO-muh: "silence"]. 2025 B.C. One of Ishmael's twelve sons. Genesis 25:14.

E

EBAL [EE-bahl: "bare"]. 1950 B.C. A son of Shobal, a Horite chief. Genesis 36:23; 1 Chronicles 1:40.

EBED [EE-bed: "servant"]

1. 1150 B.C. A resident of Shechem who conspired against Abimelech. Judges 9:26–35.

2. 450 B.C. A man who returned to Judah with Ezra after the Exile. Ezra 8:6.

EBED-MELECH [EE-bed-MEL-ahk: "king-servant"]. 600 B.C. An Ethiopian who served King Zedekiah but freed Jeremiah from imprisonment in a cistern. Jeremiah 38:7–13; 39:15–18.

EBER [EE-buhr: "crossover" or "other side"]

1. B.C. date unknown. An ancestor of Abraham. Genesis 10:21, 25; 11:14–17; 1 Chronicles 1:18–25.

2. B.C. date unknown. Listed only in the genealogy of Gad in 1 Chronicles 5:13.

3. B.C. date unknown. Head of a Benjamite family. 1 Chronicles 8:12.

4. B.C. date unknown. Head of another Benjamite family listed in 1 Chronicles 8:22.

5. 500 B.C. Head of a priestly family after the Exile. Nehemiah 12:20.

EBIASAPH [uh-BI-uh-saf: "my father has gathered"]. B.C. date unknown. Ancestor of Heman the temple musician. 1 Chronicles 6:23, 37; 9:19. Called Abiasaph in Exodus 6:24.

EDEN [EE-duhn: "delight"]

1. 725 B.C. A Levite who helped purify the temple during Hezekiah's reign. 2 Chronicles 29:12.

2. 700 B.C. A Levite who distributed offerings among the priests during Hezekiah's reign. 2 Chronicles 31:15. Probably the same as Eden 1.

EDER [EE-duhr: "helper"]

1. B.C. date unknown. Listed in the genealogy of Benjamin in 1 Chronicles 8:15.

2. B.C. date unknown. A Levite descended from Merari. 1 Chronicles 23:23; 24:30.

EDOM [EE-duhm: "red"]. 1950 B.C. Nickname of Esau who sold his inheritance for some red stew. Genesis 25:30.

EGLON [EG-lahn: "circle"]. 1334–1316 B.C. A king of Moab who dominated Israel for eighteen years during the age of the judges. Judges 3:12–25.

EHI [EE-hi]. One of ten sons of Benjamin. Genesis 46:21. The same as Ahiram in Numbers 26:38 and Aharah in 1 Chronicles 8:1.

EHUD [EE-hud]

1. 1316–1235 B.C. The judge who slew King Eglon and delivered Israel from the Moabites. Judges 3:15–31.

2. B.C. date unknown. Listed in the genealogy in 1 Chronicles 7:10; 8:6. Possibly the same as Ehud 1.

EKER [EC-kuhr: "root"]. B.C. data unknown. Listed in the genealogy of Judah in 1 Chronicles 2:27.

ELAH [EE-luh: "oak"]

1. 975 B.C. Father of Shimei, one of Solomon's twelve district governors. 1 Kings 4:18.

2. B.C. date unknown. A chief of Edom descended from Esau. Genesis 36:41; 1 Chronicles 1:52.

3. 1375 B.C. One of three sons of Caleb, who was one of the spies sent into Canaan by Moses. 1 Chronicles 4:15.

4. 886–885 B.C. The fourth king of the northern kingdom of Israel, the son and successor of Baasha. 2 Kings 18:8–14.

5. 775 B.C. Father of Hoshea, who assassinated Pekah and became the last king of Israel. 2 Kings 15:30; 17:1.

6. B.C. date unknown. A Benjamite who settled in Jerusalem after the Exile. 1 Chronicles 9:8.

ELAM [EE-luhm: "highland"]

1. B.C. date unknown. Firstborn son of Shem. The name identifies a people

listed in the table of nations. Genesis 10:22; 1 Chronicles 1:17.

2. B.C. date unknown. Listed only in the genealogy of Benjamin in 1 Chronicles 8:24.

3. 1000 B.C. One of the seven sons of Meshelemiah, who was a grandson of Asaph and gatekeeper in David's time. 1 Chronicles 26:3.

4. B.C. date unknown. Ancestor of a family that returned to Judah with Zerubbabel. Ezra 2:7; 8:7; Nehemiah 7:12.

5. B.C. date unknown. Ancestor of another family that returned from the Exile with Zerubbabel. Ezra 2:31; Nehemiah 7:34.

6. B.C. date unknown. Ancestor of some who took foreign wives after the Exile. Ezra 10:26. Probably the same as either Elam 4 or 5.

7. 450 B.C. A Jewish leader who signed the covenant renewal with God in Nehemiah's time, probably with the name of the family's ancestor (see Elam 4 and 5). Nehemiah 10:14.

8. 450 B.C. A Levite in the choir at the dedication of Jerusalem's wall. Nehemiah 12:42.

ELASAH [EL-uh-suh: "God has made"]

1. 600 B.C. A man who delivered Jeremiah's latter to the exiles in Babylon. Jeremiah 29:3.

2. 450 B.C. A descendant of Pashhur who took a foreign wife after the Exile. Ezra 10:22.

ELDAAH [el-DAY-uh]. 1975 B.C. A son of Midian and grandson of Abraham. Genesis 25:4; 1 Chronicles 1:33.

ELDAD [EL-dad: "God has loved" or "God is a friend"]. 1450 B.C. One of two named elders of Israel who were given the gift of prophesy in Moses' time. Numbers 11:26, 27.

ELEAD [EL-ee-ad: "God has testified"]. 1800 B.C. A son of Ephraim who was killed by men of Gath. 1 Chronicles 7:21.

ELEADAH [EL-ea-AY-duh: "God has adorned"]. B.C. date unknown. Listed in the genealogy of Ephraim in 1 Chronicles 7:20.

ELEASAH [EL-ee-AY-suh: "God has made"]

1. B.C. date unknown. Listed in the genealogy of Jerahmeel. 1 Chronicles 2:40.

2. B.C. date unknown. A descendant of Saul. 1 Chronicles 8:37; 9:43.

ELEAZAR [EL-ee-AY-zuhr: "God has helped"]

1. B.C. date unknown. Great-grandson of Levi, listed in 1 Chronicles 23:21, 22.

2. 1400 B.C. The son of Aaron who became high priest after Aaron's death. Exodus 6:23–25; Leviticus 10:6–16.

3. 1000 B.C. A son of Abinadab, at whose house the ark was kept for twenty years. 1 Samuel 7:1.

4. 1000 B.C. One of three chief leaders of David's military. 2 Samuel 23:9, 10.

5. 450 B.C. A priest who helped weigh the sacred temple articles in Ezra's time. Ezra 8:33.

6. 450 B.C. A descendant of Parosh who took a foreign wife after the Exile. Ezra 10:25.

7. 450 B.C. A priest in the choir at the dedication of Jerusalem's wall. Nehemiah 12:42.

8. B.C. date unknown. An ancestor of Christ listed in the genealogy in Matthew 1:15.

ELHANAN [el-HAY-nuhn: "God is gracious"]

1. 1000 B.C. A warrior who killed Lahmi, the brother of Goliath. 2 Samuel 21:19; 1 Chronicles 20:5.

2. 1000 B.C. One of David's top military men. 2 Samuel 23:24; 1 Chronicles 11:26.

ELI [EE-li: "Yahweh is exalted"]. 1120–1080 B.C. The high priest who trained Samuel during his childhood. 1 Samuel 1—4.

ELIAB [ee-LI-uhb: "God is father"]

1. 1475 B.C. The father of Dathan and Abiram, who rebelled against Moses. Numbers 16:1, 12.

2. 1450 B.C. Leader of the tribe of Zebulun during the Exodus. Numbers 1:9.

3. B.C. date unknown. An ancestor of Samuel listed in the genealogy of Levi in 1 Chronicles 6:27. Called Elihu in 1 Samuel 1:1 and Eliel in 1 Chronicles 6:34.

4. 1025 B.C. David's oldest brother. 1 Samuel 16:6; 17:13, 28; 1 Chronicles 2:13; 2 Chronicles 11:18.

5. 1000 B.C. A Gadite who joined David's army at Ziklag. 1 Chronicles 12:9.

6. 1000 B.C. A Levite minister of music. 1 Chronicles 15:18, 20; 16:5.

ELIADA [ee-LI-ah-duh: "God knows"]

1. 1000 B.C. A son of David. 2 Samuel 5:16; 1 Chronicles 3:8. Called Beeliada in 1 Chronicles 14:7.

2. 950 B.C. Father of Rezon, a Syrian king and enemy of Solomon. 1 Kings 11:23.

3. 875 B.C. A military commander under Jehoshaphat. 2 Chronicles 17:17.

ELIAHBA [ee-LI-ah-buh: "God hides"]. 1000 B.C. One of David's war heroes. 2 Samuel 23:32; 1 Chronicles 11:33.

ELIAKIM [ee-LI-uh-kim: "God raises up"]

1. B.C. date unknown. An ancestor of Christ listed in Luke's genealogy. Luke 3:30.

2. 700 B.C. Palace administrator under Hezekiah's palace administrator at the siege of Jerusalem by the Assyrians. 2 Kings 18:18, 26, 37; 19:2; Isaiah 22:20; 36:3, 11, 22; 37:2.

3. 609–598 B.C. The son of Josiah whose name was changed to Jehoiakim when he was made king of Judah by Pharaoh Necho. 2 Kings 23:34; 2 Chronicles 36:4.

4. 450 B.C. A priest who sang in the choir at the dedication of the wall of Jerusalem. Nehemiah 12:41.

5. B.C. date unknown. An ancestor of Christ listed in Matthew's genealogy. Matthew 1:13.

ELIAM [ee-LI-um: "God is kinsman"]

1. 1000 B.C. Father of Bathsheba. 2 Samuel 11:3. Called Ammiel in 1 Chronicles 3:5.

2. Son of Ahithophel and one of David's military elite. 2 Samuel 23:34. Called Ahiah in 1 Chronicles 11:38.

ELIASAPH [ea-LI-uh-saf: "God has added"]

1. 1450 B.C. Leader of the tribe of Gad during the Exodus. Numbers 1:14.

2. 1450 B.C. A Levite clan leader in Moses' time. Numbers 3:24.

ELIASHIB [ae-LI-uh-shib: "God restores"]

1. 1000 B.C. Head of the eleventh of the original twenty-four priestly divisions in David's time. 1 Chronicles 24:12.

2. 475 B.C. High priest who angered Nehemiah by providing living quarters for the pagan Tobiah within the temple compound. Ezra 10:6; Nehemiah 3:1, 20; 13:4–9.

3. 450 B.C. A Levite who took a foreign wife after the Exile. Ezra 10:24.

4. 450 B.C. A descendant of Zattu who married a foreign woman after the return to Judah. Ezra 10:27.

5. 450 B.C. Another man who was guilty of intermarriage with pagans after the Exile. Ezra 10:36.

6. 1000 B.C. One of the military heroes of David's day. 2 Samuel 23:24; 1 Chronicles 11:26.

ELIATHAH [ee-LI-ah-thuh: "God has come"]. 1000 B.C. A son of Heman who was a minister of music. 1 Chronicles 25:4, 27.

ELIDAD [ee-LI-dad: "God has loved"]. 1400 B.C. The leader from the tribe of Benjamin that Moses appointed to help divide the land of Canaan. Numbers 34:21.

ELIEHOENAI [ee-LI-uh-HO-ea-ni: "toward Yahweh are my eyes"]

1. 975 B.C. A gatekeeper in David's time. 1 Chronicles 26:3.

2. 450 B.C. A man who returned to Judah with Ezra after the Exile. Ezra 8:4.

ELIEL [ee-LI-uhl: "my God is God"]

1. B.C. date unknown. Head of a family of the half-tribe of Manasseh. 1 Chronicles 5:24.

2. B.C. date unknown. A Levite in the line of Heman, a temple musician. 1 Chronicles 6:34. Called Eliab in 1 Chronicles 6:27 and Elihu in 1 Samuel 1:1.

3. and 4. B.C. date unknown. Two listed in Benjamin's genealogy in 1 Chronicles 8:20, 22.

5. 1000 B.C. One of David's military elite. 1 Chronicles 11:46.

6. 1000 B.C. Another of David's mighty men. 1 Chronicles 11:47.

7. 1000 B.C. A military commander who joined David's army at Ziklag. 1 Chronicles 12:11. Possibly the same as Eliel 5 or 6.

8. 1000 B.C. A chief Levite who helped David bring the ark to Jerusalem. 1 Chronicles 15:9, 11.

9. 725 B.C. A supervisor under Conaniah the Levite. who oversaw storage of temple offerings in Hezekiah's time. 2 Chronicles 31:13.

ELIENAI [el-eh-EE-ni: "toward Yahweh are my eyes"]. B.C. date unknown. Listed in the genealogy of Benjamin in 1 Chronicles 8:20.

ELIEZER [el-eh-EE-zuhr: "God is help"]

1. 2100 B.C. Abraham's chief steward. Genesis 15:2.

2. 1825 B.C. A son of Becher, Benjamin's second son. 1 Chronicles 7:8.

3. 1450 B.C. Second son of Moses. Exodus 18:4; 1 Chronicles 23:15, 17; 26:25.

4. 1000 B.C. A priest who blew a trumpet as the ark was brought to Jerusalem by David. 1 Chronicles 15:24.

5. 1000 B.C. Officer over the tribe of Reuben in David's day. 1 Chronicles 27:16.

6. 850 B.C. He prophesied against Jehoshaphat. 2 Chronicles 20:37.

7. B.C. date unknown. An ancestor of Christ listed in Luke's genealogy. Luke 3:29.

8. 450 B.C. A leader Ezra sent to bring Levites from Casiphia to serve in the Jerusalem temple. Ezra 8:16.

9. 450 B.C. A priest who took a foreign wife after the Exile. Ezra 10:18.

10. 450 B.C. A Levite who married a foreign woman after the Exile. Ezra 10:23.

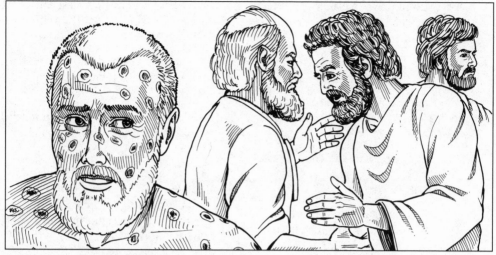

Eliphaz and his friends abandoned trying to comfort Job in favor of trying to convince Job that he had sinned.

❖

11. 450 B.C. A descendant of Harim who was also guilty of intermarriage. Ezra 10:31.

ELIHOREPH [el-uh-HOHR-uhf: "God's autumn"(?)]. 950 B.C. A secretary of Solomon. 1 Kings 4:3.

ELIHU [el-LI-hoo: "he is my God"]

1. B.C. date unknown. A young man who corrected Job and his three friends. Job 32—37.

2. B.C. date unknown. An ancestor of the prophet Samuel. 1 Samuel 1:1. Called Eliab in 1 Chronicles 6:27 and Eliel in 1 Chronicles 6:34.

3. 1000 B.C. A warrior of Manasseh who joined David's army at Ziklag. 1 Chronicles 12:20.

4. 1000 B.C. A descendant of Obed-Edom and a gatekeeper in David's time. 1 Chronicles 26:7, 8.

5. 1000 B.C. Older brother of David and officer over the tribe of Judah. 1 Chronicles 27:18. Called Eliab in 1 Samuel 16:6; 1 Chronicles 2:13.

ELIJAH [ee-LI-juh: "Yahweh is my God"]

1. 875 B.C. The most prominent prophet of his time who confronted the evil King Ahab and Queen Jezebel when they tried to establish Baal worship as Israel's religion. 1 Kings 17—19, 21; 2 Kings 1; 2.

2. B.C. date unknown. Listed in the genealogy of Benjamin in 1 Chronicles 8:27.

3. 450 B.C. A priest who took a foreign wife after the Exile. Ezra 10:21.

4. 450 B.C. A descendant of Elam who also married a foreign woman after the Exile. Ezra 10:26.

ELIKA [ee-LI-kuh]. 1000 B.C. One of David's mighty men. 2 Samuel 23:25.

ELIMELECH [el-LIM-uh-lek: "God is king"]. 1100 B.C. Husband of Naomi and father-in-law of Ruth. Ruth 1:2; 4:3, 9.

ELIOENAI [EL-ee-oh-EE-ni: "toward Yahweh are my eyes"]

1. 1825 B.C. One of nine sons of Becher, the son of Benjamin. 1 Chronicles 7:8.

2. B.C. date unknown. A clan leader listed in the genealogy of Simeon. 1 Chronicles 4:36.

3. 450 B.C. A priest who married a foreign wife after the Exile. Ezra 10:22.

4. 450 B.C. A descendant of Pashur who took a foreign wife after the Exile. Ezra 10:27.

5. 450 B.C. A priest in the choir at the dedication of Jerusalem's wall. Nehemiah 12:41.

6. B.C. date unknown. A descendant of Zerubbabel listed in the line of David after the Exile. 1 Chronicles 3:23, 24.

ELIPHAL [el-LI-fuhl: "God has judged"]. 1000 B.C. One of David's military heroes. 1 Chronicles 11:35. Called Eliphelet in 2 Samuel 23:34.

ELIPHAZ [EL-uh-faz: "God is victorious"(?)]

1. B.C. date unknown. One of the three friends who argued with Job concerning the cause of his suffering. Job 4; 15; 22; 42:7–9.

2. 1925 B.C. A son of Esau by his wife Adah. Genesis 36:4; 1 Chronicles 1:35, 36.

ELIPHELEH [e-LIF-uh-leh: "may God distinguish him"]. 1000 B.C. A Levite appointed to play the harp before the ark as David brought it to Jerusalem. 1 Chronicles 15:18, 21.

ELIPHELET [uh-LIF-uh-let: "God is deliverance"]

1. 1000 B.C. A military hero in David's army. 2 Samuel 23:34. Called Eliphal in 1 Chronicles 11:35.

2 and 3. 975 B.C. Two sons of David born in Jerusalem. 2 Samuel 5:16; 1 Chronicles 3:6, 8; 14:7. The first is called Elpelet in 1 Chronicles 14:5.

4. B.C. date unknown. A descendant of Jonathan, son of Saul, listed in 1 Chronicles 8:39.

5. 450 B.C. A descendant of Adonikam who returned to Judah with Ezra. Ezra 8:13.

6. 450 B.C. A descendant of Hashum who took a foreign wife after the Exile. Ezra 10:33.

ELISHA [ee-LI-shuh: "God is salvation"]. 850 B.C. The successor of Elijah as Israel's leading prophet during the reigns of Joram, Jehu, Jehoahaz, and Joash. 2 Kings 1—9, 13.

ELISHAH [ee-LI-shuh: "God is salvation"]. B.C. date unknown. A great-grandson of Noah listed in the table of nations in Genesis 10:4.

ELISHAMA [ee-LISH-ah-muh: "God has heard"]

1. 1450 B.C. Leader of the tribe of Ephraim at the time of the Exodus, and grandfather of Joshua. Numbers 1:10; 1 Chronicles 7:26.

2. B.C. date unknown. Listed in the genealogy of Jerahmeel, a descendant of Judah. 1 Chronicles 2:41.

3. 975 B.C. A son of David born in Jerusalem. 2 Samuel 5:16; 1 Chronicles 3:8; 14:7.

4. 875 B.C. A priest who brought the Law to all Judah during Jehoshaphat's reign. 2 Chronicles 17:8.

5. 600 B.C. Grandfather of Ishmael, who assassinated Gedaliah, the governor of Judah. 2 Kings 25:25; Jeremiah 41:1.

6. 500 B.C. A secretary of King Jehoiakim. Jeremiah 36:12, 20.

ELISHAPHAT [ee-LISH-uh-fat: "God has judged"]. 850 B.C. A military commander who agreed with Jehoiada the priest to overthrow Athaliah. 2 Chronicles 23:1.

ELISHUA [el-uh-SHOO-uh: "God is salvation]. 975 B.C. A son of David born in Jerusalem. 1 Chronicles 14:5.

ELIUD [ee-LI-uhd: "God my praise"]. B.C. date unknown. An ancestor of Christ descended from Zerubbabel. Matthew 1:14, 15.

ELIZAPHAN [el-uh-ZAY-fan: "God has protected"]

1. 1450 B.C. A Levite clan leader during the Exodus. Numbers 3:30; 1 Chronicles 15:8. Called Elzaphan in Exodus 6:22; Leviticus 10:4.

2. 1400 B.C. The leader from the tribe of Zebulun whom Moses appointed to help divide the land of Canaan. Numbers 34:25.

ELIZUR [el-LI-zuhr; "God is a rock"]. 1450 B.C. Leader of the tribe of Reuben at the time of the Exodus. Numbers 1:5.

ELKANAH [el-KAY-nuh: "God has taken possession"]

1. B.C. date unknown. A Levite listed in Exodus 6:24; 1 Chronicles 6:23, 25, 36.

2. B.C. date unknown. An ancestor of Samuel listed in Levi's genealogy. 1 Chronicles 6:26.

3. 1100 B.C. The father of Samuel the judge. 1 Samuel 1; 2:11.

4. 1000 B.C. A Korahite who joined David's army at Ziklag. 1 Chronicles 12:6.

5. 1000 B.C. A Levite who served as doorkeeper for the tabernacle. 1 Chronicles 15:23. Possibly the same as Elkanah 4.

6. 750 B.C. An officer who was second in authority to King Ahaz. He was killed in battle. 2 Chronicles 28:7.

7. B.C. date unknown. An ancestor of Berekiah, who settled in Jerusalem after the Exile. 1 Chronicles 9:16.

ELMADAM [el-MAY-duhm]. B.C. date unknown. An ancestor of Christ. Luke 3:26.

ELNAAM [el-NAY-uhm: "God is pleasant, delightful"]. 1025 B.C. Father of two of David's military elite. 1 Chronicles 11:46.

ELNATHAN [el-NAY-thuhn: "God has given"]

1. 600 B.C. A servant of Jehoiakim. 2 Kings 24:8; Jeremiah 26:22; 36:12, 25.

2, 3, and 4. 450 B.C. Two Jewish leaders and one scholar sent by Ezra to bring Levites from Casiphia to serve in the temple. Ezra 8:16.

ELON [EE-lahn: "oak, terebinth"]

1. 1950 B.C. The father of Basemath, a wife of Esau. Genesis 26:34; 36:2.

2. 1850 B.C. Son of Zebulun and ancestor of his own clan. Genesis 46:14; Numbers 26:26.

3. 1100 B.C. A judge who ruled in Israel for ten years. Judges 12:11, 12.

ELPAAL [el-PAY-uhl: "God has wrought"]. B.C. date unknown. Listed in the genealogy in 1 Chronicles 6:11, 12, 18.

ELPELET [el-PAY-let: "God is deliverance"]. 975 B.C. A son of David born in Jerusalem. 1 Chronicles 14:5. Called Eliphelet in 2 Samuel 5:16; 1 Chronicles 3:6.

ELUZAI [ee-LOO-zi: "God is my strength"]. 1000 B.C. A kinsman of Saul who joined David at Ziklag. 1 Chronicles 12:5.

ELYMAS [EL-uh-muhs: "sorcerer"]. A.D. 50. Nickname of Bar-Jesus, a false Jewish prophet at Paphos who was temporarily blinded for opposing Paul. Acts 13:6–11.

ELZABAD [el-ZAY-bad: "God has given"]

1. 1000 B.C. A man who joined David at Ziklag. 1 Chronicles 12:12.

2. 975 B.C. A Levite who served as a gatekeeper at the temple. 1 Chronicles 26:7.

ELZAPHAN [el-ZAY-fan: "God has protected"]. 1450 B.C. A kinsman of Moses. Exodus 6:22; Leviticus 10:4. Called Elizaphan in Numbers 3:30.

ENAN [EE-nuhn: possibly "fountain"]. 1475 B.C. Father of Ahira, leader of the tribe of Naphtali during the Exodus. Numbers 1:15; 10:27.

ENOCH [EE-nuhk: possibly "initiated"]

1. B.C. date unknown. Son of Cain. Genesis 4:17.

2. B.C. date unknown. A righteous man who was taken directly to heaven without dying. Genesis 5:18–24; Hebrews 11:5.

ENOS [EE-nahs: "man, mankind"]. B.C. date unknown. An ancestor of Christ. Luke 3:38. Same as Enosh.

ENOSH [EE-nahsh: "man: mankind"]. B.C. date unknown. A son of Seth, the son of Adam. Genesis 4:26; 5:6–11.

EPAPHRAS [EP-uh-fras: contracted form of Epaphroditus, "handsome, charming"]. A.D. 60. A Christian leader at the Colossian church and prisoner with Paul in Rome. Colossians 1:7; 4:12: Philemon 23.

EPAPHRODITUS   [eh-PAF-roh-DI-tuhs: "handsome, charming"]. A.D. 60. A Christian who brought Paul a gift from the Philippian church. Philippians 2:25; 4:18.

EPAENETUS [eh-PEE-nuh-tuhs: "praised"]. A.D. 55. A person greeted by Paul in Romans as the first convert in Asia. Romans 16:5.

EPHAH [EE-fah]

1. B.C. date unknown. A grandson of Abraham. Genesis 25:4.

2. B.C. date unknown. A son of Jahdai listed in 1 Chronicles 2:47.

EPHAI [EE-fi]. 625 B.C. The father of some Jews who remained in Judah after the Exile. Jeremiah 40:8.

EPHER [EE-fuhr: "young deer"]

1. 1975 B.C. A son of Midian and grandson of Abraham. Genesis 25:4; 1 Chronicles 1:33.

2. B.C. date unknown. Listed in the genealogy of Judah. 1 Chronicles 4:17.

3. 750 B.C. Head of a family taken into exile by Tiglath-Pileser, king of Assyria. 1 Chronicles 5:24.

EPHLAL [EF-lal]. B.C. date unknown. Listed in the genealogy of Judah. 1 Chronicles 2:37.

EPHOD [EE-fahd]. B.C. date unknown. Father of Hanniel, whom Moses appointed to help divide the land of Canaan. Numbers 34:23.

EPHRAIM [EF-ray-uhm: "fruitful"]. 1850 B.C. Second son of Joseph and his Egyptian wife, Asenath. Ancestor of one of the twelve tribes of Israel. Genesis 41:52; 46:20.

EPHRON [EE-frahn: "fawn"(?)]. 2025 B.C. A Hittite from whom Abraham purchased a burial cave for Sarah. Genesis 23:8–17; 25:10.

ER [UHR: "watcher"]

1. 1875 B.C. The firstborn son of Judah. Genesis 38:3–7; 46:12; 1 Chronicles 2:3.

2. B.C. date unknown. A descendant of Judah. 1 Chronicles 4:21.

3. B.C. date unknown. An ancestor of Christ listed in Luke's genealogy. Luke 3:28.

ERAN [EE-ran]. B.C. date unknown. A descendant of Ephraim and ancestor of the Eranites. Numbers 26:36.

ERASTUS [uh-RAS-tuhs: "beloved"]

1. A.D. 55. A Christian sent by Paul with Timothy to Macedonia. Acts 19:22.

2. A.D. 55. Director of public works in Corinth who sent greetings to the church in Rome. Romans 16:23.

3. A.D. 65. A Christian whom Paul left in Corinth. 2 Timothy 4:20. Possibly the same as Erastus 1 or 2.

ERI [EE-ri: "watchful"]. 1875 B.C. One of seven sons of Gad, son of Jacob. Genesis 46:16; Numbers 26:16.

ESARHADDON [eh-zuhr-HAD-uhn; "Assur has given a brother"]. 680–669 B.C. Succeeded Sennacherib as king of Assyria. 2 Kings 19:37; Ezra 4:2; Isaiah 37:38.

ESAU [EE-saw: "hairy"]. 1950 B.C. The older twin of Jacob, who traded away the Abrahamic covenant for a bowl of stew. His descendants later became known as the Edomites. Genesis 25–27; 36.

ESH-BAAL [ESH-bay-uhl: "servant of Baal"]. 1005–1003 B.C. Son and temporary successor of Saul. 1 Chronicles 8:33; 9:39. Same as Ishbosheth.

ESHBAN [ESH-ban]. 1925 B.C. Listed in the genealogy of Esau. Genesis 36:26; 1 Chronicles 1:41.

ESHCOL [ESH-kohl: "cluster of grapes"]. 2100 B.C. An Amorite who helped Abraham defeat the raiders and rescue Lot. Genesis 14:13, 24.

ESHEK [EE-shek: "oppressor"]. B.C. date unknown. A descendant of Jonathan, son of Saul. 1 Chronicles 8:39.

ESHTEMOA [ESH-tuh-MOH-uh: "listening post"]

1. B.C. date unknown. Listed in the genealogy of Judah. 1 Chronicles 4:17.

2. B.C. date unknown. Listed in the genealogy of Judah in 1 Chronicles 4:19.

ESHTON [ESH-tuhn]. B.C. date unknown. Listed in the genealogy of Judah in 1 Chronicles 4:11, 12.

ESLI [ES-li]. B.C. date unknown. An ancestor of Christ, listed in Luke. Luke 3:25.

ETAM [EE-tuhm: "lair of wild beasts"]. B.C. date unknown. Listed in the genealogy of Judah in 1 Chronicles 4:3. Or perhaps the name of a town.

ETHAN [EE-thuhn: "enduring"]

1. B.C. date unknown., A wise man surpassed by Solomon, and author of Psalm 89. 1 Kings 4:31; 1 Chronicles 2:6, 8.

2. B.C. date unknown. A Levite listed in the genealogy of Asaph the minister of music. 1 Chronicles 6:42.

3. 1000 B.C. A chief minister of music in David's time. 1 Chronicles 6:44.

ETHBAAL [ETH-bay-uhl: "with Baal"]. 875 B.C. King of Sidon and father of Jezebel, wife of Ahab. 1 Kings 16:31.

ETHNAN [ETH-nuhn: "hire" or "gift"]. B.C. date unknown. Listed in the genealogy of Judah. 1 Chronicles 4:7.

ETHNI [ETH-ni: "gift"]. B.C. date unknown. An ancestor of Asaph, David's minister of music. 1 Chronicles 6:41.

EUBULUS [yoo-BYOO-luhs: "good counsel"]. A.D. 65. A Christian who sent greetings to Timothy. 2 Timothy 4:21.

EUTYCHUS [YOO-tuh-kuhs: "fortunate"]. A.D. 55. A young man who was miraculously restored to life by Paul. Acts 20:9–12.

EVI [EE-vi: "desire"]. 1400 B.C. A king of Midian defeated and executed by the Israelites. Numbers 31:8; Joshua 13:21.

EVIL-MERODACH [EE-vuhl MAIR-uh-dahk: "man of (the god) Marduk"]. 562–560 B.C. Successor of Nebuchadnezzar as king of the Babylonian Empire. He released Jehoiachin from prison. 2 Kings 25:27–30; Jeremiah 52:31–34.

EZBAI [EZ-bi: "shining, beautiful"]. 1000 B.C. Father of Naarai, one of David's military elite. 1 Chronicles 11:37.

EZBON [EZ-bahn]

1. 1875 B.C. A son of Gad listed in Genesis 46:16.

2. 1825 B.C. Firstborn son of Bela, son of Benjamin. 1 Chronicles 7:7.

EZEKIEL [ee-ZEE-kee-uhl: "God strengthens"]. 575 B.C. A major prophet whose message is recorded in the Book of Ezekiel.

EZER [EE-zuhr: "help"]

1. 1975 B.C. A Horite chief who lived in Seir in Esau's time. Genesis 36:21, 27, 30; 1 Chronicles 1:38, 42.

2. 1800 B.C. A son of Ephraim slain by men of Gath when caught stealing cattle. 1 Chronicles 7:21.

3. B.C. date unknown. Listed in the genealogy of Judah. 1 Chronicles 4:4.

4. 1000 B.C. Chief of the Gadites who joined David's army at Ziklag. 1 Chronicles 12:9.

5. 450 B.C. A Levite who helped repair the wall of Jerusalem. Nehemiah 3:19.

6. 450 B.C. A priest in the choir at the dedication of Jerusalem's wall. Nehemiah 12:42.

EZRA [EZ-ruh: "Yahweh helps"]

1. 530 B.C. A priest who returned to Judah with Zerubbabel after the Exile. Nehemiah 12:1, 13. Same as Azariah in Nehemiah 10:2.

2. 450 B.C. A priest and scribe, the traditional author of the books of Ezra and Nehemiah. Ezra led a second return of exiles to Judah in 458 B.C. and taught God's Law. Ezra.

EZRAH [EZ-ruh: "Yahweh helps"]. B.C. date unknown. Listed in the genealogy of Judah. 1 Chronicles 4:17.

EZRI [EZ-ri: "my help"]. 975 B.C. David's overseer of farm workers on the royal lands. 1 Chronicles 27:26.

F

FELIX [FEE-liks: "happy"]. A.D. 60. Roman governor of Judea who tried Paul in Caesarea. Acts 23:23—24:27.

FESTUS [FES-tuhs]. A.D. 60. Successor of Felix as governor of Judea, he continued Paul's trial. When Paul appealed to Caesar, Festus ordered him sent to Rome for trial. Acts 24:27; 25; 26:24–32.

FORTUNATUS [FOHR-choo-NAH-tuhs: "fortunate"]. A.D. 55. A Christian from the church at Corinth who visited Paul in Rome. 1 Corinthians 16:17

G

GAAL [GAY-uhl: "scarab"]. 1125 B.C. A man of Shechem who incited a rebellion against Abimelech. Judges 9:26–41.

GABBAI [GAB-i: "collector"]. 450 B.C. A man who settled in Jerusalem after the Exile. Nehemiah 11:8.

GAD [GAD: "fortune"]

1. 1875 B.C. Seventh son of Jacob and ancestor of one of the twelve tribes of Israel. Genesis 30:11.

2. 1000 B.C. A prophet who served and advised David. According to 1 Chronicles 29:29, he also recorded the events of David's reign. 1 Samuel 22:5; 2 Samuel 24:11–19; 1 Chronicles 21:9–19; 2 Chronicles 29:25.

GADDI [GAD-i: "my fortune"]. 1450 B.C. A man of Manasseh sent by Moses to explore the land of Canaan. Numbers 13:11.

GADDIEL [GAD-ee-uhl: "fortune of God"]. 1450 B.C. Representative of the tribe of Zebulun chosen by Moses to explore the land of Canaan. Numbers 13:10.

GADI [GAD-I: "my fortune"]. 775 B.C. Father of Menahem, who assassinated Shallum and succeeded him as king of Israel. 2 Kings 15:14, 17.

GAHAM [GAY-ham]. 2050 B.C. A son of Nahor, Abraham's brother. Genesis 22:24.

GAHAR [GAY-hahr]. B.C. date unknown. Head of a family of temple servants that returned to Judah with Zerubbabel after the Exile. Ezra 2:47

GAIUS [GAY-yuhs]

1. A.D. 55. A companion of Paul from Macedonia. Seized by the crowd during the riot in Ephesus. Acts 19:29.

2. A.D. 55. A Christian from Derbe who traveled with Paul. Acts 20:4.

3. A.D. 55. A Christian at Corinth, in whose home Paul stayed when he wrote his letter to the Romans. Romans 16:23.

4. A. D. 50. A Corinthian Christian whom Paul baptized. 1 Corinthians 1:14. Likely the same as Gaius 3.

5. A.D. 90. One to whom 3 John is addressed. 3 John 1.

GALAL [GAY-lal: "rolling"]

1. 450 B.C. A Levite who settled in Jerusalem after the Exile. 1 Chronicles 9:15.

2. B.C. date unknown. Ancestor of Obadiah (called Abda in Nehemiah 11:17). A Levite who settled in Jerusalem after the Exile. 1 Chronicles 9:16; Nehemiah 11:17.

GALLIO [GAL-ee-oh]. A.D. 50. Proconsul of Achaia who ruled that charges against Paul in Corinth were matters of Jewish rather than Roman law. Acts 18:12–17.

GAMALIEL [guh-MAY-lee-uhl: "God is my reward "]

1. 1450 B.C. Leader of the tribe of Manasseh at the time of the Exodus. Numbers 1:10; 7:54–59.

2. A.D. 35. A respected Pharisee who taught Paul Old Testament law. When Peter and the apostles were called before the Sanhedrin, Gamaliel persuaded the court to release the apostles by arguing that "if their purpose or activity is of human origin, it will fall." Acts 5:33–40; 22:3.

GAMUL [GAY-mul: "weaned"(?)]. 1000 B.C. Head of the twenty-second division of priests in David's time. 1 Chronicles 24:17.

GAREB [GAIR-eb: "scabrous"]. 1000 B.C. One of David's mighty men. 2 Samuel 23:38; 1 Chronicles 11:40.

GATAM [GAY-tuhm: "burnt valley"(?)]. 1875 B.C. An Edomite chief. Genesis 36:11, 16.

GAZEZ [GAY-ziz: "shearer"]

1. A descendant of Judah listed in the genealogy in 1 Chronicles 2:46.

2. B.C. date unknown. A grandson of Caleb listed in the genealogy of Judah in 1 Chronicles 2:46.

GAZZAM [GAZ-uhm]. B.C. date unknown. Ancestor of a family of temple servants that returned to Judah with Zerubbabel after the Exile. Ezra 2:48; Nehemiah 7:51.

GEBER [GEE-buhr: "man;" "strong one"]. 950 B.C. One of Solomon's twelve district governors. 1 Kings 4:19.

GEDALIAH [ged-uh-LI-uh: "Yahweh is great"]

1. 1000 B.C. A minister of music in David's time. 1 Chronicles 25:3, 9.

2. B.C. date unknown. Ancestor of Zephaniah the prophet. Zephaniah 1:1.

3. 600 B.C. An official of Zedekiah who threw Jeremiah into a cistern to die. Jeremiah 38:1–6.

4. 587 B..C. Appointed governor of Judah by Nebuchadnezzar after the fall of Jerusalem. He was assassinated after two months in office. 2 Kings 25:22–25; Jeremiah 39:14; 40:5—41:18.

5. 450 B.C. A priest who took a foreign wife after the Exile. Ezra 10:18.

GEDOR [GEE-dohr: "wall"]

1. B.C. date unknown. Listed in the genealogy of Judah in 1 Chronicles 4:4. Possibly the town of Gedor is intended.

2. B.C. date unknown. A descendant of Judah. 1 Chronicles 4:18.

3. 1075 B.C. The grandfather of Saul. 1 Chronicles 8:31; 9:37.

GEHAZI [guh-HAY-zi: "valley of vision"]. 850 B.C. The servant of Elisha who was stricken with leprosy. 2 Kings 4:12–37; 5:19–27; 8:4, 5.

GEMALLI [guh-MAL-i: "camel driver"(?)]. 1475 B.C. Father of Ammiel, the leader from the tribe of Dan sent by Moses to explore the land of Canaan. Numbers 13:12.

GEMARIAH [gem-uh-RI-uh: "Yahweh has accomplished"]

1. 600 B.C. An official of Jehoiakim. Gemariah urged the king not to burn Jeremiah's scroll of prophecies. Jeremiah 36:10–25.

2. 600 B.C. One of the emissaries of King Zedekiah who delivered Jeremiah's message to the exiles in Babylon. Jeremiah 29:3.

GENUBATH [guh-NOO-bath]. 925 B.C. Son of Hadad the Edomite by the sister-in-law of the pharaoh of Egypt. 1 Kings 11:20.

GERA [GEER-uh]

1. 1850 B.C. A son of Benjamin, listed in Genesis 46:21.

2. and 3. 1825 B.C. Two sons of Bela, the first son of Benjamin. 1 Chronicles 8:3–7.

4. 1350 B.C. Father of Ehud, the judge who delivered Israel from the Moabites. Judges 3:15. Possibly an ancestor of or the same as Gera 1, 2, or 3.

5. 1000 B.C. Ancestor of Shimei who cursed David when the king fled from Absalom. 2 Samuel 16:5; 19:16–18; 1 Kings 2:8.

GERSHOM [GUHR-shuhm: "an alien there"]

1. 1450 B.C. First son of Moses. Exodus 2:22; 18:3.

2. B.C. date unknown. Ancestor of Jonathan whose family violated God's law by serving as priests for the Danites. Likely the same as Gershom 1.

Greed motivated Gehazi, the servant of Elisha, to run after Namaan and beg money and clothing for himself.

3. 450 B.C. A descendant of Phinehas who returned to Judah with Ezra. Ezra 8:2.

GERSHON [GUHR-shuhn]. 1875 B.C. First son of Levi. Genesis 46:11; Exodus 6:16, 17; 1 Chronicles 6.

GESHAN [GESH-uhn]. B.C. date unknown. Listed in the genealogy of Judah. 1 Chronicles 2:47.

GESHEM [GESH-uhm: "rainstorm"]. 450 B.C. An Arab enemy of Nehemiah who opposed reconstructing the wall of Jerusalem. Nehemiah 2:19; 6:1–7.

GETHER [GEE-thuhr]. B.C. date unknown. A grandson of Shem, son of Noah. Genesis 10:23.

GEUEL [GOO-uhl]. 1450 B.C. A representative of the tribe of Gad chosen to explore the land of Canaan. Numbers 13:15.

GIBBAR [GIB-ahr: "mighty"]. B.C. date unknown. Ancestor of a family that returned to Judah with Zerubbabel. Ezra 2:20.

GIBEA [GIB-ee-uh: "hill; highlander"]. B.C. date unknown. Grandson of Caleb listed in the genealogy of Judah in 1 Chronicles 2:49.

GIDDALTI [guh-DAL-ti: "I have magnified (God)"]. 1000 B.C. A minister of music in David's time. 1 Chronicles 25:4, 29.

GIDDEL [GID-uhl: "very great"]

1. 950 B.C. A temple servant of Solomon. Some of his descendants returned to Judah with Zerubbabel. Ezra 2:56; Nehemiah 7:58.

2. B.C. date unknown. Ancestor of temple servants who returned to Judah with Zerubbabel. Ezra 2:47; Nehemiah 7:49.

GIDEON [GID-se-uhn: "hewer" (i.e., great warrior)]. Ruled in Israel as a judge, about 1169–1129.

GIDEONI [gid-ee-OH-nee: "hewer"]. 1450 B.C. Father of Abidan, leader of the tribe of Benjamin at the time of the Exodus. Numbers 1:11.

GILALAI [guh-LAY-li]. 450 B.C. A priest who played music at the dedication of the wall of Jerusalem. Nehemiah 12:36.

GILEAD [GIL-ee-ad]

1. 1825 B.C. Grandson of Manasseh and ancestor of the Gileadite clan. Numbers 26:29, 30.

2. 1125 B.C. Father of Jephthah the judge. Judges 11:1, 2.

3. B.C. date unknown. Listed in the genealogy of Gad. 1 Chronicles 5:14.

GINATH [GI-nath]. 900 B.C. Father of Tibni who competed unsuccessfully with Omri to become the sixth king of Israel. 1 Kings 16:21, 22.

GINNETHON [GIN-uh-thahn]

1. 525 B.C. A chief priest who returned to Judah with Zerubbabel. Nehemiah 12:4, 16.

2. 450 B.C. A priest who signed the covenant renewal with God, probably with the name of his family's founder. Nehemiah 10:6.

GISHPA [GISH-puh]. 450 B.C. A Levite who supervised the temple servants in Nehemiah's time. Nehemiah 11:21.

GOG [GAHG]

1. B.C. date unknown. Listed in the genealogy of Reuben. 1 Chronicles 5:4.

2. B.C. date unknown. Prophesied prince of Meshach and Tubal who will lead a great army against Israel at history's end. Ezekiel 38, 39.

GOLIATH [goh-LI-uhth]

1. 1025 B.C. The giant Philistine champion whom David killed with a stone from his sling. 1 Samuel 17.

2. 1000 B.C. A second giant killed by Elhanan. Possibly the son of Goliath 1. 2 Samuel 21:19. Note however that 1 Chronicles 20:5 indicates "Lahmi, brother of Goliath."

GOMER [GOH-muhr]. B.C. date unknown. Son of Japheth. Possibly a nation or people. Genesis 10:2, 3.

GUNI [GOO-ni]

1. 1850 B.C. A son of Naphtali, listed with the descendants of Jacob. Genesis 46:24; Numbers 26:48.

2. B.C. date unknown. Listed in the genealogy of Gad. 1 Chronicles 5:15.

H

HAAHASHTARI [HAY-uh-HASH-tuh-ri]. B.C. date unknown. A family listed in the genealogy of Judah. 1 Chronicles 4:6.

HABAKKUK [huh-BAK-uhk: "embracer" or "wrestler"]. 600 B.C. A prophet whose words are recorded in the Book of Habakkuk.

HABAZZINIAH [HAB-uh-zuh-NI-uh]. 650 B.C. Grandfather of Jaazaniah the Recabite. Jeremiah 35:3.

HACHALIAH [HAK-uh-LI-uh]. 475 B.C. Father of Nehemiah. Nehemiah 1:1; 10:1.

HACHMONI [HAK-moh-ni: "wise"]. B.C. date unknown. The family name of Jehiel, who cared for the sons of King David. 1 Chronicles 27:32. The text should probably read "the Hachmonite" as in 1 Chronicles 11:11.

HADAD [HAY-dad: "thunderer" (weather god)]

1. B.C. date unknown. A son of Ishmael, son of Abraham and Hagar. Genesis 25:15.

2. B.C. date unknown. A pre-Israelite king listed among the rulers of Edom. Genesis 36:35, 36.

3. B.C. date unknown. Another Edomite king. Genesis 36:39.

4. 950 B.C. An Edomite prince who was an enemy of Solomon. 1 Kings 11:14–25.

HADADEZER [HAY-dad-EE-zuhr: "Hadad is help"]. 1000 B.C. King of Zobah defeated by David. 2 Samuel 8:3–12; 1 Chronicles 18:3–10.

HADLAI [HAD-li]. 775 B.C. Father of Amasa, a leader during Pekah's rule. 2 Chronicles 28:12.

HADORAM [huh-DOHR-uhm: "Hadad is exalted"]

1. B.C. date unknown. A son of Joktan listed in the table of nations in Genesis 10:27.

2. 975 B.C. A son of the king of Hamath sent to David with a gift after the defeat of the king of Zobah. 1 Chronicles 18:10. Called Joram in 2 Samuel 8:10.

HAGAB [HAY-gab: "locust"]. B.C. date unknown. Ancestor of a family of temple servants who returned to Judah with Zerubbabel. Ezra 2:46.

HAGABA [HAG-uh-buh: "locust"]. B.C. date unknown. Ancestor of exiles who accompanied Zerubbabel to Judah. Nehemiah 7:48. Called Hagabah in Ezra 2:45.

HAGABAH [HAG-uh-buh: "locust"]. B.C. date unknown. Ancestor of some temple servants. Ezra 2:45.

HAGGAI [HAG-i: "born on a feast day"]. 525 B.C. A prophet who exhorted completing rebuilding the Jerusalem temple. See Book of Haggai.

HAGGEDOLIM [HAG-uh-DOH-lim: "the great man"]. 475 B.C. Father of a priest who settled in Jerusalem after the Exile. Nehemiah 11:14.

HAGGI [HAG-i: "born on a feast day"]. 1875 B.C. Second son of Gad. Genesis 46:16; Numbers 26:15.

HAGGIAH [hah-GI-uh: "feast of Yahweh"]. B.C. date unknown. Listed in the genealogy of Levi. 1 Chronicles 6:30.

HAGRI [HAG-ri]. 1025 B.C. Father of Mibhar, one of David's military commanders. 1 Chronicles 11:38.

HAKKATAN [HAK-uh-tan: "the little one"]. 475 B.C. His son Johanan returned to Judah with Ezra. Ezra 8:12.

HAKKOZ [HAK-ahz: "thorn"]

1. 1000 B.C. Head of the seventh division of priests in David's time. 1 Chronicles 24:10.

2. B.C. date unknown. Ancestor of priests who were unable to demonstrate their Israelite descent. Ezra 2:61; Nehemiah 7:63.

3. B.C. date unknown. Ancestor of Meremoth, who helped rebuild the wall of Jerusalem. Nehemiah 3:4, 21. All three may be the same person.

HAKUPHA [huh-KOO-fuh: "crooked"]. B.C. date unknown. Ancestor of temple servants who returned to Judah with Zerubbabel after the Exile. Ezra 2:51; Nehemiah 7:53.

HALLOHESH [hah-LOH-hesh: "the whisperer"]. 475 B.C. A leader whose son, Shallum, helped rebuild the wall of Jerusalem. Hallohesh signed the covenant renewal pact with God after the Exile. Nehemiah 3:12; 10:24.

HAM [HAM]. B.C. date unknown. Second of the three sons of Noah. Genesis 5:32; 7:13; 9:18–27.

HAMAN [HAY-muhn]. 475 B.C. The Persian nobleman who plotted to massacre all Jews in the empire. Esther 3—9.

HAMMEDATHA [HAM-uh-DAY-thuh]. 500 B.C. Father of Haman, above. Esther 3:1: 8:5; 9:24.

HAMOR [HAY-mohr: "ass"]. 1925 B.C. Father of Shechem, who raped Dinah, the daughter of Jacob. Simeon and Levi killed him and his son. Genesis 33:19—34:26.

HAMUEL [HAM-yoo-uhl]. B.C. date unknown. Listed only in the genealogy of Simeon. 1 Chronicles 4:26.

HAMUL [HAY-muhl: "spared"]. 1850 B.C. A grandson of Judah. Genesis 46:12; Numbers 26:21.

HANAMEL [HAN-uh-mehl: "grace of God"]. 600 B.C. A cousin from whom Jeremiah bought a field at Anathoth. Jeremiah 32:6–12.

HANAN [HAY-nuhn: "grace"]

1. B.C. date unknown. Listed in the genealogy of Benjamin in 1 Chronicles 8:23.

2. 1000 B.C. One of David's mighty men. 1 Chronicles 11:43.

3. B.C. date unknown. A descendant of Jonathan, son of Saul. 1 Chronicles 8:38; 9:44.

4. B.C. date unknown. Ancestor of a family of temple servants that returned to Judah with Zerubbabel. Ezra 2:46; Nehemiah 7:49.

5. 625 B.C. The sons of Hanan had a room in the temple. Jeremiah 35:4.

6. 450 B.C. A Levite who helped Ezra instruct the people in the Law. Nehemiah 8:7.

7. 450 B.C. A Levite who signed the covenant renewal with God in Nehemiah's time. Nehemiah 10:10. Possibly the same as Hanan 6.

8. and 9. 450 B.C. Two Jews who signed the covenant renewal pact with God after the Exile. Nehemiah 10:22, 26.

10. 425 B.C. Son of Zaccur appointed by Nehemiah as an assistant treasurer in the temple. Nehemiah 13:13.

HANANI [huh-NAY-nee: "gracious"]

1. 975 B.C. A son of Heman, a minister of music for David. 1 Chronicles 25:4, 25.

2. 900 B.C. A seer who prophesied against Asa and was thrown in prison. 1 Kings 16:1, 7; 2 Chronicles 16:7–10; 19:2.

3. 450 B.C. A priest who took a pagan wife after the Exile. Ezra 10:20.

4. 450 B.C. A brother of Nehemiah. Between his two terms as governor, Nehemiah left his brother in charge of Jerusalem. Nehemiah 1:2; 7:2.

5. 450 B.C. A priest and musician at the dedication of the wall of Jerusalem. Nehemiah 12:36.

HANANIAH [HAN-uh-NI-uh: "Yahweh is gracious"]

1. B.C. date unknown. Listed in the genealogy of Benjamin. 1 Chronicles 8:24.

2. 975 B.C. A musician in David's time. 1 Chronicles 25:4, 23.

3. 775 B.C. A royal official and military commander under Uzziah. 2 Chronicles 26:11.

4. 650 B.C. Grandfather of Irijah, the captain who imprisoned Jeremiah at the fall of Jerusalem. Jeremiah 37:13.

5. 600 B.C. Father of an official of King Jehoiakim. Jeremiah 36:12.

6. 600 B.C. A false prophet who opposed Jeremiah and died within a year in accord with Jeremiah's prophecy. Jeremiah 28.

7. 600 B.C. One of Daniel's three Jewish friends taken with him to Babylon. His name was changed to Shadrach when

he entered Nebuchadnezzar's service. Daniel 1:6–19.

8. 500 B.C. A son of Zerubbabel listed in the genealogy of the royal line of Judah after the Exile. 1 Chronicles 3:19, 21.

9. 500 B.C. Head of a priestly family in Joiakim's time. Nehemiah 12:12.

10. 450 B.C. A Jew who took a foreign wife after the Exile. Ezra 10:28.

11. 450 B.C. A perfume maker who helped repair the wall of Jerusalem. Nehemiah 3:8.

12. 450 B.C. Another who helped rebuild the wall of Jerusalem. Nehemiah 3:30.

13. 450 B.C. Commander who shared authority in Jerusalem with Nehemiah's brother while Nehemiah was away. Nehemiah 7:2. However, it is possible Hananiah is another name for Hanani, brother of Nehemiah.

14. 450 B.C. A leader who signed the covenant renewal with God in Nehemiah's time. Nehemiah 10:23.

15. 450 B.C. A priest who played the trumpet at the dedication of the Jerusalem wall. Nehemiah 12:41.

HANNIEL [HAN-ee-uhl: "God is gracious"]

1. 1400 B.C. The leader from the tribe of Manasseh appointed to help divide the land of Canaan. Numbers 34:23.

2. B.C. date unknown. Listed in the genealogy of Asher. 1 Chronicles 7:39.

HANOCH [HAY-nahk]

1. 1950 B.C. One of five sons of Midian, son of Abraham. Genesis 25:4; 1 Chronicles 1:33.

2. 1900 B.C. First son of Reuben, Jacob's eldest son. Genesis 46:9; Numbers 26:5.

HANUN [HAY-nuhn: "gracious"]

1. 1000 B.C. Son and successor of Nahash, king of the Ammonites, who went to war with David. 2 Samuel 10:1; 1 Chronicles 19:2.

2. 450 B.C. One who helped repair the walls of Jerusalem. Nehemiah 3:13.

3. 450 B.C. Another who worked on the walls of Jerusalem. Nehemiah 3:30.

HAPPIZZEZ [HAP-uh-zehz]. 1000 B.C. Head of the eighteenth division of priests in David's time. 1 Chronicles 24:15.

HARAN [HAIR-uhn]

1. 2100 B.C. Younger brother of Abraham and the father of Lot. Genesis 11:26–31.

2. B.C. date unknown. Listed in the genealogy of Judah. 1 Chronicles 2:46.

3. B.C. date unknown. A descendant of Gershon, son of Levi. 1 Chronicles 23:9.

HARBONA [hahr-BOH-nuh]. 475 B.C. One of seven eunuchs who served King Xerxes. Esther 1:10; 7:9.

HAREPH [HAHR-ef]. B.C. date unknown. Listed in the genealogy of Judah. 1 Chronicles 2:51.

HARHAIAH [hahr-HAY-uh: "Yahweh protects"]. 475 B.C. Father of Uzziel, who helped rebuild the wall of Jerusalem. Nehemiah 3:8.

HARHAS [HAHR-hahs: possibly "splendor"]. 675 B.C. Grandfather of Shallum, husband of the prophetess Huldah. 2 Kings 22:14. Called Hasrah in 2 Chronicles 34:22.

HARHUR [HAHR-huhr]. B.C. date unknown. Ancestor of a family of temple servants that returned to Judah after the Exile. Ezra 2:51; Nehemiah 7:53.

HARIM [HAIR-uhm: "consecrated"]

1. 1000 B.C. Head of the third division of priests in David's time. 1 Chronicles 24:8.

2. B.C. date unknown. Ancestor of a family returning to Judah after the Exile. Ezra 2:32; Nehemiah 7:35.

3. B.C. date unknown. Ancestor of a priestly family that returned from Exile. Ezra 2:39; 10:21; Nehemiah 7:42; 10:5; 12:15. Possibly the same as Harim 1.

4. B.C. date unknown. Ancestor of some who took foreign wives after the Exile. Ezra 10:31. Probably the same as Harim 2.

5. 450 B.C. A Jewish leader who signed the covenant renewal pact with God in Nehemiah's time, possibly with the name of a family ancestor (Harim 2?). Nehemiah 10:27.

HARIPH [HAIR-if]

1. B.C. date unknown. Ancestor of a family that returned to Judah with Zerubbabel. Nehemiah 7:24.

2. 450 B.C. A leader who sealed the covenant renewal in Nehemiah's time, possibly with the name of a family ancestor (compare Hariph 1). Nehemiah 10:19.

HARNEPHER [HAHR-nuh-fuhr]. B.C. date unknown. Listed in the genealogy of Asher. 1 Chronicles 7:36.

HAROEH [huh-ROH-uh: "the seer"]. B.C. date unknown. A descendant of Caleb listed in the genealogy of Judah. 1 Chronicles 2:52.

HARSHA [HAHR-shuh]. B.C. date unknown. Ancestor of a family of temple servants that returned from Exile. Ezra 2:52; Nehemiah 7:54.

HARUM [HAIR-uhm]. B.C. date unknown. Listed in the genealogy of Judah in 1 Chronicles 4:8.

HARUMAPH [huh-ROO-mahf: "slit-nose"]. 475 B.C. Father of Jedaiah, who helped rebuild Jerusalem after the Exile. Nehemiah 3:10.

HARUZ [HAIR-uhz]. 700 B.C. Father of Meshullemeth, wife of King Manasseh. 2 Kings 21:19.

HASADIAH [HAS-uh-DI-uh: "Yahweh is kind"]. 425 B.C. A son of Zerubbabel. 1 Chronicles 3:20.

HASHABIAH [HASH-uh-BI-uh: "Yahweh has taken account"]

1. B.C. date unknown. Listed in the genealogy of Ethan, one of David's chief ministers of music. 1 Chronicles 6:45.

2. 975 B.C. Head of the twelfth division of musicians in David's time. 1 Chronicles 25:3, 19.

3. 975 B.C. One of David's officials. 1 Chronicles 26:30.

4. 975 B.C. An officer over the tribe of Levi in David's time. 1 Chronicles 27:17.

5. 625 B.C. A chief Levite during the reign of Josiah. 2 Chronicles 35:9.

6. B.C. date unknown. Ancestor of a Levite who settled in Jerusalem after the Exile. 1 Chronicles 9:14; Nehemiah 11:15.

7. B.C. date unknown. Ancestor of Uzzi, chief of the Levites in Jerusalem in Nehemiah's time. Nehemiah 11:22.

8. 500 B.C. Head of a priestly family. Nehemiah 12:21.

9. 450 B.C. A Levite who returned with Ezra to Judah after the Exile. He signed the covenant renewal pact with God. Ezra 8:19, 24; Nehemiah 10:11; 12:24.

10. 450 B.C. He helped repair Jerusalem's wall in his district after the Exile. Nehemiah 3:17.

HASHABNAH [huh-SHAB-nuh]. 450 B.C. A leader who signed the covenant renewal pact in Nehemiah's time. Nehemiah 10:25.

HASHABNIAH [HASH-uhb-NEE-uh]

1. 475 B.C. Father of Hattush, who helped repair Jerusalem's walls. Nehemiah 3:10.

2. 450 B.C. One of the Levites who led Israel in prayer prior to the covenant renewal. Nehemiah 9:5.

HASHBADANA [hash-BAD-duh-nuh]. 450 B.C. He stood to Ezra's left when Ezra read the Law to all the people. Nehemiah 8:4.

HASHEM [HAY-shehm]. 1000 B.C. One of David's military elite. 1 Chronicles 11:34.

HASHUBAH [huh-SHOO-buh: "considera-tion"]. 425 B.C. A son of Zerubbabel, governor of Judah. 1 Chronicles 3:20.

HASHUM [HAY-shuhm]

1. B.C. date unknown. Ancestor head of a family that returned to Judah after the Exile. Ezra 2:19; Nehemiah 7:22.

2. B.C. date unknown. Ancestor of some who took foreign wives after the Exile. Ezra 10:33. Possibly the same as Hashum 1.

3. 450 B.C. He stood to the left of Ezra the scribe at the reading of the Law. Nehemiah 8:4.

4. 450 B.C. A Jewish leader who signed the covenant renewal with God, probably with the name of a family ancestor (see. Hashum 1) Nehemiah 10:18.

HASRAH [HAZ-ruh]. 675 B.C. Grandfather of Shallum, husband of the prophetess Huldah. 2 Chronicles 34:22. Called Harhas in 2 Kings 22:14.

HASSENAAH [has-uh-NAY-uh]. B.C. date unknown. Ancestor of some who rebuilt the Fish Gate in Jerusalem's wall. Nehemiah 3:3. Probably the same as Senaah in Ezra 2:35; Nehemiah 7:38.

HASSENUAH [HAS-uh-NOO-uh]. B.C. date unknown. Ancestor of Sallu, a Benjamite who settled in Jerusalem after the Exile. 1 Chronicles 9:7.

HASSHUB [HASH-uhb: "considerate"]

1. 475 B.C. Father of Shemaiah, a Levite who settled in Jerusalem after the Exile. 1 Chronicles 9:14; Nehemiah 11:15.

2 and 3. 450 B.C. Two who helped rebuild the wall of Jerusalem. Nehemiah 3:11, 23.

4. 450 B.C. One who signed the pact of covenant renewal in Nehemiah's time. Nehemiah 10:23. Possibly the same as Hasshub 2 or 3.

HASSOPHERETH [huh-SAHF-uh-reth]. 950 B.C. A servant of Solomon whose descendants returned to Judah with Zerubbabel. Ezra 2:55. Called Sophereth in the parallel text in Nehemiah 7:57.

HASUPHA [huh-SOO-fuh]. 950 B.C. A servant of Solomon, whose descendants returned to Judah after the Exile. Ezra 2:43; Nehemiah 7:46.

HATHACH [HAY-thak]. 475 B.C.. A eunuch assigned to attend Esther in Xerxes's court. Esther 4:5–9.

HATHATH [HAY-thath]. 350 B.C. Son of Othniel the judge, named in 1 Chronicles 4:13.

HATIPHA [huh-TI-fuh: "seized, captive"]. B.C. date unknown. Ancestor of temple servants who returned to Judah with Zerubbabel. Ezra 2:54; Nehemiah 7:45.

HATITA [huh-TI-tuh]. B.C. date unknown. Ancestral head of a family of temple gatekeepers that returned to Judah after the Exile. Ezra 2:42; Nehemiah 7:45.

HATTIL [HAT-uhl]. 950 B.C. A servant of Solomon whose descendants returned to Judah after the Exile. Ezra 2:57; Nehemiah 7:59.

HATTUSH [HAT-uhsh]

1. 525 B.C. A chief priest who returned to Judah with Zerubbabel. Nehemiah 12:2.

2. 450 B.C. A descendant of Shecaniah who returned to Judah with Ezra. 1 Chronicles 3:22; Ezra 8:2.

3. 450 B.C. Son of Hashabneiah, who helped repair the walls of Jerusalem. Nehemiah 3:10. Possibly the same as Hattush 1.

4. 450 B.C. A priest who signed the covenant renewal pact with God, possibly with the name of his family ancestor (see Hattush 1). Nehemiah 10:4.

HAVILAH [HAV-uh-luh: "sandy"]

1. B.C. date unknown. A son of Cush listed in the table of nations in Genesis 10:7.

2. B.C. date unknown. A descendant of Shem listed in the table of nations in Genesis 10:29.

HAZAEL [HAY-zee-uhl: "God sees"]. 850 B.C. An official of Ben-Hadad, king of Syria who murdered the ill king and usurped the throne. 1 Kings 19:15–17; 2 Kings 8:8–15; 13:3, 22–25.

HAZAIAH [huh-ZAY-yuh: "Yahweh sees"]. B.C. date unknown. Ancestor of a Judahite who settled in Jerusalem after the Exile. Nehemiah 11:5.

HAZARMAVETH   [hay-zuhr-MAY-veth: "court of death"]. B.C. date unknown.

A descendant of Shem listed in the table of nations in Genesis 10:26.

HAZIEL [HAY-zee-uhl: "God sees"]. B.C. date unknown. A family head listed in the genealogy of Gershon, son of Levi, in 1 Chronicles 23:9.

HAZO [HAY-zoo]. 2075 B.C. A son of Nahor, the brother of Abraham. Genesis 22:22.

HAZZOBEBAH [HAZ-oh-BEE-buh]. B.C. date unknown. Listed in the genealogy of Judah in 1 Chronicles 4:8.

HEBER [HEE-buhr: "companion"]

1. 1850 B.C. A grandson of Asher. Genesis 46:17; 1 Chronicles 7:31, 32.

2. 1225 B.C. A Kenite descended from Moses' brother-in-law. His wife, Jael, killed Sisera, commander of a Canaanite army. Judges 4:11, 17; 5:24.

3. B.C. date unknown. Listed in the genealogy of Judah. 1 Chronicles 4:18.

4. B.C. date unknown. Listed in the genealogy of Benjamin. 1 Chronicles 8:17.

HEBRON [HEB-ruhn: "league, association"]

1. 1850 B.C. A grandson of Levi. Exodus 6:18; Numbers 3:19.

2. B.C. date unknown. Listed only in the genealogy of Caleb. 1 Chronicles 2:42, 43.

HEGAI [HEHG-I]. 475 B.C. The eunuch King Xerxes put in charge of his harem. Esther 2:3, 8, 15.

HELDAI [HEL-di]

1. 975 B.C. Commander of the twelfth division of David's army. 1 Chronicles 27:15. Probably same as Heled, one of David's thirty mighty men (1 Chron. 11:30).

2. 525 B.C. One who brought gold and silver to the Jews who returned to Judah from Exile. Zechariah 6:10, 14.

HELED [HEE-lehd]. 1000 B.C. One of David's top thirty military men. 2 Samuel 23:29: 1 Chronicles 11:30. Probably the same as Heldai 1.

HELEK [HEE-lehk: "portion, lot"]. B.C. date unknown. Ancestor of one of Manasseh's clans. Numbers 26:30.

HELEM [HEE-luhm]. B.C. date unknown. Listed in the genealogy of Asher. 1 Chronicles 7:35.

HELEZ [HEE-lehz]

1. 1000 B.C. One of David's top thirty military men. 2 Samuel 23:26; 1 Chronicles 11:27; 27:10.

2. B.C. date unknown. Listed in the genealogy of Judah. 1 Chronicles 2:39.

HELI [HEE-li]. 25 B.C. Father of Joseph listed in the genealogy of Christ in Luke 3:23.

HELKAI [HEL-ki: shortened form of Helkiah, "Yahweh is my portion"]. 500 B.C. Head of a priestly family who returned to Judah after the Exile. Nehemiah 12:15.

HELON [HEE-lahn: "strength, valor"]. 1475 B.C. Father of Eliab, leader of the tribe of Zebulun at the time of the Exodus. Numbers 1:9.

HEMAN [HEE-muhn: "faithful"]

1. B.C. date unknown. A wise man whom Solomon exceeded in wisdom. 1 Kings 4:31; 1 Chronicles 2:6. Author of Psalm 88.

2. 1000 B.C. Levite seer who was one of David's chief ministers of music. 1 Chronicles 6:33; 15:17–19; 25:1–6.

HEMDAN [HEM-dan]. 1925 B.C. KJV: Amram (1 Chron. 1:41); RSV: Hamran

(1 Chron. 1:41). Firstborn son of Dishon, a Horite chief in Esau's time. Genesis 36:26; 1 Chronicles 1:41.

HEN [HEN: "favor"]. 525 B.C. A son of Zephaniah. Likely the same as Josiah in v. 10. According to the NIV, the word may possibly be rendered "the gracious one."

HENADAD [HEN-uh-dad: "favor of Hadad" (a weather deity)]. B.C. date unknown. Ancestor of a Levite family that helped rebuild the temple after the Exile. Ezra 3:9; Nehemiah 3:18, 24; 10:9.

HEPHER [HEE-fuhr]

1. B.C. date unknown. Ancestral head of a clan in the tribe of Manasseh. Numbers 26:32, 33; 27:1; Joshua 17:2, 3.

2. B.C. date unknown. Listed in the genealogy of Judah. 1 Chronicles 4:6.

3. 1000 B.C. One of David's top thirty military men. 1 Chronicles 11:36.

HERESH [HEER-esh]. 450 B.C. A Levite who settled in Jerusalem after the Exile. 1 Chronicles 9:15.

HERMAS [HUHR-muhs]. A.D. 55. A Christian whom Paul greeted in his letter to the Romans. Romans 16:14.

HERMES [HUHR-meez]. A.D. 55. A Roman Christian to whom Paul sent greetings. Romans 16:14.

HERMOGENES [huhr-MAHJ-uh-neez; "born of Hermes"]. A.D. 65. A believer who deserted Paul. 2 Timothy 1:15.

HEROD [HAIR-uhd]

1. 37–4 B.C. Herod the Great, the king of the Jews who slaughtered the children of Bethlehem in an attempt to kill the young Jesus. Matthew 2; Luke 1:5.

2. 4 B.C.–A.D. 39. Herod Antipas, a son of Herod the Great and tetrarch of Galilee

and Perea during Jesus' ministry. He mocked Christ before returning him to Pilate, Matthew 14:1–11; Mark 6:14–29; Luke 3:19, 20; 23:6–15.

3. A.D. 25. Herod Philip, another son of Herod the Great; the first husband of Herodias and father of Salome. Matthew 14:3; Mark 6:17.

4. 4 B.C.–A.D. 34. Herod Philip, a son of Herod the Great and Cleopatra of Jerusalem. Luke 3:1.

5. A.D. 37–44. Herod Agrippa I, a grandson of Herod the Great. As king of Judea, he persecuted the early church and put the apostle James to death and imprisoned Peter.

6. A.D. 50–100. Herod Agrippa II, son and successor of Agrippa I. He advised Festus concerning the trial of Paul. Acts 24:35

HERODION [huh-ROH-dee-uhn]. A.D. 55. A relative whom Paul greeted in Romans 16:11.

HEZEKIAH [HEZ-uh-KI-uh: "Yahweh is my strength"]

1. 728–697 B.C. The king of Judah whose religious reforms provided the basis for deliverance from an Assyrian army. 2 Kings 18—20; 2 Chronicles 29—32; Isaiah 36—39.

2. B.C. date unknown. Ancestor of Zephaniah the prophet. Zephaniah 1:1.

3. 525 B.C. Head of a family that returned to Judah with Zerubbabel. Ezra 2:16; Nehemiah 7:21.

4. 450 B.C. One who signed the pact of covenant renewal with God, possibly with the name of an ancestor (see Hezekiah 3). Nehemiah 10:17.

HEZION [HEZ-ee-uhn]. 950 B.C. Grandfather of Ben-Hadad, the king of Syria (Aram). 1 Kings 15:18.

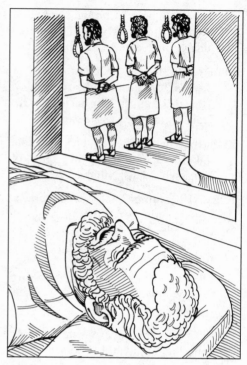

Herod the Great planned to have hundreds of leading Jews executed on the day of his death to keep the populace from rejoicing that he was gone.

HEZIR [HEZ-uhr]

1. 1000 B.C. Head of the seventeenth division of priests in David's time. 1 Chronicles 24:15.

2. 450 B.C. A Jewish leader who signed the covenant renewal with God. Nehemiah 10:20.

HEZRO [HEZ-roh]. 1000 B.C. One of David's top thirty military men. 2 Samuel 23:35; 1 Chronicles 11:37.

HEZRON [HEZ-ruhn]

1. 1875 B.C. A son of Reuben, who was the first son of Jacob. Genesis 46:9; Exodus 6:14; 1 Chronicles 5:3.

2. 1825 B.C. Grandson of Judah, the son of Jacob. Genesis 46:12; Ruth 4:18; 1 Chronicles 2:9, 21, 24. He is listed in

the genealogies of Christ in Matthew 1:3 and Luke 3:33.

HIDDAI [HID-i]. 1000 B.C. One of David's top thirty military commanders. 2 Samuel 23:30. Called Hurai in 1 Chronicles 11:32.

HIEL [HI-uhl]. 875 B.C. The man of Bethel who rebuilt Jericho at the cost of the lives of his eldest and youngest sons. 1 Kings 16:34.

HILKIAH [hil-KI-uh: "Yahweh is my portion"]

1. B.C. date unknown. A Levite listed in the genealogy of Ethan, a minister of music in David's time. 1 Chronicles 6:45.

2. 975 B.C. A Levite and temple gatekeeper in David's time. 1 Chronicles 26:11.

3. 725 B.C. Father of Eliakim, Hezekiah's palace administrator. 2 Kings 18:18; Isaiah 22:20.

4. 625 B.C. The high priest who discovered a lost Book of the Law in the temple during the reign of King Josiah. 2 Kings 22; 23:4, 24; 1 Chronicles 6:13; 2 Chronicles 34.

5. 625 B.C. Father of Jeremiah the prophet. Jeremiah 1:1.

6. 600 B.C. Father of an ambassador to Babylon in the time of Zedekiah. Jeremiah 29:3.

7. 525 B.C. A chief priest who returned to Judah with Zerubbabel. Nehemiah 12:7, 21.

8. 475 B.C. Father of a priest who settled in Jerusalem in Nehemiah's time. 1 Chronicles 9:11; Nehemiah 11:11.

9. 450 B.C. He stood to the right as Ezra read God's Law to the people. Nehemiah 8:4.

HILLEL [HIL-ehl]. 1100 B.C. Father of Abdon, a minor judge. Judges 12:13, 15.

HIRAH [HI-ruh]. 1900 B.C. A man from Adullam with whom Judah stayed. Genesis 38:1, 12.

HIRAM [HI-ruhm: shortened form of Ahiram, "my brother is exalted"]. 975 B.C. King of Tyre who was an ally of David and Solomon. 2 Samuel 5:11; 1 Kings 5:8.

HIZKI [HIZ-ki: shortened form of Hezekiah]. B.C. date unknown. Listed in the genealogy of Benjamin. 1 Chronicles 8:17.

HIZKIAH [hiz-KI-uh: "Yahweh is my strength"]. B.C. date unknown. A descendant of Zerubbabel in the genealogy of David's royal line. 1 Chronicles 3:23.

HOBAB [HOH-bahb: "beloved"]. 1450 B.C. Son of Reuel the Midianite and Moses' brother-in-law. Numbers 10:29; Judges 4:11.

HOBAIAH [hoh-BI-uh: "Yahweh has hidden"]. B.C. date unknown. Ancestor of a family of priests that returned to Judah after the Exile. Ezra 2:61; Nehemiah 7:63.

HOD [HAHD: "majesty"]. B.C. date unknown. Listed in the genealogy of Asher. 1 Chronicles 7:37.

HODAVIAH [HAHD-uh-VI-uh: "honorer of Yahweh"]

1. B.C. date unknown. Ancestor of a Levite family that returned to Judah after the Exile. Ezra 2:40; Nehemiah 7:43.

2. 750 B.C. Head of a family in the tribe of Manasseh. 1 Chronicles 5:24.

3. B.C. date unknown. Ancestor of a Benjamite who settled in Jerusalem after the Exile. 1 Chronicles 9:7.

4. B.C. date unknown. Descendant of Zerubbabel listed in the genealogy of the royal line. 1 Chronicles 3:24.

HODIAH [hoh-DI-uh: "splendor of Yahweh"]

1. B.C. date unknown. Listed in the genealogy of Judah. 1 Chronicles 4:19.

2. 450 B.C. A Levite who interpreted for the people while Ezra the scribe read the Law. Nehemiah 8:7; 9:5.

3 and 4. 450 B.C. Two Levites who signed the covenant renewal pact with God. Nehemiah 10:10, 13. Either may be the same as Hodiah 2.

5. 450 B.C. A leader who signed the covenant renewal pact with God in Nehemiah's time. Nehemiah 10:18.

HOHAM [HOH-ham]. 1400 B.C. King of Hebron who joined four other Amorite kings to attack Gibeon during the conquest of Canaan. Joshua 10:3.

HOMAM [HON-mam]. 1950 B.C. A son of Lotan, a Horite chief in Esau's time. 1 Chronicles 1:39. Called Hemam in Genesis 36:22.

HOPHNI [HAHF-ni]. 1130 B.C. One of the two unholy sons of Eli, who served as priest at the tabernacle until he died on the same day his sons were killed. 1 Samuel 1:3; 2—4.

HOPHRA [HAHF-ruh]. 589–570 B.C. Egyptian Pharaoh who marched against Nebuchadnezzar to aid Zedekiah, but withdrew, permitting Nebuchadnezzar's army to take Jerusalem. Jeremiah 37:5–8; 44:30.

HORAM [HOH-ram]. 1400 B.C. A king of Gezer defeated by Joshua. Joshua 10:33.

HORI [HOHR-i)

1. 1950 B.C. First son of Lotan and grandson of Seir, a Horite chief. Genesis 36:22.

2. 1475 B.C. Father of Shaphat, the Simeonite leader Moses sent to explore the land of Canaan. Numbers 13:5.

HOSAH [HON-suh: "refuge"]. 1000 B.C. A chief temple gatekeeper in the time of David. 1 Chronicles 16:38.

HOSEA [hoh-ZAY-uh: "Yahweh has saved"]. 750 B.C. A prophet whose words are recorded in the Book of Hosea.

HOSHAIAH [hoh-SHAY-yuh: "Yahweh has saved"]

1. 625 B.C. Father of Azariah who begged Jeremiah to seek the will of God for those left in Judah after Jerusalem fell. Jeremiah 42:1; 43:2.

2. 450 B.C. A leader at the dedication of the rebuilt walls of Jerusalem. Nehemiah 12:32.

HOSHAMA [HOSH-ab-mub: "Yahweh has heard"]. 550 B.C. A son or grandson of Jehoiachin, listed in the genealogy of the royal line after the Exile. 1 Chronicles 3:18.

HOSHEA [hob-SHEE-uh: "may Yahweh save"]

1. 1450 B.C. The leader whose name was changed by Moses to Joshua. Numbers 13:8, 16.

2. 1000 B.C. Officer over the tribe of Ephraim in David's day. 1 Chronicles 27:20.

3. 732–723 B.C. The last king of Israel, who assassinated Pekah and took the throne. 2 Kings 15:30; 17:1–6.

4. 450 B.C. A leader who signed the covenant renewal pact with God. Nehemiah 10:23.

HOTHAM [HOH-thuhm].

1. B.C. date unknown. Listed in the genealogy of Asher. 1 Chronicles 7:32.

2. 1025 B.C. Father of two members of David's military elite. 1 Chronicles 11:44.

HOTHIR [HOH-thur: "abundance"]. 975 B.C. A temple musician in David's time. 1 Chronicles 25:4.

HUBBAH [HUH-buh]. B.C. date unknown. Listed in the genealogy of Ashur. 1 Chronicles 7:34.

HUL [HUL]. B.C. date unknown. A grandson of Shem listed in the table of nations. Genesis 10:23.

HUPHAM [HOO-fhum: "coast dweller"]. Head of a Benjamite clan. Numbers 26:39.

HUPPAH [HUP-uh: "protection"]. Head of the thirteenth division of priests in David's time. 1 Chronicles 24:13.

HUPPIM [HUP-ihm: "coastal people"]. A Benjamite listed in Genesis 46:21.

HUR [HURH]

1. 1500 B.C. Son of Caleb and grandfather of the chief artisan who constructed the tabernacle. Exodus 31:2

2. 1450 B.C. He held up one of Moses' hands so the Israelites might win a battle. Exodus 17:10–12.

3. 1400 B.C. A king of Midian defeated by the Israelites. Numbers 31:8; Joshua 13:21.

4. 475 B.C. Father of a man who helped repair Jerusalem's walls in Nehemiah's time. Nehemiah 3:9.

HURAI [HYOOR-i]. One of David's thirty chief military men. 1 Chronicles 11:32.

HURAM [HYOOR-uhm]

1. 1825 B.C. A grandson of Benjamin. 1 Chronicles 8:5.

2. 950 B.C. The metalworker who cast the bronze pillars that stood before Solomon's temple. 1 Kings 7:13–45; 2 Chronicles 2:13.

HURI [HYOOR-i]. B.C. date unknown. Listed in the genealogy of Gad. 1 Chronicles 5:4

HUSHAH [HOO-shuh]. B.C. date unknown. Listed in the genealogy of Judah. 1 Chronicles 4:4

HUSHAI [HOO-shi]

1. 975 B.C. The counselor of David whose advice led Absalom to adopt a strategy that led to his defeat. 2 Samuel 15:32–37; 16:15—17:16.

2. 975 B.C. The father of one of Solomon's twelve district governors. Likely the same as Hushai 1. 1 Kings 4:16.

HUSHAM [HOO-shuhm]. B.C. date unknown. A king of Edom descended from Esau. Genesis 36:34, 35.

HUSHIM [HOO-shim]. 1875 B.C. A grandson of Jacob. Genesis 46:23. Called Shuham in Numbers 26:42.

HYMENAEUS [HI-muh-NEE-uhs]. A.D. 65. A false teacher condemned by Paul for heretical teaching. 1 Timothy 1:20; 2 Timothy 2:17.

I

IBHAR [IB-hahr: "God chooses"]. 975 B.C. A son of David born in Jerusalem. 2 Samuel 5:15.

IBNEIAH [ib-NEE-yuh: "Yahweh builds up"]. 450 B.C. A Benjamite who settled in Jerusalem after the Exile. 1 Chronicles 9:8.

IBNIJAH [ib-NI-juh: "Yahweh builds up"]. B.C. date unknown. Ancestor of a Benjamite who settled in Jerusalem after its wall was rebuilt. 1 Chronicles 9:8.

IBRI [ib-REE: "a Hebrew"]. 1000 B.C. Listed among the Levites in David's time. 1 Chronicles 24:27.

IBZAN [IB-zan: "swift"(?)]. Ruled 1078–1072 B.C.(?) A judge from Bethlehem who ruled in Israel for seven years. Judges 12:8–10.

ICHABOD [IK-uh-bahd: "no glory"]. 1050 B.C. Son of Phinehas and grandson of Eli, born shortly after their deaths. 1 Samuel 4:21; 14:3.

IDBASH [ID-bash: "honey-sweet"]. B.C. date unknown. Listed in the genealogy of Judah. 1 Chronicles 4:3.

IDDO [ID-oh: "beloved" or "adorned" (1, 2), "timely" (3)]

1. B.C. date unknown. A descendant of Levi. 1 Chronicles 6:21. Probably the same as Adaiah in 1 Chronicles 6:41.

2. 1000 B.C. Chief of the tribe of Manasseh in Gilead. 1 Chronicles 27:21.

3. 975 B.C. Father of Abinadab, a district governor who married a daughter of Solomon. 1 Kings 4:14.

4. 900 B.C. A seer whose records were used in writing the Book of Chronicles. 2 Chronicles 9:29; 12:15; 13:22.

5. 575 B.C. Grandfather of Zechariah the prophet. Ezra 5:1; Zechariah 1:1.

6. 525 B.C. A chief priest who returned to Judah with Zerubbabel after the Exile. Nehemiah 12:4, 16.

7. 450 B.C. Leader of the Levites at Casiphia who provided servants for the rebuilt Jerusalem temple. Ezra 8:17.

IEZER [i-EE-zuhr: shortened form of Abiazer]. B.C. date unknown. Ancestor of a clan of Manasseh. Numbers 26:30.

IGAL [I-gal: "may God redeem"]

1. 1450 B.C. The representative of the tribe of Issachar whom Moses assigned to spy out Canaan. Numbers 13:7.

2. 1000 B.C. One of David's thirty military elite. 2 Samuel 23:36.

3. B.C. date unknown. A descendant of Zerubbabel in the royal line. 1 Chronicles 3:22.

IGDALIAH [IG-duh-LI-uh: "Yahweh is great"]. B.C. date unknown. He is called "a man of God," suggesting that he was a prophet. Jeremiah 35:4.

IKKESH [IK-esh: "crooked"]. 1025 B.C. The father of Ira, one of David's thirty mighty men. 2 Samuel 23:26; 1 Chronicles 11:28; 27:9.

ILAI [I-li]. 1000 B.C. One of David's thirty military elite. 1 Chronicles 11:29. Called Zalmon in 2 Samuel 23:28.

IMLA [IM-luh: "fullness"(?)]. 900 B.C. Father of Micaiah, the prophet who predicted the death of Ahab. 1 Kings 22:8, 9; 2 Chronicles 18:7, 8.

IMMANUEL [ih-MAN-yoo-el: "with us is God"]. Name given in Isaiah 7:14 to a child to be born of the virgin. The name was subsequently given to Jesus. Isaiah 8:8, 10; Matthew 1:23.

IMMER [IM-uhr: "lamb"]

1. 1000 B.C. Head of the sixteenth priestly division in David's time. 1 Chronicles 24:14.

2. B.C. date unknown. Ancestor of a priestly family that returned to Judah after the Exile. Ezra 2:37; 10:20; Nehemiah 7:40.

3. B.C. date unknown. Ancestor of a priest who settled in Jerusalem after the Exile. 1 Chronicles 9:12; Nehemiah 11:13.

4. 625 B.C. Father of Pashur, a temple official who had Jeremiah beaten and put in stocks. Jeremiah 20:1.

IMNA [IM-nuh]. B.C. date unknown. Listed only in the genealogy of Asher. 1 Chronicles 7:35.

IMNAH [IM-nuh]

1. 1875 B.C. Firstborn son of Asher. Genesis 46:17; [Jimnah]. Numbers 26:44.

2. 725 B.C. Chief gatekeeper of the East Gate in Hezekiah's time. 2 Chronicles 31:14.

IMRAH [IM-ruh]. B.C. date unknown. Listed in the genealogy of Asher. 1 Chronicles 7:36.

IMRI [IM-ri]

1. B.C. date unknown. Ancestor of a Judahite who settled in Jerusalem after the Exile. 1 Chronicles 9:4.

2. 475 B.C. Father of Zaccur, who helped rebuild the wall of Jerusalem. Nehemiah 3:2.

IPHDEIAH [if-DEE-yuh: "Yahweh redeems"]. Listed in the genealogy of Benjamin. 1 Chronicles 8:25.

IR [EER]. B.C. date unknown. A descendant of Benjamin. 1 Chronicles 7:12.

IRA [I-ruh]

1. 1000 B.C. Although not a descendant of Aaron, he is called David's priest. 2 Samuel 20:26.

2. 1000 B.C. One of the military elite called David's thirty mighty men. 2 Samuel 23:26; 1 Chronicles 11:28; 27:9.

3. 1000 B.C. The Ithrite, also among David's thirty military heroes. 2 Samuel 23:38; 1 Chronicles 11:40.

IRAD [I-rad] B.C. date unknown. Son of Enoch and grandson of Cain. Genesis 4:18.

IRAM [I-ram]. B.C. date unknown. A chief of Edom descended from Esau. Genesis 36:43.

IRI [I-ri]. B.C. date unknown. Listed in the genealogy of Benjamin. 1 Chronicles 7:7.

IRIJAH [i-RI-juh: "Yahweh sees"]. 800 B.C. Captain of the guard who arrested Jeremiah and charged him with deserting to the Babylonians. Jeremiah 37:13, 14.

IR-NAHASH [ur-NAY-hash]. B.C. date unknown. Probably a mistranslation, "the city of Nahesh." 1 Chronicles 4:12.

IRU [I-roo]. 1425 B.C. A son of Caleb, the spy sent by Moses to explore Canaan. 1 Chronicles 4:15.

ISAAC [I-zik: "laughing" or "he laughed"]. 2066 B.C. The son of Abraham who inherited the covenant promises. Genesis 21—28.

ISAIAH [I-ZAY-yuh: "Yahweh is salvation"]. 739–701 B.C. The prophet who authored the Book of Isaiah. 2 Kings 19; 20; 2 Chronicles 26; 32.

ISHBAH [ISH-buh]. B.C. date unknown. Listed in the genealogy of Judah. 1 Chronicles 4:17.

ISHBAK [ISH-bak]. 2000 B.C. A son of Abraham by Keturah, his second wife. Genesis 25:2.

ISHBI-BENOB [ISH-bi-BE-nahb: "dweller at Nob"]. 1000 B.C. A Philistine warrior who tried to kill King David but was slain by Abishai. 2 Samuel 21:16.

ISHBOSHETH [Ish-BOSH-eth: "man of shame"]. 1000 B.C. A son of Saul who was made king of Israel by Abner. 2 Samuel 2. Also called Esh-Baal in 1 Chronicles 8:33.

ISHHOD [ISH-hahd]. B.C. date unknown. Listed only in the genealogy of Manasseh. 1 Chronicles 7:18.

ISHI [ISH-i: "my husband"]

1. B.C. date unknown. Listed in the genealogy of Jerahmeel of Judah. 1 Chronicles 2:31.

2. B.C. date unknown. Listed in the genealogy of Judah in 1 Chronicles 4:20.

3. B.C. date unknown. Ancestor of Simeonites who drove the Amalekites from Seir's hill country. 1 Chronicles 4:42, 43.

4. 750 B.C. Head of a family taken into exile by Tiglath-Pileser of Assyria. 1 Chronicles 5:24.

ISHIJAH [ish-I-juh]. 450 B.C. A man who took a pagan wife after the Exile. Ezra 10:31.

ISHMA [ISH-muh]. B.C. date unknown. Listed in the genealogy of Judah. 1 Chronicles 4:3.

ISHMAEL [ISH-may-uhl: "God heard"]

1. 2050 B.C. The son of Abraham by Hagar. After being expelled from Abraham's household, Ishmael, too, became a great people. Genesis 16; 17; 25:12–18.

2. B.C. date unknown. A descendant of Jonathan, son of Saul. 1 Chronicles 8:38.

3. 900 B.C. He was a judge appointed by Jehoshaphat. 2 Chronicles 19:11.

4. 850 B.C. An army officer who helped Jehoiada overthrow Athaliah and install Joash as king of Judah. 2 Chronicles 23:1.

5. 575 B.C. He assassinated Gedaliah, whom Nebuchadnezzar had appointed to govern Judah after the fall of Jerusalem. 2 Kings 25:23–26; Jeremiah 40:7—41:16.

6. 450 B.C. A priest who took a pagan wife after the Exile. Ezra 10:22

ISHMAIAH [ish-MAY-uh: "Yahweh hears"]

1. 1000 B.C. A Gibeonite who joined David at Ziklag and became one of David's top thirty military men. 1 Chronicles 12:4.

2. 1000 B.C. Chief of the tribe of Zebulun in David's time. 1 Chronicles 27:19.

ISHMERAI [ISH-muh-ri: "guard, protector"]. B.C. date unknown. Listed in the genealogy of Benjamin. 1 Chronicles 8:18.

ISHPAH [ISH-puh]. B.C. date unknown. Listed in the genealogy of Benjamin. 1 Chronicles 8:16.

ISHPAN [ISH-pan]. B.C. date unknown. A descendant of Benjamin. 1 Chronicles 8:22.

ISHVAH [ISH-vuh]. 1875 B.C. One of four sons of Asher. 1 Chronicles 7:30.

ISHVI [ISH-vi: "equal"]

1. 1875 B.C. A son of Asher. Genesis 46:17; Numbers 26:44.

3. Ruled Israel 1005–1003 B.C. Alternate name of Ishbosheth, son and successor of Saul. 1 Samuel 14:49.

ISMACHIAH [IZ-muh-KI-uh: "Yahweh sustains"]. 725 B.C. A temple official working with tithes and offerings. 2 Chronicles 31:13.

ISRAEL [IZ-ree-uhl: "God perseveres" or "he struggles with God"(?)]. Name God gave to Jacob, ancestor of the Israelites. Genesis 32:28; 35:10; 1 Kings 18:31.

ISSACHAR [IS-uh-kahr]

1. 1900 B.C. Fifth of the six sons born to Jacob by his first wife, Leah, and ancestor of one of the twelve tribes of Israel. Genesis 30:18; 35:23; 46:13; 49:14.

2. 975 B.C. A son of Obed-Edom who was a gatekeeper in David's time. 1 Chronicles 26:5.

ISSHIAH [ish-I-uh]

1. B.C. date unknown. Listed in the genealogy of Issachar. 1 Chronicles 7:3.

2. B.C. date unknown. Listed in the genealogy of Levi. 1 Chronicles 24:21.

3. B.C. date unknown. Listed in the genealogy of Levi. 1 Chronicles 23:20 24:25.

4. 1000 B.C. One of David's top thirty warriors. 1 Chronicles 12:6

ITHAI [ITH-i]. 1000 B.C. Another of David's top thirty military men. 2 Samuel 23:29; 1 Chronicles 11:31.

ITHAMAR [ITH-uh-mahr]. 1400 B.C. One of Aaron's four sons. Exodus 6:23.

ITHIEL [ITH-ee-uhl: "God is with me"(?)]

1. B.C. date unknown. A man to whom Agur's proverbs were directed. Proverbs 30:1.

2. B.C. date unknown. Ancestor of a Benjamite who settled in Jerusalem after its walls were rebuilt. Nehemiah 11:7.

ITHMAH [ITH-muh]. 1000 B.C. A Moabite numbered as one of David's thirty mighty men. 1 Chronicles 11:46.

ITHRAN [ITH-ran]

1. 1900 B.C. Son of a Horite chief in Esau's time. Genesis 36:26.

2. B.C. date unknown. Listed in the genealogy of Asher. 1 Chronicles 7:37.

ITHREAM [ITH-ree-uhm]. 975 B.C. A son of David by his wife Eglah. 2 Samuel 3:5.

ITTAI [IT-i]. 975 B.C. A Philistine mercenary who served David during Absalom's rebellion. 2 Samuel 15:19–22.

IZHAR [IZ-hahr: "shine forth"(?)]. B.C. date unknown. A descendent of Kohath, son of Levi. Exodus 6:18–21; Numbers 3:19.

IZLIAH [iz-LI-uh]. B.C. date unknown. Listed in the genealogy of Benjamin. 1 Chronicles 8:18.

IZRAHIAH [IZ-ruh-HI-uh: "Yahweh shines forth"]. B.C. date unknown. Listed in the genealogy of Issachar. 1 Chronicles 7:3.

IZRI [IZ-ri]. 1000 B.C. Head of the fourth division of priests in David's time. 1 Chronicles 25:11.

IZZIAH [iz-I-uh: "Yahweh purifies"]. 450 B.C. A man who took a pagan wife after the Exile. Ezra 10:25.

J

JAAKOBAH [JAY-uh-KOH-buh: "may God protect"]. 725 B.C. A leader who helped defeat the Amalekites during Hezekiah's reign. 1 Chronicles 4:36.

JAALA [JAY-ah-luh: "ibex" or "mountain goat"]. 950 B.C. A servant of Solomon whose descendants returned to Judah after the Exile. Ezra 2:56; Nehemiah 7:58.

JAALAM [JAY-luhm: "young man"(?)]. 1925 B.C. A son of Esau. Genesis 36:5, 14, 18.

JAARE-OREGIM [JAY-uh-ree-OHR-uh-kim]. 975 B.C. Father of Elhanan, who killed Goliath the Gittite, according to 1 Chronicles 20:5. 2 Samuel 21:19 is a corruption of the original text.

JAARESHIAH [JAIR-uh-SHI-uh]. B.C. date unknown. Listed in the genealogy of Benjamin. 1 Chronicles 8:27.

JAASIEL [jay-AY-zee-uhl: "God does" or "God makes"]

1. 1000 B.C. A hero among the thirty military men called David's mighty men. 1 Chronicles 11:47.

2. 1000 B.C. An officer over the tribe of Benjamin in David's time. 1 Chronicles 27:21.

JAASU [JAY-uh-soo: "maker" or "doer"]. 450 B.C. Man who took a pagan wife after the Exile. Ezra 10:37.

JAAZANIAH [jay-AZ-uh-NI-uh: "Yahweh hears"]

1. 600 B.C. Son of Shaphan, an Israelite elder seen offering incense to an idol in a vision of Ezekiel. Ezekiel 8:11.

2. 600 B.C. An Israelite leader seen giving false advice in one of Ezekiel's visions. Ezekiel 11:1.

3. 575 B.C. A military leader who aided Gedaliah after he was made governor by Nebuchadnezzar. Jeremiah 40:8.

4. 575 B.C. A Recabite who refused to drink when offered wine by Jeremiah the prophet. Jeremiah 35:3.

JAAZIAH [JAY-uh-ZI-uh: "Yahweh strengthens"]. B.C. date unknown. Ancestor of some Levites of David's time. 1 Chronicles 24:26, 27.

JAAZIEL [jay-AY-zee-uhl: "God strengthens"]. 1000 B.C. A Levite who played the lyre as David brought the ark of the covenant to Jerusalem. 1 Chronicles 15:18. Called Aziel in 15:20.

JABAL [JAY-buhl]. B.C. date unknown. Son of Lamech said to be the first nomad who traveled with livestock. Genesis 4:20.

JABESH [JAY-besh: "dry"]. 752 B.C. Father of Shallum, who murdered King Zechariah of Israel and succeeded him as king. 2 Kings 15:10–14.

JABEZ [JAY-bez]. B.C. date unknown. A man who called on God and received His blessing. 1 Chronicles 4:9, 10.

JABIN [JAY-bin: "intelligent" or "discerning"]

1. 1400 B.C. King of Hazor who led Canaanite forces against Joshua. He was defeated and killed. Joshua 11:1–11.

2. 1225 B.C. Another Canaanite king of Hazor, who oppressed Israel for twenty years before Deborah and Barak defeated his army. Judges 4; Psalm 83:9.

JACHAN [JAY-kuhn]. B.C. date unknown. Ancestor of a Gadite family. 1 Chronicles 5:13.

JACOB [JAY-kuhb: "supplanter"]

1. 1950 B.C. The son of Isaac and Rebekah and twin of Esau, who inherited God's covenant promises. Genesis 25—50.

2. 25 B.C. Father of Joseph, the husband of Mary the mother of Jesus. Matthew 1:16.

JADA [JAY-duh: "caring"]. Listed in the genealogy of Judah. 1 Chronicles 2:28, 32.

JADAH [JAY-duh: "honeycomb"]. B.C. date unknown. A descendant of Jonathan, son of Saul. 1 Chronicles 9:42. Called Jehoaddah in 1 Chronicles 8:36.

JADDAI [JAD-i: "beloved"]. 450 B.C. One who took a pagan wife after the Exile. Ezra 10:43.

JADDUA [JAD-oo-uh: "known"]

1. 450 B.C. A Jewish leader who signed the covenant renewal pact with God. Nehemiah 10:21.

2. 400 B.C. High priest during the reign of Darius the Persian. Nehemiah 12:22. According to Josephus, he was high priest in 331 B.C. when Alexander the Great entered Jerusalem.

JADON [JAY-dahn]. 450 B.C. A man who helped repair the walls of Jerusalem. Nehemiah 3:7.

JAHATH [JAY-hath: "God will snatch up"]

1. B.C. date unknown. Listed in the genealogy of Judah in 1 Chronicles 4:2.

2. B.C. date unknown. An ancestor of Asaph, the chief minister of music in David's time. 1 Chronicles 6:43.

3. B.C. date unknown. A descendant of Gershon, Levi's son. 1 Chronicles 23:10. Possibly Jahath 2.

4. 975 B.C. A Levite family in the time of David. 1 Chronicles 24:22.

5. 625 B.C. A Levite who supervised repair of the temple during Josiah's reign. 2 Chronicles 34:12.

JAHAZIAH [jay-huh-ZIGH-uh: "Yahweh sees"]. 450 B.C. He opposed Ezra's insistence that the Israelites divorce their pagan wives. Ezra 10:15.

JAHAZIEL [juh-HAY-zee-uhl: "God sees"]

1. 1000 B.C. A Benjamite who joined David at Ziklag. 1 Chronicles 12:4.

2. 1000 B.C. A priest who blew the trumpet as David brought the ark of the covenant into Jerusalem. 1 Chronicles 16:6.

3. 975 B.C. A Levite family in the time of David. 1 Chronicles 23:19; 24:33.

4. 875 B.C. A priest who prophesied promising King Jehoshaphat victory over Moabite and Ammonite invaders. 2 Chronicles 20:14–17.

5. 475 B.C. Father of Shecaniah, who returned to Judah with Ezra. Ezra 8:5.

JAHDAI [JAH-di: "leader" or "Yahweh leads"]. B.C. date unknown. Listed among the clans of Caleb, a descendant of Judah. 1 Chronicles 2:47.

JAHDIEL [JAH-dee-uhl: "God gives joy"]. 750 B.C. Head of a family taken into exile by the Assyrians. 1 Chronicles 5:24.

JAHDO [JAH-doh]. B.C. date unknown. Listed in the genealogy of Gad. 1 Chronicles 5:14.

JAHLEEL [JAH-lee-uhl: "God waits"]. 1875 B.C. A grandson of Jacob. Genesis 46:14; Numbers 26:26.

JAHMAI [JAH-mi: "Yahweh protects"]. B.C. date unknown. Listed in the genealogy of Issachar. 1 Chronicles 7:2.

JAHZEEL [JAH-zee-uhl: "God apportions"]. B.C. date unknown. Ancestor of one of the clans of Naphtali. Genesis 46:24. Called Jaziel in 1 Chronicles 7:13.

JAHZERAH [JAH-zuh-ruh]. B.C. date unknown. Ancestor of a priest who settled in Jerusalem after the Exile. 1 Chronicles 9:12. Called Ahzai in Nehemiah 11:13.

JAHZIEL [JAH-zee-uhl: "God apportions"]. 1875 B.C. First son of Naphtali. 1 Chronicles 7:13.

JAIR [JAIR: "may he shine forth" or "he enlightens"]

1. 1400 B.C. A descendant of Manasseh who captured Amorite towns and renamed them "settlements of Jair." Numbers 32:41; Deuteronomy 3:14; Joshua 13:30; 1 Chronicles 2:22, 23.

2. 1100 B.C. A Gileadite who led Israel for twenty-two years. Possibly a descendant of Jair 1. Judges 10:3–5.

3. 975 B.C. Father of Elhanan, who killed the brother of Goliath. 1 Chronicles 20:5. Also called Jaare-Oregim in 2 Samuel 21:19.

4. 525 B.C. The father of Mordecai, Esther's uncle. Esther 2:5.

JAIRUS [JAIR-uhs: "he will enlighten"]. A.D. 30. The synagogue ruler whose daughter Jesus raised from the dead. Mark 5:21–43; Luke 8:40–56.

JAKEH [JAY-kuh]. B.C. date unknown. Father of Agur, the author of Proverbs 30.

JAKIM [JAY-kim: "he will establish"]

1. B.C. date unknown. Listed in the genealogy of Benjamin. 1 Chronicles 8:19.

2. 975 B.C. Head of the twelfth division of priests in David's day. 1 Chronicles 24:12.

JAKIN [JAY-kin: "he will establish"]

1. 1900 B.C. A grandson of Jacob. Genesis 46:10; Numbers 26:12. Called Jarib in 1 Chronicles 4:24.

2. 975 B.C. Head of the twenty-first division of priests in David's day. 1 Chronicles 24:17.

3. 450 B.C. A priest who settled in Jerusalem after the Exile. 1 Chronicles 9:10; Nehemiah 11:10.

JALON [JAY-lahn]. B.C. date unknown. Listed only in the genealogy of Judah in 1 Chronicles 4:17.

JAMBRES [JAM-brees]. 1450 B.C. The traditional name of one of the Egyptian sorcerers who imitated some of Moses' miracles before Pharaoh. 2 Timothy 3:8.

JAMES [JAYMZ: Greek form of Jacob]

1. A.D. 1. Father of the apostle Judas (not Judas Iscariot). Luke 6:16; Acts 1:13.

2. A.D. 25. The apostle, who was the son of Zebedee and brother of John. He was executed by Herod Agrippa I. Matthew 4:21; 10:2; Acts 12:2.

3. A.D. 25. Son of Alphaeus, one of the apostles. Matthew 10:3; Acts 1:13. Matthew also called him "son of Alphaeus."

4. A.D. 30. James the younger, son of Mary and brother of Joses. Matthew 27:56; Mark 15:40; 16:1. Possibly the same as James 2.

5. A.D. 30. The Lord's brother, he was a leader in the early church, and author of the Book of James. Matthew 13:55; Mark 6:3; Acts 15:13; 21:18; Galatians 1:19; 2:9.

JAMIN [JAY-mim]

1. 1900 B.C. A grandson of Jacob. Genesis 46:10; Numbers 26:12.

2. B.C. date unknown. Listed in the genealogy of Judah. 1 Chronicles 2:27.

3. 450 B.C. A Levite who helped Ezra instruct the people in the Law. Nehemiah 8:7.

JAMLECH [JAM-lak: "may God give dominion"]. B.C. date unknown. Listed in the genealogy of Simeon. 1 Chronicles 4:34.

JANAI [JAY-ni: "may God answer"]. B.C. date unknown). Listed in the genealogy of Gad. 1 Chronicles 5:12.

JANNA [JAN-i]. B.C. date unknown. Listed in the genealogy of Jesus in Luke 3:24.

JANNES [JAN-ez: "seducer "(?)]. 1450 B.C. Traditionally one of the Egyptian sorcerers who mimicked some of Moses' miracles. The magicians are unnamed in the Old Testament (see Exodus 7:11, 22). 2 Timothy 3:8.

JAPHETH [JAY-feth: "may God enlarge"]. B.C. date not known. Son of Noah and brother of Shem and Ham. Genesis 5:32; 9:18–27; 10:2.

JAPHIA [ja-FI-uh]

1. 1400 B.C. King of Lachish defeated and executed by Joshua. Joshua 10:3.

2. 975 B.C. A son of David, born in Jerusalem. 2 Samuel 5:15; 1 Chronicles 3:7.

JAPHLET [JAF-luht]. B.C. date unknown. Listed in the genealogy of Asher. 1 Chronicles 7:32–33.

JARED [JAIR-uhd: "descent"]. B.C. date unknown. Father of Enoch and an ancestor of Noah. Genesis 5:15–20; 1 Chronicles 1:2; Luke 3:37.

JARHA [JAR-hah]. B.C. date unknown]. An Egyptian listed in the genealogy of Judah in 1 Chronicles 2:34, 35.

JARIB [JAIR-uhb: "he contends"]

1. B.C. date unknown. A son or descendant of Simeon. 1 Chronicles 4:24. Called Jachin in Genesis 46:10.

2. 450 B.C. Sent by Ezra to Casiphia to enlist Levites to serve at the temple. Ezra 8:16.

3. 450 B.C. A descendant of Jeshua the high priest who took a pagan wife after the Exile. Ezra 10:18.

JAROAH [juh-ROH-uh]. B.C. date unknown. Listed in the genealogy of Gad. 1 Chronicles 5:14.

JASHER [JAY-shahr: "upright"]. B.C. date unknown. Author of the Book of Jashar, quoted two times in the Old Testament. Joshua 10:13; 2 Samuel 1:18. Jashar may be a poetic name for Israel itself.

JASHEN [JAY-shuhn]. 1025 B.C. Father of two of David's mighty men. 2 Samuel 23:32. Called "Hashem the Gizonite" in 1 Chronicles 11:34.

JASHOBEAM [juh-SHOH-bee-uhm]

1. 1000 B.C. Chief of the three who led David's thirty mighty men. 1 Chronicles 11:11. Called Josheb-Basshebeth the Tachmonite in 2 Samuel 23:8.

2. 1000 B.C. A Korahite of the tribe of Benjamin who joined David at Ziklag. 1 Chronicles 12:6.

3. 975 B.C. A Judahite who led the first division of David's army. 1 Chronicles 27:2.

JASHUB [JAY-shuhb: "may he return"]

1. 1875 B.C. A grandson of Jacob. Genesis 46:13; Numbers 26:24; 1 Chronicles 7:1.

2. 450 B.C. One who took a pagan wife after the Exile. Ezra 10:29.

JASON [JAY-suhn: "healing"]

1. A.D. 50. A Thessalonian Christian attacked by townsmen for letting Paul and Silas stay in his house. Acts 17:5–9.

2. A.D. 55. A relative of Paul who sent greetings to the church in Rome. Romans 16:21. Possibly the same as Jason 1.

JATHNIEL [JATH-nee-el]. 975 B.C. A son of a chief gatekeeper in David's day. 1 Chronicles 26:2.

JAVAN [JAY-vuhn]. B.C. date unknown. A son of Japheth, son of Noah, listed in the table of nations. Genesis 10:2, 4. The name corresponds etymologically to Ionia and is associated with the Greeks and Macedonians.

JAZIZ [JAY-ziz]. 1000 B.C. The man who oversaw the flocks of King David. 1 Chronicles 27:31.

JEATHERAI [jee-ATH-uh-ri]. B.C. date unknown. Listed in the genealogy of Levi. 1 Chronicles 6:21.

JEBERECHIAH [juh-BAIR-uh-KI-uh: "Yahweh blesses"]. 725 B.C. Father of Zechariah, a witness to one of Isaiah's prophecies. Isaiah 8:2.

JECONIAH [JEK-uh-NI-uh]. 597 B.C. Alternate name of Jehoiachin, king of Judah. Matthew 1:11, 12.

JEDAIAH [jeh-DAY-yuh: "Yahweh has favored"]

1. 1000 B.C. Head of the second division of priests in David's day. 1 Chronicles 24:7.

2. B.C. date unknown. Ancestor of a family of priests that returned to Judah with Zerubbabel. Ezra 2:36; Nehemiah 7:39.

3. B.C. date unknown. Ancestor of Ziza, a Simeonite chief in Hezekiah's time. 1 Chronicles 4:37.

4. and 5. 525 B.C. Two priests who returned to Judah with Zerubbabel. Nehemiah 12:6, 7, 19, 21.

6. 525 B.C. He transported gold and silver to Jerusalem from Babylon. Zechariah 6:10, 14. Possibly the same as either 4 or 5.

7. 450 B.C. A man who helped repair the wall of Jerusalem. Nehemiah 3:10.

8. 450 B.C. A priest who settled in Jerusalem after the Exile. 1 Chronicles 9:10; Nehemiah 11:10.

JEDIAEL [jeh-DI-uhl: "God knows"]

1. B.C. date unknown. Descendant of Benjamin listed in 1 Chronicles 7:6, 10, 11.

2. 1000 B.C. One of David's military elite, the "thirty." 1 Chronicles 11:45.

3. 1000 B.C. A man who joined David at Ziklag. 1 Chronicles 12:20. Possibly the same as Jediael 2.

4. 975 B.C. A temple gatekeeper. 1 Chronicles 26:2.

JEDIDIAH [JED-uh-DI-uh: "beloved of Yahweh"]. 950 B.C. The name God gave to Solomon at his birth through Nathan the prophet. 2 Samuel 12:25.

JEDUTHUN [jeh-DOO-thuhn]

1. 1000 B.C. A chief minister of music in David's day. 1 Chronicles 9:16; 25:1–6; Nehemiah 11:17. Called Ethan in 1 Chronicles 6:44; 15:17.

2. 1025 B.C. Father of Obed-Edom, a chief gatekeeper in David's day. 1 Chronicles 16:38.

JEHALLELEL [jeh-HAL-uh-lel: "may God shine forth"]

1. B.C. date unknown. Listed in the genealogy of Judah. 1 Chronicles 4:16.

2. 725 B.C. Father of a Levite who helped purify the temple in Hezekiah's time. 2 Chronicles 29:12.

JEHATH [JEE-hath: "God will snatch up"]. B.C. date unknown. Listed in the genealogy of Levi. 1 Chronicles 6:20. Called Jahath in 1 Chronicles 6:43.

JEHDEIAH [jeh-DEE-yuh: "may Yahweh rejoice"]

1. 975 B.C. A Levite who served during the time of David. 1 Chronicles 24:20.

2. 975 B.C. An official in charge of King David's donkeys. 1 Chronicles 27:30.

JEHEZEKEL [jeh-HEZ-uh-kel: "God strengthens"]. 975 B.C. Head of the twelfth division of priests in David's day. 1 Chronicles 24:16.

JEHIAH [jeh-HI-uh: "Yahweh lives"]. 1000 B.C. A gatekeeper when David brought the ark of the covenant to Jerusalem. 1 Chronicles 15:24.

JEHIEL [jeh-HI-uhl: "God lives"]

1. 1000 B.C. A Levite assigned to play the lyre before the ark of the covenant when it was brought to Jerusalem. 1 Chronicles 15:18, 20; 16:5.

2. 1000 B.C. A Levite descended from Gershon who handled funds gathered for building of the Jerusalem temple. 1 Chronicles 23:8; 29:8. Called Jehieli in 1 Chronicles 26:21.

3. 975 B.C. Caretaker of King David's sons. 1 Chronicles 27:32.

4. 850 B.C. A younger brother of Jehoram who was executed when Jehoram became king of Judah. 2 Chronicles 21:2.

5. 725 B.C. A descendant of Heman the seer who served in the temple during

the reign of Hezekiah. 2 Chronicles 29:14: 31:13.

6. 625 B.C. Chief administrator of the temple during the reign of Josiah. 1 Chronicles 35:8.

7. 475 B.C. Father of Obadiah, who returned to Judah with Ezra. Ezra 8:9.

8. 475 B.C. Father of Shecaniah, who supported Ezra's reform. Ezra 10:2–4.

9. 450 B.C. A priest who took a pagan wife after the Exile. Ezra 10:21.

10. 460 B.C. A descendant of Elam who also married a pagan after the Exile. Ezra 10:26. Probably the same as 8.

JEHIELI [jeh-HI-uh-li]. 975 B.C. A Levite in charge of the temple treasury in David's day. 1 Chronicles 26:21. Same as Jehiel 2.

JEHIZKIAH [JEE-hiz-KI-uh: "Yahweh strengthens"]. 750 B.C. An Ephraimite who opposed the enslavement of prisoners taken in Israel's war with Judah. 2 Chronicles 28:12.

JEHOADDAH [juh-HOH-uh-duh]. B.C. date unknown. A descendant of Jonathan, son of Saul. 1 Chronicles 8:36.

JEHOAHAZ [juh-HOH-uh-haz: "Yahweh has grasped"]

1. 814–798 B.C. Son and successor of Jehu, king of Israel. 2 Kings 13:1–9.

2. 608 B.C. Son and successor of Josiah, king of Judah. 2 Kings 23:30–34; 2 Chronicles 36:1–4. Called Shallum in 1 Chronicles 3:15 and Jeremiah 22:11.

JEHOASH [juh-HOH-ash: "Yahweh has given"]. 798–782 B.C. Son and successor of Jehoahaz, eleventh king of Israel. 2 Kings 13:9–25. Called Joash in 2 Chronicles 25:17–25; Hosea 1:1; Amos 1:1.

JEHOHANAN [jeh-hoh-HAY-nuhn: "Yahweh is gracious"]

1. 975 B.C. A son of Meshelemiah, listed among the temple gatekeepers. 1 Chronicles 26:3.

2. 875 B.C. A military commander under Jehoshaphat king of Judah. 2 Chronicles 17:15.

3. 875 B.C. Father of Ishmael, a military officer who helped Jehoiada overthrow Athaliah to make Joash king of Judah. 2 Chronicles 23:1. Probably the same as 2.

4. 775 B.C. Father of Azariah, a leader who opposed enslavement of captives from Judah. 2 Chronicles 28:12.

5. 500 B.C. Head of the priestly family of Amariah. Nehemiah 12:13.

6. 450 B.C. High priest in Ezra's time. Ezra 10:6. Same as Johanan in Nehemiah 12:22, 23 and Jonathan in Nehemiah 12:11.

7. 450 B.C. A man who took a pagan wife after the Exile. Ezra 10:28.

8. 450 B.C. Son of Tobiah, an enemy of Nehemiah. Nehemiah 6:18.

9. 450 B.C. A priest who shared in the dedication of Jerusalem's wall. Nehemiah 12:42.

JEHOIACHIN [jeh-HOY-ah-kin: "Yahweh will establish"]. 597 B.C. The nineteenth king of Judah, who reigned for only three months. 2 Kings 24:8–17: 2 Chronicles 36:8–10; Jeremiah 22:24–30; 52:31–34.

JEHOIADA [jeh-HOY-ah-duh: "Yahweh knows"]

1. 1000 B.C. Father of Benaiah, the officer in charge of David's bodyguard and commander of Solomon's army. 2 Samuel 8:18; 23:20–23; 1 Chronicles 11:22–24.

2. 1000 B.C. A descendant of Aaron who joined David at Hebron. 1 Chronicles 12:27.

3. 975 B.C. Son of Benaiah and an adviser of David. 1 Chronicles 27:34.

4. 850 B.C. The priest who saved Joash and organized the overthrow of Queen Athaliah. 2 Kings 11; 12; 2 Chronicles 23; 24.

5. 600 B.C. A priest at the Jerusalem temple who was replaced by Zephaniah. Jeremiah 29:26.

6. 450 B.C. A man who helped repair the wall of Jerusalem. Nehemiah 3:6.

JEHOIAKIM [jeh-HOY-ah-kim: "Yahweh raises up"]. 609–598 B.C. The eighteenth king of Judah, whose name was changed from Eliakim by Pharaoh Necho. 2 Kings 23:34—24:6; 2 Chronicles 36:4–8; Jeremiah 22:18; 26:21–23; 36.

JEHOIARIB [jeh-HOY-ah-rib: "Yahweh contends"]

1. 975 B.C. Head of the first division of priests in David's time. 1 Chronicles 24:7.

2. 450 B.C. A priest who settled in Jerusalem after the Exile.

JEHONADAB [juh-HAHN-uh-dab: "Yahweh is noble" or "Yahweh is liberal"]. 850 B.C. A Recabite who joined the king of Israel in destroying the family of Ahab. 2 Kings 10:15–23. Possibly the same as Jonadab son of Recab in Jeremiah 35:6–19.

JEHONATHAN [juh-HAHN-ah-thuhn: "Yahweh has given"]

1. 875 B.C. A Levite Jehoshaphat sent to teach the Law throughout Judah. 2 Chronicles 17:8.

2. 500 B.C. Head of a priestly family in the days of Joiakim the high priest. Nehemiah 12:18.

JEHORAM [juh-HOHR-uhm: "Yahweh is exalted"]

1. 853–841 B.C. Son and successor of Jehoshaphat of Judah, who married Athaliah, a daughter of Ahab. 2 Kings 8:16–24; 2 Chronicles 21.

2. 850 B.C. A priest sent by King Jehoshaphat to teach God's Law throughout Judah. 2 Chronicles 17:8.

JEHOSHAPHAT [juh-HAHSH-uh-fat: "Yahweh has judged"]

1. 975 B.C. Son of Ahilud, official recorder of David and Solomon. 2 Samuel 8:16; 20:24; 1 Kings 4:3.

2. 950 B.C. One of Solomon's twelve district governors. 1 Kings 4:17.

3. Reigned 872–848 B.C. Son and successor of Asa, third king of Judah. 1 Kings 22; 2 Chronicles 17:1—21:3.

4. 875 B.C. Father of Jehu, the tenth king of Israel. 2 Kings 9:2, 14.

JEHOZABAD [juh-HOH-zuh-bad: "Yahweh gives"]

1. 975 B.C. A temple gatekeeper in David's day. 1 Chronicles 26:4.

2. 875 B.C. A military commander who served under Jehoshaphat. 2 Chronicles 17:18.

3. 800 B.C. An official who murdered King Joash. 2 Kings 12:21; 2 Chronicles 24:26.

JEHOZADAK [juh-HOH-zuh-dak: "Yahweh is righteous"]. 575 B.C. Father of Jeshua (Joshua), high priest when the Jews returned to Judah with Zerubbabel. 1 Chronicles 6:14, 15; Haggai 1:1; Zechariah 6:11. Called Jozadak in Ezra and Nehemiah.

JEHU [JEE-hoo: "he Is Yahweh"]

1. B.C. date unknown. Listed in the genealogy of Judah. 1 Chronicles 2:38.

2. 1000 B.C. A Benjamite who defected from Saul's army to David. 1 Chronicles. 12:3.

3. 900 B.C. A man who prophesied against Baasha, king of Israel. He later opposed Jehoshaphat's alliance with Ahab. 1 Kings 16:1–7, 12; 2 Chronicles 19:2, 3.

4. 841–814 B.C. A military commander anointed king of Israel by both Elijah and Elisha, who ended Baal worship in Israel. 1 Kings 19:16, 17; 2 Kings 9, 10; 2 Chronicles 22.

5. 725 B.C. Head of a Simeonite family during Hezekiah's reign. 1 Chronicles 4:35.

JEHUCAL [juh-HOO-kuhl: "Yahweh is powerful"]. 600 B.C. An official of Zedekiah who threw Jeremiah into a cistern to die. Jeremiah 37:3.

JEHUDI [juh-HOO-di]. 600 B.C. The official sent by King Jehoiakim to get the scroll containing Jeremiah's prophecies. Jeremiah 36:14, 21–23.

JEIEL [jeh-I-uhl]

1. B.C. date unknown. Head of a clan of Reubenites listed in 1 Chronicles 5:7.

2. 1125 B.C. Great-grandfather of King Saul. 1 Chronicles 8:29; 9:35.

3. 1000 B.C. He and his brother Shama were members of David's top thirty military men. 1 Chronicles 11:44.

4. 1000 B.C. A Levite who was a gatekeeper and musician when the ark of the covenant was brought to Jerusalem. 1 Chronicles 15:18, 21; 16:5.

5. 1000 B.C. Another Levite who played music before the ark of the covenant. 1 Chronicles 16:5.

6. B.C. date unknown. A descendant of Asaph who prophesied before King Jehoshaphat. 2 Chronicles 20:14.

7. 775 B.C. Secretary of King Uzziah of Judah. 2 Chronicles 26:11.

8. 725 B.C. A Levite who helped purify the temple in Hezekiah's time. 2 Chronicles 29:13.

9. 650 B.C. A chief Levite in Josiah's day. 2 Chronicles 35:9.

10. 450 B.C. A man who took a pagan wife after the Exile. Ezra 10:43.

JEKAMEAM [JEK-uh-MEE-uhm]. 975 B.C. A Levite listed in 1 Chronicles 23:19; 1 Chronicles 24:23.

JEKAMIAH [JEK-uh-MI-uh: "may Yahweh establish"]

1. B.C. date unknown. Listed in the genealogy of Judah. 1 Chronicles 2:41.

2. 550 B.C. A son of Jehoiachin listed in the genealogy of the royal line. 1 Chronicles 3:18.

JEKUTHIEL [juh-KOO-thee-uhl]. B.C. date unknown. Listed in the genealogy of Judah. 1 Chronicles 4:18.

JEMUEL [JEM-yoo-uhl]. 1900 B.C. First son of Simeon, listed in Genesis 46:10. Called Nemuel in Numbers 28:12; 1 Chronicles 4:24.

JEPHTHAH [JEF-thuh: "he opens"]. 1085–1079 B.C. The judge who delivered Israel from the Ammonites and ruled for six years. Judges 11:1—12:7; Hebrews 11:32.

JEPHUNNEH [juh-FUN-uh]

1. 1475 B.C. Father of Caleb the spy. Numbers 13:6; 1 Chronicles 4:15.

2. B.C. date unknown. Listed in the genealogy of Asher. 1 Chronicles 7:38.

JERAH [JEER-uh: "moon"]. B.C. date unknown. A descendant of Shem, listed in the table of nations. Genesis 10:26.

JERAHMEEL [juh-RAH-mee-uhl: "may God have mercy"]

1. B.C. date unknown. One of the three through whom the genealogy of Judah is traced. 1 Chronicles 2:9, 25–27.

2. 975 B.C. A Levite in David's time. 1 Chronicles 24:29.

3. 600 B.C. He was commanded by King Jehoiakim to arrest Baruch and Jeremiah. Jeremiah 36:26.

JERED [JEER-ed]. B.C. date unknown. Father of a Gedor listed only in the genealogy of Judah. 1 Chronicles 4:18.

JEREMAI [JAIR-uh-mi]. 450 B.C. A descendant of Hashum who took a pagan wife after the Exile. Ezra 10:33.

JEREMIAH [JAIR-uh-MI-uh: "Yahweh lifts up"]

1. 1000 B.C. A warrior who joined David's army at Ziklag. 1 Chronicles 12:4.

2. and 3. 1000 B.C. Two Gadite warriors who also joined David at Ziklag. 1 Chronicles 12:10, 13.

4. 875 B.C. Father of Hamutal, the mother of Jehoahaz, eleventh king of Israel. 2 Kings 23:31; 24:18.

5. 750 B.C. Head of an Israelite family taken into exile by Assyria. 1 Chronicles 5:24.

6. 625 B.C. The great prophet who lived the last years of Judah and predicted both Jerusalem's fall and the return of the Jews to Judah some seventy years later. Author of books of Jeremiah and Lamentations. 2 Chronicles 35:25; 36:21, 22; Ezra 1:1; Jeremiah 1—52; Matthew 2:17; 16:14; 27:9.

7. 600 B.C. A Recabite, father of Jaazaniah. Jeremiah 35:3.

8. 525 B.C. A priest who returned to Judah after the Exile. Nehemiah 12:1, 12.

9. 450 B.C. A priest who signed the renewal covenant with God. Nehemiah 10:2. Possibly the same as Jeremiah 8.

10. 450 B.C. A leader who took part in the dedication of the wall of Jerusalem. Nehemiah 12:34.

JEREMOTH [JAIR-uh-mahht: "swollen"]

1. B.C. date unknown. A descendant of Becher, son of Benjamin. Listed in 1 Chronicles 7:8.

2. B.C. date unknown. Listed in the genealogy of Benjamin. 1 Chronicles 8:14.

3. 975 B.C. A Levite of the time of David. 1 Chronicles 23:23.

4. 5, and 6. 450 B.C. Three who took pagan wives after the Exile. Ezra 10:26, 27, 29.

JERIAH [juh-RI-uh: "Yahweh sees"(?)]. 975 B.C. A Levite of Hebron in David's day. 1 Chronicles 23:19; 24:23.

JERIBAI [JAIR-uh-bi]. 1000 B.C. One of two sons of Elnaam listed among David's military elite. 1 Chronicles 11:46.

JERIEL [JEER-ee-uhl: "God sees"(?)]. B.C. date unknown. Listed in the genealogy of Issachar. 1 Chronicles 7:2.

JERIMOTH [JAIR-uh-mahht: "swollen"]

1. 1850 B.C. A grandson of Benjamin. Listed in listed in 1 Chronicles 7:7.

2. 1000 B.C. A Benjamite who joined David's army at Ziklag. 1 Chronicles 12:5.

3. 975 B.C. A Levite of the time of David. 1 Chronicles 23:23; 24:30.

4. 975 B.C. A minister of music appointed by David. 1 Chronicles 25:4, 22.

5. 975 B.C. Officer over the tribe of Naphtali in David's time. 1 Chronicles 27:19.

6. 950 B.C. A son of David and father of Mahalath, wife of King Rehoboam. 2 Chronicles 11:18.

7. 725 B.C. A Levite who worked in the temple treasury in Hezekiah's time. 2 Chronicles 31:13.

JEROBOAM [JAIR-uh-BOH-uhm: "may the people increase"]

1. 930–909 B.C. Jeroboam I; the first king of Israel following the division of the kingdom. 1 Kings 11:26—14:20; 2 Chronicles 10, 13.

2. 793—753 B.C. Jeroboam II, the thirteenth king of Israel. 2 Kings 14:16–29: Amos 7:9–11.

JEROHAM [juh-ROH-ham]

1. 1125 B.C. The father of Elkanah, the husband of Hannah and father of Samuel. Samuel 1:1; 1 Chronicles 6:27, 34.

2. B.C. date unknown. Listed in the genealogy of Benjamin. 1 Chronicles 8:27.

3. B.C. date unknown. Ancestor of a Benjamite who settled in Jerusalem after the Exile. 1 Chronicles 9:8.

4. 475 B.C. Father of Adaiah, a priest who settled in Jerusalem after the Exile. 1 Chronicles 9:12; Nehemiah 11:12.

5. 1000 B.C. Father of two Benjamite warriors who joined David at Ziklag. 1 Chronicles 12:7.

6. 975 B.C. Father of Azarel, officer over the tribe of Dan in David's time. 1 Chronicles 27:22.

7. 850 B.C. Father of Azariah, an army officer who helped overthrow Athaliah. 2 Chronicles 23:1.

JERUBBAAL [JAIR-uhb-BAY-uhl: "let Baal contend"]. 1169–1129 B.C. Name given to Gideon the judge after his destruction of an altar of Baal. Judges 6—8.

JERUBBESHETH [JUR-uhb-BEH-sheh: "let shame contend"]. 1169–1129 B.C. Alternate form of Jerubbaal, substituting the word "shame" for "Baal" to avoid speaking the name of the false deity. 2 Samuel 11:21. See Gideon.

JESHAIAH [jeh-SHAY-yuh: "Yahweh has saved"]

1. B.C. date unknown. A descendant of Moses who served in the treasury in David's time. 1 Chronicles 26:25.

2. 975 B.C. A minister of music in David's time. 1 Chronicles 25:3, 15.

3. B.C. date unknown. Ancestor of a Benjamite who settled in Jerusalem after the Exile. Nehemiah 11:7.

4. 450 B.C. A descendant of Elam who returned to Judah with Ezra. Ezra 8:7.

5. 450 B.C. A Levite who returned to Judah with Ezra. Ezra 8:19.

6. B.C. date unknown. A descendant of Zerubbabel listed in the genealogy of the royal line. 1 Chronicles 3:21.

JESHARELAH [JES-uh-REE-luh]. 975 B.C. A son of Asaph and minister of music appointed by David. 1 Chronicles 25:14.

JESHEBEAB [juh-SHEB-ee-ah]. 975 B.C. Head of the fourteenth division of priests in David's day. 1 Chronicles 24:13.

JESHER [JEH-shuhr: "uprightness"(?)]. B.C. date unknown. Listed in the genealogy of Judah in 1 Chronicles 1:18.

JESHISHAI [jeh-SHISH-i: "aged"(?)]. B.C. date unknown. Listed in the genealogy of Gad. 1 Chronicles 5:14.

JESHOHAIAH [JESH-uh-HAY-yuh: "Yahweh humbles"]. 725 B.C. A

Simeonite leader during the reign of Hezekiah. 1 Chronicles 4:36.

JESHUA [JESH-oo-uh: "Yahweh is salvation"]

1. 975 B.C. Head of the 9th division of priests in David's time. 1 Chronicles 24:11; Ezra 2:36; Nehemiah 7:39.

2. 725 B.C. A priest who helped distribute the priests' portion in Hezekiah's time. 2 Chronicles 31:15.

3. B.C. date unknown. An ancestor of some who returned to Judah with Zerubbabel. Ezra 2:6; Nehemiah 7:11.

4. 525 B.C. The high priest who returned to Judah with Zerubbabel. Ezra 2:2; 3:2–8; 5:2; 10:18; Nehemiah 7:7. Called Joshua in Haggai and Zechariah.

5. 525 B.C. A Levite who returned to Judah with Zerubbabel and taught God's Law. Ezra 2:40; 3:9; Nehemiah 7:43; 9:4, 5; 12:8, 24.

6. 475 B.C. Father of Jozabad, a Levite in Ezra's time. Ezra 8:33.

7. 475 B.C. Ruler at Mizpah in Nehemiah's time. Nehemiah 3:19.

8. 450 B.C. A Levite who signed the covenant of renewal, possibly with the name of his family's founder. Nehemiah 10:9.

JESHURUN [JESH-uh-ruhn: "upright"]. Name ascribed to Israel by Moses in personifying national history and relationship with God. Deuteronomy 32:15; 33:5, 26; Isaiah 44:2.

JESIMIEL [jeh-SIM-ee-uhl: "may God establish"]. 725 B.C. Head of a Simeonite family during the reign of Hezekiah. 1 Chronicles 4:36.

JESSE [JES-ee]. 1050 B.C. Father of King David and an ancestor of Jesus Christ.

Ruth 4:17, 22; 1 Samuel 16:1–13; 17:12–19.

JESUS [JEE-zuhs: Gk. form of Joshua, "Yahweh is salvation"]

1. 4 B.C.-A.D. 30. The Son of God incarnate. His name, Jesus, comes from a Hebrew word meaning "savior" or "Yahweh saves."

2. A.D. 60. A Christian who with Paul sent greetings to the church at Colosse. Colossians 4:11. Also called Justus.

JETHER [JEE-thuhr: "abundance"]

1. B.C. date unknown. Listed in the genealogy of Judah. 1 Chronicles 2:32.

2. B.C. date unknown. Listed in the genealogy of Judah. 1 Chronicles 4:17.

3. B.C. date unknown. Listed in the genealogy of Asher. 1 Chronicles 7:38.

4. 1150 B.C. Oldest son of Gideon the judge. Judges 8:20.

5. 1000 B.C. Husband of Abigail, David's sister, and father of Amasa, the commander of Absalom's army who was killed by Joab. 2 Samuel 17:25; 1 Kings 2:5, 32; 1 Chronicles 2:17.

JETHETH [JEE-theth]. B.C. date unknown. An Edomite chief descended from Esau. Genesis 36:40.

JETHRO [JETH-roh: "excellence"]. 1500 B.C. Priest of Midian and father of Zipporah, Moses' wife. Exodus 3:1; 4:18; 18:1–27. Called Reuel in Exodus 2:18; Numbers 10:29.

JETUR [JEE-tuhr]. 2025 B.C. A son of Ishmael. Genesis 25:15. Ancestor of an Ishmaelite tribe (1 Chron. 1:31).

JEUEL [JOO-uhl]

1. 450 B.C. A Judahite who settled in Jerusalem after the Exile. 1 Chronicles 9:6.

2. 450 B.C. A man who returned to Judah with Ezra. Ezra 8:13.

JEUSH [JEE-uhsh]

1. 1925 B.C. A son of Esau. Genesis 36:5, 14, 18.

2. B.C. date unknown. Listed in the genealogy of Benjamin. 1 Chronicles 7:10.

3. 975 B.C. Head of a Levite family. 1 Chronicles 23:10, 11.

4. 900 B.C. A son of Rehoboam, the successor of Solomon. 2 Chronicles 11:19.

5. B.C. date unknown. A descendant of Jonathan, son of Saul. 1 Chronicles 8:39.

JEUZ [JEE-uhz]. B.C. date unknown. Listed in the genealogy of Benjamin. 1 Chronicles 8:10.

JEZANIAH [JEZ-uh-NI-uh: "Yahweh hears"]. 600 B.C. Army officer who disregarded the guidance of Jeremiah the prophet after the death of Gedaliah. Jeremiah 42:1. Called Jaazaniah in 2 Kings 25:23; Jeremiah 40:6.

JEZER [JEE-zuhr]. 1875 B.C. A son of Naphtali. Genesis 46:24; Numbers 26:49.

JEZIEL [JEE-zee-uhl: "God unites"(?)]. 1000 B.C. The son of a man who joined David's army at Ziklag. 1 Chronicles 12:3.

JEZRAHIAH [JEZ-ruh-HI-uh]. 450 B.C. Leader of the choir at the dedication of the walls of Jerusalem. Nehemiah 12:42.

JEZREEL [JEZ-ree-uhl: "God sows"]

1. B.C. date unknown. Listed in the genealogy of Judah. 1 Chronicles 4:3.

2. 700 B.C. Symbolic name given to the son of Hosea as a sign of the coming judgment of Jehu. Hosea 1:4.

Joab's murder of the northern general, Abner, was in part revenge for the death of a brother in battle. But Joab's primary motive was probably to preserve his position as commander of David's army.

JIBSAM [IB-sam: "fragrant"]. B.C. date unknown. Listed in the genealogy of Issachar. 1 Chronicles 7:2.

JIDLAPH [JID-laf]. 2075 B.C. A son of Nahor the brother of Abraham. Genesis 22:22.

JOAB [JOH-ab: "Yahweh is father"]

1. 1000 B.C. The relentless commander of David's army. 2 Samuel 2:13–32.

2. B.C. date unknown. Listed in the genealogy of Judah. 1 Chronicles 4:14.

3. B.C. date unknown. Ancestor of some who returned to Judah with Zerubbabel and Ezra. Ezra 2:6; Nehemiah 7:11.

JOAH [JOH-uh: "Yahweh is brother"]

1. B.C. date unknown. Listed in the genealogy of Levi. 1 Chronicles 6:21.

2. 975 B.C. Head of a family of temple gatekeepers in David's time. 1 Chronicles 26:4.

3. 725 B.C. A Levite who helped purify the temple during the reign of Hezekiah. 2 Chronicles 29:12.

4. 700 B.C. An official of Hezekiah in besieged Jerusalem who spoke with the Assyrian envoy. 2 Kings 18:18–37: Isaiah 36:3–22.

5. 625 B.C. An official whom Josiah sent to help repair the temple. 2 Chronicles 34:8.

JOAHAZ [JOH-uh-haz: "Yahweh has grasped"]. 625 B.C. Father of Josiah's recorder. 2 Chronicles 34:8.

JOANAS [joh-AN-us]. B.C. date unknown. Listed in the genealogy of Christ in Luke 3:27.

JOASH [JOH-ash: Yahweh has given"]

1. 1850 B.C. A grandson of Benjamin. 1 Chronicles 7:8.

2. B.C. date unknown. Listed in the genealogy of Judah. 1 Chronicles 4:22.

3. 1100 B.C. Father of Gideon, the judge. Judges 6:11.

4. 1000 B.C. Another who joined David's army at Ziklag. 1 Chronicles 12:3.

5. 975 B.C. An official in charge of David's olive oil. 1 Chronicles 27:28.

6. 850 B.C. A son of Ahab who held Micaiah the prophet prisoner. 1 Kings 22:26; 2 Chronicles 18:25.

7. 835–796 B.C. The eighth king of Judah, crowned as a child. 2 Chronicles 24.

JOB [JOHB: meaning uncertain]. B.C. date unknown. The righteous man whose sufferings are explored in the Book of Job. Job 1—42; Ezekiel 14:14, 20; James 5:11.

JOBAB [JOH-bab]

1. B.C. date unknown. Sons of Joktan listed in the table of nations. Genesis 10:29; 1 Chronicles 1:23.

2. A pre-Israelite king of Edom. Genesis 36:33, 34; 1 Chronicles 1:44, 45.

3. 1400 B.C. King who joined other Canaanite kings to battle Joshua. Joshua 11:1.

4 and 5. B.C. dates unknown. Two listed in the genealogy of Benjamin. 1 Chronicles 8:9, 18.

JODA [JOH-duh]. B.C. date unknown. A descendant of Zerubbabel and ancestor of Christ. Luke 3:26.

JOED [JOH-ed: "Yahweh is witness"]. B.C. date unknown. Ancestor of a Benjamite who settled in Jerusalem after the Exile. Nehemiah 11:7.

JOEL [JOH-uhl: "Yahweh is God"]

1. B.C. date unknown. Listed in the genealogy of Issachar. 1 Chronicles 7:3.

2. B.C. date unknown. Listed in the genealogy of Reuben. 1 Chronicles 5:4, 8.

3. B.C. date unknown. A Gadite chief. 1 Chronicles 5:12.

4. B.C. date unknown. Ancestor of Samuel. 1 Chronicles 6:36.

5. 1050 B.C. First son of Samuel. 1 Samuel 8:2: 1 Chronicles 6:28, 33.

6. 1000 B.C. A Benjamite who joined David at Ziklag. 1 Chronicles 4:35.

7. 1000 B.C. A military commander, one of David's elite corps of thirty. 1 Chronicles 11:38.

8. 1000 B.C. A Levite in David's time. 1 Chronicles 15:7, 11,

9. 975 B.C. A man appointed a temple treasurer by David. 1 Chronicles 23:8: 26:22.

10. 975 B.C. Officer over the tribe of Manasseh in David's day. 1 Chronicles 27:20.

11. B.C. date unknown. A prophet whose words are recorded in the Book of Joel. Joel 1:1; Acts 2:16.

12. 725 B.C. A Levite who helped purify the temple in Hezekiah's time. 2 Chronicles 29:12.

13. 450 B.C. A man who married a pagan wife after the Exile. Ezra 10:43.

14. 450 B.C. A Benjamite chief who settled in Jerusalem after the Exile. Nehemiah 11:9.

JOELAH [joh-EE-luh]. 1000 B.C. A Benjamite who joined David's army at Ziklag. 1 Chronicles 12:7.

JOEZER [joh-EE-zuhr: "Yahweh is help"]. 1000 B.C. A warrior who joined David at Ziklag. 1 Chronicles 12:6.

JOGLI [JAHG-li]. 1425 B.C. The representative from the tribe of Dan appointed to help divide the land of Canaan. Numbers 34:22.

JOHA [JOH-uh]

1. B.C. date unknown. Listed in the genealogy of Benjamin. 1 Chronicles 8:16.

2. 1000 B.C. One of David's top thirty military men. 1 Chronicles 11:45.

JOHANAN [joh-HAY-nuhn: "Yahweh is gracious"]

1. 1000 B.C. A relative of Saul who defected to David's army at Ziklag. 1 Chronicles 12:4.

2. 1000 B.C. A Gadite who also joined David at Ziklag. 1 Chronicles 12:12.

3. 950 B.C. Great-grandson of Zadok, priest to David and Solomon. 1 Chronicles 6:9, 10.

4. 825 B.C. First son of Josiah, who did not succeed his father on Judah's throne. 1 Chronicles 3:15.

5. 575 B.C. An army officer who warned Gedaliah of a plot to assassinate him. See 2 Kings 25:23; Jeremiah 40:8, 13–16; 41:11—43:7.

6. 450 B.C. A man who returned to Judah with Ezra. Ezra 8:12.

7. 400 B.C. A high priest during the reign of Darius the Persian. Nehemiah 12:22, 23. Called Jonathan in Nehemiah 12:11.

8. B.C. date unknown. A descendant of Zerubbabel listed in the genealogy of the royal line. 1 Chronicles 3:24.

JOHN [JAHN: shortened form of Jehohanan, "God is gracious"]

1. A.D. 1. Father of Peter the apostle. John 1:40; 21:15–17. Also called Jonah.

2. A.D. 25. John the Baptist, the forerunner of Jesus. Matthew 3:1-14; 14:1–12; Luke 1:13–17, 57–63; John 1:6–40.

3. A.D. 25. Son of Zebedee and brother of James, one of Jesus' inner circle of apostles and author of the Gospel of John, three Epistles of John, and Revelation. Matthew 4:21; 10:2; Acts 1:13; Galatians 2:9.

4. A.D. 30. John Mark, a young disciple of Jesus and author of the Gospel of Mark. Acts 12:12, 25; 15:37–39.

5. A.D. 35. A relative of Annas the priest who was involved in the trial of Peter and John before the Sanhedrin. Acts 4:6.

JOIADA [JOY-uh-duh: "Yahweh knows"]. 425 B.C. In the line of high priests who returned to Judah after the Exile. Nehemiah 12:10, 11, 22; 13:28.

JOIAKIM [JOY-uh-kim; shortened form of Jehoiakim]. 500 B.C. In the line of high priests through the return to Judah after the Exile. Nehemiah 12:10, 12, 26.

JOIARIB [JOY-uh-rib: shortened form of Jehoiarib]

1. B.C. date unknown. Ancestor of a Benjamite who settled in Jerusalem after the Exile. Nehemiah 11:5.

2. 525 B.C. A priest who returned to Judah after the Exile. Nehemiah 12:6, 19.

3. 450 B.C. A priest whose son settled in Jerusalem. Nehemiah 11:10. Possibly same as Joiarib 2.

4. 450 B.C. A man who was sent by Ezra to enlist Levites to serve at the Jerusalem temple. Ezra 8:16.

JOKIM [JOH-kim: "Yahweh raises up"]. B.C. date unknown. A descendant of Judah, listed in 1 Chronicles 4:22.

JOKSHAN [JAHK-shan]. 2000 B.C. A son born to Abraham after Sarah's death. Genesis 25:2, 3.

JOKTAN [JAHK-tan]. B.C. date unknown. A descendant of Shem listed in the table of nations. Genesis 10:25–29.

JONADAB [JOH-nuh-dab: "Yahweh is noble"]

1. 1000 B.C. A nephew of David who suggested David's son Amnon seduce Amnon's half-sister, Tamar. 2 Samuel 13:5.

2. B.C. date unknown. Ancestor of the Recabites whose command to abstain from wine was followed by his descendants. Jeremiah 35:6–19.

JONAH [JOH-nuh: "dove"].

1. 775 B.C. The prophet whose story is recorded in the Book of Jonah. 2 Kings 14:25; Jonah 1—4; Matthew 12:39–41; Luke 11:29–32.

2. A.D. 1. Father of the apostle Peter. Matthew 16:17.

JONAN [JOH-nuhn]. B.C. date unknown. Listed in the genealogy of Jesus. Luke 3:30.

JONATHAN [JAHN-uh-thuhn: "Yahweh has given"]

1. B.C. date unknown. Listed in the genealogy of Judah. 1 Chronicles 2:32, 33.

2. B.C. date unknown. A descendant of Moses [not Aaron]. who became a household priest for Micah and later the tribe of Dan. Judges 17:7—18:6; 18:17–31.

3. 1025 B.C. Uncle of David who served him as a scribe and counselor. 1 Chronicles 27:32.

4. 1025 B.C. The eldest son of Saul and a close friend of David. 1 Samuel 13:16—14:49; 18–20; 23:16–18; 31:2.

5. 1000 B.C. Son of Abiathar, a high priest in David's time. 2 Samuel 15:27, 36; 17:17–20; 1 Kings 1:42–43.

6. 1000 B.C. One of David's top thirty military men. 2 Samuel 23:32; 1 Chronicles 11:34.

7. 975 B.C. Son of David's brother who also killed a giant from Gath. 2 Samuel 21:21; 1 Chronicles 20:7.

8. 975 B.C. Son of Uzziah who was in charge of town storehouses in David's time. 1 Chronicles 27:25.

9. 600 B.C. Secretary of Zedekiah, king of Judah, in whose house Jeremiah was temporarily imprisoned. Jeremiah 37:15, 20.

10. 575 B.C. A military officer when Gedaliah was governor of Judah. Jeremiah 40:8.

11. 500 B.C. Head of a priestly family. Nehemiah 12:14.

12. 475 B.C. Father of Ebed, a man who returned to Judah with Ezra. Ezra 8:6.

13. 450 B.C. Father of a priest who took part in the dedication of the wall of Jerusalem. Nehemiah 12:35.

14. 450 B.C. A man who opposed Ezra's plan to divorce the pagan wives taken after the Exile. Ezra 10:15.

15. 400 B.C. Descendant of Jeshua the high priest. Nehemiah 12:11. Called Johanan in Nehemiah 12:22, 23.

JORAH [JOHR-uh]. B.C. date unknown. Ancestor of a family that returned to Judah after the Exile. Ezra 2:18. Called Hariph in Nehemiah 7:24.

JORAI [JOHR-i]. B.C. date unknown. Listed in the genealogy of Gad. 1 Chronicles 5:13.

JORAM [JOHR-uhm: "Yahweh is exalted"]

1. B.C. date unknown. Ancestor of a Levite who served as treasurer in King David's time. 1 Chronicles 26:25.

2. 1000 B.C. Son of the king of Hamath, who congratulated David after a victory. 2 Samuel 8:10.

3. 852–841 B.C. Son of Ahab, who became king of Israel. 2 Kings 1:17; 3; 9:14–29 .

4. 853–841 B.C. Alternate name of Jehoram, son and successor of Jehoshaphat, who is listed in the genealogy of Christ in Matthew 1:8.

JORIM [JOHR-im: "Yahweh is exalted"]. B.C. date unknown. Listed in the genealogy of Christ. Luke 3:29.

JORKOAM [johr-KOE-uhm]. B.C. date unknown. Listed in the genealogy of Judah. 1 Chronicles 2:44.

JOSECH [JOH-zek]. B.C. date unknown. A descendant of Zerubbabel found only in the genealogy of Christ. Luke 3:26.

It was common for fathers to teach their children their trade. This is why many believe that Jesus worked as a carpenter until He began His public ministry.

JOSEPH [JOH-suhf: "may God add"]

1. 1900 B.C. The son of Jacob and Rachel who was sold into slavery by his brothers. Genesis 30:24, 25; 37; 39—50.

2. 1475 B.C. Father of a man Moses sent to spy out Canaan. Numbers 13:7.

3. 975 B.C. A son of Asaph. 1 Chronicles 25:2, 9.

4. B.C. date unknown. A descendant of David listed in the genealogy of Christ. Luke 3:30.

5. 500 B.C. Head of a family of priests. Nehemiah 12:14.

6. 450 B.C. A Jew who took a pagan wife after the Exile. Ezra 10:42.

7. B.C. date unknown. A descendant of Zerubbabel listed in the genealogy of Christ. Luke 3:24.

8. A.D. 1. The carpenter husband of Mary, the mother of Jesus. Matthew 1:16—2:19; Luke 1:27; 2:4–16.

9. A.D. 25. A brother of Jesus. Matthew 13:55. Called Joses in Mark 6:3.

10. A.D. 30. Joseph of Arimathea, in whose tomb Jesus was buried. Mark 15:43–45; John 19:38–42.

11. A.D. 35. Joseph called Barsabbas. One of two considered to replace Judas Iscariot. Acts 1:23.

12. A.D. 35. The given name of Barnabas. Acts 4:36. See Barnabas.

JOSES [JOH-seez]

1. A.D. 25. A brother of Jesus. Mark 6:3. Called Joseph in Matthew 13:55.

2. A.D. 30. The brother of James the younger. Mark 15:40, 47.

JOSHAH [JAHSH-uh: "Yahweh's gift"]. 725 B.C. A clan leader listed in the genealogy of Simeon. 1 Chronicles 4:34.

JOSHAPHAT [JAHSH-uh-fat: "Yahweh has judged"]

1. 1000 B.C. One of David's thirty mighty men. 1 Chronicles 11:43.

2. 1000 B.C. A priest who blew the trumpet when the ark was brought into Jerusalem. 1 Chronicles 15:24.

JOSHAVIAH [JAHSH-uh-VI-uh]. 1000 B.C. One of two brothers listed among David's military elite. 1 Chronicles 11:46.

JOSHBEKASHAH [JAHSH-buh-KAY-shuh]. 975 B.C. A son of one of David's ministers of music. 1 Chronicles 25:4, 24.

JOSHEB-BASSHEBETH [JOH-shuhb-bah-SHEE-buht]. 1000 B.C. Chief of the three commanders over David's thirty military leaders. 2 Samuel 23:8.

JOSHIBIAH [JAHSH-uh-BI-uh: "Yahweh caused to dwell"]. 750(?) B.C. Father of a Simeonite clan leader. 1 Chronicles 4:35.

JOSHUA [JAHSH-oo-uh: "Yahweh is salvation"]

1. 1450 B.C. The godly man who led Israel after the death of Moses and conquered Canaan. Exodus 17:9–14; Numbers 13:8, 16; Deuteronomy 31:7, 14, 23; Joshua 1—24.

2. 1075 B.C. A man who owned a field in Beth Shemesh. 1 Samuel 6:14–18.

3. 625 B.C. Governor of Jerusalem during the reign of Josiah. 2 Kings 23:8.

4. 525 B.C. The high priest at the time of the return from exile in Babylonia. Haggai 1; Zechariah 3.

5. B.C. date unknown. Listed in the genealogy of Jesus. Luke 3:29.

JOSIAH [joh-SI-uh: "Yahweh supports"]

1. 640–609 B.C. A pious king of Judah who purged idolatry from Judah and renewed the covenant with God. 2 Kings 22:1–23; 30; 1 Chronicles 3:14, 15; 2 Chronicles 34; 35.

2. 525 B.C. Son of Zephaniah, a contemporary of Zechariah the prophet. Zechariah 6:10.

JOSIPHIAH [JAHS-uh-FI-uh: "Yahweh adds"]. 450 B.C. Father of a group that returned to Judah with Ezra. Ezra 8:10.

JOTHAM [JAH-thuhm: "Yahweh is perfect"]

1. B.C. date unknown. Listed in the genealogy of Judah. 1 Chronicles 2:47.

2. 1125 B.C. The youngest of Gideon's seventy sons, who escaped when

Abimelech murdered their brothers. Judges 9:5–21, 57.

3. 750–735 B.C. The son and successor of Uzziah king of Judah. 2 Kings 15:5, 7, 32–38: 2 Chronicles 27:1–9.

JOZABAD [JAHZ-uh-bad: "Yahweh has bestowed"]

1. 1000 B.C. A Benjamite who defected to David at Ziklag. 1 Chronicles 12:4.

2. and 3. 1000 B.C. Two military commanders who joined David with their men. 1 Chronicles 12:20.

4. 800 B.C. An official who assassinated Joash at Beth Millo. 2 Kings 12:21.

5. 725 B.C. A Levite who helped distribute temple offerings in the reign of Hezekiah. 2 Chronicles 31:13.

6. 625 B.C. A chief Levite in the time of Josiah. 2 Chronicles 35:9.

7. 450 B.C. A Levite who helped weigh the sacred temple vessels returned to Judah from Babylon. Ezra 8:33.

8. 450 B.C. A priest who took a pagan wife after the Exile. Ezra 10:22.

9. 450 B.C. A Levite who took a pagan wife after the Exile. Ezra 10:23.

10. 450 B.C. A Levite who instructed the people in God's Law. Nehemiah 8:7.

11. 450 B.C. A chief Levite who settled in Jerusalem after the Exile. Nehemiah 11:16.

JOZADAK [JAHZ-uh-dak: "Yahweh is righteous"]. 575 B.C. Father of the high priest of the first return from exile. Ezra 3:2, 8. Called Jehozadak in Haggai 1:1; Zechariah 6:11.

JUBAL [JOO-bahl]. B.C. date unknown. The original developer of music and musical instruments. Genesis 4:21.

JUDAH [JOO-duh: "praise"]

1. 900 B.C. Fourth of the six sons of Jacob and Leah, and ancestor of the tribe of Judah, to which David and Jesus both belonged. Genesis 29:35; 35:23; 37:26.

2. B.C. date unknown. Listed in the genealogy of Jesus. Luke 3:30.

3. 525 B.C. A Levite who returned to Judah with Zerubbabel. Nehemiah 12:8.

4. 450 B.C. A Levite who took a pagan wife after the Exile. Ezra 10:23.

5. 450 B.C. A Benjamite who settled in Jerusalem after the Exile. Nehemiah 11:9.

6. 450 B.C. A participant in the dedication of the wall of Jerusalem. Nehemiah 12:34.

7. 450 B.C. A priest who played music to celebrate the dedication of the rebuilt wall of Jerusalem. Nehemiah 12:36.

JUDAS [JOO-duhs: "praise"]. A form of Judah.

1. 5 B.C. Judas the Galilean, who fomented a rebellion against Rome. Acts 5:37.

2. B.C. 25. A brother of Jesus, notable as the author of Jude. Matthew 13:55; Mark 6:3.

3. A.D. 25. Son of James, one of the twelve apostles. Luke 6:16; Acts 1:13. Possibly the same as Thaddeus.

4. A.D. 30. Judas Iscariot, the apostle who betrayed Christ for thirty silver coins. Matthew 26:14–25, 47–50: 27:3–10; Acts 1:16–25.

5. A.D. 35. Saul of Tarsus (Paul) stayed at his home after being temporarily blinded on the road to Damascus. Acts 9:11.

6. A.D. 50. Judas called Barsabbas, a prophet in the church in Jerusalem sent with Silas to Antioch. Acts 15:22–32.

JUDE [JOOD: a form of Judah]. A.D. 65. Younger brother of Jesus and author of the Book of Jude. Called Judas in Matthew 13:55 and Mark 6:3.

JULIUS [JOOL-yuhs]. A.D. 60. A centurion who brought Paul to Rome to stand trial. Acts 27:1, 3.

JUNIA [JOO-nee-uh]. A.D. 55. A Christian who was imprisoned with Paul. Romans 16:7.

JUSHAB-HESED [JOO-shuhb-HEE-suhd: "loving-kindness is returned"]. 500 B.C. A man listed in the genealogy of the royal line. 1 Chronicles 3:20.

JUSTUS [JUS-tuhs: "just"]

1. A.D. 35. Latin name of Joseph, also called Barsabbas. Acts 1:23.

2. A.D. 55. See Titus Justus.

3. A.D. 60. Latin name of a Christian companion of Paul. Colossians 4:11.

K

KADMIEL [KAD-mee-uhl: "God is ancient"(?)]

1. 525 B.C. Head of a family of Levites that returned to Judah after the Exile. Ezra 2:40; 3:9; Nehemiah 7:43.

2. 450 B.C. A Levite who helped lead worship. Nehemiah 9:4, 5; 12:24.

3. 450 B.C. A Levite who signed the pact of covenant renewal in Nehemiah's time. Nehemiah 10:9.

KALLAI [KALi: "swift"(?)]. 500 B.C. Head of a priestly family. Nehemiah 12:20.

KAREAH [kuh-REE-uh: "bald head"]. 625 B.C. Father of two military men allied with Gedaliah after the fall of Jerusalem. 2 Kings 25:23: Jeremiah 40:8; 41:16.

KEDAR [KEE-duhr: "powerful" or "dark, swarthy"]. B.C. date unknown. A son of Ishmael. Genesis 25:13.

KEDEMAH [KED-uh-muh: "eastward"]. B.C. date unknown. Last of the sons of Ishmael. Genesis 25:15.

KEDORLAOMER [KED-ohr-lay-OH-muhr]. 2100 B.C. King of Elam who led a coalition that defeated the kings of Sodom and Gomorrah. Genesis 14.

KEILAH [kuh-I-luh]. B.C. date unknown. Listed in the genealogy of Judah. 1 Chronicles 4:19.

KELAIAH [kuh-LAY-yuh]. 450 B.C. A Levite who took a pagan wife after the Exile. Ezra 10:23.

KELAL [KEE-lal: "perfection"]. 450 B.C. A man who married a pagan woman after the Exile. Ezra 10:30.

KELITA [kuh-LI-tuh: possibly "dwarf"]

1. 450 B.C. A Levite guilty of intermarriage with pagan women. Ezra 10:23. Also called Kelaiah.

2. 450 B.C. A Levite who helped Ezra teach the Law. Nehemiah 8:7.

3. 450 B.C. A Levite who signed the renewal covenant with God. Nehemiah 10:10. Probably all three are the same man.

KELUB [KEE-lub]

1. B.C. date unknown. Listed in the genealogy of Judah. 1 Chronicles 4:11.

2. 1025 B.C. Father of the man who supervised field workers on David's royal lands. 1 Chronicles 27:26.

KELUHI [KEL-uh-hi]. 450 B.C. One of those who married pagan women after the Exile. Ezra 10:35.

KEMUEL [KEM-yoo-uhl]

1. 2050 B.C. A nephew of Abraham. Genesis 22:21.

2. 1400 B.C. The Ephraimite Moses assigned to help divide the land of Canaan. Numbers 34:24.

3. 1000 B.C. Father of the leader of the tribe of Levi in David's day. 1 Chronicles 27:17.

KENAANAH [kuh-NAY-uh-nuh]

1. B.C. date unknown. Listed in the genealogy of Benjamin. 1 Chronicles 7:10.

2. 875 B.C. Father of Zedekiah, a false prophet who opposed Micaiah the prophet in Ahab's time. 1 Kings 22:11, 24; 2 Chronicles 18:10, 23.

KENAN [KEE-nuhn]. B.C. date unknown. Listed in the genealogy of Adam's line before the Flood. Genesis 5:9–14; Called Cainan in Luke 3:37.

KENANI [kuh-NAY-ni]. 450 B.C. A Levite who led the community confession of sins. Nehemiah 9:4.

KENANIAH [KEN-uh-NI-uh: "establish by Yahweh"]

1. 1000 B.C. A Levite who led singers celebrating the entrance of the ark into Jerusalem. 1 Chronicles 15:22, 27.

2. 975 B.C. A Levite who served in David's administration. 1 Chronicles 26:29.

KENAZ [KEE-naz: "hunting"]

1. 1875 B.C. An Edomite chief who was the grandson of Esau. Genesis 36:11, 15, 42.

2. 1425 B.C. Younger brother of Caleb the spy and father of Othniel the judge. Judges 1:13; 3:9–11; 1 Chronicles 4:13.

3. 1400 B.C. Grandson of Caleb the spy. 1 Chronicles 4:15.

KERAN [KEER-uhn]. 1925 B.C. A brother of one of Esau's wives. Genesis 36:26.

KEROS [KEER-ahs: "fortress"]. B.C. date unknown. Ancestral head of a family of temple servants that returned to Judah after the Exile. Ezra 2:44; Nehemiah 7:47.

KESED [KEH-sed]. 2050 B.C. A son of Nahor, Abraham's brother. Genesis 22:22.

KILION [KIL-ee-uhn: "pining"]. B.C. date unknown. Son of Naomi, who died in Moab. Ruth 1:2, 5.

KIMHAM [KIM-ham]. 1000 B.C. A kinsman of Barzillai who was give a post at court as a reward for Barzillai's aid to David during Absalom's rebellion. 2 Samuel 19:37–40.

KISH [KISH: "bow" or "power"]

1. 1100 B.C. Listed in the genealogy of Benjamin. Perhaps the uncle of Kish, father of Saul. 1 Chronicles 8:30; 9:36.

2. 1075 B.C. The father of King Saul. 1 Samuel 9:1–5; 14:51.

3. B.C. date unknown. Listed in the genealogy of Levi. 1 Chronicles 23:21, 22; 24:29.

4. 725 B.C. A Levite who helped purify the temple in Hezekiah's time. 2 Chronicles 29:12.

5. B.C. date unknown. An ancestor of Mordecai, the uncle of Esther. Esther 2:5.

KISHI [KISH-i]. 1025 B.C. The father of Ethan, a chief minister of music in David's time. 1 Chronicles 6:44. Called Kushaiah in 1 Chronicles 15:17.

KISLON [KIZ-lahn]. 1400 B.C. Father of Elidad, the representative of Benjamin whom Moses appointed to help divide the land of Canaan. Numbers 34:21.

KITTIM [KIT-im]. B.C. date unknown. Listed in the table of nations, possibly the ancestor of the people of Cyprus. Genesis 10:4.

KOHATH [KOH-hath]. 1875 B.C. An ancestor of Moses and Aaron. Genesis 46:11; Exodus 6:16–18; 1 Chronicles 6.

KOLAIAH [koh-LAY-yuh: "voice of Yahweh"]

1. 625 B.C. Father of Ahab, a false prophet among the Babylonian exiles. Jeremiah 29:21.

2. B.C. date unknown. Ancestor of a Benjamite who resettled in Jerusalem after the Exile. Nehemiah 11:7.

KORAH [KOHR-uh: "bald"]

1. 1900 B.C. A son of Esau. Genesis 36:5, 14, 18.

2. 1875 B.C. A grandson of Esau and an Edomite chief. Genesis 36:16.

3. B.C. date unknown. Listed in the genealogy of Judah. 1 Chronicles 2:43.

4. 1450 B.C. The Levite leader of a rebellion against Moses. Exodus 6:21–24; Numbers 16; 26:9–11; Jude 11.

KORE [KOHR-ee: "quail"(?)]

1. 1000 B.C. A son of Asaph whose descendants served as temple gate-keepers. 1 Chronicles 9:19; 26:1.

2. 725 B.C. A Levite in charge of distributing temple offerings in Hezekiah's time. 2 Chronicles 31:14.

KOZ [KAHZ: "thorn"]. B.C. date unknown. Listed in the genealogy of Judah. 1 Chronicles 4:8.

KUSHAIAH [koo-SHAY-yuh: "bow of Yahweh"]. 1025 B.C. Father of a chief minister of music in David's day. 1 Chronicles 15:17. Called Kishi in 1 Chronicles 6:44.

L

LAADAH [LAY-uh-duh]. B.C. date unknown. Listed in the genealogy of Judah. 1 Chronicles 4:21.

LAADAN [LAY-duhn]

1. B.C. date unknown. An ancestor of Joshua, hero of the conquest of Canaan. 1 Chronicles 7:26.

2. B.C. date unknown. A descendant of Gershon. 1 Chronicles 23:7–9; 26:21. Called Libni in 1 Chronicles 6:17, 20.

LABAN [LAY-buhn: "white"]. 2000 B.C. The brother of Rebekah and father of Rachel and Leah. Genesis 25:20; 27:43; 29–31.

LAEL [LAY-uhl: "belonging to God"]. 1475 B.C. Father of a leader of the Gershonites at the time of the Exodus. Numbers 3:24.

LAHAD [LAY-had]. B.C. date unknown. Listed in the genealogy of Judah. 1 Chronicles 4:2.

LAHMI [LAH-mi]. 975 B.C. The giant brother of Goliath, killed by Elhanan. 1 Chronicles 20:5.

LAISH [LAY-ish: "lion"]. 1050 B.C. Father of Palti to whom Saul gave David's wife Michal. 1 Samuel 25:44; 2 Samuel 3:15.

LAMECH [LAY-mek: "strong youth"(?)]

1. B.C. date unknown. A descendant of Cain; he was the first recorded polygamist. Genesis 4:18–24.

2. B.C. date unknown. Father of Noah. Genesis 5:25–31.

LAPIDOTH [LAP-uh-dahth: "flames, torches"(?)]. 1225 B.C. Husband of Deborah the prophetess and judge. Judges 4:4.

LAZARUS [LAZ-uh-ruhs: "God has helped"]

1. The beggar in Christ's story of the rich man and poor man in the afterlife. Luke 16:19–31.

2. A.D. 30. The brother of Martha and Mary whom Jesus raised from the dead. John 11; 12.

LEBANA [luh-BAY-nuh: "white"]. B.C. date unknown. Ancestor of a family of temple servants that returned to Judah after the Exile. Nehemiah 7:48.

LEBANAH [luh-BAH-nuh: "white"]. B.C. date unknown. Ancestor of temple servants. Ezra 2:45. See Lebana.

LECAH [LEE-kuh: "walking"]. B.C. date unknown. Listed in the genealogy of Judah. 1 Chronicles 4:21.

LEMUEL [lem-YOO-uhl: "devoted to God"]. B.C. date unknown. A king identified as the author of Proverbs 31:1–9. Tradition identifies him as Solomon or Hezekiah.

LEVI [LEE-vi: "joined"]

1. 1900 B.C. Son of Jacob by Leah. Ancestor of one of the twelve tribes of Israel. Genesis 29:34; 34:25–31; 1 Chronicles 6.

2 and 3. B.C. dates unknown. Two ancestors of Christ descended from David. Luke 3:24, 29.

4. A.D. 30. The tax collector who became Matthew the apostle. Mark 2:14–17; Luke 5:27–32.

LIBNI [LIB-ni: "white"(?)]

1. B.C. date unknown. A descendant of Levi and ancestor of his own clan. Exodus 6:17; 1 Chronicles 6:17, 20. Called Laadan in 1 Chronicles 23:7–9.

2. B.C. date unknown. Listed in the genealogy of Levi. 1 Chronicles 6:29.

LIKHI [LIK-hi]. B.C. date unknown. Listed in the genealogy of Manasseh. 1 Chronicles 7:19.

LINUS [LI-nuhs]. A.D. 65. A Christian who sent greetings to Timothy. 2 Timothy 4:21.

LO-AMMI [LOH-AM-i: "not my people"]. 725 B.C. Name given the second son of the prophet Hosea, as a sign of God's rejection of the northern kingdom. Hosea 1:9.

LOT [LAHT: "covering"]. 2100 B.C. The nephew of Abraham. Genesis 13, 19.

LOTAN [LOH-tan]. 1975 B.C. A Horite chief who lived in Seir in Esau's time. Genesis 36:20, 22, 29.

LUCIUS [LOO-shuhs: "light"]

1. A.D. 45. A Christian from Cyrene, a leader of the early church at Antioch. Acts 13:1.

2. A.D. 55. A relative of Paul who sent greetings to the Roman church. Romans 16:21. Possibly same as Lucius 1.

LUD [LUD]. B.C. date unknown. A son of Shem, and ancestor of a Semitic nation, probably Lydia. Genesis 10:22.

LUKE [shortened form of Lucas: "light"]. A.D. 50. The author of the books of Luke and Acts. Colossians 4:14; 2 Timothy 4:11; Philemon 24.

LYSANIAS [lih-SAY-nee-uhs]. A.D. 25. Tetrarch of Abilene when John the Baptist began his ministry. Luke 3:1.

LYSIAS [LIS-ee-uhs]. A.D. 60. Roman officer in command of the Jerusalem garrison who saved Paul when a mob sought his life. Acts 21:31—23:30; 24:7, 22.

M

MAACAH [MAY-uh-kuh: "oppression"]

1. 2050 B.C. A son of Nahor. Genesis 22:24.

2. 1025 B.C. Father of one of David's chief thirty military men. 1 Chronicles 11:43.

3. 1025 B.C. Father of Achish, king of Philistine Gath. 1 Kings 2:39. Called Maoch in 1 Samuel 27:2.

4. 1000 B.C. Father of the officer over the tribe of Simeon in David's day. 1 Chronicles 27:16.

MAADAI [MAY-uh-di: "Yahweh is an ornament"]. 450 B.C. He married a pagan wife after the Exile. Ezra 10:34.

MAADIAH [MAY-uh-DI-uh: "Yahweh is an ornament"]. 525 B.C. Head of a priestly family that returned to Jerusalem after the Exile. Nehemiah 12:5, 17.

MAAI [MAY-i: "compassionate"]. 450 B.C. A musician at the dedication of the walls of Jerusalem. Nehemiah 12:36.

MAASAI [MAY-uh-si: "work of Yahweh"]. 450 B.C. A priest who settled in Jerusalem after the Exile. 1 Chronicles 9:12. Called Amashsai in Nehemiah 11:13.

MAASEIAH [MAY-uh-SEE-yuh: "work of Yahweh"]

1. 1000 B.C. A Levite who played the lyre as David brought the ark to Jerusalem. 1 Chronicles 15:18, 20.

2. 850 B.C. A military commander who helped Jehoiada overthrow Queen Athaliah. 2 Chronicles 23:1.

3. 800 B.C. A military officer under Uzziah, king of Judah. 2 Chronicles 26:11.

4. 725 B.C. A son of King Ahaz slain in battle with Pekah, king of Israel. 2 Chronicles 28:7.

5. 625 B.C. Governor of Jerusalem who helped Josiah repair the temple. 2 Chronicles 34:8.

6. 625 B.C. Father of Zephaniah, a priest during the reign of Zedekiah. Jeremiah 21:1; 29:25; 37:3.

7. 625 B.C. Father of Zedekiah, a false prophet among the exiles in Babylon. Jeremiah 29:21.

8. 600 B.C. A doorkeeper at the temple during the reign of Zedekiah. Jeremiah 35:4.

9. 475 B.C. Father of Azariah, who helped repair the wall of Jerusalem. Nehemiah 3:23.

10. 11, and 12. 450 B.C. Three priests who took foreign wives in Ezra's time. Ezra 10:18, 21, 22.

13. 450 B.C. A man who married a pagan woman. Ezra 10:30.

14. 450 B.C. A man who stood at Ezra's right as he read the Law to the people. Nehemiah 8:4.

15. 450 B.C. A Levite who instructed the people in the Law. Nehemiah 8:7.

16. 450 B.C. A Jewish leader who signed the covenant renewal pact with God. Nehemiah 10:25.

17. 450 B.C. A Judahite who settled in Jerusalem after the Exile. Nehemiah 11:5.

18. 450 B.C. The ancestor of a man who settled in Jerusalem. Nehemiah 11:7.

19. and 20. 450 B.C. Two priests in the choir at the dedication of the walls of Jerusalem. Nehemiah 12:41, 42.

MAATH [MAY-ath: "small"]. B.C. date unknown. A descendant of Zerubbabel listed in the genealogy of Jesus. Luke 3:26.

MAAZ [MAY-az]. B.C. date unknown. Listed in the genealogy of Judah. 1 Chronicles 2:27.

MAAZIAH [MAY-uh-ZI-uh]

1. 975 B.C. Head of the twenty-fourth division of priests in David's day. 1 Chronicles 24:18.

2. 450 B.C. A priest who signed the covenant renewal pact. Nehemiah 10:8.

MACHBANAI [mak-BAN-i]. 1000 B.C. A Gadite warrior who joined David's army at Ziklag. 1 Chronicles 12:13.

MACHBENAH [mak-BEE-nuh]. B.C. date unknown. Listed in the genealogy of Judah. 1 Chronicles 2:49.

MACHNADEBAI [mak-NAD-uh-bi]. 450 B.C. He married a pagan wife after the Exile. Ezra 10:40.

MADAI [MAY-di]. B.C. date unknown. A son of Japheth listed in the table of nations. Genesis 10:2; 1 Chronicles 1:5. Ancestor of the Medes.

MAGDIEL [MAG-dee-uhl]. B.C. date unknown. An Edomite chief descended from Esau. Genesis 36:43; 1 Chronicles 1:54.

MAGOG [MAY-gahg]. B.C. date unknown. A son of Japheth listed in the table of nations. Genesis 10:2. In Revelation 20:8 "Magog" stands for nations opposed to God's people.

MAGOR-MISSABIB [MAY-gohr-MIS-uh-bib: "terror on every side"]. 600 B.C. Symbolic name given to the priest Pashhur by Jeremiah. Jeremiah 20:3.

MAGPIASH [MAG-pee-ash: "moth killer"(?)]. 450 B.C. A leader who signed a pact of covenant renewal. Nehemiah 10:20.

MAHALALEL [muh-HAL-uh-lel: "God is praise" or "God shines forth"]

1. B.C. date unknown. Ancestor of Noah listed in the genealogy of Christ. Genesis 5:12–17; Luke 3:37.

2. B.C. date unknown. Ancestor of a Judahite who settled in Jerusalem after the Exile. Nehemiah 11:4.

MAHARAI [MAY-huh-ri: "impetuous"(?)]. 1000 B.C. A military hero and one of David's soldiers. 2 Samuel 23:28; 1 Chronicles 11:30; 27:13.

MAHATH [MAY-hath: "snatching"(?)]

1. B.C. date unknown. Listed in the genealogy of Heman the seer. 1 Chronicles 6:35.

2. 725 B.C. A Levite who served in the temple in Hezekiah's time. 2 Chronicles 29:12; 31:13.

MAHAZIOTH [muh-HAY-zee-ahth: "visions"]. 975 B.C. A minister of music in David's time. 1 Chronicles 25:4, 30.

MAHER-SHALAL-HASH-BAZ [MAY-huhr-SHAL-uhl-HASH-baz: "the spoil speeds, the prey hastens"]. 725 B.C. Symbolic name given to one of Isaiah's sons signifying that Syria and the northern kingdom would soon be destroyed by Assyria. Isaiah 8:1, 3.

MAHLAH [MAH-luh: "weak, sickly"]. 1800 B.C. Great-grandson of Manasseh. 1 Chronicles 7:18.

MAHLI [MAH-li: "weak, sickly"]

1. B.C. date unknown. A descendant of Levi. 1 Chronicles 6:19; 23:21; 24:26.

2. B.C. date unknown. Listed in the genealogies of Levi. 1 Chronicles 6:47; 23:23; 24:30.

MAHLON [MAH-luhn]. 1100 B.C. Son of Elimelech and Naomi, and the first husband of Ruth. Ruth 1:2, 5; 4:10.

MAHOL [MAY-hahl: "dance"]. B.C. date unknown. Ancestor of four wise man who were exceeded in wisdom by Solomon. 1 Kings 4:31. "Sons of Mahol" may be the name of a guild or organization.

MAHSEIAH [mah-SEE-yuh: "Yahweh is a refuge"]. 650 B.C. Grandfather of

Seraiah and Baruch the scribe. Jeremiah 32:12; 51:59.

MAKI [MAY-ki]. 1475 B.C. Father of the representative of the tribe of Gad assigned to spy out Canaan. Numbers 13:15.

MAKIR [MAY-keer: "sold"]

1. 1825 B.C. Firstborn son of Manasseh, son of Jacob. Genesis 50:23; Numbers 26:29; 1 Chronicles 7:14–17.

2. 975 B.C. A man in whose house Jonathan's son Mephibosheth lived. 2 Samuel 9:4, 5; 17:27.

MALACHI [MAL-uh-ki: "my messenger" or "angel"]. 450 B.C. A prophet whose words are recorded in the Book of Malachi, the last book of the Old Testament.

MALCAM [MAL-kam: "their king"]. B.C. date unknown. Listed in the genealogy of Benjamin. 1 Chronicles 8:9.

MALCHUS [MAL-kuhs: "ruler"]. A.D. 30. The high priest's servant, whose ear Peter cut off. John 18:10.

MALKIEL [MAL-kee-uhl: "God is king"]. A descendant of Gad. Genesis 46:17; Numbers 26:45.

MALKIJAH [mal-KI-juh: "Yahweh is king"].

1. B.C. date unknown. Listed in the genealogy of Asaph, the chief minister of music in David's court. 1 Chronicles 6:40.

2. 975 B.C. Head of the fifth division of priests in David's day. 1 Chronicles 24:9.

3. 600 B.C. Father of Pashur, an official of Zedekiah who threw Jeremiah into a cistern to die. Jeremiah 21:1 [Melchiah]; 38:1 [Malchiah].

4. 600 B.C. Son of Zedekiah who owned the cistern into which Jeremiah was flung. Jeremiah 38:6.

5. B.C. date unknown. Ancestor of a priest who settled in Jerusalem in

The prophet Malachi was scandalized that the Israelites offered crippled and sick animals to God. His book underlines the spiritual state of the Jewish community at the end of the Old Testament.

Nehemiah's time. 1 Chronicles 9:12; Nehemiah 11:12.

6. and 7. 450 B.C. Two who wed pagan wives after the Exile. Ezra 10:25.

8. 450 B.C. A descendant of Harim who married pagan wives. He also contributed to the rebuilding of Jerusalem's wall. Ezra 10:31; Nehemiah 3:11.

9. 450 B.C. A Recabite who helped repair the wall of Jerusalem. Nehemiah 3:14.

10. 450 B.C. A goldsmith who also worked reconstructing the wall. Nehemiah 3:31.

11. 450 B.C. One who stood to Ezra's left as he read the Law. Nehemiah 8:4.

12. 450 B.C. A priest who signed the covenant renewal with God.

Nehemiah 10:3. Possibly the same as number 11.

13. 450 B.C. A priest who sang in the choir at the dedication of the wall of Jerusalem. Nehemiah 12:42. Possibly the same as numbers 11 or 12.

MALKIRAM [mal-KI-ruhm: "my king is exalted"]. A son of Jehoiachin, listed in the genealogy of the royal line. 1 Chronicles 3:18.

MALKI-SHUA [MAL-kih-SHOO-uh: "the king saves"]. 1025 B.C. Third son of Saul, killed with his father in battle with the Philistines. 1 Samuel 14:49; 31:2; 1 Chronicles 8:33; 10:2.

MALLOTHI [MAL-uh-thi: "Yahweh has spoken"]. 975 B.C. Head of the nineteenth division of temple singers. 1 Chronicles 25:4, 26.

MALLUCH [MAL-uhk: "counselor"]

1. B.C. date unknown. An ancestor of Ethan, a chief minister of music in David's day. 1 Chronicles 6:44.

2. 525 B.C. A priest who returned to Judah after the Exile. Nehemiah 12:2, 14.

3. and 4. 450 B.C. Two who wed pagan wives after the Exile. Ezra 10:29, 32.

5. 450 B.C. A priest who signed the covenant renewal, possibly with the name of a family ancestor (see Malluch 2). Nehemiah 10:4.

6. 450 B.C. A leader who signed the covenant renewal with God after the Exile. Nehemiah 10:27.

MAMRE [MAM-ree: "strength"]. 2100 B.C. An Amorite allied with Abram. Genesis 14:13, 24.

MANAEN [MAN-ee-uhn: "comforter"]. A.D. 45. One of the prophets and teachers of the church in Antioch. Acts 13:1.

MANAHATH [MAN-uh-hath]. 1950 B.C. Son of a Horite chief who lived in the land of Seir in Esau's time. Genesis 36:23.

MANASSEH [muh-NAS-uh: "one who causes forgetfulness"]

1. 1850 B.C. First son of Joseph, adopted by Jacob as an heir. Genesis 41:51; 48; Numbers 26:28–34; Matthew 1:10.

2. 697–642 B.C. Son and successor of Hezekiah who abandoned his father's pious ways. 2 Kings 21:1–18; 2 Chronicles 33:1–23.

3. and 4. 450 B.C. Two who wed foreign wives after the Exile. Ezra 10:30, 33.

MANOAH [muh-NOH-uh: "rest"]. 1125 B.C. The father of Samson. Judges 13.

MAOCH [MAY-ahk: "poor"]. 1025 B.C. Father of Achish, the Philistine king of Gath with whom David and his men took refuge from Saul. 1 Samuel 27:2. Called Maachah in 1 Kings 2:39.

MAON [MAY-ahn: "dwelling"]. B.C. date unknown. Listed in the genealogy of Judah. 1 Chronicles 2:45.

MARESHAH [muh-REE-shuh]

1. B.C. date unknown. Listed in the genealogy of Judah. 1 Chronicles 2:42.

2. B.C. date unknown. Listed in the genealogy of Judah. 1 Chronicles 4:21.

MARK [MAHRK: "large hammer"]. A.D. 45. Son of Mary of Jerusalem, notable as author of the Gospel bearing his name. Acts 12:12, 25; 15:37–39; Colossians 4:10; 2 Timothy 4:11; 1 Peter 5:13.

MARSENA [mahr-SEE-nuh]. 475 B.C. One of seven nobles who advised King Xerxes. Esther 1:14.

MASSA [MAS-uh: "burden"]. 2025 B.C. A son of Ishmael. Genesis 25:14.

MATRI [MAY-tri: "rainy"]. B.C. date unknown. Ancestral head of the

Benjamite clan from which Saul was chosen as king of Israel. 1 Samuel 10:21.

MATTAN [MAT-uhn: "gift"]

1. 850 B.C. Priest of Baal slain during the overthrow of Queen Athaliah. 2 Kings 11:18; 2 Chronicles 23:17.

2. 825 B.C. Father of an official of Zedekiah who threw Jeremiah into a cistern to die. Jeremiah 38:1.

MATTANIAH [MAT-uh-NI-uh: "gift of Yahweh"]

1. 975 B.C. Head of the ninth division of singers appointed by David. 1 Chronicles 25:4, 16.

2. B.C. date unknown. A descendant of Asaph and ancestor of Jahaziel, who prophesied before King Jehoshaphat. 2 Chronicles 20:14.

3. B.C. date unknown. An ancestor of Zechariah, a priest at the dedication of the wall of Jerusalem. Nehemiah 12:35.

4. B.C. date unknown. Another Levite whose descendants settled in Jerusalem after the Exile. 1 Chronicles 9:15; Nehemiah 11:17, 22. Possibly the same as Mattaniah 3.

5. 725 B.C. Another Levite descended from Asaph who helped purify the temple in Hezekiah's time. 2 Chronicles 29:13.

6. 597–587 B.C. Last king of Judah, whose name was changed to Zedekiah by Nebuchadnezzar. 2 Kings 24:17.

7. 525 B.C. A Levite who returned to Judah after the Exile. Nehemiah 12:8.

8. 500 B.C. Grandfather of an assistant to those in charge of the temple store-rooms in Nehemiah's time. Nehemiah 13:13. Possibly the same as Mattaniah 7.

9. 500 B.C. A temple gatekeeper in the time of Joiakim the high priest. Nehemiah 12:25.

10. 11, 12, and 13. 450 B.C. Four who married pagan wives after the Exile. Ezra 10:26, 27, 30, 37.

MATTATHA [MAT-uh-thuh: "gift"]. B.C. date unknown. A descendant of David listed in the genealogy of Jesus. Luke 3:31.

MATTATHIAS [MAT-uh-THI-uhs: "gift of Yahweh"]

1. and 2. B.C. dates unknown. Two descendants of Zerubbabel listed in the genealogy of Jesus. Luke 3:25, 26.

MATTATTAH [MAT-uh-tuh]. 450 B.C. A man who divorced his pagan wife when confronted by Ezra. Ezra 10:33.

MATTENAI [MAT-uh-ni: "gift of Yahweh"]

1. 500 B.C. A priest when Joiakim was high priest. Nehemiah 12:19.

2. and 3. Two who took pagan wives after the Exile. Ezra 10:33, 37.

MATTHAN [MATH-an: "gift"]. 50 B.C. Grandfather of Joseph the husband of Mary, in the genealogy of Jesus in Matthew 1:15. Possibly the same as Matthat in Luke 3:24.

MATTHAT [MATH-at: "gift"]

1. B.C. date unknown. Listed in the genealogy of Jesus in Luke 3:29.

2. 50 B.C. Grandfather of Joseph in Luke's genealogy of Jesus. Luke 3:24. See Matthan.

MATTHEW [MATH-yoo: shortened form of "gift of Yahweh"]. A.D. 25. One of the twelve apostles, the author of the Gospel bearing his name. Matthew 9:9–13; 10:3; Acts 1:13.

MATTHIAS [muh-THI-uhs: shortened form of "gift of Yahweh"]. A.D. 30. Chosen to become the twelfth apostle in place of Judas Iscariot. Acts 1:21–26.

MATTITHIAH [MAT-uh-THI-uh: "gift of Yahweh"]

1. 1000 B.C. A Levite who played the harp as the ark was brought into Jerusalem. 1 Chronicles 15:18, 21; 16:5.

2. 975 B.C. Head of the fourteenth division of temple singers in David's day. 1 Chronicles 25:3, 21.

3. 450 B.C. A Levite in charge of the bread offerings in Nehemiah's time. 1 Chronicles 9:31.

4. 450 B.C. A man who took a pagan wife after the Exile. Ezra 10:43.

5. 450 B.C. One who stood to Ezra's right when Ezra read the Law. Nehemiah 8:4. Possibly the same as 3.

MEBUNNAI [mah-BUN-i]. 1000 B.C. One of David's top thirty mighty men. 2 Samuel 23:27. Called Sibbechai in 2 Samuel 21:18; 1 Chronicles 11:29; 20:4; 27:11.

MEDAD [MEE-dad: "loved"(?)]. 1450 B.C. An Israelite elder who prophesied in the camp in Moses' time. Numbers 11:26, 27.

MEDAN [MEE-dan]. 2000 B.C. A son of Abraham by Keturah. Genesis 25:2.

MEHETABEL [muh-HET-uh-bel: "God is doing good"]. 500 B.C. Grandfather of the traitor Shemaiah who tried to trick Nehemiah into committing sacrilege. Nehemiah 6:10.

MEHIDA [muh-HI-duh: "famous"]. B.C. date unknown. Ancestor of a family of temple servants who returned to Judah after the Exile. Ezra 2:52; 1 Chronicles 4:11.

MEHIR [MEE-huhr]. B.C. date unknown. Listed in the genealogy of Judah. 1 Chronicles 4:11.

MEHUJAEL [meh-HOO-jee-uhl: "God is smiting"]. B.C. date unknown. A descendant of Cain. Genesis 4:18.

MEHUMAN [meh-HOO-muhn]. 475 B.C. One of seven eunuchs who served King Xerxes. Esther 1:10.

MELATIAH [MEL-uh-TI-uh: "Yahweh has delivered"]. 450 B.C. A man who helped repair the wall of Jerusalem. Nehemiah 3:7.

MELCHIZEDEK [mel-KIZ-uh-dek: "king of righteousness"]. 2100 B.C. Priest-king of Jerusalem who blessed Abram after his defeat of Kedorlaomer and his allies. Genesis 14:18–20; Ps. 110:4; Hebrews 5—7.

MELEA [MEE-lee-uh]. B.C. date unknown. A descendant of David listed in the genealogy of Christ. Luke 3:31.

MELECH [MEE-lek: "king"]. B.C. date unknown. A descendant of Jonathan, son of Saul. 1 Chronicles 8:35; 9:41.

MELKI [MEL-ki: "my king"]

1. and 2. B.C. date unknown. Two ancestors of Christ listed in Luke's genealogy. Luke 3:24, 28.

MEMUCAN [meh-MOO-kuhn]. 475 B.C. One of seven nobles who advised King Xerxes (Ahasuerus). Esther 1:14–21.

MENAHEM [MEN-uh-hem: "comforter"]. 752–742 B.C. He assassinated Shallum and seized the throne of the northern kingdom. 2 Kings 15:14–22.

MENNA [MEN-uh]. B.C. date unknown. A descendant of David, listed in the genealogy of Christ. Luke 3:31.

MEONOTHAI [mee-AHN-uh-thi: "my dwelling"]. 1350 B.C. Son of Othniel the judge, listed in the genealogy of Judah. 1 Chronicles 4:13, 14.

MEPHIBOSHETH [meh-FIB-oh-sheth: "he scatters shame," i.e., "idol breaker"]

1. 1000 B.C. Lame son of Jonathan, son of Saul. After the death of Jonathan, David gave Mephibosheth Saul's estate, and thereafter Mephibosheth ate at the king's table. 2 Samuel 4:4; 9:6–13; 16:1–4; 19:24–30.

2. 1000 B.C. A son of Saul by his concubine Rizpah. 2 Samuel 21:8.

MERAIAH [muh-RAY-yuh]. 500 B.C. Head of a priestly family when Joiakim was high priest. Nehemiah 12:12.

MERAIOTH [muh-RAY-ahth]

1. 1100 B.C. Descendant of Aaron, and ancestor of a number of significant priests—grandfather of Ahitub, and great-grandfather of Zadock, David's high priest. 1 Chronicles 6:6, 7, 52; Ezra 7:3.

2. B.C. date unknown. Ancestor of Azariah, a priest who settled in Jerusalem in Nehemiah's time. 1 Chronicles 9:11; Nehemiah 11:11.

MERARI [muhr-AHR-i: "bitter" (?)]. 1875 B.C. Son of Levi and ancestor of a Levite clan. Genesis 46:11; Numbers 3:17, 33–37; 1 Chronicles 6.

MERED [MEER-ed: "rebel"]. B.C. date unknown. Listed in the genealogy of Judah. 1 Chronicles 4:17, 18.

MEREMOTH [MAIR-uh-mahth]

1. 525 B.C. A priest who returned to Judah after the Exile. Nehemiah 12:3, 15.

2. 450 B.C. A priest who helped weigh the sacred vessels of silver and gold. Ezra 8:33; Nehemiah 3:4, 21.

3. 450 B.C. One who wed a pagan wife after the Exile. Ezra 10:36.

4. 450 B.C. A priest who signed the pact of covenant renewal. Nehemiah 10:5. Possibly the same as 1 or 2.

MERES [MEER-ez: "worthy"]. 475 B.C. One of seven nobles of Persia who advised King Xerxes. Esther 1:14.

MERIB-BAAL [MAIR-ib-BAY-uhl: "Baal contends"]. 1000 B.C. Original name of Jonathan's son, Mephibosheth. 1 Chronicles 8:34; 9:40.

MERODACH-BALADAN [MAIR-uh-dak-BAL-uh-duhn: "Marduk has given a son"]. 725 B.C. Babylonian king who sent a gift to Hezekiah after he recovered from an illness. 2 Kings 20:12–19; Isaiah 39:1–8.

MESHA [MEE-shuh]

1. B.C. date unknown. The first son of Caleb. 1 Chronicles 2:42.

2. B.C. date unknown. Listed in the genealogy of Benjamin. 1 Chronicles 8:9.

3. 650 B.C. King of Moab who successfully rebelled against Ahaziah, son of King Ahab. 2 Kings 3:4.

MESHACH [MEE-shak]. 600 B.C. Babylonian name given to Mishael, one of the three young Jewish captives trained in Babylon with Daniel. Daniel 1:7; 2:49; 3.

MESHECH [MEE-shek: "long; tall"]

1. B.C. date unknown. A son of Japheth listed in the table of nations. Genesis 10:2.

2. B.C. date unknown. A son of Aram listed in the table of nations. Genesis 10:23.

MESHELEMIAH [muh-SHEL-uh-MI-uh: "Yahweh repays"]. B.C. date unknown. A Levite appointed as a gatekeeper by David. 1 Chronicles 9:21; 26:1, 2, 9.

MESHEZABEL [muh-SHEZ-uh-bel: "God delivers"]

1. 500 B.C. Grandfather of a man who helped rebuild the wall of Jerusalem. Nehemiah 3:4.

2. 475 B.C. A Judahite, father of Pethahiah. Nehemiah 10:24.

3. 450 B.C. A leader who sealed the covenant renewal pact with God. Nehemiah 10:21.

MESHILLEMITH [muh-SHIL-uh-mith]. B.C. date unknown. Ancestor of a priest who settled in Jerusalem after the Exile. 1 Chronicles 9:12. Called Meshillemoth in Nehemiah 11:13.

MESHILLEMOTH [muh-SHIL-uh-mohth]

1. B.C. date unknown. Ancestor of a priest who lived in Jerusalem in Nehemiah's time. Nehemiah 11:13.

2. 775 B.C. Father of Berekiah, a leader who opposed the enslavement of prisoners from Judah. 2 Chronicles 28:12.

MESHOBAB [muh-SHOH-bab]. 725 B.C. A tribal leader in the time of Hezekiah. 1 Chronicles 4:34.

MESHULLAM [muh-SHOO-luhm: "reconciliation" or "friendship"]

1. B.C. date unknown. Listed in the genealogy of Benjamin. 1 Chronicles 8:17.

2. B.C. date unknown. Head of a Gadite family. 1 Chronicles 5:13.

3. B.C. date unknown. Ancestor of a priest who settled in Jerusalem after the Exile. 1 Chronicles 9:12.

4. 675 B.C. Grandfather of Shaphan, secretary of King Josiah. 2 Kings 22:3.

5. 650 B.C. A descendant of Zadok, David's high priest. 1 Chronicles 9:11; Nehemiah 11:11. Called Shallum in 1 Chronicles 6:12, 13; Ezra 7:2.

6. 625 B.C. A Levite who supervised the restoration of the temple in Josiah's time. 2 Chronicles 34:12.

7. 500 B.C. Son of Zerubbabel, listed in the royal genealogy. 1 Chronicles 3:19.

8. and 9. 500 B.C. Two priests when Joiakim was high priest. Nehemiah 12:13, 16.

10. 500 B.C. A Levite gatekeeper in the time of Joiakim. Nehemiah 12:25.

11. 475 B.C. Father of a Benjamite who settled in Jerusalem after the Exile. 1 Chronicles 9:7; Nehemiah 11:7.

12. 450 B.C. A Benjamite who settled in Jerusalem after the Exile. 1 Chronicles 9:8.

13. 450 B.C. A Jewish leader who returned to Judah with Ezra. Ezra 8:16.

14. 450 B.C. One who opposed Ezra's demand that pagan wives be divorced. Ezra 10:15.

15. 450 B.C. A Jew who wed a pagan wife after the Exile. Ezra 10:29.

16. 450 B.C. A priest who made repairs on the wall of Jerusalem. Nehemiah 3:4, 30; 6:18.

17. 450 B.C. One who helped repair the wall of Jerusalem. Nehemiah 3:6.

18. 450 B.C. He stood to Ezra's left at the public reading of the Law. Nehemiah 8:4.

19. 450 B.C. A priest who signed the pact of covenant renewal. Nehemiah 10:7.

20. 450 B.C. A leader who signed the covenant renewal pact. Nehemiah 10:20. Possibly the same as 13.

21. 450 B.C. A leader who took part in the dedication of Jerusalem's wall. Nehemiah 12:33.

METHUSELAH [muh-THOO-suh-luh: "man of the javelin"]. B.C. date unknown. Longest-lived person recorded in the Bible. Genesis 5:21–27; Luke 3:37.

METHUSHAEL [muh-THOO-shee-uhl: "man of God"(?)]. A descendant of

Cain and father of Lamech. Genesis 4:18.

MEUNIM [me-YOO-nim]. B.C. date unknown. Ancestor of a family of temple servants that returned to Judah after the Exile. Ezra 2:50; Nehemiah 7:52.

ME-ZAHAB [MEH-zay-hab]. B.C. date unknown. Grandfather of Mahatabel, wife of Hadad, an Edomite king. Genesis 36:39; 1 Chronicles 1:50.

MIBHAR [MIE-bahr: "choice"]. 1000 B.C. One of David's military heroes. 1 Chronicles 11:38.

MIBSAM [MIB-suhm: "sweet odor"]

1. 2025 B.C. A son of Ishmael. Genesis 25:13; 1 Chronicles 1:29.

2. B.C. date unknown. Listed in the genealogy of Simeon. 1 Chronicles 4:25.

MIBZAR [MIB-zahr: "fortress"]. B.C. date unknown. An Edomite chief descended from Esau. Genesis 36:42; 1 Chronicles 1:53.

MICA [MI-kuh: "who is like Yahweh?"]

1. B.C. date unknown. An ancestor of Uzzi, chief Levite in Jerusalem after the Exile. 1 Chronicles 9:15; Nehemiah 11:17, 22. Called Micaiah in Nehemiah 12:35 .

2. 450 B.C. A Levite who signed the pact of covenant renewal, possibly with the name of a family ancestor. Nehemiah 10:11.

MICAH [MI-kuh: "who is like Yahweh?"]

1. B.C. date unknown. An Ephraimite who employed a Levite as family priest in the days of the Judges. Judges 17, 18.

2. B.C. date unknown. Listed in the genealogy of Reuben. 1 Chronicles 5:5.

3. 975 B.C. Son of Mephibosheth and great-grandson of Saul. 1 Chronicles 8:34, 35; 9:40, 41.

4. 975 B.C. A Levite of David's time. 1 Chronicles 23:20.

5. 725 B.C. Micah of Moresheth, the prophet whose words are recorded in the Book of Micah. Jeremiah 26; Micah 1:1.

6. 650 B.C. Father of Abdon, who was sent by Josiah to seek guidance from Huldah the prophetess. 2 Chronicles 34:20.

MICAIAH [mih-KAY-yuh: "who is like Yahweh?"]

1. 875 B.C. A prophet who revealed the truth to Ahab concerning God's intent to see the king dead in battle. 1 Kings 22; 2 Chronicles 18.

2. 875 B.C. A Levite Jehoshaphat commissioned to teach God's Law throughout Judah. 2 Chronicles 17:7.

3. B.C. date unknown. An ancestor of Zechariah, a Levite who took part in the dedication of Jerusalem's wall. Nehemiah 12:35. Same as Mica 2.

4. 650 B.C. Father of Acbor, an official Josiah sent to seek counsel of the prophetess Huldah. 2 Kings 22:12. Called Micah, father of Abdon, in 2 Chronicles 34:20.

5. 600 B.C. A man who reported Jeremiah to the king for treasonous preaching. Jeremiah 36:11–13.

6. 450 B.C. A priest who sang at the dedication of Jerusalem's wall. Nehemiah 12:41.

MICHA [MI-kuh: "who i s like Yahweh?"]. 975 B.C. Son of Mephibosheth, the son of Jonathan. 2 Samuel 9:12. Called Micah in 1 Chronicles 8:34, 35; 9:40, 41.

MICHAEL [MI-kuhi: "who is like God?"]

1. The archangel who is the protector of the Jewish people. Daniel 10:13, 21; 12:1; Jude 9; Revelation 12:7.

2. 1475 B.C. Father of Sether, the representative of the tribe of Asher whom Moses sent to spy out the land of Canaan. Numbers 13:13.

3. B.C. date unknown. Listed in the genealogy of Issachar. 1 Chronicles 7:3.

4. and 5. B.C. dates unknown. Two listed only in the genealogy of Gad. 1 Chronicles 5:13, 14.

6. B.C. date unknown. Ancestor of Asaph, chief minister of music in David's time. 1 Chronicles 6:40.

7. B.C. date unknown. Listed in the genealogy of Benjamin. 1 Chronicles 8:16.

8. 1000 B.C. A man who joined David at Ziklag. 1 Chronicles 12:20.

9. 1000 B.C. Father of a leader of the tribe of Issachar in David's day. 1 Chronicles 27:18.

10. 850 B.C. A son of Jehoshaphat, king of Judah. 2 Chronicles 21:2–4.

11. 475 B.C. Father of Zebadiah, head of a family that returned to Judah with Ezra. Ezra 8:8.

MICHRI [MIK-ri]. B.C. date unknown. Ancestor of Elah, a Benjamite who settled in Jerusalem after the Exile. 1 Chronicles 9:8.

MIDIAN [MID-ee-uhn]. 2000 B.C. A son of Abraham and ancestor of the Midianites. Genesis 25:2, 4.

MIJAMIN [MIJ-uh-min: "of the right hand," i.e., fortunate]

1. 975 B.C. Head of the sixth division of priests in David's day. 1 Chronicles 24:9.

2. 525 B.C. A priest who returned to Judah after the Exile. Nehemiah 12:5. Called Minjamin in Nehemiah 12:17, 41.

3. 450 B.C. A man who married a pagan woman after the Exile. Ezra 10:25.

4. 450 B.C. A priest who sealed the covenant renewal with God. Nehemiah 10:7. Possibly the same as #2.

MIKLOTH [MIK-lahth]

1. 1100 B.C. A man listed in the genealogy of Saul. 1 Chronicles 8:32; 9:37, 38.

2. 975 B.C. Commander of the division of David's army that served during the second month. 1 Chronicles 27:4.

MIKNEIAH [mik-NEE-yuh: "Yahweh possesses"]. 1000 B.C. A Levite who played the harp as the ark was brought into Jerusalem. 1 Chronicles 15:18, 21.

MILALAI [MIL-uh-li]. 450 B.C. A Levite musician at the dedication of Jerusalem's walls. Nehemiah 12:36.

MINIAMIN [MIN-yuh-min: "of the right hand"]

1. 725 S.C. A priest who helped distribute temple offerings. 2 Chronicles 31:15.

2. 525 B.C. A priest who returned to Judah after the Exile. Nehemiah 12:17, 41. Called Mijamin in Nehemiah 12:5.

MINJAMIN [Minj-uh-min]. 450 B.C. A priest who played the trumpet at the dedication of Jerusalem's walls. Nehemiah 12:41.

MIRIAM [MEER-ee-uhm: "loved by Yahweh"]. B.C. date unknown. Listed in the genealogy of Judah. 1 Chronicles 4:17.

MIRMAH [MUHR-muh]. B.C. date unknown. Listed in the genealogy of Benjamin. 1 Chronicles 8:10.

MISHAEL [MISH-ee-uhl: "who is what God is?"]

1. 1450 B.C. A kinsman of Moses and Aaron who removed the bodies of Aaron's sons, Nadab and Abihu, after they had been struck dead before the sanctuary. Exodus 6:22; Leviticus 10:4.

2. 600 B.C. Birth name of Meshach, one of Daniel's three companions in Babylon. Daniel 1:6, 7, 19; 2:17. See Meshach.

3. 450 B.C. One who stood at Ezra's left at the reading of the Law. Nehemiah 8:4.

MISHAM [MI-sham]. B.C. date unknown. Listed in the genealogy of Benjamin. 1 Chronicles 8:12.

MISHMA [MISH-muh]

1. 2025 B.C. A son of Ishmael and ancestor of a tribe. Genesis 25:14.

2. B.C. date unknown. Listed in the genealogy of Simeon. 1 Chronicles 4:25, 26.

MISHMANNAH [MISH-man-uh]. 1000 B.C. Gadite leader who joined David's army at Ziklag. 1 Chronicles 12:10.

MISPAR [MIS-pahr]. B.C. date unknown. Ancestor of a family that returned to Jerusalem after the Exile. Ezra 2:2. Called Mispereth in Nehemiah 7:7.

MISPERETH [MIS-puhr-eth]. B.C. date unknown. Ancestor of a post-exilic family. Nehemiah 7:7. See Mispar.

MITHREDATH [MITH-ruh-dath: "gift of Mithra"]

1. 525 B.C. Treasurer of Cyrus, king of Persia. Ezra 1:8.

2. 450 B.C. An official of the Trans-Euphrates province who opposed the rebuilding of Jerusalem. Ezra 4:7.

MIZRAIM [MIZ-ray-uhm]. B.C. date unknown. A son of Ham listed in the table of nations. Genesis 10:6, 13. Probably the ancestral source of the Egyptians.

MIZZAH [MIZ-uh: "terror"(?)]. 1875 B.C. A grandson of Esau, and an Edomite chief. Genesis 36:13, 17.

MNASON [NAY-suhn]. A.D. 60. A Christian from Cyprus who offered his home as a base for Paul and his fellow missionaries. Acts 21:16.

MOAB [MOH-ab: "from my father"]. 2025 B.C. Son of Lot by incest with his eldest daughter. Ancestor of the Moabites. Genesis 19:37.

MOADIAH [mo-uh-DI-uh]. 525 B.C. A priest who returned to Judah after the Exile. Nehemiah 12:5, 17.

MOLID [MOH-lid]. B.C. date unknown. Listed in the genealogy of Judah. 1 Chronicles 2:29.

MORDECAI [MOHR-duh-ki]

1. 525 B.C. A man who returned to Judah after the Exile. Ezra 2:2; Nehemiah 7:7.

2. 475 B.C. A Benjamite deported to Babylon with Jeconiah whose cousin Esther became wife of King Xerxes. Esther 2—10.

MOSES [MOH-zuhs: "drawn-out"]. B.C. 1450. The great leader God chose to bring His people out of Egypt and give them the Law at Sinai, and to author the first five books of the Old Testament.

MOZA [MOH-zuh]

1. B.C. date unknown. A son of Caleb listed in the genealogy of Judah. 1 Chronicles 2:46.

2. B.C. date unknown. A Benjamite descended from Jonathan, son of Saul. 1 Chronicles 8:36, 37; 9:42, 43.

MUPPIM [MUP-im]. 1825 B.C. A descendant of Benjamin. Genesis 46:21. Called Shupham in Numbers 26:39 and Shephuphan in 1 Chronicles 8:5.

MUSHI [MOO-shi]. B.C. date unknown. Ancestor of a Levite clan. Exodus 6:19; Numbers 3:20; 1 Chronicles 23:21, 23.

N

NAAM [NAY-uhm: "pleasant"]. B.C. 1425. A son of Caleb the spy, listed in the genealogy of Judah. 1 Chronicles 4:15.

NAAMAN [NAY-uh-muhn: "pleasantness"]

1. 1825 B.C. A son of Bela, firstborn son of Benjamin. Genesis 46:21; Numbers 26:40; 1 Chronicles 8:4.

2. 850 B.C. Syrian commander healed of leprosy by Elisha the prophet. 2 Kings 5; Luke 4:27.

3. B.C. date unknown. Listed in the genealogy of Benjamin. 1 Chronicles 8:7.

NAARAI [NAY-uh-ri]. 1000 B.C. A military commander, one of David's mighty men. Chronicles 11:37. Called Paarai the Arbite in 2 Samuel 23:35.

NABAL [NAY-buhl: "foolish"]. 1025 B.C. A wealthy man who earned David's ire and God's punishment by denying hospitality to David and his men. 1 Samuel 25.

NABOTH [NAY-bahth: "a sprout"]. 875 B.C. He refused to sell his ancestral land to King Ahab and was subsequently murdered judicially by Jezebel. 1 Kings 21:1–19; 2 Kings 9:21–26.

NACON [NAY-kahn]. 1000 B.C. Owner of a threshing floor near which Uzzah was struck dead for touching the ark. 2 Samuel 6:8. Called Chidon in 1 Chronicles 13:9.

NADAB [NAY-dab: "liberal"]

1. 1450 B.C. First son of Aaron, who was immolated for offering "unauthorized fire" before the Lord. Exodus 6:23; Leviticus 10:1, 2.

2. B.C. date unknown. Listed in the genealogy of Judah. 1 Chronicles 2:28–30.

3. 1100 B.C. A son of Jeiel and probably a grand-uncle of Saul. 1 Chronicles 8:30; 9:36.

4. 909–908 B.C. The son and successor of Jeroboam I, who was assassinated in the second year of his reign. 1 Kings 15:25–31.

NAGGAI [NAG-I]. Listed in the genealogy of Jesus in Luke 3:25.

NAHAM [NAY-ham: "comfort"]. B.C. date unknown. Listed in the genealogy of Judah. 1 Chronicles 4:19.

NAHAMANI [NAY-huh-MAY-ni: "compassionate"]. 525 B.C. A leader who returned to Judah after the Exile. Nehemiah 7:7.

NAHARAI [NAY-uh-ri]. 1000 B.C. A military officer and one of David's thirty mighty men. 2 Samuel 23:37; 1 Chronicles 11:39.

NAHASH [NAY-hash: "serpent"]

1. 1050 B.C. Ammonite king who attacked Jabesh Gilead and was defeated by Saul. 1 Samuel 11:1–3; 12:12.

2. 1000 B.C. Ammonite ruler who befriended David. 2 Samuel 10:2; 17:27; 1 Chronicles 19:1, 2.

3. 1000 B.C. Father of Abigail and Zeruiah, sisters of David. An alternate name for Jesse or a former husband of Jesse's wife. 2 Samuel 17:25.

NAHATH [NAY-hath]

1. 1875 B.C. A grandson of Esau. Genesis 36:13, 17.

2. B.C. date unknown. An ancestor of Samuel, listed in the genealogy of Levi. 1 Chronicles 6:26.

3. 725 B.C. A Levite who served in the temple during the reign of Hezekiah. 2 Chronicles 31:13.

NAHBI [NAH-bi]. 1450 B.C. The representative of the tribe of Naphtali whom Moses sent to explore Canaan. Numbers 13:14.

NAHOR [NAY-hohr]

1. B.C. date unknown. Ancestor of Abraham. Genesis 11:22–25; Luke 3:34.

2. 2150 B.C. A brother of Abraham and grandfather of Rebekah. Genesis 11:28–29; 22:20–23.

NAHSHON [NAH-shahn]. 1450 B.C. Brother-in-law of Aaron and leader of the tribe of Judah at the time of the Exodus. Ancestor of David and Christ. Exodus 6:23; Numbers 1:7; 1 Chronicles 2:10, 11; Matthew 1:4; Luke 3:32.

NAHUM [NAY-hum: "comforter"]

1. 650 B.C. A prophet whose words are recorded in the Book of Nahum.

2. B.C. date unknown. An ancestor of Christ. Luke 3:25.

NAPHISH [NAY-fish]. 2025 B.C. A son of Ishmael and ancestor of an Ishmaelite tribe. Genesis 25:15; 1 Chronicles 1:31; 5:19.

NAPHTALI [NAF-tuh-li: "wrestle"]. 2000 B.C. Sixth son of Jacob and ancestral source of one of the twelve tribes of Israel. Genesis 30:8; 46:24; 49:21; 1 Chronicles 7:13.

NARCISSUS [nahr-SIS-uhs]. A.D. 55. Head of a household, some of whom were Christians. Romans 16:11.

NATHAN [NAY-thuhn: "gift"]

1. B.C. date unknown. Listed in the genealogy of Judah. 1 Chronicles 2:36.

2. 1025 B.C. A man from Zobah and father of Igal, one of David's mighty men. 2 Samuel 23:36; 1 Chronicles 11:38.

3. 1000 B.C. The court prophet who confronted David concerning his adultery with Bathsheba. 2 Samuel 7:1–17; 12:1–15, 25; 1 Kings 1:8–45; 1 Chronicles 29:29.

4. 975 B.C. A son born to David in Jerusalem. 2 Samuel 5:14; 1 Chronicles 3:5; Zechariah 12:12; Luke 3:31.

5. 975 B.C. Father of Azariah and Zabud, two of Solomon's officials. 1 Kings 4:5. Possibly the same as Nathan 3 or 4.

6. 450 B.C. A leader Ezra sent to enlist Levites for the post-exilic temple. Ezra 8:16.

7. 450 B.C. A man who wed a pagan wife after the Exile. Ezra 10:39.

NATHANAEL [nuh-THAN-ee-uhl: "God has given"]. A.D. 30. A Galilean called to be a disciple of Christ. John 1:45–49; 21:2. Some identify him with Bartholomew.

NATHAN-MELECH [NAY-thuhn-MEL-ek: "king's gift"]. 625 B.C. An official during the reign of Josiah, king of Judah. 2 Kings 23:11.

NEARIAH [NEE-uh-RI-uh]

1. 725 B.C. A Simeonite leader who invaded the hill country of Seir in the time of Hezekiah. 1 Chronicles 4:42.

2. B.C. date unknown. A descendant of Zerubbabel listed in the genealogy of the royal line. 1 Chronicles 3:22, 23.

NEBAI [NEE-bi] 450 B.C. A leader who signed the covenant renewal pact. Nehemiah 10:19.

NEBAIOTH [neh-BAY-yahth]. 2025 B.C. First son of Ishmael and ancestor of a North Arabian tribe. Genesis 25:13; Isaiah 60:7.

NEBAT [NEE-bat]. 950 B.C. Father of Jeroboam I. 1 Kings 11:26; 12:2, 15.

NEBO [NEE-boh; "to announce" or "height"]

1. A Babylonian deity, god of wisdom, mentioned in Isaiah's prophecy of Babylon's fall. Isaiah 46:1.

2. B.C. date unknown. Ancestor of some who took foreign wives after the Exile. Ezra 10:43.

NEBO-SARSEKIM [NEE-boh-SAHR-suh-kim]. 600 B.C. An official of Nebuchadnezzar at the fall of Jerusalem. Jeremiah 39:3.

NEBUCHADNEZZAR [NEB-uh-kuhd-NEZ-urh: "may Nebo protect my boundary"]. 60–62 B.C. The powerful king who captured Jerusalem and deported the Jews to Babylon. 2 Kings 24; 25; 2 Chronicles 36; Daniel 1—4.

NEBUSHAZBAN [NEB-uh-SHAZ-ban: "Nebo deliver me"]. 600 B.C. A chief Babylonian officer instructed by Nebuchadnezzar to free Jeremiah following the fall of Jerusalem. Jeremiah 39:13.

NEBUZARADAN [NEB-uh-zahr-AY-duhn: "Nebo has given offspring"]. 600 B.C. Commander of the imperial guard under Nebuchadnezzar. 2 Kings 25:8–20; Jeremiah 39:9–14; 52:12–30.

NECHO [NEE-koh]. 600–595 B.C. The pharaoh who killed King Josiah at Megiddo; later he made Jehoiakim king of Judah. He was defeated by Nebuchadnezzar in 605 B.C. 2 Kings 23:29–35; 2 Chronicles 35:20–26; Jeremiah 46:2.

NEDABIAH [NED-uh-BI-uh: "Yahweh is willing"]. 550 B.C. A son of Jehoiachin, listed in the genealogy of the royal line. 1 Chronicles 3:18.

NEHEMIAH [NEE-uh-MI-uh: "Yahweh comforts"]

1. 525 B.C. He returned to Judah after the Exile. Ezra 2:2; Nehemiah 7:7.

2. 450 B.C. The Jewish governor of Judah under whose leadership the walls of Jerusalem were rebuilt. Nehemiah 1—13.

3. 450 B.C. He helped repair the wall of Jerusalem. Nehemiah 3:16.

NEHUM [NEE-hum]. 525 B.C. One who returned to Judah after the Exile. Nehemiah 7:7. Called Rehum in Ezra 2:2.

NEKODA [neh-KOH-duh]

1. B.C. date unknown. Ancestor of a family of temple servants that returned to Judah after the Exile. Ezra 2:48; Nehemiah 7:50.

2. B.C. date unknown. Ancestor of returned exiles who were unable to prove Israelite descent. Ezra 2:60; Nehemiah 7:62.

NEMUEL [NEM-yoo-uhl]

1. 1875 B.C. A son of Simeon and ancestor of a clan. Numbers 26:12; 1 Chronicles 4:24. Called Jemuel in Genesis 46:10 and Exodus 6:15.

2. 1425 B.C. Brother of Dathan and Abiram, who rebelled against Moses. Numbers 26:9.

NEPHEG [NEE-fag: "sprout"]

1. B.C. date unknown. A Levite listed in the family record of Moses and Aaron. Exodus 6:21.

2. 975 B.C. A son of David born in Jerusalem. 2 Samuel 5:15.

NEPHUSIM [neh-FOO-sim]. Ancestor of temple servants who returned to Judah after the Exile. Ezra 2:50; Nehemiah 7:52. Probably the same as Naphish.

NER [NUHR: "tight" or "lamp"]

1. 1100 B.C. Grandfather of King Saul. 1 Chronicles 8:33.

2. 1100 B.C. Father of Abner, uncle or grand-uncle of Saul. 1 Samuel 14:50, 51; 26:5, 14. He may possibly be the same as Ner 1.

NEREUS [NEER-ee-uhs]. A.D. 55. A Roman Christian mentioned by Paul. Romans 16:15.

NERGAL-SHAREZER [NUHR-gahl-shahr-EE-zuhr: "may Nergal protect the king"]. 600 B.C. A Babylonian official present at the fall of Jerusalem. Jeremiah 39:3, 13.

NERI [NEER-i: shortened form of Nariah]. B.C. date unknown. Listed in the genealogy of Jesus. Luke 3:27.

NERIAH [nuh-RI-uh: "Yahweh is light"]. 625 B.C. Father of Baruch and Seraiah, who served Jeremiah the prophet. Jeremiah 32:12, 16; 51:59.

NETHANEL [nuh-THAN-uhl: "gift of God"]

1. 1450 B.C. Leader of the tribe of Issachar during the Exodus. Numbers 1:8.

2. 1025 B.C. A son of Jesse and older brother of David. 1 Chronicles 2:14.

3. 1000 B.C. A priest who blew the trumpet as the ark was brought into Jerusalem. 1 Chronicles 15:24.

4. 1000 B.C. A Levite, father of Shamaiah the scribe. 1 Chronicles 24:6.

5. 975 B.C. A temple gatekeeper appointed by David. 1 Chronicles 26:4.

6. 875 B.C. An official Jehoshaphat commissioned to teach God's Law throughout Judah. 2 Chronicles 17:7.

7. 625 B.C. A chief Levite who provided offerings for the Passover celebration in Josiah's time. 2 Chronicles 35:9.

8. 500 B.C. Head of a priestly family when Joiakim was high priest. Nehemiah 12:21.

9. 450 B.C. A priest who wed a pagan wife after the Exile. Ezra 10:22.

10. 450 B.C. A Levite who played an instrument at the dedication of Jerusalem's wall. Nehemiah 12:36.

NETHANIAH [NETH-uh-NI-uh: "gift of Yahweh"]

1. 975 B.C. A temple singer. 1 Chronicles 25:2, 12.

2. 875 B.C. A Levite who instructed people in the Law in Jehoshaphat's time. 2 Chronicles 17:8.

3. 600 B.C. Father of Jehudi, an official of Jehoiakim. Jeremiah 36:14.

4. 575 B.C. Father of Ishmael, the military officer who murdered Gedaliah, governor of Judah. 2 Kings 25:23, 25; Jeremiah 40:8; 41:18.

NEZIAH [nah-ZI-uh: "faithful"]. B.C. date unknown. Ancestor of a family of temple servants that returned to Judah after the Exile. Ezra 2:54; Nehemiah 7:56.

NICANOR [ni-KAY-nohr: "conqueror"]. A.D. 35. One of seven chosen to oversee distribution of food to Christian widows in Jerusalem. Acts 6:5.

NICODEMUS [NIK-uh-DEE-muhs: "conqueror of the people"]. A.D. 30. A Pharisee and member of the Sanhedrin who was told by Jesus that he must be "born again." John 3:1–21; 7:50–52; 19:39.

NICOLAS [NIK-uh-luhs: "conqueror of the people"]. A.D. 35. One of the seven men appointed to distribute food to the poor in the Jerusalem church. Acts 6:5.

NIGER [NI-juhr: "black"]. A.D. 45. Surnamed Simeon, he was a prophet and teacher of the church at Antioch. Acts 13:1.

NIMROD [NIM-rahd]. B.C. date unknown. Renowned warrior and hunter listed in the table of nations. He established a kingdom in Babylonia and founded many ancient cities, among them, Erech, Babel, Akkad, and Nineveh. Genesis 10:8–12; Micah 5:6.

NIMSHI [NIM-shi]. 900 B.C. Grandfather of Jehu, king of Israel. 1 Kings 19:16; 2 Kings 9:2, 14, 20.

NOADIAH [NOH-uh-DI-uh: "Yahweh assembles"]. 450 B.C. A Levite who helped weigh sacred temple vessels. Ezra 8:33.

NOAH [NOH-uh: "rest" or "comfort"]. B.C. date unknown. The righteous man who built an ark in which he and his family survived the Genesis Flood. Genesis 5:28–32; 6:8—9:29; Matthew 24:37, 38; Hebrews 11:7.

NOBAH [NOH-buh]. 1400 B.C. A man who took Kenath and renamed it Nobah after himself. Numbers 32:42.

NODAB [NOH-dab]. B.C. date unknown. Ancestor of an Arabian tribe defeated by the tribes of Reuben, Gad, and Manasseh. 1 Chronicles 5:19.

NOGAH [NOH-guh: "splendor"]. 975 B.C. A son born to David in Jerusalem. 1 Chronicles 3:7; 14:6.

NOHAH [NOH-hah: "rest"]. 1850 B.C. Listed as a son of Benjamin in 1 Chronicles 8:2, but omitted in Genesis 46:21.

NUN [NUN: "fish"]. 1475 B.C. The father of Joshua. Exodus 33:11; Joshua 1:1; 1 Chronicles 7:27.

NYMPHAS [NIM-fuhs]. A.D. 80. A Christian whose house served as a church. Colossians 4:15. It is uncertain whether Nymphas was a man or a woman.

O

OBADIAH [OH-buh-DI-uh: "servant of Yahweh"]

1. B.C. date unknown. Listed in the genealogy of Issachar. 1 Chronicles 7:3.

2. 1000 B.C. A Gadite leader who joined David at Ziklag. 1 Chronicles 12:9.

3. 1000 B.C. Father of a leader of the tribe of Zebulun in David's day. 1 Chronicles 27:19.

4. 875 B.C. An officer Jehoshaphat sent throughout Judah to instruct the people in the Law. 2 Chronicles 17:7.

5. 875 B.C. Devout follower of Yahweh in charge of Ahab's palace. 1 Kings 18:1–16.

6. B.C. date unknown. A descendant of Jonathan, son of Saul. 1 Chronicles 8:38; 9:44.

7. 625 B.C. A Levite who supervised the restoration of the temple for King Josiah. 2 Chronicles 34:12.

8. 500 B.C. A chief gatekeeper who served in the days of Joiakim. Nehemiah 12:25.

9. Sixth-century prophet whose prophecy against Edom is recorded in the Book of Obadiah.

10. B.C. date unknown. A descendant of Zerubbabel listed in the genealogy Judah. 1 Chronicles 3:21.

11. 450 B.C. A Levite descended from Jeduthun, a minister of music. 1 Chronicles 9:16. Called Abda in Nehemiah 11:17.

12. 450 B.C. Head of a family that returned to Judah after the Exile. Ezra 8:9.

13. 450 B.C. A priest who signed the covenant renewal pact in Nehemiah's time. Nehemiah 10:5.

OBAL [OH-buhl]. B.C. date unknown. Son of Joktan listed in the table of nations; ancestor of an Arabian tribe. Genesis 10:28; 1 Chronicles 1:22.

OBED [OH-bed: "worshiper" or "servant"]

1. 1075 B.C. Son of Ruth and Boaz, and grandfather of David. Ruth 4:17, 21, 22; 1 Chronicles 2:12.

2. B.C. date unknown. Listed in the genealogy of Judah. 1 Chronicles 2:37, 38.

3. 1000 B.C. One of David's top thirty military men. 1 Chronicles 11:47.

4. 975 B.C. A temple gatekeeper. 1 Chronicles 26:7.

5. 875 B.C. Father of Azariah, a military commander who helped Jehoiada overthrow Queen Athaliah. 2 Chronicles 23:1.

OBED-EDOM [OH-bed-EE-duhm: "servant of Edom"]

1. 1000 B.C. A man of Gath in whose yard the ark of the Lord remained for three months. 2 Samuel 6:10–12; 1 Chronicles 13:13, 14; 15:25.

2. 1000 B.C. A chief gatekeeper appointed by David. 1 Chronicles 15:18, 24; 16:5, 38; 26:4–8.

3. 800 B.C. Temple treasurer in the time of Amaziah, king of Judah. 2 Chronicles 25:24.

OBIL [OH-bil: "camel driver"]. 975 B.C. An Ishmaelite who supervised King David's camels. 1 Chronicles 27:30.

OCRAN [AHK-rahn: "trouble"]. 1450 B.C. Father of Pagiel, leader of the tribe of Asher during the Exodus. Numbers 1:13.

ODED [OH-dad: "restorer"]

1. 925 B.C. Father of Azariah, a prophet who encouraged King Asa to seek the Lord. 2 Chronicles 15:1–8.

2. 750 B.C. A prophet who opposed the enslavement of captives Pekah took in his war with Ahab, king of Judah. 2 Chronicles 28:9–11.

OG [AHG]. 1400 B.C. Amorite king defeated by the Israelites under Moses. Numbers 21:33–35; Deuteronomy 3:1–13.

OHAD [OH-had]. 1875 B.C. A son of Simeon. Genesis 46:10; Exodus 6:15.

OHEL [OH-hel: "tent"]. 500 B.C. A son of Zerubbabel listed in the genealogy of the royal line. 1 Chronicles 3:20.

OHOLIAB [oh-HOH-lee-ab: "father's tent"]. 1450 B.C. A Danite craftsman who assisted Bezalel in constructing the tabernacle and making its furnishings. Exodus 31:6; 35:34—36:2.

OHOLIBAMAH [oh-HOH-lih-BAH-muh: "tent of the high place"]. B.C. date unknown. An Edomite chief descended from Esau. Genesis 36:41.

OLYMPAS [oh-LIM-puhs]. A.D. 55. A Roman Christian to whom Paul sent greetings. Romans 16:15.

OMAR [OH-mahr]. 1875 B.C. A grandson of Esau. Genesis 36:11, 15.

OMRI [AHM-ree]

1. B.C. date unknown. Listed in the genealogy of Benjamin. 1 Chronicles 7:8.

2. 975 B.C. Officer over the tribe of Issachar in David's day. 1 Chronicles 27:18.

3. 885–874 B.C. The commander of King Elah's army who became king of Israel after Zimri murdered Elah. He founded Samaria, capital of the northern kingdom. 1 Kings 16:16–29.

4. B.C. date unknown. Ancestor of a man who settled in Jerusalem after the Exile. 1 Chronicles 9:4.

ON [AHN: "strength"]. 1450 B.C. A Reubenite leader who joined Korah's rebellion against Moses. Numbers 16:1.

ONAM [OH-nam: "vigorous"]

1. 1950 B.C. A son of Shobal, a Horite chief of Seir in Esau's time. Genesis 36:23.

2. B.C. date unknown. Listed in the genealogy of Judah. 1 Chronicles 2:26, 28.

ONAN [OH-nan: "vigorous"]. 1875 B.C. Second son of Judah, slain by the Lord for his disobedience. Genesis 38:4, 8, 9; 46:12.

ONESIMUS [oh-NES-ih-muhs: "profitable"]. A.D. 60. A runaway slave on whose behalf Paul wrote a letter to his master, Philemon. Colossians 4:9; Philemon 10.

ONESIPHORUS [on-uh-SIF-uh-ruhs: "profit-bringer"]. A.D. 65. A Christian who ministered to Paul during his imprisonment in Rome. 2 Timothy 1:16; 4:19.

OPHIR [OH-fuhr: "rich"]. B.C. date unknown. A son of Joktan, listed in the table of nations. Genesis 10:29.

OPHRAH [AHF-ruh: "fawn"]. 1350 B.C. A grandson of Othniel, listed in the genealogy of Judah. 1 Chronicles 4:14.

OREB [OHR-eb: "raven"]. 1175 B.C. A Midianite leader put to death by Gideon's forces. Judges 7:25; 8:3; Psalm 83:11.

OREN [OHR-en: "fir tree"]. B.C. date unknown. Listed in the genealogy of Judah. 1 Chronicles 2:25.

OTHNI [AHTH-ni]. 975 B.C. A man who served as a temple gatekeeper. 1 Chronicles 26:7.

OTHNIEL [AHTH-nee-uhl: "God is might"(?)]. 1374–1334 B.C. The first judge of Israel following the death of Joshua. Joshua 15:17, 18; Judges 1:13, 14; 3:7–11; 1 Chronicles 4:13.

OZEM [OH-zuhm]

1. B.C. date unknown. Listed in the genealogy of Judah. 1 Chronicles 2:25.

2. 1025 B.C. Sixth son of Jesse and older brother of David. 1 Chronicles 2:15.

OZNI [AHZ-ni]. 1875 B.C. Ancestor of a Gadite clan. Numbers 26:16. Same as Ezbon, son of Gad, in Genesis 46:16.

P

PAARAI [PAY-uh-ri]. 1000 B.C. One of David's thirty mighty men. 2 Samuel 23:35. Called Naarai in 1 Chronicles 11:37.

PADON [PAY-dahn: "redemption"]. B.C. date unknown. Ancestor of a family of temple servants that returned to Judah with Zerubbabel. Ezra 2:44; Nehemiah 7:47.

PAGIEL [PAY-gee-uhl]. 1450 B.C. Leader of the tribe of Asher at the time of the Exodus. Numbers 1:13; 7:72–77.

PAHATH-MOAB [PAY-hath-MOH-ab: "ruler of Moab"]

1. B.C. date unknown. Ancestor of a family that returned to Judah after the Exile. The name may be a title. Ezra 2:6; 8:4; Nehemiah 3:11.

2. 450 B.C. A leader who sealed the covenant renewal pact with God, probably with the name of his family

ancestor (see Pahath-Moab 1). Nehemiah 10:14.

PALAL [PAY-lal: "judge"]. 450 B.C. A man who helped rebuild the walls of Jerusalem. Nehemiah 3:25.

PALLU [PAL-oo: "distinguished"]. 1900 B.C. Second son of the patriarch Reuben, Jacob's son. Genesis 46:9; Exodus 6:14; Numbers 26:5.

PALTI [PAL-ti: "Yahweh delivers"]. 1400 B.C. The representative of the tribe of Benjamin whom Moses sent to explore Canaan. Numbers 13:9.

PALTIEL [PAL-tee-uhl: "God delivers"]

1. 1400 B.C. Representative of the tribe of Issachar who helped divide the land of Canaan. Numbers 34:26.

2. 1025 B.C. A Benjamite to whom Saul gave his daughter Michal, although she was David's wife. 2 Samuel 3:15.

PARMASHTA [pahr-MASH-tuh]. 475 B.C. One of ten sons of Haman hanged by Mordecai. Esther 9:9.

PARMENAS [PAHR-muh-nuhs: "steadfast"]. A.D. 35. One of seven appointed to distribute food among the poor. Acts 6:5.

PARNACH [PAHR-nak: "gifted"(?)]. 1425 B.C. Father of the Zebulun appointed to assist in dividing the land of Canaan. Numbers 34:25.

PAROSH [PAIR-ahsh]

1. B.C. date unknown. Ancestor of a postexilic family. Ezra 2:3; 8:3; 10:25; Nehemiah 3:25.

2. 450 B.C. A leader who signed the covenant renewal pact with God, probably with the name of a family ancestor (see Parosh 1). Nehemiah 10:14.

PARSHANDATHA [pahr-shan-DAY-thuh]. 475 B.C. A son of Haman put to death by the Jews of Shushan. Esther 9:7.

PARUAH [puh-ROO-uh: "blooming"]. 975 B.C. Father of one of Solomon's district governors. 1 Kings 4:17.

PASACH [PAY-sak]. B.C. date unknown. Listed in the genealogy of Asher. 1 Chronicles 7:33.

PASEAH [puh-SEE-uh: "limping"]

1. B.C. date unknown. Listed in the genealogy of Judah. 1 Chronicles 4:12.

2. B.C. date unknown. Ancestor of a family of temple servants that returned to Judah with Zerubbabel. Ezra 2:49; Nehemiah 7:51.

3. 475 B.C. Father of one of the builders of the walls of Jerusalem. Nehemiah 3:6.

PASHHUR [PASH-hur]

1. B.C. date unknown. Ancestral head of a priestly family that returned to Judah after the Exile. Ezra 2:38; 10:22; Nehemiah 7:41.

2. 625 B.C. Father of Gedaliah, one of the officials who threw Jeremiah into a cistern. Jeremiah 38:1. Possibly the same as Pashhur 3 or 4.

3. 600 B.C. A priest who put Jeremiah in stocks. Jeremiah gave him the symbolic name, "Magor-Missabib," "terror on every side." Jeremiah 20:1–6.

4. 600 B.C. One of the officials who threw Jeremiah into a cistern to die. Jeremiah 21:1; 38:1.

5. B.C. date unknown. Ancestor of a priest who settled in Jerusalem after the Exile. 1 Chronicles 9:12; Nehemiah 11:12. Probably the same as Pashhur 4.

6. 450 B.C. A priest who signed the covenant renewal pact, possibly with the name of his family ancestor (see Pashhur 1). Nehemiah 10:3.

PATROBAS [PAT-ruh-buhs: "paternal"]. A.D. 55. A Roman Christian to whom Paul sent greetings. Romans 16:14.

PAUL [PAWL: "little"] A.D. 35. A Pharisee who mercilessly persecuted the early Christians until his miraculous conversion on the road to Damascus. Author of thirteen New Testament epistles. Also know by his Jewish name of Saul. Acts 7:57, 58; 8:1–3; 9:1–28.

PEDAHEL [PED-uh-hal: "God has redeemed"]. 1400 B.C. The representative from the tribe of Naphtali appointed to help assign inheritances in Canaan. Numbers 34:28.

PEDAHZUR [peh-DAH-zuhr: "the rock has redeemed"]. 1475 B.C. Father of Gamaliel, leader of the tribe of Manasseh during the Exodus. Numbers 1:10.

PEDAIAH [puh-DAY-yuh: "Yahweh has redeemed"]

1. 1000 B.C. Father of the officer over half the tribe of Manasseh in David's day. 1 Chronicles 27:20.

2. 650 B.C. Grandfather of King Jehoiakim. 2 Kings 23:36.

3. 550 B.C. A son of Jeconiah. He is listed as the father of Zerubbabel in the post-exilic genealogy of the royal line. Elsewhere his brother Shealtiel is given as Zerubbabel's father. (See. Ezra 3:2; Nehemiah 12:1). 1 Chronicles 3:18, 19.

4. B.C. date unknown. Ancestor of a Benjamite who settled in Jerusalem after the Exile. Nehemiah 11:7.

5. 450 B.C. He helped rebuild Jerusalem's walls. Nehemiah 3:25.

6. 450 B.C. He stood to the left of Ezra at the reading of the Law. Nehemiah 8:4.

7. 425 B.C. A Levite put in charge of food storage by Nehemiah. Nehemiah 13:13. Possibly the same as Pedaiah 5 or 6.

PEKAH [PEE-kuh: "he opens" or "he sees"]. 752–732 B.C. A military officer who assassinated King Pekahiah and seized the throne of Israel. 2 Kings 15:25–31; 16:5; 2 Chronicles 28:6; Isaiah 7:1.

PEKAHIAH [PEH-kuh-HI-uh: "Yahweh opens" or "Yahweh sees"]. 742–740 B.C. Son and successor of Menahem, king of Israel. 2 Kings 15:22–26.

PELAIAH [puh-LAY-yuh: "Yahweh is marvelous"]

1. 450 B.C. A Levite who translated the Hebrew into Aramaic as Ezra read the Law to the people. Nehemiah 8:7.

2. 450 B.C. A Levite who signed the covenant renewal pact in Nehemiah's time. Nehemiah 10:10. Possibly the same as Pelaiah 1.

3. B.C. date unknown. A descendant of Zerubbabel, listed in the genealogy of the royal line. 1 Chronicles 3:24.

PELALIAH [PEL-uh-LI-uh: "Yahweh judges"]. B.C. date unknown. Ancestor of a priest who settled in Jerusalem after the Exile. Nehemiah 11:12.

PELATIAH [PEL-uh-TI-uh: "Yahweh delivers")

1. 725 B.C. A leader of the Simeonites who defeated the remaining Amalekites in the hill country of Seir. 1 Chronicles 4:42.

2. 600 B.C. A leader in Jerusalem who gave "wicked advice." Pelatiah fell dead as Ezekiel prophesied. Ezekiel 11:1–13.

3. B.C. date unknown. A descendant of Zerubbabel listed in the genealogy of the royal line. 1 Chronicles 3:21.

4. 450 B.C. A Jewish leader who sealed the covenant renewal pact in Nehemiah's time. Nehemiah 10:22.

PELEG [PEE-leg: "division" or "channel"]. B.C. date unknown. A descendant of Shem and ancestor of Abraham. Genesis 10:25; 11:16–19; Luke 3:35.

PELET [PEE-let: "deliverance"]

1. B.C. date unknown. A Judahite, listed in the genealogy of Caleb. 1 Chronicles 2:47.

2. 1000 B.C. One of the two brothers who joined David's army at Ziklag. 1 Chronicles 12:3.

PELETH [PEE-lath: "swiftness"]

1. 1475 B.C. Father of On, a Reubenite who rebelled against Moses. Numbers 16:1.

2. B.C. date unknown. Listed in the genealogy of Judah. 1 Chronicles 2:33.

PENUEL [peh-NOO-uhl: "face of God"]

1. B.C. date unknown. Listed in the genealogy of Judah. 1 Chronicles 4:4.

2. B.C. date unknown. Listed in the genealogy of Benjamin. 1 Chronicles 8:25.

PERESH [PEER-ash]. B.C. date unknown. Listed in the genealogy of Manasseh. 1 Chronicles 7:16.

PEREZ [PEER-ez: "bursting forth"]. 1850 B.C. One of the twin sons born to Judah by his daughter-in-law, Tamar. He was an ancestor of Christ. Genesis 38:29; 46:12; Matthew 1:3.

PERIDA [puh-RI-duh: "divided"] B.C. date unknown. A servant of Solomon and ancestor of a family that returned to Judah with Zerubbabel. Nehemiah 7:57. Called Peruda in Ezra 2:55.

PERUDA [puh-ROO-duh]. B.C. date unknown. His descendants returned to Judah after the Exile. Ezra 2:55.

PETER [PEE-tuhr: "rock"]. A.D. 30. The prominent apostle who denied Christ three times and later became a leader in the early church. Author of the two epistles that bear his name. Matthew 16:13–23; 26:32–46, 69–75; John 21; Acts 1—5; 9:32–42; 15.

PETHAHIAH [PETH-uh-HI-uh: "Yahweh opens up"]

1. 975 B.C. Appointed by David to be head of the nineteenth division of priests. 1 Chronicles 24:16.

2. 450 B.C. A Levite who wed a pagan wife after the Exile. Ezra 10:23.

3. 450 B.C. A Levite who led public confession at the ceremony of covenant renewal. Nehemiah 9:5. Probably the same as Pethahiah 2.

4. 450 B.C. A Judahite agent of King Artaxerxes "in all affairs relating to the people." Nehemiah 11:24.

PETHUEL [puh-THOO-uhl]. B.C. date unknown. Father of Joel the prophet. Joel 1:1.

PEULTHAI [pee-UHL-thi]. 975 B.C. A gatekeeper appointed by David. 1 Chronicles 26:5.

PHANUEL [fuh-NOO-uhl]. 75 B.C. Father of Anna the prophetess. Luke 2:36.

PHARAOH [FAIR-oh: "great house"]. Royal title of Egyptian rulers. See Hophra, Necho.

PHICHOL [FI-kahl]. 2050 B.C. Philistine commander of Abimelech's army in the time of Abraham and Isaac. Genesis 21:22–32; 26:26. Many scholars believe this is a title, like Abimelech, and two persons are referred to.

PHILEMON [fi-LEE-muhn: "friendship"]. A.D. 60. An important Christian to whom Paul wrote concerning his slave, Onesimus. Philemon 1.

PHILETUS [fi-LEE-tuhs: "beloved"]. A.D. 65. A heretical teacher in the church at Ephesus. 2 Timothy 2:17.

PHILIP [FIL-ip: "lover of horses"]

1. A.D. 25. Herod Philip I, first husband of Herodias. He was the father of Salome, who asked for the head of John the Baptist. Matthew 14:3; Mark 6:17.

2. 4 B.C.-A.D. 34. Herod Philip II, tetrarch of Iturea and Trachonitis. Unlike his brother's, his reign was peaceful and benevolent. Luke 3:1.

3. A.D. 30. One of the twelve apostles. Like Andrew and Peter, he was from the town of Bethsaida. Matthew 10:3; John 1:43–48; 6:5–7; 12:21, 22: 14:8, 9; Acts 1:13.

4. A.D. 35. Notable as Philip the evangelist: one of the seven deacons of the church at Jerusalem. Acts 6:5; 8:4–13, 26–40; 21:8.

PHILOLOGUS [fi-LAHL-uh-guhs: "lover of learning"]. A.D. 55. A Roman Christian greeted by Paul. Romans 16:15.

PHINEHAS [FIN-ee-uhs: "mouth of brass"]

1. 1400 B.C. Righteous and zealous grandson of Aaron. Exodus 6:25; Numbers 25:7–13; Joshua 22:13–34.

2. 1100 B.C. One of the wicked sons of Eli against whom Samuel prophesied. 1 Samuel 1:3; 2:12–17, 22–36; 3:11–13; 4:11–22.

3. 475 B.C. Father of Eleazar, a priest who helped weigh out the sacred temple articles. Ezra 8:33.

PHLEGON [FLEG-ahn: "burning"]. A.D.55. A Roman Christian to whom Paul sent greetings. Romans 16:14.

PHYGELLUS [fi-JEL-uhs: "fugitive"]. A.D. 65. He deserted Paul in Asia. 2 Timothy 1:15.

PILATE [PI-luht: "javelin-carrier"]. A.D. 26–36. Roman procurator of Judea by whom Christ was tried. Matthew

The wealthy Philemon welcomes his runaway slave back as a brother. Early Christians counted on the spiritual transformation of individuals to right society's wrongs.

❖

27; Luke 13:1; 23; John 18:29—19:38.

PILDASH [PIL-dash]. 2050 B.C. A son of Nahor, brother of Abraham. Genesis 22:22.

PILHA [PIL-hah]. 450 B.C. A Jewish leader who signed the covenant renewal pact of Nehemiah's time. Nehemiah 10:24.

PILTAI [PIL-ti: "Yahweh delivers"]. 500 B.C. Head of a priestly family in the time of Joiakim the high priest. Nehemiah 12:17.

PINON [PI-nahn]. B.C. date unknown. An Edomite chief descended from Esau. Genesis 36:41.

PIRAM [PI-ruhm]. 1400 B.C. Amorite king who joined Adoni-zedek in an attack on Gibeon. Joshua 10:3.

PISPAH [PIS-puh]. B.C. date unknown. Listed in the genealogy of Asher. 1 Chronicles 7:38.

PITHON [PI-thahn]. 950 B.C. A great-grandson of Saul's son, Jonathan. 1 Chronicles 8:35; 9:41.

POCHERETH [PAHK-uh-reth]. Ancestral head of a family that returned to Judah with Zerubbabel. Ezra 2:57; Nehemiah 7:59.

PONTIUS [PAHN-shuhs]. A.D. 26–36. Roman family name. See Pilate.

PORATHA [pohr-AY-thuh]. 475 B.C. A son of Haman, executed by the Jews at Shushan. Esther 9:8.

PORCIUS [POHR-shee-uhs]. See Festus.

POTIPHAR [PAHT-ih-fuhr: "whom (the sun god) Re has given"]. 1875 B.C. Prominent Egyptian whose wife made false accusations against Joseph, and who then threw Joseph into prison. Genesis 37:36; 39:1.

POTI-PHERAH [pah-TIF-uhr-uh: "given by the sun god"]. 1800 B.C. Egyptian priest of On, father of Asenath the wife of Joseph. Genesis 41:45, 50.

PROCHORUS [PRAH-kohr-uhs]. A.D. 35. One of the seven deacons appointed to oversee the church's daily distribution of food in Jerusalem. Acts 6:5.

PUAH [POO–uh]

1. 1875 B.C. A son of Issachar and head of a clan. Genesis 46:13; Numbers 26:23.

2. 1150 B.C. Father of Tola, a judge who led Israel for twenty-three years. Judges 10:1.

PUBLIUS [PUB-lee-uhs]. A.D. 60. The chief official on Malta, who showed hospitality to Paul after his shipwreck. Acts 28:7.

PUDENS [POO-denz: "modest"]. A.D. 65. A Christian who added his greetings to Paul's second letter to Timothy. 2 Timothy 4:21.

PUL [PUL or POOL]. See Tiglath-Pileser.

PURAH [PYOOR-uh]. 1175 B.C. Servant who accompanied Gideon in his night reconnaissance of the Midianite camp. Judges 7:10, 11.

PUT [PUT]. A son of Ham listed in the table of nations. Genesis 10:6. Identified with Libya.

PUTIEL [POO-tee-uhl]. 1425 B.C. Father-in-law of Eleazar, a son of Aaron. Exodus 6:25.

PYRRHUS [PEER-uhs: "fiery red"]. A.D. 25. Father of Sopater, a companion of Paul. Acts 20:4.

Q

QUARTUS [KWOHR-tus: "fourth"]. A.D.55. A Christian in Corinth who sent greetings to the Roman church through Paul. Romans 16:23.

QUIRINIUS [kwh-RIN-ee-uhs]. 5 B.C. Roman governor of Syria at the time of Jesus' birth. Luke 2:2.

R

RAAMAH [RAY-uh-muh: "thunder" or "trembling"]. B.C. date unknown. A descendant of Ham, listed in the table of nations. Genesis 10:7.

RAAMIAH [RAY-uh-MI-uh: "Yahweh has thundered"(?)]. 525 B.C. One of twelve Israelite leaders who returned to Judah with Zerubbabel. Nehemiah 7:7. Same as Reelaiah in Ezra 2:2.

RADDAI [RAD-i]. 1025 B.C. An older brother of David. 1 Chronicles 2:14.

RAHAM [RAY-ham: "mercy, love"]. B.C. date unknown. Listed in the genealogy of Caleb. 1 Chronicles 2:44.

RAKEM [RAY-kuhm]. B.C. date unknown. Listed in the genealogy of Manasseh. 1 Chronicles 7:16.

RAM [RAM]

1. B.C. date unknown. Head of the family of Elihu, who argued with Job. Job 32:2.

2. B.C. date unknown. An ancestor of David and Christ. Ruth 4:19;1 Chronicles 2:9, 10; Luke 3:33.

3. B.C. date unknown. First son of Jerahmeel, a descendant of Judah. 1 Chronicles 2:25, 27.

RAMIAH [ruh-MI-uh: "Yahweh is high"]. 450 B.C. He married a pagan wife after the Exile. Ezra 10:25.

RAPHA [RAY-fuh]

1. B.C. date unknown. Ancestor of the Philistine giants killed in battle in David's time. 2 Samuel 21:16–22; 1 Chronicles 20:6–8.

2. 1825 B.C. The last son of Benjamin. 1 Chronicles 8:2. His name is omitted in Genesis 46:21.

RAPHAH [RAY-fuh]. B.C. date unknown. A descendant of Saul through Jonathan. 1 Chronicles 8:37. Called Rephaiah in 1 Chronicles 9:43.

RAPHU [RAY-foo: "healed"]. 1475 B.C. Father of the representative of the tribe of Benjamin whom Moses sent to spy out the land of Canaan. Numbers 13:9.

REAIAH [rea-AY-yuh: "Yahweh has seen"]

1. B.C. date unknown. Listed in the genealogy of Judah. 1 Chronicles 4:2.

2. B.C. date unknown. Listed in the genealogy of Reuben. 1 Chronicles 5:5.

3. B.C. date unknown. Ancestor of a family of temple servants that returned to Judah with Zerubbabel. Ezra 2:47; Nehemiah 7:50.

REBA [REE-buh]. 1400 B.C. One of the five Midianite kings killed by the Israelites under Moses. Numbers 31:8; Joshua 13:21.

RECHAB [REE-kab: "horseman"]

1. B.C. date unknown. Founder of the Rechabites, who gave up wine and lived as nomads. 2 Kings 10:15, 23; 1 Chronicles 2:55; Jeremiah 35.

2. 1000 B.C. He and his brother assassinated Ishbosheth, son of Saul. 2 Samuel 4:2–12.

3. 475 B.C. Father of Malkijah, who helped repair the walls of Jerusalem. Nehemiah 3:14. Possibly the same as Rechab 1.

REELAIAH [REE-uh-LAY-yuh]. 525 B.C. He returned to Judah with Zerubbabel. Ezra 2:2. Called Raamiah in Nehemiah 7:7.

REGEM [REE-guhm: "friend"]. B.C. date unknown. Listed in the genealogy of Caleb. 1 Chronicles 2:47.

REGEM-MELECH [REE-guhm-MEH-lak: "royal friend"]. 525 B.C. Member of a delegation sent to ask the priests whether fasting to commemorate the temple's destruction should be continued. Zechariah 7:2.

REHABIAH [REE-huh-BI-uh: "Yahweh has made wide"]. 1425 B.C. A grandson of Moses. 1 Chronicles 23:17; 24:21; 26:25.

REHOB [REE-hahb: "broad: open"]

1. 1025 B.C. Father of Hadadezer, the king of Zobah defeated in battle by David. 2 Samuel 8:3, 12.

2. 450 B.C. A Levite who sealed the covenant renewal pact in Nehemiah's time. Nehemiah 10:11.

REHOBOAM [REE-huh-BOH-uhm]. 931–913 B.C. The son and successor of

Solomon, whose foolishness led to division of the united Hebrew kingdom. 1 Kings 12; 14:21–31; 2 Chronicles 10:12.

REHUM [REE-hum: "merciful"]

1. 525 B.C. A leader who accompanied Zerubbabel in the return to Judah. Ezra 2:2. Called Nehum in Nehemiah 7:7.

2. 525 B.C. A chief priest who returned to Judah with Zerubbabel. Nehemiah 12:3.

3. 450 B.C. A Persian officer who co-authored a letter to Artaxerxes opposing the rebuilding of Jerusalem. Ezra 4:6–23.

4. 450 B.C. He helped repair the walls of Jerusalem. Nehemiah 3:17.

5. 450 B.C. A Jewish leader who sealed the covenant renewal pact in Nehemiah's time. Nehemiah 10:25.

REI [REE-i: "friendly"]. 975 B.C. A loyal friend of David. 1 Kings 1:8.

REKEM [REE-kuhm: "friendship"]

1. 1400 B.C. One of five kings of Midian killed in battle with the Israelites under Moses. Numbers 31:8; Joshua 13:21.

2. B.C. date unknown. A descendant of Caleb listed in the genealogy of Judah. 1 Chronicles 2:43, 44.

REMALIAH [REM-uh-LI-uh: "Yahweh adorns"]. 775 B.C. Father of Pekah, king of Israel. 2 Kings 15:25.

REPHAEL [REF-ay-el: "God heals"]. 975 B.C. A man who served as a tabernacle gatekeeper in David's time. 1 Chronicles 26:7.

REPHAH [REE-fuh: "healing" or "support"]. B.C. date unknown. Listed in the genealogy of Ephraim. 1 Chronicles 7:25.

REPHAIAH [reh-FAY-yuh: "Yahweh heals"]

1. B.C. date unknown. Listed in the genealogy of Issachar. 1 Chronicles 7:2.

2. B.C. date unknown. A descendant of Saul through Jonathan. 1 Chronicles 9:43. Called Raphah in 1 Chronicles 8:37.

3. 725 B.C. A Simeonite leader who fought against the Amalekites in Hezekiah's time. 1 Chronicles 4:42.

4. B.C. date unknown. A descendant of David listed in the genealogy of the royal line. 1 Chronicles 3:21.

5. 450 B.C. He helped repair the wall of Jerusalem. Nehemiah 3:9.

RESHEPH [REE-shaf: "flame"]. B.C. date unknown. Listed in the genealogy of Ephraim. 1 Chronicles 7:25.

REU [REE-oo: "friendship"]. B.C. date unknown. An ancestor of Abraham. Genesis 11:18–21; Luke 3:35.

REUBEN [ROO-ben: "see, a son"]. 1900 B.C. First son of Jacob, by his wife Leah, and ancestor of one of the twelve tribes of Israel. Genesis 29:32; 35:22, 23; 37:21–29; 49:3, 4.

REUEL [ROO-uhl: "friend of God"]

1. 1925 B.C. A son of Esau. Genesis 36:4, 10–17.

2. 1500 B.C. Midianite priest who gave his daughter Zipporah to Moses in marriage. Exodus 2:18; Numbers 10:29. Also called Jethro.

3. B.C. date unknown. Ancestor of a man who settled in Jerusalem after the Exile. 1 Chronicles 9:8.

REZIN (REE-zin)

1. 750 B.C. A king of Syria who warred against Jotham and Ahaz. He was executed by Tiglath-Pileser, king of

Assyria. 2 Kings 15:37; 16:5–9: Isaiah 7:1–8.

2. B.C. date unknown. Ancestor of a family of temple servants that returned to Judah after the Exile. Ezra 2:48; Nehemiah 7:50.

REZON [REE-zuhn: "prince"]. 950 B.C. A man of Zobah who became king of Damascus and founded a dynasty of Syrian rulers. 1 Kings 11:23–25. Probably the same as Hezion in 1 Kings 15:18.

RHESA [REE-suh]. 500 B.C. Listed in Luke's genealogy of Jesus. Luke 3:27.

RIBAI [RI-bi]. 1025 B.C. Father of one of David's mighty men. 2 Samuel 23:29; 1 Chronicles 11:31.

RIMMON [RIM-ahn: "pomegranate"]. 1025 B.C. The father of Rechab and Baanah, the murderers of Ishbosheth, son of Saul. 2 Samuel 4:2–9.

RINNAH [RIN-uh: "praise to God"]. B.C. date unknown. Listed in the genealogy of Judah. 1 Chronicles 4:20.

RIPHATH [RI-fath]. B.C. date unknown. A descendant of Japhath listed in the table of nations. Genesis 10:3; 1 Chronicles 1:6.

RIZIA [rih-ZI-uh]. B.C. date unknown. Listed in the genealogy of Asher. 1 Chronicles 7:39.

RODANIM [ROH-duh-nim]. B.C. date unknown. A descendant of Japheth listed in the table of nations. Genesis 10:4; 1 Chronicles 1:7.

ROHGAH [ROH-guh]. B.C. date unknown. Listed in the genealogy of Asher. 1 Chronicles 7:34.

ROMAMTI-EZER [roh-MAM-tih-EE-zuhr: "highest help"]. 970 B.C. Head of the twenty-fourth division of temple singers. 1 Chronicles 25:4, 31.

ROSH [RAHSH: "head"]. 1825 B.C. A son or grandson of Benjamin. Genesis 46:21.

RUFUS [ROO-fuhs: "red"]

1. A.D. 50. A brother of Alexander and son of Simon of Cyrene, the man who carried the cross for Christ. Mark 15:21.

2. A.D. 55. A Christian who was greeted by Paul in his letter to the Roman church. Romans 16:13. Possibly the same as Rufus 1.

S

SABTA [SAB-tuh]. B.C. date unknown. A Hamite listed in the table of nations. 1 Chronicles 1:9.

SABTAH [SAB-tuh]. B.C. date unknown. Listed in the table of nations. Genesis 10:7. See Sabta.

SABTECHAH [SAB-tuh-kuh]. B.C. date unknown. Last of the sons of Cush listed in the table of nations. Genesis 10:7.

SACAR [SAY-kahr]

1. 1025 B.C. Father of Ahiam, one of David's thirty mighty men. 1 Chronicles 11:35. Called Sharar in 2 Samuel 23:33.

2. 975 B.C. A gatekeeper in David's day. 1 Chronicles 26:4.

SACHIAH [suh-KI-uh]. B.C. date unknown. Listed in the genealogy of Benjamin. 1 Chronicles 8:10.

SALLAI [SAL-i]. 450 B.C. A man who settled in Jerusalem after the Exile. Nehemiah 11:8.

SALLU [SAL-oo]

1. 525 B.C. A priest who returned to Judah with Zerubbabel after the Exile. Nehemiah 12:7, 20.

2. 450 B.C. A Benjamite listed among the residents of Jerusalem after its walls

were rebuilt. 1 Chronicles 9:7; Nehemiah 11:7.

SALMA [SAL-muh: "strength"]. B.C. date unknown. A descendant of Caleb and founder of Bethlehem. 1 Chronicles 2:51, 54.

SALMON [SAL-muhn: "clothing"]. B.C. date unknown. Ancestor of Boaz, the second husband of Ruth. Ruth 4:20, 21; Matthew 1:4, 5: Luke 3:32.

SALU [SAY-loo]. 1425 B.C. Father of Zimri, who was slain with his Midianite paramour by Phinehas. Numbers 25:14.

SAMLAH [SAM-luh: "garment"]. B.C. date unknown. A pre-Israelite king of Edom. Genesis 36:36, 37.

SAMSON [SAM-suhn: "sun's man" or "distinguished"]. 1095–1075 B.C. History's strongest man, who served as a judge for twenty years. Judges 13—16; Hebrews 11:32.

SAMUEL [SAM-yoo-uhl: "name of God" or "God hears"]. 1063–1043 B.C. Notable as a prophet and the last judge of Israel. 1 Samuel 1:20–28; 3; 4; 7—13; 15; 16; 28:3–16; 1 Chronicles 6:27, 28.

SANBALLAT [san-BAL-uht: "Sin (the god) has given life"]. 450 B.C. A Samaritan who opposed the rebuilding of Jerusalem's wall in Nehemiah's time. According to Egyptian papyri, he became governor of Samaria. Nehemiah 2:10, 19; 6:1–14; 13:28.

SAPH [SAF]. 975 B.C. A descendant of Philistine giants, killed by Sibbecai. 2 Samuel 21:18. Called Sippai in 1 Chronicles 20:4.

SARAPH [SAIR-uhf]. B.C. date unknown. A Judahite who ruled in Moab. 1 Chronicles 4:22.

SARGON [SAHR-gahn: "the king is legitimate"]. 722–705 B.C. Sargon II, son of Tiglath-Pileser and successor of his brother, Shalmaneser II, king of Assyria. He conquered Samaria and deported the Israelites. Mentioned by name only in Isaiah 20:1.

SAUL [SAWL: "asked"]

1. 1043–1010 B.C. The first king of Israel. 1 Samuel 9—31.

2. A.D. 35. Hebrew name of the apostle Paul. Acts 7:58—8:3; 9:1—30:13.

SCEVA [SEE-vuh]. A.D. 55. A Jewish priest in Ephesus whose sons attempted to invoke the name of Jesus to cast out evil spirits. Acts 19:14.

SEBA [SEE-buh]. B.C. date unknown. Listed in the table of nations. Genesis 10:7.

SECUNDUS [Seh-KUN-duhs: "second"]. A.D. 55. A Thessalonian Christian and companion of Paul during part of his third missionary journey. Acts 20:4.

SEGUB [SEE-gub]

1. B.C. date unknown. Listed only in the genealogy of Judah. 1 Chronicles 2:21, 22.

2. 850 B.C. Youngest son of Hiel, who died when his father rebuilt Jericho. 1 Kings 16:34. (See Josh. 6:26.)

SEIR [SEER]. B.C. date unknown. Ancestor of the inhabitants of the land of Seir. Genesis 36:20.

SELED [SEE-led]. B.C. date unknown. Listed in the genealogy of Jerahmeel, a descendant of Judah. 1 Chronicles 2:30.

SEMACHIAH [SEM-uh-KI-uh: "Yahweh has sustained"]. 975 B.C. A Levite who served as tabernacle gatekeeper in David's time. 1 Chronicles 26:7.

SEMEI [SEM-ee-i]. B.C. date unknown. Listed in the genealogy of Christ in Luke 3:26.

9. 609–608 B.C. Another name for Jehoahaz, son and successor of Josiah, king of Judah. 1 Chronicles 3:15; Jeremiah 22:11.

10. B.C. date unknown. Ancestor of a family of gatekeepers that returned to Judah after the Exile. Ezra 2:42; Nehemiah 7:45.

11. 450 B.C. A chief gatekeeper at the temple in Jerusalem after the Exile. 1 Chronicles 9:17, 19, 31.

12. 450 B.C. A gatekeeper listed among the Levites who took pagan wives after the Exile. Ezra 10:24.

13. 450 B.C. A descendant of Binnui, he also took a pagan wife after the Exile. Ezra 10:42.

14. 450 B.C. He and his daughters helped repair the walls of Jerusalem. Nehemiah 3:12.

SHALLUN [SHAL-uhn]. 450 B.C. One who helped repair the wall of Jerusalem in Nehemiah's day. Nehemiah 3:15.

SHALMAI [SHAL-mi]. B.C. date unknown. Ancestor of a family of temple servants that returned to Judah with Zerubbabel. Ezra 2:46.

SHALMAN [SHAL-muhn]. B.C. date unknown. He sacked Beth Arbel, but is mentioned only in Hosea 10:14. Perhaps another name for Shalmaneser of Assyria, or the Moabite king Salmans.

SHALMANESER [SHAL-muh-NEE-zuhr: "Sulman (the god) is chief"]. 727–722 B.C. Shalmaneser II, son and successor of Tiglath-Pileser, king of Assyria. 2 Kings 17:36; 18:9.

SHAMA [SHAY-muh: "he has heard"]. 1000 B.C. He and his brother were members of David's military elite. 1 Chronicles 11:44.

SHAMGAR [SHAM-gahr]. B.C. date unknown. A judge who "killed six hundred men of the Philistines with an ox goad." Judges 3:31; 5:6.

SHAMHUTH [SHAM-huth]. 975 B.C. Commander of the fifth division of David's army. 1 Chronicles 27:8.

SHAMIR [SHAY-muhr: "sharp point; thorn"]. 1000 B.C. A Levite family in David's time. 1 Chronicles 24:24.

SHAMMA [SHAM-uh]. B.C. date unknown. Listed only in the genealogy of Asher. 1 Chronicles 7:37.

SHAMMAH [SHAM-uh: "desolation, waste"]

1. 1875 B.C. An Edomite chief, the grandson of Esau. Genesis 36:13, 17.

2. 1025 B.C. An older brother of David. 1 Samuel 16:9; 17:13. Also called Shimea (1 Chron. 2:13; 20:7) and Shimeah (2 Sam. 13:3, 32).

3. 1000 B.C. One of the three leaders of the military elite known as David's mighty men. 2 Samuel 23:11, 12, 33. Called Shageh in 1 Chronicles 11:34.

4. 1000 B.C. Another member of David's thirty mighty men. 2 Samuel 23:25. Called Shammoth in 1 Chronicles 11:27.

SHAMMAI [SHAM-i]

1. B.C. date unknown. A Judahite listed in the genealogy of Jerahmeel. 1 Chronicles 2:28, 32.

2. B.C. date unknown. Listed in the genealogy of the clans of Caleb. 1 Chronicles 2:44, 45.

3. B.C. date unknown. Listed in the genealogy of Judah. 1 Chronicles 4:17.

SHAMMOTH [SHAM-ahth]. 1000 B.C. One of David's mighty men. 1 Chronicles 11:27. Listed as Shammah in 2 Samuel 23:25.

Secretaries were scribes, trained to record in writing the thoughts and words of those who hired them.

SHAMMUA [SHAM-moo-uh: "renowned"]

1. 1400 B.C. Representative of the tribe of Reuben sent by Moses to spy out the land of Canaan. Numbers 13:4.

2. 975 B.C. A son of David and Bathsheba born in Jerusalem. 2 Samuel 5:14; 1 Chronicles 3:5.

3. B.C. date unknown. Ancestor of a Levite who settled in Jerusalem after the Exile. Nehemiah 11:17. Called Shemaiah in 1 Chronicles 9:16.

4. 500 B.C. Head of a priestly family in the time of Joiakim. Nehemiah 12:18.

SHAMSHERAI [SHAM-shuh-ri]. B.C. date unknown. Listed in the genealogy of Benjamin. 1 Chronicles 8:26.

SHAPHAM [SHAY-fuhm]. 750 B.C. A chief Gadite who lived in Bashan. 1 Chronicles 5:12.

SHAPHAN [SHAY-fuhn: "rock badger"]

1. 650 B.C. Grandfather of Gedaliah the governor. 2 Kings 22:12; Jeremiah 26:24; 40:5, 11.

2. 625 B.C. Secretary of Josiah, who brought the king the rediscovered Book of the Law. 2 Kings 22:3–14; 25:22; 2 Chronicles 34:8–21; Jeremiah 36:10–12.

3. 625 B.C. Father of a man who took Jeremiah's letter to the exiles in Babylon. Jeremiah 29:3. Possibly the same as Shaphan 1 or 2.

4. 625 B.C. Father of one of seventy idolaters seen by Ezekiel in the Jerusalem temple. Ezekiel 8:11.

SHAPHAT [SHAF-at: "judged"]

1. 1450 B.C. Representative of the tribe of Simeon whom Moses sent to explore the land of Canaan. Numbers 13:5.

2. 975 B.C. An official of David in charge of royal herds. 1 Chronicles 27:29.

3. 875 B.C. Father of Elisha the prophet. 1 Kings 10:16, 19.

4. B.C. date unknown. A descendant of Zerubbabel listed in the genealogy of the royal line. 1 Chronicles 3:22.

5. 750 B.C. A Gadite chief who lived in Bashan. 1 Chronicles 5:12.

SHARAI [SHAIR-i]. 450 B.C. He took a pagan wife after the Exile. Ezra 10:40.

SHARAR [SHAR-ahr]. 1000 B.C. Father of a member of David's military elite. 2 Samuel 23:33. Called Sacar in 1 Chronicles 11:35.

SHAREZER [shuh-REE-zuhr: "he has protected the king"]

1. 675 B.C. A son of Sennacherib, king of Assyria, who helped murder his father in 681 B.C. 2 Kings 19:37; Isaiah 37:38.

2. 525 B.C. A man sent by the people of Bethel to consult priests and prophets in Jerusalem regarding the practice of ritual fasting. Zechariah 7:2.

SHASHAI [SHAY-shi: "noble"]. 450 B.C. A descendant of Binnui who divorced a pagan wife in Ezra's time. Ezra 10:40.

SHASHAK [SHAY-shak]. B.C. date unknown. Listed in the genealogy of Benjamin. 1 Chronicles 8:14, 25.

SHAUL [SHAWL: variant of Saul]

1. 1875 B.C. A son of Simeon by a Canaanite woman. Genesis 46:10; Numbers 26:13; 1 Chronicles 4:24.

2. B.C. date unknown. A pre-Israelite king of Edom. Genesis 36:37, 38.

3. B.C. date unknown. A man listed in the genealogy of Levi. 1 Chronicles 6:24.

SHAVSHA [SHAV-shuh]. 975 B.C. Secretary of King David. 1 Chronicles 18:16. See Seraiah 3.

SHEAL [SHEE-uhl: "request"]. 450 B.C. One who wed a pagan wife after the Exile. Ezra 10:29.

SHEALTIEL [shea-AL-tee-uhl]. 550 B.C. Eldest son of Jehoiachin and father of Zerubbabel. His brother Pedaiah is identified as the father of Zerubbabel in 1 Chronicles 3:17. It is likely that Shealtiel adopted him or that Zerubbabel was born as the result of a Levirate marriage. Ezra 3:2; Haggai 1:1; Matthew 1:12; Luke 3:27.

SHEARIAH [SHEE-uh-RI-uh: "Yahweh considers"]. A descendant of Jonathan, son of Saul. 1 Chronicles 5:38; 9:44.

SHEAR-JASHUB [SHEER-JAH-shub: "a remnant shall return"]. 725 B.C. Symbolic name of Isaiah's first son, foreshadowing the restoration of the Jews after the Exile. Isaiah 7:3.

SHEBA [SHEE-buh: "oath"]

1. B.C. date unknown. Listed in the table of nations. Genesis 10:7.

2. B.C. date unknown. A descendant of Shem listed in the table of nations. Genesis 10:28.

3. B.C. date unknown. A descendant of Abraham and Keturah. Genesis 25:3.

4. 975 B.C. A Benjamite who instigated a brief and unsuccessful rebellion against David. 2 Samuel 20.

5. 750 B.C. Head of a Gadite family during the time of Jotham. 1 Chronicles 5:13.

SHEBANIAH [sheb-uh-NI-uh]

1. 1000 B.C. A priest who blew the trumpet before the ark of the covenant as David brought it into Jerusalem. 1 Chronicles 15:24.

2. 400 B.C. A Levite involved in the ceremony of covenant renewal in Nehemiah's time. Nehemiah 9:4, 5.

3. 400 B.C. A priest who sealed the covenant renewal pact with God. Nehemiah 10:4.

4. and 5. 400 B.C. Two Levites who also put their seals upon the covenant

renewal pact. Nehemiah 10:10, 12. Either may be the same as Shebaniah 2.

SHEBER [SHEE-buhr: "breach"(?)]. B.C. date unknown. A son of Caleb by his concubine. In the genealogy of Judah in 1 Chronicles 2:48.

SHEBNA [SHEB-nuh: "youthfulness"(?)]. 725 B.C. Secretary of Hezekiah whom Eliakim replaced as palace administrator. 2 Kings 18:18—19:2; Isaiah 22:15-21; 36:3—37:2.

SHECANIAH [SHEK-uh-NI-uh: "dweller with Yahweh"]

1. 975 B.C. Head of the tenth division of priests in David's day. 1 Chronicles 24:11.

2. 725 B.C. A priest who helped distribute contributions among his priestly brethren. 2 Chronicles 31:15.

3. 525 B.C. A priest who returned to Judah with Zerubbabel. Nehemiah 12:3.

4. B.C. date unknown. Ancestor of a descendant of David who returned to Judah with Ezra. Ezra 8:3.

5. B.C. date unknown. A descendant of Zerubbabel listed in the royal line. 1 Chronicles 3:21, 22. Probably the same as #4.

6. 475 B.C. Father of Shemaiah, who helped repair the wall of Jerusalem. Nehemiah 3:29.

7. 450 B.C. Head of a family that returned to Judah with Ezra. Ezra 8:5.

8. 450 B.C. One who supported Ezra's reform requiring the divorce of pagan wives. Ezra 10:2-5.

9. 450 B.C. Father-in-law of Tobiah the Ammonite, an enemy of Nehemiah. Nehemiah 6:18.

SHECHEM [SHEK-uhm: "shoulder"]

1. 1000 B.C. He raped Dinah, the daughter of Jacob. Genesis 34:2.

2. B.C. date unknown. A descendant of Manasseh and head of a clan. Numbers 26:31; Joshua 17:2.

3. B.C. date unknown. Listed in the genealogy of Manasseh. 1 Chronicles 7:19.

SHEDEUR [SHED-ee-uhr: "shedder of light"]. 1475 B.C. Father of Elizur, leader of the tribe of Reuben at the time of the Exodus. Numbers 1:5.

SHEHARIAH [SHEH-huh-RI-uh]. B.C. date unknown. Listed in the genealogy of Benjamin. 1 Chronicles 8:26.

SHELAH [SHEE-luh]

1. B.C. date unknown. A descendant of Shem and an ancestor of Abraham. Genesis 10:24; 11:12-15; 1 Chronicles 1:18, 24; Luke 3:35.

2. 1850 B.C. Third son of Judah, promised but never married to Tamar. Genesis 38:5, 11-26; Numbers 26:20; 1 Chronicles 4:21.

SHELEMIAH [SHEL-uh-MI-uh: "Yahweh is recompense"]

1. 975 B.C. He was selected to guard the East Gate of the sanctuary in David's time. 1 Chronicles 26:14. Called Meshelemiah in 1 Chronicles 26:1, 2.

2. 650 B.C. Sent by the officials of Jehoiakim to seize the scroll of Jeremiah's prophecies. Jeremiah 36:14.

3. 625 B.C. Father of an official of Zedekiah who threw Jeremiah into a cistern. Jeremiah 37:3; 38:1.

4. 625 B.C. Father of the captain who arrested Jeremiah. Jeremiah 37:13.

5. 600 B.C. He was sent by King Jehoiakim to arrest Baruch and Jeremiah. Jeremiah 36:26.

6. 475 B.C. Father of a man who rebuilt a section of Jerusalem's wall. Nehemiah 3:30.

7. and 8. 450 B.C. Two of Binnui's descendants who divorced pagan wives in Ezra's time. Ezra 10:39, 41.

9. 425 B.C. A priest appointed as a temple treasurer by Nehemiah. Nehemiah 13:13.

SHELEPH [SHEE-lef]. B.C. date unknown. A descendant of Shem listed in the table of nations. Genesis 10:26.

SHELESH [SHEE-lash]. B.C. date unknown. Listed in the genealogy of Asher. 1 Chronicles 7:35.

SHELOMI [shuh-LOH-mi: "peace"]. 1425 B.C. Father of the representative of the tribe of Asher appointed by Moses to help assign inheritances in Canaan. Numbers 34:27.

SHELOMITH [shuh-LOH-mith: "peaceful"]

1. B.C. date unknown. A Levite descended from Izhar. 1 Chronicles 23:18. Called Shelomoth in 1 Chronicles 24:22.

2. 975 B.C. He was made treasurer of the valuables in the temple. 1 Chronicles 26:25–28.

3. 900 B.C. Son or daughter of King Rehoboam. 2 Chronicles 11:20.

4. 450 B.C. Head of a family that returned to Judah with Ezra. Ezra 8:10.

SHELOMOTH [shuh-LOH-mahth: "peaceful"]

1. 1000 B.C. Head of a family of Levites mentioned in David's day. 1 Chronicles 23:9.

2. B.C. date unknown. Listed in the genealogy of Levi. 1 Chronicles 24:22. See Shelomith 1.

SHELUMIEL [shuh-LOO-mee-uhl: "God is peace"]. 1450 B.C. Leader of the tribe of Simeon during the Exodus. Numbers 1:6.

SHEM [SHEM: "name" or "renown"]. B.C. date unknown. Son of Noah and ancestor of the Semitic peoples. Genesis 5:32; 9:23–27; 10:21, 22; 11:10, 11.

SHEMA [SHEE-muh: "fame: rumor"]

1. B.C. date unknown. A descendant of Caleb listed in the genealogy of Judah. 1 Chronicles 2:43, 44.

2. B.C. date unknown. Listed in the genealogy of Reuben. 1 Chronicles 5:8.

3. B.C. date unknown. Head of a Benjamite family who helped defeat the Philistines of Gath. 1 Chronicles 8:13.

4. 450 B.C. He stood at Ezra's right at the reading of the Law. Nehemiah 8:4.

SHEMAAH [shuh-MAY-uh: "fame"]. 1025 B.C. A Benjamite whose two sons joined David at Ziklag. 1 Chronicles 12:3.

SHEMAIAH [shuh-MAY-yuh: "Yahweh hears"]

1. B.C. date unknown. Ancestor of a Simeonite who lived during the reign of Hezekiah. 1 Chronicles 4:37.

2. B.C. date unknown. Listed in the genealogy of Reuben. 1 Chronicles 5:4.

3. 1000 B.C. A chief Levite who helped bring the ark of the covenant to Jerusalem. 1 Chronicles 15:8, 11.

4. 975 B.C.. A Levite scribe who recorded the divisions of the priests in David's day. 1 Chronicles 24:6.

5. 975 B.C. Head of a family of tabernacle gatekeepers in David's time. 1 Chronicles 26:4, 6, 7.

6. 925 B.C. A prophet who told Rehoboam not to go to war against the

ten northern tribes after their rebellion. 1 Kings 12:22–24; 2 Chronicles 11:2–4; 12:5–8, 15.

7. 875 B.C. A Levite sent by Jehoshaphat to teach the Law throughout Judah. 2 Chronicles 17:8.

8. 725 B.C. A Levite who helped purify the temple in Hezekiah's time. 2 Chronicles 29:14.

9. 725 B.C. An assistant to Kore, a Levite in charge of distributing offerings among the towns of the priests. 2 Chronicles 31:15.

10. 625 B.C. A chief Levite who contributed to the Passover celebration during Josiah's religious revival. 2 Chronicles 35:9.

11. 625 B.C. Father of Uriah, a prophet killed by Jehoiakim. Jeremiah 26:20.

12. 625 B.C. Father of an official of Jehoiakim who urged the king not to burn the scroll of Jeremiah. Jeremiah 36:12.

13. 600 B.C. A false prophet among the exiles and an opponent of Jeremiah. Jeremiah 29:24–32.

14. B.C. date unknown. A Levite descended from Asaph. Nehemiah 12:36.

15. 525 B.C. A priest who returned to Judah with Zerubbabel after the Exile. Nehemiah 10:8; 12:6, 18.

16. 475 B.C. Father of a man who settled in Jerusalem in Nehemiah's time. 1 Chronicles 9:16. Called Shammua in Nehemiah 11:17.

17. 450 B.C. A Levite who settled in Jerusalem after the Exile. 1 Chronicles 9:14; Nehemiah 11:15.

18. 450 B.C. He returned to Judah with Ezra after the Exile. Ezra 8:13.

19. 450 B.C. He was sent as part of a delegation to retrieve Levites to serve at the temple in Jerusalem. Ezra 8:16.

20. 450 B.C. A priest who took a pagan wife after the Exile. Ezra 10:21.

21. 450 B.C. A man required to put away his pagan wife in Ezra's time. Ezra 10:31.

22. 450 B.C. He helped rebuild the wall in Nehemiah's time. Nehemiah 3:29.

23. 450 B.C. A false prophet hired by Tobiah and Sanballat to try to frighten Nehemiah into an act of sacrilege. Nehemiah 6:10–13.

24. 450 B.C. A priest who signed the renewal covenant pact in Nehemiah's time, possibly with the name of a family ancestor (see Shemaiah 15). Nehemiah 10:8.

25. 450 B.C. A leader who participated in dedicating the rebuilt wall of Jerusalem. Nehemiah 12:34.

26. 450 B.C. A musician in the procession at the dedication of Jerusalem's wall. Nehemiah 12:35.

27. 450 B.C. A priest in one of the choirs at the dedication of the wall. Nehemiah 12:42.

28. B.C. date unknown. A descendant of Zerubbabel listed in the genealogy of the royal line. 1 Chronicles 3:22.

SHEMARIAH [SHEM-uh-RI-uh: "Yahweh keeps"]

1. 1000 B.C. A Benjamite warrior who defected to David at Ziklag. 1 Chronicles 12:5.

2. 900 B.C. A son of King Rehoboam of Judah. 2 Chronicles 11:19.

3. and 4. 450 B.C. Two men who took pagan wives after the Exile. Ezra 10:32, 41.

SHEMEBER [shem-EE-buhr]. 2100 B.C. A king allied with the kings of Sodom and Gomorrah in the defeat by Chedorlaomer. Genesis 14:2.

SHEMED [SHEE-med: "destruction"]. B.C. date unknown. Builder of the towns of Ono and Lod, listed in the genealogy of Benjamin. 1 Chronicles 8:12.

SHEMER [SHEE-muhr: "watch"]

1. An ancestor of Ethan, a chief minister of music in David's day. 1 Chronicles 6:46.

2. 875 B.C. Owner of the hill on which Omri built the city of Samaria. 1 Kings 16:24.

SHEMIDA [shuh-MI-duh]. B.C. date unknown. Ancestor of a clan of Manasseh. Numbers 26:32; 1 Chronicles 7:19.

SHEMIRAMOTH [shuh-MEER-uh-mahth]

1. 1000 B.C. A Levite who played the lyre while the ark of the covenant was brought into Jerusalem. 1 Chronicles 15:18, 20; 16:5.

2. 875 B.C. A Levite sent by King Jehoshaphat to teach the Law in the cities of Judah. 2 Chronicles 17:8.

SHEMUEL [SHEM-yoo-uhl: variant form of Samuel]. 1400 B.C. The representative of the tribe of Simeon appointed to help assign inheritances in the land of Canaan. Numbers 34:20.

SHENAZZAR [shuh-NAZ-uhr]. 550 B.C. A son of Jehoiachin. 1 Chronicles 3:18.

SHEPHATIAH [SHEF-uh-TI-uh: "Yahweh is judge"]

1. 1000 B.C. A Benjamite who joined David at Ziklag. 1 Chronicles 12:5.

2. 975 B.C. A son born to David in Hebron. 2 Samuel 3:4; 1 Chronicles 3:3.

3. 975 B.C. Officer over the tribe of Simeon in David's time. 1 Chronicles 27:16.

4. 950 B.C. A servant of Solomon whose descendants returned to Judah with Zerubbabel. Ezra 2:57; Nehemiah 7:59.

5. 850 B.C. A son of Jehoshaphat and younger brother of Jehoram. 2 Chronicles 21:2.

6. B.C. date unknown. Ancestor of a family whose members returned to Judah with Zerubbabel and Ezra. Ezra 2:4; 8:8; Nehemiah 7:9.

7. B.C. date unknown. Ancestor of a Judahite who settled in Jerusalem in Nehemiah's time. Nehemiah 11:4.

8. 600 B.C. One of the officials of Zedekiah who threw Jeremiah into a cistern to die. Jeremiah 38:1.

9. 475 B.C. Father of a Benjamite who settled in Jerusalem after the Exile. 1 Chronicles 9:8.

SHEPHO [SHEE-foh]. 1950 B.C. A son of Shobal, a Horite chief in Esau's time. Genesis 36:23; 1 Chronicles 1:40 .

SHEPHUPHAN [sheh-FOO-fan]. 1825 B.C. A grandson of Benjamin. 1 Chronicles 8:5. Called Shupham in Numbers 26:39; possibly the same as Muppim in Genesis 46:21.

SHEREBIAH [SHAIR-uh-BI-uh]

1. 525 B.C. A Levite who returned to Judah with Zerubbabel after the Exile. Nehemiah 12:8.

2. 450 B.C. Head of a Levite family recruited by Ezra to serve at the Jerusalem temple. Ezra 8:18, 24; Nehemiah 8:7; 9:4, 5.

3. 450 B.C. A Levite who sealed the covenant renewal pact in Nehemiah's time. Nehemiah 10:12.

4. 450 B.C. A chief Levite when Eliashib was high priest. Nehemiah 12:24. Probably the same as #2.

SHERESH [SHEER-esh]. B.C. date unknown. Listed only in the genealogy of Manasseh. 1 Chronicles 7:16.

SHESHAI [SHEE-shi]. 1450 B.C. A giant who was driven out of Hebron by Caleb. Numbers 13:22; Joshua 15:14; Judges 1:10.

SHESHAN [SHEE-shan]. B.C. date unknown. A descendant of Judah who had no sons. He gave his daughter to his adopted Egyptian slave to continue his line. 1 Chronicles 2:31, 34, 35.

SHESHBAZZAR [shesh-BAZ-uhr]. 525 B.C. A prince of Judah who brought the sacred temple vessels to Jerusalem when Cyrus decreed the rebuilding of the temple. He was appointed governor over Judah. Ezra 1:8, 11; 5:14, 16. Possibly the Persian name of Zerubbabel.

SHETH [SHETH: "tumult"(?)]. B.C. date unknown. A descriptive name given to the Moabites in Balaam's fourth oracle. Numbers 24:17.

SHETHAR [SHEE-thahr]. 475 B.C. One of seven nobles who advised King Xerxes. Esther 1:14.

SHETHAR-BOZNAI [SHEE-thahr-BAHZ-ni]. 525 B.C. A Persian official who sent a letter to King Darius opposing the rebuilding of the temple. Ezra 5:3, 6; 6:6, 13.

SHEVA [SHEE-vuh]

1. B.C. date unknown. Son of Caleb by his concubine, Maachah; listed in the genealogy of Judah. 1 Chronicles 2:49.

2. 1000 B.C. David's secretary. 2 Samuel 20:25. See Seraiah 3.

SHILHI [SHIL-hi]. 925 B.C. Grandfather of Jehoshaphat, king of Judah. 1 Kings 22:42.

SHILLEM [SHIL-uhm]. 1875 B.C. A grandson of Jacob and ancestral head of a clan. Genesis 46:24; Numbers 26:49.

SHILONI [SHY-loan-ih] B.C. date unknown. Ancestors of a Judahite who settled in Jerusalem after the Exile. Nehemiah 11:5.

SHILSHAH [SHIL-shuh]. B.C. date unknown. Listed in the genealogy of Asher. 1 Chronicles 7:37.

SHIMEA [SHIM-ee-uh: "fame" or "God has heard"]

1. B.C. date unknown. Listed only in the genealogy of Levi. 1 Chronicles 6:30.

2. 1075 B.C. A Levite descended from Gershon and grandfather of Asaph, a chief minister of music in David's day. 1 Chronicles 6:39.

3. 1025 B.C. An older brother of David. 1 Chronicles 2:13; 20:7. Also called Shammah (1 Sam. 16:9), and Shimeah (2 Sam. 13:3, 32; 21:21).

SHIMEAH [SHIM-ee-uh: "fame" or "God has heard"]

1. 1070 B.C. A relative of King Saul who lived in Jerusalem. 1 Chronicles 8:32. Called Shimeam in 1 Chronicles 9:38.

2. 1025 B.C. A brother of David. 2 Samuel 13:3, 32; 21:21.

SHIMEAM [SHIM-ee-uhm: "fame" or "God has heard"]. 1075 B.C. An uncle of Kish, father of Saul. 1 Chronicles 9:38. See Shimeah 1.

SHIMEI [SHIM-ee-I: "Yahweh hear me"]

1. 1850 B.C. A son of Gershon son of Levi; ancestral head of a Levite clan. Exodus 6:17; Numbers 3:18; 1 Chronicles 23:7–10; Zechariah 12:13.

2. B.C. date unknown. Listed in the genealogy of Simeon. 1 Chronicles 4:26, 27.

3. B.C. date unknown. Listed in the genealogy of Reuben. 1 Chronicles 5:4.

4. B.C. date unknown. Listed in the genealogy of Levi. 1 Chronicles 6:29.

5. B.C. date unknown. Listed in the genealogy of Heman, a chief minister of music in David's day. 1 Chronicles 6:42.

6. B.C. date unknown. Listed in the genealogy of Benjamin. 1 Chronicles 8:21.

7. B.C. date unknown. A Levite descended from Gershon. 1 Chronicles 23:9. Possibly the same as #5.

8. B.C. date unknown. A descendant of Kish and ancestor of Mordecai. Esther 2:5.

9. 975 B.C. A kinsman of Saul who cursed David as he fled from Absalom. 2 Samuel 16:5–13; 19:16–23; 1 Kings 2:8, 9, 36–46.

10. 975 B.C. An officer of David who remained loyal when Adonijah attempted to seize the throne. 1 Kings 1:8.

11. 975 B.C. A son of Jeduthun and head of the tenth division of ministers of music in David's time. 1 Chronicles 25:3, 17.

12. 975 B.C. Overseer of King David's vineyards. 1 Chronicles 27:27.

13. 950 B.C. One of Solomon's twelve district governors. 1 Kings 4:18.

14. 725 B.C. He helped purify the temple in Hezekiah's time. 2 Chronicles 29:14.

15. 725 B.C. Brother of Cononiah and next in rank in charge of the temple treasury. 2 Chronicles 31:12, 13. Possibly the same as Shimei 14.

16. 525 B.C. Grandson of Jehoiachin, listed in the genealogy of the royal line. 1 Chronicles 3:19.

17. 450 B.C. A Levite who took a pagan wife after the Exile. Ezra 10:23.

18 and 19. 450 B.C. Two more men who took pagan wives after the Exile. Ezra 10:33, 38.

SHIMEON [SHIM-ee-uhn: "hearing" or "(God) has heard"]. 450 B.C. He divorced his pagan wife in Ezra's time. Ezra 10:31.

SHIMON [SHI-muhn]. B.C. date unknown. Listed in the genealogy of Judah. 1 Chronicles 4:20.

SHIMRATH [SHIM-rath: "watch"]. B.C. date unknown. Listed in the genealogy of Benjamin. 1 Chronicles 8:21.

SHIMRI [SHIM-ri: "(Yahweh) watches"]

1. B.C. date unknown. Listed in the genealogy of Simeon. 1 Chronicles 4:37.

2. 1025 B.C. Father of one of David's mighty men. 1 Chronicles 11:45.

3. 975 B.C. He was among the tabernacle gatekeepers in David's time. 1 Chronicles 26:10.

4. 725 B.C. A Levite who helped purify the temple in Hezekiah's day. 2 Chronicles 29:13.

SHIMRON [SHIM-rahn: "a guard"]. 1875 B.C. Fourth son of Issachar and ancestral head of a clan. Genesis 46:13; Numbers 26:24.

SHIMSHAI [SHIM-shi]. 450 B.C. A Persian secretary who helped write a letter to Artaxerxes, king of Persia, opposing the rebuilding of Jerusalem's walls. Ezra 4:6–23.

SHINAB [SHI-nab]. 2100 B.C. King who rebelled against Chedorlaomer and was defeated. Genesis 14:2.

SHIPHI [SHI-fi]. 750 B.C. Father of Ziza, a Simeonite who lived in the days of Hezekiah. 1 Chronicles 4:37.

SHIPHTAN (SHIF-tan: 'lodge"]. 1420 B.C. Father of an Ephraimite leader appointed by Moses to help divide the land of Canaan. Numbers 34:24.

SHISHA [SHI-shuh]. 975 B.C. Father of Solomon's secretaries, Elihoreph and Ahijah. 1 Kings 4:3.

SHISHAK [SHI-shak]. 925 B.C. Egyptian pharaoh and founder of the twenty-second dynasty. 1 Kings 11:40; 14:25; 2 Chronicles 12:2–9.

SHITRAI [SHI-tri]. 975 B.C. A man in charge of the flocks that grazed in Sharon. 1 Chronicles 27:29.

SHIZA [SHI-zuh]. 1025 B.C. The father of one of David's thirty mighty men. 1 Chronicles 11:42.

SHOBAB [SHOH-bab]

1. B.C. date unknown. A son of Caleb, a descendant of Judah. 1 Chronicles 2:18.

2. 975 B.C. A son born to David in Jerusalem. 2 Samuel 5:14; 1 Chronicles 3:5; 14:4.

SHOBACH [SHOH-bak]. 975 B.C. Syrian commander of Hadadezer's army, defeated and killed in battle against King David. 2 Samuel 10:16–18. Called Shophach in 1 Chronicles 19:16–18.

SHOBAI [SHOH-bi]. B.C. date unknown. Ancestor of a family of temple gate-keepers that returned to Judah after the Exile. Ezra 2:42; Nehemiah 7:45.

SHOBAL [SHOH-buhl]

1. 1975 B.C. A Horite chief living in the land of Seir in Ezra's time. Genesis 36:20, 23, 29.

2. B.C. date unknown. A descendant of Caleb who founded Kirjath Jearim. 1 Chronicles 2:50–52.

3. B.C. date unknown. Ancestor of clans listed in the genealogy of Judah. 1 Chronicles 4:1, 2. Probably the same as Shobal 2.

SHOBEK [SHOH-bek]. 450 B.C. A leader who signed the covenant renewal pact in Nehemiah's time. Nehemiah 10:24.

SHOBI [SHOH-bi]. 975 B.C. A prince of Ammon who brought David food as he fled from Absalom. 2 Samuel 17:27.

SHOHAM [SHOH-ham]. 1000 B.C. Head of a family of Levites who served in David's time. 1 Chronicles 24:27.

SHOMER [SHOH-muhr. "keeper: watcher"]. B.C. date unknown. Listed in the genealogy of Asher. 1 Chronicles 7:32, 34.

SHOPHACH [SHOH-fak]. 975 B.C. General of the Syrian army who was slain by David. 1 Chronicles 19:16–18.

SHUA [SHOO-uh: "prosperity"]. 1925 B.C. Canaanite whose daughter married Judah, son of Jacob. Genesis 38:2, 12.

SHUAH [SHOO-uh: "depression"]. 2000 B.C. A son of Abraham by Keturah. Genesis 25:2.

SHUAL [SHOO-uhl: "fox" or "jackal"]. B.C. date unknown. Listed only in the genealogy of Asher. 1 Chronicles 7:36.

SHUBAEL [SHOO-bay-uhl: "God's captive"]

1. B.C. date unknown. A Levite descended from Amram. 1 Chronicles 24:20.

2. 1000 B.C. A Levite descended from Gershom, son of Moses: in charge of the treasuries in David's time. 1 Chronicles 23:16; 26:24.

3. 575 B.C. A son of Heman and head of the thirteenth division of singers in David's time. 1 Chronicles 25:20.

SHUHAH [SHOO-huh: "depression"]. B.C. date unknown. Listed only in the genealogy of the clans of Judah. 1 Chronicles 4:11.

SHUHAM [SHOO-ham]. 1875 B.C. A son of Dan and ancestor of the Shuhamite clan. Numbers 26:42. Called Hushim in Genesis 46:23.

SHUNI [SHOO-ni]. 1875 B.C. A son of Gad and ancestral head of a clan. Genesis 45:16; Numbers 26:15.

SHUPHAM [SHOO-fam) 1825 B.C. A son or grandson of Benjamin. Numbers 26:39. Called Shephuphan in 1 Chronicles 8:5.

SHUPPIM [SHUP-im]. 975 B.C. A gatekeeper in the days of David. 1 Chronicles 26:16.

SHUTHELAH [SHOO-thuh-luh]

1. 1850 B.C. A son of Ephraim and ancestor of the clans of Ephraim. Numbers 26:35, 36; 1 Chronicles 7:20.

2. B.C. date unknown. Another descended from Ephraim, son of Joseph. 1 Chronicles 7:21.

SIA [SI-uh]. B.C. date unknown. Ancestor of a post-exilic family of temple servants. Nehemiah 7:47.

SIAHA [SI-uh-huh]. B.C. date unknown. Ancestor of a family of temple servants that returned to Judah with Zerubbabel. Ezra 2:44.

SIBBECHAI [SIB-uh-ki: "Yahweh intervenes"]. One of David's mighty men who also slew a Philistine giant. 2 Samuel 21:18; 1 Chronicles 11:29; 27:11.

SIHON [SI-hahn]. 1425 B.C. An Amorite king who denied the Israelites passage through his territory and was killed in the subsequent battle. Numbers 21:21–34: Deuteronomy 2:24–30.

SILAS [SI-luhs. form of Silvanus or Saul]. A Christian chosen by the Jerusalem church to accompany Paul and Barnabas to Antioch. Acts 15:22–40; 16:19–29; 17:15; 2 Corinthians 1:19.

SIMEON [SIM-ee-uhn: "he hears" or "hearing"]

1. 1900 B.C. Son of Jacob and head of one of the twelve tribes of Israel. Genesis 29–33; 34:25–30; 49:5–7.

2. B.C. date unknown. A descendant of David and an ancestor of Jesus Christ. Luke 3:30.

3. 5 B.C. A devout Jew in Jerusalem who recognized the child Jesus as the Messiah. Luke 2:25–35.

4. A.D. 45. One of the prophets and teachers of the church in Antioch; also called Niger. Acts 13:1.

SIMON [SI-muhn: "he hears" or "hearing"]

1. A.D. 1. Father of Judas Iscariot, the betrayer of Christ. John 6:71: 13:2, 26.

2. A.D. 25. Given name of the apostle Peter. Matthew 4:18; 16:17; Mark 3:16. See Peter, page 165, 332.

3. A.D. 25. Simon the Zealot, notable as one of the twelve apostles. Matthew 10:4; Luke 6:15.

4. A.D. 25. A brother of Christ. Matthew 13:55; Mark 6:3.

5. A.D. 25. A Pharisee in whose house Jesus' feet were anointed. Luke 7:36–50.

6. A.D. 30. A leper in Bethany in whose house Jesus was anointed with perfume shortly before His crucifixion. Matthew 26:6; Mark 14:3.

7. A.D. 30. A man from Cyrene who was forced to carry the cross to the place of Christ's crucifixion. Mark 15:21; Luke 23:26.

8. A.D. 35. Simon Magus, a renowned sorcerer in Samaria who tried to buy the miraculous powers of the apostles Peter and John. Acts 8:9–24.

9. A.D. 35. A tanner with whom Peter stayed while he was in Joppa. Acts 9:43; 10:6, 32.

SIPPAI [SIP-i]. 1000 B.C. A Philistine champion who was killed in combat by Sibbecai. 1 Chronicles 20:4. Called Saph in 2 Samuel 21:18.

SISERA [SIS-uhr-uh]

1. 1225 B.C. Commander of the army of Jabin, Canaanite king of Hazor. Judges 4; 5:20–30.

2. B.C. date unknown. Ancestor of a family of temple servants that returned to Judah with Zerubbabel. Ezra 2:53; Nehemiah 7:55.

SISMAI (SIS-mi]. B.C. date unknown. Listed in the genealogy of Judah. 1 Chronicles 2:40.

SITHRI [SITH-ri: "Yahweh is protection"]. B.C. date unknown. A Levite listed in the family record of Moses and Aaron. Exodus 6:22.

SO [SOH]. 725 B.C. A king of Egypt, to whom Hoshea appealed when he rebelled against Assyria. 2 Kings 17:4.

SOCO [SOC-oh: "thorny"]. B.C. date unknown. A descendant of Judah. 1 Chronicles 4:18.

SODI [SOH-di]. 1475 B.C. Father of Gaddiel, the representative of the tribe of Zebulun sent to spy out the land of Canaan. Numbers 13:10.

SOLOMON [SAHL-uh-muhn: "peaceable"]. 970–930 B.C. The son and successor of King David, renowned for his wisdom. 2 Samuel 12:24; 25; 1 Kings 1—11; 2 Chronicles 9:31; Matthew 1:6, 7.

SOPATER [SOH-pah-tuhr]. A.D. 55. A man who accompanied Paul from Greece to Jerusalem. Acts 20:4. Possibly the same as Sosipater.

SOPHERETH [SAHF-uh-reth]. 950 B.C. A servant of Solomon whose descendants returned to Judah after the Exile. Ezra 2:55; Nehemiah 7:57.

SOSIPATER [soh-SIP-uh-tuhr: "defending one's father"]. A.D. 55. One who sent greetings to the Roman church through Paul. Paul called him "my relative," meaning he was a Jew. Romans 16:21. He may be the same as Sopater.

SOSTHENES [SAHS-thuh-naez]

1. A.D. 55. Ruler of the synagogue at Corinth when the Jews took Paul to court. When the case was dismissed against Paul, Sosthenes was seized and beaten by the crowd in an act of anti-Semitism. Acts 18:17.

2. A.D. 55. A Christian mentioned in the salutation of 1 Corinthians. He may be identical to Sosthenes 1, converted after the incident in Corinth. 1 Corinthians 1:1.

SOTAI [SOH-ti]. 950 B.C. Ancestor of a family of Solomon's servants that returned to Judah with Zerubbabel. Ezra 2:55; Nehemiah 7:57.

STACHYS [STAY-kis: "head of grain"]. A.D. 55. A Christian at Rome greeted by Paul as his "dear friend." Romans 16:9.

STEPHANAS [STEF-uh-nuhs: "crown"]. A.D. 60. A Christian convert from Achaia whose household was baptized by Paul at Corinth. 1 Corinthians 1:16; 16:15–17.

STEPHEN [STEE-vuhn: "crown"]. A.D. 35. Foremost of the seven deacons appointed by the Jerusalem church and the first Christian martyr. Acts 6:5—8:2.

SUAH [SOO-uh]. B.C. date unknown. Listed in the genealogy of Asher. 1 Chronicles 7:36.

SUSI [SOO-si]. 1475 B.C. Father of the representative from the tribe of Manasseh whom Moses sent to spy out the land of Canaan. Numbers 13:11.

T

TABALIAH [TAB-uh-LI-uh: "Yahweh has purified"(?)]. 975 B.C. A tabernacle gatekeeper in David's day. 1 Chronicles 26:11.

TABBAOTH [TAB-ay-ahth: "rings"]. B.C. date unknown. Ancestor of a family of temple servants that returned to Judah with Zerubbabel. Ezra 2:43; Nehemiah 7:46.

TABEL [TAY-bee-uhl: "God is good"]

1. 775 B.C. Father of a man whom Rezin, king of Damascus, and Pekah, king of Israel, planned to set up as a puppet king in Judah after deposing Ahaz. Isaiah 7:6.

2. 450 B.C. An official in Samaria who joined in sending a letter to Artaxerxes opposing rebuilding Jerusalem's walls. Ezra 4:7.

TABRIMMON [tab-RIM-ahn: "Rimmon (the deity) is good"]. 925 B.C. Father of Ben-Hadad I, king of Syria. 1 Kings 15:18.

TAHAN (TAY-han]

1. B.C. date unknown. Ancestor of an Ephraimite clan. Numbers 26:35.

2. B.C. date unknown. A descendant of Ephraim listed in 1 Chronicles 7:25.

TAHASH [TA-hash]. 2050 B.C. A son of Abraham's brother Nahor. Genesis 22:24.

TAHATH [TAY-hath]

1. B.C. date unknown. A Kohathite listed in the genealogy of Levi. 1 Chronicles 6:24, 37.

2 and 3. B.C. dates unknown. Two men listed in the genealogy of Ephraim. 1 Chronicles 7:20.

TAHREA [TAH-ree-uh]. B.C. date unknown. A descendant of Saul. 1 Chronicles 9:41. Called Tarea in 1 Chronicles 8:35.

TALMAI [TAL-mi]

1. 1400 B.C. One of the three sons of Anak and head of a clan driven out of Hebron by Caleb. Numbers 13:22; Joshua 15:14; Judges 1:10.

2. 1025 B.C. King of Geshur and father of Maacah, the wife of David and mother of Absalom. 2 Samuel 3:3; 13:37.

TALMON [TAL-mahn]

1. B.C. date unknown. Ancestor of a family of gatekeepers that returned to Judah with Zerubbabel. Ezra 2:42; Nehemiah 7:45.

2. 450 B.C. A gatekeeper among the Levites who settled in Jerusalem in Ezra's day. 1 Chronicles 9:17; Nehemiah 11:19; 12:25.

TANHUMETH [tan-HOO-meth: "comfort"]. 625 B.C. Father of a military officer who joined Gedaliah at Mizpah. 2 Kings 25:23; Jeremiah 40:8.

TAPPUAH [TAP-poo-uh]. B.C. date unknown. A descendent of Caleb listed in the genealogy of Judah. 1 Chronicles 2:43.

TAREA [TAIR-ee-uh]. B.C. date unknown. Great-grandson of Jonathan, son of Saul. 1 Chronicles 8:35.

TARSHISH [TAHR-shish]

1. B.C. date unknown. A son of Javan listed in the table of nations. Genesis 10:4.

2. B.C. date unknown. Listed only in the genealogy of Benjamin. 1 Chronicles 7:10.

3. 475 B.C. One of seven nobles who advised King Xerxes. Esther 1:14.

TATTENAI [TAT-uh-ni]. 500 B.C. A Persian governor of the territory west of the Euphrates ordered by King Darius to help the Jews rebuild the temple. Ezra 5:3—6:13.

TEBAH [TEE-buh]. 2050 B.C. Son of Abraham's brother Nahor. Genesis 22:24.

TEHINNAH [tuh-HIN-uh: "supplication"]. B.C. date unknown. Founder of the city of Ir-Nahash, listed in the genealogy of Judah. 1 Chronicles 4:12.

TELAH [TEE-luh]. B.C. date unknown. Listed only in the genealogy of Ephraim. 1 Chronicles 7:25.

TELEM [TEE-lem]. 450 B.C. A gatekeeper who wed a pagan wife after the Exile. Ezra 10:24.

TEMA [TEE-muh: "south"]. 2025 B.C. A son of Ishmael. Genesis 25:15.

TEMAH [TEE-muh]. B.C. date unknown. Ancestor of a family of temple servants that returned to Judah after the Exile. Ezra 2:53; Nehemiah 7:55.

TEMAN [TEE-muhn: "south"]

1. 1875 B.C. A grandson of Esau. Genesis 36:11, 15; 1 Chronicles 1:36.

2. B.C. date unknown. An Edomite chief descended from Esau. Genesis 36:42.

TEMENI [TEM-uh-ni: "fortunate"]. B.C. date unknown. Listed in the genealogy of Judah. 1 Chronicles 4:6.

TERAH [TEER-uh]. 2200 B.C. Father of Abraham, Nahor, and Haran. Genesis 11:24–32; Luke 3:34.

TERESH [TEER-esh]. 475 B.C. A bodyguard of Xerxes who conspired to assassinate the king. Esther 2:21; 6:2.

TERTIUS [TUHR-shee-uhs: "third"]. A.D. 55. The person to whom Paul dictated his letter to the Romans. Romans 16:22.

TERTULLUS [tuhr-TUL-uhs: diminutive of Tertius]. A.D. 60. Lawyer hired by the Jews to prosecute Paul before Felix, the Roman governor of Judea. Acts 24:1–8.

THADDAEUS [THAD-ee-uhs]. A.D. 30. One of the twelve apostles. Matthew 10:3; Mark 3:18. Possibly the same as Judas the son of James, in Luke 6:16; John 14:22; Acts 1:13.

THEOPHILUS [thee-AHF-uh-luhs: "loved by God"]. A.D. 60. The person, otherwise unknown, to whom Luke dedicated his Gospel and the Book of Acts. Luke 1:3; Acts 1:1.

THEUDAS [THYOO-duhs: "gift of God" (?)]. B.C. date unknown. Leader of a short-lived rebellion against the Romans, referred to by Gamaliel. Acts 5:36.

THOMAS [TAHM-uhs: "twin"]. A.D. 25. The apostle who refused to believe in the resurrection until he saw Christ with his own eyes. Matthew 10:3; John 11:16; 14:1–6; 20:24–29; Acts 1:13.

TIBERIUS [ti-BEER-ee-us]. Claudius Caesar Augustus, Roman emperor from A.D. 14–37. Luke 3:1.

TIBNI [TIB-ni]. 885–880 B.C. He unsuccessfully challenged Omri for the throne of Israel after the death of Zimri. 1 Kings 16:21, 22.

TIDAL [TI-duhi]. 2000 B.C. King of Golim who joined a coalition to raid the area around the Dead Sea, plundering Sodom and Gomorrah. Genesis 14:1–17.

TIGLATH-PILESER [TIG-leth-pih-LEE-zuhr]. 744–727 B.C. Tiglath-Pileser III, the king of Assyria under whom Assyria returned to international power. 2 Kings 15:19, 20, 29; 16:7–10; 1 Chronicles 5:6, 26; 2 Chronicles 28:16–21. Also called Pul.

TIKVAH [TIK-vuh: "hope"]

1. 650 B.C. Father of Shallum, husband of Huldah the prophetess. 2 Kings 22:14. Called Tokhath in 2 Chronicles 34:22.

2. 475 B.C. Father of Jahaziah, who disputed Ezra's reform requiring the divorce of pagan wives among the Jews. Ezra 10:15.

TILON [TI-lahn]. B.C. date unknown. Listed in the genealogy of Judah. 1 Chronicles 4:20.

TIMAEUS [tih-MAY-uhs]. A.D. 1. Father of Bartimaeus, the blind beggar of Jericho whom Christ healed. Mark 10:46.

TIMNA [TIM-nuh: "restraining"]. B.C. date unknown. An Edomite chief descended from Esau. Genesis 36:40; 1 Chronicles 1:51.

TIMON [TI-mahn]. A.D. 35. One of seven chosen by the church in Jerusalem to minister to the poor. Acts 6:5.

TIMOTHY [TIM-uh-thee: "honored by God" or "honoring God"]. A.D. 50. A member of Paul's missionary team who became a second-generation leader of the church. Acts 16:1–3; 17:14, 15; 20:4; 1 Corinthians 4:17; 1 Timothy 1—6; 2 Timothy 1—4.

TIRAS [TI-ruhs]. B.C. date unknown. A son of Japheth listed in the table of nations. Genesis 10:2.

TIRHAKAH [tuhr-HAY-kuh]. 700 B.C. A king of Egypt and Ethiopia who promised but failed to deliver aid to Hezekiah. 2 Kings 19:9; Isaiah 37:9.

TIRHANAH [tuhr-HAY-nuh]. B.C. date unknown. A son of Caleb. 1 Chronicles 2:48.

Titus proved more effective in his ministry than did Timothy, and Paul sent him on more difficult missions. It was Titus's mission to Crete that was the occasion for Paul to write the letter that we now have in our New Testament.

TIRIA [TEER-ee-uh]. B.C. date unknown. Listed in the genealogy of Judah. 1 Chronicles 4:16.

TITIUS JUSTUS [TIT-ee-us JUS-tuhs]. A.D. 55. A Christian in Corinth with whom Paul stayed. Acts 18:7.

TITUS [TI-tuhs]. A.D. 55. A Greek convert who was entrusted by Paul with missions in Corinth and Crete. 2 Corinthians 2:13; 7:6–15; 8:6, 16–24; Titus 1—3.

TOAH [TOH-uh]. B.C. date unknown. An ancestor of Samuel. 1 Chronicles 6:34. Called Nahath in 1 Chronicles 6:26 and Tohu in 1 Samuel 1:1.

TOBADONIJAH [TAHB-ad-oh-NI-juh: "the Lord Yahweh is good"]. 875 B.C. A Levite who taught the Law throughout Judah during the reign of Jehoshaphat. 2 Chronicles 17:8.

TOBIAH [toh-BI-uh: "Yahwah is good"]

1. B.C. date unknown. Ancestor of some who returned to Judah with Zerubbabel but could not prove Israelite descent. Ezra 2:60; Nehemiah 7:62.

2. 450 B.C. An Ammonite official who with Sanballat opposed Nehemiah's reconstruction of Jerusalem. Nehemiah 2:10, 19; 4:1–8; 6; 13:4–8.

TOBIJAH [tob-BI-juh: "Yahweh is good"]

1. 875 B.C. A Levite sent by Jehoshaphat to teach the Law in the towns of Judah. 2 Chronicles 17:8.

2. 525 B.C. A Jewish exile among those who brought the gold and silver from Babylon used to make a crown for the high priest. Zechariah 6:10–14.

TOGARMAH [toh-GAHR-muh]. B.C. date unknown. Listed in the table of nations. Genesis 10:3.

TOHU [TOH-hoo]. B.C. date unknown. An ancestor of Samuel. 1 Samuel 1:1. See Toah.

TOKHATH [TAHK-hath]. 650 B.C. Father of Shallum, the husband of Huldah the prophetess. 2 Chronicles 34:22. Called Tikvah in 2 Kings 22:14.

TOLA [TOH-luh]

1. 1875 B.C. First son of Issachar, among those who went into Egypt with Jacob. Genesis 46:13; Numbers 26:23; 1 Chronicles 7:1, 2.

2. 1100 B.C. A minor judge who led Israel for twenty-three years. Judges 10:1, 2.

TOU [TOH-oo]. 1000 B.C. King of Hamath who sent his son to congratulate David on his victory over Hadadezer, their mutual enemy. 2 Samuel 8:9, 10; 1 Chronicles 18:9, 10.

TROPHIMUS [TROHF-ih-muhs: "nourishing"]. A.D. 55. A Christian convert from Ephesus who was one of Paul's traveling companions. Acts 20:4; 21:29; 2 Timothy 4:20.

TUBAL [TOO-bahl]. B.C. date unknown. Listed in the table of nations. Genesis 10:2.

TUBAL-CAIN [TOO-bahl-CAYN]. B.C. date unknown. A son of Lamech and a master metalworker. Genesis 4:22.

TYCHICUS [TIK-ih-kuhs: "fortuitous"]. A.D. 60. An Asian Christian who traveled with Paul and served as his messenger during Paul's imprisonment in Rome. Acts 20:4; Ephesians 6:21; Colossians 4:7; 2 Timothy 4:12.

TYRANNUS [tuh-RAN-uhs: "tyrant"]. A.D. date unknown. An Ephesian in whose school Paul taught daily for two years. Acts 19:9.

U

UCAL [OO-kuhl]. B.C. date unknown. One of two men to whom Agur addressed his sayings. Proverbs 30:1.

UEL [OO-uhl: "will of God"]. 450 B.C. A man who took a pagan wife after the Exile. Ezra 10:34.

ULAM [OO-lam: "first"]

1. B.C. date unknown. Listed only in the genealogy of Manasseh. 1 Chronicles 7:16, 17.

2. B.C. date unknown. A descendant of Jonathan whose sons are described as "brave warriors who could handle the bow." 1 Chronicles 8:39, 40.

ULLA [UL-uh]. B.C. date unknown. Listed in the genealogy of Asher. 1 Chronicles 7:39.

UNNI [UN-i]

1. 1000 B.C. A Levite who played the lyre in the procession before the ark of the covenant. 1 Chronicles 15:18, 20.

2. 525 B.C. A Levite who returned to Judah with Zerubbabel after the Exile. Nehemiah 12:9.

UR [UHR: "flame"]. 1025 B.C. Father of one of David's mighty men. 1 Chronicles 11:35.

URBANUS [uhr-BAY-nuhs: "pleasant, urbane"]. A.D. 55. A Roman Christian to whom Paul sent greetings. Romans 16:9.

URI [YOOR-i: "fiery" or "enlightened"]

1. 1475 B.C. Father of Bezalel, the head craftsmen empowered by God to build the tabernacle. Exodus 31:2; 1 Chronicles 2:20.

2. 1000 B.C. Father of Geber, governor of Gilead in Solomon's time. 1 Kings 4:19.

3. 450 B.C. A Levite who took a pagan wife after the return from the Exile. Ezra 10:24.

URIAH [yoor-I-uh: "Yahweh is light"]

1. 1000 B.C. The righteous husband of Bathsheba and a Hittite officer in David's army. 2 Samuel 11:2–12; 10; 23:39.

2. 750 B.C. A chief priest during the reign of Ahaz, who constructed an Assyrian altar in the temple. 2 Kings 16:10–16.

3. 750 B.C. A priest in Ahaz's time who served as a witness to a prophecy of Isaiah. Isaiah 8:2. Probably the same as Uriah 2.

4. 600 B.C. A prophet from Kirjath Jearim who was put to death by Jehoiakim. Jeremiah 26:20–23.

5. 475 B.C. Father of a priest who helped Ezra weigh out the sacred articles for the temple. Ezra 8:33; Nehemiah 3:4, 21.

6. 450 B.C. One who stood to Ezra's right at the reading of the Law. Nehemiah 8:4.

URIEL [YOOR-ee-el: "God is light"]

1. 1000 B.C. A Levite during the time of David. 1 Chronicles 6:24; 1 Chronicles 15:5, 11.

2. 975 B.C. His daughter, Michaiah, was the mother of Abijah, king of Judah. 2 Chronicles 13:2.

UTHAI [YOU-thi]

1. 450 B.C. A Judahite who settled in Jerusalem after the Exile. 1 Chronicles 9:4.

2. 450 B.C. Head of a family that returned to Judah with Ezra. Ezra 8:14.

UZ [UZ]

1. B.C. date unknown. Listed in the table of nations. Genesis 10:23; 1 Chronicles 1:17.

2. 2050 B.C. Son of Nahor. Genesis 22:21.

3. 2050 B.C. A son of Dishan, a Horite chief who lived in the land of Seir in Esau's time. Genesis 36:28.

UZAI [UZ-i]. 475 B.C. Father of Palal, who helped rebuild the walls of Jerusalem. Nehemiah 3:25.

UZAL [OO-zuhl]. Listed among the Semites in the table of nations. Genesis 10:27.

UZZA [UZ-uh: "strength"]

1. B.C. date unknown. Listed in the genealogy of Benjamin. 1 Chronicles 8:7.

2. B.C. date unknown. Ancestor of a family of temple servants that returned to Judah after the Exile. Ezra 2:49; Nehemiah 7:51.

UZZAH [UZ-uh: "strength"]

1. B.C. date unknown. A Levite descended from Merari. 1 Chronicles 6:29.

2. 1000 B.C. A man who was struck dead by God when he violated God's Law and touched the ark. 2 Samuel 6:3–8; 1 Chronicles 13:7–11.

UZZI [UZ-i: "my strength"]

1. B.C. date unknown. A descendent of Issachar. 1 Chronicles 7:2, 3.

2. B.C. date unknown. A descendent of Benjamin. 1 Chronicles 7:7.

3. B.C. date unknown. A priest in the line of Eleazar, son of Aaron. 1 Chronicles 6:6, 51; Ezra 7:4.

4. B.C. date unknown. Descendant of Benjamin who settled in Jerusalem in Ezra's time. 1 Chronicles 9:8.

5. 500 B.C. Head of a priestly family in the time of Joiakim the high priest. Nehemiah 12:19.

6. 450 B.C. A descendant of Asaph and chief Levite in Jerusalem. Nehemiah 11:22.

7. 450 B.C. A Levite involved in the dedication of the wall of Jerusalem. Nehemiah 12:42.

UZZIA [uh-ZI-uh: "Yahweh is my strength"]. 1000 B.C. One of David's thirty mighty men. 1 Chronicles 11:44.

UZZIAH [uh-ZI-uh: "Yahweh is my strength"]

1. 1000 B.C. Father of Jonathan, an officer of King David. 1 Chronicles 27:25.

2. B.C. date unknown. A Levite descended from Kohath. 1 Chronicles 6:24.

3. 790–739 B.C. The son and successor of Amaziah, king of Judah. 2 Kings 15:13, 30–34; 2 Chronicles 26; Matthew 1:9.

4. 475 B.C. Father of Athaiah, a Judahite who settled in Jerusalem in Nehemiah's time. Nehemiah 11:4.

5. 450 B.C. A priest who divorced his pagan wife in the time of Ezra. Ezra 10:21.

UZZIEL [uh-ZI-uhl: "God is my strength"]

1. B.C. date unknown. Listed in the genealogy of Benjamin. 1 Chronicles 7:7.

2. B.C. date unknown. Ancestor of the Uzzielites. Exodus 6:18, 22; Leviticus 10:4; 1 Chronicles 15:10; 23:20.

3. 975 B.C. A son of Heman, the king's seer and a minister of music in David's time. 1 Chronicles 25:4. Called Azarel in 25:18.

4. 725 B.C. A Simeonite leader among those who invaded the land of Seir. 1 Chronicles 4:42.

5. 725 B.C. A Levite who helped purify the temple in Hezekiah's time. 2 Chronicles 29:14.

6. 450 B.C. A goldsmith who helped rebuild Jerusalem's walls in Nehemiah's time. Nehemiah 3:8.

V

VAJEZATHA [VI-zuh-thuh]. 475 B.C. One of the ten sons of Haman executed by the Jews in Shushan. Esther 9:9.

VANIAH [vuh-NI-uh]. 450 B.C. Listed as one who took a pagan wife after the Exile. Ezra 10:36.

VOPHSI [VAHF-si]. 1475 B.C. The representative from the tribe of Naphtali whom Moses sent to explore the land of Canaan. Numbers 13:14.

W, X, Y, Z

XERXES [ZERK-seez]. 485–484 B.C. Xerxes I, the son and successor of Darius the

Great. He was the king of Persia who divorced Vashti and married Esther. Ezra 4:6; Esther 1—10; Daniel 9:1. See Ahasuerus.

ZAAVAN [ZAY-uh-van: "fearful"(?)]. 1950 B.C. A Horite chief in Esau's time. Genesis 36:27; 1 Chronicles 1:42.

ZABAD [ZAY-bad: "gift" or "endowment"]

1. B.C. date unknown. Listed in the genealogy of Ephraim. 1 Chronicles 7:21.

2. B.C. date unknown. Listed only in the genealogy of Jerahmeel in 1 Chronicles 2:36, 37.

3. 1000 B.C. One of David's thirty mighty men. 1 Chronicles 11:41. Possibly the same as Zabad 2.

4. 800 B.C. An official of Joash who plotted to assassinate the king. 2 Chronicles 24:25, 26; 25:3.

5, 6, and 7. 450 B.C. Three men who pledged to divorce their pagan wives. Ezra 10:27, 33, 43.

ZABBAI [ZAB-I]

1. 475 B.C. Father of Baruch, who helped rebuild Jerusalem's walls. Nehemiah 3:20.

2. 450 B.C. One who took a pagan wife after the Exile. Ezra 10:28.

ZABDI [ZAB-di: "Yahweh has given"]

1. B.C. date unknown. Listed in the genealogy of Benjamin. 1 Chronicles 8:19.

2. 975 B.C. An overseer in charge of King David's wine cellars. 1 Chronicles 27:27.

3. B.C. date unknown. A Levite descended from Asaph. Nehemiah 11:17. Also called Zichri (1 Chron. 9:15) and Zaccur (1 Chron. 25:2, 10; Neh. 12:35).

Although small of stature, Zacchaeus proved to be a great Christian. His return of funds he had gained by fraud, and additional gifts to the poor, showed that his conversion to Christ was genuine.

ZABDIEL [ZAB-dee-uhl: "God has given"]

1. 1025 B.C. Father of one of the three chiefs of David's mighty men and commander of the first division of his army. 1 Chronicles 27:2.

2. 450 B.C. Chief of the priests who settled in Jerusalem after the Exile. Nehemiah 11:14.

ZABUD [ZAY-buhd: "bestowed"]. 950 B.C. A priest and personal advisor to King Solomon. 1 Kings 4:5.

ZACCAI [ZAK-I]. B.C. date unknown. Ancestor of a family that returned to Judah with Zerubbabel. Ezra 2:9; Nehemiah 7:14.

ZACCHAEUS [ze-KEE-uhs: "pure"]. A.D. 30. A wealthy but dishonest tax collector in Jericho who became a follower of Jesus. Luke 19:1–10.

ZACCUR [ZAK-uhr: "remembered"]

1. 1475 B.C. Father of Shammua, representative of the tribe of Reuben whom Moses sent to explore the land of Canaan. Numbers 13:4.

2. B.C. date unknown. Listed in the genealogy of Simeon. 1 Chronicles 4:26.

3. B.C. date unknown. A Levite descended from Merari. 1 Chronicles 24:27.

4. 975 B.C. A son of Asaph and head of the third division of ministers of music. 1 Chronicles 25:2, 10; Nehemiah 12:35. See Zabdi 3.

5. 450 B.C. He returned to Judah with Ezra after the Exile. Ezra 8:14.

6. 450 B.C. He helped reconstruct the walls of Jerusalem. Nehemiah 3:2.

7. 450 B.C. A Levite who signed the covenant renewal pact. Nehemiah 10:12.

8. 450 B.C. Father of Hanan, assistant to the temple treasurer. Nehemiah 13:13.

ZADOK [ZAY-dahk: "righteous"]

1. 1000 B.C. A high priest who was totally loyal to David. 2 Samuel 8:17; 15:24–35; 1 Kings 1:8, 32–45; 1 Chronicles 12:28; 27:17.

2. 800 B.C. Maternal grandfather of the mother of Jotham, king of Judah. 2 Kings 15:33; 2 Chronicles 27:1.

3. B.C. date unknown. A descendant of Zadok, the high priest in David's time. 1 Chronicles 6:12; 9:11; Ezra 7:2.

4. 450 B.C. One who helped repair the wall of Jerusalem. Nehemiah 3:4.

5. 450 B.C. A priest who also helped with Jerusalem's reconstruction. Nehemiah 3:29.

6. 450 B.C. A leader who sealed the covenant renewal pact in Nehemiah's time. Nehemiah 10:21. Probably the same as Zadok 4.

7. 425 B.C. A scribe among those put in charge of the temple treasury by Nehemiah. Nehemiah 13:13.

8. B.C. date unknown. A descendant of Zerubbabel and ancestor of Christ. Matthew 1:14.

ZAHAM [ZAY-ham]. 900 B.C. A son of King Rehoboam and David's granddaughter Mahalath. 2 Chronicles 11:19.

ZALAPH [ZAY-laf]. 475 B.C. Father of Hanun, a rebuilder of Jerusalem's walls. Nehemiah 3:30.

ZALMON [ZAL-muhn]. 1000 B.C. Among the military elite known as David's mighty men. 2 Samuel 23:28.

ZALMUNNA [zal-MUN-uh: "deprived of shade (protection)"]. 1175 B.C. A king of Midian pursued and put to death by Gideon. Judges 8:5–21; Psalm 83:11. See also Zebah.

ZANOAH [zuh-NO-uh]. B.C. date unknown. Listed in the genealogy of Judah. 1 Chronicles 4:18.

ZAPHNATH-PAANEAH [ZAF-nath-puh-NEE-uh: "the god speaks and he lives" or "sustainer of the land"(?)]. 1875 B.C. Name Pharaoh gave Joseph after he interpreted the pharaoh's dream. Genesis 41:45. See Joseph #1.

ZATTU [ZAT-oo]

1. B.C. date unknown. Ancestor of a family whose members returned to Judah with Zerubbabel and Ezra. Ezra 2:8; 10:27; Nehemiah 7:13.

2. 450 B.C. A Jewish leader who signed the covenant renewal pact of Nehemiah's time, probably with the name of his family ancestor. Nehemiah 10:14.

ZAZA [ZAY-zuh]. B.C. date unknown. Listed only in the genealogy of Jerahmeel. 1 Chronicles 2:33.

ZEBADIAH [ZEB-uh-DI-uh: "Yahweh has bestowed"]

1. and 2. B.C. dates unknown. Listed in the genealogy of Benjamin. 1 Chronicles 8:15, 17.

3. 1000 B.C. A Benjamite warrior who with his brother joined David's army at Ziklag. 1 Chronicles 12:7.

4. 975 B.C. A tabernacle gatekeeper. 1 Chronicles 26:2.

5. 975 B.C. The commander of the fourth division of David's army. 1 Chronicles 27:7.

6. 875 B.C. A Levite sent by King Jehoshaphat to teach the Law throughout Judah. 2 Chronicles 17:8.

7. 850 B.C. Leader in Jehoshaphat's day who was made judge of all matters pertaining to the king. 2 Chronicles 19:11.

8. 450 B.C. Head of a family group that returned to Judah with Ezra. Ezra 8:8.

9. 450 B.C. A priest who wed a pagan wife after the Exile. Ezra 10:20.

ZEBAH [ZEE-buh: "sacrifice"]. A Midianite king who oppressed Israel until defeated and put to death by Gideon. Judges 8:5–21; Psalm 83:11.

ZEBEDEE [ZEB-uh-dee: "gift of Yahweh" (?)]. A.D. 1. A wealthy fisherman on the sea of Galilee, the father of the apostles James and John. Matthew 4:21; Mark 1:19, 20; Luke 5:9, 10.

ZEBINA [zuh-BI-nuh: "purchased"]. 450 B.C. A Jew who took a pagan wife after the Exile. Ezra 10:43.

ZEBUL [ZEE-buhl: "dwelling"]. 1125 B.C. Governor of Shechem allied with Abimelech. Judges 9:28–41.

ZEBULUN [ZEB-yoo-luhn: "dwelling" or "honor"]. 2000 B.C. Son of Jacob by his wife Leah; ancestor of one of the twelve tribes of Israel. Genesis 30:20; 46:14; 49:13.

ZECHARIAH [ZEK-uh-RI-uh: "Yahweh remembers"]

1. B.C. date unknown. Listed in the genealogy of Reuben. 1 Chronicles 5:7.

2. 1100 B.C. A relative of Saul. 1 Chronicles 9:37. Called Zekar in 1 Chronicles 8:31.

3. 1000 B.C. A Levite musician who played the lyre as the ark was brought into Jerusalem. 1 Chronicles 15:18, 20; 16:5.

4. 1000 B.C. A priest who blew the trumpet in the procession before the ark. 1 Chronicles 15:24.

5. 1000 B.C. The head of a Levite family listed among the Levites of David's day. 1 Chronicles 24:25. Possibly the same as Zechariah 3.

6. 975 B.C. Head of a division of temple gatekeepers. 1 Chronicles 26:2, 14.

7. 975 B.C. Also a Levite gatekeeper. 1 Chronicles 26:11.

8. 975 B.C. Officer over the tribe of Manasseh in David's time. 1 Chronicles 27:21.

9. 875 B.C. An official sent by King Jehoshaphat to teach the Law in the towns of Judah. 2 Chronicles 17:7.

10. 875 B.C. A Levite who prophesied before Jehoshaphat. 2 Chronicles 20:14.

11. 850 B.C. A son of Jehoshaphat put to death when his brother Jehoram ascended to the throne of Judah. 2 Chronicles 21:2.

12. 800 B.C. Son of Jehoiada the priest, who was executed for prophesying against Joash for turning to idolatry. 2 Chronicles 24:20.

13. 775 B.C. Mentor who led King Uzziah to seek God during the early years of his reign. 2 Chronicles 26:5.

14. 775 B.C. Father of Abijah, the mother of King Hezekiah. 2 Kings 18:2; 2 Chronicles 29:1.

15. 753 B.C. Son and successor of Jeroboam II, king of Israel. He reigned in Samaria six months before Shallum, who took the throne, assassinated him. 2 Kings 14:29; 15:8–12.

16. 750 B.C. He served as a reliable witness for the prophet Isaiah. Isaiah 8:2.

17. 725 B.C. A Levite who took part in the purification of the temple in Hezekiah's time. 2 Chronicles 29:13.

18. 625 B.C. A Levite who served as a supervisor during the reconstruction of the temple in Josiah's time. 2 Chronicles 34:12.

19. 625 B.C. A temple administrator who contributed to the Passover celebration in Josiah's time. 2 Chronicles 35:8.

20. B.C. date unknown. Ancestor of a priest who settled in Jerusalem after the Exile. Nehemiah 11:12.

21. B.C. date unknown. Ancestor of Athaiah, who settled in Jerusalem in Nehemiah's time. Nehemiah 11:4.

22. B.C. date unknown. Ancestor of another descendant of Judah who resettled in Jerusalem. Nehemiah 11:5.

23. 525 B.C. Zechariah the prophet, whose visions are recorded in the Book of Zechariah. Nehemiah 12:16; Zechariah 1—14.

24. B.C. date unknown. A prophet, son of Berekiah, said by Christ to have been killed between the altar and the temple. Matthew 23:35; Luke 11:51. Likely Zechariah 12 or 23.

25. 500 B.C. Head of a priestly family in the days of Joiakim the high priest. Nehemiah 12:16.

26. and 27. 450 B.C. Two Jewish leaders who returned to Judah with Ezra. Ezra 8:3, 11.

28. 450 B.C. A leader sent by Ezra with a delegation to recruit Levites to serve in the temple. Ezra 8:16. Possibly Zechariah 26 or 27.

29. 450 B.C. One who wed a pagan wife after the Exile. Ezra 10:26.

30. 450 B.C. One who stood to Ezra's left at the public reading of the Law. Nehemiah 8:4.

31. 450 B.C. A temple gatekeeper. Either he or his descendants settled in Jerusalem after the Exile. 1 Chronicles 9:21. Possibly Zechariah 6.

32. 450 B.C. A Levite who was among the musicians at the dedication of Jerusalem's wall. Nehemiah 12:35.

33. 450 B.C. A priest who blew the trumpet at the dedication of the wall. Nehemiah 12:41.

34. 5 B.C. The father of John the Baptist. Luke 1:5–25, 57–79. Also called Zacharias.

ZEDEKIAH [ZED-uh-KI-uh: "Yahweh is my righteousness"]

1. 850 B.C. One of four hundred false prophets who, in opposition to the prophet Micaiah, assured Ahab he would be victorious against Syria. 1 Kings 22:11, 24; 2 Chronicles 18:10, 23.

2. 800 B.C. A false prophet among the exiles in Babylon; Jeremiah predicted he would be put to death by Nebuchadnezzar. Jeremiah 29:21–23.

3. 800 B.C. An official of Jehoiakim, king of Judah. Jeremiah 36:12.

4. 597–586 B.C. The son of Josiah who became the last king of Judah. 2 Kings 24:17—25:7; 1 Chronicles 3:15, 16; Jeremiah 21; 34; 37:1—39:7.

5. 450 B.C. A priest who signed the covenant renewal pact in Nehemiah's time. Nehemiah 10:1.

ZEEB [ZEE-eb: "wolf"]. 1175 B.C. A Midianite leader put to death by the Ephraimites led by Gideon. Judges 7:25; 8:3; Psalm 83:11.

ZEKER [ZEE-kuhr: "fame" or "remembrance"]. 1100 B.C. Listed in the genealogy of Saul. 1 Chronicles 8:31. See Zechariah 2.

ZELEK [ZEE-luhk: "fissure"]. 1000 B.C. An Ammonite among David's mighty men. 2 Samuel 23:37; 1 Chronicles 11:39.

ZELOPHEHAD [zeh-LOH-fuh-had]. 1450 B.C. Because he had no sons, his daughters were given his inheritance and Israel's inheritance laws were modified. Numbers 26:33; 27:1–11; 36:1–13.

ZEMIRAH [zuh-MI-ruh]. B.C. date unknown. A descendant of Benjamin. 1 Chronicles 7:8.

ZENAS [ZEE-nuhs]. A.D. 65. A Christian missionary in Crete skilled in Roman or Jewish law. Titus 3:13.

ZEPHANIAH [ZEF-uh-NI-uh: "Yahweh has hidden" or "Yahweh has treasured"]

1. B.C. date unknown. Listed in the genealogy of Heman, a minister of music in David's day. 1 Chronicles 6:36.

2. 625 B.C. A prophet whose words are recorded in the Book of Zephaniah.

3. 600 B.C. A chief priest in Jerusalem during the reign of Zedekiah who was executed by Nebuchadnezzar. 2 Kings 25:18–21; Jeremiah 21:1; 29:25–32.

4. 550 B.C. Father of Josiah and Hen, who returned to Judah after the Exile. Zechariah 6:10, 14.

ZEPHO [ZEE-foh: "watch"]. 1875 B.C. A grandson of Esau and an Edomite chief. Genesis 36:11, 15; 1 Chronicles 1:36 .

ZEPHON [ZEE-fahn: "watching"(?)]. 1875 B.C. First son of Gad, with those who entered Egypt with Jacob. Genesis 46:16; Numbers 26:15.

ZERAH [ZEER-uh: "shining" or "risen"(?)]

1. 1875 B.C. A grandson of Esau and an Edomite chief. Genesis 36:13, 17.

2. 1825 B.C. A son of Judah by Tamar and twin brother of Perez. Genesis 38:30; 46:12; Numbers 26:20; 1 Chronicles 2:4, 6; Matthew 1:3.

3. B.C. date unknown. A descendant of Simeon. Numbers 26:13; 1 Chronicles 4:24. Possibly the same as Zohar, son of Simeon.

4. B.C. date unknown. Father of Bela, a king of Edom. Genesis 36:33.

5. B.C. date unknown. Ancestor of Asaph, a chief minister of music in David's time. 1 Chronicles 6:21, 41.

6. 900 B.C. A Cushite (Ethiopian) king who led a powerful army against Asa

and was defeated. 2 Chronicles 14:9–15.

ZERAHIAH [ZAIR-uh-HI-uh: "Yahweh has come forth"]

1. B.C. date unknown. An ancestor of Ezra the scribe. 1 Chronicles 6:6, 51; Ezra 7:4.

2. 475 B.C. Father of Eliehoenai, who returned to Judah with Ezra. Ezra 8:4.

ZERETH [ZEER-ath: "brilliance"(?)]. B.C. date unknown. Listed in the genealogy of Judah. 1 Chronicles 4:7.

ZERI [ZEER-i]. 975 B.C. A son of Jeduthun and head of a division of temple singers. 1 Chronicles 25:3.

ZEROR [ZEER-ohr]. B.C. date unknown. An ancestor of Saul. 1 Samuel 9:1.

ZERUBBABEL [zuh-RUB-uh-buhl: "seed of Babylon"]. 525 B.C. The prince of Judah who led the first return of the Jews to Judah after the Exile. 1 Chronicles 3:19; Ezra 2:1; 2; 3:1—4:5; 5; Nehemiah 7:7; 12:1, 47; Matthew 1:12, 13.

ZETHAM [ZE-thuhm: "olive tree"]. B.C. date unknown. A Levite who served as a temple treasurer in David's time. 1 Chronicles 23:8; 26:22.

ZETHAN [ZEE-thuhn: "olive tree"]. B.C. date unknown. Listed in the genealogy of Benjamin. 1 Chronicles 7:10.

ZETHAR [ZEE-thehr: "victor"(?)]. 475 B.C. One of the seven eunuchs who served King Xerxes. Esther 1:10.

ZIA [ZI-uh: "trembling"(?)]. B.C. date unknown. Listed in the genealogy of Gad. 1 Chronicles 5:13.

ZIBA [ZI-buh: "plant"]. 1000 B.C. A servant of Saul whom King David instructed to cultivate Saul's estates for the benefit of Mephibosheth, the lame son of Jonathan. 2 Samuel 9:1–13: 16:1–4; 19:17, 26–30.

ZIBEON [ZIB-ee-uhn: "hyena"]. 1975 B.C. Grandfather of one of Esau's wives. Genesis 36:2, 14, 20, 24.

ZIBIA [ZIB-ee-uh: "gazelle"]. B.C. date unknown. Listed in the genealogy of Benjamin. 1 Chronicles 8:9.

ZICRI [ZIK-ri: "remembered"]

1. B.C. date unknown. A Levite listed in the family of Moses and Aaron. Exodus 6:21.

2. 3, and 4. B.C. dates unknown. Three men listed in the genealogy of Benjamin. 1 Chronicles 8:19, 23, 27.

5. 1025 B.C. Father of Shelomith, a leading Levite in David's time. 1 Chronicles 26:25.

6. 1000 B.C. Father of Eliezer, officer over the tribe of Reuben. 1 Chronicles 27:16.

7. 975 B.C. Son of Asaph and ancestor of a Levite who settled in Jerusalem after the Exile. 1 Chronicles 9:15. See Zabdi 3.

8. 900 B.C. Father of Amasiah, commander of an army of Judahites under Jehoshaphat. 2 Chronicles 17:16.

9. 875 B.C. Father of Elishaphat, a military commander who aided Jehoiada in the overthrow of Athaliah. 2 Chronicles 23:1.

10. 750 B.C. An warrior who killed Maaseiah, son of King Ahaz. 2 Chronicles 28:7.

11. 500 B.C. Head of a priestly family in the time of Joiakim the high priest. Nehemiah 12:17.

12. 475 B.C. Father of Joel, chief officer over the Benjamites in Nehemiah's time. Nehemiah 11:9.

ZIHA [ZI-huh]

1. B.C. date unknown. Ancestor of a family of temple servants that returned to Judah with Zerubbabel. Ezra 2:43; Nehemiah 7:46.

2. 450 B.C. Overseer of temple servants in Nehemiah's time. Nehemiah 11:21.

ZILLETHAI [ZIL-uh-thi: "shadow, protection"]

1. B.C. date unknown. Listed only in the genealogy of Benjamin. 1 Chronicles 8:20.

2. 1000 B.C. A military leader who joined David's army at Ziklag. 1 Chronicles 12:20.

ZIMMAH [ZIM-uh]

1. B.C. date unknown. A Levite descended from Gershon. 1 Chronicles 6:20, 42.

2. 750 B.C. Father of Joah, who helped purify the temple in Hezekiah's time. 2 Chronicles 29:12.

ZIMRAN [ZIM-ran: "fame"(?)]. 2000 B.C. First son of Abraham by Keturah. Genesis 25:2.

ZIMRI [ZIM-ri]

1. 1400 B.C. A Simeonite leader who was slain by Phinehas, grandson of Aaron, for his adultery with a Midianite woman. Numbers 25:6–14.

2. B.C. date unknown. Ancestor of a Judahite family. Joshua 7:1, 17, 18; 1 Chronicles 2:6.

3. B.C. date unknown. A Benjamite descended from Jonathan, son of Saul. 1 Chronicles 8:36; 9:42.

4. 885 B.C. A military officer who killed King Elah and his family, seizing the throne of Israel. 1 Kings 16:9–20.

ZIPH [ZIF]

1. B.C. date unknown. Grandson of Caleb. 1 Chronicles 2:42.

2. B.C. date unknown. Listed in the genealogy of Judah. 1 Chronicles 4:16.

ZIPHAH [ZIF-uh]. B.C. date unknown. A son of Jehallelel. 1 Chronicles 4:16.

ZIPPOR [ZIP-ohr: "bird"]. 1425 B.C. Father of Balak, the Moabite king who opposed the Israelites in Moses' time. Numbers 22:2.

ZIZA [ZI-zuh]

1. B.C. date unknown. A Levite listed in the genealogy of the Gershonite clan. 1 Chronicles 23:10, 11.

2. 900 B.C. Son of Rehoboam and Maacah. 2 Chronicles 11:20.

3. 725 B.C. A Simeonite leader who lived in the time of Hezekiah. 1 Chronicles 4:37.

ZOHAR [ZOH-hahr]

1. 2025 B.C. Father of Ephron, the Hittite who sold Abraham a field with a cave to use as a family burial site. Genesis 23:8; 25:9.

2. 1875 B.C. A son of Simeon who accompanied Jacob's family to Egypt. Genesis 46:10; Exodus 6:15. Probably the same as Zerah 3.

3. B.C. date unknown. Listed in the genealogy of Judah. 1 Chronicles 4:7.

ZOHETH [ZOH-heth]. B.C. date unknown. Listed in the genealogy of Judah. 1 Chronicles 4:20.

ZOPHAH [ZOH-fuh]. B.C. date unknown. Listed in the genealogy of Asher. 1 Chronicles 7:35, 36.

ZOPHAI [ZOH-fi]. B.C. date unknown. A Levite descended from Kohath. 1 Chronicles 6:26. Called Zuph in v.35.

ZOPHAR [ZOH-fuhr]. B.C. date unknown. One of the three friends of Job who came to comfort Job and soon began to argue with him. Job 2:11; 11; 20; 42:9.

ZUAR [ZOO-uhr: "little"]. 1475 B.C. Father of Eliab, leader of the tribe of Issachar during the Exodus. Numbers 1:8.

ZUPH [ZUF: "honeycomb"]. B.C. date unknown. An ancestor of Samuel, a Levite who lived in the hill country of Ephraim. 1 Samuel 1:1; 1 Chronicles 6:35. See Zophai.

ZUR [ZUHR: "rock"]

1. 1425 B.C. A Midianite king whose daughter was slain by Phinehas, grandson of Aaron. He himself was later killed in battle with Israel. Numbers 25:15; 31:8.

2. 1100 B.C. A Benjamite listed in the genealogy of Saul. 1 Chronicles 8:30.

ZURIEL [ZUHR-ee-uhl: "God is a rock"]. 1450 B.C. Leader of the Merarite clans during the Exodus. Numbers 3:35.

ZURISHADDAI [ZUHR-ih-SHAD-i: "the Almighty is a rock"]. 1475 B.C. Father of the leader of the tribe of Simeon during the Exodus. Numbers 1:6.

EXPOSITORY INDEX

An expository index organizes information by topic and guides the reader to Bible verses and book pages which are critical to understanding the subject. It does not list every verse referred to in the book, but seeks to identify key verses. It does not list every mention of a topic in the book, but directs the reader to pages where a topic is discussed in some depth. Thus an expository index helps the reader avoid the frustration of looking up verses in the Bible or the book, only to discover that they contribute in only a small way to one's understanding of the subject.

This expository index organizes references to men by topic. Topics and sub-topics are identified in the left-hand column. Key Bible verses and passages are listed in the center column under "Scriptures." The far right column identifies pages in this book where the topic is covered.

In most instances, several of the key verses in the "Scriptures" column will be discussed on the book pages referred to. Very often additional verses will be referred to on the pages where the topic is covered. Our goal is to help you keep in focus the critical Bible verses and passages. Similarly, the book pages referred to are only those which make a significant contribution to understanding a topic, not every page on which a topic may be mentioned.

Please note that material under sub-topics is sometimes organized chronologically by the sequence of appearance in Scripture, and sometimes alphabetically, depending upon which organization will be most helpful in understanding and locating information.

MEN GIVEN EXTENDED TREATMENT

NAME	PAGES	NAME	PAGES
Aaron	138-140	Cyrus	137
Abednego	149-150	Daniel	95-98
Abihu	150-151	David	43-57
Abimelech	151	Doeg	153
Abraham	10-25	Elijah	85-88
Absalom	151-152	Elisha	88-89
Adam	1-10	Enoch	146-147
Ahab	121-124	Esau	70-71
Aquila	213	Ezekiel	93-95
Balaam	152-153	Ezra	140-142
Barnabas	204-206	Gedaliah	147
Baruch	145	Gideon	103-105
Boaz	145-146	Haman	153-154
Caiaphas	199-200	Hezekiah	128-130
Cain	153	Hushai	147-148
Caleb	146	Isaac	66-68

TOPIC	SCRIPTURE	PAGES
Jacob and wives	Gen. 29; 30	73
Solomon and wives	1 Kings 11	117
JUDGES		102-103
LEADER/FOLLOWER RELATIONSHIPS		
Barnabas and John Mark	Acts 15	210
Hezekiah and Judah		130
Joshua and Israelites	Josh. 23; 24	81
Moses and Israelites	Ex 5; 16-17; Num. 11; 14	29-42
Moses and Israelites	Num. 26-36	42
Paul and co-workers		181
Paul and John Mark	Acts 15	210
Paul and Timothy		214-215
Paul and young Christians		180-181
Peter and other apostles		174
Peter and other disciples		169
Pilate and the Jews	John 19	201
Samson and Israelites	Judg. 15	107
Samuel and Israelites	1 Sam. 7	110
MAN/WOMAN RELATIONSHIPS		
Boaz and women	Ruth	145-146
Importance of	Gen. 2	5-6
Distortion of	Gen. 3	9
Job and women	Job 31	63-64
Samson and women	Judg. 16	107
Solomon and women	1 Kings 11	117
NAMELESS MEN IN THE GOSPELS		202-203
PRIESTHOOD		137-138
PRAYER		
Of Abraham	Gen. 18	22
Of Daniel	Dan. 6	97
Of Ezra	Ezra 8	141
Of Hezekiah	2 Chron. 32	129-130
Of Jacob	Gen. 30	72
Of James		212
Of Joshua	Josh. 10	80-81
Of Moses	Ex. 32	34-35
Of Moses	Num. 11	40-41
Of Solomon	1 Kings 3	116
PROPHETS	Deut. 13; 18	82-83

TOPIC	SCRIPTURE	PAGES
REAL MEN	Gen. 2; 3	6
RELATIONSHIP WITH GOD		
Brings changes		189-190
Deepening	Ex. 33:13-23	35-36
Denial of	Matt. 26	172-173
Dependence on for guidance	1 Sam. 23	50
Disobedience		
By Saul	1 Sam. 13; 15	113-114
By Moses	Num. 20	37-38
ENCOURAGEMENT OF	1 Sam. 26; 2 Sam. 6	50-51
EMPOWERMENT	Judg. 6	104
ESTABLISH	Ex 3:1-4:17	32
FAITH BASED	Gen. 15:6; Rom. 4	14-15
FAITHFULNESS IN PRAYER	Dan. 6; 9	87
FALL FROM	1 Kings 11	117
FEAR OF GOD	1 Kings 21	122-123
FLAWS IN	Ex. 34:29-34; Num. 20:1-12	36-38
FOCUS ON WORSHIP	2 Chron. 29-31	128-129
Growth in	Matt. 14	170-172
INADEQUATE KNOWLEDGE	Job	65
IN CHILDHOOD		
Of David	1 Sam. 16	46-47
Of Samuel	1 Sam. 2	109-110
Obedience	Josh. 1; 7	80-81
PROMISE BASED	1 Sam. 17	50
REJECTION OF		
By Jeroboam I	1 Kings 12	120-121
By Judas	Mark 14	191-193
RELIANCE ON	Ezra 8; Neh. 8	141
REPENTANCE FOR SIN	2 Sam. 12	52
REQUEST FOR SIGNS	Judg.	104-105
RESPECT FOR	Ex. 5-7	33-34
RESPONSE TO REVELATION		
By David	Ps. 8	49-50
By Josiah	2 Kings 22	131
By Joshua	Joshua 1	80

TOPIC	SCRIPTURE	PAGES
By Pharaoh	Ex. 7-14	134-135
By Solomon	1 Kings 3; 8	116-117
Second chances		
Given to Jonah	Jonah 1-4	90-91
Given to Peter	John 21	173-174
Tested	Ex. 5:1-7:7	33
Transforming power	Ex. 32:1-14	34-35
Uncertainty about	John 14; 20	190-191
Worship:		
Encouragement of	1 Sam. 26; 2 Sam. 6	50-51
Commitment to		
By Josiah	2 Kings 22	131
By David	Ps. 23	44-45
Satan	Job 1; 2	64-65
Sidebars		
"David" in prophecy		45
Role of the occult in the ancient world		114
Baal-Melqart		122
John's Gospel		188
Josephus on the Pharisees		198-199
Matthew's Gospel		189
Mark's Gospel		210
Political and religious factions in the First Century		163
Saul's commission		177
Which animals were on the ark?		61
Son/parent relationships		
Jesus and parents	Luke 2	160
Moses and his mother	Ex. 2:1-10	27-28, 31
Samson and parents	Judg. 13; 14	106
Samuel and mother	1 Sam. 1; 2	109
Uncle/nephew relationships		
Abraham and Lot	Gen. 12-14; 18; 19	21-22
Laban and Jacob	Gen. 28-31	69-70, 72
Work		
An overemphasis on	Gen. 3	9-10
As toil	Gen. 3	9
Meaningful	Gen. 3	6

SCRIPTURE INDEX

(Bible references are in boldface type, followed by the pages on which they appear in this book.)

GENESIS

1—2, 2, 4; **1—5**, 220; **1**, 2, 3; **1:26–27**, 2, 3; **1:26**, 3; **2**, 3, 6; **2:1—5:5**, 1; **2:7–25**, 2; **2:7**, 3; **2:8–20**, 4; **2:9**, 5; **2:15**, 5; **2:17**, 5, 6; **2:18**, 5; **2:19**, 5; **2:20**, 5; **2:21–24**, 5; **2:23**, 6; **3**, 10; **3:1–10**, 1; **3:1–19**, 6; **3:6**, 6; **3:7**, 10; **3:8**, 8, 10; **3:10**, 10; **3:12**, 10; **3:16**, 8; **3:17–18**, 8; **3:17–19**, 9; **3:17**, 8, 9; **3:18**, 8; **3:19**, 8, 9; **3:21**, 10; 4, 217, 245; **4:17**, 256; **4:18–24**, 298; **4:18**, 275, 305, 308; **4:20**, 278; **4:21**, 295; **4:22**, 344; **4:25–26**, 327; **4:26**, 256; **5—9**, 58; **5**, 60; **5:1–3**, 3; **5:6–11**, 256; **5:9–14**, 297; **5:12–17**, 301; **5:15–20**, 280; **5:18–24**, 256; **5:21–27**, 307; **5:21**, 146; **5:24**, 146; **5:25–31**, 298; **5:28–32**, 315; **5:32**, 263, 280, 333;

6—7, 61; **6—9**, 58; **6:3**, 60; **6:5**, 60; **6:8—9:29**, 315; **6:8**, 60; **6:9**, 60; **6:11–22**, 60; **7:1—8:14**, 61; **7:10**, 61; **7:13**, 263; **8:14**, 61; **8:15—9:29**, 61; **8:20–22**, 61; **9:1–7**, 61; **9:5–6**, 3; **9:6–7**, 61; **9:6**, 61; **9:8–17**, 61; **9:8–28**, 61; **9:18–27**, 245, 263, 280; **9:22**, 62; **9:23–27**, 333; **10:2–3**, 262; **10:2**, 280, 281, 301, 306, 343, 344; **10:3**, 233, 325, 344; **10:4**, 254, 281, 298, 325, 341; **10:5–18**, 245; **10:6–8**, 246; **10:6**, 245, 310, 322; **10:7**, 247, 268, 322, 325, 326, 331; **10:8–12**, 315; **10:13**, 310; **10:21–22**, 333; **10:21**, 249; **10:22–23**, 230; **10:22**, 232, 233, 250, 299; **10:23**, 261, 273, 306, 345; **10:24**, 232, 332; **10:25–29**, 292; **10:25**, 249, 320; **10:26**, 226, 268, 285, 333; **10:27**, 248, 263, 345; **10:28**, 218, 316, 331; **10:29**, 268, 290, 317;

11, 16; **11:10–11**, 333; **11:12–15**, 332; **11:14–17**, 249; **11:16–19**, 320; **11:18–21**, 324; **11:20–23**, 327; **11:22–25**, 312; **11:24–32**, 342; **11:26–31**, 265; **11:27–28**, 21; **11:28–29**, 312; **11:31**, 16; **12—14**, 21; **12—15**, 15; **12—24**, 10; **12**, 11, 12; **12:1–3**, 11, 12, 16; **12:1–5**, 16; **12:1–7**, 1; **12:1**, 16; **12:2**, 74; **12:6–8**, 16; **12:7**, 11, 12; **12:10**, 16; **12:11–20**, 16; **12:14–20**, 133;

13—21, 22; **13**, 16, 21, 22, 299; **13:6**, 21; **13:8**, 21; **13:10**, 21; **13:13**, 21; **13:15**, 17; **14**, 17, 21, 229, 296; **14:1–17**, 342; **14:1**, 231; **14:2**, 242, 244, 335, 337; **14:9**, 231; **14:13**, 230, 257, 303; **14:18–20**, 305; **14:22–23**, 17; **14:24**, 230, 257, 303; **15**, 17, 22; **15:1**, 17; **15:2**, 252; **15:5**, 14, 17; **15:6**, 11, 14; **15:7**, 1; **16—17**, 276; **16—24**, 18; **16**, 18; **16:1–6**, 22; **16:2**, 22; **16:5**, 23; **16:16**, 23; **17:1–9**, 18; **17:5**, 18; **17:9–27**, 18; **17:19–21**, 66, 67; **18—19**, 21, 22; **18**, 18, 22; **19**, 299; **19:37**, 310; **19:38**, 241; **20**, 19, 22; **20:1–18**, 218; **20:11**, 19;

21—28, 275; **21**, 23; **21:1–14**, 19; **21:3–12**, 66, 67; **21:11**, 19, 23; **21:13**, 19; **21:22–32**, 320; **21:22–34**, 218; **22**, 19, 24, 66; **22:2**, 24; **22:3**, 19; **22:5**, 19; **22:20–23**, 312; **22:21**, 230, 245, 297, 345; **22:22–23**, 243; **22:22**, 268, 289, 297, 321; **22:24**, 259, 299, 341, 342; **23**, 20; **23:8–17**, 256; **23:8**, 353; **24—28**, 66; **24**, 20, 67; **24:2**, 21; **24:3–4**, 21; **24:7**, 20, 21; **24:15**, 243; **24:50**, 243; **24:67**, 67; **25—27**, 257; **25—35**, 68; **25—50**, 278; **25:1–11**, 21; **25:2–3**, 292; **25:2**, 275, 305, 309, 338, 353; **25:3**, 247, 331; **25:4**, 217, 250, 256, 265, 309; **25:7–8**, 23; **25:9**, 23, 353; **25:10**, 256; **25:12–18**, 276; **25:13**, 220, 296, 308, 313; **25:14**, 248, 303, 310; **25:15**, 262, 288, 296, 312, 342; **25:19–26**, 71; **25:20**, 298; **25:27–34**, 69; **25:29–34**, 71; **25:30**, 249;

26, 67; **26:1–33**, 218; **26:23–25**, 67; **26:26–31**, 225; **26:26**, 320; **26:34**, 229, 240, 255; **27:1–41**, 69; **27:20**, 67; **27:33**, 67; **27:43**, 298; **28—31**, 69; **28:10–22**, 71; **28:20**, 71; **29—30**, 73; **29—31**, 298; **29—33**, 339; **29:32**, 73, 324; **29:33**, 73; **29:34**, 73, 299; **29:35**, 295; **30:6**, 247; **30:8**, 312; **30:11**, 259; **30:13**, 233; **30:18**, 276; **30:20**, 349; **30:24–25**, 293; **30:25–43**, 72; **31**, 66; **32—35**, 70; **32:1–12**, 72; **32:10–12**, 72; **32:22–32**, 72; **32:28**, 276; **33:9**, 71; **33:19—34:26**, 264; **34:2**, 332; **34:25–30**, 339; **34:25–31**, 299; **35**, 66; **35:10**, 276; **35:18**, 241, 242; **35:22–23**, 324; **35:23**, 276, 295; **35:24**, 241; **35:25**, 247; **35:26**, 233;

36, 257; **36:2**, 255, 352; **36:4**, 254, 324; **36:5**, 277, 289, 298; **36:10–17**, 324; **36:11**,